Religion in Social Context

in Europe and America,

1200-1700

Medieval and Renaissance Texts and Studies

Volume 238

RELIGION IN SOCIAL CONTEXT

IN EUROPE AND AMERICA,

1200-1700

by

Richard C. Trexler

Arizona Center for Medieval and Renaissance Studies
Tempe, Arizona
2002

Library of Congress Cataloging-in-Publication Data
Trexler, Richard C., 1932–

    Religion in social context in Europe and America, 1200–1700 / by Richard C. Trexler.

       p. cm. — (Medieval and Renaissance texts and studies ; v. 238)
    ISBN 0–86698–280–9 (alk. paper)
    1. Europe — Religious life and customs. 2. New Spain — Religious life and customs. I. Title. II. Medieval & Renaissance Texts & Studies (Series) ; v. 238.

BR735.T74 2002
270--dc21   2002018437

For

Rab, Tony, and Klaus

CONTENTS

ACKNOWLEDGMENTS

It is in the nature of a book of collected papers that the debts incurred by the writer are many. They stretch in this case over a third of a century. But they are also diffuse: the friends and scholars who helped me with an article on fourteenth-century Florence belong to a demographic almost wholly different from the one that provided help with the study of the Aztecs. For this reason, with one exception I will limit my (many) expressions of thanks to those contained in individual chapters of the work that follows.

But a special note of thanks is due Klaus Schreiner. He not only invited me to teach a semester in Bielefeld, Germany, but repeatedly asked me to present papers to conferences he organized in that country, three of which are reprinted in the present work. Schreiner's kindness made it possible for me, after a long absence, to tap again into the roots of my education as a historian (I had done all my graduate work in that blessed country). Klaus's invitations to conferences brought me into contact with some of the best of European scholarship, and the classroom he provided introduced me to his own fine students. Finally, they, and Klaus himself, have become my friends. What could be more gratifying?

Institutions have played an important role in my ability to do the work contained in this volume. I will mention three of them. First, the Department of Art History at the University of California at Los Angeles made me its Art Council Professor for two terms in 1987. I researched the evangelical magi with an excellent group of students, who gave me many of the ideas regarding them used in the chapters of this book. And I have more recently benefited from two research grants, a John Paul Getty Senior Research Grant in the History of Art and a Henry Luce Fellowship at the National Humanities Center. My thanks to them all.

INTRODUCTION

Go to class and ask students what is their religious affiliation. Then discover in the course of, say, lectures on the Reformation that virtually none of them understands the first thing about the teachings of their particular religion. It has always been so. The fact is that none but a whimsical minority of the devotees of any religion have any concept of their group's teachings or of how they are different from any other. And yet those who go to a church, temple, or mosque can describe to you their devotional practices and perhaps even how others' practices are different from their own.

Go to any bookstore and seek out the "religion" section. You will discover that what is contained in such sections are books about the teachings of different religions and works on so-called spirituality, or lucubrations of particular understandings of how the authors love and need their God, in other words, precisely those things our students know nothing about. What you will almost certainly not find are works that deal with the practice of religions, either past or present, which the same students are most likely to know about. The few books on that subject are found under "social science."

Finally, consider the power of the word "religion." Some years ago I was perplexed to find that William A. Christian's book *Local Religion in Sixteenth-Century Spain* had been translated into Spanish with the title *La religiosidad local en la España de Felipe II* (1992). On my next visit to Spain, thumbing through the "religion" section in bookstores and dictionaries, I discovered that the Spanish word "religion" referred to clerical liturgy and dogma, while "religiosity," which has a definite negative denotation in Spanish as in English, refers to lay religious sentiments and practices.

The thread that links the previous observations is that a predominantly clerical understanding of religion as reflective still reigns, one that has never penetrated to the body of the laity, whose own (allegedly non-reflective) behavior is belittled as something less. The thread that unites most of the articles in this book, on the other hand, is the author's belief in the fundamental importance of what people — both laity and clergy — do in the religious sphere. This sphere is much more vast than the space within any house of God. It recognizes profanation as the step before and after sacralization, both inherently religious processes. That behavior, I submit, has almost nothing to do with what a clergy — whether ordained or not — thinks, important as that thoughtful discussion may be to understanding that clergy's, if not the laity's, corporate behavior.

The best way to understand the character and specificity of any religion is, therefore, to watch devotees' behavior, and that means observing the patterns they follow, the rituals, in short, which indeed identify what are rather communities of behavior than of belief. That ritual, usually of the laity, is another abiding interest of the author, to be revealed in the following chapters.

This is not to say that each of these religions, on examination, does not have processes in common with other religions, and my book is, as shown in the table of contents, organized around just such commonalities. I begin with three chapters under the heading Roman Catholicism, ones best characterized as church history. I turn then decisively to God-Making, a process of constructing those deities whose power and vulnerability will remain the ultimate explanation for that culture's world of experience. In various ways, all four of my examples concern the evangelical magi through whose actions the Christian God was first shaped. Matthew inserted the story into his gospel to provide an outside or foreign legitimation for the claim that the Infant was a king and, once the wise men were converted into kings in the Middle Ages, offered a standard means of showing that European rulers themselves vouchsafed God and his clergy's *bona fides*. Visions would fill out their persons and, in the New World, the story in procession would lead the native gentiles to the correct, Christian and Spanish, altars, to worship the natives' own infant. All the while, the profile of the adored child was enriched, embellished, and moulded by these processional, theatrical, and stable images of the outside savants, whose story was believable because as foreigners they had no interest in lying.

Just as surely do religions engage in Saint-Making, that is, through processions, prayers, and theatrical commemorations converting dead human beings into communication sources for intercession and of knowledge about the devotees' own futures. The present book offers two specific cases of this process, of which the first is little known outside Mexico. As early as 1540, the story of the three boys of Tlaxcala "who died for Jesus" was being fashioned by interested Franciscans into a legend which has reached such a point at the end of the last millennium that these boys have been beatified by the pope. Yet what becomes evident after a careful study of the earliest sources is that, leaving the friaries to which the friars had kidnapped them, these boys had gone out to physically attack and abuse their ("pagan") parents, killing one of them, and regularly ransacked the homes of these same parents and other relatives because there were "idols" in their parents' residences. Not only that: the archbishop of Mexico praised this comportment, for it was, after all, the goal of the churchmen to turn the children against their recalcitrant elders so as to spread the faith. None of this has much to do with the story told today of these "innocent" beatific boys, but that is the point. "The Three Boys of Tlaxcala" is a hagiographic construction.

But the pinnacle of all such constructions is surely what was done to the memory of Francis of Assisi after his death. As my different contributions to the Francis story show, his renunciation of the world as a young man, the story of his so-called stigmata, his death, and finally the *translatio* of his cadaver to the new Basilica of San Francesco, when studied without ideological blinkers, all appear in a much different light from the image given by orthodoxy. The most important narrative constructor of that orthodoxy was certainly Thomas of Celano, who wrote two decisively different *Lives* of Francis to please two different generations in his order's life. A close study of his and Elias' — the first order general — stories of Francis, especially those regarding his death and *translatio*, will show how serious and ongoing the making of a saint really is. Because a central purpose of such constructions is to provide an image for worship, which, being false, is idolatrous, the historian has the duty to unravel the past and to present it in a truthful image, the best that the sources in all their complexity and contradiction will allow.

Next I observe that many religions have a group of Religious Structures whose behavioral actualizations have much in common with one another. This book examines a few such structures, such as learning how to pray, dressing supernaturals, and talking to them. And finally comes a set of chapters dedicated to gendering as religious practice, a more recent interest of mine. As they are carried out by any particular religion, all of these activities obviously manifest peculiarly distinct edges and contours, and those particularities certainly receive their due in what follows. But it will no longer do to speak of the "magic" and "superstition" of such practices only because one is blissfully unaware of kindred practices in other societies and cultures. As I argue in my chapter on the berdache, a native American who his life long played a woman's role, we indeed cannot allow our own presentist preoccupations to dictate our language and shape our study of the past. Believing as I do in the universalities behind the multi-faceted variety of particular religious and socioreligious acts, I hope at least while observing and respecting these particularities to have paid decent attention to their underlying universalistic substrates.

All but one of the chapters in the present book have appeared, or are about to appear, elsewhere. The one exception is a re-edition of an early print under the title "An Early Printed Text Against Homosexual Behavior, c. 1485," a paper published here for the first time. Yet that does not tell the whole story. Fully eight chapters of this book appear here in English for the first time, having been originally published in another language. They include "The Gender and Number of the Evangelical Magi," "Dreams of the Three Kings," "Ludic Life in New Spain: The Emperor and his Three Kings," "At the Right Hand of God: Organization of Life by the Holy Dead in New Spain," "Dressing and Undressing Images: An Analytic Sketch," "Bending Over Backwards: Prayer Posture and Sexual Posture in Traditional Europe and America," "The Talking Image: An Attempt at Typology Using Spanish Sources of the Sixteenth Century," and "Dressing Like a Woman: The Case of the Berdache."

Nor do the articles appear here without some changes. I have of course corrected previous typos and misspellings, and added bibliography pertaining to the subjects covered. In one chapter I present a significantly different edition of a previous article. Owing to space needs, the original publication of "From the Mouths of Babes" was in fact an abridged version of what I had written. The present edition presents my original text, which lays out my thesis at greater length, with much more documentary evidence than was earlier possible.

At one point in the proceedings that follow, our sources reveal that in the period of the Spanish conquest of the Americas, lay and clerical Christians consulted the native Gods to learn their future in the dangerous land that was not yet fully their own. One explanation put forward at the time for this heterodox practice was that the Christian God did not tell the future and that his devotees must not ask it. With whose help do *we* then tell the past, as our muse beckons us to do? I have made my choice. It is the principle of profanity before, and after, it has lapsed into the sacred.

ROMAN CATHOLICISM

Diocesan Synods in
Late Medieval Italy*

THE VITALITY OF SYNODS OR GATHERINGS of diocesan clergy in the pre-modern period has traditionally been measured by the presence or absence of bodies of episcopal law that were approved at such meetings. For historically, such laws, when dated, have furnished the easiest evidence that synods had indeed been held. C. R. Cheney has observed that the golden age of episcopal legislation was the late twelfth and thirteenth centuries, whence date the basic codes or statutes or constitutions of so many dioceses. Later years, Cheney says, witnessed some additions to these books of diocesan law, but few large-scale revisions right up until the eve of the Council of Trent.[1] Further, no new papal legal codifications appeared

---

* This essay appeared previously in *Vescovi e diocesi in Italia dal* XIV *alla metà del* XVI *secolo*, ed. G. de Sandre Gasparini, A. Rigon, F. Trolese, and G. M. Varanini, *Atti del VII Convegno di Storia della Chiesa in Italia*, 2 vols. (Rome, 1990), 1:295–335.
    [1] C. R. Cheney, *English Synodalia of the Thirteenth Century* (Oxford, 1968 [1st ed.: 1941]), 34–44. The same point from a French perspective in O. Pontal, *Les statuts synodaux*, Typologie des sources du moyen âge occidental, fasc. 11, A-III.1 (Turnhout, 1975): 68–69. The provincial council of Florence in 1516–1517 (in J.-D. Mansi, *Sacrorum conciliorum nova et amplissima collectio* [Florence and Venice, 1759–1798], 35, c. 215–318) and the synod(s) in Verona that Bishop Giberti presumably held after 1527 to approve his constitutions (in his *Opera*, ed. P. and H. Ballerini [Verona, 1733], 1–153) are the conspicuous exceptions to this diocesan lethargy before Trent. In his biography of Giberti,

after the council of Vienne (1311), though the decrees of the councils of Constance (1414–1418) and Basel (1431–1445) had some marginal significance for the dioceses. What is true for the rest of Europe certainly applies to Italy as well: the late middle ages were not a period of legislative splendor at the diocesan level, and thus not one where synods featured legislative activity.

Trent provided much new papal law to be brought to the attention of clergy and laity, giving a new lease on life to the ancient institution of the episcopal synod. Yet Hinschius is our authority for the notion that the synod soon enough resumed its decline, because now the printing press could communicate a bishop's wishes to his clergy and laity at less expense and risk.[2] Especially in Italian ecclesiastical historiography, the synod has always been viewed as a means of downward, not lateral, communication: a means by which a bishop, or his vicar, communicated with his diocese.

Recently, scholars have come to recognize that many synods were held in late medieval Europe that had no new constitutions or episcopal law emanating from them. Giuseppina De Sandre specifically made this claim for the Veneto at the conference where the present paper was presented. It is wrong to think that because there were few new constitutions, there were few synods. After all, the requirement of a minimum annual synod instituted in 1215 by Lateran IV was specifically maintained by the council of Basel in 1433 and by Lateran V in 1515.[3] The expectation was there. And in France, actual practice as well as norms aimed at two annual synods rather than one.[4] England had similar goals and practices.[5]

A. Prosperi does not, however, record such synods: *Tra evangelismo e controriforma: G. M. Giberti (1495–1543)* (Rome, 1969).

[2] P. Hinschius, *System des katholischen Kirchenrechts mit besonderer Rucksicht auf Deutschland*, vol. 3 (Graz, 1959), 597–99; C. Black, "Perugia and Post-Tridentine Church Reform," *Journal of Ecclesiastical History* 35 (1984): 436–38; P. Prodi, *Il cardinale Gabriele Paleotti (1522–1597)*, 2 vols. (Rome, 1959–1967), 2:152–61.

[3] *Conciliorum oecumenicorum decreta* (hereafter *COD*), ed. J. Alberigo et al. (Bologna, 1973), respectively 236–37, 473–75, 631. For Trent, see *COD*, 761–62.

[4] See the lists in Pontal, *Statuts synodaux*; further, A. Artonne, "Les synodes diocésains d'Arles de 1410 à 1570," *Revue d'histoire de l'Eglise de France* 41 (1955): 76–84. Yet P. Adam, *La vie paroissiale en France au XIVe siècle* (Paris, 1964), 5–7, found that most French synods in the period were held before 1350.

[5] See for example M. Aston, *Thomas Arundel. A Study of Church Life in the Reign of Richard II* (Oxford, 1967); D. M. Owen, "Synods in the Diocese of Ely in the latter Middle Ages and the Sixteenth Century," *Studies in Church History* 3 (1966): 217–22.

Now students are finding that in the Italian peninsula as well, synods were more common than previously thought. At Bologna, for example, Paolo Prodi has established an impressive list of such gatherings, while Enrico Peverada has found more synods than expected in Ferrara. Florence too has been found to have had several synods.[6] The conference where this paper was originally delivered has also added many more synods without proclamations of constitutions to the diocesan lists. It is all but certain that as greater use is made of state archives in the study of ecclesiastical history, it will be determined that diocesan synods were not unusual in the late middle ages.

What interpretation can be put on this information? A ready answer lies all too close at hand: these synods must have been dedicated to the *reformatio morum* which the prelates who held them stated to be their purpose-in short, more evidence for defenders of the church that it was already reforming when Luther appeared. Not only an older polemical scholarship, but also moderns like Peverada and Gorini remain ready to see synods by definition as reform-minded, precisely because they tend to view the synod as exclusively episcopal, and mainly legislative, in inspiration.[7]

The purpose of the present essay is to broaden and deepen our under-

---

[6] Prodi, *Il cardinale*, 2:152–53, found synods in 1455, 1481, 1482, 1483, 1486, 1535, 1549, 1551, 1556, 1559, and 1564; E. Peverada, "Sinodi ferraresi quattrocenteschi," *Analecta Pomposiana* 5 (1980): 137–59; R. C. Trexler, *Synodal Law in Florence and Fiesole, 1306–1518* (Vatican City, 1971); D. Peterson, "Archbishop Antoninus: Florence and the Church in the Earlier Fifteenth Century," Ph.D. diss., Cornell University, 1985.

[7] Peverada, "Sinodi ferraresi"; A. Gorini, "L'azione pastorale dei vescovi in Italia nell'epoca di San Felice da Cantalice (1510/1515–1587): linee e problemi, sez. 2 a," published in the conference *Atti: S. Felice da Cantalice, i suoi tempi, il culto e la diocesi di Cittaducale dalle origini alla canonizzazione del santo (Rieti-Cantalice-Cittaducale, 28 agosto–3 settembre 1987)*. Whether at law a gathering of the diocesan clergy *sede vacante* was called a synod is an open question. Recent work on such gatherings is by A. Rigon, "Le elezioni nel processo di sviluppo delle istituzioni ecclesiastiche a Padova tra XII e XIII secolo," *Mélanges de l'École française de Rome. Moyen âge-Temps modernes* 89 (1977), 377–99. Rigon found the Paduan fraternity of parochial priests *representing* the secular clergy at such gatherings *interregnum*: Rigon, "L'associazionismo del clero in una città medioevale. Origine e primi sviluppi della 'Fratalea cappellanorum' di Padova (XII-XIII sec.)," in *Pievi, parrocchie e clero nel Veneto dal X al XV secolo*, ed. P. Sambin (Venice, 1987), 95–180, 145–47. In 1401 Boniface IX ordered the cathedral canons to "convoke" to a "convocatio sive congregatio" (and not a synod) the whole Florentine diocesan clergy, exempt and non-exempt, to publish his bull that had transferred the former Florentine bishop to another diocese: B. Sanesi, "Episodi fiorentini dello scisma d'Occidente," *La scuola cattolica* 73 (1945): 433–53.

standing of the inspiration and purposes of synods during the late middle ages, and to lay out avenues of research for future study. It seems important to do this because, to be brief, it is hard to find bishops in synod in this age doing the traditional things scholars suppose bishops in synod to have done. Not only were new bodies of law rarely being pronounced, but other asserted purposes of synods are missing as well.[8] There is little evidence that late medieval Italian synods had much of a judicial function, for example. If for no other reason, this was so because reserve of cases by the papacy — ones listed in re-editions of diocesan constitutions — had robbed the bishops of much of their judicial competence in such matters.[9] Thirdly, the evidence is scant that bishops or their vicars held synods to correct faults they had found in preceding diocesan visitations. I can find little actual connection between visitations and synods in this age.[10] Fourth, with one exception, I can find no evidence that the synods were particularly spiritual in character: types of seminaries before the fact, in Pontal's view, where clerks might be exposed to legal and moral training of a kind.[11] In general, Italian synods in this age were not operating as

---

[8] The first discrete treatise on the subject of synods contains a lengthy list of such episcopal duties, including those listed in what follows; H. De Bottis, *Tractatus de synodo episcopi, et de statutis episcopi synodalibus* (Lyon, 1529).

[9] See e.g., C. Pazzi, *Constitutiones synodales cleri Florentini* (Florence, 1508 [stil. flor.]), c. K2r–K6v; P. Caiazza, "Sinodi pre-tridentini in diocesi di Amalfi," *Rassegna del Centro di cultura e storia amalfitana* 6 (1986): 15.

[10] Botti has synods appointing *testes synodales* to investigate moral problems in the diocese and referring them to the bishop, but he makes no mention of the latter's visitation or of these problems being subsequently aired in synod: Botti, *Tractatus*, c. 24v, 25r, 26r. See Cheney, *English Synodalia*, 5–6; recent work on visitations makes no mention of synods at all: U. Mazzone and A. Turchini, *Le visite pastorali* (Bologna, 1985), 146–48. Giberti refers to what he had seen in past visits, but as noted, it is not clear this constitution (bk. I, ch. 22) was read in synod: cited in J. Olin, *The Catholic Reformation: Savonarola to Ignatius Loyola* (New York, 1969), 141.

[11] O. Pontal, "Le rôle du synode diocésain et des statuts synodaux dans la formation du clergé," in *Les évêques, les clercs et le roi (1250–1300)* (Fanjeaux, 1972), 336–59. In 1375 the archbishop of Genoa required "quod omnes abbates priores prepositi et archipresbiteri constituciones istas infra duos menses habeant, capelanis sibi subiectis semel vel bis in anno eas declarent et exponant ne per ignorantiam aliqui se excusent. Capellani autem sub pena solidorum 10 ad plebem suam veniant quando archipresbiter pro ipsis constitucionibus exponendis ipsos duxerit advocandos. Volumus etiam quod omnes ipsi suffraganei nostri ipsas constituciones et maxime illi qui provinciam totam respiciunt secum defferant, et in sinodo suo legi et publicari faciant, ordinantes quod in tota sua diocesi habeantur et observentur": see D. Cambiaso, "Sinodi genovesi antichi," *Atti della reale Deputazione di storia patria per la Liguria* (n.s. of the *Atti della Società ligure di storia patria* 4) 68 (1939): 87. See also A. D'Addario, "Il problema 'de vita et moribus

they are usually said to have done.

If on the one hand there seems to have been a larger number of synods than anticipated, and on the other hand few of them show bishops doing the accustomed things, we must entertain the notion that we have failed to grasp their full functionality. Scholars may have too narrowly embedded synods in ecclesiastical and moral considerations seen from the top down. The first monographic writer on synods, Enrico de' Botti, definitely erred in this way. In his view, an "episcopal synod held to collect money or because of ambition or something similar can't properly be called a synod" ("synodum episcopi factam ob congregandas pecunias vel ob ambitionem seu aliam similem causam non proprie dici synodum").[12] It is time, I think, to dismiss such moralisms and begin again by thinking of a synod simply as a gathering of diocesan clergy.

This paper argues that in fact taxation was a central matter of concern at synods in the late middle ages, silent though previous works on synods have been on the subject. Secular authorities had long used political gatherings like parliaments and estates to raise taxes, and popes had in fact never been indifferent to the actions of their clergy when they assembled in such gatherings or synods. This essay will show that money was much discussed in late medieval synods. To put the matter provocatively: limiting ourselves for the moment just to downward communications, everyone recognizes that synods were used to propagate papal law in Italy. Yet scholars in the peninsula have not thought much about how the popes announced, and facilitated the collection of, their taxes.

In turn, questions about the connection between clerical taxation and synods lead us to redefine the corporate nature of the "clergy" that was taxed in synod. This essay will maintain that rather than individual clerks appearing at synod on the command of their bishop, the clergy appeared in groups, representing larger groups, at least alongside or lateral to the bishop in synod, but in any case not merely individually beneath him. A closer examination of the clergy in synod will show that they sometimes came together as a corporation under the presumption that what touched all had to be at least discussed, and at most decided, by all.

---

clericorum' nella diocesi di Firenze. Legislazione canonica e civile, e iniziative spontanee, fra XIV e XVI secolo," in *Chiesa e società dal secolo IV ai nostri giorni* (Rome, 1979), 2:383–414.

[12] Botti, *Tractatus*, c. 2r. Yet Botti saw the collection of the so-called "synodal" impost as part of the synod; *Tractatus*, c. 26r.

Thus my first and second aims in this essay are to determine what the clergy was and who "the clergy" in synod was. Then I want to provide some assessment of how these late medieval gatherings fit into the great political movements of the time. For any discussion of synods in this age must view them against the backdrop of the Great Schism, of the period of Conciliarism, and of the anti-conciliar, so-called Renaissance popes. In short, church history at this time was dominated precisely by questions about the legitimacy of clerical gatherings or synods. In one writer's words, this period saw a reactivation *at all levels* of the traditional federative structure of the church, including synods.[13]

Thus the history of episcopal synods in this period must be seen through the prism (1) of the secular powers' attempts to nationalize their clergies during the Great Schism, when ecclesiastical authorities were weak; (2) as part of the larger history of church councils in this period; and (3) as impacted by the papacy's attempts to regain its supremacy over the Councils. Little if any attention has been paid to these factors in the previous study of synods. The same must be said about the place that money had in these gatherings. Taxation was central at this time for states, conciliarists, and popes, all of whom used fiscal enticements to win over their clergies during the Schism.

Synodal Imposts

At the beginning of the Duecento, Boncompagno da Signa enumerated the names of episcopal imposts on the clergy:

> Nota, quod huiuscemodi denarii in quibusdam partibus appellantur synodales, in quibusdam denarii visitationis, in quibusdam collecte, in quibusdam procurationes, in quibusdam testiales, in quibusdam denarii de circa, in quibusdam denarii obedientie, et cathedrales, aut denarii de cathedratico, et in illis partibus vocantur annuales, in quibus annualiter solvuntur.[14]

---

[13] W. Krämer, *Konsens und Rezeption. Verfassungsprinzipien der Kirche im Basler Konziliarismus* (Münster 1980), 180. Further, the radical conciliarist Simon de Cramaud brought into his work the representational notion from Gratian that priests were like Christ's disciples: *De substractione obediencie*, ed. H. Kaminsky (Cambridge, MA, 1984), 11.

[14] C. DuCange, *Glossarium mediae et infimae latinitatis, s.v.* "Synodus." The list does not include all such grants. For example, aids or caritative subsidies are not mentioned.

Within this list is a workable distinction between two types of taxes. Some taxes were directly related to a gathering or meeting of some type, and could not be raised without the meeting. For example, before they were commuted to cash, procurations had been the expenses incurred by a prelate and paid in kind to him by a subordinate beneficiary when the former visited and met with the latter in his benefice.[15] Again, the synodals Boncompagno mentions were a type of demonstrative tribute bishops from earliest times required from clerks when the latter attended synods at the *seat* of the diocese.[16]

Since there has been no systematic work that I know of on the praxis of such taxes, there is no way at present to know just how important these sums might have been to bishops. The synodals were substantive enough to make their collection a stipulated part of an English vicar-general's duties.[17] But quantitative documentation on this tax is unusual, except for those apparently anomalous, poorly understood cases when the synodal tax surfaces in the papal archives because it became linked to the papal tax called Peter's Pence and thus fell due to a pope rather than to a bishop.[18] I would hazard the guess, however, that bishops did not call synods primarily to raise sums of money due them by virtue of the synod itself.

The so-called visitational "procurations," on the other hand, have left some pronounced tracks for the simple reason that they became a source of papal profit. As I have indicated, procurations began as bishops' rights to expenses when they visited. Then the prelates sought license from Rome to allow them to claim such procurations even if only their delegates, rather than they personally, visited the diocese or some parts of it. Next the papacy conceded such licenses on the condition that the bishop split the take with the apostolic camera. Papal collectors, in turn, claimed their part directly from the hapless beneficiaries rather than from the bish-

---

[15] C. Samaran and G. Mollat, *La fiscalité pontificale en France au XIVe siècle* (Paris, 1965), 34–47; W. Lunt, *Papal Revenues in the Middle Ages*, 2 vols. (New York, 1934), 1:107–11.

[16] As will be noted below, the tax called the *cathedraticus* was not quite identical to the synodal, at least in its origins: Botti, *Tractatus*, c. 26r.

[17] A. Hamilton-Thompson, *The English Clergy and their Organization in the Later Middle Ages* (Oxford, 1947), 190, 195. See further O. Pontal, "Le synode diocésain et son cérémonial du XIIe au XIVe siécle," *L'Année canonique* 4 (1970): 56; Cheney, *English Synodalia*, 4.

[18] Lunt, *Papal Revenues*, 2:81.

ops. Soon enough, the apostolic camera forbade bishops to collect other procurations until the cameral collectors got what was due them. "The more procurations, the more visitations," said Samaran and Mollat, referring to the benefit the bishops originally hoped to gain by visiting their dioceses.[19] "No procurations, no visits," Favier put it, meaning that if there was no procurational income, bishops would not bother visiting benefices.[20] Thus when reformers cut back on the size of procurations, visitations stopped.

But the "meeting taxes" as a genre only scratch the surface of those imposts which the clergy might have to pay at or after synods. For the synod or clerical assembly was long established, probably all over Europe, as a convenient forum in which to impose, distribute, and at times collect other kinds of taxes. Already in the eleventh century, Peter Damian is found praising a bishop of Gubbio because at his annual synod, "nullus exsuetae oblationis vel exeniorum canonem a clericis exigi permittebat."[21] Obviously, synods called by bishops had for centuries been associated with the raising of other types of monies.

It is usually said that one such tax I shall list here, the *cathedraticus*, was the same as the synodal, a type of "gathering tax." And indeed, in many usages it was just that and no more.[22] Yet considering that the term refers to the bishop's chair (*cathedra*) rather than to a gathering or synod, one may suspect that this impost was originally linked to that prelate's investiture, when he first sat in the chair. Thus the *auxilium et subsidium* the bishop of Florence in 1305 said was owed him and his successors on the occasion of *possesso* may originally have been called a *cathedraticus*.[23] Indeed, when Archbishop Antonino Pierozzi first took that same

---

[19] Samaran and Mollat, *Fiscalité pontificale*, 34–47.

[20] J. Favier, *Les finances pontificales à l'époque du grand schisme d'Occident, 1378–1409* (Paris, 1966), 217–21.

[21] DuCange, *Glossarium, s.v.* "Synodus."

[22] Thus in the Florentine Council of 1516–1517: Mansi, *Sacrorum conciliorum* 35, c. 230; and in Bologna: Prodi, *Il cardinale*, 2:160.

[23] "Taxamus, ut duo milia florenorum auri sint et dici valeant moderatum subsidium, ad quod solum de iure prestandum in posterum clerici Florentine civitatis et diocesis suis episcopis quando primo de curia ad Florentinam Ecclesiam veniunt teneantur. Et si ultra . . . iniustum denuntiamus": Trexler, *Synodal Law*, 6–7. A synod held in 1492 in Nocera five days after a new bishop's *possessio* was mainly to impose caritative subsidy on all benefices, while another held in 1496 was solely for financial matters, among which was a caritative subsidy "pro creatione noviter facta de domino episcopo": G. Sigismondi, "Tre sinodi diocesani sul finire del sec. XV," *Bollettino ecclesiastico ufficiale per la diocesi*

chair in 1446, the language evokes such an origin, combining as it does the words "synod" and "cathedra" into the notion that the first synod was the first time the bishop sat in his chair: Pierozzi was said to have been "presented to the clergy, synodally congregated in the cathedral church of Florence."[24]

Another document, this one from the diocese of Arezzo, shows that in that see, synods were necessary to raise any such subsidy, here labelled "caritative," from the clergy, and not just a subsidy at the *possesso*. In a letter of 1461, Girolamo Aliotti wrote to the bishop of Arezzo informing him that his vicar had held a diocesan synod a month before for the purpose of raising a caritative subsidy. Aliotti reminded the bishop that according to "synodal constitutions approved long ago by the pope," a maximum of 500 florins could be raised in caritative subsidy at any one time. In the letter, Aliotti also noted that while the vicar had the right to convoke some 600 persons in synod, he had allowed the use of proxies (*voces*), so that only 130 actually needed to attend.[25] Obviously, in that way a great deal of expense had been spared. What is important at this point, however, is that a synod was the proper, perhaps necessary place to impose, if not to gain consent for, other types of taxation besides a synodal or a *cathedraticus*.

Once this insight is integrated into one's view of a synod, evidence begins to spring from the sources, and indeed at the conference where this paper was first delivered, various colleagues in their comments added to my insight. Angelo Turchini showed the bishop of Faenza convoking a synod in 1312 "per trattare dell'estimo del clero," and Mario Sensi noted a 1351 synod at Città di Castello called to lay imposts to cover costs. Not the least significant of such evidence is that which shows the use of synods to deal with papal taxes, for example Turchini's reference at that conference to a synod called by the bishop of Bertinoro in 1371 to discuss the collection practices of papal *nuncii* in the diocese. In Genoa in 1385, the imposition of a papal tax led to the calling of a synod for the purpose of organizing a new assessment of ecclesiastical properties for the collection.

---

di Nocera e Gualdo 5 (1942): 73–74, nn. 9–10. Mario Sensi kindly brought this article to my attention.

[24] R. Morçay, *Saint Antonin Archevêque de Florence (1398–1495)* (Paris, 1914), 438.

[25] H. Aliotti, *Epistolae et opuscula*, 2 vols. (Arezzo, 1769), 1:437–38. Cf. the papal limit set on Aretine episcopal subsidies to that the Florentine bishop set on his predecessor in 1305, cited above. The canonical guidelines were firm, but did not impose precise limits for such taxation: *Corpus iuris canonici*, X.III.39.6 (1179).

The synod appointed four assessors, who ultimately drew up a cartulary assessing all benefices.[26] Florentine synods of 1427 and 1429 were called for discreetly financial purposes linked to the papacy.[27] Another interesting set of cases is included in the synodal records of the diocese of Nocera and Gualdo. One synod of 1496 was called to deal with finances and for that purpose alone. A papal subsidy having been imposed on all diocesan benefices, it was decided in synod, even while the clergy appointed three diocesan exactors of the papal subsidy, to appeal to Rome against the cameral treasurer who had demanded the amount. Still another synod of that diocese in 1498 repeated just such business, in addition to the clergy appointing new revisors of the diocesan *liber beneficiorum*. In summary, to the mind of their student Sigismondi, these synods were "brought together only and exclusively for financial questions."[28] There seems little doubt that this process of using synods for financial problems will be everywhere discovered once students' eyes are opened to the mundane truth about them. This must have been an old practice, beginning long before the period of the Great Schism and lasting long after it.

Thus bishops and, less directly, popes could and did demand and collect a wide variety of fees from subject clerks gathered in synods. On the other hand, the use of synods by *secular* rulers to impose taxes on the clergy is to date poorly studied in Italy. But abroad, the matter is different. Our texts are first of all in France, where diocesan synods had been used in Langue d'Oc since the twelfth century as a platform for imposing the Peace of God — and thus doubtless as a way to raise the taxes to pay the soldiers who enforced that Peace.[29]

Then between 1294 and 1305, during the famous struggle with Boniface VIII, Philip the Fair raised money to fight his adversary by convoking the French clergy on several different occasions and requesting grants from it without first gaining the pope's approval. To be sure, it sometimes seems

---

[26] Cambiaso, "Sinodi genovesi," 48.

[27] R. Ristori, "L'arcivescovo Amerigo Corsini e la sua controversia con il clero florentino (1427–29)," *Interpres* 1 (1978): 276–81.

[28] Sigismondi, "Tre sinodi diocesani," 74–75, 80.

[29] T. Bisson, *Assemblies and Representation in Languedoc in the Thirteenth Century* (Princeton, 1964), chap. 3, 102ff. The basic canon law was the decree of Lateran IV forbidding secular taxation of churches without approval by ecclesiastical superiors: COD, 255. The English clergy sometimes justified refusal to grant aid to the king by reference to this law: E. Kemp, *Counsel and Consent. Aspects of the Government of the Church as Exemplified in the History of the English Provincial Synods* (London, 1961), 73.

that not individual diocesan clergy, but prelates from the ecclesiastical provinces, or even from regions comprising several provinces, or indeed from northern, and then southern France, were those usually involved in these meetings. Still, many of these prelates did operate with procuratorial powers from their home clergy, a fact of some importance, as will be seen.[30] And at least once during these years, the crown specifically called the lower clergy to a provincial council — that of Bourges in 1296 — to consult on tax impositions.[31] Finally, somewhat later, in both 1351 and 1374, we find bishops ordered to call synods before the convoking of provincial councils, so that the local clergy could not later plead ignorance.[32] There may have been much more involvement of the diocesan clergy in royal taxation procedures than we know about at present.

Yet even if the "clergy" that met with the officials of Philip the Fair were usually prelatial, the political dynamics of these meetings are of some interest, because they involved the clergy in bargaining with the crown. Knowing that the king depended on them in his fight with Boniface, the clergy repeatedly wrung concessions from Philip in exchange for their support. One such concession made by the king in 1297 was that any aid to him could be collected only by churchmen.[33] Strayer was direct in assessing the constitutional import of such trades. It was an admission that the clergy played a role in government.[34]

So systematic was the relation between royal concessions and taxation of the clergy in these ecclesiastical meetings that historians of French institutions tend to see them as protorepresentative institutions, where the king could *de facto*, if not always admittedly *de iure*, raise money only with the consent of his subject clergy.[35] Philip the Fair saw the dilemma, and recognized that when crown and pope could work together in taxing the clergy, the latter was defenseless. Once Clement V became pope in 1305, Philip moved to regain his power over his clergy. Philip had decided that to avoid concessions to the clergy, "it was better for the government to

---

[30] See J. Strayer and C. Taylor, *Studies in Early French Taxation* (Cambridge, MA, 1939), especially Strayer's chapter on "Consent to Taxation under Philip the Fair," 24–43.

[31] Kemp, *Counsel and Consent*, 58.

[32] Kemp, *Counsel and Consent*, 55.

[33] Strayer and Taylor, *Studies*, 31.

[34] Strayer and Taylor, *Studies*, 34.

[35] Strayer and Taylor, *Studies*, 34.

get its grants from the pope even if [the pope] demanded a share of the proceeds."[36]

The identical processes involving the use by secular powers of clerical gatherings for fiscal purposes are to be found in England, but the involvement of the lower clergy there is much better documented and much more visible and substantial. The historical process began in the early thirteenth century, with clergies in synods consulting on the distribution and size of papal taxes. In defending their refusal simply to levy the taxes on their clergy without such gatherings, local bishops cited the principle of *quod omnes tangit* before papal tax collectors.[37]

When popes importuned the two archbishops for such taxes, the latter in turn called provincial councils that, when dealing with such fiscal matters, came to be called convocations. The famous English convocations were simply provincial synods or councils, called together for fiscal purposes. Put differently, a convocation was the fiscal part of a council, the "council" its non-fiscal part.[38] Preparatory work for these meetings was often done at diocesan synods, including the appointment of leaders of that clergy, but also representatives from the lower clergy itself, to attend the councils.[39] Such convocations in turn became the standard locus used by the crown to obtain monies from its clergies.

Here is the particular interest of these gatherings for us. As in France, so in England the crown recognized that the clergy had no duty to grant aids, so it tried to obtain in advance the good will of the pope, who might encourage the local clergies to contribute. That then required clerical deliberation at different levels. The highest level was in convocation. As

---

[36] Strayer and Taylor, *Studies*, 24, 42.

[37] Here is the famous passage of Matthew Paris, uttered to the papal nuncio at Reading: "Cui, inito consilio, responderunt episcopi, quod nullo modo tam importabile onus, quod universalem tangebat ecclesiam, subirent, sine prolixi consilii diligenti deliberatione," and further: "Et quod principaliter tangit, ab omnibus comprobetur, ut sic melius ecclesia relevetur, et singuli minus praegraventur": the passages are in his *Chronica Major* (London, 1857), respectively 4:10–11, 376. W. Lunt was not sure such things had actually been said: "The Consent of the English Lower Clergy to Taxation during the Reign of Henry III," in *Persecution and Liberty. Essays in Honor of George Lincoln Burr* (New York, 1931), 129; cf. Kemp, *Counsel and Consent*, 69. Aston, *Thomas Arundel*, 68–82, is excellent on the diocesan synods of the time, and especially on those of Ely, where the principal of *quod omnes tangit* was alive and well. As will be seen, so was it in Florence, Italy.

[38] Kemp, *Counsel and Consent*, 60–61, 104–5.

[39] Kemp, *Counsel and Consent*, 71, 76–77, 146–47; Lunt, "Consent," 165.

in France, so in England the actual presence of the lower clergy at these provincial or national gatherings was not common. Kemp found only two cases in the thirteenth century.[40] But some historians have seen that presence of the lower clergy in convocation as the very root of English parliamentary govemment![41]

Yet as the same author points out, in many other cases besides these two the consent of the lower clergy had already been obtained at local, diocesan synods.[42] Here was the common level of consultation, for as one bishop told his monarch requiring aid, "sine assensu eorundem clerico-rum," no grant was possible.[43] In 1270 a council called by the king conceded him a crusade subsidy, but only after the lower clergies in diocesan synods had debated the matter and agreed.[44] In 1282 Edward I, ready to ask for taxes in convocation, ordained that the diocesan clergies first meet separately so they would know what was impending, and so they would elect proctors to the council.[45]

Thus as in France, so in England the crown fostered the consultation of the lower clergy through its representatives as a way of legitimating its demands, but also as a means to counterbalance the authority of the great prelates, especially when it asked for aid without having first obtained papal agreement.[46]

In summary, synods were commonly held in England in the thirteenth and fourteenth century to consider royal, as well as ecclesiastical, requests for aids. These synods often appointed representatives to attend provincial councils which while they might be said to aim at *reformatio morum*, were in fact sometimes little more than a standard route for royal taxation of the clergy.[47] Lastly, it goes without saying that here, as in France and

---

[40] Kemp, *Counsel and Consent*, 73.

[41] The classic study is E. Barker, *The Dominican Order and Convocation* (Oxford, 1913). The works of Lunt and Kemp cited here are glosses on the questions Barker raised.

[42] Kemp, *Counsel and Consent*, 73.

[43] Lunt, "Consent," 168.

[44] Kemp, *Counsel and Consent*, 71.

[45] Kemp, *Counsel and Consent*, 76–77.

[46] Lunt, "Consent," 169.

[47] See the interesting case in 1342 where an archbishop called a "convocation" for 9 October and a "council" for 14 October to meet in the same place: Kemp, *Counsel and Consent*, 104–5. Clearly, this was in effect one gathering. In his "Sinodi ferraresi," Peverada found a similar phenomenon of legal but not factual separateness at Ferrara: see below.

elsewhere, the clergy did not grant aids without bargaining for rights.

There has been no intention in the preceding paragraphs to deal seriously with these northern institutions, but only to make it seem irresistible that, *mutatis mutandis*, Italian rulers must have used diocesan synods to raise taxes in similar ways. It defies the imagination, for example, to think of the archbishops of Milan building their state without making use of these instrumentalities. But as with so much else in Italian ecclesiastical history, the subject requires study: did the north Italian communes use clerical gatherings to impose, distribute, and collect communal taxes, and more generally, to weaken prelatial opposition to comunal goals?[48] This and many other questions regarding clerical gatherings spring to mind the moment we put aside the authoritarian notion that synods were merely episcopal instruments for reforming manners.

In the very rhetoric of the bishops themselves, the importance of their clergies in synod to episcopal attempts to raise, distribute, and collect taxes is evident. It far outstrips the attention scholarly literature on synods has accorded the fisc. A certain Trecento patriarch of Aquileia left no doubt why he celebrated "synodalia concilia quasi annis singulis." "Recordare," he wrote, "quantos labores, tribulationes, expensas et pericula sustinuimus in recuperatione et defensione jurium et bonorum Aquileiensis ecclesie."[49] Obviously the prelate wanted money, and needed the clergy in synod to that end.

Who Was the Clergy in Synod?

We come now to the crucial problem of determining who was the "clergy" that was called to synod. In northern Europe, it is generally said that all priests were not required to come to synods: either only the beneficed clergy, or clergy with cure of souls, or indeed only the prelates or dignitaries, are said to have been ordered in.[50] Alas, for the Italian dioceses, no detailed information seems to have been ferreted out at this point. No notifications of those required to attend are known to me, as Pontal has found at Amiens,[51] no lists of those contumacious clerks who failed to attend synods, like those Artonne found at Arles, have been

---

[48] Cf. R. Trexler, *Church and Community 1200–1600. Studies in the History of Florence and New Spain* (Rome, 1987), 245–88.

[49] G. Mantese, *Memorie storiche della Chiesa vicentina*, vol. 3.1 (Vicenza, 1958), 151.

[50] Cheney, *English Synodalia*, 13–14; Pontal, *Statuts synodaux*, 27.

[51] Pontal, "Le rôle du synode," 55.

located.[52] I have found but one comparable list: one of those who attended a Genoese diocesan synod in 1311.[53] Until much more documentation of this type is unearthed, the simplest matters about Italian synods will remain obscure.

But because of the importance I attach to taxation and finance in such clerical gatherings, I want to suggest that even if the persons on such lists were to be identified only as individuals or as holders of individual benefices or rectorates, it is a priori improbable that "the clergy" of Italian dioceses came to synod as such atomized individuals, which is the universal assumption made by the authoritarian historiography in question. My evidence will indeed show that the clerks came in groups, or as individuals representing groups, or at a minimum, that they acted as groups in synod. My hypothesis is that, not much different from the English clergy in wanting to avoid being lambs on the altar of prelatial taxation,[54] Italian clergies in synod formed a corporate body or bodies, a confraternity or group of confraternities, *representing* larger groups of clerks.

Unfortunately, in all his pathfinding work on clerical confraternities, Gilles Meersseman did not ask if clerical confraternities were ever identical with or even related to "the clergy" or any of its parts *in synod*.[55] I believe they were. As Cosimo Fonseca has put it, the problem is then to determine how voluntary associations like clerical confraternities "inserted themselves into the ambit of local ecclesiastical structures."[56] In two steps, I want to suggest the surprising degree to which a corporate identity of the clergy seems to me to be involved in synods.

At the first step, I want simply to establish that parts of the secular clergy, which might, as we shall see later, legally define themselves as corporations (*societates*) — that is, as entities capable of owning property whether they did or not — were being *represented* in synods. Pievanal priests in northern Italy appointed and empowered proctors to represent or

---

[52] Artonne, "Synodes diocésains," 82.

[53] Cambiaso, "Sinodi genovesi," 20.

[54] The extensive research on representation within the English synodal tradition is of course not encountered in Cheney, *English Synodalia*, for he tended to see the synod as an authoritarian exercise of the bishops, but in the work by Lunt, "Consent," and Kemp, *Counsel and Consent*.

[55] G. G. Meersseman, "Die Klerikervereine von Karl dem Grossen bis Innocenz III," *Zeitschrift für schweizerische Kirchengeschichte*," 46 (1952): 1–42, 81–112; Meersseman, *Ordo fraternitatis. Confraternite e pietà dei laici nel medioevo*, vol. 1 (Rome, 1977).

[56] C. D. Fonseca, " 'Congregationes clericorum et sacerdotum' a Napoli nei secoli XI e XII," in *La vita comune del clero nei secoli XI e XII* (Milan, 1962), 2:266–67.

act for them at synod. A notarial register at Genoa, for example, shows seven parish rectors of a *pieve*, unable to attend a synod like nine other colleagues, constituting the pieve's archpriest or pievano as their proctor.[57] In 1323 the priests of the pieve of Impruneta outside Florence appointed their pievano as their proctor to represent them in a synod scheduled at Florence.[58] Thus when in 1327 the bishop of Florence ordered the pievano of Impruneta to come to general synod on August 4 to hear synodal constitutions read and "to confirm or infringe" these constitutions, it may be assumed that the pievano proceeded to synod armed with the proxies of the priests of the whole pieve, whom he represented.[59] Synodal constitutions must often have been approved in part by clerks representing other clerks.

Another document from Impruneta shows that this type of representation definitely extended to financial matters. During a five-month episcopal interregnum in 1309, the rectors and chaplains of the pieve of Impruneta appointed their pievano as their proctor, to appear before one of the Florentine canons.[60] According to the document of procuration, the pievano was first obliged to swear to observe certain statutes and ordinances that had been made by the *clerum florentinum et clericos florentinos*. Second, the pievano had to swear before that same Florentine canon not to impose any imposts on the *clerum et clericos* of the city and diocese of Florence "unless this act was first approved by a majority of voters *ad pissides et ballotas*."[61] Clearly, at least at this date the clerks of the suburbs were uniting with those in the city in a clerical body whose proctors gathered to resist some type of impost.

And if the *clerus* of a diocese corporately resisted imposts, it insisted on its time-honored right to distribute what it agreed to. In France and England, a bishop, commune, or pope might levy an impost of a certain global

[57] Cambiaso, "Sinodi genovesi," 21 (1311).

[58] *Archivio di Stato di Firenze* (hereafter ASF), *Not. antecos.*, B 1343 (1321–48), at the date 24 January.

[59] ASF, *Not. antecos.*, B 1343, at the date 3 August. It is worth mentioning that in 1435 an episcopal bursar paid the "clergy of Florence" for themselves having paid messengers to announce a synod to one and all clergy: *Archivio Arcivescovile di Firenze, Mensa*, 5, fol. 54v.

[60] ASF, *Not. antecos.*, B 1340 (1296–1347), fol. 297. Note that a pievano did not have rights of proctor simply by virtue of his ecclesiastical office: B. Tierney, *Foundations of the Conciliar Theory. The Contribution of the Medieval Canonists from Gratian to the Great Schism* (Cambridge, MA, 1955), 117–19.

[61] ASF, *Not antecos.*, B 1340 (1296–1347), fol. 297r.

amount on the clergy, but they left the actual distribution of the sum among the clergy to its members.[62] That was the case for ecclesiastial taxation in parts of Italy, as we have seen, but the matter was similar for taxes imposed by secular governments. Thus in 1328 the *clerus florentinus* in convocation asked the episcopal vicar to allow its officials to deliberate on a communal impost, and asked the same vicar to associate a member of the clergy to himself in its distribution.[63] Again, in a government document of 1392, the *clerus florentinus* is seen assessing and distributing a tax that the government had imposed.[64]

Terms like *clerus florentinus, clerus aretinus,* and so on, could therefore refer to no mere collection of individuals, but to a corporate body whose gathered proctors followed voting procedures and had the ability to accept oaths and distribute taxes. As we know from a document of 1301, they also had the right to appoint proctors among themselves. In that year, indeed, the *clerus florentinus* was clearly divided between a body within and a body outside the city, each appointing separate proctors who underwent separate syndication of their incomes and expenses as new proctors were appointed.[65] The logical next step, the appointment of a proctor to represent the whole diocesan clergy in negotiating with a bishop ("presente ed accettante il mandato ad agire e procurare tutte le pratiche del clero stesso"), is found in a Genoese document of 1311.[66]

Finally, these syndics or proctors of diocesan clergies represented their constituencies toward the outside. A prominent example of this took place in 1300 at the time the papal bull *Super cathedram* was published. The rise of the Mendicant orders had seriously compromised the secular clergy's access to incomes from divine services, including of course testamental monies for masses. The secular clergy acted as a body in defending its rights. In Florence, for instance, the "syndics and proctors of the clergy of the whole city and diocese of Florence" (actually two priors, a rector, and a chaplain from the city) appeared with the bull *Super cathedram* in chapter at the Dominican convent of Santa Maria Novella and the Franciscan friary of Santa Croce. They published and left each convent a copy of this

[62] Strayer, *Studies,* 31 (1297); N. Valois, *La France et le grand schisme d'Occident,* 4 vols. (Paris, 1896–1902), 2:290; 3:313.

[63] ASF, *Not. antecos.,* G 106 (1326–30), fol. 105r (3 August).

[64] ASF, *Provvisioni,* 82, fols. 217rv (11 October).

[65] ASF, *Not. antecos.,* B 1341 (1300–40), fol. 119r.

[66] Cambiaso, "Sinodi genovesi," 21–22.

document, which reasserted the seculars' prerogatives in this area of divine services.[67] This secular clergy was not unorganized in the defense of its rights.

We come now to the second step in the study of clerical representation, the so-called congregations or companies or confraternities or gilds of the clergy, which I believe to have effectively often acted as the clergy in synod. From as early as 1110, priests are found in synod "cum omnibus confratribus suis," or otherwise identified with certain congregations.[68] Meersseman emphasized one purpose for these companies, the desire to procure proper burial for their members.[69] But in the light of much recent research dealing with the character of these associations, it is clear that Meersseman's model was faulty. If I may anticipate and simplify: the fault lay in emphasizing intent rather than operation — in juxtaposing "confraternities" with pious intents that looked inward, to "corporations" with worldly ones operating outwardly.

A superior model has been put forward by Antonio Rigon, in articles that appeared at the time of this conference.[70] Studying clerical groups in the Veneto, Rigon has shown just how tied to particular churches and territories these organizations were. In short, to the unsuspecting observer, they look like no more than diocesan subdivisions, basically uniting all the priests, or clerks, of a given area. Yet appearances may deceive. For example, Rigon maintains that while on the Venetian terra firma these groups *represented* local clergies before bishops, in Venice itself, he says, the famous nine congregations did not. Rigon is aware of the improbability of

---

[67] ASF, Not. antecos., L 76 (1298–1327), fols. 17v–19v (22 April); on *Super cathedram*, see further Trexler, *Church and Community*, 289–337.

[68] A. Samaritani, "Circoscrizioni battesimali, distrettuazioni pastorali, congregazioni chiericali nel medioevo ferrarese," *Analecta Pomposiana* 4 (1978), 153; Samaritani, "Il 'conventus' e le congregazioni chiericali di Ferrara tra analoghe istituzioni ecclesiastiche nei secoli X–XV," *Ravennatensia* 7 (1979): 168, and 172 for an archpriest at synod, "de congregatione S. Clementis." See recently W. Bowsky, "The Confraternity of Priests and San Lorenzo of Florence: A Church, a Parish, and a Clerical Brotherhood," *Ricerche Storiche* 27 (1997): 53–92.

[69] Meersseman, *Ordo*, 183.

[70] A. Rigon, "Le congregazioni del clero urbano in area veneta (XII–XV sec.)," in *Le mouvement confraternel au moyen-âge. France, Italie, Suisse* (Rome, 1987), 343–60; Rigon, "L'associazionismo." I want to thank Rigon for alerting me to these new and extremely rich articles, so they could be included in the present paper. See now also his *Clero e città. "Fratalea cappellanorum" parroci, cura d'anime in Padova dal XII al XV secolo* (Padua, 1988).

this latter statement, for in the fifteenth century there is irrefutable evidence that these groups, which have a distinct territorial character, were closely, and at this time customarily, linked administratively to the bishops.[71]

But the heart of Rigon's model is what interests me, for it identifies what must have been the fundamental gild characteristic of most such groups. A gild of priests was more reliable than any individual priest in producing masses and producing them right. With greater surety than any single priest, a gild of priests, which might mean all the priests of one parish, all the priests of a region, or even all the priests of a town,[72] could be expected to say masses commissioned by the laity. In some areas, equity between priests also inspired these groups. For example, Luigi Passerini documents a clerical confraternity founded in Florence in 1373 which allowed rural priests, who because of their distant residences were usually cut off from urban alms, to say their share of the masses commissioned by the rich urban burghers.[73]

It was presumably the reliable saying of these masses that first allowed the brothers of such confraternities to raise the money to bury their kind. In short, the pious desire to bury one's dead was probably first entertained once the profits from a reliable performance of divine services by a corporation became apparent. Certain laity left legacies to such confraternities for that purpose, and that endowment paid for the social services.

The linkage between pious activity and corporative possession of properties is, I think, characteristic. Holdings could be vast. Verona's clerical voluntary association, for example, was so potent that in the twelfth century its possessions were protected by the emperor and the pope.[74] Needless to say, such activities and such riches attracted the attention of

---

[71] Rigon, "Le congregazioni," 348.

[72] "Omnes clerici Verulane civitatis sint in una fraternitate"; Meersseman, *Ordo*, 179. The variety of clerical confraternities is only now being explored with due attention; for organizational variety, see especially Rigon, "Le congregazioni." In twelfth-century Padua the city's rectors formally entrusted the administration of their benefices to the voluntary association or *congregatio seu universitas cappellanorum* [i.e., rectors] *civitatis Padue*: Meersseman, *Ordo*, 186.

[73] L. Passerini, *Storia degli stabilimenti di beneficenza e d'istruzione elementare gratuita della città di Firenze* (Florence, 1853), 530. An article by A. D'Addario, "Compagnie di preti in Firenze nei secoli XV e XVI," apparently did not appear as scheduled in *Chiesa e società dal secolo IV ai nostri giorni* (above, n. 11).

[74] Meersseman, *Ordo*, 186. On the extent of these properties, see now Rigon, "L'associazionismo."

ecclesiastical authorities. For on the one side, these groups were effectively engaged in the cure of souls, which was an episcopal responsibility, while on the other their incomes from masses and burials and the like were owed, in part, to the prelates.[75] It is time to posit as being close, and at times as being identical to each other, the secular clergy brought together as beneficiaries, and the secular clergy organized in confraternities.

No one doubts that in that age, clerical organizations varied greatly, and that this variety must be taken into account. What helps in re-imagining the structures of the secular clergy at this time, however, is to downplay alleged differences between "corporations" and "confraternities," which are modern constructions. Instead, the similar legal characteristics of both types need emphasis: they were both legally capable of holding property. Units of the secular clergy seemingly acting within the category of beneficed clerks could, quite as easily as secular clerks banding together to insure fraternal burial, convert themselves into corporations (*societates*) for the purpose of accepting legacies and defending rights to such properties, even if the purpose of such property was not to build endowment but only to pay taxes and meet expenses.[76] Thus the priests of a pieve might readily convert themselves into *societates et fraternitates* when the occasion demanded.[77] This same record shows further that the *societas* of one pieve might expand to offer membership to brothers from outside the pieve. In 1331, some priests belonging to the *societas* of the pieve of Impruneta actually had their benefices in the neighboring pievi of Antella and Incisa.[78] Third, at the peak of the pyramid, such groups might meld into a *societas* at the diocesan level. This was the case with the *societas cleri florentini*.[79]

In my view, such a *societas* of the clergy carried effortlessly over to the synodal context. In effect, the *societas cleri florentini* just mentioned was no different from the term *clerus florentinus*, and the terms are used inter-

---

[75] On the episcopal claim for portions on such funds, see Trexler, "Bishop's Portion," in his *Church and Community*.

[76] On this distinction, see P. Prodi, "The Application of the Tridentine Decrees: The Organization of the Diocese of Bologna during the Episcopate of Cardinal Gabriele Paleotti," in *The Late Italian Renaissance, 1525–1630*, ed. E. Cochrane (New York, 1970), 236.

[77] Cf. ASF, *Not. antecos.*, A 354, at the date 5 May 1348. This *societas* included priests and laity.

[78] ASF, *Not. antecos.*, B 1345 (1327–32), fol. 226v.

[79] ASF, *Not antecos.*, S 96 (1332–33), fols. 190v–194v.

changeably in the document under consideration: the term *clerus floren-*
tinus is written in the margin to refer to the *societas cleri* referred to in the
text proper.[80] In short, the relation between property-holding corporations of clerks or priests, and the (sometimes incorporated [*societates*]) synodal clergy assembled in their role as beneficiaries or curates — both
groups composed, as must be emphasized, of much the same personnel —
was apparently so tight that differences seem mirror tricks. Indeed, in
1311, the main clerical confraternity in Florence was called a "society of
the synod": the *universitas vel societas sinodi civitatis florentine.*[81]

In pursuing this hypothesis, researchers should not imagine that episcopal documents will readily be found to reflect the existence of incorporated clerical interest groups in synod. Samaritani has noted that the
general law does not refer to such clerical corporations.[82] It was obviously
in the interest of the bishops to ignore such corporatism, and it can no
more be expected that these prelates would herald such groups than that
a student of Italian city politics should expect communal records to name
the confraternities from which we know city councilmen at times got their
marching instructions.[83] Still today, pressure groups and lobbying groups
go unmentioned in official records, important as they are to the formation
of policy. Modern policy makers, like medieval bishops, use such groups,
but at the same time they fear their potential.

Plus ça change. . . . As sparse as have been studies of the relations
between incorporated clergy and bishops in Italy, there is evidence for
both episcopal fear and episcopal utilization of self-conscious clerical corporations. Thus archbishop Federigo Visconti seems to have had a clerical
confraternity in mind when his Duecento Pisan statutes warned against
any clerical "coniurationem vel conspirationem vel colligationem."[84] A
Florentine bishop of 1311 was clear and forceful on this point. He recognized the newly founded *congregatio clericorum* as a body that was designed
to remember dead clerks. Yet fearing the clerical conspiracies arising from

---

[80] ASF, *Not. antecos.,* S 96 (1332–33), fols. 190v–194v.

[81] G. Richa, *Notizie istoriche delle chiese florentine* (Florence, 1757), 5:296; cf. Trexler,
Synodal Law, 370.

[82] Samaritani, "Circoscrizioni," 158.

[83] On Tuscan confraternities and the formation of stances in city councils, see N.
Rubinstein, *The Government of Florence under the Medici (1434 to 1494)* (Oxford, 1966),
118–19.

[84] E. Virgili, "Il sinodo dell'arcivescovo Federigo Visconti (1258)," *Bollettino storico
pisano* 44–45 (1975–76): 480.

its meetings, he turned about in the same document and forbade the brothers to meet unless they were called by the *procuratores cleri florentini*.
That is, elected officials of the *clerus florentinus* alone might permit a
clerical confraternity to meet![85] It must be suspected that, by any other
name, this clerical confraternity, the only one in Florence at the time, was
nothing more than the synod of clergy. Indeed, as we have seen "the
synod of the clergy" meant in some cases the confraternity. And why not?
Our tendency to divide and subdivide legal groups easily obscures the fact
that we are talking about the same individual clerks moving from one to
the other. A bishop of Lucca knew what was involved, and acted simply.
In a constitution of 1351, he forbade the Lucchese clergy from assembling
without his approval.[86]

Let me reconstruct. Italian synods of the late middle ages met perhaps
to agree to, and certainly to distribute, both secular and ecclesiastical taxes
as a matter of course. In these synods, formal representation was widely
used within the synodal clergy, toward the bishop and his vicars, and toward the communes. The corporations appointing such syndics and proctors, which often call themselves *societates*, are similar to clerical confraternities. Clerical confraternities in many venues essentially incorporated
in themselves a large part of the clerical patrimony, upon which prelates
could and did draw for support.

A central problem with this hypothesis is that one needs evidence of
the presence, or force, of such confraternities in synodal gatherings, understand though one may why bishops did not like to refer to them as
opposite numbers. That is, one needs to find direct evidence either that
such clerical corporations *de facto* did participate in synod, or that clerks
were behaving in synod following the wishes of their confraternities.

The types of evidence I wish to present are two. First, Antonio Rigon
has now demonstrated something first suspected by Enrico Peverada: some
synodal constitutions are copied from the statutes of clerical confraternities. Most striking: the Paduan statutes of the brotherhood of parish
rectors of 1285 dealing with the life of the clergy, the defense of their
parochial rights, the celebration of funerals, and so forth, were copied
word for word in the synodal constitutions of 1339 — without their source

---

[85] Trexler, *Synodal Law*, 294–95. On the *procuratores* of the whole clergy, see above,
at n. 66, and further below, where proctors of the Florentine Clergy are called the "head
of the clergy."

[86] P. Dinelli, *Dei sinodi della diocesi di Lucca* (Lucca, 1834), 76.

being recognized, of course.[87] The lesson of this discovery is clear: one influence of early statutes of clerical confraternities has to be sought in so-called "episcopal" constitutions.

Alas, Rigon did not suggest that his discovery indicated that the clergy in the brotherhood and the urban clergy in the synods were one and the same. That does not necessarily follow, of course: synodal statutes were often copied across diocesan lines, which did not mean the clerks were the same. What is needed to further our inquiry is evidence of a complementarity of confraternal and synodal activity.

In this regard, I would reach back to an earlier determination that concerned the difference between a "council" and a "convocation": medieval lawyers, anxious to maintain distinctions, might encourage the calling of what might seem two meetings for two different bodies, but what was in fact one continuing gathering of the same people. In Ferrara, Samaritani found the *conventus* of priests asking the bishop on 11 March 1335 to approve their election of a new leader (archpriest) — no small indication in itself of the role of that city's bishop in a clerical corporation's inner life. But what Peverada realized was that the day on which that election probably took place — 10 March, the first Friday in Lent — was the day on which the diocesan synod was to be held, according to constitutions promulgated only three years earlier. In short, the clerical confraternity had probably acted in, or lateral to, the synod, without saying so in its request to the bishop.[88] Thus a comparison of dates in different confraternities' histories to those of known events in synodal history would be important.

If one asks what would most likely be the quotidian link between such corporations and the bishops, the answer must surely be: the financial officials of the confraternities and those of the *clerus* in synod might be the same. Clerical bodies that distributed taxes and clerical bodies that held properties that could facilitate tax payments must have had the same fiscal officials. Remember that in several areas, these corporations were simply brotherhoods of all the priests, so that they had an irresistible representational quality in synod.

---

[87] Peverada noted that the terminology of the 1461 Roman synodal legislation was similar to the language of the famous *Romana fraternitas*; "Il vescovo Francesco de Lignamine e il sinodo del clero romano del 1461," *Analecta Pomposiana* 4 (1978): 222, n. 133. See now Rigon, "L'associazionismo," 152–62.

[88] Peverada, "Sinodi ferraresi," 144; Samaritani, "Circoscrizioni," 161.

Where would one look for such officials? At Ferrara, they are perhaps to be sought in the officials of the same *conventus presbiterorum* that brought together the urban clergy with cure of souls. Peverada found these officials little different from the syndics and accountants (*massari*) the clergy elected in synod in the early fifteenth century.[89] In other places, I suspect they are to be found among a type of official called *sapienti del clero*. In an *intervento* at the conference where this paper was read, Antonio Rigon noted that at Padua and Vicenza, such officials ended as an overarching financial administration for the whole exempt and non-exempt diocesan clergy.[90] The question is if officials of that name are first to be found in the voluntary associations of some clergies.

Let me summarize. The evidence of corporate solidarity among the clergy in the face of demands from outside is widespread throughout northern Italy by 1300. The more research is done, the stronger that solidarity seems. The documents showing the regular election of proctors and syndics of the clergy, who on the one hand seem to have serviced the financial needs of the bishops, while on the other they obviously were meant to protect the clergy, point to the type of confraternal clergy we believe had often *de facto* acted as "the clergy in synod."

Scholars have long emphasized that a bishop did not have to call a synod to publish his constitutions.[91] Nor was a synod required for any other particular reason than to fulfill the requirements of papal law. Therefore, high and late medieval synods have been generally represented as passive gatherings. But another picture emerges the moment we raise that element of synodal activity — taxation — which was not talked about in polite company, and once we recognize that synods were above all clerical convocations and not merely expressions of episcopal wishes.

Scholars have not recognized that the clergy of certain dioceses came to synod with a corporate, property-holding identity. This is of course not to say that clerical corporations were the legal basis of the clergy in synod. Quite the contrary, in episcopal documentation that clergy is indeed usually assumed to be unincorporated.

Yet students of the Italian cities know just how central confraternities

---

[89] Peverada, "Sinodi ferraresi," 144.

[90] Rigon has promised to publish the fourteenth-century documentation on this institution. For post-Tridentine *sapienti*, who are lawyers and not accountants, see further below.

[91] E.g., recently Trexler, *Synodal Law*, 6.

were to the exercise of power at the communal level. Often, the confraternities were precisely the loci where men bound themselves to vote a certain way in public councils which formally forbade precisely such "conspiracies." It can not have been much different with clerical confraternities in relation to diocesan government. And in general, the bishops must have preferred it that way. Even today, industry often prefers to deal with labor through the latter's trade unions rather than with individual workers. The risk that the clergy would go off on its own had to be run.

Schismatic Synods

The evidence has shown that in Italy as elsewhere, the clergy was an important incorporated body long before the Great Schism. And despite the early-fifteenth century notion that a certain type of clerical gathering — a council of bishops — was more authoritative than the pronouncements of any lord, it cannot be said that the conciliarism of Pisa, Constance, and Basel was responsible for a move from clerical passivity to activity. The incorporated clergy had long guarded its interest. Nor would the period of the Schism be the first when Italian secular lords thought to raise money from the clergy in synod.

Yet it would be foolhardy indeed to deny the obvious: that the history of diocesan synods was affected by the Great Schism. In France and northwestern Europe alone, many a synod gathered to determine no less than that clergy's allegiance to one pope or another.[92] As we shall see, not even the badly researched history of the Italian churches can deny us the insight that it must have been much the same in the peninsula. In what follows, I will concentrate on just two characteristic effects of the Schism on synodal history.

The first effect is that the so-called territorial states of the period of the Schism were able to assemble and to tax ecclesiastical units according to communal or dominion boundaries rather than diocesan ones — in effect redrawing synodal circumscriptions — there being no ecclesiastical authority powerful enough to resist them. In France this was not new: since the time of Philip the Fair, the regional character of clerical assemblies had commonly been made to agree with the needs of the monarchy.[93]

---

[92] For national councils in France to this end, see Valois, *France et le grand schisme*, 1:103–4; 3:27–28, 103, 148–50, 173, 279; an assembly of the Flemish clergy: 1:258; a synod to this end in Liège: 1:274–76; at Metz: 1:285; and at Avignon: 3:319.

[93] F. Lot and R. Fawtier (eds.), *Histoire des institutions françaises au moyen âge*, vol. 3,

But in northern Italy, such evidence has not heretofore been collected or interpreted. We know how secular *signori* resented priests subject to them going out of their lands, even if the lands were within the diocese of the town.[94] But we do not have the literature which would let us watch the same *signori* rearranging the lands of the synod, so to speak: not even for Milan, where because of the prince-signore, geographical rearrangements of dioceses and synodal circumscriptions must have been easy.

But the Florentine evidence can be shown to possess this motif. On 6 or 7 February 1409, for example, the government of Florence according to one chronicler assembled a "grand council" of 120 doctors *from the [secular] dominion of Florence* at the episcopal palace which, after three days, declared Pope Gregory XII to be a heretic and left his obedience.[95] A diarist, on the other hand, put the same news into synodal language. Giovanni di Pagolo Morelli says that the commune ended its obedience to Gregory on 1 February, and that "poi, a dì 6 detto, si fece conciliuzzo in vescovado, dove fu richiesto *tutto il chericato di Firenze, contado e distretto.* E utimamente diterminarono l'ubbidienza si potea levare di buona coscienza."[96] The emphasis upon secular borders is unmistakable. Probably clergy were present whose churches were within the dominion, but who themselves were subject to bishops whose sees were outside the Florentine dominion.

In addition to calling synods or councils to determine or legitimate ecclesiastical obediences, communes in this period readily *taxed* clergies according to state borders and interests rather than diocesan ones. How the communes could use gatherings of the clergy in the pursuit of such fiscal interests will soon be clear. Taxing clergy according to secular borders could avoid the bothersome distinction between the secular and the regular clergy, which complicated taxation when done within a purely ecclesiastical framework. There is some indication that communes pursued strategies to facilitate this type of taxation. For example, communes tried to place their citizens as bishops of surrounding dioceses. Then with the

---

Institutions ecclésiastiques (Paris, 1962), 360; Bisson, *Assemblies and Representation*, passim.

[94] See e.g., a 1533 Gonzaga letter to Bishop Giberti of Verona, protesting "che quelli che habbitano nel mio dominio siano citati fuori di esso": Prosperi, *Tra evangelismo e controriforma*, 208.

[95] *Cronica volgare di anonimo fiorentino dall'anno 1385 a 1409, già attribuita a Piero di Giovanni Minerbetti*, ed. E. Bellondi in *Rerum Italicarum Scriptores* (hereafter *RIS*), n. ed., 27.2 (hereafter Ps.-Minerbetti), 377.

[96] G. Morelli, *Ricordi* (Florence, 1956), 526–27.

assistance of those fellow citizens, a commune might well implement its insistence that it had a right to tax all clergy within its own sovereign borders.[97]

Taxing clergy within secular borders rather than ecclesiastical ones certainly might be useful to the papacies of the Schism. The principle was well established, as we know. In the end, in Strayer's words, Philip the Fair had found it "better ... to get its grants from the pope even if he demanded a share of the proceeds. ..." When pope and king were in accord, he continues, "the French clergy gained no important concessions. ..."[98] That is, at a time when clerical independence was possible because of papal schism, agreements with communes might be apropos.

Did the French king want papal approval to tax his clergy? Clement VII was ready to barter.[99] Did the Florentines wish to erase their enormous debt to the papacy incurred as the result of their war with Gregory XI? Clement was not the only pontiff ready to oblige.[100] In the early fifteenth century, the communes also made it a condition of their support for a particular pontiff that he allow the communes to impose large caritative subsidies on their clergy. The popes responded by permitting the imposts as long as a certain portion fed the small treasuries of the Schism popes.[101]

In those half dozen or so Italian cities that had consolidated their public debt, that financial institution, in some areas in place, be it noted, well before the Schism, furnished another powerful incentive for popes to go along with the process of territorialization. It was less significant that several individual pontiffs of the period of the Schism and councils had important investments in these so-called *monti*, investments made at times by the communes for the pontiffs to render the latter dependent on the former.[102] More important was the fact that communes under pressure for money to fight wars coerced their clergies to invest in the public debt, so that over time, the clergy at all levels was rendered dependent on a secular organization of its investments.

---

[97] For a recent discussion with regard to this question, see R. Bizzocchi, *Chiesa e potere nella Toscana del Quattrocento* (Bologna, 1987), 195–244.

[98] Strayer, *Studies*, 42–43.

[99] Valois, *France*, 1:110.

[100] Ps.-Minerbetti, 46–47, 376.

[101] See in general Favier, *Finances pontificales*.

[102] See e.g., J. Kirshner, "Papa Eugenio IV e il Monte comune," *Archivio storico italiano* 127 (1969): 339–82.

The Great Schism turned these *monti* into papal instruments of combat with their opponents. Pontiffs seeking legitimacy encouraged communes to seize beneficial incomes held by those of other obediences, and in one case at least even licensed a commune to deposit all beneficial incomes from vacancies into consolidated public debts until a rightful pope was defined by a council.[103] The net result of such clerical deposits in communal consolidated public debts was similar to what scholars have long recognized it was for the laity. The clergy *of the dominion* saw its identity in the commune increasingly more than it did in their dioceses.

A detailed knowledge of how these administrative transformations came about in different Italian sees is still beyond our reach, so daunting has the problem of the financial relations of Italian communes with the Schismatic popes proved. Our understanding is further complicated by the fact that the popes after the Schism set about reversing some of the statist innovations of that period.

But some indications that these changes did have long-lasting effects are evident. The durability of the new concordats of the Schism period are well known, as are the new provisions for recycling ecclesiastical wealth back into the secular economy.[104] But these matters are less pertinent to our inquiry than this: well after the Schism and the councils, popes are found imposing a crusading tax on the clergy not of a diocese, but on those "sub dominio et iurisdictione comunis," as in one Florentine example of the mid-1440s.[105] Bishop Antonino Pierozzi was referring to the clergy *of the (secular) dominion* when he refers to his role as an apostolic commissioner "ad imponendum et exigendum *a clero florentino*" in 1454.[106] There is an unmistakable tendency for writers referring to the "Florentine clergy" in this age to mean in fact all clerks within the Florentine state, and not merely those within the diocese.

It need hardly be said that what is outlined above is relevant only for certain types of political and ecclesiastical entities in Italy.[107] Of more concern to me would be a protest that such political and economic struc-

---

[103] ASF, *Prov.*, 105, fols. 232v–33v (12 December 1415).

[104] N. Rodolico, *Stato e Chiesa in Toscana durante la reggenza lorenese (1737–1765)* (Florence, 1972), chap. 5.

[105] C. C. Calzolai, *Frate Antonino Pierozzi dei domenicani arcivescovo di Firenze* (Rome, 1960), 233.

[106] Calzolai, *Frate Antonino Pierozzi*, 216.

[107] For that variety, see D. Hay, *The Church in Italy in the Fifteenth Century* (Cambridge, 1977).

tures as I have sketched above are not really germane to a study of synods. For that would mean my point has been missed. The correct approach to studying synods is *not* to adopt some preordained legal notion of what they are, and not to insist, with Enrico de' Botti, that a synod by definition must be called by a bishop not to raise money, but for *reformatio morum*.[108]

Rather, assembled clergy is our subject. Such clerks came together with particular statutes and classes. The clergy in synod has a certain relation not only to the bishop and the cathedral canons, but also to lay communal faction, which needs to be ascertained. At every step, the assembled clergy has to be inserted into the social, political, and cultural history of which it was a part. As what follows will show, in no instance is historical context more significant than in studying the synods of the period of the Schism and councils.

The Florentine Constitutions of the Clergy

Certainly the most striking document of the synodal tradition of the late middle ages are the so-called *constitutiones synodales cleri florentini*, which I published some years ago.[109] The pending publications of another scholar interested in these constitutions will add to our understanding of their effect, but they will not, alas, resolve any more than did I important questions about their immediate background and date.[110] Lacking that detail, what will be most useful here will be to characterize the constitutions in relation to the synodal traditions and problems we have been studying.

These constitutions represent, in many ways, a logical progression in the history of the synod. In studying Bolognese ecclesiastical institutions after ihe Council of Trent, Paolo Prodi thought he had found a new "rapporto più stretto tra vescovo e clero (almeno per i rapporti giuridici)," which he explained by an allegedly new institution of representation, an *organismo rappresentativo*.[111] As we shall see, such institutions are clearly

---

[108] See above.

[109] Trexler, *Synodal Law*, 349–71.

[110] I am grateful to David Peterson for graciously making the following articles available to me before publication: "Conciliarism, Republicanism and Corporatism: the 1415–1420 Constitution of the Florentine Clergy," *Renaissance Quarterly* 42 (1989): 183–229; see also his still-unpublished "Florence's *universitas cleri* in the Early Fifteenth Century." See also Ristori, "L'arcivescovo Amerigo Corsini," 273–84.

[111] Prodi, *Il cardinale*, 2:157.

found in the Florentine constitutions of a century and a half earlier. Clerical representation was, however, obviously not new in the Quattrocento.

Yet on the other hand, it will also be evident that there are some new
things about this Florentine clerical document, things inexplicable apart
from the Great Schism which inspired them. It is to be hoped that once
other scholars recognize how radical these constitutions can be, they will
be able to identify comparable documents in other diocesan traditions. For
now, even the contemporary label *constitutiones cleri* seems unusual, if not
unheralded: we recall that the *clerus florentinus* had its own statutes and
ordinances as early as 1309.[112] Such comparative work will, in turn, lead
us to a better understanding of how the great tradition of the Councils of
Pisa, Constance, and Basel affected the small tradition of the diocesan
synods.

The 31 rubrics of these *constitutiones cleri florentini*, distinguished there-
in from the *constitutiones episcopales*,[113] were probably written between
1415 and 1420. Their author(s) is unknown: the very identity of the *nos*
who commands (*statuimus*) is not clear. The purpose of this legislation is,
however, not in doubt. On the authority of the clergy itself, the constitutions sanction or newly establish a series of representative standing bodies
for the diocesan clergy as a whole. Gone are the days, it is intimated,
when only the urban clergy made decisions for the clergy of the whole
diocese!

These standing bodies range from the 11 *procuratores cleri florentini*, said
to be the *capi* of the clergy and to meet monthly,[114] through a group of
11 counsellors of the clergy[115] up to a *maior consilium* of 66 meeting
twice a year.[116]

The justification the constitutions give for appointing the *procuratores
cleri florentini* is, surprisingly, that it would be monstrous rather than hu-

---

[112] See above, text at n. 61. Mantese's reference to "statuti del clero urbano" in
Vicenza in 1439 is a misnomer; on inspection, the statutes are actually for cathedral
canons' benefices with cura: Mantese, *Memorie*, 3.1:641–59. Once adopted, the name
"constitutiones sinodales cleri Florentini" was not discarded after the Schism. Archbishop Cosimo Pazzi used it as the title of his re-edition of the basic episcopal constitutions in 1509 (Florence 1508 *stil. flor.*).

[113] Trexler, *Synodal Law*, 365.

[114] Trexler, *Synodal Law*, 349.

[115] Trexler, *Synodal Law*, 350.

[116] Trexler, *Synodal Law*, 360–61; cf. G. Ferri, "La 'Romana fraternitas'," *Archivio
della r. Società romana di storia patria* 26 (1903): 459.

man to be acephalic.[117] So much for the idea that the bishop was head of the clergy! The grand council, in turn, was thought of as equivalent to the clergy itself, as the significant formula *maior consilium sive clerus* clearly shows.[118] And assembled, this grand council was thought equivalent in authority to a synod of the *universitas sive sinodus generalis iamdicte civitatis et diocesis.*[119] It is interesting that the opposition to post-Tridentine bishops' attempts to impose that council's legislation almost always came from the cathedral canons.[120] In this earlier crisis of authority, the officers of the whole synodal clergy, in which the cathedral canons had only 1/11th representation, had stepped to the foreground.

For the de facto purpose of this Florentine clerical superstructure was to defend the clergy against outside forces. To this end, three lawyers, *doctores egregii et in advocationibus periti et experti,* were to be appointed to annual positions to act as legal proctors at law.[121] The potential adversaries were the laws *contra libertatem ecclesiasticam* of the commune,[122] papal taxation,[123] and, if necessary, present and future bishops of Florence.[124] Though the clergy might gather in the episcopal palace,[125] meetings of the grand council were to be called by the clergy not the bishop, although he or his vicar could attend if they wanted to.[126]

There is, however, a certain reticence displayed in the constitutions about meetings of the whole clergy. It may be that this document is evidence that synods actually lost out to a leaner, more responsive representation of the clergy through standing bodies. It can be no accident, for instance, that nowhere in the constitutions is it said that the latter were themselves products of such a general synod. And there is more. Rubric 30

---

[117] Trexler, *Synodal Law*, 349.

[118] Trexler, *Synodal Law*, 354, 363.

[119] Trexler, *Synodal Law*, 361, and 370 for the *universalis et generalis sinodus totius civitatis et diocesis Florentine.*

[120] See Prodi, "Application of the Tridentine Decrees," 226–41; Prosperi, *Tra evangelismo e controriforma;* C. Cairns, *Domenico Bollani, Bishop of Brescia. Devotion to Church and State in the Republic of Venice in the Sixteenth Century* (Nieuwkoop, 1976).

[121] Trexler, *Synodal Law*, 369. Such legal officials are called *sapienti* or *savi del clero* in post-Tridentine Bologna (Prodi, *Il cardinale,* 2:157), and in Brescia (Cairns, *Bollani,* 171).

[122] Trexler, *Synodal Law*, 354.

[123] Trexler, *Synodal Law*, 353.

[124] Trexler, *Synodal Law*, 352–53, 365.

[125] Trexler, *Synodal Law*, 354.

[126] Trexler, *Synodal Law*, 354.

notes that the canon law requires an "episcopal synod" annually, yet noting how much trouble an annual synod was for clergy and laity, this rubric ordered May meetings of the *universalis et generalis sinodus totius civitatis et diocesis florentine* only once every five years, to meet where the proctors of the clergy desired.[127] I suspect this means that the bishop could call an episcopal synod when he liked, but that following these present constitutions, synods of the clergy were to be summoned by its leaders only quinquennially.

Indeed it is precisely the windows of opportunity for representation which the Schism directly or indirectly created that are so interesting. For here in Florence it transpires that in fact, the leaders of the clergy were less ready to assemble synods than was the bishop. In 1427, seeking to override the influence of the clerical officials provided for in their *constitutiones*, Amerigo Corsini appealed over their heads precisely to a synod of the whole clergy. And what was the principle that the archbishop Amerigo Corsini used to justify calling this synod in 1427, whose purpose was to discuss the revision of assessments on benefices? No less than *quod omnes tangit*, a legal principle especially favored in conciliar times.[128] And after the matter had been fully discussed in synod, the bishop again invoked the principle of *quod omnes tangit* to justify the vote of the synod's assembled members.[129]

Thus the radical *constitutiones*, whose long-range impact on the clergy is yet unknown, and possibly minimal, can be explained only in the particular historical context of the Schism and the Councils. First, the clergy had been heavily taxed by both the commune and the papacy, who at times effectively conspired with each other in the manner outlined above, to the detriment of a helpless clergy. Second, as I pointed out in my edition and as Peterson has elaborated upon by analyzing the writings of the canonist and bishop of Florence Francesco Zabarella, this document is unimaginable apart from notions of conciliar authority current in Europe at

---

[127] Trexler, *Synodal Law*, 370–71.

[128] "Finem commode habere non posset nisi quos negotium tangeret consentirent et insuper approbarent": Ristori, "L'arcivescovo Amerigo Corsini," 281.

[129] "Archiepiscopus, auditis consulentibus, ut quod omnes tangebat ab omnibus approbari contingeret, nonnulla de dictis prepositis, ut moris et antique consuetudinis dicti cleri existebat, inter congregatos in sinodo ad fabas nigras et albas, ut sic libere possent votum suum exprimere, proponi et micti fecit ad partitum": Ristori, "L'arcivescovo Amerigo Corsini," 282. Cf. Y. M.-J. Congar, "Quod omnes tangit, ab omnibus tractari et approbari debet," *Revue historique de droit français et étranger* 36 (1958): 210–59.

the time.[130] Finally, Florence's republican character was important. Indeed the writers of these constitutions were so aware of the symmetry between republican office-holding as practiced in this commune, and the *clerus florentinus* as structured in these constitutions, that they "imitated" the Florentine magistrates in having the clerical proctors' office begin on January 1[131] and claimed that the 11 proctors of the clergy had a power and authority over the clergy similar (*ad instar*) to that of the eight lords prior over Florence.[132]

And yet for all that, the constitutions did not spring from the head of Zeus. We met the *procuratores cleri florentini*, whose office is put forward in this document as if unexampled, a century and more before, at least in name. And we have also heard before about the clergy's need to defend itself against its enemies, beginning by a serious participation in fiscal decisions. Radical as they sound, in short, these constitutions will only fall into place once the history of clerical representations in synod, in Tuscany and elsewhere in Italy, is taken seriously.

What was the fate of other Italian urban clergies during the Schism and conciliar period? Did some follow Florence in organizing themselves to resist coordinated taxations by communes and popes? Or was Florence imitating someone else? As far as I can see, questions of this type, which assume that the political and social contexts of synods need to be understood, have scarcely been asked. They need to be.

I have been suggesting a new approach to studying gatherings of the clergy, which may be summed up in the notion that a clergy is a social and political body. Teleological or moralistic notions about how "real" synods *ought* to work should not shape inquiries.[133] First, I have emphasized the importance of financial matters in studying gatherings of the clergy: such matters indeed give synodal participants their common identity. This seems obvious, and yet it has been all but completely neglected by previous scholarship, as if synods were a qualitatively different type of political gathering. Second, the link between synodal groups and clerical

---

[130] Peterson, "Conciliarism."

[131] "Cum secundum legittimas sanctiones magistratuum officia initient in kalendis Ianuarii tanquam anni principio, qui nos eos imitantes in hoc . . .": Trexler, *Synodal Law*, 351.

[132] Trexler, *Synodal Law*, 352.

[133] Such moralisms are obviously not limited to Italian historiography. Hay's *Church in Italy* spends much time judging the "Renaissance church": see for example page 20, for his distinction between "good" and "bad" bishops.

confraternities, to which no one denies a *social* identity, needs close attention. This would include studies of the member lists of the confraternities in relation to their diocesan offices and roles. It would test my hypothesis that to an unrecognized extent, the synodal clergy was organized long before the Great Schism, even if, perhaps only for lack of study, that synodal clergy seems to give strong signs of assuming an independent authority only during that Schism and the conciliar period.

From such focuses a third point derives, and deserves a last consideration: the question of *reformatio morum.* In their introduction, the 1516–1517 provincial constitutions of Florence[134] made the traditional point that the moral state of the metropolis was bad because, due to episcopal absenteeism, no synod had been held in Florence for half a century[135] (this from Giulio de' Medici!). I believe that in fact, there is really no reason at all to assume that this linkage is correct. It might be that the fewer the synods, the better the moral condition of the dioceses in question, not only after, as indicated by Hinschius, but perhaps also before the age of printing.

Just as one municipality thought that good order required priests to leave town the minute a synod was over,[136] so synods might seem problematic from the clerks' point of view as well. That is intimated in the radical constitutions of the Florentine clergy referred to above. The bishop of Florence apologized to his synod in 1427 for burdening them by calling the meeting.[137] We recall Girolamo Aliotti of Arezzo as well praising the episcopal vicar for radically reducing the number of clerks in synod through proxies, implicity because that saved the clergy both time and money.[138]

Not surprising. It was a truism of early modern Europe that the clerical as well as the noble estate feared being summoned to court just as much as they feared the authorities visiting their benefices or fiefs. Thus at the

---

[134] The council ended but did not begin in 1517, as is generally said. A diary entry dated 15 October 1516 says it was scheduled to open the following 18th: *Istorie di Giovanni Cambi, cittadino fiorentino,* in *Delizie degli eruditi toscani,* ed. Ildefonso da San Luigi, 24 vols. (Florence, 1770–1789), 22:102. A. D'Addario's dating of 1519 is fanciful (*Il problema,* 402).

[135] Mansi, *Sacrorum conciliorum,* 35:216, 230.

[136] Early fourteenth-century Bruges: J. Toussaert, *Le sentiment religieux en Flandre à la fin du moyen âge* (Paris, 1963), 556.

[137] Ristori, "L'arcivescovo Amerigo Corsini," 281.

[138] See also Toussaert, *Le sentiment religieux,* 555.

very least, any assertion of a link between the holding of synods and the moral status of either the clergy or laity should be greeted with healthy skepticism.

After all, in 1516 and 1517 the archbishop of Florence who complained about absenteeism was himself absent in Rome when his synod was held, and he left the _reformatio morum_ to his vicar.[139] It is unknown what taxes were raised at the council, and how the clergy defended itself against its prelates. It is certainly unclear that the clergy or laity improved because of the meeting.

---

[139] Mansi, _Sacrorum conciliorum_, 35:215.

A Medieval Census:
The *Liber Divisionis**

IN THE AVIGNON REGISTERS of the Vatican Archive (reg. 204, fols. 429–507) there is preserved a document of distinctive value for historians of the fourteenth century. It is a census ordered by Gregory XI to determine the legal status of the inhabitants of the city of Avignon. The first modern notice of the document was given by Denifle in 1885.[1] Since then, many historians have utilized it, but it remained for Bernard Guillemain in his work *La cour pontificale d'Avignon (1309–1376)* (Paris, 1962) to first exploit some of its manifold possibilities.

One aspect of the *liber* which was long of no apparent difficulty to its examiners has been its date. True, it is not dated specifically, but both external and internal evidence allow the correct date to be determined. In the first place, the title of the document in the original writing is to be read:

Liber divisionis cortesanorum et civium romane curie et civitatis Avinionensis, facte de novo, de mandato Gregorii XI, ad certitudinem curiarum et ne amodo de earum subditis valeat hesitare.

* This essay appeared previously in *Medievalia et Humanistica* 17 (1966): 82–85.
[1] *Archiv für Literatur- und Kirchengeschichte* 1 (1885): 627–30.

In addition, on the first page of the census proper (fol. 429r), in a much later writing, is the somewhat different formulation:

> Liber divisionis cortesanorum et civium existentium in civitate Avinionensi post recessum romane curie, facte de mandato Gregorii XI.

Thereto, at several places within the census, the day and date (minus year) on which the counting took place in the different parishes are given.[2]

Despite and because of these leads, the *liber* has been almost uniformly misdated. It is the purpose of this paper to determine the correct date of the census.

Using the universal calendar, all but one of the several direct chronological indications contained in the census determine that, in the 1370s — Gregory ruled from 1370 to 1378 — the census could have taken place only in 1371 or 1376. Nonetheless, the year 1378 has found general favor among historians.

Besides being chronologically impossible, August to November 1378 is historically improbable. Gregory had died in March of that year. His successor Urban VI, the first Italian pope in three-quarters of a century, was faced almost from the beginning of his reign with a revolt within the college of cardinals, one which soon led to the Great Schism. With the Avignonese cardinals in open revolt against the Roman see and with the election of an Avignonese pope in the offing, a census of inhabitants was most unlikely.

What of 1376 as a date of compilation? It must be discarded upon consideration of the fact that in the *liber*, 252 Florentines (family units) are identified by name or company. All contemporary sources, however, concur that these same Florentines had been driven "like dogs" from the city on 31 March 1376. Is it probable that so many went to the census office in August of 1376?[3]

Another factor negating 1376 are the actual dates on which the census was taken in relation to the activities of Gregory XI at the same time.

---

[2] *Liber:* Sat. 16 Aug. (fol. 443r); Wed. 20 Aug. (fol. 446r); Thur. 21 Aug. (fol. 452v); Thur. 21 Aug. (fol. 458r); Fri. 22 Aug. (fol. 462v); Fri. 22 Aug. (fol. 467r); Sat. 23 Aug. (fol. 469r); Sat. 23 Aug. (fol. 474r); Mon. 25 Aug. (fol. 484r); Tues. 26 Aug. (fol. 487r); Tues. 27 Aug. (fol. 496r). The italicized "7" should in the text doubtless read "sexto" instead of "septo."

[3] No. See my dissertation, *Economic, Political, and Religious Effects of the Papal Interdict on Florence, 1376–1378* (Frankfurt am Main, 1964), 25–45.

When Gregory decided to return to Rome, he ordered on 23 August 1376 that a census be taken *after* his departure.[4] But the greatest part of the counting in our *liber* had already been accomplished by this time. Gregory's order of 23 August certainly could not, in short, have had as a result a census already well underway eleven days before. Besides, according to Gregory's order, it was to take place *post recessum romane curie*. The *liber divisionis* was already nearing completion at the date (not year) of Gregory's departure, 13 September. Clearly, the census which we possess is not the one requested by Gregory in 1376.

The grounds for past error in determining the date lie mainly in the interpretation of the title. In the first place, most writers have used the original formulation of the fourteenth century, which states simply that the *liber* contains a new division of courtiers and citizens ordered by Gregory XI. Then they have read the modern writing, which contains the important addition that the *liber* is of courtiers and citizens residing (*existentium*) in Avignon *after the departure of the curia*, this done also by command of Gregory. The conclusion has been irresistible that the *recessum* spoken of was that of Gregory XI. The departure of the curia referred to in this second formulation was, in fact, that of Urban V in 1367.

Just before Urban departed for Rome in this year, a papal order was published stipulating that all "curiales" who chose to remain on the Rhone would from thenceforth in perpetuity be considered citizens of Avignon, and could no longer designate themselves courtiers. The pope commanded at this date that a census be taken after his departure to determine the number and condition of those who remained.[5] It cannot be determined if this census was actually made between his departure for Rome and his return to Avignon and subsequent death (19 December 1370). We know only that a "new division" was made by his successor.

With the return to Avignon and the election of a new pope, the legal status of the contingent which had stayed doubtlessly developed into a polemic. Legally the matter was clear: according to Urban's ordinance, all who had stayed on the Rhone after 1367 should be citizens in perpetuity. But citizenship was a burden. It meant a different tax category, eligibility for military service or comparable contribution. In addition, the courtier stood under the judicial authority of a papal official, a more attractive status than that of the citizen, who was subject to the communal authorities.

---

[4] B. Guillemain, *La cour pontificale d'Avignon (1309–1376)* (Paris, 1962), 654.

[5] Guillemain, *La cour pontificale*, 653.

And now, most important, the curia was again in Avignon. What possible advantage in citizenship?[6]

One resident, asked if he was a citizen or courtier, told the counter: "de isto remanet dubium, quia audivit dici de bulla pape Urbani; tamen intentio erat et vult esse cortisanus."[7]

The confusion which arose on the return of the curia in 1370 was indeed the reason for the new census, for on the original title page, the census is said to have been taken "ad certitudinem curiarum et ne amodo de earum subditis valeat hesitare."[8]

Certainly these two citations point to 1371. Why would our merchant have "heard of the bull of pope Urban" six or eight years after his death?[9]

The calendar, then, shows that the document could have been written only in 1371 or 1376. Induction shows the latter date to be improbable. Finally, information given in the census on specific persons conclusively sets the date of compilation at 1371.[10]

---

[6] The differences in status are sketched by Guillemain, *La cour pontificale*, 635–42.

[7] *Liber*, fol. 437r.

[8] *Liber*, front cover before fol. 429.

[9] C. Tihon's affirmation of this date in the *Bulletin de l'institut historique belge de Rome* (1922): 184, has remained unnoticed. I thank him for referring me to this note. Part of the documentation given here results from his subsequent assistance.

[10] (1) "Johannes coqus domini Cardinalis Caniglacho" (fol. 431r): this prelate died 20 June 1373: K. Eubel, *Hierarchia Catholica Medii Aevi* (Pavia, 1952), 1:19. (2) "Guillelmus Golgari, coqus dom. Jerolomitani" (fol. 477v): the cardinal of Jerusalem died 27 August 1372: Eubel, *Hierarchia Catholica Medii Aevi*, 1:21. (3) "Christoforus Geri Gazzi, campsor de Florentia" (fol. 470r): this banker in curia died in 1375: K. H. Schäfer, *Die Ausgaben der apostolischen Kammer unter den Päpsten Urban V und Gregor XI* (Paderborn, 1937), 617. (4) "Narduccius Lapi, merciarius de Florentia" (fol. 484v): this man died in 1373: Schäfer, *Ausgaben*, 614; his widow was involved in a lawsuit in Avignon in 1376: *Archivio Segreto Vaticano* (hereafter ASV), *Reg. Avin.* 201, fols. 171v, 172r. (5) The following identified as *de Florentia* fled in March 1376 from Avignon and were on the Arno in February and March 1378: "Johannes Chiari, campsor" (fol. 484v), "Leonardus Clari, campsor" (fol. 485v), "Alamannus Andree Ghetti" (fol. 485r), "Domenicus Johannis, merciarius" (fol. 485v), "Franciscus Chiti" (fol. 494v), "Bartolommeus Jacobi de Adimaris" (fol. 441r); ASF, *Mercanzia*, vol. 1173 (no pagination), 6 February, 13 March 1378 (new style). (6) "Thomasus Monis pro se et societate Albertorum Antiquorum" (fol. 486v): he was the agent in curia for the Alberti Antiqui until 1373, at which time he was replaced by Filippo Marsili, who is *not* in the census. Tommaso does not reappear in the papal records after this date: Schäfer, *Ausgaben*, 481, 484. (7) "Guido de Cavalcantibus pro se et societate Albertorum Novorum" (fol. 486v): this merchant also ceased to represent his company in curia. In later years, its representative was Scolaio dei Spini: Schäfer, *Ausgaben*, 536, 605. (8) "Franciscus Marchi de Prato, Flor. dioc., merciarius, pro se et Toro Berti, eius socio, de Florentia" (fol. 487v): Toro's business relationship with

Such a detailed foundation for the correct date is dictated principally by the critical dates involved: the period of the return to Rome by the two popes. Whether the census was done in 1371 or '76 or '78 is of import, and the erroneous date is so generally accepted and utilized as to require this extensive treatment. Of specific importance to this writer is that the large Florentine contingent recorded in the census was not in fact there after the expulsion order of 31 March 1376. A bare handful remained. Conclusion of an incorrect date has in the case of Guillemain's work negatively affected his interpretation of the decade's events and the demography of Avignon during that period.[11]

One further point is in need of clarification. This concerns just what segment of the population of Avignon was counted. The title of the document would indicate that it was a general census of the inhabitants (*habitantes*) both native and foreign. M. Guillemain rejects this, believing rather that only those were counted who previously had opted for courtiership, and then had stayed in Avignon when the pope went to Rome.[12] To buttress his argument, he states that no family originally of Avignon whose name appears in censuses of citizens made in 1358–1360 is recorded in the census in question.[13]

This writer does not have access to the earlier censuses. And yet Guillemain's estimation of the contents of this list as being of original courtiers may be in need of modification. One learns from his tabulation that there are 139 in the list whose origin is Avignon or its diocese. This is no list of foreign *curiales*.

Guillemain's second point, that only those were counted who had remained in Avignon after the pope's departure, is essentially wrong because of the date of compilation he uses: Gregory went to Rome never to return; Urban did return. As a result of the attendant confusion of legal status, as we have seen, the census was taken in 1371. The confusion made it necessary to count even those who had in fact returned to Rome with Urban in 1367, or had in some way served him there, only to return

---

Datini of Prato ended in 1372: I. Origo, *The Merchant of Prato* (New York, 1957), 104.

[11] For a summary of the massive work of Guillemain, see now C. E. Perrin, "La cour pontificale d'Avignon (1309–1376)," *Revue Historique* 232 (1964): 361–78, especially 374.

[12] Guillemain, *La cour pontificale*, 656.

[13] Guillemain, *La cour pontificale*, 656.

to the Rhone with the pope in 1370. The census abounds with such individuals.[14]

The evidence seems to indicate that the census was meant to include all *habitantes*, that is inhabitants not having the legal status of citizens, whether native or foreign, whether they had left the city or not. One further limitation is necessary: the counting was done less than one year after the curia returned to Avignon, and it is probably safe to say that the totals have little cumulative value. Sizable numbers who had left in 1367–1368 for Rome had not returned, at least at the date of census. It should also be noted that few employees of the curia were counted. Including employees of the cardinals, twelve in this category have come to my attention. Finally, a comparison of this census with the membership lists of the fraternity of Notre-Dame de la Major in Avignon, which were compiled in these years, reveals that several scores of Florentines were enrolled in the confraternity, but were not counted in the census.[15] The incompleteness of the census is so marked, the disinclination of the businessmen of the time to be registered so evident as to limit its value, a value further reduced by the fact of its composition in a period of "transition" of merchants and curia from Rome to Avignon. With these limits in mind, however, historians, and especially Joëlle Rollo-Koster, have continued to find the *liber divisionis* of great value.[16]

---

[14] E.g., among those already mentioned Tommaso di Mone and Guido dei Cavalcanti: see respectively Schäfer, *Ausgaben*, 121, 214, 241, 248, and Y. Renouard, "Le compagnie commerciali fiorentini del Trecento," *Archivio storico italiano* 96 (1938): 60. On Matteo di Metto (fol. 469r) see Schäfer, *Ausgaben*, 213, 245. On "Johannes Jordani, pillicierius de Florentia" see Schäfer, *Ausgaben*, 239ff., 252. A non-Florentine in this category is "Johannes Ravenesi, dioc. Camiensis, coqus dom. nostri pape" (fol. 485r); his presence in Rome is shown by Schäfer, *Ausgaben*, 366.

[15] Particulars on these lists are given by Guillemain, *La cour pontificale*, 596ff.

[16] See her "The People of Curial Avignon: A Critical Edition of the *Liber Divisionis* and the lists of Matriculation of the Confraternity of Notre Dame la Majour," Ph.D. diss., State University of New York at Binghamton, 1992, and, among her articles, "*Mercator florentinensis* and Others: Immigration in Papal Avignon," in *Urban and Rural Communities in the South of France*, ed. K. L. Reyerson and J. Drendel (Leiden, 1998), 73–100.

Rome on the Eve of
the Great Schism[*]

POPE GREGORY XI (1370–1378) had intended from the beginning of his
reign to move the papal court from Avignon to Rome. The most serious
obstacles stood between intention and realization. The majority of the
sacred college was French and antagonistic to the plan. The French king
and his brother, the duke of Anjou, were steadfastly opposed. The security
of the papal possessions on the Rhone was questionable. If Gregory
moved, disorders in Avignon and the surrounding countryside might arise.
Even more disheartening, the Papal States in Italy certainly provided no
secure residence and source of income for the papal court.

Gregory's persistence in the face of such difficulties awes the reader of
his diplomatic correspondence. A strong sense of religious mission com-
bined with the politician's feeling for the realities of power. When in
December of 1375 the cities of the Papal States revolted to the cry of
Libertà! and Rome itself seemed about to follow suit, Gregory, rather than
hesitate, urged on the preparations for his departure. Leaving Avignon in
September 1376, he entered Rome triumphantly on 17 January 1377.
Fifteen months later he was dead, and Rome became the scene of bitter

---

[*] This essay appeared previously in *Speculum* 42 (1967): 489–509.

rivalry between the new Italian pope (Urban VI) and the cardinalate which had elected him. The Great Schism of the church was beginning.

These last fifteen months of Gregory's life have remained clouded in obscurity.[1] The original papal registers are gone, and all that remains are copies of a relatively small number of the pontiff's letters from 1377 and 1378.[2] On the basis of the scant information contained in these letters, the researcher would despair of shedding much light on this short period, important as it is. For certainly the period in Rome immediately prior to the outbreak of the Great Schism is of the highest importance to historical understanding. Luckily, certain individuals involved in the events of 1378 felt the historical significance of this moment. In the collection of depositions made by participants and witnesses to the events of the Schism, main stress was placed on the events after the death of Gregory, but a careful reading uncovers worthwhile amounts of information relating to the last year of the pope's life.[3] Finally, remnants of court hearings in Rome during this same period have survived to cast much light on inner-Roman affairs.[4] Through a combination of these three sources, this paper

---

[1] The sparse literature devoted to Gregory XI has recently been enlarged by A. Pléssier's *Grégoire XI, ramène la Papauté à Rome* (Tulle, 1962). The best estimate of the pope's character is still found in G. Mollat, *The Popes at Avignon* (New York, 1965), 168–71. On the type of court which Gregory brought to Rome, see B. Guillemain, *La cour pontificale d'Avignon (1309–1376)* (Paris, 1962). Research on Gregory's later years has concentrated on the return to Rome, and largely ignored the period after this return; see L. Mirot, *La politique pontificale et la rétour du Sainte-Siège à Rome en 1376* (Paris, 1899); J. Kirsch, *Die Rückkehr der Päpste Urban V und Gregor XI von Avignon nach Rom* (Paderborn, 1898); and finally A. Alessandrini, "Il ritorno dei Papi da Avignone e S. Caterina da Siena," *Archivio della r. Società Romana di Storia Patria* (hereafter *ASRSP*) 56 (1933): 1–131.

[2] L. Mirot and H. Jassemin, eds., *Lettres sécrètes et curiales du Pape Grégoire XI (1370–1378) relatives à la France* (Paris, 1935–1957); G. Mollat, ed., *Lettres sécrètes et curiales du Pape Gregoire XI (1370–1378) interéssant les pays autres que la France* (Paris, 1962–1965).

[3] I have used the sizable number of depositions printed in L. Gayet, *Le grand schisme d'Occident* (Florence–Berlin, 1889) and M. Seidlmayer, *Die Anfänge des grossen abendländischen Schisma* (Münster, 1940).

[4] A small section of the records was edited by G. Palmieri, "Processi contra i Fiorentini in occasione della venuta in Roma di Gregorio XI," *Spicilegio Vaticano* 1 (1890), 33–59. *Archivio Segreto Vaticano* (hereafter *ASV*), *Collectiones*, 433, fols. 152–238 contains the entire extant hearings. On Rome at this period, see M. Antonelli, "La dominazione pontificia nel Patrimonio negli ultimi venti anni del periodo Avignonese," *ASRSP* 30 (1907): 269–332; 31 (1908): 121–68, 315–55; E. Dupré-Theseider, *I papi di Avignone e la questione Romana* (Florence, 1939).

proposes to show more clearly than hitherto the nature of the forces at work in Rome before the outbreak of the Schism.

Running through the history of Rome in the fourteenth century, through the months of Gregory's stay in and around Rome, and of course dominating Roman policy and emotions during the hectic days after Urban VI's election in April 1378, was the anxious concern of the *popolo romano* for a pope and curia domiciled in the Eternal City. The revolt of the cities of the Papal States against the rule of the cardinal-legates in late 1375[5] had put a new weapon into the hands of the Romans. The threat of Roman revolt was a political circumstance of capital importance, not to be ignored by the court in Avignon. Florence, the leading spirit in the revolt of the Italian cities, demanded from December 1375 on that the Romans achieve their liberty by expelling the papal officials. The humanist chancellor Salutati's letter to the Romans of 4 January 1376 provides an example of this pressure at the time of the revolts:

> Deus benignus ... erexit oppressos contra fedissam tyrannidem Gallicorum ... Ob quid, fratres karissimi, cum omnes ad libertatem naturaliter incendantur, vos solum ex debito hereditario quodam jure obligamini ad studia libertatis. ... Quocirca insurgite et vos inclitum Italiae nedum caput, sed totius orbis domitor populus contra tantam tyrannidem, fovete populos, expellite abominationem de Italiae finibus et libertatem cupientes protegite, et si quos vel ignavia, vel iugum fortius duriusve sub servitate continet, excitate. Haec sunt opera merita Romanorum. ... Non illos [curiales] enim nostra utilitas, sed dominandi cupiditas in Italiam evocavit. Nolite decipi in nectares verborum, sed prout diximus, Italiam nostram, quam optimi progenitores vestri universo orbi multa impensa sanguinis praefecerunt, saltem nolite pati barbaris et exteris gentibus subjacere.[6]

The chancellor stressed in this letter the "Italian" nature of the undertaking against the French "tyrants." But he also recognized the peculiar "Roman" interests of the *popolo romano*. They should not be taken in by the pope's decision to come to Rome; their interests would be better

---

[5] For bibliography on this war, I refer the reader to G. Brucker, *Florentine Politics and Society, 1343–1378* (Princeton, 1962), 410f.

[6] Bibliothèque Nationale de Paris, Ms. lat. 1463, fols. 41rv.

guarded by freedom from the papal court than by submisison to it; the coming of the pope would be the end of Roman liberty. Doubtless hard points to sell! To paraphrase a recent English statesman: Some liberty! Some submission! For surely Rome stood to gain immensely in wealth and political influence if the curia returned to the city. One could worry about communal liberties later. The Florentine government was of course aware of the overwhelming desire of the Romans to have the papal court once again within the city, and its subsequent letters to the Romans became ever more insistent:

> Ubi est ille priscus vigor, quo se Romanus populus dignum putabat, dignus et erat hostium contestatione rerum omnium dominator? Cogitate liberationis Italiae gloriam vobis coelesti dispositionibus et consensu omnium hominum reservari ...?[7]

A revolt of the Roman citizenry would have been invaluable to Florentine and League polity. By effectively shutting the door to Gregory's return, it would have paved the way for the allied city-states to consolidate their communal liberty from the papacy and papalist factions. It is not clear whether the Florentines counted on such a revolt of the Romans. In any case, instability in the Eternal City might have served the same purpose, and these letters, overtly propagandistic in nature, had this objective.

Roman policy after the revolt in the Papal States as before attempted to attract the court to the city and keep it there. Letters such as Salutati's were potent instruments in encouraging Gregory's speedy return, but the Romans were not above using threats of their own manufacture to pressure the supreme pontiff. One knowledgeable individual, the *capitano* of the Castel Sant' Angelo in Rome, remembered being sent to the shores of the Tiber in late 1375 to secure possession of the fortress for the church and to dissuade the Romans from the "spiritual scandal" they were preparing. According to Pierre Rostaing, certain circles in the city, with the encouragement of the anti-papal cities to the north, planned to elect an antipope from among the Roman citizenry. Indeed, the "abbot of Cassino" had already agreed to exercise the office if the Roman citizens so desired. Rostaing alleges that he and many other servants of the church urged Gregory to return immediately to avoid such a scandal. According to him, the Roman Cardinal Tebaldeschi, papal legate in the city, thought

---

[7] Paris, Ms. lat. 1463, fol. 42r (letter of 1 February 1376).

it necessary to write the pontiff that if the return was not immediate, "spirituale scandalum ecclesie indubie sentiebat paratum."[8]

Rostaing was not the only one to write about the schismatic plot. Both he and the inquisitor of Aragon, who was in Avignon in the summer of 1376, mention that a Roman embassy had been received by the pope at this time. Besides requesting his return, the ambassadors had made it clear that if he did not do so quickly, "the Romans would provide themselves with a pope who would live in Rome with them."[9]

Taken at face value, these statements are quite striking. Schism was in the air in Rome and Italy long before 1378, when the French cardinals divided the church. But can these accounts be accepted? Both of the authors were anti-Urbanists and consequently anti-Roman when the split in the church became final in 1378.[10] It would have been in their interest to claim that not only had the Romans forced the election of an Italian pope in 1378, but as Rostaing explicitly states: "Before the advent of our Holy Lord Gregory, the desire of the Roman citizenry to possess the papacy existed."[11] The motivation of these two authors may be clear, yet this is no sufficient reason to discredit their story completely. "Even faction exaggerates, rather than invents."[12] Both were present at the events they described. Furthermore, it is not difficult to imagine in the supercharged ethnocentric atmosphere of Italian *libertà* that the idea of schism would be broached: Italian piety and glory in place of Gallic duplicity, rapine, and general barbarism.

---

[8] Gayet, *Le grand Schisme*, 1:156f. (Pièce Justificative, xxiv). The allusion of Rostaing to support for the "scandal" by the rebel cities and Florence ("etiam cum inductione illorum de Italia") cannot be validated through other available sources. Two letters from the Florentine chancery written precisely at this critical juncture lack any hint of support for schism: ASF, *Lettere missive*, 15, fol. 76v (1 August 1376); 17, fols. 55rv (14 August 1376).

[9] The inquisitor Nicholas Eymerich's deposition is found in Gayet, *Le grand Schisme*, 1:118f (P.J., xx); Rostaing refers to the embassy in Gayet, *Le grand Schisme*, 157. The pope himself had sent emissaries to the Romans to reassure them. The Mantuan ambassador to the court notes in a letter of 17 July of this summer: "Demum Franciscus de Ursinis die XI presentis mensis recesit et vadit ad Urbem ad confortandum Romanos et ad intimandum Romanis motum pape . . .": A. Segrè (ed.), "I dispacci di Cristoforo da Piacenza, procuratore mantovano alla corte pontificale," *Archivio Storico Italiano* (hereafter *ASI*), ser. 5, 43 (1909): 92.

[10] Analysis of the reliability of these individuals can be found in Seidlmayer, *Anfänge des grossen abendländischen Schisma*, and in W. Ullman, *Origins of the Great Schism* (London, 1948).

[11] Gayet, *Le grand Schisme*, 1:157.

[12] E. Gibbon, *The Decline and Fall of the Roman Empire*, chap. IV, n. 1.

There was certainly a deep antipathy felt from both sides. One might question the sincerity of the Florentine chancery's chauvinism, but there is no doubting the patent dislike of Rostaing (though Italian born) for the Italians, nor the disdain of Italian chroniclers of all things French. In the coming months, even the pope will not be above asking his Breton mercenaries where their pride of race is.[13] "Gentes de ecclesia" will appear as synonymous with "ultramontani" in papal records.[14] Indeed the word Ghibelline will be used in the papal courts to mean *supporter* of the heavily French papal court.[15] Threat of schism rooted in deep-seated chauvinism loomed ominously on the Roman horizon well before an Italian pope and a French cardinalate bitterly attacked each other at the beginning of the Great Schism. When the pope touched Italian soil at Corneto in December 1376, he and his compatriots were entering a hostile country.

Florence and the League cities did their utmost to disrupt the pope's return. On the home front, they initiated the systematic seizure of church properties.[16] On the military front, influential Florentine counsellors urged that "the war be carried whereever the pope be . . . ," that is, into the Patrimony.[17] But sending troops of the League into Roman territories would have created a delicate situation for Florentine diplomacy, which could not afford to alienate the Romans. In the first place, even though the Romans would not revolt, it was in the interest of the Florentines to maintain tension in the city between papal court and *Campidoglio*. Driving the Romans into the hands of the curia in order to protect their lands would compromise any possibility Florence had of influencing Roman politics in the future.[18] There was a second consideration: as a result of Florentine leadership of the revolt in the States of the Church, the pope had interdicted wherever the Florentines resided, in any city of Christendom. Rome had been slow in publishing the papal strictures against the Tuscans and never made more than a half-hearted attempt to drive the

---

[13] "Ubi fides, ubi nobilitas, ubi devotio Gallicorum . . .": Paris, Ms. lat. 4128, p. 334 (letter of 31 August 1377).

[14] ASV, *Collectiones* 488, fol. 166r.

[15] ASV, *Collectiones* 488, fol. 210r.

[16] R. Trexler, *Economic, Political, and Religious Effects of the Papal Interdict on Florence, 1376–1378* (Frankfurt am Main, 1964), 118f.

[17] ASF, *Consulte e Pratiche*, xiv, fol. 89; cf. also fol. 94r for like sentiments.

[18] "Super equitando territorium Romanorum, est periculosum, provocando Romanos et reprehensibile pro persona pape, qui est vicarius Christi": ASF, *Consulte e Pratiche*, fol. 138r, cited in Brucker, *Florentine Politics*, 312.

Florentine merchants and artisans from the city.[19] Since it was essential for the Signoria of Florence to retain as many Florentines in the city as possible for spying and agitating, Roman goodwill had to be retained.

The decision was taken to limit as much as possible the operation of League mercenaries in the Patrimony. An ambassador was dispatched to the Roman authorities in November, assuring them that in the future, the northern cities would try to restrain their soldiery.[20] For the rest, the Signoria deplored the Romans' unwillingness to "seize their liberty" before Gregory entered the city. In a letter of Christmas Day 1376, chancellor Salutati warned the *banderesi*, or citizen militia, not to disband, as the pope was demanding as part of the treaty which was to regulate the relationship of city and court. For what reason does he demand this, asked Salutati, if not to "extirpate the central point of Roman liberty."

> While it is possible, while there is still time, while the oppressor of your domestic liberty is not yet served within your walls, we pray you, Roman citizenry, who have your salvation in your hands, to consult your liberty. Even if we are forced to follow, we are ready to lend all our power for your liberty as if it were for our own liberty and health. We are aware that once your citizenry comes under the yoke, although it would seem soft at first, it would be difficult to escape.[21]

The chancellor's words were not completely wasted, for the *banderesi* continued to function, the guardians of city interests and the cautious observers of curial action.

All sources agree that the reception of Gregory XI into the Eternal City on 17 January 1377 was festive. A new era had opened for Rome, so many thought. But a closer look shows that anxiety for the future mingled with the cries of *viva il papa!* The grounds for this apprehension may be summed up as follows: the war; the animosity between Roman *popolo* and

---

[19] See Trexler, *Effects of the Papal Interdict*, 87–98.

[20] *Archivio di Stato, Siena* (hereafter *ASS*), *Concistoro*, reg. 1789, n. 24, a letter of 7 November from the Sienese ambassador to Florence, detailing the embassy. A Florentine diarist states that the messenger, Jacopo Folchi, did not complete the embassy due to inability to gain safe-conduct: *Diario d'Anonimo fiorentino*, ed. A. Gherardi, in *Cronache dei secoli XIII e XIV, Documenti di Storia Italiana* 6 (Florence, 1876), 325 (entry of 26 November 1376).

[21] *Lini Coluci Pieri Salutati Epistolae*, ed. J. Rigaccio (Florence, 1742), 1:58f.

Roman territorial nobility; the ties of several of these powerful nobles with the papal court; the French nationality of the pope, the majority of the cardinalate, and most of his military lieutenants; and behind it all, anxiety to hold a pope.

To speak of the "military operations" of this period would be overstatement. Rome and many other cities of Italy were faced with often uncontrolled and always unpredictable bands of mercenaries roaming the northern half of the peninsula more eager for plunder and subsidies than for battle. Of the several groups of foreign soldiers, two should be identified: one a large army of Bretons, the other a mixed group both indigenous and foreign under the English captain John Hawkwood. The first of these groups had been sent into Italy by the pope in May 1376 to regain the cities lost to the church through revolt. The other was also more or less committed to papal subsidies. The inability to retain and control both, but especially the Bretons, was one of the signal failures of papal policy. These "barbarians" weakened the moral as well as the military position of the papacy by such acts as the terrible sack of the city of Cesena in February 1377. "No one wants to believe any more" is a mild example from the chronicles of the feelings of many. "Papa Guastamondo," so one spoke of the pope in these early months of 1377.[22]

The Roman *popolo* shuddered with the rest of Italy at the inability of the pope to control these troops. But what if the pope did succeed in successfully directing their activities? Was it not possible that he might direct them against the popular government of the city itself? It seemed logical to many Romans that a French pope would gladly use French (Breton) mercenaries to crush the communal government of Rome, that speck of popular sovereignty marring a clean slate of papal control.

Popular government gave rise to other dangers. The Romans feared that the territorial nobility around Rome would utilize the papacy to seize power for itself. Noble families such as the di Vico, Colonna, Orsini, and Gaetani were, in the minds of the *cittadini*, natural allies of the papacy.[23] Roman *popolo* policy had to prevent any group of nobles from making all too closed a front with the curia.

The announcement that Gregory and his court planned to spend the long summer months of 1377 at Anagni caused great uneasiness in the city. Once

---

[22] Trexler, *Effects of the Papal Interdict*, 137.

[23] Mollat traces this turmoil between *popolani* and nobles in *The Popes at Avignon*, 125–33, 146–60.

removed from the surveillance of Roman eyes, the pope could prepare a
variety of military adventures against the city. All the worse, once Gregory
had left the city he might decide to remain away, or even take the
extreme step of returning to Avignon. The city well remembered that
Urban V, scarcely returned to Rome in 1367, came to prefer the Patrimony as a safer residence; it was from his residence in Viterbo that he had
then returned to Avignon. Ambassadors had been sent, there had been
pleading, but the earlier pope had "escaped." Was this to be repeated?[24]

And what if the pope were to die away from the city? There would be
no way to prevent the French cardinals, "questi ladri limosini," from
electing another French pope or themselves removing the curia back to
Avignon. The Romans certainly had wider ends than keeping the pope;
Gregory's frail health meant that the citizens looked forward from the
moment he reached Italy to *making* one, and that "romano, o almeno
Italiano."

The Mantuan ambassador in Rome wrote in late April 1377:

> Nam credo quod die octava mensis junii [dominus noster] ibit Ad-
> naniam et ibi stabit usque ad medium mensem septembris. Aliqui
> dicunt quod curia remanebit in Urbe.[25]

To the uncertainty of papal plans is added the inexactness of the ambassador's words. Are we to understand that some thought the pope, but not
the curia, would go to Anagni? By any interpretation, one point is clear
from another source: the Romans sought absolute guarantees that Gregory
would return. There were doubts that the Romans would let him leave the
city at all. Indeed, "permission" was only granted, says the inquisitor
Eymerich, when the pontiff placed himself in the power and hands of the
Romans and promised them that he would promptly and infallibly return
at the end of the summer.[26] The sources make no mention of material

---

[24] Mollat, *The Popes at Avignon*, 158ff.

[25] Segrè, "Dispacci," *ASI* 44 (1909): 261.

[26] "Postquam autem D. Gregorius papa Romam ivisset, ibique hyemasset et estivare
propter aeris intemperiem extra Romam in civitate Anagnie cum DD. cardinalium collegio decrevisset, dubitatum multum extitit et a multis ultramontanis, et deponens ipse
dubitantium unus fuit, quod romani non permitterent Urbem exire antefactum D. N. papam, nec, ut dicebatur, tunc utique permisissent, nisi quia idem D. Gregorius posuit personam suam in posse et manibus romanorum, certificando et promittendo eis, quod illa
estate transacta, ad Urbem infallibiliter et protinus remearet": Gayet, *Le grand schisme*,
1:119.

guarantees, though one may suspect that the wealth stored within the Castel Sant'Angelo formed such surety.

Gregory left for Anagni on schedule. We find the papal chancery publishing from that town 12 July. In the months that followed, the pope busied himself with extensive peace negotiations with the Florentines and other League diplomats.[27] At the same time he tried to marshal the Breton mercenaries for an assault on the city of Florence itself. By this means he hoped to force his chief antagonist to bargain for peace at a high price.[28] But events displayed the weakness of his position. John Hawkwood had recently deserted the papacy to serve the League. Now all the more reliant on the Bretons, Gregory found himself the less capable of utilizing their arms. Writing to one of his agents on 24 July, the pope was sure of a resounding success since, as he said, the city of Florence contained "few if any troops."[29] One month later, the failure of his plan was clear. The Bretons had defected.[30] Worse, they were looting and burning cities loyal to the church, making even the movements of the curia hazardous. To round off the disaster, the delicate deliberations with the Florentines had collapsed. Gregory was convinced that Florentine money had been at work in corrupting the Bretons. He wrote to Charles V suggesting that the Breton terror in the Patrimony was the turning point in the negotiations: the Florentines, he intimated, saw no reason to make peace with an enemy so destitute in its own bailiwick.[31]

"We see no remedy, if not the miraculous intervention of God."[32] In Gregory's own words we find the tone of depression which marks the last seven months of his reign. The only apparent way to control the mercenaries was to rehire them, and the absurdity of this move did not escape

---

[27] Most of the scanty information on these negotiations is found in Brucker, _Florentine Politics_, 327–31.

[28] "Per quam sperabamus aut totaliter triumphare aut ad pacem nobis honorabilem devenire . . .": Paris, Ms. lat. 4128, p. 385 (undated letter to Charles V of ca. 8 October).

[29] Paris, Ms. lat. 4128, p. 317 (letter of 24 August). See also Mirot, _Lettres_, no. 2036 (letter of 25 July).

[30] Paris, Ms. lat. 4128, p. 317. See also Mirot, _Lettres_, nos. 2048, 2049, 2050, 2056, 2060.

[31] Paris, Ms. lat. 4128, pp. 385–90 contains the above information (letter to Charles V). Much the same information is contained in a letter to the duke of Anjou of 12 October: Mirot, _Lettres_, no. 2060.

[32] Paris, Ms. lat. 4128, pp. 385–90.

him. Nor did the reengagement of the Bretons bring peace to the Patrimony. On 5 September they were ravaging the countryside just fourteen
miles from Rome itself.[33]

Under these conditions, it is not surprising to find murmuring in the
Eternal City. Was it not true, asked the Romans, that the mercenaries
who were threatening Rome and its territory were in the hire of the pope?
Was it not possible, they conjectured, that this destruction was at the
pope's bidding? Cardinal Lagier, sent to the city in September to advise
the pope on conditions there, wrote in the most pessimistic terms. The
Romans were incensed, he reported, at the depredations of the Bretons.
There was even talk of the pope and cardinals being killed. The cardinal
advised Gregory not to come to Rome until the Bretons had left the Patrimony.[34] Scarcely nine months in Italy and the Supreme Pontiff found
his life in danger.

Gregory is said at this point to have wanted to return to Avignon,[35]
certainly an understandable reaction to this series of disasters. Another
source states that the pope considered some move other than a return to
Rome. He allegedly made inquiries as to a suitable winter residence for
himself and the curia.[36] Whatever the truth of these stories, they should
be recorded, since they certainly circulated in Rome in the early fall.

Watchful Romans perceived in October a grave new threat to domestic
tranquility. Gregory was entering into peace negotiations with an avowed
enemy of the Roman *popolo*, Francesco di Vico. Vico had been the most
prominent Roman territorial noble to join the Florentine League in late
1375. Throughout the following two years his troops had often committed
depredations in Roman territory. Peace with Vico was unpalatable and,
some thought, dangerous to the *popolo*, which had struggled with the fami-

---

[33] ASS, *Concistoro*, reg. 1792, no. 6 (letter of Sienese ambassador in Rome of 6
September).

[34] Cardinal Lagier says he wrote the pope: "quod quia Britones transibant per terram
Romanam aliqua dampna dantes, quod erat murmur, quod papa et cardinales occideren-
tur, et quod non veniret, nisi Britones essent extra patrimonium": Seidlmayer, *Anfänge
des grossen abendländischen Schisma*, 328f.

[35] "Et tunc papa voluit redire Avinionem": Seidlmayer, *Anfänge des grossen abendländischen Schisma*, 328f. The deposition of Lagier was written in 1380. Another witness
in Rome spoke of the pope's intention to return to Avignon: Gayet, *Le grand Schisme*,
1:67 (P.J. xviii, deposition of Tommaso Ammannati of Pistoia, later cardinal of Naples).

[36] The Aragonese inquisitor mentions this: Gayet, *Le grand Schisme*, 1:119.

ly Di Vico for decades.[37] Once at peace with the papacy, Vico could use his arms to crush the liberty of the city.

But there is no evidence that the pontiff had any other reason for making peace with Vico than to partially pacify the Patrimony. Negotiations between pope and noble were ultimately successful, and on 30 October the parties agreed to peace, subject to the treaty's approval by the *popolo romano*, a necessary cosignatory.[38]

Gregory himself carried the tentative treaty to Rome when, after long hesitation, he left his summer residence and returned to the Eternal City on 7 November. The Mantuan ambassador was there, and speaks of the pope being received "gratanter et cum maximo honore."[39] The mood in fact was more somber, and even the ambassador's words have a stiff and formal ring. Florentine eyewitnesses sized up the atmosphere:

Quod Britones non erant concordis cum domino nostro papa, et quod populus romanus stabat male cum dicto domino nostro propter pacem fiendam cum prefecto.[40]

The pope brought an unwanted peace, but more important, he brought himself. The Romans whispered that they owed his return only to his failure to find a winter residence outside the city. No wonder that with these suspicions, many Romans agreed then and there that Gregory must at no time, summer or otherwise, be allowed to leave the city.[41]

The avid desire of the Romans to control the movements of the curia has been a main theme of the inquiry to this point. As has already been mentioned, there are basic questions to be raised as to the veracity of certain witnesses to these events. To repeat, it was in the interest of anti-Urbanists in 1379 and 1380 to paint the Romans of 1377–1378 in the darkest colors. We may doubt isolated points: did the pope really express

---

[37] On Giovanni di Vico, see Mollat, *The Popes at Avignon*, 131ff.

[38] F. Gregorovius, *Geschichte der Stadt Rom im Mittelalter* (Stuttgart, 1912), 6:476f.

[39] Segrè, "Dispacci," *ASI* 44 (1909): 262.

[40] "Prefect" was an honorary title held by the di Vico": ASV, *Collectiones*, 433, fol. 235r. Cristoforo da Piacenza states in a letter of November that "Romani potius contentantur de guerra, quam de pace cum prefeto, papa totius oppositus. . . ." Indeed they at this very time appointed as their captain Count Petro de Anquilarra, "qui diti prefeti est antiquus inimicus": Segrè, "Dispacci," *ASI* 44 (1909): 263f. Peace with Vico was not "perfeta" until 7 December: Segrè, "Dispacci," *ASI* 44 (1909): 267 (letter of 31 December).

[41] "Quod non permitterent papam Urbem exire deinceps etiam in estate": Gayet, *Le grand Schisme*, 1:119 (deposition of Eymerich).

a desire to return to Avignon? Had the Romans allowed him to go to Anagni only under oath and then decided upon his return never again to allow it? By citations of papal letters and reports of witnesses writing at the time, it has been shown that the music was there, if indeed the words sometimes failed. There is a strong case for asserting that while what the Romans permitted may be in question, they were in fact the permitting party. Roman determination to retain the papacy made Gregory's *de jure* signory over the city far less than effective.

At this point, however, the historian is able to pierce the cloudy atmosphere of apprehension in the city and describe quite clearly certain of the plans and goals of some of the influential *popolani*. The source for this inside look is a series of depositions given before Roman civil courts by various Florentines seized in the Eternal City in December 1377. The hearings were held the following month.[42]

What were Florentines doing in Rome in late 1377? It will be remembered that Florentine interests dictated the retention of spies in the city, and that the Romans had shown little interest in fully expelling them. True, the papal interdict against their habitation had been published in August 1376, but many stayed.[43] The series of documents referred to shows that in December 1377 there were in Rome over thirty individuals originating from the dioceses of Florence and Fiesole. Cover for their presence was provided in three ways: some had become Roman citizens,[44] others circulated with safe-conducts,[45] while still others seem to have paid protection money to the Capitol itself.[46] Many, perhaps most of these individuals, simply stayed in the city to preserve the only existence their mature lives had known. Others were in the city for political reasons, and it is with this aspect of their presence that we have to do.

This is, however, to state the case too simply. Niccolò di Lippo, for example, had been established in Rome for twenty-five years. Not only did he have Roman citizenship papers, he was also was in the top echelons of

---

[42] For archival references, see above, n. 5.

[43] Trexler, *Effects of the Papal Interdict*, 88, 93.

[44] The case of Niccolò di Lippo may serve as an example: ASV, *Collectiones*, 433, fol. 204r.

[45] E.g., Guccio Albizzi: ASV, *Collectiones*, 433, fols. 210rv. Another case is that of Buonaccorso Pitti: *Cronica di Buonaccorso Pitti*, ed. A. Bacchi della Lega (Bologna, 1905), 42f.

[46] Examples: ASV, *Collectiones*, 433, fols. 221r, 226r.

the merchant class of the city. And it was to this side of his activity that he alluded when he was questioned in January.[47] But his political activity came into the open soon enough. Niccolò was, in fact, in constant touch with the Florentine government, "explorandam et significandam Florentie diversis vicibus."[48] With his contacts in merchandising, Niccolò was in an excellent position for such work. And there is evidence that his and other knowledgeable Florentines' advice to the Eight of War in Florence was seriously weighed. According to our prime informer on these political activities, many letters were sent to the Eight of War in Florence urging this group to write to the Capitol. They should warn the Romans that unless they could arrive at a scheme to bring about peace between Florence and the pope, Florence would consider the Romans enemies and would send its forces into Roman territory, indeed, all the way to Rome.[49] For previously stated reasons, the Florentine chancery could not and did not write such an ultimatum; but such advice helps the reader of Salutati's letters to understand the serious undertones of these rhetorical showpieces.

The *concittadini* in Rome were used for much more than information. The evidence makes clear that, at least from the spring of 1377, sizable sums of money were being sent to these individuals to be distributed among Romans they thought sympathetic or corruptible. The aim of these activities was to bring about a revolt in the city against the papal regime. This goal was pursued in two ways:

> Omnes florentini qui sunt vel erant tunc Rome dicebant tam per plateas quam per tabernas et alia loca omnia mala que cognare poterant Romanis contra dominum nostrum papam et statum ecclesie ad finem quod inflammarent populum Romanum contra dictum dominum nostrum et ecclesiam predictam.[50]

Verbal subversion was thus the first method. But it was in itself obviously insufficient. The purpose of these stirrings was to prime the Romans' distrust of the curia for successful exploitation when the time for organized

---

[47] Niccolò's business activities are examined in Trexler, *Effects of the Papal Interdict*, 88ff.

[48] ASV, *Collectiones*, 433, fol. 234v. Unless otherwise stated, information on Florentine political activities in the city was obtained from a confession of one Bartolommeo Folchi, a Florentine born in Lastra near Florence. The deposition was given 27 January 1378; ASV, *Collectiones*, 433, fols. 234r–238r.

[49] ASV, *Collectiones*, 433, fol. 234r.

[50] ASV, *Collectiones*, 433, fol. 234r.

revolt came. The second aim of Florentine activity in the city was to bring such a plot into being, and it was here that most of the money was used.

Who were the Romans approached by the Florentines? What was the consideration paid them? For what purpose were they paid? We can first distinguish *popolani* within the city paid to "talk against the pope," if possible bring about a revolt from within, and if not to prepare the citizenry to rise when the call to arms was carried into the city from without. Seven Roman *popolani* were named by our informer as having received money. The highest priced conspirator was one Ser Johannes de Cessis, who received two hundred florins, while the six others received a total of five hundred florins.[51] Five other *popolani* were named as co-conspirators, but apparently received no payment.[52] All of the plotters were, however, to receive a sizable sum if and when a revolt took place in the city. Three hundred florins each were to be paid to all but two: Renzolus Seronis was to receive five hundred florins, "Dominus Johannes de Sessis" was to obtain the large sum of two thousand florins.[53]

In his many letters to the Roman Capitol, the Florentine chancellor consistently invoked the *libertà* of the citizens of Rome. One might think this a call for the popular forces of the city to rise, and the Signoria of Florence had nothing against such an interpretation or such an uprising. Florence was by no means, however, a champion of government by the *popolo*. In the Papal States its goal had been the expulsion of papal governments; in Rome, expulsion of the curia itself was its goal. While popular government (liberty) remained its propaganda line, it showed no hesitation in aligning itself with the territorial nobility around Rome in order to bring about revolt in the city.

---

[51] Simon "Zigii," Antonius Bellihominis, Renzolus Seronis, and Tucius Tamarochi received 100 florins each; Colla "Batat" and Colla Grifi received 50 florins each: ASV, *Collectiones*, 433, fol. 236v.

[52] The source mentions none; their names are Stephanus Cavadoro, Matteus the butcher, one Nicholas Griffoli, and two spicers, Martinus and Narduccius: ASV, *Collectiones*, 433, fol. 235r.

[53] ASV, *Collectiones*, 433, fol. 235r. This must have been an important personage to have warranted such a bribe, and yet I have been unable to ascertain his identity. Dominus or ser Johannes "de Sessis, de Cessis, Chessis," as his name is variously written, may be one "Johannes Cessi de Capucinis de Urbe, canonicus ecclesie Lateranensis": cf. Mirot, *Lettres*, nos. 1030, 1031. An attractive but unfounded assumption would be to identify him with Giovanni Cenci, and to identify "Narduccius spetiator" with "Nardus spetiator" (cf. note 52). Cenci was captain-general and chancellor of the popular government, Nardo leader of the *banderesi*. Both were key leaders of the *popolo* in the disturbances after Gregory's death.

Who were the nobles successfully approached by the Florentines? The key figure was Buccio di Giordano Orsini, lord of Narni. His role is succinctly stated by the Florentine informer:

Et tractatus erat talis quod dominus Johannes Agut debebat equitare prope Romam et tunc isti supradicti [the urban plotters] debebant incipere rumorem contra forensses et ita cito quod Johannes appropinquasset Romam Buccius Jordani debebat intrare Romam et incipere rumorem unus cum prenominatis tam florentinis quam aliis.[54]

That such a coup might have meant the substitution of noble for papal rule in the city was of little concern to the Florentines. Indeed, they courted not only certain of the Orsini, but also Petruccio Colonna, ruler of Palestrina. One thousand florins were given him for his adherence to Florentine forces at this time.[55]

The complicated negotiations in this plot were carried out by six Florentines active in Rome and its environs.[56] It was at all times a risky business. At first the money used in these dealings was held in the bank of Marco di Matteo of Siena. But when in April (?) of 1377 whispers of an anti-curial conspiracy were first heard in the city, the *campsor* Marco fled the city, the money being handed over to the Florentine Niccolò di Lippo.[57] This merchant then distributed these monies among the plotters under cover of an elaborate series of letters of exchange and pawns of an ostensible business nature.[58]

---

[54] "Johannes Agut" is the English captain John Hawkwood: ASV, *Collectiones*, 433, fol. 235v.

[55] One of the agents "tractabat et tractarit cum Petrucio de Columna qui tenebat Penistruam, ut ipse Petrucius intraret ligam. ... Et dictus Petrucius in dicto tractatu petebat quod haberet primo quod intrare in dicta liga pro fortifficando Penestrinam et alias terras suas ac pro munitionibus per eum fiendis 10,000 fl. Tamen habuit per manus dicti Gregorii Ferantini et Chatalini de Infangatis de Florentia, familiari dicti Petrucii, nomine dicte comitatis ... M fl.": ASV, *Collectiones*, 433, fol. 237r. Other nobles approached, but rejecting the overtures, were Giordano de Marino Orsini and Luca Savelli: ASV, *Collectiones*, 433, fol. 238r.

[56] Niccolò di Lippo received a salary of 25 florins per month; Piero Conradi and Gregorio Ferrantini and the subsequent informer Bartolommeo Folchi 20 florins per month; the informer did not know the salary of Guccio Albizzi, while any wage paid to Brunetto Brandini goes unmentioned: ASV, *Collectiones*, 433, ff. 236r, 238r.

[57] ASV, *Collectiones*, 433, fols. 234rv.

[58] The money promised in the event of an actual revolt was to be on deposit (*poni ad cambium*) at the Roman banks of Andrea Tici of Pistoia and Bartolommeo Tignosso

Coordination of the plot in the area of the Patrimony was accom-plished by the Florentine Guccio Albizzi, who for months was in a par-ticularly strategic position for his undercover work: he was in the service of Gomez Albornoz, senator of Rome and one of the pope's chief military leaders![59]

Coordination with Florence itself was of course all-important. At the end of October 1377, the situation on the Tiber seemed urgent enough to send one of the Florentines to the banks of the Arno. The man selected was Bartolommeo Folchi di Lastra. Leaving Rome on 26 October, he brought to the war commissioners in Florence an assessment of the Roman situation at that time, as compiled by Niccolò di Lippo, Gregorio Ferran-tini, Brunetto Brandini, and Piero di Conrado. Conditions were ripe for execution of the plan, they wrote. The Bretons were at odds with the pope, as were the Romans, who murmured against his peace attempts with Francesco di Vico. When Bartolommeo went to Florence, the pontiff was still at Anagni, and the emissary urged the Eight of War to send John Hawk-wood into the Patrimony and to the city of Rome to incite a revolt.[60]

Bartolommeo returned to Rome without the prospect of an immediate uprising. The Eight had advised him that Hawkwood had decided to go into winter quarters. The military maneuver would have to be put off until the spring, when the mercenary troops would move south to bring the plot to fruition. The Florentine government warned, however, against letting the threads of the conspiracy loose:

Non obstante predicta ambaxiata deberet loqui omnibus preno-minatis tam Romanis quam aliis Florentinis nominatis ut ipsi bene vellent stare attenti nec ipsos vellet cedere ad expectandum se-

---

of Pisa: ASV, *Collectiones*, 433, fol. 238r. The story Niccolò told the tribunal on 2 January, before the Florentines stood accused by the public confession of Bartolommeo on 28 January, was that his financial dealings had been concerned with dissolving his business interests for fear of papal reprisals. Account had to be made for the possession of incriminating letters and goods by such as Simone di Egidio and Antonio Belliuomini, who, as we have seen (cf. above, n. 52), were involved in the conspiracy: ASV, *Collec-tiones*, 433, fols. 203r–204r. Some of the leading merchants in Rome were compromised in this affair. Niccolò had "sold" his holdings to the Romans Cecco Serragone, Cola di Paolo, Cecco di Luca, and Guillelmo dei Rubeis: ASV, *Collectiones*, 433, fol. 203r. All four were important members of the merchants' organization. The first three had been or were consuls of that organization: *Statuti dei Mercanti di Roma*, ed. G. Gatti (Rome, 1887), 99, 104.

[59] ASV, *Collectiones*, 433, fol. 234r.
[60] ASV, *Collectiones*, 433, fol. 235v.

cundum ordinem datum et quod eis bene attendentur omnia pro-
missa nec dubitent.[61]

Nor did the plot collapse. It was too crucial to Florence. In the Arno
city itself factional warfare was leading towards revolt, and peace with the
papacy had become a prime necessity.[62] Gregory had to be forced to the
bargaining table by Roman revolt. The ambassador Bartolommeo told a
papal court in January, in fully revealing the plot, that "... tota spes florentinorum erat in istis de Urssinis videlicet pro parte Bucii ..."[63] and
again that "... tota spes dictorum florentinorum erat et ad huc est quod
iste tractatus videlicet quod rumor fiat in Roma et ellevetur contra statum
domini nostri papae."[64]

If we add the information given by the informer Bartolommeo to that
already cited of the Mantuan ambassador and other witnesses to the return
of Gregory in November 1377, we possess a fairly well-defined picture of
Rome at this time: suspicion of papal duplicity on one side, fear of Roman
revolt and intrigues on the other; determination to retain the power of the
Capitol on one side, an equal awareness in the curia that the Capitol tolerated the presence of Florentines in the city,[65] enemies whose object
was the subversion of papal rule.

The last four months in the life of Gregory XI were to be no quieter
than the previous eleven. Far from being a calm before the storm of
Urban's election, they were filled with a turbulence even the sparseness of
the sources cannot disguise. Early in December, a Florentine recently
arrived in the Eternal City was seized by Roman authorities and incar-
cerated in the Castel Sant'Angelo. The news of his arrest reached the
Arno on the tenth,[66] and on the following day another messenger left

---

[61] ASV, *Collectiones*, 433, fols. 235v, 237v.

[62] On the turmoil and peace feeling in Florence at this time, see Brucker, *Florentine
Politics*, 310–35.

[63] ASV, *Collectiones*, 433, fol. 235v.

[64] ASV, *Collectiones*, 433, fol. 237v.

[65] Examples of Florentines paying money to the Capitol are cited above, n. 46.

[66] Considering what we know of Florentine political activity in Rome, the story
which circulated on the Arno may appear quaint. The anonymous diarist heard that a
relative of Vieri di Cambio Medici "era ito a Roma, perche doveva avere dal Cardinale
[of Marmoutier] fiorini 500 d'oro. Onde il Cardinale disse a quel giovani: Va 'in cotale
luogo per essi; e 'l Cardinale il fecie appostare e pigliare, e fu preso in sul Ponte di S.
Piero i' Roma. Ed annogli posto di taglia XII milia fiorini d'oro, e annolo i Brettoni. Ora
vedete chi e' sono questi ischericati ladri": *Diario d'Anonimo*, 345.

Florence, apparently to secure the quick release of the first.[67] But it was too late. The conspiratorial purpose of the captured Florentine's trip to Rome had become evident, and soon details of the plot were in the hands of papal authorities. On the seventeenth, Gregory published his hardest interdict against his enemies.[68] Two days later, the dragnet for Florentines was out.

On the nineteenth, the news raced through the city. The hosteler Antonio da Castro Nuovo later told how he had sent his wife outside his hostel to find out the cause of the commotion. "Florentini capiuntur," she cried, and fled. Her husband was imprisoned. Another Florentine told how two fellow workers had run to their master on that Saturday. "What are you going to do now that the Florentines are under arrest and their property is gone?" Unwilling at first to come to grips with the crisis, the master nevertheless moved quickly once convinced of its earnestness. He went with his goods to a neighbor's house, where he hid the rest of the day. That night he fled the city with two workers and went to the town of Palestrina "since he was and is a servant of Petruccio Colonna."[69]

Several of the Florentines directly involved in the plot seem to have escaped, while one, Guccio Albizzi, fled to Orbetello, where he sought a new safe-conduct to return to the city. According to one report, he was willing to offer up to one hundred florins for the paper.[70] Niccolò di Lippo was captured, as was the erstwhile ambassador Bartolommeo di Lastra.

Who was the individual whose arrest had set off this chain of events? We know only that he was a *nipote* of Vieri di Cambio Medici, a leading Florentine banker.[71] The name of the captured *cursor* was of secondary importance to the curialists; his function was neatly summed up by a prelate whose authority is unimpeachable: the arrested man was a Florentine merchant

---

[67] The messenger, Monte d'Andrea, was an employee of the Datini firm at the time: Palmieri, "Processi," 57 and Trexler, *Effects of the Papal Interdict*, 95.

[68] Trexler, *Effects of the Papal Interdict*, 92.

[69] Trexler, *Effects of the Papal Interdict*, 92f; ASV, *Collectiones*, 433, fol. 207r.

[70] ASV, *Collectiones*, 433, fol. 210r.

[71] See above, n. 66. It might well be that it was through Vieri's bank that the money for Florentine subversion found its way to Rome. On Vieri, see R. de Roover, "Gli antecedenti del Banco Mediceo e l'azienda bancaria di messer Vieri di Cambio de' Medici," *ASI* 123 (1965): 3–13.

qui venerat Romam ad dandum pecunias romanis, et ad incitandum eos, ut moverent rumorem, et interficerent Gregorium et omnes cardinales.[72]

We may well doubt the extreme conclusion, but must remember that talk of killing pope and cardinals was reported to have already been heard in Rome in September.[73]

The removal of the Florentine cancer from the Roman body politic, far from assuaging the tension in the city, may have served only to increase the mutual suspicion between Capitol and curia. A recurrent question put to the Florentines by papal prosecutors in January concerned the degree of complicity of officers of the Capitol with them. The evidence of complicity is sketchy; the suspicion is marked.

Thus not only were the relations between Romans and curia tension-filled long before the fatal days of April, but the friction between the Roman city government and the curia, so marked a feature of the period of the election in April, was also evident before the death of the reigning pontiff.[74] Indeed these suspicions expressed in the hearings of January preceded the onset of the illness which finally led to Gregory's death.

It was at the end of January 1378 that Gregory was confined by his physicians. Eight weeks of suffering lay ahead of him, weeks of powerlessness for the once energetic pontiff, of frenetic activity among the Romans, whose hour of decision was drawing near.

The papal physician had no sooner sent his patient to bed than a rumor swept the city that the pope had but three days to live.[75] Another had it that the pope was already dead, but that the fact was being hidden by the cardinals. The pope's physician was sought out, but neither rumors

---

[72] Gayet, *Le grand Schisme*, 1:170; this is a marginalium added to a deposition by the hand of the collector and editor of the *libri de schismate*, Martin de Zalva, bishop of Pamplona. His expertise in this matter issued from his position as one of the curial judges of the Florentines. Cf. his position as presiding judge in the hearing of Lorenzo di Lapo: ASV, *Instrumenta Miscellanea*, 2982. On the judge, see Seidlmayer, *Die Anfänge des grossen abendländischen Schisma*, 197f.

[73] The trials of the Florentines were conducted by a special court in January. Until the 27th, the last recorded hearing, interviewed Florentines and suspected Romans steadfastly maintained their ignorance of a conspiracy. But the confession of Bartolommeo di Lastra of that date brought the whole matter into the open. These depositions comprise ASV, *Collectiones*, 433, fols. 208r–238r.

[74] See below, and above, n. 46.

[75] Gayet, *Le grand Schisme*, 1:19 (reported by Johannes Vinrosini).

nor medical advice were sufficient for the Romans.[76] A delegation of city leaders was formed. They determined at any cost to see the pope, who had for some time neither made public appearances nor held audiences. It was necessary to know the truth. The interview was duly held, and returning from the pope's chambers the Roman delegation was overhead to say:

> The pope will not escape. The time has come to show ourselves good Romans. We must see to the arrangements so that this time, the papacy remains with the Italians and the Romans.[77]

At about this time, the Romans started to gather in secret to discuss the illness of Gregory and its implications. When we ask what specifically was said at these meetings, which were the more frequently held as the pope's death neared, we meet with a most difficult task of interpretation, since no two depositions are alike. With some simplification, three lines of argument may be stated: (1) the Romans met to discuss ways to prevent the ultramontane cardinals from executing a coup in the election of the new pope (a Roman point of view);[78] (2) the subject of the meetings was how best to insure the election of a Roman, or at least an Italian pope (a moderate French position);[79] (3) discussion centered around preparations for the killing or arrest of the French before or upon the death of the pope (the radical Clementine view).

If the Roman atmosphere in the months prior to the fatal illness of Gregory has been accurately gauged, it may be assumed that *all* these considerations were taken up at these meetings. There is good authority for asserting that even the murder of the ultramontane cardinals was pondered. The *camerarius* of the Roman Cardinal Tebaldeschi told of a meeting of certain Italian cardinals and city officials in his master's house *ante obitum pape Gregorii*, in which "aliquid tractabatur, quod interficerentur

---

[76] Gayet, *Le grand Schisme*, 1:22.

[77] Gayet, *Le grand Schisme*, 1:20f. (report of the bishop of Assisi). When this interview took place cannot be ascertained. Perhaps it would be best to place it in February, at the time that the first clandestine meetings of the Romans to discuss the future in light of the pope's condition were reported. Pierre Rostaing stated that from the beginning of March on, the Romans inquired as to the condition of the pope *de hora in horam*: Gayet, *Le grand Schisme*, 1:158.

[78] Of sixteen cardinals in the city at the time, only four were Italian. Details of this Roman concern are contained in the deposition of Bartolommeo de Zabriciis: Gayet, *Le grand Schisme*, 1:92–95.

[79] This is the most common assertion; *inter alia*, cf. Gayet, *Le grand Schisme*, 1:20f., 26, 28.

cardinales ultramontani." A member of the Urbanite wing of the schism would scarcely report this without there being some truth in it.[80] A Clementine prelate referring to the contemplated murder of the cardinals was the inquisitor of Aragon. He related how, from the beginning of February on, the non-Italians discussed with great concern a report that

> nonnulli romani voluerunt sibi et Urbi tribunum perficere in rectorem, et hoc ad finem, ut deponens ipse tunc Rome a pluribus audivit, quatenus oportunitate adepta, interficerent Ultramontanos et potissime DD. cardinales, hac, ut dicebatur, ex causa ut pontifex romanus in Roma cum Romanis perpetuo remaneret.[81]

It will be remembered that this was just after the extent of the plot of the Florentines with Roman cohorts, "ut [Romani] moverent rumorem, et interficerent Gregorium et omnes cardinales," had been revealed in the papal courts.[82] The concern of the ultramontanes is not surprising.[83]

It was in the midst of these anxious moments for the ultramontanes that an attempt was made to crush the city government. Our information is scant. On 21 February, a diarist in Florence reports:

> Oggi, a' dì 21 di febbraio 1377, si disse in Firenze come il Papa trattava i' Roma con Conte di Fonda e con Iacopo Savelli, di levare i Banderesi di Roma. Onde il popolo, sentendo questo fatto,

---

[80] Gayet, *Le grand Schisme*, 1:26. Romans mulling over the Schism in 1379 were heard to remark: "Certe si nos interfecissemus ultramontanos, non evenisset aliquid ex istis": Gayet, *Le grand Schisme*, 1:27 (reported by the *camerarius* of cardinal Tebaldeschi). The Cardinal du Puy (Marmoutier) asserted in his deposition that "vivente adhuc S. M. D. Gregorio papa XI, antequam esset infirmus sua qua decessit, unus cardinalis romanus conspiravit in mortem suam, cupiens ut in Urbe romana, de qua ipse erat oriundus et in qua plures et potentiores habebat amicos, celebraretur romani pontificis electio, ad finem quod ipse posset esse papa, et hoc scivit dictus D. Gregorius ante mortem suam. . . ." The two Roman cardinals were Tebaldeschi and Orsini. Although this cardinal's assertion is suspect because of its extreme nature and because he was perhaps the most radical Italophobe among the ultramontanes, it may be that he was in fact referring to the secret meeting at Tebaldeschi's residence. For du Puy's deposition, see Gayet, *Le grand Schisme*, 2:162.

[81] Gayet, *Le grand Schisme*, 1:120.

[82] Cf. above, n. 72.

[83] Although the focus of this paper lies in strictly Roman attitudes and conditions, it should be mentioned that not only Romans came together in these conclaves. Bartolommeo de Zabriciis, the Bishop of Rouen and a strong Urbanite, reports that the Limousin cardinals congregated (Gayet, *Le grand Schisme*, 1:92); that in another meeting they consulted with Roman city officials (93); and that all the cardinals met with the same officials, *Gregorius in extremis* (94).

sì levorono u' romore addosso al Papa. Onde il Papa si fuggì in
Castello Santagniolo, ed ebbe gran paura. E que' principi s'us-
cirono di Roma, per paura del popolo. Non sa come la cosa si
riuscirà.[84]

On 4 March, the Signoria wrote of "discordia, quam nuper [papa] cum
Romanis habet."[85] What had actually happened? One other reference to
this apparent conspiracy of a papaphilic nobility has come to my attention. A seicento historian, whose sources apparently do not include the
diarist, described the event:

Fu di questi medesimi giorni scoperto un trattato in Roma, guidata,
come dicono, da Luca Savelli, e dal Conte di Fondi, per dare a
terra il Reggimento de' Banderesi, ed ucciderne quanti più po-
tevano; e vogliano, che fosse fatto ad instanza de' Ministri del
Papa, che per arco si trovava in Anagni, benchè poco dopo se ne
tornasse a Roma; al qual trattato avevano congiurato più di 400
uomini.[86]

The historian Pellini continues that the citizens, who were well satisfied with their officials, killed some of the plotters and drove the rest
from the city. The cardinals were seized with fear and fled to the Castel
Sant'Angelo, where they stayed until the "pretence of the pope" was
done with.[87]

Was the pope actually involved,[88] or only his "ministers?" The Romans, with Gregory abed, would have made no distinction. The real question is whether the papal party was involved at all. Circumstantial evidence points in that direction. More important, the population obviously
thought the curia was involved.[89]

---

[84] *Diario d'Anonimo*, 349.

[85] *Lini Coluci*, 1:146f. (letter to John Hawkwood).

[86] P. Pellini, *Dell' Historia di Perugia di* . . . (Venice, 1664), parte I, libro 9 (p. 1206).

[87] Pellini, *Perugia*, 1206.

[88] There is a cryptic sentence in a letter dispatched by Gregory on 2 March which
has no apparent reference to the context: "Lucas enim de nocte fugiit, quod credimus
pro meliori fuisse." Further reference will be made to this important letter. Suffice here
to remark that "Luca" may be Luca Savelli, named by the diarist as one of the plotters,
while his brother Jacopo is named by Pellini. Both were in the church camp at this time:
Mirot, *Lettres*, no. 2119.

[89] Backing for such an attempt could not have been lacking among the ultramontanes. This was, as we have seen, a time when rumors abounded that they were to be
killed. Consider also posterior events: after Gregory died, and it was a question of guard-

Under these conditions, even the suggestion of removing the sick pope to the healthier air of Anagni was enough to infuriate the population at large.[90] Had there not already been talk this year that the pope planned to remove to Avignon?[91] Conditions in the Eternal City at this point can only be described as murderous. The infuriated Romans poured the blood of the noble conspirators on the streets, while judging the ultramontanes as subverters of the *libertà* of the Capitol. The cardinals, leaving the Castel Sant'Angelo after their terrified flight there, could no longer feel at ease in the streets of Rome.

Their anxiety did not ease. A little more than a week after their flight to the castle came a new threat to the lives of the foreign cardinals. In the latter part of February, word reached the cardinal of Amiens and the bishop of Vich (Catalonia) that their lives were endangered by a group of plotters. A housewoman, *pietate humana quadam ducta*, warned the latter not to venture out of his house, specifically on Sunday the 28th. On this day the Romans celebrated the festival of the *ludus bovum* on Mount Testaccio. Curia and *popolo* were to be present, and it was planned in the midst of the festivities to seize the Capitol, excite the people, and proceed to kill the ultramontanes.[92]

Not without unintended humor, our source notes that despite the fact that the plot was discovered, and the leader captured and publicly decapitated before the festival day, the bishop remained indoors on that day. Who were these Roman conspirators? Their leader was one Antonio de' Malavolti, who according to one source was a poor vineyard worker (*puta-*

---

ing the election consistory, the cardinals asked specifically for the Counts of Nola and Fondi, "amicos suos de quibus confidebant" (Gayet, *Le grand Schisme*, 1:4). It was rumored that the Count of Fondi, Onorato Gaetani, had advised the cardinals not to hold the consistory in the city at all, but outside (Gayet, *Le grand Schisme*, 1:27). It is no surprise, then, that when the *banderesi* published a decree before the election ordering all lay nobles to leave the city on pain of death, Gaetani, along with the Count of Nola, was specifically mentioned (Gayet, *Le grand Schisme*, 1:122). Gaetani subsequently allied himself with the French cardinals at Anagni against Urban VI and the city. Finally, it will be recalled that Luca Savelli had refused any part in the Florentine plot (above, n. 55). In light of this evidence, circumstantial as it may be, it is improbable that some part of the ultramontanes did not conspire with the nobles.

[90] "Statim murmur in populo furioso fuit . . .": Gayet, *Le grand Schisme*, 1:158 (report of Pierre Rostaing).

[91] "Ut dicebant deliberaverat ipso anno a Roma recedere et ad Avinionem se transferre": Gayet, *Le grand Schisme*, 1:67 (report of Tommaso Ammannati).

[92] Gayet, *Le grand Schisme*, 1:120f. (report of Eymerich).

tor vinorum). His associates, whom he accused under questioning, were likewise vinedressers (*fossatores vinorum*).[93] The evidence suggests that the plot was conceived "in fantasia." While Eymerich purported to espy behind the plan to kill the cardinals a determination "to keep the pope in Rome perpetually,"[94] another ultramontane saw no more than the desire *ut haberent thesauros* of the curia.[95] So it may have been; in such a distraught city the wildest fantasy might have become grim reality.

The long months since the pontiff first entered Rome had not been wanting in high drama. The history of the latter part of Gregory's reign, far from being an unimportant lacuna between the end of the Avignonese papacy and the Great Schism, provides a key to the understanding of the events which followed his demise. Schism had been threatened by the Romans if Gregory did not return. Once he had, the citizens set about controlling his movements and those of the French cardinals. The popular government maintained itself as an independent force for just this purpose, as well as to prevent an alliance of hostile Roman nobles with the ultramontanes. Rome was once more a world capital, and under no circumstances were its citizens prepared to allow the removal of the curia to again degrade it to a second-class Italian town. To guarantee papal residence in Rome after the ailing pontiff's death, some citizens, encouraged by Florence, talked of murdering the foreign cardinals. Plots against the ultramontanes were matched by a vain attempt of the Roman nobility, allied with ultramontane curialists, to crush the city's independence. The forces at work in these months were those which soon after formed the drama of the election of Urban VI and the outbreak of the Great Schism.

Two days before the *ludus bovum*, Gregory XI addressed to his peace commissioner in the north one of his last missives.

> We are forced to wonder from whence have come the reports which you say have been related to you. For this city has been so quiet since you left, that we can indicate nothing new at all.

True, he goes on, there has been a plotter caught and executed, but even

---

[93] Seidlmayer, *Anfänge des grossen abendländischen Schisma*, 328f. (report of Lagier). The name of the conspirator was mentioned by the pope in a letter of 2 March: Mirot, *Lettres*, no. 2119.

[94] Gayet, *Le grand schisme*, 2:120f.

[95] Seidlmayer, *Anfänge des grossen abendländischen Schisma*, 328.

this on demand of the *popolo*. "We therefore, blessed by the divine clemency, enjoy the prosperity brought by the charm of repose."[96]

The careful reader recognizes at once a letter written to be read by a wider audience than a papal confidant. What could have been more harmful to the pope than to have had reports of disorders in Rome again destroy peace talks? The city of Rome was not quiet. The attitude of the Romans to the execution was other than Gregory averred. Eymerich tells us that the execution of the conspirator fomented the greatest odium against the ultramontanes.[97]

The pope was not at peace, but in the throes of a painful disease. The day after this letter was written was Ash Wednesday, and the Supreme Pontiff heard Mass in public. It was his first public appearance in some time, and the last of his eventful life.[98] It is as if he died on this day, for the records, while continuing to speak of preparation for a new pope, largely ignore the dying man in the Vatican.

In considering the election of Gregory's successor Urban, and the split in the church which followed, we ignore the events here narrated at our peril. What is the force of the information presented in this paper? In what way could it modify our views of the events which followed?

The election of Urban VI on 8 April 1378 was accomplished under conditions of extreme unrest in the Eternal City. And yet it was months before the cardinals expressed corporate doubt as to the election's validity. The election had been constrained by the tumultuous actions of the *popolo romano*, the argument of the cardinals now ran, and consequently Urban was not a true pope. After five centuries of debate, the consensus of scholarly opinion defends Urban's claim, pointing out that the cardinals did not contest the legality of the election for three months, while notifying their kings and princes of the free election of Urban.[99] It should be pointed

---

[96] Mirot, *Lettres*, no. 2119. In this letter one finds the reference to "Lucas" noted previously (above, n. 88).

[97] "Que justitie executio contra DD. cardinalium collegium et ultramontanos et presertim contra D. Ambianensem majoris odii fomitem ministravit": Gayet, *Le grand Schisme*, 1:120f.

[98] Gayet, *Le grand Schisme*, 1:66 (report of Ammannati).

[99] There is nothing surprising in this. The evidence suggests that the cardinals had decided to make the best of an irregular situation. That they vouched for the freedom of the election and attended Urban proves neither the election's freedom nor their own conviction, but simply their willingness to respond to the situation. The cardinals' "intentions" are the keynote of a perceptive recent analysis by O. Přerovský, *L'elezione di Urbano VI e l'insorgere dello scisma d'Occidente* (Rome, 1960). On this basis the author in

out, however, that what the cardinals did *after* the election is of limited substantive value in ascertaining whether Urban was freely elected or not. That can be decided only by examining the election itself, and the events anterior to the election.

The election took place in Rome. The internal conditions there have been analysed in some detail, and those conditions would appear to have ruled out the election of a Frenchman.[100] If so, they thus ruled out a free election.

"Constraint" is not easily definable. Were the French cardinals not in Italy by the constraint of Gregory? Was not the very existence of an independent city government in Rome constraint? If the cardinals had left the city to hold the election in the territory of the Count of Fondi, as that noble had suggested to them, would they not have been under noble constraint instead of popular? Were not the cardinals however constrained to remain in Rome until after the election by the fact that otherwise their wealth, much of which was stored in the Castel Sant'Angelo, might have been lost? Was not the holding of the election *in Italy*, not to mention Rome, constraint, given the makeup of the college of cardinals?

Posing the question of constraint in this extreme fashion serves one purpose: it concentrates our attention on the situation *before* the election. The Urbanite church historian von Pastor recognized at one point that this was the crux of the matter: he stated that the cardinals' fear of the Roman mob postdated the election.[101] In other words, evidence of fear prior to the election would be symptomatic of constraint. The findings of this paper make clear, however, that the cardinals did fear for their lives

---

his conclusion calls the election "viziata e poi convalidata." K. A. Fink states that the election was "weder absolut gültig noch absolut ungültig": "Zur Beurteilung des grossen abendländischen Schismas," *Zeitschrift für Kirchengeschichte* 73 (1962): 338. This revisionism is based on events after Gregory's death, and especially after the election of Urban. The latter author suggests: ". . . die Wahl ist nicht mit dem Wahlakt völlig erledigt, sondern erfordert auch die oft lange Zeit in Anspruch nehmende Anerkennung": Fink, "Beurteilung," 338.

[100] Certain scholars have suggested that the election of Urban was a foregone conclusion from the very start (A. Flick, *The Decline of the Medieval Church*, vol. 1 [New York, 1930], 255). This may well be the case. As we have seen, meetings of the different factions of cardinals had been held since early February, when Gregory's impending death had become clear. Two months were sufficient to decide on a new pope. There is also evidence of a split in the cardinalate (Flick, *Decline*, 1:253–56). But that Urban may have been assured of election before the convocation does not mean that the election was without constraint. It may have been constraint which made the choice an easy one.

[101] L. von Pastor, *Geschichte der Päpste*, vol. 1 (Freiburg, 1955), 119.

months before the election, and with good reason. Further, the general atmosphere of the city, among French and Italians alike, was one of fear and anxiety.

The Romans had been long determined to have a pope who "would live in Rome with them." From November 1377 on, they held Gregory a virtual prisoner within the city. Certain Romans talked of killing the ultramontane cardinals from September of the same year, a move which would have guaranteed the election of an Italian. Florentine money fostered such plans; the French cardinals had little doubt that Florentines and well-placed Romans considered the possible elimination of the "Gallic wolves" desirable. Repeated rumors of such plots filled the city from then on, rumors not without foundation in fact.

Forced early in February to flee to the Castel Sant'Angelo to escape Roman wrath, the ultramontanes were constrained soon after returning to their residences to remain within, as another plot against them boiled up at the end of the month. And through all of the fright, the cardinals realized that the government of the city was their worst enemy. In many ways, it was the *banderesi* of the Capitol who "saw to the arrangements" for a new pope as much as the cardinals themselves. The Capitol had tolerated the presence of Florentine spies. It was the city government which banned the noble friends of the ultramontane cardinals from the city while allowing it to be filled by crowds of outside peasants as the consistory neared.

In the light of conditions in Rome on the eve of the election, it is improbable that the election of a new pope could have been accomplished without constraint. Captives of a situation beyond their control, they rightly feared the intrigues of those Romans who had long considered killing them as well as the mob which twice before Gregory's death had forced them into the asylum of their homes or their fortress of Sant' Angelo. Quite apart from the events of 8 April, this is not the stuff of which free elections are made.

GOD-MAKING

The Gender and Number of
the Evangelical Magi*

TO EXPLORE THE NUMBER AND GENDER of the evangelical magi might seem to be an antiquarian, even a silly, adventure.[1] Were these intellectuals from the east, who bore the three gifts to King Jesus in Bethlehem, not evidently males? And even if the evangelist Matthew did not specify how many there were, it has been clear since the sixth century that they were assumed to have been three, one per gift. In fact, from the time that in the writing of Caesarius of Arles they definitively became the Three Kings, and no longer mere savants, their trinity has been definite. For all that, it seems to me that often, even though three Kings are always represented in medieval art, we are meant to see, to recall, and to experience only two persons or groups, and that one of the two is not just male.

Why does this matter for any but art historians? First, the question of number is important because the Three Kings were thought of as the

---

* This essay appeared previously in *Mundus in imagine: Bildersprache und Lebenswelten im Mittelalter: Festgabe für Klaus Schreiner*, ed. A. Löther, Ulrich Meier, N. Schnitzler, G. Schwerhoff, and G. Signori (Munich, 1996), 205–17.

[1] Details of the argument below, reproduction of related images, and more bibliographical detail can be found in R. Trexler, *The Journey of the Magi: Meanings in History of a Christian Story* (Princeton, 1997). In addition to other magian materials in the present collection, see also Trexler, "Les mages à la fin du moyen âge," *Cahiers du centre de recherches historiques* 5 (1990): 39–51.

whole of the world recognizing one god. Thus their number is a figure of the plurality medieval people imagined the world to be. The number of magi can therefore encode some fundamental information about how Christians partition their experience of cultural and social order. For instance, the personalities making up this triadic notion of the Three Kings, or those making up the famous medieval orders of those who pray, fight, and work, are always imagined only as males.

Second, female gender seems missing from representations of the Three Kings. Carl Jung long ago suggested that the so-called Holy Trinity of Christianity — and the magi have always functioned as a figure of that Holy Trinity — may actually conceal a fourth god to represent the female or evil principle, because without it, comprehension of the divinity is impossible.

Third, it is becomingly increasingly clear that in drama and the fine arts, images of the Three Kings in medieval times often functioned as representations of public triumph — either Christian, royal, or papal — following in the footsteps of the Roman triumphs, which were the figural predecessor of Adorations of the Magi. By extension, the context of a Journey or of an Adoration of the Three Kings implied and implies the participation of all those who watched and imitated the acts of the triumphant magi. As an example, in the Middle Ages the comportment of the magi at prayer served as an example for those following in their processional train, that is, in their Journey. The Adoration of the Kings is a high political representation about power and control.

Fourth, it is well known that different medieval princes liked to have themselves painted or carved as *one* of the magi. How then to do it? Obviously, they had to divert attention from the other two kings in the representation. Thus to recapitulate, principles of sovereignty, gender, and proper order vied to make three seem two or four, male seem female, plurality seem unitary. Whereas on the surface the magi seem to conform to the strong tripartite tendency in the male Indo-European mentality or to the West's tenacious idea that male society had three estates of priests, nobles, and workers, our examination will show that other models of the magi have long competed with the conventional triadic model.

The Emergence and Character of a Real King as Third King

It is now thought that the first extant visual representation of the magi dates from during or after the reign of Constantine (d. 336), and that that representation glossed the political success of this first Christian emperor at the Milvian bridge. Thus the very beginnings of magi representations are linked to politics, and through the mosaics of Justinian's church at San Vitale in Ravenna and (implicitly) Charlemagne's Pfalzkappelle in Aachen, that linkage moved directly into the medieval representation of sovereignty in the west.

There was, however, a problem. Unless the reigning monarch was to be portrayed not as a magus but as the theocratic single star of Bethlehem itself (as in the West Otto III did choose to be), there was no convincing way to represent his full sovereignty while he was just one, and only one, of several magi. Alternately, there was no satisfactory way to represent a sovereign couple, man and woman, in this format. One sees this difficulty clearly in the mosaics of San Vitale, where the emperor Justinian and the empress Theodora stand near each other, but the Three Kings with their presents are shown only on the empress's dress. It proved difficult to replace givers of three gifts with two living sovereigns.

I would suggest that the inability of the magi to represent single authority is the most important reason why in the Byzantine empire, the magi practically never attained royal status. And while in the West the Kings did eventually attain some individuality, in the East they also long remained nameless, uncrowned heralds or ambassadors exhibiting little or no individual personality. Thus in several Ravennese and Roman sarcophagi of the sixth century, the deceased is pictured as a fourth personage behind three such identical ambassadors, almost as if they are one, supplicating for another.

The Living and the Dead Kings

A quite different solution for this sovereignty problem, however, was found in the West, one which opened the gates to the charismatic representation of the reigning monarch. This was his representation as a magus who was the hereditary descendant of dead forebearers. Why not picture the magi kings as three generations of one dynasty, thus converting an ecumenical image into a national or familial one?

Adorations showing Habsburg dynastic kin as the Kings are well known from sixteenth-century art, but it is not generally recognized that at a much earlier point, this practice originally distinguished one living from two dead magi, all of the same family. We see it first in Apulia, in the age of the Hohenstaufen. In a laud addressed to Frederick II, Nicholas of Bari around 1235 referred to Frederick's grandfather Barbarossa and then to his father, Henry VI, both deceased. Then he states that "these three emperors are like the three magi, who came with gifts to adore god and man. But here is the youngest [adolescentior] of the three, over whom the child Jesus has laid his happy hands and his sacrosanct arms."[2] Clearly, Nicholas visually links an Adoration scene to the coronation of the emperor!

The emphasis on the third and youngest magus is a recognized, but dimly understood phenomenon in late medieval and early modern European Adorations. In effect, Nicholas of Bari's remarkable emphasis upon the Hohenstaufen dynasty works politically by highlighting its one living sovereign. Already in the high Middle Ages, therefore, two dead magi are imagined as legitimating a single living ruler. Alternately, in the Wilton diptych of c. 1395 (London, National Gallery), we see in magian format one dead ancestor and a dead patron saint commending the one live King, Richard II. It can be said that in this approach, the ruler is privileged over the dynasty, the individual over the collectivity, the living one over the dead many. Precisely such a discourse about the old and the young, and the dead and the living, is the background needed to understand the images of the third magus generated in the late Middle Ages.

The Exotic Magus

The emergence of magi images that show a dichotomy between life and death was but one expression of a larger dichotomy between inside and outside, the conventional and the exotic. Of course, the essence of the magi story was that they came from the outside exotic east to legitimate the western King Jesus. Yet the essence of a *cult* is domestication; that is, worship of a particular set of divinities in a certain time and place is intended to control those divinities in that context. So even as the magi offerants became insiders, a certain outside character had to be maintained. Let us subdivide this polarization by age and color. In both, the first two kings represent the established inside authority, while the third king becomes an exotic figure unrepresentative of the mature community that is offering to the child.

---

[2] "Profecto hii tres imperatores sunt quasi tres magi, qui venerunt cum muneribus deum et hominem adorare, sed hic est adolescentior illis tribus, super quem puer Ihesus felices manus posuit et brachiola sacrosancta": Rudolf M. Kloos, "Nikolaus von Bari, eine neue Quelle zur Entwicklung der Kaiseridee unter Friedrich II," *Deutsches Archiv für Erforschung des Mittelalters* 11 (1954–1955): 171. The laud's magian content was introduced into the magi literature by F. O. Büttner, *Imitatio Pietatis. Motive der christlichen Ikonographie als Modelle zur Verähnlichung* (Berlin, 1983), 27.

The emergence of a brilliant youth at times strikingly different from the two often lackluster older kings can already be seen at the beginning of the thirteenth century, in a monument erected to honor the deposit of the bones of the magi in the cathedral of Cologne. Though a fourth, rather than a third magus, the late twelfth-century, brilliant gold image of the pretender Philip of Swabia, the patron of this masterwork, on the great magi shrine in Cologne (where the magi are said to be buried) (fig. 1), already breathes a youthful future, which will transform that magus into an exotic prince. Note further that the four kings stand beneath only three archways. Obviously, the patron had projected himself into the picture only after its architecture had been established.

In hundreds of paintings and in sculpture, a youthful *third* king will become the true visual crown of the work, rather than just one-third of the cosmos worshiping Jesus, as he usually appears in literature. If the two other kings are bearded, the third is not; in Italy the youthful third king is commonly blond, though blond hair was not usual in Italy. The third king sometimes wears rakishly short clothes revealing the full length of livery colors; the others feature ankle-length cloaks. He wears Asiatic clothing, they do not, and so forth. Nowhere, indeed, is the youth king quite as exotic as in Italy, and particularly in Tuscany the third king dominates many an adoration. Sometimes, as in the Strozzi altarpiece of Gentile da Fabriano, a youth's knighting seems to be the occasion for the whole adoration, while in other cases a child's baptism may be commemorated, as I believe is the baptism, on Epiphany 1449, of Lorenzo de' Medici, the blond king in Benozzo Gozzoli's famous Journey of the Magi in the Medici Palace in Florence. The realistic countenance of this charming young prince contrasts at times so much with the stock figures of the first and second kings as to make us think less of Three Kings than of one or at most two.

Indeed a mid-fifteenth century story from Erlau, marvelously refashioned in an early sixteenth-century Milanese source, *conceives* merely two, not Three Kings![3] According to what the Milanese Veronica of Binasco (1445–1497) saw in her vision of c. 1490, on approaching the child the three magi began to argue over who would adore him first. In the end, she says, the youngest of the three approached and kissed the infant's feet

---

[3] See the Erlau play (*ludus magorum*) in the edition of K. F. Kummer (Hildesheim, 1977), 15–30.

Figure 1.
Adoration of the Kings, first half of the twelfth century.
Cathedral of Cologne, Shrine of the Three Kings.

first. Then "the others did the same," though it is not said in which order. Veronica then saw "that the youngest king, who had done his adoration first, was seen, amazingly" — and here note the wording well — "*to
have turned older and to have become of one age with the other two.*"[4] A
moment's reflection reveals that in this mental slip, the writer conceived
of the two older kings as being of identical age. The axis of the whole
story was the difference between "age" and "youth."

We come now to perhaps the most powerful of the dichotomies in
magi representations, that of color. It was Neenah Hamilton, I believe,
who first noted how Italian Adorations and Journeys clung to white third
kings even as fifteenth-century German and Flemish painters began to feature a black prince.[5] In some areas of Europe, color was replacing age as
a statement of exoticism. An important observation is in place here. Many
real kings were represented as third kings in European Journeys and Adorations of the Magi, but with one possible exception — a Moor painted by
Juan de Flandre who, because the painting may represent the fall of
Granada to the Catholic Kings in 1492, may show the just-deposed King
Boabdil — I presently know of no non-white king in magi art (not even the
famous Mansa Musa) who is meant to represent an actual ruler, and indeed
the brown or black color of such figures sometimes appears without a
crown or its equivalent. Almost exclusively, the black or Moorish king of
European painting is meant to provide, one on one, a stark exotic contrast
to two often prosaic white kings.

That color bifurcation does not really change with the discovery of the
New World. True, from the end of the sixteenth century the notion that
the Kings represented the three *races* (rather than the old three conti-
nents) is current; one more symbolic triad to add to the great literary storehouse! But in fact, even after the discovery of the Indian world, rarely did
artists clearly represent an Asian, a black, and a white king; I have yet to
find a pre-modern painting of the magi where two of the kings are not, effectively, white. At first glance the Blankenberger Altar (attributed to the
Master of the Fröndenberger Altar, Münster Landesmuseum) appears to

---

[4] "At reges specie corporis praestantes fuisse dicebat Veronica, aureis vestibus usque
ad genua indutos, iunioremque regem, qui primus adoraverat, veluti effectum seniorem &
unius aetatis cum reliquis duobus demirans intuita est": *Acta Sanctorum*, 1 January
(Venice, 1734), 906.

[5] N. Hamilton, *Die Darstellung der Anbetung der heiligen drei Könige in der toskanischen
Malerei von Giotto bis Lionardo* (Strassburg, 1901); cf. also P. H. Kaplan, *The Rise of the
Black Magus in Western Art* (Ann Arbor, 1983).

show two black kings, but on closer examination both these kings have white hands to accompany their black faces. Obviously both these kings originally had white faces which were later repainted over, perhaps to achieve a mask-like effect, as the magi were often shown in theatre pieces.

Once we are aware how commonly this third king is the center of visual attention, we may surmise that more fundamentally than youth, it is exoticism, the outside, that is at the root of things. A black king in a magi painting is indeed usually the youngest king, for instance, but that is not always the case. What does unify the white, the black and the occasional Asiatic third kings, is rather the astonishing opulence of their dress. At times we can almost blink and substitute a black for a white youth, each of comparable opulence. Is it possible that there is cultural criticism here: jaded lecherous youth, or the darkness of the devil?

Regarding one object of ornamentation, however, there is an important limit to be drawn between the white and black or moorish third magus. That object is earrings. At first, the fact that many black kings wear earrings confirms our thesis that the third king is at times the exotic pole of a dualistic representation of a nominal trilogy of magi. Indeed it is the blacks' exoticism even more than their rank that protrudes, for in the Bosch Epiphany among others, not just black princes but their servants are made to wear earrings. And there are other, often much older paintings in which white third kings have black servants wearring earrings.

What is at work here is an ancient stereotype. At least as far back as the Satyricon, Europeans have associated pierced ears and earrings with the "Arabians." With this the limits of comparison have been reached, for despite an extensive search, I cannot find a single young white king (or older one for that matter) who sports earrings, not even in the seventeenth century, when earrings did come to be worn by white males in other pictorial vehicles. To repeat: if many Adorations pit the young against the old, many others pit colored against white. The exoticism of one's own youth was one thing; that of blacks or Asians was quite another!

Despite the limits of a comparison between black and white third magi, I do believe their common rakishness is important. Keep in mind that in one persistent Syrian tradition, the magi were thought of as practitioners of black magic whose subsequent fealty to Jesus amounted to a recognition that magic had been conquered by religion. Is it going too far to suggest that the third king at times represents not the conversion of the young or the black to goodness, but the abiding evil of being young or black, or at least some level of moral inferiority? Recalling Jung's notion, we may not want to dismiss the idea.

Recall that already in antiquity and from the fifteenth century forward, exegesis contrasted Matthew's (good smart gentile) magi with Luke's (bad dumb Jewish) shepherds. Also bear in mind that in fifteenth-century illuminations, the magi might be imagined as the good divine worshippers over and against a Manichean bad set of black magi monsters worshipping the devil.[6] The Adoration of the Magi might in fact be imagined as the civilized opposite to a state of nature, in which wild men and animals worshipped disorder. The dualism implicit in these imaginings thus call upon us to rethink the unquestioned notion of magian triadism.

A closer examination of some painted scenes of the magi encourages us in this direction, and in fact to discover a bipolarism within the social group of the magi themselves. Sometimes, in fact, these third kings, totally self-sufficient, turn away from the Christ child, even mount a stand, to advertise themselves! (fig. 2). It is indeed usually the third king and not the first or second who invites the audience into the charmed circle! It is almost as if their very liveliness and earthiness leads to damnable excess.

The Gender of the Three Kings

After life and death, youth and age, white and black, we come now finally to gender. On the surface, the story of the magi seems an exclusively macho sacred story par excellence, in which — if we except Mary always virgin — there is in effect no room for the womanly. For in it, a group of men accord international diplomatic recognition as king to the infant whom they see to have male genitalia[7] — just as a pope was thought tested for full manhood before his coronation.

And yet here again, things are not always as they seem. The actual medieval and modern celebration of the feast of the Kings on 5 and 6 January commonly had a strong female component. The election not only of a King, but also of a Queen for the Day was fairly common, and in Italy and Germany, the divinities of the day were predominantly women, Befana and Berchte. Let us then look harder for the women in representations of the magi.

---

[6] Cf. in J. Devisse and M. Mollat, *The Image of the Black in Western Art*, vol. 2, part 2 (New York, 1979).

[7] L. Steinberg, *The Sexuality of Christ in Renaissance Art and in Modern Oblivion* (New York, 1983); R. Trexler, "Gendering Jesus Crucified," in *Iconography at the Crossroads*, ed. B. Cassidy (Princeton, 1993), 107–19.

Figure 2.
Anonymous master, *Adoration of the Kings*, ca. 1550.
Bob Jones University.

What we find in the first place are certain works in which the male magi are symmetrically balanced by a group of females. A sculpture in the Münster Landesmuseum shows the Three Kings together with Joseph, with two women each standing at both their sides. Sometimes a group of women, placed alongside Mary and the sibyls or midwives, seems to greet the male magian trio. It is rare on the other hand to see a set of female magi alongside the male ones. Perhaps the most striking representation of this type is in the famous Ortenberg Altar (ca. 1430, Hessische Landesmuseum, Darmstadt), where opposite the adoration of the magi on one panel is another with women adoring Mary in a larger, separate scene. Surely the artist, in preparing this panel for a nunnery, wanted to say that the Adoration of the Magi showed males submitting to Jesus, but that women also did so independently. The Ortenberg concept was then enlarged upon by Holbein the Elder, who shows three Queens by themselves in a type of Adoration scene (The Fountain of Life, Museu Nacional de Arte Antiga, Lisbon).

Where then did such inspirations for female magi come from? In terms of biblical exegesis, the answer may be that in the Middle Ages the visit of the Queen of Sheba to Solomon was usually considered a prefiguration of the visit of the magi to Jesus; figural similes to the Adoration often speak to that typology. But André Chastel went deeper, and got closer to the truth. In an important article early in his career, he showed that the Solomon/Sheba image was meant to contrast maleness with femaleness, reason with passion, nurture with nature, etc.[8] My contribution to that insight is that the magi as well were meant to project precisely such binary, not triadic, oppositions.

I would take that argument one step further. It is certainly true that in the long list of fundamental human polarities the story of the magi does speak to — riches against poverty, power against powerlessness, age against infancy, and so forth — the dichotomy male/female does, admittedly, seem to have played a limited role. There are relatively few works in which women, including Mary, are overtly important to the dynamics of adoration. Yet when we look more closely, we may perceive in some of the qualities of the third king traits which contemporaries identified with femaleness, or effeminacy.

---

[8] A. Chastel, "La légende de la Reine de Saba," in his Fables, Formes, Figures, vol. 1 (Paris, 1978), 61–101. Cf. also J. Lassner, Demonizing the Queen of Sheba: Boundaries of Gender and Culture in Postbiblical Judaism and Medieval Islam (Chicago, 1993).

We have already seen that within their own pictorial tradition, the magi, in the person of the third magus, are themselves not devoid of that type of sexual or gender polarization. This prince, sometimes far from preparing to adore Jesus, actually can be seen strutting his stuff for spectators, a type of dandy behavior contemporaries identified not just with youth but with women. Both the characterological and conventional physical bearings of females are often encountered. The third king not only wears earrings, but fantastically ornate clothing, a behavior that was punished in women. In Soest, in fact, we find a third king who not only wears what appears to be a woman's crown, but also an unmistakably female veil (fig. 3)! Perhaps the veil and the crown are intended to refer to a marriage alliance of this (virginal?) king.[9] A close examination of this still mysterious painting further reveals that the face of this originally white king was apparently later painted brown.

Convincing evidence of the trend toward effeminacy in representations of the third king is contained in a painting of an anonymous, so-called Antwerp Mannerist, which seems to show him as a woman (fig. 4). Such a representation certainly belongs within a larger early modern context in which John the Evangelist, for example, can be shown with lovely hair and curves and even female breasts, perhaps best exemplified in the work of Jacques Bellanges (d. 1616), who regularly painted the apostles as effeminate if not as women. But let us remain with the Three Kings. The early modern trend toward effeminate or even womanly third kings is important even if in magian representations such womanly maguses remain ephemeral.

In any case, my argument remains at the structural level, rather than resting on a merely anecdotal identification of any given third king as effeminate or female. I have tried to call attention to a propensity on the part of some artists to have us remember their magi as singles or as a duet, though they may appear as a trio. As we approach our conclusion, we can speculate on the probable reasons for this dualistic tendency. Certainly intellectual principles are relevant: the moral of the magi story itself is rooted in dualistic oppositions of supernatural and natural, rich and poor, old vs. infantile, etc. Political struggle is also relevant: obviously, the medieval church-state struggle was often reflected in magi scenes, secular

---

[9] Cf. J. Boswell, *Same-Sex Unions in Premodern Europe* (New York, 1994), 185, 203–8.

Figure 3.
Anonymous master, *Adoration of the Kings*,
Church of Maria zur Wiese.
Soest. Bildarchiv Foto Marburg, Arch.-Nr. 192.457.

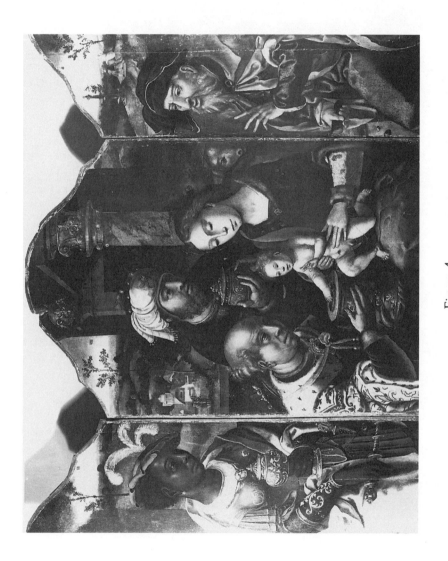

Figure 4.
Anonymous master, *Adoration of the Kings*, ca. 1550.
Palermo, National Gallery.

kings demonstrably kneeling before Jesus — as should latter-day princes before the vicar of Christ.

But there is one other polar phenomenon that was at work in the back of our artists' minds, and that is the polarity of play and work, succeeding each other at different times of the year. It was common for social groups to elect a play king and even a queen consort for the Christmas season, and sometimes specifically for the feast of the Epiphany and the banquets that, along with Herod or Star plays, were such an important part of that feast.[10] The exotic king of some magi paintings may indeed represent the play king, or queen, elected for these days. He sometimes did wear the most outlandish clothing, indeed could seem a most unroyal prince, as in the famous Adoration of Peter Breugel (fig. 5).

But where was the line separating play and reality? Take the case of Borso d'Este, duke of Ferrara. Beginning in 1476 and for a generation thereafter, on the nights of 4 and 5 January this prince rode from his castle into town on his way, he said, to Bethlehem. The inhabitants of palazzo after palazzo in town left rich gifts of food, precious metals, and other objects at their doors for the duke, who would, he said, present them to the infant. But in truth, Borso was raising taxes or tribute. Yet like legions of other feigned magi, the prince of Ferrara enlivened these nights by singing and begging for gifts for the infant. A world of contradictions, of seeming and being. Two worlds (not three) really, mediating between the one and the other.

To conclude, let me state my position on the significance of the discovery of such dualism among the magi. In the iconography of the Three Kings, the figure of the rake or androgyne often represents the people's ability to reproduce biologically. The stiff first two kings, on the contrary, only want to maintain and pass on the established patriarchy of Western societies of that age. For certainly, in these paintings it is the androgyne rake who represents the biological reproduction of the races, and not the stiff first and second kings, who merely want to maintain, or culturally reproduce, the existing patriarchy of Western societies. At bottom, in the iconography of the magi conflict and not consensus around the crèche may be represented. I have not shown that one needs the presence of women, or of magicians, to pray successfully, but rather that negation, the

---

[10] See now A. van Wagenberg-ter Hoeven, *Het Driekoningenfeest: De uitbeelding van een populair thema in de beeldende kunst von de zeventiende eeuw* (Amsterdam, 1997).

Figure 5.
Peter Bruegel the Elder, *Adoration of the Kings*, ca. 1560.
London, National Gallery: detail.

conflict of denied women and youth with their lords, is life. Males like Matthew reached into space and fetched outside magi to prove their lord is king and god. Yet with that power from outside, there came the danger of youth, the threat of woman.

Dreams of the Three Kings[*]

> Moreover, he must be well thought of by outsiders.
> (1 Tim. 3)

OF THE MANY DREAMS AND VISIONS regarding the history of Jesus' birth, from the political point of view none are as important as those of Matthew. The dreams of this evangelist begin with an "angel of the lord" who appears to Joseph and reports to him that the Holy Ghost has made Mary pregnant (1.20–21). Appearances to the contrary, Jesus is legitimate and no bastard.[1] They end when presumably the same "angel of the lord" reappears to a sleeping Joseph and orders him to flee to Egypt with Mary and the child (2.13). The wise men who had come from the east and given gifts to Jesus, the king of the Jews, form the substance of a third dream, interposed between the two events already mentioned. After having adored the infant and fallen asleep, these wise men from the east were warned by unknown persons in a dream not to return to Herod in Jeru-

[*] This essay appeared previously in *Träume im Mittelalter: Ikonologische Studien*, ed. A. Paravicini-Bagliani and G. Stabile (Stuttgart, 1989), 55–71.
[1] For this reason Joseph was important for Nativity and Epiphany plays: N. King, *Mittelalterliche Dreikönigsspiele: Eine Grundlagenarbeit zu den lateinischen, deutschen und französischen Dreikönigsspielen und -spielszenen bis zum Ende des 16. Jhs.*, 2 vols. (Fribourg/Schweiz, 1979), 165. I thank Peter Arnade and Daniel Williman for their help with this paper.

salem, but rather to reach their homeland by another road (2.12).[2] Matthew had introduced the magi into his account so as to legitimate the child among the Jews (so that it would "be recognized by outsiders", as Paul had said: 1 Tim. 3). Now their successful flight back to their homeland meant that Jesus' reputation in the pagan world would survive indefinitely. Indeed to the present day ancestors of these wise men from the east are said to rule in Paradise. They or their kin regularly descend from the clouds to save an endangered world just as once upon a time their predecessors traveled west to announce the legitimacy of the savior of the world.[3]

It is fitting that the three wise men's appearance in the Bible ends with a dream or a vision, for in medieval tradition as well their story is enveloped in the world of dreams and visions. Together or singly the Three Kings, as they are generally called in the medieval millennium, gazed up at an unusual heavenly body. Some thought that it was a star in or over which a baby was imaged, while others claimed that the three variously aged Kings each saw in that star a Jesus of his own age, so that each effectively saw himself![4] Furthermore, the appearance of the Kings in the stall or grotto was considered the actual beginning and condition of Jesus' own "epiphany" into a God-King, as this revelation was called. From the beginning, and through the Middle Ages — when the Three Kings everywhere were associated with predictions for the New Year — down to modern times, when first Anna-Katharina Emmerich and more recently Theresa Neumann continued to contribute to our knowledge of the Wise Men, the history of the Three Kings has been elaborated upon and strengthened by extrabiblical visions.[5]

Dreams and visions also served to legitimate events or conditions in the real, waking world, especially when they came upon the pious while

---

[2] "Et responso accepto in somnis ne redirent ad Herodem, per aliam viam reversi sunt in regionem suam. Qui cum recessissent, ecce angelus Domini apparuit in somnis Ioseph, dicens: 'Surge et accipe puerum et matrem eius, et fuge in Aegyptum. . . .' " The intervention is always said to have been that of an angel, who in at least one medieval play was identified as Raphael: King, *Mittelalterliche Dreikönigsspiele*, 170.

[3] A. Tomas, *Shambhala: Oasis of Light* (London, 1977).

[4] This Eastern theme was known in the West at the latest through the story of Marco Polo; see the text in U. Monneret de Villard, *Le leggende orientali sui magi evangelici* (Vatican City, 1952), 82, and further 35 (the eighth-century *Chronicle of Zuqnin*) and 77 (a late medieval Armenian text).

[5] For Epiphanic prophecies, see A. Van Gennep, *Manuel de folklore français contemporain*, tom. I, vol. 8 (Paris, 1988), 3531 and seq.

they were in a receptive mode. And since Matthew left to our imagination practically everything about these legitimating kings — they are the only representatives of philosopher-kings in the New Testament — it is not surprising to find that pious people in the twelfth century began to retrieve from their unconscious vital statistics regarding the Three Kings. Presumably other, older, dreamers preceded those who are the subjects of our article in enriching our knowledge about the Kings, but alas, the extant dreamers we will rely on did not admit to the inspiration of their elders.[6] It was taken for granted that they were the dreamers' own dreams, and in his classic seventeenth-century compilation of all traditions regarding the Three Kings, the Jesuit Hermann Crombach regularly cited these persons — almost all women and thus outsiders just as the Kings had been — together with more conventional sources as authorities for biographical information regarding the Kings. In fact, just a few years ago, in 1941, in an attempt to legitimate a modern uncoverer of the magian past, the Augustinian Helmut Fahsel declared:

> And the report of the gospel being so short, that little bit moves our feelings and excites us to want to learn more about these Kings. Written tradition gives us one possibility, but also the revelations of saints and seers, and among them the most extensive and descriptive [are those] of the servant of God, Anna Katharina Emmerich.[7]

---

[6] The first detailed description of the personalities of the magi is in the so-called Pseudo-Bede, which is now dated to the late eighth century and was perhaps Irish; the text is in R. E. McNally, "The Three Holy Kings in Early Irish Latin Writing," in *Kyriakon: Festschrift Johannes Quasten*, ed. P. Granfield and J. A. Jungmann, vol. 2 (Münster, 1970), 669–70; P. H. D. Kaplan, *The Rise of the Black Magus in Western Art* (Ann Arbor, 1985), 32f. Ps.-Bede gives no source for his information, but it might be a painting. See for example the description of the second magus by the clerk Agnello of Ravenna (d. 842). This text is a first-hand description of the mosaic of the Kings in the church of Sant'Apollinare Nuovo, Ravenna. The scribe says that his sixth-century predecessor, bishop Agnello, "magorum historiam perfecte ornavit, et sua effigies mechanico opere oculis inserta est": see the text, compared to the Ps.-Bede, in G. Zappert, "Epiphania: ein Beitrag zur christlichen Kunstarchäologie," in *Sitzungsberichte der philosophisch-historischen Klasse der kaiserlichen Akademie der Wissenschaften* 21 (1856): 338f. Since such "perfect" paintings often produced dreams or visions, it is possible that this inspired the Ps.-Bede as well. A noteworthy, curious medieval legend held that the magi had a painter in their retinue, who recorded the Adoration: Monneret de Villard, *Leggende orientali*, 108.

[7] *Die heiligen Drei Könige in der Legende und nach den Visionen der Anna Katherina Emmerich* (Basel, 1941), 5. Emmerich herself may have ascribed this type of authority to romantic genius. Referring to Clemens von Brentano, who transcribed (or manufactured!)

The three main questions of this article are first, the role that such dreams and visions played in our increasing "knowledge" of the Three Kings during the high and late Middle Ages, then how these spiritual images related to the material realities of the time, and finally what these visions tell us about the political understanding of the history of the Three Kings.

The earliest documented dreamer was one Elisabeth, the sainted young *magistra* of the nuns of the double monastery of Schönau, near Rhenish St. Goarshausen, a house whose church had been dedicated on Epiphany, the feast of the Kings (6 January). A protegée of Hildegard of Bingen, Elisabeth (1129–1164) is best known for her visions of the Eleven Thousand Virgins, a legend which spread at a crucial point in the history of Cologne.[8] But her less well known picturesque descriptions of the Kings also came to light at a decisive point in the city's history. After he had written to his flock on 12 June 1164 to tell them that he had come into possession of the relics of the "three magi and kings," the imperial chancellor and archbishop of Cologne Rainald von Dassel returned to his see on 23 July 1164.[9] A new cult of the so-called "Three Kings of Cologne," outfitted

---

the visions, she said: "Dieser Mann schreibt dies nich so sehr aus sich; er hat die Gnade Gottes dazu. Es kann es kein Mensch als er; es ist, als sähe er es selbst": Fahsel, *Drei Könige*, 16. H. Crombach, *Primitiae Gentium seu Historia SS. Trium Regum Magorum* (Cologne, 1654), 167, 398, 835, 839.

[8] B. Newman, *Sister of Wisdom: St. Hildegard's Theology of the Feminine* (Berkeley, 1987), 36. For the dedication, see F. W. E. Roth, *Die Visionen der hl. Elisabeth und die Schriften der Äkbert und Emecho von Schönau* (Brünn, 1884), 176. Elisabeth's head is still in the parish church of Schönau; N. Del Re, "Schönau, Elisabetta di," *Bibliotheca Sanctorum*, vol. 11 (Rome, 1968), 730f. In 1156 a Roman cemetery was unearthed in Cologne that allegedly contained the remains of the Virgins: T. A. Archer, "Ursulines," *Encyclopaedia Britannica*, 11th ed. (New York, 1911), 804.

[9] None of the legends regarding the magi appears to have known at the time that the relics of the Three Kings were actually in Milan, whence they then allegedly were brought to Cologne: P. J. Geary, "I magi e Milano," in *Millennio Ambrosiano*, ed. C. Bertelli (Milan, 1988), 78–92. On the cult, see H. Hofmann, *Die hl. Drei Könige: Zur Heiligenverehrung im kirchlichen, gesellschaftlichen und politischen Leben des Mittelalters* (Bonn, 1975); *Die Heiligen Drei Könige, Darstellung und Verehrung: Katalog zur Ausstellung des Wallraf-Richartz-Museums in der Josef-Haubrich-Kunsthalle, Köln, 1 Dezember 1982 bis 30. Januar 1983*, ed. R. Budde (Cologne, 1982); *Achthundert Jahre Verehrung der Heiligen Drei Könige, 1164–1964*, in *Kölner Domblatt: Jahrbuch des Zentral-Dombauvereins 23 and 24* (1964), and the classic work by H. Kehrer, *Die heiligen Drei Könige in Literatur und Kunst*, 2 vols. (Leipzig, 1908–1909). Barbarossa's and Reinald's attempt to establish a link between the Hohenstaufen and Charlemagne is well known: R. Folz, *Le souvenir et la Légende de Charlemagne dans l'Empire germanique médiéval* (Paris, 1950). A direct interest of Barbarossa in the cult of the magi has not yet been established. For that of his grandson, however, see below at n. 48.

with a fantastic pre-history, suddenly achieved an importance of the first order, which was nourished by the city, its bishop, and perhaps also by the young emperor, Frederick Barbarossa.

According to the record of Elisabeth's visions that were made by her brother Egbert (d. 1184), the abbot of Schönau and a follower of Barbarossa, Elisabeth in ecstasy saw the Three Kings on 6 January 1154 (Epiphany) and on the same feast the following year.[10] Although according to tradition she died on 18 June 1165, today it is thought that Elisabeth died exactly one year earlier, thus just one month before the relics of the Three Kings entered the city of Cologne in triumph (23 July 1164). If one assumes that Elisabeth indeed had the vision and admits that her brother came up with the later dating, then it must be suspected that the nun's visions survived because of the cultic sensation caused by the archbishop in 1164.

As we shall see, the content of the visions strengthens this idea. Let us say up front that no matter how important her visions would appear to later researchers into the life of the Three Kings, they really added nothing to the existing visual canon. As Paul Kaplan has emphasized, while a so-called prayer of the late twelfth or early thirteenth century from Schönau as well as one or two phrases of the nun Herrad von Hohenburg (d. 1195) upriver in Alsace did contribute something to the older descriptions of the Three Kings, to the best of our knowledge Elisabeth's visions did not.[11]

Still, what Elisabeth saw is interesting, because her visions, instead of merely describing a personal picture, raise the question of the relations between the Kings and the child, which is equivalent to some extent to the question of relations between worldly and church power. She describes types of comportment which, transcending our image of a static Adoration that we hold in our visual memory, give us a new insight into the contemporary understanding of that moment. Thus in her first vision the nun saw on one Epiphany evening Mary sitting on a throne with the child. This was of course not a realistic picture of Mary and child in the grotto, but as we will later see, it was one well known in the art and theatre of the time.

---

[10] *Acta Sanctorum* (hereafter *AS*), June (vol. 3) 18 (Antwerp, 1701), 618, 624.

[11] Kaplan, *Rise*, 29, referring to the text in Roth, *Visionen der hl. Elisabeth*, 176. But Kaplan exaggerates in characterizing this description as a prayer. It stands in part before those prayers and clearly comes from a narrative source and is not really hortatory. See Herrad's slightly varied contemporary description in her *Hortus Deliciarum: Reconstruction* (London, 1979), 150.

Then, on the following morning, during mass, Elisabeth saw the Kings kneel down together and, "taking the crowns from their heads, they offered them into the hands [of Jesus] and then received them back from them."[12] Such coronations or decrownings were a standard means of describing the relations between heaven and earth, and before as well as long after Elisabeth the Adoration of the Three Kings played a role in visually representing these relations (figs. 6, 8, 9, 10).[13]

Then in the Epiphany vision bearing a date of 1155, Elisabeth in ecstasy saw in her mind's eye three *viri* come forward "with royal ornament" so as to adore the child. On their approach, the second and third of these men offered their gifts to Jesus with gestures that would have been familiar to Elisabeth from the visual tradition of this scene, but the behavior of the first king she mentioned did not follow that tradition. This man "extended a large gold coin with the picture of a royal on it and put it in Jesus' hand." At first glance, it might appear to mean that the first king handed over his own image to the child. But Elisabeth and her brother could rather have been referring to the royal image, that is, to the profile of Frederick Barbarossa, who in the moment of this vision was indeed the German King, if not yet emperor.[14]

---

[12] "In circumcisione domini & epiphania visiones vidi dominicae diei, sed evidentius in epiphania. Tunc etiam in prima vespera vidi tres reges coronatos stantes ante thronum: & accedentes, adoraverunt flexis genibus ante filium hominis & tollentes coronas de capitibus suis, obtulerunt eas in manus ipsius; rursusque eas ab ipso receperunt. In die ad missam, rursus eosdem tres vidi, adorantes coram domino Jesu: & munuscula nescio quae lucida in manus ejus dare visi sunt": AS, June (vol. 3, 18), 618. Here Elisabeth surely also saw the deacons and subdeacons participating in the solemn mass of Epiphany.

[13] For these fourteenth-century miniatures, kindly brought to my attention by Debra Pincus, see *The Corpus of the Miniatures in the Manuscripts of Decretum Gratiani* (Rome, 1975), 45. They illustrate Gratian's first distinction relating to the foundations of divine and human law and power.

[14] After Frederick had been crowned King of Germany on 9 March 1152 at Aachen, Pope Hadrian IV crowned him emperor on 18 June 1155 in Rome. One can assume that on this latter occasion Barbarossa gifted Hadrian with the usual imperial gift of gold in the form of such coins. For such coronation gifts at the end of the twelfth century, see *Die Ordines für die Weihe und Krönung des Kaisers und der Kaiserin*, ed. R. Elze (Hannover, 1960), 62; for the "tresdecim bisantes aureos" of the French see *The Coronation Book of Charles V of France*, ed. E. S. Dewick (London, 1899), 43. Elisabeth's second vision: "In epiphania quoque domini, multiplicavit dominus gratiam suam in me, vidi in spiritu dominam meam & parvulum ejus, quasi in domo quadam longe posita commorantes. Et ecce tres viri, regalem habentes decorem, introierunt illuc, & flexis genibus adoraverunt coram puero. Unus autem ex illis proferens numisma aureum magnum, quasi imagine regia signatum, obtulit in manus ipsius. Similiter & alii duo accedentes, munera sua in vasculis quibusdam reverenter obtulerunt": AS, June (vol. 3, 18), 624. See also Hofmann,

Figure 6.
Majesty, fourteenth century.
Madrid, National Library, Ms. Vitr. 21.2, fol. 5v.

Figure 7.
Adoration of the Three Kings, c. 1470.
Munich, Bavarian National Museum: relief.

Figure 8.
Adoration of the Magi, fourteenth century.
Madrid, National Library, Ms. Vitr. 21.2, fol. 6r.

Figure 9.
Adoration of the Three Kings, tenth century.
London: British Library, Ms. Add. 49 598, fol. 24v.

Let us insist again that none of these moments in Elisabeth's dreams concurs with the visual canon of the Adoration or was later taken into it. Perhaps this can be most easily demonstrated if we focus on the royal image. Certainly rulers used the iconography of the Three Kings to vaunt their own brilliance and magnificence, and the "gold" that the first king offered to the child in painted Adorations appears in coins of surprisingly diverse forms, from eucharistic hosts to ducats lined up in gold chests (fig. 7) to Adorations that are framed by dynastic coins and medals.[15] But I have seen no picture that shows the image of a ruler on such an offered coin or medal. Nor can I find this type of gold gift in any of the liturgical Kings plays of the time. Thus Elisabeth's vision naively describes the dual adoration or apotheosis of real-life rulers as the center point of the Adoration, even if the latter's visual tradition, for whatever reason, failed to carry on this secular glorification in such simplicity.

Turning now to Elisabeth's other visions, we begin with the obvious: any time that crowns were surrendered and then returned to their original owners, significant problems of sovereignty were in play. In the case of representations of the Three Kings, these problems touch on the relative authority of state and church, which were respectively embodied in the Kings and in the child with Mary.[16] In the liturgical dramas of this age, wood sculptures of the divine Mary and Child sat on church altars to accept the gifts of the faithful, beginning with the Three Kings, who indeed bore the title of "the first fruits" of the pagan world.[17]

Now there were some established historical or legendary models for the

---

Heilige Drei Könige, 150f., who also imagines this was a royal image. Further background: in 1159 Barbarossa recognized his first anti-pope, Victor IV (1159–1164); his second, Paschal III, entered office in 1164, the year of Elisabeth's death and of the entry of the kings into Cologne.

[15] Like those in the Book of Hours of Manuel of Portugal, of the early sixteenth century; on this ruler and painting see J. Barreira, *Arte Portugese: Pinture* (Lisbon, 1948), 204, and Trexler, *Journey*, 134. Regarding eucharistic coins, see G. Ellard, "Bread in the Form of a Penny," *Theological Studies* 4 (1943): 319–46. In the c. 1480 Swabian altar painting of the Adoration in the Bavarian National Museum, a King holds a gold chest with four rows of coins.

[16] At times the pope was equated with the child Jesus; see R. Trexler, *Public Life in Renaissance Florence* (New York, 1980), 439 and n. 111.

[17] See the photographs in I. H. Forsyth, *The Throne of Wisdom: Wood Sculptures of the Madonna in Romanesque France* (Princeton, 1972), and also her "Magi and Majesty: A Study of Romanesque Sculpture and Liturgical Drama," *Art Bulletin* 50 (1968): 215–22.

surrender and recapturing of crowns seen by Elisabeth. First of all, the literature of this period is full of kings who offered up their crowns and other insignia. The most famous is the story of the humble King Canute of England: he was so impressed by his own incapacity to still the waves compared to God's power to do so that he never again wore a crown. Instead he promptly crowned a statue of the crucified Jesus, thus receiving nothing back as did Elisabeth's Kings.[18]

A second comparable practice, still encountered in the age of Elisabeth and Barbarossa, was the so-called *coronatum* or *Festkrönung*. According to Schramm, on the days of the year when the emperor attended festive divine services, and especially on Christmas, Easter, and Pentecost, the ruling prelate of the area took the royal crown from the altar of a church near the main church and crowned the ruler, who then bore it in procession to the main church, where a mass was then celebrated.[19]

Still, note that in this *Festkrönung* the king did not, as did Elisabeth's Three Kings, surrender his crown before entering the church. This third comparable practice, which obeyed the Pauline prohibition against men having anything on their head (1 Cor. 11.14), obviously came from the East to the West. Schramm documented already in fifth-century Constantinople what Constantine Porphyrogenitus's *De Ceremoniis* would transcribe in the tenth: after the Byzantine emperor had taken off his diadem upon entering Haghia Sophia on Christmas, he was in fact recrowned by the patriarch upon leaving the church.[20] Perhaps the diadem lay openly upon the altar during divine services.

---

[18] Cited in R. Deshman, "*Christus rex et magi reges:* Kingship and Christology in Ottonian and Anglo-Saxon Art," *Frühmittelalterlichen Studien* 10 (1976): 404f. For so-called votive crowns, which in being given over to the Gods were not taken directly from the rulers' heads, see P. E. Schramm, *Herrschaftszeichen und Staatssymbolik* (Stuttgart, 1956), 910–12.

[19] It is not clear just how public these cyclical coronations were: Schramm, *Herrschaftszeichen*, 915f. Cf. the story that Barbarossa had sworn that he would not wear his crown until Milan had fallen to his army, with the result that between 1159 and 1162 there were no *Festkrönungen*. The prophecy of the Anti-Christ should also be mentioned: Karl Hauck related it to Barbarossa's royal coronation in 1152: Schramm, *Herrschaftszeichen*, 918.

[20] Constantine VII Porphyrogenitus, *Le livre des cérémonies*, ed. A. Vogt, vol. 1 (Paris, 1967), 31 (I, 2); Schramm, *Herrschaftszeichen*, 917. For the important Byzantine Nativity theme and the song: "Christ was born who, emperor, crowned you," see O. Treitinger, *Die oströmische Kaiser- und Reichsidee nach ihrer Gestaltung im höfischen Zeremoniell* (Bad Homburg, 1969), 114. Note that when Pope Leo crowned Charlemagne on Christmas 800, the crowd cried that he had been "crowned by God": R. Folz, *The Coronation of Charlemagne, 25 December 800* (London, 1974), 25.

Yet the public surrender of a crown by one ruler to another, who then publicly gave it back, was not, as Robert Deshman presumed, the generally accepted practice. Referring to the old tribute ritual of the *aurum corona-rium*, this scholar directs our attention to the Adoration scene in the Benedictional of Aethelwold of England (c. 975), where the first king appears to give over their diadems to the child (fig. 10). But note well that the actual crowns of the Kings remain fast on the heads of the rulers.[21] I assume that this is so not only because western rulers of the time wore their crowns on their heads while in church, as Schramm claims, but also because rulers hesitated to give up the power that was embodied in their crowns.

Because Elisabeth envisioned the gesticulation of a mutual exchange, while paintings present precise moments in time, it is difficult to assert without reserve that her vision left no echo at all in subsequent art. Let us pursue this problem by introducing some comparable images. First, there are in fact many Adorations that show kings taking off or laying down their crowns. One of the earliest is the Klosterneuburg altar painting of 1181 by Nicholas of Verdun, in which the lead king has taken off his crown and laid it on his bent knee, presumably a sign of respect rather than of surrender.[22] But many other paintings, though of later date, show that the oldest king has laid his crown down on the floor, or "at the foot of Jesus," as Georg Zappert has said.[23] This deposition of the crown on the ground before a ruler is clearly an expression of respect, reciprocated by the child, who in some cases can be seen to bless each royal.[24]

Having referred to Adoration scenes that are comparable to Elisabeth's visions, we must be clear what the visual archive does not show. First, although the symbolic content of the Matthew story is the legitimation of Jesus by the Three Kings, it is not surprising that no known image shows a king crowning the child Jesus — as Canute and other European rulers are known to have crowned the Crucified and his crosses. Second, I know of no picture that shows the child Jesus holding a crown or any other symbol

---

[21] Deshman, "*Christus rex*," 380f.

[22] Reproduced in Kehrer, *Heilige Drei Könige*, 2:142.

[23] See his list of such works in "Epiphania," 336. In the eastern *Chronicle of Zuqnin* the magi also "lay" their crowns at Jesus' feet, "because the eternal empire belongs to him": Monneret de Villard, *Leggende orientali*, 39.

[24] The Latin can be interpreted to mean that Jesus then blessed each of the *kings*, but each of the *crowns* might also be suggested; see the text below, at n. 51. For the emperor and empress who were urged to *deponere* their crowns during a Roman coronation, see the late twelfth-century *ordo* in Elze, *Ordines*, 46.

Figure 10.
The Coronation of Louix XIV and an Adoration of the Magi, 1652.
France, Royal Almanach.

of rule belonging to those who adore him, and thus none shows Jesus handing over any such symbol of rule to a ruler. Third, no picture I know of shows the child Jesus crowning or recrowning one of the Kings, especially surprising given the undoubted association of the theme of the Three Kings to royal coronations.[25] In short, it is difficult to find in Adorations evidence of ruler reciprocity among these kings, or evidence of Jesus, who in these Adorations represents the church, crowning these secular rulers.

Yet perhaps such evidence can be found in another area. For if few if any paintings or sculptures of the Three Kings appear to have survived that refer dramatically to the fundamental problems of royal and ecclesiastical power — as if to say that no ruler would do business with a child, whether he was a God or not — there was in Elisabeth's time another area of experience alongside the *Festkrönung* that could have influenced her vision. I am referring to the liturgical drama of the Three Kings that was performed in churches on the feast of Epiphany. To judge from Herrad of Hohenburg's *Hortus deliciarum*, this drama must have been customarily performed in the Rhineland after 1164, when the Kings' relics reached Cologne, which is also the year of Elisabeth's death.[26] Perhaps Elisabeth saw in such theatre how the clerics playing the Kings approached the altar so as to gift the wood or stone Mary with Child seated on the Throne of Wisdom.[27] Or perhaps she saw something even more closely resembling her vision. According to Crombach, the Kings laid down their crowns

---

[25] That is, *a deo coronatus*. Yet the problematic text in the Vita of Veronica of Binasco (n. 50) requires attention. There is, further, a rich tradition in which particular kings were crowned by older Jesuses and by godfathers, if not by children: P. E. Schramm and F. Mütherich, *Denkmale der deutschen Könige und Kaiser* (Munich, 1962), 258, 315, 326, 329. A theme of perfect reciprocity, in which the child Jesus gifts the Kings from his own possessions (relics!), appears to be almost exclusively eastern: see Monneret de Villard, *Leggende orientali*, 107, where the Kings receive some of Jesus' swaddling clothes.

[26] For Herrad's long denunciation of plays in churches and especially those dealing with the magi — obviously familiar to both her and her readers — see her *Hortus Deliciarum. Reconstruction*, 491f. See also the more general denunciations of such plays by Elisabeth's contemporary Gerhoh of Reichersberg in K. Young, *The Drama of the Medieval Church*, vol. 2 (Oxford, 1933), 524f. When the Star plays began in Cologne is disputed; Norbert King could find no medieval evidence: "Ein Magierspiel im Kölner Dom?," *Kölner Domblatt* 36–37 (1975): 23–34.

[27] The text (at no. 12) makes it sound as if Elisabeth was in church with the throne actually before her when she saw the magi approach him. For this Throne of Wisdom, see Forsyth, *Throne of Wisdom* (above n. 18).

together with their gifts on the altar in an ancient but alas undated play from Besançon.[28]

If this latter magi play also does not state how the kings got their crowns back — as did Elisabeth's Kings get theirs back from Jesus — a comparable rite, the crowing of a play king, may give us an answer. This ritual was usually the most important coronation during Christmastide. Following the biblical rubric of inversion — "He has put down the mighty from their thrones, and exalted those of low degree" (Lk. 1.52) — in many areas during Twelve Nights power was transferred from a real to a festive king (for example, to a Boy Bishop), and within this upside-down kingdom from one canonical or societal group to another. Although these happenings are better documented in the later Middle Ages, they were surely in place at the earlier point we are studying. Gerhoh von Reicherberg's complaints and Herrad von Hohenburg's dull denunciations of such strange festive kings lead me to suspect that such transferrals of office were already customary in the Rhineland during Elisabeth's lifetime.[29]

The symbolic agent for this transferral could be a miter or a crown. In the course of a ritual the old ruler laid his crown on an altar, a crown which then found its way to the head of a new ruler, who, aided by his cortège, became responsible for the execution of the festival.[30] I do not know if the wooden child on the Throne of Wisdom, at whose side stood a living minister, was the source of the renewed power not only of the festive Three Kings but also that of the lord of the festival. Nor can I do more than speculate that the inspiration for Elisabeth's coins bearing the royal face may have been the cheap coins that were usually passed out in such celebrations. One can only assume that the theatrical festive images produced by the church, with their special emphasis upon the Three Kings, were, along with royal *Festkrönungen*, another source for Elisabeth's imaginings.

Other, less interesting Epiphany visions follow those of Elisabeth of

---

[28] "Postea pergunt ante maius altare; ibique flexis genibus offerunt sua munera cum coronis ... super altare": Crombach, *Primitiae Gentium*, 732–34, analyzed in Young, *Drama*, 2:40.

[29] Already mentioned above, n. 26.

[30] To elaborate on this is beyond the scope of this paper. Already in the early tenth century we find boys in the monastery of Sankt Gall choosing a festive king: *Monumenta Germaniae Historica: Scriptores*, vol. 2 (Hannover, 1829), 91. At the time of Elisabeth, boy bishops were elected in Germany just as in France were lords or kings of fools. For this material see E. K. Chambers, *The Medieval Stage*, 2 vols. (Oxford, 1903), 1:278, 336f.

Schönau. The daydreams of the blessed Walthenus, abbot of the Scottish
Cistercian abbey of Melrose (1159–1214), deserve special mention, because
his biographer made the determination, surprising in a clergyman, that this
holy man in ecstasy one Epiphany evening "*saw* the whole *text* of the
lord's Epiphany."[31] In short, the writer has his hero see each picture of
the magi story as recorded in Matthew, but clerically describes it as the
Kings' text.

Then toward the end of the thirteenth century a Franciscan nun in
Vienna by the name of Agnes Blannbekin or Blambeck imagined the
crowned Kings during their Journey. For thirteen days, she says, they rode
along on the most unusual horses; the scribe recording her words decides
these were camels. Following her revelation, she told her clerical director
what she had seen of the clothing of each King, in the process detailing
some important variations from the customary. Each King wore a cloak as
he rode along, which fell down over the rear end of the animal he rode,
while over their tunic and over-tunic each King was enveloped in a different colored coat, "exactly the way the apostles are painted."[32]

I have already shown that earlier literary details about the exterior
appearance of the Kings, as in the Pseudo-Bede, might actually be descriptions either of visions or of paintings, as seems the case here. I would only

---

[31] My italics. At night in the choir, during psalms, "cecidit in mentis excessum, vid-
itque in spiritu, sicut evangelica prodit historia, totum apparitionis dominice textum . . .
regum ab oriente cum magno apparatu venientium cursu praevio praeducem . . . & demum in somnis divinitus admonitos per aliam viam, quam advenerant, in regionem suam
reversos. . . ." Later he was happy, "nam singulis annis in vigilia theophaniae, cum col-
lecta illa recitaretur, scilicet 'Corda nostra splendor futurae festivitatis illustret etc.,' largo
lacrymatum sed mellifluo ex visionis hujus recordatione, rigabatur profluvio": see the *vita*
of Jordan in *AS*, August (1) 3 (Antwerp, 1733), 263f. Note that there is no biblical basis
for the visionary's "great retinue."

[32] My italics. "In hac quoque revelatione vidit magos ab oriente venientes et, ut sit,
quibusdam equis, quales nunquam vidit, unde creduntur fuisse dromedarii. Quilibet eorum
habuit manticam magnam & plenam post tergum in equo: ea quoque, quae erant victui
necessaria, secum deferebant: & stella magna eos antecedebat in aere satis prope terram.
Incedebant autem coronati, in tredecim diebus de loco suo usque ad puerum pervenerunt.
Primus rex et senior indutus erat per totum albis vestibus, tunica scilicet et supertunicali,
et chlamyde, quam chlamidem circumdabat sibi, sicut depinguntur apostoli. Eodem modo
& alii induti erant, excepto, quod secundus sive medius habuit vestes bicolores, id est,
colore jacynthino & nigro permixto, & ultimus habuit vestes rubeas": *Ven. Agnetis Blannbekin . . . vita et revelationes auc. anon. ordinis minorum e celebri conventu Sanctae Crucis
Wiennensis* (Vienna, 1731), 242. Note that the magi are portrayed as prefigurers of the
Apostles. See R. Strauss, *Studien zur Mystik in Österreich, mit besonderer Berücksichtigung
von Agnes Blambeck* (diss., University of Vienna, 1948).

add that while the male visionary Walthenus saw biblical words become pictures, the male biographer of Agnes Blannbekin has her visions emerge from other pictures.

These traditions of dreams and visions of the Three Kings continue in the *Gesta Romanorum*, a compilation of moral *exempla* from the early fourteenth century. In one of these the Danish king, Canute, seems to exactly repeat the behavior of the Three Kings, in the process demonstrating that medieval rulers experienced a certain solidarity with their ancient pagan brothers. During his pilgrimage to Cologne *cum comitatu solemni* — one evoking the arrival of the ashen Three Kings themselves in 1164 — the nordic ruler distributed liberal alms to the poor and to churches. After arriving at the famous shrine of the magi, the prince presented to the Kings the three crowns he had brought with him, following an already established Cologne tradition.[33] Then on the evening before his departure for home he dreamed . . . just as had the Kings. In this dream each King had placed the crown given him by Canute on his head. Then each of the Three Kings told their "brother" the Danish king his future; the Kings were of course famous as heavenly astrologers and for their predictions during Twelfth Night.[34] In this dream each King gave the Dane a monstrance filled respectively with the gold of wisdom, the myrrh of penance, and the incense of forgiveness. The Dane found all three monstrances beside him when he awoke.

What is so striking in this dream or vision, as it is also named, is the actual surrender and retrieval of the crowns. After they were at first laid at the shrine, then in the dream they were taken off by the Kings, to then finally be symbolically returned to their royal gifter in the monstrances. In the end the king was promised that he would remain on his earthly throne for twenty-three more years, at which point he would enter into the heavenly kingdom.[35] Here again is the reciprocity experienced by Elisabeth.

---

[33] Perhaps Otto IV introduced this practice on Epiphany: Hofmann, *Die Heiligen Drei Könige*, 305. It is noteworthy that although the image of the Journey of the Magi was used as a context for large distribution of alms in medieval and early modern theatre, this Franciscan innovation (see e.g., the Ps.-Bonaventure text) rarely found its way into paintings of the Kings.

[34] See the text in the next note, along with the promise that he would live another twenty-three years. This detail tends to show that the story was a typical backdated prophecy that referred to an actual nordic king.

[35] See the text in *Gesta Romanorum*, ed. H. Oesterly (Hildesheim, 1963), 345f. (cap. 47, *de tribus regibus*). It says that the king would return home happier and richer than he had come, and that after twenty-three years "jugiter in celestibus nobiscum regnabis,"

At this time the cult of the magi was obviously also a cult for earthly kings, and through magi pictures, representations, and plays contemporaries dealt with the problem of their own rulers' legitimacy. Elisabeth has Jesus legitimate the Three Kings, while these in turn insured a long life for their Danish brother and indirectly for his descendants. Robert Folz and others have emphasized that exactly in the time of Elisabeth different European rulers canonized the holy founders of their various realms.[36] Yet nothing could afford a descendant greater legitimacy than to know that through dreams, his ancestry could be traced back to the very Three Kings who had visited the savior child himself.

The importance that the *Gesta Romanorum* obviously assigned to the solidarity between kings leads us to turn our attention to the relations among them. We shall neglect the so influential visionary Bridget of Sweden (1303–1373) because, while she was the inspiration for some important book illuminations that showed her looking in on the crib, she has almost nothing to say about the Three Kings.[37] But an important Roman visionary, Francesca de' Ponziani or "Romana" (1384–1440), does afford us a last medieval insight into our continuing problem of the relations of the Kings to the child, of the state to the church. The contribution of this woman to the tradition is the more interesting because the city of Rome, even though it did boast a famous crib in the church of Santa Maria in Trastevere, and was in fact the locus of many of Francesca's visions, actually had very little or no city cult to the Kings. While during the previous century first Milan and Pavia and then Florence had developed such cults, which were very important to the political and artistic identity of these cities, in medieval and early modern Rome nothing comparable is encountered.[38]

In another context a student of Francesca's Three Kings visions would insist on the importance they attached to poverty. In them the gifts of the

---

notable evidence that earthly kings associated collegially with the Three Kings in heaven. In fact, at death the king had indeed earned heaven.

[36] Folz, *Souvenir*, 203–5.

[37] She says only that the child smiled at the magi: J. Jorgensen, *Saint Bridget of Sweden*, vol. 2 (London, 1954), 260. Interestingly, the illuminations in question transform the bright light that Bridget envisioned behind the child into the Star of Bethlehem: *Medieval and Renaissance Miniatures from the National Gallery of Art* (Washington, DC, 1975), 58–60, Pl. 5.

[38] Background is in R. Trexler, "The Magi Enter Florence: The Ubriachi of Florence and Venice," now in my *Church and Community, 1200–1600: Studies in the History of Florence and New Spain* (Rome, 1987), 75–167.

magi were said to be welcome because the holy family was poor, and yet soon enough Mary distributed what she did not need to others. Both while in and outside her trances Francesca was sure the magi were now in heaven because of their generosity.[39] Another student might want to dwell instead on the new information Francesca brought to light about the magi's knowledge. They knew about Moses and the burning bush and looked to the heavens to find the Star, because they were familiar with the prophecies of the Sibyls about the birth of the savior, etc.[40] A third student might dwell on the fact that Francesca's visionary Kings sang songs of praise of a quasi-liturgical type, allowing us to suspect that in contemporary Rome there were at least liturgico-dramatic presentations of the Adoration.[41] Indeed Francesca's scribe, almost as if he was composing a play, tells us how the Kings just lay down for a short nap, when they saw the three angels, the first of whom warned them in their dreams to go home by another way, *as can be read in Matthew's gospel.*[42]

For our present purpose, however, what is important is that Francesca clarifies the range of the behavior that she witnessed during the Adoration: the Three Kings bowed their heads to the child's feet. She says that after kneeling down, the last king, Melchior, was restrained by respect and fear from approaching the virgin and child more closely, but that the middle king, Balthazar, got up from kneeling and approached the child, who promptly moved his foot forward so that the monarch could kiss it.[43]

---

[39] Mary thanks the magi "ut veniretis visitatum nostram paupertatem" in her vision no. 16, of 1432; see the *Vita* of Giovanni Mariotti in *AS*, March (2) 9 (Antwerp, 1668), 113. As regards the "munera vero et oblationes non modici valoris, quas secum actulerant relinquentes, ipsa virgo excellentissima et misericordiosissima pauperibus distribuere precipiebat," see the 1440 witness in *I processi inediti per Francesca Bussa dei Ponziani (Santa Francesca Romana), 1440–1453*, ed. P. T. Lugano (Vatican City, 1945), 64. Her 1433 vision (no. 46), which appeared first while she was passive and then continued while she was active, assured her that the Three Kings were in heaven, and so she promptly prayed to them there: *AS*, March (2, 9), 136.

[40] "Dixit etiam, quomodo illi magi bene sciebant, qualiter Moyses viderat rubum ardere & non comburi; sciebant etiam dicta prophetarum de incarnatione dominica prophetantium & ideo steterunt cum magno affectu in illo orientali monte simul cum aliis spectatoribus, ut viderent signum novae stellae. Et priusquam vidissent stellam, fuerunt declarati in eorum mentibus, quod redemptor era iam natus, & descendentibus ipsis de monte apparuit eis stella": *AS*, March (2, 9), 135f. (no. 46).

[41] The lauds that each magus sang for mother and child in Francesca's vision no. 16 (1432), are in *AS*, March (2, 9), 113.

[42] "Ut legitur in evangelio Macthei": Lugano, *Processi*, 64.

[43] "Aliis vero antiquior Gaspar adhuc genibus flexis stans, magna cum reverentia pedibus Verbi humanati caput submisit: ipsum autem Verbum divinum suum sanctissi-

A king kissing the foot of the child is a common enough scene found in many Adorations. But what is most important in this visionary scene is what Francesca saw the first magus do. According to our source Caspar got up off his knees and then "threw his head down beneath the foot of the Word That Became Flesh. This holy Word [then] put his most holy foot down on the head [of Caspar]."[44]

Thus Francesca's scribe left little doubt that the actual original model for the theme of the Three Kings in Christian art — the submission of foreign princes beneath the foot of the Roman imperial ruler in a demonstration of dependency which in its servility was intended to appear almost feminine — was still in place as a conventional meaning of the Adoration of the Kings. In fact an important ceremonial even in papal history, the submission of Roger Guiscard to Honorius II in 1125, shows that since antiquity, the papacy had maintained the practice of placing the papal foot on the neck of subjects.[45]

As a Roman, Francesca obviously knew that kissing the papal foot was an important and often disputed sign of papal lordship in contemporary Roman ritual. And in fact papal supremacy is stressed in other parts of her magi visions.[46] Yet again, this vision of rigid subordination never seems

---

mum pedem super eius caput posuit. Balthassari vera stanti adhuc genu flexo, & pedes dei altissimi filii osculare volenti, ipse dei & virginis filius pedem aliquantulum extensum ad os applicuit. Tertius vero rex adhuc etiam genuflexus, prae reverentia & timore verbi incarnati, noluit se approximare": AS, March (2, 9), 113 (no. 16). Then they all sat down and admired Virgin and child. The significance of the third king not approaching Mother and child is examined below, at n. 52, and in Trexler, Journey, 100.

[44] See the text in the previous note.

[45] "E il papa gli puose il calcio in sul collo e disse il verso del psaltero [91.13] che dice: 'Super aspidem et basiliscum ambulabis, et conculcabis leonem et draconem'; e cio detto, gli perdono, e fecelo levare, e basciollo in segno di pace": Croniche di Giovanni, Matteo e Filippo Villani (Triest, 1857), Giovanni: bk. 4, cap. 34; further B. Schimmelpfennig, Die Zeremonienbücher der Römischen Kurie im Mittelalter (Tübingen, 1973), 206f., and in the index "pes pape." More generally, for the foot of the Roman emperor on the neck of the barbarians as a model for magi iconography, see A. Grabar, L'Empereur dans l'art byzantin: Recherches sur l'art officiel de l'empire d'Orient (Paris, 1936). For the metaphoric and behavioral effeminizing of the victim, see R. Trexler, " 'Correre la Terra': Collective Insults in the Late Middle Ages," in R. Trexler, Dependence in Context in Renaissance Florence (Binghamton, 1994), 113–70.

[46] Note especially the papal twist that she gave her spiritual director of the description of Mary's crown. It begins: "in una eadem erant tres coronae, una super aliam": AS, March (2, 9), 112 (no. 15). For the famous earlier case of the humiliated emperor Henry IV who in 1077 kissed the feet of the pope, see G. Villani, Croniche, bk. 4, cap. 27. Naturally, an emperor's foot might also be kissed: M. Villani, Croniche, bk. 4, cap. 53 (1355).

to have entered the visual repertory. I have encountered no Adoration in which Jesus actually puts his foot down on the head of a King.

We turn now finally from the King-child relationship in these dreams and visions to the relations between the Kings themselves, as they were first articulated in the Danish dream in the *Gesta Romanorum*. We wish to sketch the problematic within which these relationships can be understood. At first it would appear that the cult of the magi was a monarchical cult for rulers, since it emphasizes royal values. Yet there are facts in the way. In Constantinople the magi remained wise men or at most ambassadors of a great Eastern monarch, rather than ever having become Kings as in the West, and in Rome itself, the magi had at best an unimportant cult. Perhaps the cult could only have gotten off the ground in these two absolutistic centers if their rulers had been identified with Jesus and not with the Kings, or only if they had developed the ecumenic notion of many kings and nations submitting themselves to the pope or the Byzantine ruler. It is well known that the emperor Otto II did actually cultivate an identification between himself and either Jesus or God the Father, but more generally, in the West such a solution never caught on.[47]

A solution to this problem — that there were Three biblical Kings but only one worldly king to be honored — was, however, in reach, for a secular ruler if not for an elected pope. This was to represent the Three Kings as three generations of a dynasty and thus to convert an ecumenical into a national or familial image. Adorations that show a dynastic relationship between the Kings are well known from a later time, but it is not generally recognized how early this interpretation was conceived and described. It emerged in Apulia in the age of the Hohenstaufen. In a laud written around 1235 to honor Frederick II, Nicholas of Bari refers first to Frederick's dead grandfather Barbarossa and then to his father, Henry VI. Then he states: "These three emperors are like the Three Kings who came with gifts to honor the man-god. But here is the youngest (*adolescentior*) of the three, over whom the child Jesus has extended his godly hands and his most holy arms."[48]

---

[47] Many representations of the provinces that paid tribute to the Ottonians and to certain previous rulers are reproduced in Schramm and Mütherich, *Denkmale*, 259, 297, 320, 323, 326, 329.

[48] "Magnus dominus avus suus, quia imperator romanus, magnus dominus pater, quia imperator et rex Sicilie, ipse maximus, quia imperator romanus, rex Iherusalem et Sicilie. Profecto hii tres imperatores sunt quasi tres magi, qui venerunt cum muneribus deum et hominem adorare, sed hic est adolescentior illis tribus, super quem puer Ihesus felices

Emphasizing the third or youngest King is a well enough known practice in late medieval and early modern Adorations, but one that is insuffi-
ciently understood. Nicholas of Bari's presentation stands out especially
because he emphasizes the one living in relation to the two dead members
of the dynasty. Thus already in the high Middle Ages a writer dwelled on
two dead Kings to legitimate the single living one. One can say that Bari
privileged the ruler over the dynasty, the individual over the community,
the one living over the many dead. Thus the ghosts of Epiphanies past,
who are there in dreams, are pitted against the real material power of the
living monarch, whom we see, touch, and fear. Precisely this reflection on
the Young vs. the Old and the Dead vs. the Living is what is necessary for
us to understand the images created by the last of the medieval visionaries
of the Kings.

The nun Veronica, who spent the greater part of her life (1445-1497)
in the convent of Binasco, about halfway between Milan and Pavia —
cities that were both associated with important cults to the magi —, had
visions of the Three Kings that, like those of Francesca Romana, almost
certainly derived from street- and church-theatre.[49] After in these visions
being carried east by the angels, Veronica saw the Three Kings journeying
westward together, and got a good overview of the multiplicity of wild
animals in their great retinue. In our mind's eye we can almost picture a
great contemporary street cavalcade in a Milanese feast of the Epiphany.[50] Veronica then describes how Mary stood up to greet the Kings as
they entered her room, how Jesus' legs were bare while his upper body was
covered over, and how each of the Kings genuflected thrice as he approached the child.

At this point the action becomes important for our inquiry, for it
shows a third King starkly at variance from the retiring prince in Fran-

---

manus posuit et brachiola sacrosancta": printed first by R. M. Kloos, "Nikolaus von Bari,
eine neue Quelle zur Entwicklung der Kaiseridee unter Friedrich II," *Deutsches Archiv für
Erforschung des Mittelalters* 2 (1954-55): 171. The contents of the royal laud is also in
F. O. Büttner, *Imitatio Pietatis: Motive der christlichen Ikonographie als Modelle zur Verähnlichung* (Berlin, 1983), 27. Note especially the reference to oiling in the laying on of the
hands.

[49] For the theatrical background see also R. Trexler, "Triumph and Mourning,"
elsewhere in this volume.

[50] The vision emerged during developing phases of ecstasy, which began in private
and then continued at different point during the mass. The *vita*, by Isidoro Isolani (c.
1518), is in AS, Jan. (1, 13), 906 (cap. 4).

cesca Romana's scene. According to the nun of Binasco the Three began endlessly to debate as to who would adore the child first. Finally she says: "The youngest of the three approached first, kissed the feet of the child and then took the crown from his head so as to lay it at the child's feet. Then he put [the crown] back on his head, whereupon Jesus blessed him. The others did the same."[51] After reporting that each of the imposing Kings was dressed in gold down to his knees, she emphasized that "amazingly, the youngest king, who had done his adoration first, seemed to have grown old, appearing to have reached the same age as the two others."[52] Obviously, the latter two kings were conceived as being of one age. In her subsequent description of the dream in which the magi were ordered to go home by another way, Veronica has nothing so interesting as this curious history of the ageing at the point of gifting, not even her story that a rabid Herod on hearing of the magi's offerings promised gifts to anyone who would arrest the Kings.[53]

The inspiration for Veronica's story of the two ages derives from a particular theatrical tradition associated with the town of Erlau, the details of which I cannot enter into here, in which the magi, as in Veronica's vision, were of only two different ages and not three. In this dramatic tradition the young King, who wishes to be old and thus adore the child first,

---

[51] "Anteaquam reges infantulum contingentes adorarent ter genu flexere, diuque ad invicem disputarunt, quis eorum prior adoraret; denique iunior primus accessit, pedes infantis exosculans & quam capite gestabat coronam ante pedes infantuli solo reponens, quem Iesus infans benedixit. Sic quoque egere ceteri": *Vita*, cap. 4.

[52] "At reges specie corporis praestantes fuisse dicebat Veronica, aureis vestibus usque ad genua indutos, iunioremque regem, qui primus adoraverat, veluti effectum seniorem & unius aetatis cum reliquis duobus demirans intuita est": *Vita*, cap. 4.

[53] "Posteaquam recessere magi, una tantum nocte per vicina hospitia demorati sunt. Vidit autem Veronicae spiritus angelum domini in somnis apparentem regibus, ac mandantem ne redirent ad Herodem. Quo responso accepto, per aliam viam reversi sunt in regionem suam. Post regum abscessum angelus domini mentem Veronicae ad locum ubi Herodes erat perduxit. Vehementer iratus videbatur una cum omnibus qui aderant, quod abeuntes magi ad se reversi minime fuissent. Iussit quoque per praecones omnibus nuntiari, ut quicumque inventos reges ad se perducerent magnis muneribus donarentur. Post haec ad corporeos usus rediens Veronicae mens sorores vesperas iam magna ex parte decantavisse comperit": *Vita*, cap. 4. Note Galvano Fiamma's theatrical variant on the phrase "go home by another way" in his description of a 1336 Milanese festival: "Et angelus alatus eis dixit, quod non redirent per contratam Sancti Laurentii, sed per portam Romanam; quod & factum fuit": *Rerum Italicarum Scriptores*, old ed. vol. 12 (Milan, 1728), 1017f.

exchanges with the eldest of the trio perhaps a mask or becomes older in some other marvelous way.[54]

We do not have space here to show that at one level Veronica's vision was also linked to the painterly tradition. At first sight that appears unlikely, for in that tradition the old man has almost exclusive precedence, and if there are cases in which the youngest king comes second, he is in fact never shown as being first in line to adore. But when we look again at the visual record we can verify that while the Kings may always be three, they may be shown as having only two ages. Or expressed differently, in such Adorations the Kings are shown typologically dualistic, as being only Old and Young.[55] To express myself still more directly: within this duet, the young King is individualized in a vital and lively fashion — going so far as to be shown sometimes as almost soft or womanly — while the other two Kings often appear similar and lifeless.[56]

A western king could in fact allow himself to be represented within such a format. His painter could show two kings as lifeless or as in heaven, while representing his patron — the youngest and actual ruler — at the center of attention, embodying so to speak the latter of the King's two bodies.[57] Just as Matthew legitimated the poor infant as the King of the Jews by reference to authoritative outsiders, so medieval dreamers could legitimate their kings by linking this dynastic element of age progression to

---

[54] In the various non-liturgical plays in which the Kings dispute over who should worship Jesus first, the oldest wins in all but one. In the Erlau play (1400–1440), the youngest King demands but also wins not only this precedence but also the age itself (i.e., a mask) of the oldest King along with his virtues, while the oldest King gains the youth of the youngest: King, *Mittelalterliche Dreikönigsspiele*, 130f., and 253, n. 203, for a list of the plays in which such disputes emerge. A masked King is almost certainly shown in the Berlin drawing reproduced in W. W. S. Cook, "The Earliest Painted Panels of Catalonia (VI)," *Art Bulletin* 10 (1928): 320 (fig. 16). A fifteenth-century legend from Brixen (not far from Milan) also shows a successful "jung künig dy grosse begierd, das er der elter wär, dar umb das er des ersten ophert": King, *Mittelalterliche Dreikönigsspiele*, 131. Recall that in certain eastern traditions the Kings (of different ages) saw in the Star the Jesus of their individual age group: Monneret de Villard, *Leggende orientali*, 35, 77.

[55] These hypotheses are argued in mature form in Trexler, *Journey of the Magi*.

[56] The exotic third king is established no later than Gentile da Fabriano's Adoration of 1423, and is a commonplace among the later Antwerp Mannerists. Büttner (*Imitatio*, 29) is mistaken when he says that usually it is the older King who has the most individualized features; in fact, he is usually quite stereotyped. This artistic habit of individualizing one king emerges at about the same time that Margaret of Navarre for the first time dwells on the specific psychological quality of each of them: see the text in King, *Mittelalterliche Dreikönigsspiele*, 144f.

[57] E. H. Kantorowicz, *The King's Two Bodies* (Princeton, 1957).

the iconography of the Three Kings. The coins that "were similar to the royal face" could remain legal tender after the person represented had died.

Yet here again, another magi theme that emerged in dreams and visions — that of Veronica — left no direct echo in art, as if painting and sculpture were too solemn or "decent" a means of expression to be open to such temporary politico-festive ends. "He has put down the mightly," indeed! It is the silence of the pictures that makes the representations of the visionaries so interesting. They, perhaps more than the pictures, referred directly to the dynamic relation between child and Kings (that is, between church and state) and between the Kings themselves, that is, between those living and those dead, those young and those old.

But dreams about the Three Kings were far from over. There was still so much to learn about these wise men! That is, actual political relations change with time and thus make it possible for the "Journey" and "Adoration" to change with them. For example, the changing nature of the control that male scribes had over the women who imagined the Three Kings can explain why a dreamer of the enlightened twentieth century — Theresa Neumann — was the first visionary to see the wife of one of the Kings accompanying him to Bethlehem! Indeed, in Neumann's report the decor and ornament of that queen's clothing is made to seem greater than that worn by her husband.[58] Now, if we were to limit ourselves to emphasizing the importance of women in modern images of the Adoration, we might falsely presume that female elements were absent in the iconography of the earlier magi. First, while we usually think of festive kings during Twelve Nights, at least in the late Middle Ages queens of the bean, for example, may have been quite as prominent.[59] And while doubtless the male prophets of Israel have strongly informed our image of

---

[58] In the sources of traditional Europe, I could find only one indication that a King was married: King, *Mittelalterliche Dreikönigsspiele*, 135. Neumann's innovative vision of Balthazar's wife, with her four court ladies on the Journey, is in F. Gerlich, *Die stigmatisierte Therese Neumann von Konnersreuth* (Munich, 1929), 225–28. But for medieval women and men who imagined Jesus as woman, see C. Walker Bynum, *Jesus as Mother* (Berkeley, 1982), and the information in Newman, *Sister of Wisdom*, 238–71. For the Kings' inspection of the child to see if it was truly male, see the various pictures in L. Steinberg, *The Sexuality of Christ in Renaissance Art and in Modern Oblivion* (New York, 1983).

[59] For example, the first visual representation of a Christmas festive ruler known to me is in fact a fifteenth-century woman Queen of the Bean, Adelaide of Savoy: see M. Vloberg, *Les Noëls de France* (Grenoble, 1938), 175.

the importance of the child's birth, the female sibyls played a quite comparable role in the medieval imagination.[60]

But still more pregnant with meaning: what appears on the surface to be a discretely male iconography of the magi, *deponentes potentes*, actually comes to grips with the presumed female principle of dependency and subordination. Just as contemporaries in attempting to describe the relation between state and church could draw up an image of a gray old King interacting with a mere infant, so too, so as to describe the relation between rulers, they subversively produced a young King with a vitality that they withheld from the elder ones. Some of these transformations of dependents into *potentes* surely were not apt for representation in the pictorial tradition. And yet, in the end the vitality, sweep, and exoticism of this last magus occasionally produced a female or effeminate note: Sir Woman, the often extravagantly dressed third King who, if a black, was even fitted with earrings, and who, shamelessly, pushed ahead of his elders! A carnival dream, indeed.

---

[60] The Tiburtine sibyl — a woman — was the best-known prophet of the Nativity, and many considered her a predecessor of the magi: see the text above, n. 41.

Triumph and Mourning in
North Italian Magi Art[*]

FOR SOME TIME I HAVE BEEN STUDYING the political and social significance of the Christian story of the magi or wise men.[1] Called the Three
Kings since the sixth century, these men are said to have followed a star
to Bethlehem, there worshipped King Jesus, and then returned home to
spread Christianity among the gentiles. The magi story is significant because it describes a set of ideas and a type of legitimating behavior both in
past times, when people have evoked it in art, festive life, oral tradition,
and literature, and in the present, whenever scholars still call such past activities to our attention, as I do now. To be taken seriously, any movement, like Christianity, must first and last be recognized by outside savants

---

[*] This essay appreared previously in *Art and Politics in Late Medieval and Early
Renaissance Italy*, ed. C. Rosenberg (Notre Dame, 1990), 38–66.
[1] R. Trexler, "The Magi Enter Florence: The Ubriachi of Florence and Venice," in
R. Trexler, *Church and Community, 1200–1600. Studies in the History of Florence and New
Spain* (Rome, 1987), 75–167; R. Trexler and Mary E. Lewis, "Two Captains and Three
Kings: New Light on the Medici Chapel," in *Church and Community*, 169–244; R. Trexler, "La vie ludique dans la Nouvelle Espagne. L'empereur et ses trois rois," in *Church
and Community*, 493–510, and in English elsewhere in the present collection; R. Trexler,
Public Life in Renaissance Florence (New York, 1980; Ithaca, 1990), passim. I would like
to thank Ilka Kloten and Debra Pincus for their help, and my former collaborator Lewis
for her inspiration.

or princes who come inside. Thus did the magi legitimize Jesus at Bethlehem, in the traditional Christian telling.

In my view, this magi theme belongs to a select group of Christian stories whose essences powerfully relate art to life processes at a fundamental
narrative-structural level, and identifying such themes must be a priority
of cultural historians who hope to relate their "objects" to broad social
and political realities. I call such life-pictures "iconographs." Like certain
other stories in Christian history such as the marriage of Jesus' parents and
Francis of Assisi's renunciation of his father and property,[2] the Journey
and Adoration of the Magi continually lend themselves first to the *pictorial*
reproduction of contemporary discourses about the structure and activity
of the body *social* — this iconograph talks, after all, about differences,
mediated by the gifts of the magi, between rich and poor, urban and rural,
old and young, exotic and quotidian, and so on.

But second, still today that same story of the magi in legions of school
plays, parades, and even adult processions continues to lend itself to the
mirroring or reproduction in *festive* behavior of *political* activities in Christian nations. This story, in short, not only has left pictures about past social structures and relations, but, politics being process, it still allows any
given political process to be acted out in a recognized and legitimate process (procession) — the Journey of the Magi — thus making politics.

The present essay is an attempt to understand the story of the magi as
one type of journey some say individuals all make: from life to afterlife.
According to André Grabar, few recognize that "the Adoration of the
Magi was the sign of the Incarnation-Redemption. [It] is the oldest image-
sign for ... collective and individual salvation, and this explains its fre-
quent appearance in funerary art from the beginning."[3] In what follows
we shall see polities send their men of power on the journey into death, so
that both can triumph over it.

---

[2] On Mary and Joseph's marriage, see C. Klapisch-Zuber, *Women, Family and Ritual
in Renaissance Italy* (Chicago, 1985), esp. chaps. 9 and 12; and on Francis, see R. Trexler,
Naked Before the Father: The Renunciation of Francis of Assisi (New York, 1989), esp. part
3, and by the same author, "Francis of Assisi, His Mother's Son," *Studi Medievali*, ser. 3,
36 (1995), 363–74, and elsewhere in the present book.

[3] Grabar continues, "It is the iconographic sign that indicates the principal argument
in favor of the salvation of each believer: the fact of the Saviour's Incarnation and his
work on earth": A. Grabar, *Christian Iconography: A Study of Its Origins* (Princeton,
1968), 11. Note that Grabar does not link the magi directly to Jesus, but to the general
resurrection.

For almost a century, historians of early Christianity have known that pictures of the Adoration of the Magi, who were first represented in the catacombs that were used for Christian burial, derive from images of the ancient Roman triumph, with its mandatory prisoners prostrate at the feet of the *imperator*.[4] Only in the last decade, however, and especially since an article by Johannes Decker in 1982, has it become clear that these oldest representations of the magi stem not from the second or third century when Christianity was a cult, as was previously thought, but that they are from the age of Constantine and thus were done under the aegis of majoritarian, imperial Christianity.[5]

When, therefore, as an example, one sees the magi in the catacomb of SS. Pietro and Marcellino look up in the sky and find not a star but the first letter or letters, the chi-rho, of "Christ,"[6] it becomes clear that the historical stimulus for the story's immediate and subsequent popularity was almost certainly the stellar story of that first Christian emperor. For Constantine, too, saw Christ's name. Eusebius's and Lactantius's story of Constantine at the Milvian Bridge seeing a Christic sign in the sky with some variant of a notation like "In this sign conquer" was one means by which to legitimate Christian political actions; making the fourth-century emperor into that for which the biblical magi had actually been searching was still more powerful.

---

[4] The two fundamental works on the origins are F. Cumont, "L'Adoration des mages et l'art triomphal de Rome," *Memorie della pontifica accademia romana di archeologia* 3 (1922–1923): 81–105 and plates; A. Grabar, *L'Empereur dans l'art byzantin. Recherches sur l'art officiel de l'empire d'Orient* (Paris, 1936); see further C. Ihm, *Die Programme der Christlichen Apsismalerei vom vierten Jahrhundert bis zur Mitte des achten Jahrhunderts* (Wiesbaden, 60), 51–55. The standard overview of the cultural history of the magi is by H. Kehrer, *Die heiligen Drei Könige in Literatur und Kunst,* 2 vols. (Leipzig, 1908–1909). More recently, see H. Hofmann, *Die Heiligen Drei Könige. Zur Heiligenverehrung im kirchlichen, gesellschaftlichen und politischen Leben des Mittelalters* (Bonn, 1975). Also important is *The Image of the Black in Western Art,* vol. 2, *From the Early Christian Era to the "Age of Discovery"* (New York, 1979), pt. 1, J. Devisse, "From the Demonic Threat to the Incarnation of Sainthood," and pt. 2, J. Devisse and M. Mollat, "Africans in the Christian Ordinance of the World (Fourteenth to Sixteenth Century)."

[5] J. Decker, "Die Huldigung der Magier in der Kunst der Spätantike," in *Die Heiligen Drei Könige — Darstellung und Verehrung. Katalog zur Ausstellung des Wallraf-Richartz-Museums in der Josef-Haubrich-Kunsthalle Köln, 1. Dezember 1982 bis 30. Januar 1983* (Cologne, 1982), 20–32.

[6] Reproduced in G. Wilpert, *Ein Cyclus Christologischer Gemälde aus der Katakombe der heiligen Petrus und Marcellinus* (Freiburg im Breisgau, 1891).

With this insight, much of the magian art from Justinian's San Vitale through Charlemagne to the famous illuminations of the Ottonians receiving reverence falls into a meaningful pattern.[7] The Spaniards and Portuguese would still be finding or playing the magi as emblems of imperial Christianity when they conquered the so-called New World in the sixteenth century.[8]

Thus, from its beginnings, the theme of the magi, from their reading of fate in the stars through their appearance in Herod's court to their majestic return to their homelands, was the iconograph par excellence for acting out secular triumph in all of Christian art. Beside it, the story of Christ's "triumphant" entry into Jerusalem on Palm Sunday was a conceit of limited use in Christian behavior. The subjects of the latter story were Jews, whom few besides hired clergy wanted to play. The story of the gentilic magi, on the other hand, lent itself to processional representation by the laity not only in pictures but in festivals. It allowed a powerful man to act politically legitimately, no matter whether he played the infant Jesus adored — as did earlier kings and even baroque popes — or one of the Three Kings as was more customary, or even if he humbly played what I shall call a "Fourth Magus," a figure almost as old as the pictorial tradition of the magi itself.[9]

It is in this latter guise that we often find powerful Christians showing themselves triumphing over death, a theme generally neglected in the literature on the magi and hence the particular subject of the present essay. A 1354 Piedmontese fresco over a grave serves as a particularly striking example of that link (fig. 11). At the top Jesus is shown in majesty among

---

[7] R. Deshman has made an important advance in comprehending the political significance of the magi in the early Middle Ages in his "*Christus rex et magi reges*: Kingship and Christology in Ottonian and Anglo-Saxon Art," *Frühmittelalterliche Studien* 10 (1976): 367–405. I have presented further evidence for the link of Constantine to the magi in my *The Journey of the Magi: Meanings in History of a Christian Story* (Princeton, 1997), 25–28.

[8] See the link between the magi theme and triumph and exploration in Devisse and Mollat, *Image of the Black*, pt. 2, passim; also Trexler, "Ludic Life in New Spain," in the present volume.

[9] Several early Christian sarcophagi show the "fourth Magus" (G. Wilpert, *I sarcofagi cristiani antichi*, 2 vols. [Rome, 1929–1930], *tavole* 177,3; 185,3; and 222,1), "... as if [he] too wants to approach [the child] to adore him": Wilpert, *Sarcofagi*, 2:285. The literary theme of the "Fourth Magus" is at least as old as Goethe's "Epiphanias." See *Goethes Werke*, ed. E. Trunz (Hamburg, 1948), 1:112–13. Among many works so titled, see recently Michel Tournier's novel, *Gaspar, Melchior et Balthazar* (Paris, 1980), translated into English as *The Four Wise Men* (New York, 1984).

Figure 11.
Fresco, c. 1354.
Vezzolano (Piedmont), Cloister, S. Maria.

the evangelists. Then, in the register below, the magi, including a fourth magus, adore Jesus. Below the magi are the Three Living and the Three Dead, and below them, finally, comes an image of the dead patron stretched out on his grave.[10]

In the work at hand, several monuments of Italian magi art, beginning with the tomb of a mid-Trecento doge, will be the objects of attention, the aim being to work out the relation of the magi to the theme of triumph over death. It ends with the mid-Quattrocento frescoes of Benozzo Gozzoli in the chapel of the Medici-Riccardi Palace in Florence.[11]

The Tomb of Doge Giovanni Dolfin

The imposing anonymous tomb of the Venetian doge Giovanni Dolfin, who died in 1361, is, along with the contemporary Piedmontese frescoes mentioned above, the first monument in late medieval Italian art I know to link the magi unambiguously to the death of a powerful man (fig. 12).[12] It was originally in the choir of the great state basilica of SS. Giovanni e Paolo, open to the view and reverence of all. Its iconography is symmetrical. In the central panel a statue of Jesus is shown being unveiled by two angels. On its left kneels a woman, presumably the *dogaressa*, and next to her is a field showing the death or Dormition of Mary. This female side of the monument obviously wants to save the *dogaressa* by linking her to the Assumed Mary. On Jesus' right kneels a man, certainly the doge

---

[10] A. Brizio, *La pittura in Piemonte. Dall'età romanica al cinquecento* (Turin, 1942), 158–59; described by I. Kloten, *Wandmalerei im Grossen Kirchenschisma. Die Cappella Bolognini in San Petronio zu Bologna* (Heidelberg, 1986), 115. The fresco is in S. Maria in Vezzolano (Piedmont). The patron was a lord of Castelnuovo. Kehrer mentions the funerary link of the magi in *Heiligen Drei Konige*, 2:221–22. D. Davisson developed the idea in "The Advent of the Magi: A Study of the Transformations in Religious Images in Italian Art 1260–1425" (Ph. D. diss., Johns Hopkins University, 1971), 227, 384–85. There is a series of late thirteenth- and fourteenth-century tombs with representations of the magi in the old cathedral of Salamanca: see A. Rodriguez G. de Ceballos, *Las catedrales de Salamanca* (Madrid, 1979), 17 and 22–25.

[11] Gozzoli's work is one that Michelangelo knew intimately. Mary Lewis and I have argued ("Two Captains and Three Kings") that Michelangelo's New Sacristy in the church of San Lorenzo in Florence was just such a magi funeral monument, in which Cosimo di Giovanni and his grandsons Lorenzo and Giuliano de' Medici are buried as though magi. The present article further contextualizes the notion of the magi in relationship to death.

[12] W. Wolters, *La scultura veneziana gotica (1300–1400)*, 2 vols. (Venice, 1976), 1:193. I am grateful to Debra Pincus for bringing this tomb to my attention.

Dolfin, and behind him is a field showing the Journey and Adoration of the Magi.

How specifically does this male field think to save the doge by associating him with the magi? The answer lies in the representation. Four men approach the mother and child, who are seated under what for all intents and purposes is the baldachin of a triumphal car or wagon. In addition to the three kings is one servant — a version of the "fourth magus" — who holds the crown for the oldest, kneeling, sovereign. Increasing one's honor by close association with real kings was a tried and true theme in Italian republican representations as well as in the magian representative tradition in general.[13] This figure probably represents the doge; being the only non-monarch, there can be little doubt that this servant is at least associated with him. In his own humble way, Dolfin states that in life — like the magi, the archetypical gift-givers of Christian tradition — he too showered gifts on poor Jesus, that is, on the church and poor for whom the babe stands. As in many similar scenes in earlier European art, the doge Dolfin claimed a right to heaven on the basis of the gifts he, and the republic for which he stood, had made to the ruler of heaven.

The Burial Chapel of Baldassare degli Ubriachi

The "capella de' tre magi," as it was named by its donor, is located off the cloister of Santa Maria Novella in Florence. It was built in the 1360s and 1370s by the Florentine messer Baldassare di Simone degli Ubriachi who, incidentally, was also active in Venice as early as 1369, when the Dolfin tomb was newly in place. Ubriachi was an important art impresario and perhaps an artist who spent a lifetime associating with and producing art for princes. Perhaps the first of these was the German emperor Charles IV, who in the same year, 1369, made Baldassare a Count Palatine. It may be at that point that messer Baldassare decided to vaunt his status by building his personal burial chapel in the Florentine Dominican complex.[14]

Gert Kreytenberg has claimed that messer Baldassare was actually the grandson of another Baldassare degli Ubriachi,[15] and that it was the lat-

---

[13] E. Muir, *Civic Ritual in Renaissance Venice* (Princeton, 1981); and Trexler, *Public Life.*

[14] All the data relevant to the chapel and its patron, including his testament, is in my biography of Ubriachi: see Trexler, *Church and Community*, 82–94, 149–60.

[15] G. Kreytenberg, "Das 'Capitulum studium' im Konvent von Santa Maria Novella," *Mitteilungen des kunsthistorischen Institutes in Florenz* 23 (1979): 237.

Figure 12.
Tomb of Doge Giovanni Dolfin, c. 1361.
Venice, SS. Giovanni e Paolo.

Figure 13.
Baldassare degli Ubriachi recommended by the magus Balthasar, 1365–1378.
Florence, Chiostro Grande, S. Maria Novella: lintel.

ter so-called "Baldassare the Elder" who built the chapel in the 1330s. I have responded elsewhere that this older Baldassare never existed; Krey-tenberg merely misread an eighteenth-century Italian document.[16] In fact, our messer Baldassare, the first in the family with that Christian name, built his chapel after 1365 and before 1378. It had come to include a marvelous lintel facing on the Chiostro Grande that shows the magus Baldassare commending the kneeling Baldassare degli Ubriachi to Mary and Child (fig. 13). Here is another type of "fourth magus." Now the orant figure of the type in the central field of the Dolfin tomb is inte-grated into the space of the magi.

Hugo Kehrer recognized long ago that any picture of an orant patron being presented to Mary and the Child is a type of Magi Adoration, and one often employed in funerary contexts. Elsewhere in the same volume, he also documents what I am calling the "fourth magus" in magi repre-sentations, some (unrecommended) person who follows or accompanies the gift-bearing trio, often with a present of his or her own.[17] Kehrer failed, however, to bring the recommended orant and the fourth magus together so as to reveal that central tributary or caritative or exchange message of such magi: the patron has gifted God and the church in life, and thus de-serves paradise. As we shall presently see, Baldassare degli Ubriachi was not finished with paying honor to his homonymous magi patrons.

The Bovi Chapel in Padua

In 1397, one Pietro, of the originally Veronese family of the Bovi, commissioned Jacopo da Verona to fresco the walls of his burial chapel in the one-time parochial church of San Michele, Padua. The patron was either Pietro di Bonaventura de' Bovi, an official of the Paduan mint, or, more probably, Pietro di Bartolomeo de' Bovi, who also may have worked

---

[16] R. Trexler, "The Ubriachi at Santa Maria Novella," *Mitteilungen des kunsthisto-rischen Institutes in Florenz* 32 (1988): 519–21. Unfortunately, two other scholars have credited Kreytenberg: E. Merlini, "Il trittico eburneo della Certosa di Pavia: iconografla e committenza," *Arte cristiana* 73 (1985): 369–84, 74 (1986): 139–54; and Kloten, *Wand-malerei*, 113, 219.

[17] Kehrer, *Heiligen Drei Könige*, 2:221–22, 143. Thus, more is involved than Elisabeth of Schönau's (d. 1164) prayer, "Pro me aurum, thus et mirram offerte deo," cited in F. Büttner, *Imitatio Pietatis. Motive christlichen Ikonographie als Modelle zur Verähnlichung* (Ber-lin, 1983), 19.

for the same mint.[18] The artist seems to have been a friend or pupil of the Paduan painter Altichiero and his Bolognese associate Jacopo Avanzi, active in Padua, and may indeed earlier have contributed to an important Altichiero Adoration frescoed in the oratory of San Giorgio in 1384. In any case, a significant Journey and Adoration of the Magi was the result of Jacopo's labor in the Bovi chapel (fig. 14).[19]

Three things strike the viewer of this Adoration. First and most unusual at this point in the tradition, the three magi are all dressed in basically the same clothes. The uniformity is almost certainly liturgical in nature, the three kings actually figuring three cathedral canons, chaplains, or schoolmen, that is, members of the ceremonial clergy. Given the fame of the Paduan Epiphany theater, in which clerics usually played the kings, I believe that this painting in part reproduces a magi play.[20]

This hypothesis is the more attractive because neither the crèche nor the magi figures but certain non-biblical individuals are the center of attention. Two august lay figures and their six retainers dominate the middle of the painting. It should be pointed out that it was not unusual in contemporary Italy for important politicians to make up the retinue of the magi in public processions.[21]

A third remarkable fact is that while the older magus kneels before the infant, the second and third kings direct their attention away from Jesus and to these august lay figures. The middle king looks at the first such figure and points out the Star *to him*, while the third king actually turns away from Jesus to look at the younger august figure and hold his hand. Without any doubt, these "fourth and fifth magi," so to speak, dominate the painting. It remains to be seen, however, if their message — that God should reciprocate terrestrial charity with heaven — is as simple as in the previous works.

That depends on who these two men are. The possibility that they are

---

[18] Davisson, "Advent," 220; and A. Medin, "I ritratti autentici di Francesco il Vecchio e di Francesco Novello da Carrara ultimi principi di Padova," *Bollettino museo civico di Padova* 11 (1908): 100–4.

[19] See recently F. D'Arcais, "Jacopo da Verona e la decorazione della cappella Bovi in S. Michele a Padova," *Arte Veneta* 27 (1973): 9–24, esp. 10. Kloten, *Wandmalerei*, 115, compares the Bovi chapel painting to the frescoes commissioned by (the mint official!) Bartolomeo Bolognini in Bologna, which are studied below.

[20] For the dramatic tradition, see *Uffici drammatici padovani*, ed. G. Vecchi (Florence, 1954).

[21] Rather than to play a king: see Trexler, *Public Life*, 423.

Figure 14.
Jacopo da Verona, *Adoration of the Magi*, 1397.
Padua, Bovi Chapel, Church of San Michele: fresco.

members of the Bovi family itself cannot, of course, be excluded; it was noted long ago that there are figures of cattle (*bovi* or *bue*) on the sleeve of the older man on the left. If that is so, the Bovi would stand to the magi as did Baldassare Ubriachi: a patron of art recommending himself through the magi. But for over a century, scholars have commonly identified the two lay figures with two generations of the ruling Carrara family of Padua, primarily because the cattle, and the motto *memor* on a sleeve, together formed the device of Francesco il Vecchio, who died a prisoner of the Visconti in 1392, shortly before the chapel was founded. By extension, the younger is said to be his son Francesco Novello, who ruled Padua from 1390 until 1405, that is, during the time the painting was executed.[22]

If this reading is correct, two important results follow. First, dynastic rulers and their polities recommended themselves in the context of other people's burial chapels. Second and inversely, chapel owners recommended themselves to and for heaven and to viewers by vaunting their association with powerful men and rulers. The historian wanting to reconstruct the "frame" of such a work should imagine this in quotidian behavioral terms. Just as signori customarily honored selected city inhabitants by going in procession to visit some activity put on by them or their group (including perhaps a magi play!), so the lords in turn, journeying to the beyond, have the chapel patrons as retinue.

The particular association between the Bovi and Carraresi is not hard to speculate upon. As has been noted, one and perhaps both known Pietros de' Bovi were mint officials. Now, not only are these Bovi not the only minters we shall see associating themselves with the magi, but there was a fundamental reason in the story of the magi itself for them to do so. Minters furnished gold coinage, the premier medium of exchange in society, and at its deepest roots, the story of the magi describes how social groups — including those in heaven with those on earth — circulate things and values. Whether we imagine the Bovi or Carraresi as the "fourth magus," therefore, the sociopolitical relevance of this iconograph to the theme of the triumph over death should now be evident.

The Certosa Triptych, Pavia

Reenter Baldassare degli Ubriachi. Concerned as we have seen about his own chapel in Florence, Baldassare about 1396 took up the task of cre-

---

[22] See Medin, "Ritratti autentici," and D'Arcais, "Jacopo da Verona."

ating, or supervising the creation of, the altarpiece for the Certosa of Pavia. Elena Merlini has recently laid out the iconographic program of this marvelous work (fig. 15): the Life of the Virgin on the left wing of the triptych, that of Jesus on the right extension, and, in the middle, most unusual in its amplitude, a field of twenty-six scenes, which is the focus of Merlini's and our attention. Merlini observes that the top fourteen sections of this field deal with the Old Testament story and legends surrounding the prophet Balaam, who was believed in the Middle Ages to have prophesied the star of the magi. The bottom twelve sections show the magi proper.[23]

Though failing to provide any new documentation, Merlini does an excellent job of summarizing and assessing existing data and views regarding the political background and content of this work. First, she addresses the question of patronage. The abbey of the Certosa, founded in 1396, was in debt to an agent of Baldassare Ubriachi in 1400, and sometime thereafter, before 1409, paid Baldassare for this work. Merlini rightly dismisses both the eighteenth-century story that the altarpiece was a gift of the French king to Gian Galeazzo Visconti, and the equally old idea that the abbey itself had commissioned the altarpiece.[24]

Merlini accepts the by now standard view that the patron of the monastery itself, Gian Galeazzo Visconti, *who wanted to be buried there*, was the work's real commissioner. As Charles Rosenberg has noted, building Charterhouses was a standard activity of great European nobles at the time.[25] Merlini's view is especially persuasive because the Visconti had an established relation to the magi cult, because that cult in turn was one of the central cults of the Ambrosian city of Milan, and perhaps especially because of the close association between Baldassare Ubriachi and the Visconti.[26]

When, then, was the work carried out? The general opinion is that it was finished around 1396, at the time that the Certosa itself was built, probably to sit on the main altar. Such a dating proves irresistible when one considers events of the time in relation to likely motivations for its construction. Merlini reviews the previous notions. Because of the profu-

---

[23] Merlini, "Trittico," 371–75; and, Trexler, *Church and Community*, 118–22.

[24] Merlini, "Trittico," 141–42.

[25] C. Rosenberg, " 'Per il bene di . . . nostra ciptà': Borso d'Este and the Certosa of Ferrara," *Renaissance Quarterly* 29 (1976): 332–34.

[26] Merlini, "Trittico," 141–44.

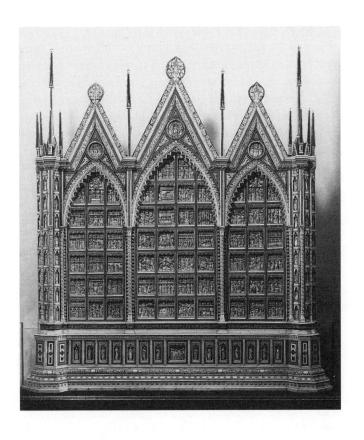

Figure 15.
Baldassare degli Ubriachi, ivory centerpiece, c. 1396.
Certosa, Pavia.

sion of fleurs-de-lis around the base of the work, Sant'Ambrogio believed that it was done in 1394, the year of a supposed treaty between Visconti and the French.[27] And another scholar has suggested that its commissioning had a domestic motivation, Gian Galeazzo's wife Caterina having ordered it as an ex-voto after a difficult birth.[28]

But, in my view, the strongest hypothesis remains that the work was commissioned to commemorate the coronation of Gian Galeazzo Visconti as the first duke of Milan by an agent of the Holy Roman Emperor. Indeed, this ducal investment can be viewed as the historical essence of the iconography of the work's central panel. *Mi spiego.*

As precisely recorded in a contemporary miniature (fig. 16), Gian Galeazzo Visconti was made a duke, and thus Milan a duchy, in a grand pomp that was held in the Lombard metropole on 5 September 1395, in the presence of many dignitaries.[29] However, an earlier event deserves as much attention. In traditional Europe, the date that was commemorated relevant to such an event was often the date the news reached a city that such an event was to take place.[30]

The news that Milan and Gian Galeazzo were to receive this honor actually arrived in Milan about 2 January 1395. On that day, Gian Galeazzo ordered that the German imperial eagle be quartered into his Viscontean arms.[31] This date is the point: it could mean that it was on the vigil

---

[27] Cited in Merlini, "Trittico," 151 n. 51. The treaty never happened: D. M. Bueno de Mesquita, *Giangaleazzo Visconti Duke of Milan* (Cambridge, 1941), 157–58.

[28] Merlini, "Trittico," 142.

[29] Trexler, *Church and Community*, 120. The primary sources for this ceremony are the Chronicon Bergomense, in the new edition of *Rerum Italicarum Scriptores* (hereafter *RIS*), vol. 16, pt. 2, 61; a contemporary letter by Gregorio Azanello to Andreolo Ansi, in the old *RIS* (hereafter *RIS*, old ed.), vol. 16, 821–26; and the description in Bernardino Corio, *Storia di Milano*, vol. 2 (Turin, 1978), 929–33. An imperial official bestowed the ducal beret and cloak.

[30] Trexler, *Public Life*, 279–90.

[31] Trexler, *Church and Community*, 169–70, n. 156. See, Merlini, "Trittico," 143, for the quartering of the French lily in the Visconti arms. The source for the imperial news is in the Pavian document of 2 January 1395, summarized by C. Santoro, *I registri dell'ufficio di provvisione del ufficio dei sindaci sotto la dominazione viscontea*, vol. 1 (Milan, 1940), 44, n. 223: "Il signore di Milano scrive ai nobili uomini il podestà, il referendario, il vicario e i XII di Provvisione di Milano, di far depingere la sua arma inquartata coll'arma imperiale." See also Bueno de Mesquita, *Giangaleazzo Visconti*, 173. With reference to "Registro civico, f. 136 a tergo," C. Giulini, however, says that it was on 4 January that the order came out: *Memorie spettanti alla storia, al governo e alla descrizione della città e campagna di Milano ne' secoli bassi*, vol. 5 (Milan, 1856), 794.

Figure 16.
Anovelo da Imbronato, *Investiture of Gian Galeazzo as Duke of Milan*.
Milan, Capitular Library, S. Ambrogio, Ms. Lat. 6, fol. 8: missal.

of Epiphany or on the "feast of the kings" itself (6 January), as that day was usually called, that the news was first celebrated by the Milanese, most probably by separate German and Visconti banners being flown together and by some new Viscontean flags (with the imperial quarter) being displayed. Since, according to tradition, a magi pageant was performed annually in Milan on these dates, and since in similar pageants it was customary to unfurl various contemporary flags while accompanying the magi to Jerusalem and Bethlehem,[32] it is easy to speculate that the magi festival of January 1395 celebrated the impending coronation of the first duke of Milan, in part by flying these mixed flags.

Thus the enormous attention given to the magi in the Ubriachi altarpiece may not just show the traditional Visconti and Milanese devotion to the kings. It may also directly refer to a particular Feast of the Magi on which a momentous event in Visconti history transpired. Not only does this thought concur with the common European understanding of the Adoration of the Magi as a coronation (did not in truth the magi essentially crown the new King of the Jews by their legitimating visit?).[33] There is a further, previously unnoticed but striking piece of evidence precisely to this effect in the triptych itself.

Merlini notes that in the segment of the triptych which she numbers "B-I-11," there is a Viscontean viper (biscione) painted in gold on the shield of one of the soldiers. She then notes elsewhere that an imperial eagle is visible once on a shield and again on a flag of what turns out to be the very same scene (fig. 17).[34] Putting two and two together, I surmise that the flags of the Empire and of the Visconti are together here to

---

[32] A glance at any collection of magi paintings shows that flags were often a feature of the festive Journey of the Magi. I must admit that Galvano Fiamma's description of the Milanese magi festival of 1336, with its statement that the celebration was held each year thereafter, is accepted at one's peril; in fact, I have still to find a description of any other magi festival held in Milan during the late Middle Ages. For Galvano, see Hofmann, Heiligen Drei Könige, 154–55.

[33] On the magi and coronations, see Hofmann, Heiligen Drei Könige, 141ff. The most striking visual confirmation of this doctrinal association are illuminations on facing pages of a Madrid manuscript of Gratian's Distinctions recently brought to my attention by Debra Pincus. On the left, divine Majesty oversees two angels crowning a pope and a king, who in turn invest their subjects; on the right is an Adoration of the Magi. They are reproduced in the present volume in the chapter "Dreams of the Three Kings."

[34] Merlini, "Trittico," 143. The contemporary miniature by Anovelo da Imbonate (fig. 16) also shows at least two distinct coats-of-arms: the Visconti viper, and one with an azure base covered with gold fleurs-de-lis. Giulini speculates that the latter is the banner of Gian Galeazzo as Count of Virtù: Memorie, 5:797.

Figure 17.
Baldassare degli Ubriachi, *Balaam is Inspired, and Blesses Israel.*
Certosa, Pavia: detail of ivory altarpiece.

commemorate the Feast of the Magi, 1395, when the two flags first flew together. The altarpiece recalls Epiphany, 1395, as well, of course, as 5 September, the day of Visconti's investment.

Once the significance of this one segment is understood, we may explain the general iconography of the central panel of the altarpiece as related to the same historical event. That iconography, as Merlini well states, is passing strange, for the story of Balaam is told in such unusual detail as to take up more space than do the magi![35] Why would the prophet receive more attention than what is prophesied?

The answer lies in the very segment — B-I-11 — we have been studying. It is as follows: Balaam is to be thought of as prophesying the coronation of Gian Galeazzo, and then blessing Visconti's arms along with those of the Empire! Now to the subject matter of the segment, which is about Balaam and not the magi. In it, soldiers bear the arms of the Empire and of the Visconti. Merlini labels this Old Testament scene: "Balaam receives divine inspiration and blesses the people of Israel." Given what we have already found, we can now ask if the Milanese are not the people of Israel. Let me pursue this hypothesis after retelling the story of Balaam.

The story is that Balak, king of Moab, feared the Israelites, who were being led out of Egypt by Moses. Wanting to destroy the Jews, he employed the famous magician Balaam to curse his enemy. Constrained by God, Balaam instead delivered oracles foretelling the future greatness of Israel and the rise of King David.[36] Worse, Balaam blessed the Jews (that is, their army) instead of cursing them. Our segment shows Balaam blessing the united arms of the Germans and the Milanese. It is fair to conclude, I think, that here the Old Testament was being made to say that imperial Milan, led by the Davidic Duke Gian Galeazzo, was a chosen people, destined for greatness now that its leader, and the city itself, had achieved princely status. Nor was this the first time that Gian Galeazzo was associated with David. Indeed, it was propagandized at the time that Gian Galeazzo Visconti wanted (like David) to become King of Italy![37]

---

[35] Merlini, "Trittico," 369–70, 373.

[36] R. Brown, *The Birth of the Messiah* (Garden City, NY, 1977), 194.

[37] King David prophesied Gian Galeazzo in Psalm 1 of the Visconti Hours (pre-1395). Throughout this work's illuminations, the association between the two princes is insistent. See *The Visconti Hours*, ed. M. Meiss (New York, 1972), BR 3, 128, and for the Balaam miniature where, within a border made up of a Visconti device, the prophet blesses Israel, see *Visconti Hours*, LF 126v–127v. For Gian Galeazzo as "the Messiah who has arrived" for Italy, see H. Baron, *The Crisis of the Early Italian Renaissance* (Princeton,

Thus, I would suggest that the great altarpiece of the Certosa features Balaam because the greatness of the Visconti and Milan — as once that of Constantine — are being prophesied at the same time as the magi.

In this work, earthly triumph stands supreme. To see that Visconti's resurrection into a blessed eternity was also in play, we have, in turn, only to fill in what is missing, and remember, as Gian Galeazzo's testament insists we do, that the prince's body was to lie near this great story of Balaam and the magi, conceivably even at the cross of the church immediately before the triptych.[38] The people would mourn, yet see and know that their ruler would live forever. Indeed they would recall that fact whenever they took part in a festive procession of the Ambrosian magi, whenever, that is, they practiced the politics of legitimation. Gian Galeazzo is not a fourth magus. Instead he is a king himself, comparable to David and in the succession of Balaam, who foresaw David, the Star, Jesus, the magi, and now, Visconti himself in paradise.

The Bolognini Chapel

The frescoes of the Bolognese painter Giovanni da Modena in the burial chapel of the Bolognini family in the basilica of San Petronio, Bologna, were done around 1410.[39] Certainly one of the most extensive cycles of magi representations in all of Christian art, this "Chapel of the Magi," as it was named, has recently been the object of an excellent dissertation by

---

1966), 37. For Milan as a second Rome and its archbishop as a second pope, see Bonvesin da la Riva, De magnalibus Mediolani. Le meraviglie di Milano, ed. Maria Corti (Milan, 1974), 15. Note that an army is being blessed in the picture. This is just what would be expected at the investment of a duke, and what transpired at the coronation of Gian Galeazzo, as we see in the miniature by Anovelo da Imbonate, which also has a characteristic stockade of military prisoners. Coronations in feudal practice were associated with battles and victories, as were knightings imagined to follow upon a victory.

[38] Merlini, "Trittico," 154, n. 75 (testament of 23 August 1397). Alas, despite the will, he did not end up buried at that location.

[39] Plans for the chapel matured in 1400, as can be reconstructed from the curious fact that the inscription in Bartolomeo's "and his heirs'" gravestone tells us the month and year (May 1400) that stone was carved. It transpires that Bartolomeo's only son Andrea died in the very same month, as we know from the latter's gravestone in the Bolognese Servite church. Thus the history of the Bolognini chapel — where Bartolomeo's gravestone was in place when he wrote his testament in 1408 — began on the occasion of his only son's death (cf. Kloten, Wandmalerei, 51 and 181).

Figure 18.
Giovanni da Modena, *History of St. Petronio.*
Bologna, Bolognini Chapel, S. Petronio: fresco.

Ilka Kloten.[40] Among much else, Kloten asked what the relations were between the patrons and paintings in this chapel and comparable work done elsewhere in Italy, just as Merlini had asked about her Pavian work.[41] I hope to show that a stark theme of triumph in the Bolognini chapel continued the pattern of magi funeral monuments that we have already reviewed.

Let us begin by sketching the chapel's whole picture program, for the eight frescoed scenes showing the magi, those great legitimators of King Jesus, command only the right wall of a chapel crammed with frescoes.[42] To the left of the entrance, opposite the magi, the wall is divided into three zones. At top is the coronation of Mary, in the middle zone sits the heavenly court, and at bottom is hell. Thus a theme of coronation is found on the left and right walls: here of Mary, there of King Jesus. The linkage was not fortuitous: these two surfaces were the only ones whose pictorial contents the patron prescribed in his testament of 10 February 1408.[43]

Yet a motif similar to coronation is again represented on the wall facing the chapel entrance (fig. 18). At the top one sees the figure of a pope who, as Kloten has convincingly argued, actually plays two different pontiffs, worshipped, be it noted, by three patrons, in Kloten's view probably members of the Bolognini family. As Pope Celestine I, the figure turns toward our right and invests with a ring St. Petronius, the first bishop of Bologna. The rest of the pictures below this register consists, in fact, of

---

[40] Kloten, *Wandmalerei*, esp. 183; "Et in sponda dicte capelle versus sero pingi debeat historia trium magorum ... et ... sacrari debeat sub nomine trium magorum": from Bolognini's testament, in L. Frati, "La cappella Bolognini nella Basilica di San Petronio a Bologna," *L'Arte* 13 (1910): 215.

[41] Kloten makes a notable circumstantial case that the silk merchant Bolognini and the banker-art impresario Baldassare Ubriachi may have known each other at Pavia or at Florence (Kloten, *Wandmalerei*, 115 and 118; and Merlini, "Trittico," 144–46). Since Ubriachi did diplomatic duty for Gian Galeazzo Visconti, it is worthwhile adding that Bolognini had diplomatic contacts with Visconti as well (A. Pini, "Bolognini, Bartolomeo," *Dizionario biografico degli Italiani* [hereafter *DBI*], vol. 11 [Rome, 1969], 332). Further, Bolognini had dual citizenship and thus a residence in Florence (Frati, "Cappella," 214).

[42] The best illustrations of the chapel are in *La Basilica di San Petronio in Bologna*, 2 vols. (Bologna, 1983–1984), the chapter by C. Volpe, "La pittura gotica. Da Lippo di Dalmasio a Giovanni da Modena," 1:213–94.

[43] Kloten, *Wandmalerei*, 183. Bartolomeo Bolognini died on 2 July 1411: Pini, "Bolognini, Bartolomeo."

scenes from the life of Petronius, the most prominent being the bishop's first triumphant entry into, or *possesso* of, Bologna.

But the other identity of this pontifical figure is not unimportant. He is the contemporary Pope John XXIII, otherwise known by the magian moniker *Baldassare* Cossa, for one sees on our left beneath the seated prelate a contemporary bishop who bears a scroll seeming to announce that this pontiff had "elected" him.[44] Cardinal legate of Bologna since August 1403, Cossa had long been the effective ruler of Bologna before being elected pope *in Bologna* by the Pisan obedience on 17 May 1410 —well after Bolognini wrote his testament, but a year before his death. Baldassare Cossa was deposed by the Council of Constance in May 1414.[45]

The fourth painted surface is difficult to see, but no less important for all that. From the chapel altar beneath the papal representation, which not only reproduces the theme of the magi but, through statues of SS. Andrew and Bartholomew, directly commemorates the death of Bartolomeo and his only begotten son, turn toward the chapel entrance. Look up from the gravestone of Bartolomeo to the inside surface of the entry arch. There, Jesus flanked by angels announces his judgment. A half figure in a mandorla, he opens his arms wide and beckons to himself the resurrected dead, who climb from their sarcophagi up the steep incline. Kloten links this scene of resurrection to the altar beneath:

> Christ shows his wounds to those who are not yet judged and [thus] announces their salvation. . . . He lets himself be recognized by the resurrected. Bartolomeo Bolognini, who rests at the feet [of Jesus], will also belong to [this group] on the last day. The hope of salvation is what is important, not judgment. The theme of resurrection is explained in the context of the grave.[46]

Thus, elegantly, Kloten sees the heavenly apotheosis of the Bolognini as the central pious desideratum in this chapel, yet did not grasp the position of the magi in the salvation strategy, although the whole chapel

---

[44] For the reading of this difficult text, see Kloten, *Wandmalerei*, 39–40.

[45] On Cossa, see A. Esch, "Das Papsttum unter der Herrschaft der Neapolitaner. Die führenden Gruppe Neapolitaner Familien an der Kurie während des Schismas 1378–1415," in *Festschrift für Hermann Heimpel*, vol. 2 (Göttingen, 1972), 757–800.

[46] Kloten, *Wandmalerei*, 94–95, 5. I cannot find a photograph of this scene. Note that the New Sacristy in Florence is dedicated to Jesus' resurrection, and that Lewis and I built our argument on the notion of the magian Medici journeying to eternal resurrection: Trexler and Lewis, "Two Captains."

is dedicated to them. While documenting the important view that the Bolognini family probably had a devotion to the magi before this chapel was painted, she missed the programmatic idea that not just Jesus, but the magi were one of Bolognini's tickets to heaven.[47] We, however, are prepared to see that Bartolomeo Bolognini was but another influential Italian who, proud of what he had given to Christ and the church, placed himself in the retinue of the magi in one way or another so as to pass through the heavenly gates, as the magi had passed the gates of Jerusalem on their way to the King of the Jews.[48] All beg for salvation with gifts.

If the logic of the magi as Bolognini's journeymen is evident, we must still ask what it was that Bartolomeo gifted the Judge, and the faithful who visited his chapel, as surety for his right to heaven. As we shall see, the answer is as it was for the Bovi of Padua: the patron's relation to his superiors and to their triumphs in time. And what a time of schisms for the church and triumphs for the communes! Yet, though Kloten's work argues that other paintings in the Bolognini chapel propagandized against the Great Schism, she neglected to say that the magi are about union, and about triumph.[49]

The notion of union over diversity in magi art almost goes without saying. Since Augustine of Hippo, the story of the magi coming not just from "the east," but from "all parts of the world," has lent itself to ecumenical ideology, as the whole "exotic" character of the iconograph in festival and art, for instance in Gozzoli's Journey of the Magi in the Medici chapel in Florence, pervasively demonstrates.[50] In the magi story, pluralities become a unity and schisms are terminated, and in no historical moment more than one with three popes could a plea for unity through a represen-

---

[47] Kloten, *Wandmalerei*, 96–98.

[48] See Domenico Ghirlandaio's Sassetti Adoration, which shows the magi passing under a triumphal arch on their way to the crib.

[49] The author does indicate in passing that Baldassare Cossa wanted to play the unifier, and that he was a force behind the calling of the Council of Pisa in 1409 which aimed at ending the Great Schism (Kloten, *Wandmalerei*, 78 and 144).

[50] On Augustine's calculated notion that the magi came from "all over the world," see Kehrer, *Heiligen Drei Könige*, 1, 34. On Gozzoli's work, see A. Beyer, "Der Zug der Magier" (diss., Frankfurt am Main, 1985), kindly shown to me by the author; and the same author's "De significatione cometae. Guglielmo De Becchis Traktat 'De Cometa' (1456) und sein Einfluss auf die bildische Kometenikonogaphie in Florenz," in *Die Kunst und das Stadium der Natur vom 14. zum 16. Jahrhundert*, ed. W. Prinz and A. Beyer (Weinheim, 1987), 181–91.

Figure 19.

Giovanni da Modena, *Journey of the Magi.*
Bologna, Bolognini Chapel, S. Petronio: fresco.

tation of the magi have been more apposite.[51] Even today Christian teachers and parents have their children perform the play of the magi to teach them a tolerant pluralism ... under one God, of course.[52]

We have already established that the theme of triumph had been central to the image's meaning from its inception in the catacombs. That theme's role in the Bolognini chapel begins, certainly, with the pictures themselves. The Journey of the Magi is shown as so many triumphal processions in three different frescoes: the departures from the East and from Jerusalem, and the march to Bethlehem (fig. 19). The enthroned pope opposite the entrance, Jesus crowning Mary on the left wall, the majestic Jesus on the inside entry arch, and St. Petronius entering Bologna beneath a palio like a conquering hero, all these scenes are triumphs.

From the beginning, I have maintained that during these ages certain Christian images were vehicles for political and social discourse, and the magi story was one of a limited number of such images offering a privileged way to study art as a political vehicle. Its significance is that, as an iconograph, it evoked and shaped the processual structures of Italian polities. Thus, from the triumphal character of the paintings, we turn to the question of magian activity in real Bolognese time.

First comes the question of the quality of the powerful persons Bartolomeo Bolognini's chapel vaunts, and of the patron's relations to them. St. Petronius presents no problem. He is the patron saint of the city of Bologna, someone all good citizens revered as they did any Infant or pope. Baldassare Cossa, appointed cardinal-legate or ersatz-pope in Bologna in 1403, long before he became pope in the same city, presents a more interesting object of devotion. Not only was he named after one of the magi; so was his brother Gaspare, an important papal representative in Bologna in these years.[53] This was certainly not the only reason Bartolomeo chose

---

[51] The magi were unity symbols as well at the Councils of Constance and Florence: see now my *Journey of the Magi*, 128.

[52] As recently as 1958, in Endicott, New York, rectors did this as part of the holiday season, each king played by children of different ancestry from the ethnic populations of this area. I owe this information to M. E. Semple, whose children were involved in such plays. Today, each Epiphany in New York City, the school children of ethnic Puerto Ricans perform a Journey of the Magi through the streets of Spanish Harlem. Led by three adult magi, many trios of children dress as the magi, emphasizing this pluralism.

[53] Gaspare is mentioned as administrator for Baldassare in Bologna by M. de Griffonibus, *Memoriale Historicum*, in *RIS*, vol. 18, pt. 2 (hereafter Griffoni), 96, 158; also in the *Corpus Chronicorum Bononiensium*, *RIS*, vol. 18, pt. 1, vol. 3 (hereafter *Corpus*), 520; further, see C. Carbonetti, "Cossa, Gaspare," *DBI*, vol. 30 (Rome, 1984), 87–88.

the magi for his chapel, but he could hardly have been oblivious of the fact that that theme flattered the prelate.

Bartolomeo's links to both the city of his birth and these magian prelates were many. The very first civil office Bolognini filled of which we are informed links him to the Bovi of Padua: Bartolomeo was supervisor of the Bolognese city mint.[54] I can do no more here than state, not demonstrate, that gold in the form of (often specific) *coins* was a standard gift of the magi in the commercial centers where so many paintings and festivals of the magi were produced.

Second, beginning in the 1390s or slightly earlier, Bartolomeo Bolognini served Bologna and later the cardinal as ambassador.[55] Need it be pointed out that the three kings were precisely on a diplomatic mission, first to Herod and then to King Jesus? In the late Middle Ages diplomatic missions might indeed be commemorated through a painting of the magi.[56]

Third, Bartolomeo was made a knight not once but three times: by the city, by a Bentivoglio, and by Cossa.[57] The vaunting of the knightly status of especially the youngest magus in many Adorations hardly needs mentioning, and on another occasion I hope to show that the investment of a knight, like the coronation of a king, was one occasion memorialized in magi paintings. Such knightly investments, incidentally, were commonly bestowed on the so-called "youth ambassador" of some Italian communes during or on the conclusion of his first mission.[58]

There is as yet no direct evidence that the brothers, as distinct from their father Giovanni, showed any devotion to the Kings or politically used them. That cannot be proven from their siblings' names: Marino and Petrillo (Esch, "Papsttum," 758).

[54] Pini, "Bolognini, Bartolomeo," 332.

[55] In 1389 a communal secretary treated Bolognini with the deference that might become an ambassador (Pini, "Bolognini, Bartolomeo"). He was a city ambassador in 1401 (Kloten, *Wandmalerei*, 13), and a legatine emissary to the pope in Rome in 1405 (Griffoni, 95, and *Corpus*, 514).

[56] As I maintain did Botticelli's Uffizi "Adoration" record an embassy to the pope of Lorenzo de' Medici: Trexler, *Public Life*, 439.

[57] On 14 March 1401, G. Bentivoglio on seizing power in Bologna made Bartolomeo a knight with twenty others (*RIS*, vol. 18, pt. 1, 473; and vol. 18, pt. 2, 90). In 1408, Cossa made him a papal counsellor and knighted him (Griffoni, 96). In June 1410, King Louis d'Anjou knighted him again (Griffoni, 98; *Corpus*, 536; and Kloten, *Wandmalerei*, 15).

[58] The young king in Gentile da Fabriano's Strozzi altarpiece is a striking example of such a knight. For a youth of the "honor class," his first diplomatic mission was an important rite of passage. On the youth ambassador, who I believe is occasionally the model for the young king in Adorations, see Trexler, *Public Life*, 292.

With all of these honors, it is no surprise that messer Bartolomeo Bolognini not only had the title of privy counsellor to Cossa, but was indeed an important political and financial arrow in the quiver of the local authorities, one of the richest and most influential citizens of Bologna.[59] There can, therefore, be little doubt that Bolognini was also prominent in the seemingly endless festive triumphs that distinguished life in Bologna in these years, events which we will presently summarize.

But first, it should be emphasized that the Bolognini and the pope filling magian roles in life does not prove that the eight magi frescoes in the Bolognini chapel consciously quote those past roles. Nor will showing that Bologna was all but overwhelmed by formal triumphal events in these years allow us to think that any particular one of them was commemorated in the art of the Bolognini chapel, any more than any particular festive drama of the magi performed in the streets and squares of Bologna in these years, if there were such, would likely have been *the* event explaining the unmistakable theatricality of some of the frescoes.[60] I cannot demonstrate that the magi painted in San Petronio memorialized a specific event. I can describe a civic experience of festive triumph in these years that, the magi story being about the triumph of civil order, the inhabitants perforce recalled again in these frescoes.

I shall distinguish those events occurring before Bolognini's testament of February 1408 — in that testament he stipulated that the chapel was to be painted with and dedicated to the magi[61] — from events after his testament up until Bartolomeo's death on 2 July 1411, that could still have affected the patron's understanding of the meaning of his chapel.[62] Then

---

[59] His wealth was a local legend, but so was his influence. On 8 February 1404, he was appointed to guard Gabione Gozzadino for the legate (Esch, "Papsttum," 761–62). In early 1405, at a government meeting called by the legate to meet the challenge of a marauding local count, Bolognini volunteered, essentially in concert with Cossa, to finance a unit of soldiers until victory over the count was achieved: *Corpus*, 511–12. He was a papal counselor in 1408: above, n. 57.

[60] Especially the one of Herod talking with his intellectuals while the magi await an audience with him. For vestiges of magi theater in Bologna, see Kloten, *Wandmalerei*, 111–13, and esp. 218, n. 40. On the link in Florence between such festival and art, see R. Hatfield, "The Compagnia de' Magi," *Journal of the Warburg and Courtauld Institutes* 33 (1970): 107–61.

[61] See above, n. 40.

[62] See above, n. 43.

I will list certain events from that death up until late 1414 when, according to Kloten, the painting was finished.[63]

Before the Testament

A. 3 September 1403. Bologna having reentered the Papal States, Baldassare celebrates his first triumphal entry into Bologna as legate or ersatz-pope. Presumably Bolognini was among the major citizens said to have honored Cossa on this occasion. "The salvation of Bologna" in one chronicler's words, this triumph was extensively described.[64] Cossa being essentially a Bolognese *condottiere*, in subsequent years many triumphs followed, each celebrating some victory for Bologna.

B. August 1407. Baldassare Cossa reenters Bologna in triumph after military victories at Forlì. Three days of celebration followed in which Bolognini may be assumed to have joined.[65] In May of the following year, just three months after Bartolomeo Bolognini wrote his testament dedicating his chapel to the three kings, the recipient of that triumph, Baldassare Cossa, invested Bartolomeo as a knight and named him one of his privy counsellors.[66]

At this time, Cossa emerged as the ecumenical leader par excellence. On 29 June 1408, he broke away from the Roman pope Gregory XII and with thirteen friendly cardinals began to plot a general council *causa tollendi sismam*.[67] What was in the headlines almost at the moment that Bolognini wrote his testament? The notion that (like some infant Jesus gathering around him multilingual magi) Cossa would unify the church.

Between Testament and Death

A. 12 January 1410. The pope elected by Cossa's Council of Pisa, Alexander V, the former archbishop of Milan, entered Bologna in great triumph as the guest of the legate and church chancellor, Baldassare Cossa. The sources spare no effort to detail the event. The *anziani* of the city rode out in the festive wagon or *carrozzo* to meet the pope. In three

---

[63] Kloten, *Wandmalerei*, 26–27.

[64] Griffoni, 92–93; and *Corpus*, 501–3.

[65] *Corpus*, 523–24.

[66] Griffoni, 96.

[67] *Corpus*, 526 (26–29 June). The Latin phrase is used when Cossa goes to Cesena on 25 February 1409, to meet with Pope Gregory; Griffoni, 97.

days of feasting, the apostolic twelve citizens carried the baldachin over the pope much as, in the Bolognini chapel, earlier Bolognese are shown carrying a baldachin over St. Petronius, first bishop of the city, and holding the reins of his horse. "The greatest happiness I believe Bologna has ever had," said one chronicler.[68] In the coming weeks, Bologna reveled as one Italian prince after another sent ambassadors to the city to recognize the new pope, and thus honor papal Bologna.

B. 26 May 1410. Pope Alexander having died in Bologna, Cossa is elected pope there by the cardinals, and on this day crowned in the very basilica of San Petronio. All this was in the midst of marvelous celebrations, for it is not often that a city other than Rome hosts the death, election, and coronation of a pope! One source exclaims, "Never had such dignity been seen in Bologna!"[69] The same source says that after the coronation "gran triunfi" of clothes and flags marched through the city.[70] Certainly Bartolomeo Bolognini, confidant of Cossa, must have shown off his status in these days, perhaps precisely the time the magi were being painted onto the wall of his chapel. For, as we have seen, in June Bolognini hosted King Louis d'Anjou in his home.[71]

A year later, on 2 July 1411, Bartolomeo died in Bologna. His frescoes of the magi had been envisioned and executed at a marvelous conjuncture of Bolognese and Bolognini honor and triumph.

From Death to the Finished Chapel

A. 27 April 1412. Bartolomeo's grandson and heir Girolamo d'Andrea Bolognini presents the first chaplain of the family chapel to the episcopal vicar, the Benedictine Giovanni di Michele, abbot of St. Procolo.[72] Thus, at this date, the decoration of the chapel of the magi must have been largely complete.

B. 6 November 1412. This same prelate, now bishop of Bologna, enters the city for his triumphal *possesso*. One of those who held the reins of the bishop's horse on that day was Marchionne (that is, Melchior), son of Gio-

---

[68] Griffoni, 97; and *Corpus*, 532–33.

[69] *Corpus*, 534.

[70] *Corpus*, 534. See also Griffoni, 98.

[71] See above, n. 57.

[72] F. Filippini, "Gli affreschi della cappella Bolognini in San Petronio," *Bollettino d'arte* 10 (1916): 193; and Frati, "Cappella Bolognini," 215.

vanni Bolognini, a brother of the deceased Bartolomeo.[73] Given this link
of the Bolognini to the new bishop, Kloten may be right that Giovanni di
Michele was indeed the bishop who in the fresco of the Bolognini chapel
seems to say he was "elected" by Pope John XXIII.[74]

C. 11 November 1413. Pope John approaches Bologna for still another
triumphal entry. He is the guest of Giovanni Bolognini, Bartolomeo's
brother and his testamental executor.[75] Thus, the papal link to the Bolognini family remaining in place, it made sense for the family chapel to
describe the new bishop's election by that pope. By the time the Cossa
pope left Bologna for the last time, on 1 October 1414, going to the
Council of Constance which imprisoned and deposed him, the painting of
the Bolognini chapel was finished.

Visitors to the chapel knelt before the altar and gravestone, beneath
which presumably lay the remains of Bartolomeo and his son Andrea. On
the facing wall, they saw how Bartolomeo had triumphed in life by serving
the great city of Bologna and its pope in a period of incredible pageantry
and civic vanity. Glancing, then, at the wall to their right and then to
their left, they saw not only scenes of Christian convention, but the journey of the Bolognini souls. Their salvation was implored on one wall by
the biblical wise men in reciprocation for the gifts Bartolomeo had bestowed on their church and city, the options of a blissful or damned eternity shown starkly on the other. Behind and above the orant, mercifully,
Jesus promised Bolognini resurrection. A comforting decorum of individual
and group history is matched by a sure and honorable future, dead history
linked to merely promised future by the procession or journey of gift-givers
through time, and across the barrier of death. What better encouragement
for that viewer to himself march out and take his place in politics!

---

[73] The deceased Bartolomeo himself had a brother named Melchior. Obviously the
family was not bereft of magian namesakes. For the brother, see Kloten, *Wandmalerei*, 97;
for Marchione, see Griffoni, 100; *Corpus*, 543; and Kloten, *Wandmalerei*, 43, for a
Bolognese writer identifying Marchione with Melchior. It may be significant that in
Florence the customary honor of holding a bishop's horse during the *possesso* belonged
to the Strozzi, a family, as is known from the Strozzi altarpiece, associated with the magi
cult (Trexler, *Public Life*, 273).

[74] Kloten, *Wandmalerei*, 40–43.

[75] Griffoni, 101; *Corpus*, 546–47; and Frati, "Cappella," 215.

On the Road to the New Sacristy

The previous pages have established that the strong association of the magi with funereal themes in early Christian art continued in Renaissance Italy. In concluding, let me dwell once more on two notions central to the task of discovering the political content in this artistic image.

The first is the notion of political space, if I may employ a new figure to repeat my leading theme. I have claimed a peculiar relevance for the magi as a political iconograph because their story lends itself both to parades and to the discourse on politics as legitimated through process or activity. In late medieval Italy, magi dramas were used as story frames for the demonstration of political structures and processes. That notion has been brought to the fore especially through our review of processional life in Bologna as background to the Bolognini chapel.

Another way of expressing this idea of space is that through magi pictures, one imagined oneself, a political animal, in the midst of the train of the magi. In my *Journey of the Magi*, I was then able to trace that notion of the Journey and Adoration of the Magi within political space beginning in the two Ravennate monuments of Sant'Apollinare Nuovo and San Vitale,[76] continuing into the chapel of the Medici-Riccardi Palace where Benozzo Gozzoli placed a viewer in the midst of the circumambulating magi, to the land in the New Sacristy, where the viewer is once more in their midst.[77] And I have been later able to extend that notion of

---

[76] In the mosaic on the left side of the choir of San Vitale, Justinian bears a gift (now we can understand the significance of the chi-rho on the shield of one of Justinian's soldiers: it was a sign the magi, as well as Justinian's imperial predecessor Constantine, had seen in the sky). Opposite Justinian is the gifting figure of Theodora (meaning "God's Gift"), with the three magi on the empress's hem bearing their gifts. To see the magian space in San Vitale, as can be done with the help of O. von Simson's brilliant *Sacred Fortress: Byzantine Art and Statecraft in Ravenna* (Princeton, 1987), recall the procession on the great southern wall of the church of Sant'Apollinare Nuovo where the virgins of the church bear their gifts behind the magi like so many fourth, fifth, sixth, etc., magi. Beneath, the faithful once actually brought their gifts to the altar. Now, ask if in San Vitale, Justinian and Theodora did not, like the servants of the magi, bear gifts behind invisible magi to Jesus (not Mary) in the apse mosaic, just as in the triumphal arch of S. Maria Maggiore in Rome, visible magi had waited on an enthroned Jesus (but not Mary).

[77] Mary Lewis and I argue that the three magi in Michelangelo's monument were Cosimo di Giovanni, buried at the cross of San Lorenzo, and Lorenzo and Giuliano di Piero, buried in the *sepultura in testa* of the New Sacristy, beneath the statues of Mother and Child and Cosmas and Damian. The two captains of Michelangelo were servants of these magi, bearing gold and frankincense (the doctors [*medici*] Cosmas and Damian bore the myrrh), just as did a servant in Gozzoli's Journey and another in Filippino Lippi's

magian space into the famous Holy Mountains of the sixteenth century where, as at Varallo, visitors once wandered through the space of the magi in Journey on their visiting that station.[78] Thus, the earlier reconstruction of the magian character of the New Sacristy will be confirmed by insisting on people's processional participation in the political life and space of the magi.

Finally, we return once more to the notion of political triumph which informed the several monuments of late medieval Italian politicians we have reviewed. The magi emerged as a subject of art at the time of Constantine, we recall. His heavenly sign, or a variant, was in fact the Star of Bethlehem seen by the magi. The link between magian iconography and secular triumph, I said, has been patent from the beginning.

Little changed on this score, as a feature of the Gozzoli paintings a millennium later shows. It is now generally agreed that a complex emblem (fig. 20) on the ceiling of the Medici-Riccardi chapel, having as its core the Bernardine JHS with protruding sun rays, stands for the Star of Bethlehem.[79] Forming the circular border around these typical rays is what passes for a laurel (=Lorenzo?) wreath of triumph. It is as if to say that not just Jesus and his church, but the Medici, or at least the kings beneath, conquer. Then, completing the figure, at four corners outside the wreath are diamond rings, the device of Piero di Cosimo, the chapel's patron.

Thus a millennium and more after the chi-rho — not a star — that was seen by the Apollonian Constantine had led the magi to Christ, so now,

---

Uffizi Adoration and many other magian servants of European art. Visitors thus stand in the space of the retinue of the magi: Trexler and Lewis, "Two Captains."

[78] I owe this information to Eugenio Battisti. On the *sacro monte*, see *Il sacro monte di Varallo*, ed. M. Bernardi (Turin, 1960), and the thoughtful characterization of its spaces by P. De Vecchi, "Annotazioni sul Calvario del sacro monte di Varallo," in *Fra rinascimento, manierismo e realtà*, ed. P. Marani (Florence, 1984), esp. 111: "non la 'cappella dei Magi,' ma il corteo dei Magi, che i pellegrini risalivano nel loro viaggio. . . ."

[79] Beyer, "De significatione," 182. Beyer did not know this "destarring" of the Star of Bethlehem had precedents. Bernardino called his monogram (which can as easily be read triumphantly as IHS ["in this sign (conquer)"] as it can be YHS ["Jesus"]) a "sun" (I. Origo, *The World of San Bernardino* [New York, 1962], 118). Before Bernardino, the visionary Bridget of Sweden in a miniature watches the infant lying in the manger on a (magian) sun or star (*Medieval and Renaissance Miniatures from the National Gallery of Art*, ed. G. Vikan [Washington, DC, 1975], xiii, 58–60). On Jesus in Medicean tradition as the *lux vera* that *in tenebris lucet*, see Trexler and Lewis, "Two Captains," in my *Church and Community*, 213. The Johannine words "lux vera" (Jn. 1.9) may also be shown on the breast of a rider behind the oldest king in Gozzoli's "Journey of the Magi."

Figure 20.
Benozzo Gozzoli, *Star of Bethlehem*.
Florence, Chapel, Medici-Riccardi Palace: fresco.

in humble Florence, the initialed sun stands again for the Star of Bethlehem, describing the laureled triumph of a more modern ruler. Those
great predecessors, the Emperors Constantine and Justinian, recognized
that myrrh, the medicine used to preserve the dead, was borne not just by
the three Marys to the tomb of Jesus, but also by the three magi to the
cave where he was born.

This much of a conceit the intellectuals in the Medici circle must certainly have communicated to their patrons: the magi kept the dead from
being forgotten. In the great magian space of the New Sacristy, beneath
another Bethlehemic star in "whose sign [one] conquers," the Medici
family would memorialize, or apotheosize, the sons and nephews of two
popes, who had so often marched in magian ranks to worship the infant
pontiff.

Ludic Life in New Spain:
The Emperor and His Three Kings*

IN SOME PARTS OF SIXTEENTH-CENTURY EUROPE, a form of urban political play developed which bonded politically disinherited males with the rising absolutistic dynasties of the continent: Play Kings from the adult lower classes and from youths of good family celebrated and theatrically fraternized with the real princes of the age. Monarchs in the pre-modern age understood that their power rested in part on the scope of their theatrical representation. Festively associating with nonpolitical urban groups, publicly crossing the line separating the worlds of real and imaginary monarchies, brought those nonpolitical kingdoms into the political realms while helping real kings subvert burgher liberties and noble privileges. The "powers" (potenze), as they were called in Italy, were intended to pose a playful threat to the kings' more political opponents. The upshot of this expanded world of festive identities, therefore, was a closer approximation

* This essay appeared previously in French in *Les Jeux à la Renaissance*, ed. J.-C. Margolin and P. Ariès (Paris, 1982), 81–93, and again in French in R. Trexler, *Church and Community 1200–1600. Studies in the History of Florence and New Spain* (Rome, 1987), 549–73.

in theatre to the actual world of struggle in early modern Europe. Public festive life was the stage where the corporate identities of the modern state could first be glimpsed.[1]

While in Europe festive confraternities dressed up as African and Indian kin to amuse their patrons, a substantially different, yet recognizably related type of play occurred in sixteenth-century America. Recently real Indian monarchs the length and breath of the New World dressed up as their old selves to integrate their nations into the international order of the Spanish monarchs and Gods. A common process of expanded representational integration was at work abroad and at home, but in the Indies the monarchs were real, and had established representational traditions. This study suggests that in the New World, the play of the magi or Three Kings, the *ludus magorum*, served as one iconologic vehicle through which its erstwhile real kings could be brought to worship at Caroline and Philippine altars.

In Europe, the story of the Three Kings had long found favor among the merchant class, and the attraction of the magi's gold would assure to the cult itself just as much popularity. Christopher Columbus himself believed that he had discovered ancient Sheba in the island of Cuba, "the country whence came the magus who offered gold."[2] Other explorers spoke of those associates of the magi St. Thomas and St. Bartholomew, who had supposedly traversed Brazil, Mexico, and Peru well before the Conquest. Still others maintained that Tarsis, said to be the homeland of the King who brought gold, was none other than America, which was so rich in the precious metal.[3] Explorers, miners, merchants, and even

---

[1] Y.-M. Bercé, *Fête et Révolte* (Paris, 1976); M. Boiteux, "Carnaval annexé: Essai de lecture d'une fête romane," *Annales E.S.C.* 32 (1977): 356–80, and by the same author: "Les Juifs dans le carnaval de la Rome moderne (XVè–XVIIIè)," *Mélanges de l'École française de Rome. Moyen Age, Temps Modernes* 88 (1976): 745–87; M. Grinberg, "Carnaval et société urbaine XIVè–XVIè siècles: le Royaume dans la ville," *Ethnologie française* 4 (1974): 215–44; N. Zemon Davis, *Society and Culture in Early Modern France* (Stanford, 1975), 97–123; R. Trexler, *Public Life in Renaissance Florence* (New York, 1980).

[2] *Journals and Other Documents on the Life and Voyage of Christopher Columbus*, ed. S. Morison (New York, 1963), 227–28; H. Hofmann, *Die heiligen Drei Könige: Zur Heiligenverehrung im kirchlichen, gesellschaftlichen und politischen Leben des Mittelalters* (Bonn, 1975); S. Boorsch, "America in Festival Presentations," in *First Images of America*, ed. F. Chiappelli, vol. 1 (Berkeley, 1976), 503–15.

[3] B. de Las Casas, *History of the Indies*, ed. A. Collard (New York, 1971), 68–69; Huamán Poma de Ayala, *Letter to a King: A Peruvian Chief's Account of Life under the Incas and under Spanish Rule*, ed. C. Dilke (New York, 1978), 104; J. de Acosta, *Historia*

interpreters and translators quickly determined that the Three Kings were at home in the West Indies.[4]

Some political aspects of the cult also contributed to its introduction into the New World. The myth of the Three Kings who moved toward a precise place of cult evoked the growing unity of diplomacy and society. In European festivals, peoples, wards, and professions had for a long time poured the riches of their games, their disguises, their discourses, and their music into the mold of this trip of the Three Kings, which usually finished with a gift or the payment of a tribute delivered by these "nations" to a sole king.[5] Could a theme like this fail to fascinate the rulers of Iberia, who brought with them their altars and a great king, or for that matter the nations, classes, and occupations of America, who sought to save their cohesion by means of processions? The myth of the Three Kings proved irresistible even for the deracinated black slaves, who sought to discover an old, and construct a new cultural community.[6] It was the same for the red men and for the whites, who sought to bring forward a public order after the Spanish law had been violently imposed. For them too the legend of the magi would prove useful. The city of Mexico soon became a figure for Jerusalem of the time of Herod, where Montezuma learned the bad news of the appearance of a new king; for its part the new capital of Peru was baptized, some said, as "the city of the Three Kings."[7] The

---

natural y moral de las Indias, bk. 1, chaps. 13 and 14, in _Obras_, ed. F. Mateos (Madrid, 1954), 22–25; J. Lafaye, _Quetzalcóatl et Guadalupe_ (Paris, 1974), 238–42. Cf. below, n. 27.

[4] On the mines, E. Parsons, _Mitla, Town of the Souls, and other Zapotec-Speaking Pueblos of Oaxaca, Mexico_ (Chicago, 1936), 202; and the merchants, V. Turner, _Dramas, Fields, and Metaphors: Symbolic Action in Human Society_ (Ithaca, 1974), 219–23, and R. Redfield, _The Folk Culture of Yucatan_ (Chicago, 1941), 243, 297–300. For the organization of a Mayo village by the magi see N. Crumbine, _El Ceremonial de Pascua y la Identidad de los Mayos de Sonora_ (Mexico City, 1974), 57–58, 141, 143–44, 152, 181, 258; for the magi in modern Mexico see G. Foster, _Culture and Conquest_ (Chicago, 1960), 187.

[5] After 1470, the Duke of Ferrara went _cercando la fortuna_ on the feast of Epiphany, and received "gifts," a form of taxation and a proof of loyalty: cf. W. Gundersheimer, _Ferrara: The Style of a Renaissance Despotism_ (Princeton, 1973), 186–87; the neighborhoods of the Florentine magi are studied in Trexler, _Public Life_, 400–4.

[6] A. Bachiller y Morales, _Los Negros_ (Barcelona, 1888), 113–19; F. Ortiz, _La Antigua Fiesta afrocubana del 'Dia de Reyes'_ (Havana, 1960). In 1609, there was fear in Mexico City of a black revolt, "que la Noche de los Reies se avian juntado, en cierta parte, muchos de ellos, y elegido Rei, y otros con titulos de duques, y condes, y otros principados, que ai en las republicas": J. de Torquemada, _Monarquia Indiana_, 3 vols. (Mexico City, 1969), 1:759 (bk. 5, chap. 70). For a rebellion c. 1540, see Torquemada, _Monarquia_, 1:610–11 (bk. 5, chap. 11), and for black kings and queens in the 1530s, below, n. 26.

[7] The first name of Lima was supposedly Ciudad de los Reyes, just as Mexico was like

monarchs of biblical history would be shown to come to Israel in a procession of perfect order, pagans though they might be, and they would return as good Christians to their homelands in just as good an order. The governors of the Indians, whether lay or ecclesiastical, and whether from Iberia or of indigenous stock, would be charged to carry out just as harmonious a procession, having their caciques pass in disciplined order from damnation to the salvation assured by Charles or Philip.[8]

I want to verify this theory of play by studying the staging of plays of the Three Magi in sixteenth-century Mexico, where though they are few in number, such plays are incomparably more rich than in the other colonies. The Nahuatl texts of two pieces — the Comedy and the Adoration of the Magi — have survived, and I will study the Spanish translations done by Paso y Troncoso. These two plays were transcribed at the end of the sixteenth and beginning of the seventeenth, but they reflect a theatrical tradition that goes back to the mid-sixteenth century.[9] Beyond these texts, there are two descriptions, the one short and the other long, of representations of the Three Kings which actually took place. For Tlaxcala, we have the c. 1540 description of the Franciscan Motolinía, and for Tlaxomulco near Guadalajara, that of another Franciscan, Alonso Ponce, in

---

Jerusalem: "Como aquellas gentes [de el Oriente] . . . , como quando entraron los Magos en Jerusalém . . . , y que como Cortés le venia á quitar la posesion de el Reino, á Motechuçuma . . . , asi tambien este Señor, y Rei Soberano, venia en habito de Rei Universal, á destruirlo, y quitarle el Reino": Torquemada, Monarquia, 1:380–81 (bk. 4, chap. 14). But according to another primary source, "Los Reyes" referred to the contemporary Spanish monarchs, and not to the magi: R. Trexler, The Journey of the Magi: Meanings in History of a Christian Story (Princeton, 1997), 238, n. 60. There is no mention of the utopic theme of the magi either in Lafaye, Quetzalcóatl, or in J. Phelan, The Millennial Kingdom of the Franciscans in the New World (Berkeley, 1970). For the battles organizing public processions in Mexico City, see J. García Icazbalceta, "La Fiesta del Pendon en México," in his Obras, vol. 2 (Mexico City, 1896), 443–51, and his Introduction to the Coloquios espirituales y sacramentales y poesias sagradas del presbitero Fernando Gonzalez de Eslava (Mexico City, 1877), xxiv–xxviii.

[8] For comparable processions in Florence, Italy during the republican and Medicean periods, see Trexler, Public Life, chaps. 11–13.

[9] Adoración de los Reyes, Auto en lingua mexicana (anonimo), ed. F. Del Paso y Troncoso (Florence, 1900) (hereafter A); Comedia de los Reyes, escrita en mexicano a principios del siglo XVII (por Agustin de la Fuente?), ed. F. Del Paso y Troncoso (Florence, 1902) (hereafter C). More accessible editions of the same are in F. Horcasitas, ed., El Teatro náhuatl: épocas novohispana y moderna (Mexico City, 1974), 253–327.

1587.[10] Combined with associated documents, these sources allow us to pursue our inquiry.

The Star is Sighted

The star that will lead to the infant savior is first glimpsed in the *Comedy of the Magi*, a text probably written in 1607 and marked by strong departures from the traditional legend.[11] In this play, the only extant Mexican account of the sighting, an otherwise unspecified "emperor" sends a "captain of the Three Magi" and two imperial vassals from his opulent court to the sacred mountain. It is the latter trio whose prayers and incense on the mountain are rewarded by sighting the star, they who then report that epochal event back to the emperor. The emperor forthwith instructs these personages to travel to the Three Kings and announce this fact. The Kings promptly come to the imperial court, and proclaim to their emperor their intention to follow the star.

The emperor opens our *Comedy* by addressing the captain and vassals: "Oh you, my nobles, my dignitaries," and the captain starts his response to the emperor with the salutation: "Oh lord, oh monarch." For Icaza these forms are "oriental," but De Bopp has shown that they correspond to the ornate Aztec salutations noted by the earliest conquerors.[12] As at that court, these forms are carefully calibrated to match the relative social standing of the parties addressed, the two vassals in this play, for example, at times speaking only to each other and to the captain but not to the emperor in whose presence they are.[13] The pattern of liturgical forms continues. When the captain and vassals climb the mountain, they pray to God: "Hail! ah, oh lord, oh God, oh Godfather." Arriving before the emperor to hear the news of the star, the Three Kings receive the former's

---

[10] Fray Toribio de Benevento, called Motolinía, *Historia de los Indios de la Nueva España*, ed. J. García Icazbalceta, in his *Colección de documentos para la historia de México*, vol. 1 (Mexico City, 1858), 70, slightly different from the description in the same author's *Memoriales*, ed. F. de Lejarza (Madrid, 1970), 50. Ponce's work was actually written by his scribe, Antonio de Ciudad Real: *Relación breve y verdadera de algunas cosas de las muchas que suciederan . . .*, (Madrid, 1873), 2:38–43 (hereafter P).

[11] R. Ricard, *La "Conquête Spirituelle" du Mexique* (Paris, 1933), 239–40. F. De Icaza, "Origenes del teatro en México," *Boletin de la Real Academia Española* 2 (1915): 59–60; J. Lockhart, *The Nahuas After the Conquest* (Stanford, 1992), 404–7.

[12] Icaza, "Origenes," 58; M. de Bopp, "Autos mexicanos del siglo XVI," *Historia Mexicana* 3 (1953): 122–23.

[13] C:109–10.

greeting: "Be welcome here, oh you three, oh you lords, you kings."[14] When the Kings reach Herod, both the *Comedy* and the play of the *Adoration* will have them address him similarly: "oh lord, oh great prince, oh Herod," with Herod replying: "oh principals, oh lords, worthy of being honored, oh knights."[15] And when the Kings finally reach the manger, the *Comedy* and the *Adoration* will show their textual interdependence by having the Kings address the child in identical terms: "oh noble, oh our lord, oh precious stone, oh rich feather, oh fine turquoise, oh bracelet."[16]

The hallucinatory effect these verbal rhythms have on the reader, not to mention on their audiences, is a mechanism intended to enforce social divisions, and we see this just as clearly in the body language the play-wrights assign to the actors. The *Comedy* has the captain and vassals incensing God on the mountain while genuflecting and kneeling.[17] The *Adoration* has the Kings promising to kiss the hand of Herod four hundred times, and when bringing news of the Kings' arrival at Jerusalem, Herod's major-domo is instructed to lift his sombrero and make three bows.[18] Once the Kings are present, Herod is to be paid reverence by his court, and he then is to see to *muchos honores* for them; after he has heard the news of the infant savior, *mucho se humillará* before these exotic monarchs.[19] This theatre with its often innovative story line is less a vehicle for teaching Bible history than for articulating and maintaining verbal and bodily signs of social hierarchy.

Assembling the Royal Retinue for the Journey

The Kings have heard the news, and they now went "to prepare their travelling bags."[20] We must picture them as assembling people and things representative of their distinct kingdoms, presumably, for it is this sociocultural specificity and variety which explains why, in the Franciscan Motolinía's words of about 1540, the festival of the magi was such a happy occasion for the Tlaxcalans. This is the feast, he explains, "in which the

---

[14] C:110.
[15] A:60.
[16] A:64; C:119–20.
[17] C:110.
[18] A:58.
[19] A:60, 62.
[20] C:113.

provinces of the peoples march out to find and adore the lord. ..."[21]
The Journey of the Magi, in short, was as much an indigenous cultural
performance as a biblical recollection, in the New World as in Europe a
summoning of local social structures to legitimate the son of a carpenter.
How much did the retinues which the Kings assembled in Mexico reflect
their actual social structures?

The sources are sparse on this score. The *Comedy* makes clear that
there was a retinue, identified by at least one banner.[22] The Kings had
come "from very far," and the 1587 description of the Tlaxomulco festival
has the Kings apparently traveling at some distance from one another, as
was proper for royal retinues and as we see in European paintings of the
time.[23]

Thus while two distinct accounts mention only one flag, the Tlaxomulco narrative shows that the Journey was sometimes a great district procession down mountains over rough roads. Indeed, this particular festive
site had witnessed the same veridical Journey every year since at least the
1550s.[24] The Tlaxomulco procession was done this way, we are told, "for
gravity," and gravity has to be seen to be appreciated. At the same festival
we learn that some five thousand Indians "assisted" (*acuden*), "as well

---

[21] Motolinía, *Memoriales*, 50, a phrase lacking in his *Historia*. Copying their master,
Mendieta and Torquemada say: "propia, suya, en la cual las *primícia* [not *provincias*] de las
gentes ó gentiles": G. Mendieta, *Historia eclesiástica indiana*, ed. J. García Icazbalceta
(Mexico City, 1971), 432 (bk. 4, chap. 19); Torquemada, *Monarquia*, 3:225 (bk. 17, chap.
7). I have chosen *provincias* because it seems right in context; I could not verify the word
in a manuscript of the *Memoriales*. Below, at n. 46, we see that Balthazar spoke the popoloco language (of the province of Tlaxcala: P:1:106, 140, 142, 261), that is, the language
of a "barbaric province." Another association of the various magi with the Indian *gentes*
is encountered c. 1640 in Parras, "la pasqua de la Epifanía, como tan propia de gentiles
que venían a reconocer a Cristo nuestro Señor, celebraron ...": A. Pérez de Ribas, *Triunfos de nuestra santa Fe entre gentes las más bárbaros y fieras del Nuevo Orbe*, in *Paginas
para la Historia de Sinaloa y Sonora*, ed. R. Cervantes Ahumada, 3 vols. (Mexico City,
1944), 3:266 (bk. 11, chap. 10). A sixteenth-century auto presents the history of the *four*
Tlaxcalan kings as the first baptized: J. Rojas Garcidueñas, ed., *El Teatro de Nueva
España en el siglo XVI* (Mexico City, 1935), 131–40, 181–221. For this legend, see C.
Gibson, *Tlaxcala in the Sixteenth Century* (Stanford, 1952), 30, 89–91. Its representation
in 1587 is below, at n. 27.
[22] "Y los vasallos, un individual llevará la estrella, uno llevará estandarte": C:113.
[23] P:40. In fact, they came from Persia.
[24] The same Indian is said to have played the role for more than thirty years: P:50.
The fact that A mentions no banner, along with several other variations, makes it improbable that P derives from A, as maintained by Ricard, "*Conquête*," 240.

[coming] from this ward as from other pueblos, because everyone in this region came together for this feast."[25] I suspect, therefore, that as in European festivals of the time so in the Mexican magi plays of this type, a mass of people started as participants, forming the retinues of the magi, and ended as audience once the monarchs had reached Jerusalem.

This argument — that the Mexican feast of the Three Kings assembled various nations or indigenous groups — is persuasive only to the extent that the kings themselves were regal figures requiring a grand retinue. As early as 1539 we have evidence that black slaves in Mexico City elected kings — and queens — to celebrate the Feast of the Kings.[26] There is no doubt that Indian military formations of "señores y principales" took part in the mock battles of *Moors and Christians* as early as 1539. It is fair to assume that such royal units of Indian society did so in the magi plays as well. For surely, if the Indians had to organize an entry for some dignitary passing through their area (and we remember that the magi play is precisely a triumphal entry), they too would have required just as exact a representation of their own social order, which put their *principales* in their proper place.[27]

---

[25] "A la cual se hallaron presentes dies ó doce frailes y muchos españoles seculares, y más de cinco mil índios, así de los de aquella guardianía, como de otros pueblos, porque todos los de aquella comarca acuden á aquella fiesta": P:43.

[26] "De negros y negras, con su rey y reina": B. Díaz del Castillo, *Historia verdadera de la conquista de la Nueva España*, ed. G. García, vol. 2 (Mexico City, 1904), 420–21 (148). They are princes represented in the battle of Moors and Christians of 1539, a play celebrating a French-Spanish peace treaty. News of the peace arrived in January (*Epistolario de Nueva España, 1505–1818*, ed. F. del Paso y Troncoso, vol. 3 [Mexico City, 1939], 243–44), and so I suspect that the king and queen were elected on Epiphany, as they were in 1609 (see above, at n. 6). We find the election of the Epiphany king *and* of the queen in Europe at the court of France, for example: J.-B. Bullet, *Du Festin du Roi-Boit* (Besançon, 1762), 1, also 6.

[27] Díaz del Castillo, *Historia*, 419–28 (148); Motolinía, *Historia*, 87–98 (bk. 1, chap. 15). Though he never visited America, López de Gómara (c. 1550) describes the Tlaxcalans during entries: "Tambien se preciaban mucho ellos mesmos de aquesto, y de la resistencia y batalla que dieron á Cortés en Teoacacinco; y así, cuando hacen fiestas ó reciben algun virey, salen al campo sesenta ó setenta mil dellos á escaramuzar, y pelean como pelearon con él": cited in *Historiadores primitivos de Indias*, ed. E. De Vedia (Madrid, 1946), 370. They showed the same political structure later, when the missionaries entered into Indian cities and villages; P:1:113, 304, 314, 366, 505–6 and passim. P saw the viceroy received into Tlaxcala in 1586 with "un tablado [con] quatro indios viejos, vestidos á lo antiguo, con coronas de reyes en las cabezas, los cuales representaban á los cuatro reyes ó cuatro cabeceras de aquella provincia de Tlaxcala que ayudaron al marqués [Cortés] del Valle tan valerosamente en la conquista de México": P:1:164. On the road from Guatemala to Chiapas, toward Coapa, Ponce saw in the homonymous church of St.

Perhaps then I am right to suppose that analogous units composed of Indians took part in similar fashion in the celebrations of the Three Kings. But there is more. Our picture of the sixteenth-century magi Journey also vividly calls to mind Mendieta's descriptions of Indian social units being marshaled and marched to church for *fiestas*. For in sixteenth-century Mexico City, one did not go to church only as an individual. One went in procession, from one's barrio or *calpulli*, under its flag. The sociopolitical infrastructure of the pre-Conquest city had been taken over wholesale by the Spaniards, and churches established in each of its four wards. As before Jesus the Indians had marched to their festivals under flags, so did they *annis domini*:

> The day before the feastday, each centenary and ventenary informed the people of the neighborhood of their responsibility, for the day was coming when they would have to sing and come to the church and house of God with flowers so as to acquit themselves of the service they owed him. ... They then went around their neighborhoods ..., crying out in loud voices for all to come out and join together in the ordained place in the said neighborhood, so that it could be seen and recognized if they were all there. ... Moving then along the road to the church, in processional order, that is, with the men in one file and the women in another, and led by an Indian who went in front with the colored taffeta standard or banner of each neighborhood [painted] with its own insignia of some saint they had taken as their patron, they went along, singing. ... When they arrived at the patio they said a prayer to the Holy Sacrament. There they were checked off against their names on tables, and those who were not there were noted, so that they would have to give them penance, which was a half dozen stripes across the shoulders.[28]

Were the flag or flags in the magi processions those of urban barrios or of rural pueblos? Only new sources can answer this question definitely, yet the circumstantial evidence argues for the following point of view: here were "the provinces of the peoples" of which Motolinía spoke (parishes,

---

Thomas, "y teníanle pintado en el altamayor con corona del rey, no supo la causa el padre Comisario [Ponce]": P:1:470.

[28] Mendieta, *Historia*, 498–99 (bk. 4, chap. 32).

whole towns, or social groups *mutatis mutandis*), coming together to adore the new lord.[29]

Bethlehem and Jerusalem

The Kings approach Jerusalem and Bethlehem, located in the patios our sources have already mentioned. The center of Indian religion during the early colonial period, these great "open-air churches," as McAndrew calls them, were large walled areas extending out from the convents of the friars much as such patios spread out from the pre-Christian temple pyramids.[30] The farthest wall of these patios was graced by gates, commonly in the form of triumphal arches, while the opposite end closing onto the church and convent often had a chapel with similar arches: the crib might be placed there when it was not placed in the church itself.[31] Leading to this patio on some festive occasions stretched what Motolinía designated as "triumphal arches" made of flowers and other exotica.[32] For the festival of the magi, two separate patio areas were used for Herod's Jerusalem and Jesus's Bethlehem, the former surrounded by signs of secular majesty and triumph, the latter "decently" decorated so as to evoke both secular and spiritual majesty. At Tlaxcala, Motolinía tells us, the paintings in the chapel featured ecclesiastical lords on one side of the crib, and secular ones next to them.[33]

Our interests require that two aspects of this patio setting be emphasized. The first is the recurrent architectural theme of triumph. The second is the name "Bethlehem." The Tlaxcalans gave the large chapel in their patio this name (even though it was built for Easter, 1539), just as the premier Indian chapel in Mexico City was named San José *de Belén* at

---

[29] See above, n. 21.

[30] J. McAndrew, *The Open-Air Churches of Sixteenth-Century Mexico* (Cambridge, MA, 1965).

[31] McAndrew, *Open-Air Churches*, 228–31. McAndrew does not take note of the triumphant nature of the tripartite arch, and cannot economically explain why the two- and four-part arches are rarely utilized: *Open-Air Churches*, 368ff. P locates the crèche: "Tenían hecho el portal de Bethlem en el patio de la puerta de la iglesia, casi arrimando á la torre de las campanas, y en él tenian puesto al Niño y á la madre y al Santo Joseph": P:2:39. At Tlaxcala, the crib was "en la iglesia," but perhaps that meant the exterior chapel: Motolinía, *Memoriales*, 50.

[32] There were ten triumphal arches, with the intervals being filled with more than a thousand other arches, according to Motolinía, *Historia*, 80, 96 (bk. 1, chap. 15). The last arch was perhaps the great arch of the gate of the patio.

[33] Motolinía, *Historia*, 84. "Cierto, el sitio donde nació (es) muy decente": A:64.

an earlier date.[34] The European magi festival had since late antiquity represented a fusion between the Roman imperial triumph and the Christian legend of the magi's triumphant entrance into Jerusalem.[35] When the magi arrived at the gates of Jerusalem, Herod would greet them as kings. When they arrived in Bethlehem, they would honor the child-king by their obeisance.

The patio which would witness this fanfare did not remain inactive as the Kings traversed their mountain roads. At least at Tlaxomulco, friars, lay Spaniards, and Indians watched an entertainment performed by other groups. Angels sang *Gloria in excelsis deo* etc. in Latin ("Goria," the scribe noted in amusement), and a host of other dance songs in their native language. Shepherds appeared and, after making their gifts to the child in Bethlehem, fell into a protracted wrestling match with each other. Then they formed a circle for a mock bullfight, their shepherds' crooks serving as bull horns to knock about those in the rodeo.[36]

Finally the Kings arrived at the gates of Jerusalem and the merriment ceased. Herod's major-domo listened to their messenger's request that his principals be admitted to the city, to then return to his master with the embassy and his impressions:

> In truth, no one has ever arrived here in this way. He is surely the first [to come here] speaking this language, with such a body [and] face. I actually am not sure this isn't idolatry![37]

Thus as in European and pre-Christian Aztec diplomatic formalities, the Kings sent a messenger, who encountered the host's major-domo with the entry request, which permission was granted along with instructions

---

[34] McAndrew, *Open-Air Churches*, 418; see also above, n. 31.

[35] See Trexler, *Public Life*, 551; and "The Magi Enter Florence: The Ubriachi of Florence and Venice," *Studies in Medieval and Renaissance History*, n.s. 1 (1978): 152–57.

[36] "Andaban tras los de la rueda como si fueran toros": P:41. Too lengthy to be reproduced here, this description can perhaps be compared to the great ritual bullfight in today's Zinacantan; E. Vogt, *Zinacantan: A Maya Community in the Highlands of Chiapas* (Cambridge, MA, 1969), 535–36. On the pre-Columbian Aztec games, see C. Duverger, *L'esprit du jeu chez les Aztèques* (Paris, 1978). The battle of the shepherds recalls the tradition of the magi who fight before arriving at the crib, and the imitation of the bulls calls to mind many European paintings of the Adoration of the Magi that show animals fighting: see e.g., C. Sterling, "Fighting Animals in the Adoration of the Magi," *Cleveland Museum of Art Bulletin* 61 (1974): 331–59, and n. 24 there for the magi as enemies one to another.

[37] A:58.

for the diplomatic reception of the visitors into the city. In the play of the *Adoration*, Herod sends his knights out of the city to accompany the Kings through its gates.[38] The Kings enter Jerusalem honorably and proceed to the palace of Herod, who awaits them on his royal throne, "con grande acompañamiento." In the midst of the most formal salutations, the Kings announce that they have lost sight of the star, and are searching for the child. Herod points the way to Bethlehem. The star reappears, and leads the Kings toward the crib.[39] Let us take a closer look at them as they cross the patio toward the birthplace of Jesus.

Did these Indian kings resemble the fabled Indian monarchs whose gold Columbus thought he had found in 1492? Our evidence on this count is slim but suggestive. The eyewitness account of 1587 notes the gravity of their bearing, while the play of the *Adoration* instructs the Kings that they were to "walk like lords."[40] Yet the *Comedy*, which was probably written down in 1607 and may be the latest of our documents, presents a less than grave reality. The play started, we recall, with the novel imperial court having all the trappings of majesty, but the Kings relatively deprived on that score. Indeed when they arrive at the emperor's court to hear the news of the star, they await their lord's pleasure on a bench![41] And when the magi arrive at the crib to present their gifts, we discover that far from being equal royal brothers, they are in fact representatives of different social classes, the lowest of whom is consigned to eternal poverty! Over the course of the sixteenth century, in short, the Indian magi may have declined, as did their nations, from proud lords to the impoverished butts of jokes.[42]

---

[38] A:59. For European entries, see *The Libro Cerimoniale of the Florentine Republic by Francesco Filarete and Angelo Manfidi*, ed. R. Trexler (Geneva, 1978). The entry of Cortés's army into Mexico in 1519 was similar: Díaz del Castillo, *Historia*, 1:259–74 (86–88).

[39] P:39–42. For the star, cf. also Motolinía, *Historia*, 70, and P:41.

[40] P:38–39; A:64.

[41] "Aparecerá los reyes; tomará asiento en sendos escaños": C:112.

[42] Mendieta and Dr. Zorita (c. 1566) bemoaned the decline of the authority of the Indian caciques because they both recognized that the preservation of social order depended upon these chiefs' cultural authority: A. de Zorita, *Breve y sumaria relación*, in *Nueva Colección de documentos para la historia de México*, ed. J. García Icazbalceta, 5 vols. (Mexico City, 1886–1892), 3:99–107, and *Nueva Colección*, 1:48–49, a letter of Mendieta to Philip II of 8 October 1565. Those accused of diminishing that authority responded that they were defending average Indians against their powerful indigenous lords.

An examination of their gifts enforces this impression, as does the apologetic manner in which they are presented. Whereas in Motolinía's account of c. 1540, the magi

... before the crib on that day offered wax, incense, doves, partridges and other birds that they had trapped especially for this day ...

as if they came from a country which abounded in goods of all sorts, the gifts of the later magi, though still precious, seem the products of a depleted society.[43] At Tlaxomulco they were seen to give "some silver jars," and in the plays we find what was in these containers.[44] In the *Adoration*, the child who had hair "which shone like gold," receives "the copal called incense" from Gaspar, who in the Comedy gives "a tiny bit of gold and silver."[45] Apologizing for his "barbaric language of Popoloco," Balthazar in the Comedy gives both myrrh and a burial shroud, and in the Adoration myrrh alone.[46] The youngest King, Melchior, gives gold in the *Adoration* and "a bit of incense and myrrh" in the *Comedy*.[47] Especially in the *Comedy* the Kings apologize, but already in the *Adoration* they have "almost nothing, just all our spirit, soul and life," or even "nothing, just what's right here."[48]

One reason for this refrain is that the magi measure their gifts against the life which one day Jesus will himself offer his father as propitiation: how could any material gift surpass such a gesture?[49] This is certainly sufficient reason to give all one has, and yet, perplexingly, the magi give their gifts to Jesus only on the condition that he will in fact take up his cross and be crucified, and thus save them.[50] In both the *Adoration* and

---

[43] Motolinía, *Historia*, 70 (bk. 1, chap. 13).

[44] P:40.

[45] A:64–65; C:120.

[46] C:120–21; A:66.

[47] A:65–66; C:121.

[48] A:66.

[49] This refrain is repeated in both plays. Just as in Europe, the star itself could be made to recall the coming sacrifice (C:111–113). For the child who placated the beloved Godfather, see A:65.

[50] "Aquí está un poquillo de oro y de plata, y esto, mientras que se cumpla tu gloriosa page (que será) cuando tengas á bien salvarnos": C:120. "Un poquillo de unguento ... para esto, oh Señor, oh Rey, ten a bien trabajar como siervo, sírvete pagar tributo": C:120.

the *Comedy*, Jesus is scheduled ultimately to pay "tribute" to his God-father, and the Kings "restitute" or "pay" Jesus for his tribute.[51] The infant is seen as at one and the same time paying his father and serving the Kings "like a slave," while the Kings both perform signs of service to Jesus and receive his promise.[52]

The person who makes these promises and accepts these gifts is, of course, Mary and not the mute Jesus, who cannot yet speak. In what is surely the most unusual point in the extant plays, the *Comedy* has Mary first recognize that the Kings deserve something in exchange for their graciousness, then look into the future like a prophetess, and finally forecast each King's future in relation to what each gave. Gaspar's gift of gold and silver is certainly meritorious and "dignas di recompensa," she says, and his fine person is one that cannot tolerate hard work. So Mary promises this King that:

> Your children will be just like what you offer, what you deign to give: gold and silver. Dear Gaspar, my dear son will give you that in return.[53]

She then recognizes that Balthazar's gift of unguent and myrrh marks him as poor, but his exertion for her son decent. His industry and courage will ultimately be rewarded:

> Because you came to greet my beloved only son, dear Balthazar, he will certainly deign to send you that which you ask with your tears.[54]

Mary's forecast for the final King was, unfortunately, not encouraging. He had given "a bit of incense and myrrh," and would, she was sure, continue to exert himself without material gain:

---

[51] Tribute: at n. 50 and A:65. Restitution and payment: A:66; C:121.

[52] Slavery: C:120. Jesus had also "empeñado" himself to the Old Testament prophets: "Hicieste tu deber tocante á ellos, que habrán ido á saber allá dias ha": A:65. In Europe, the Epiphany rituals at Ferrara (see at n. 5) show this fusion perfectly, but cf. also the case of the Duke of Bourbon Louis III, who each Epiphany personally gathered up the tributes of his officers, and then gave them to the child playing Jesus: Bullet, *Du Festin*, 7–8.

[53] Y, cierto, hay merecimento y acciones tuyas dignas de recompensa, para que te conceda favores mi amado hijo, á fin de que nos vengas fatigándote: lo que á ti sea necessario; y tus hijos . . .": C:120.

[54] "Y tú (que) eres pobre . . .": C:121.

You, poor one, will never stop working, and your children will always be poor; they will always work. Persevere, good Melchior.[55]

These prophecies, made to Indian kings, must have been meant to distinguish either between different native tribes or, more likely, between different classes within the same race. We have seen that the magi play was, after all, a tributary form linked, we believe, to the social structure of the Indians. Missionaries and bureaucrats, we emphasized, wanted to preserve not only the cultural integrity of the natives, but class distinctions within those cultures. By the early seventeenth century, most of the precious wealth of the Indies was no longer in native hands. The Offertory in the mass of the Epiphany, and the many other tribute forms of which the Spaniards disposed, had left their mark. The magi procession of Tlaxomulco, our source wrote, was marked by impoverished accoutrements, and the cultural pride of the nation was enfeebled.[56] Yet the plaintive cry to maintain social distinctions persists, even protrudes: the *Comedy* of 1607 makes the poverty of the poor King and his legions of retinue their very glory. "Giving all" to Jesus was the lot and the salvation, one hinted, of the poor Mexican *macehuales* just as it was of the impoverished festive *potenze* of Europe. The ancient octogenarian at Tlaxomulco who carried the collection basket in the *Comedy of the Magi* now comes to center stage. As he has been doing for thirty years on the feasts of Epiphany, he keeps his distance from the infant, for he is a mere porter. Putting down his now empty basket from which the Kings had taken their gifts, he turns toward the child, and . . .

. . . kneeling, speaks to him in the Mexican language itself, saying that he has nothing to offer him other than what he has on his

---

[55] C:122.

[56] This association between the magi and different social classes is unique, as far as I know; normally, one considers the Kings to have status equality among themselves. But an association between the sons of Noah and the classic Christian orders is to be found (O. Niccoli, *I sacerdoti, i guerrieri, i contadini: Storia di un immagine della società* [Turin, 1979], and J. Le Goff, "Les trois fonctions Indo-Européennes, l'historien et l'Europe féodale," *Annales E. S. C.* 34 [1979], 1027, 1214, n. 44), and the association between these sons and the magi was quite customary. Le Goff ("Trois fonctions," 1027) discusses the transformation of equal parts into unequal parts. For the transformation in Mexico, cf. De Bopp: "Los Reyes Magos se identifican evidentemente con los cencidos . . . , y los pastores se vuelven indios": "Autos," 118.

back, and the exhaustion he's endured in carrying it. All that he offers him.[57]

The plays are over. The Slaughter of the Innocents is left to our imagination.[58]

§

At the outset we asked how the Spaniards hoped to maintain the so-cial order of the Indies so as to convert and tax them without exhausting them. We answered that Christian theatre was part of the strategy. The feast of Corpus Christi was certainly the easiest vehicle to transfer the worship of a great lord like Montezuma to the one living God, but that feast had no processional iconography, as did the cult of the magi. The "provinces of the gentiles," we hypothesized, must have marched under the flags of the magi.

We have not provided conclusive evidence that through this particular play vehicle, an existing social system was captured, redirected, and its wealth systematically tapped, but we have presented substantial evidence for the notion, which only further data on the cult will prove or disprove. We know for a fact that the social units of the native tribes were repeat-edly marshaled for festive presentations, and we believe that they marched as magian retinues. We have seen Indian groups gathering their wealth for their magi to give the Christ child, and we surmise that this tribute for the churches, perhaps even for the crown, came from national or class units of the natives.[59] There is no doubt, we have shown, that in the military-religious festivities of the 1530s, real Indian lords and caciques com-manded their own native forces, so it is the more probable that Indian chiefs were substantive magi long before their descendants delighted to-day's Mexican children by playing gift-giving Kings.[60]

At the least we have raised one important question for further re-

---

[57] For the impoverished situation, see P:39. For examples of massive Indian gifts to-ward the mid-sixteenth century, see Motolinía, *Historia*, 73–75 (bk. 1, chap. 74).

[58] P:42–43.

[59] An interesting description of a tribute collection among lower-class Indian groups which, converted into a gift, was given by their caciques to high-standing Aztec lords, is in Zorita, *Relación*, 162, 220.

[60] For example, the Indians played "the army of New Spain," the Spaniards that of Spain, etc.: Motolinía, *Historia*, 87–98.

search. What happened when Spain, what happens when any colonial power imports its theatrical spaces, narratives, and tabus, and implants them into the behavior life of a colony? What happened when Indians marched to a different god, within a new mythic frame? For more than four centuries, the plays of the Indians have been viewed almost exclusively as instruments for teaching catechism, but now it is time to look at the Indian Journey as a behavioral fact and memory. Is it not profoundly irrelevant whether, as Mendieta before Ricard fretted, the Indians may have been "Christians [more] in jest [than] in truth"?[61] A noble deceit, the *ludus magorum*, lets us watch cultures and societies march in and out of the magic circle of pure play.

---

[61] Mendieta, *Historia*, 429 (bk. 1, chap. 74); Ricard, "*Conquête*," chap. 12, passim.

SAINT-MAKING

Francis of Assisi,
His Mother's Son[*]

I FIRST ADDRESSED FRANCISCAN MATTERS IN 1982, at the Walters Art Gallery in Baltimore on the occasion of an exposition of Franciscan objects honoring the eighth centenary of the saint's birth. Yet fully seven years passed before I published anything on the subject, a book entitled *Naked Before the Father: The Renunciation of Francis of Assisi* (New York, 1989). Alessandro Barbero was not so lethargic. In the immediate wake of the book's appearance, he published a long critique of it in the pages of *Studi medievali*,[1] and in the following year, 1991, again turned his attention to the book in his own monograph, *Un santo in famiglia: vocazione religiosa e resistenze sociali nell'agiografia latina medievale* (Turin, 1991).[2] This is my response to that review. I do respond because my book advances a radical new interpretation of Francis's famous renunciation, which deserves the reader's close attention. Alas, Barbero's confrontations with my *Naked Before the Father*, by (erroneously) faulting my source readings for Francis's renunciation and by repeatedly misreading my English text, may

---

[*] This essay appeared previously in *Studi medievali*, ser. 3, 36 (1995): 363–74.

[1] "La rinuncia di Francesco all'eredità paterna," *Studi medievali* 31 (1990): 837–51; as will be seen, the title of this article contains its thesis.

[2] The printing is dated September 1991. I reviewed this work in the *American Historical Review* 98 (1993): 850–51, but without mentioning his criticism of my work.

hinder readers from giving the book's total argument the weight it deserves. In the following pages, I want to correct this situation.

Naked Before the Father was written with one hagiographical leitmotif up front and clearly visible. The story of a saint (or, as here, that of his or her conversion) in fact usually contains several stories. Only the pious confound them into one, for the simple reason that, guided by a convincing story-teller, these stories are combined to project the saint as one reified object. In fact, those who write such stories, living as they do at different times and in varied contexts, change what has already been written, in part because their story, if it is to be heard or read by their own contemporaries, must conform to the interests of the patrons supporting the writer, as well as to the sentiments of the audience that hears the story told. Thus the histories of a saint are constantly reshaped, to appear a new, single history.

So forget for a moment any attempt to understand what actually happened in Francis's life. The student wishing to reach an understanding of the *true* saint begins by avoiding that most dangerous of all shoals, the conviction that there *is* such a true biography at the end of the historiographical rainbow that is accessible to the historian. No conventional, that is, no solemnly legitimate reading of a story replicates how things really were, and so the student must always be open to new readings of a saint's life. Of course he or she must begin with a serious knowledge of the social context of a writer's time, and with the question of what the interests were that might have brought any writer to vary his story from the received one. Finally, it goes without saying that such work requires the student not only to command the language of his or her sources, but those of the scholarly community with whom that student wants to discourse. These then are the historiographic grounds guiding my book, and the discussion that follows.

Naked Before the Father advances four arguments about Francis's renunciation that emerge from the study of as many types of sources or texts. The first argument is that Francis was the son of his mother by the latter's second marriage. This claim emerges from a genealogical study of thirteenth- and early fourteenth-century notarial records concerning a family that was almost certainly Francis's own. In these notarial records, one Pica has a son named Angelo. This man, identified by almost all students as Francis's brother, is in these documents uniformly referred to as "Angelo di Pica," and not as Angelo di Pietro, that is, as the son of his father, as previous writers have always assumed Pietro to have been. There is in fact no appropriate Angelo di Pietro in the notarial records. Thus I argue that in referring to Angelo as the son of his mother, the notaries were indicating that his personage and property derived from her, and not from any (living) man. The argument is further refined in the book. Pica, I believe, had been married, borne Angelo, and probably been widowed before she married Pietro di Bernardone. It was from this latter union that Francis was born.

The second argument follows from the first. The famous struggle between Pietro and his son Francis was less over the father's wealth, as has always been assumed, than it was about the mother's property. The earliest and most suggestive evidence for this view is visual in character. While almost all paintings of the scene of the renunciation in subsequent centuries exclude the mother — as if the struggle was purely male in character and implications — the first two paintings of the scene, dating in execution or in inspiration to the years soon after Francis's death and canonization, feature Pica in the scenes describing the renunciation. In effect, her presence in these primary sources establishes, I believe, that Pica and her propertied personage were serious players in the dramatic denouement of the renunciation. That was not a "decent" reading of the story for future painters and their clerical patrons, and they soon excluded her from that story.

The third argument in this book claims that the early lives of Francis (1 Celano, the Life by Julian of Speyer, the Three Companions, 2 Celano, and the definitive *Legenda maior* of Bonaventure) show a clear development or movement regarding the question of Francis's relationship to property. As a part of this general problematic, I argue that there is an observable shift away from the simple view in 1 Celano that Francis, following Jesus' admonition, renounced his goods *e basta*, to the gender-specific statement, in Bonaventure, that he precisely renounced all rights to his father's, that is, to the paternal, estate. It is this development in the written tradition that Barbero disputes, beginning with the title of his critique, and I shall return to it shortly.

A fourth argument continues in this vein: despite Bonaventure's thereafter authoritative claim of the mid-1260s that these men fought only over men's things, the earlier view of the original renunciation in painting — that the men were at odds in part because Francis might receive his mother's goods — was alive and well across Italy in the fourteenth and fifteenth centuries. Not only does a Trecento Tuscan "translation" of Bonaventure's story say just this, but so do the first two printed editions of this same translation, which appeared in Rome in 1477 and 1480 with the support of the Franciscan Pope Sixtus IV, who was pushing Bonaventure's canonization.

Thus what must appear self-evident to anyone familiar with late medieval Italian law, inheritance practices, and religious devotion was also a conventional understanding of the faithful in that earlier period. Mothers who had property could and often did leave it to sons who had entered religion, their purpose being to assure their retirement and burial in those sons' monasteries or friaries, if need be. Pietro recognized this danger to his interests, and got his son to give up any interest he had in his mother's estate. The opposite scenario makes little sense. In this historical context, sons on the outs with their fathers were out of luck: they had little chance of laying claim to a recalcitrant father's wealth when the latter chose to exclude such a son from it. Thus for Pietro to have wrung from Francis the latter's renunciation of his rights solely to his father's estate, as earlier scholarship has always assumed, would have been pointless, and the late medieval vernacular tradition recognizes this by having Pietro try to secure from Francis all rights to his wife's estate, as in the Italian "translation" mentioned above.

Naked Before the Father is not limited to these four arguments or to the handful of evidence mentioned here, and I must refer the reader to the book for details and documentation. But I do want to mention one other finding it advances because it will set the stage for understanding the general problem with Barbero's attack on my book. Apparently for the first time, *Naked Before the Father* shows that the early biographers used their stories of Francis's renunciation to gloss the well-known Franciscan debate over apostolic poverty. Whether the Franciscan order or its friars could or should own property was described in part in terms of whether Francis had owned, or merely used, property at this point in his life. One bit of source material that I use to bolster this important ancillary argument is the statement in the earliest Life (1 Celano) that Francis was twenty-five years of age when he renounced. I contend that Celano made this affirmation because twenty-five was the classical age of majority and the age at which, if it had not been accomplished beforehand, young men might automatically be emancipated from their father. Thus Celano probably recognized that his hero's age was relevant to the question of Francis's status as either a property-owning sinner or as a mere juvenile user of Pietro's usuriously earned wealth at the time that he renounced the world.

Now in his monograph, Barbero recognizes that this matter of whether Francis was or was not propertied at that point in time is of some importance, and I am gratified by that. But unfortunately, he misunderstood or at least misrepresents my position. He has me "seem to say" ("sembra rite-nere") that being twenty-five years of age, Francis was automatically eman-cipated and thus could trade and make contracts on his own. In fact I say no such thing. Instead, after insisting on the vagueness of the sources, I conclude that Celano and the Three Companions *may have* considered Francis's legal emancipation to have occurred not before, but simultaneous with, his assumption of clerical status, which was in turn simultaneous to his renunciation before the bishop of Assisi.[3] That Barbero rushed to pub-lish his misreading of my English — which I would gladly have clarified if he had asked me — is bad enough, and such misreadings will prove a pat-tern in his whole critique. Worse is that he does not realize that whether Francis owned property or not was more important to the Franciscan order than it is to the historical record of Francis's life.

The author's carelessness in this question of emancipation ("seems to say"!) allows the reader to anticipate Barbero's cavalier way of handling my exposition of more fundamental questions regarding the renunciation. What was it, for example, that Francis renounced? Barbero thinks I get this wrong too, with the result that in his eyes my whole recasting of the renunciation story comes near to total collapse. He dwells on this matter almost exclusively in his *Studi medievali* critique of late 1990, then raises it again in his 1991 monograph as being the second problem with the book, along with the emancipation argument mentioned above. Together, my failures in these two areas are so grave as to cause Barbero to warn the readers of his book that my conclusions "have to be used cautiously."[4] But is Barbero's pedantic "caution" any more justified in this second area than it was in the first? Let us see.

As stated above, I argue that the authoritative *vitae*, like the paintings, show a development over time in this area. In 1 Celano, Francis at his father's behest renounces any goods of his own into the bishop's hands (Pietro "ducit eum deinde coram episcopo civitatis, ut in ipsius manibus omnibus eius renuntians facultatibus, omnia redderet quae habebat").[5] Then some four decades later, Bonaventure has Francis renounce into the

---

[3] Trexler, *Naked*, 38; Barbero, *Un santo*, 207.

[4] Barbero, *Un santo*, 253.

[5] 1 Celano chap. VI, paragraph 14. All relevant texts are in appendices in Trexler, *Naked*.

bishop's hands "all paternal rights, and he render[ed] everything that he had" ("Tentabat deinde pater carnis filium gratiae pecunia tam nudatum ducere coram episcopo civitatis, ut in ipsius manibus facultatibus renuntiaret paternis et omnia redderet, quae habebat …").[6] Barbero disagrees with my readings of these texts. In his view 1 Celano, in the phrase *eius renuntians facultatibus,* means to say that Francis renounced the goods or faculties *of his father.* I, on the contrary, read the Celano passage to mean that Francis renounced whatever goods or faculties he himself (*eius*) had. Thus in Barbero's view there was no development over time. Bonaventure had exactly copied if not the words, then certainly the meaning, of 1 Celano.[7] In Barbero's view, this has the effect of deflating the whole notion that Francis's mother, and her estate, were at all involved in these transactions. For the genitive *eius* of the personal pronoun, says the author, can only have referred to Pietro.

Alas, Barbero here defies common sense.[8] The crucial phrase in 1 Celano that begins by saying that Francis renounces all his faculties is followed by a clause stating that Francis "rendered everything he had." Now, no one doubts that this concluding clause says that Francis renounced everything *he* had, so it is to be expected that the preceding words merely set up what the final clause emphatically echoes, and indeed, the participial phrase around *renuntians* is clearly meant to be subsumed in the clausal activity around *redderet.*[9] That is, what Francis rendered of his own in the last clause is the same or at least contains what he renounced in the previous phrase. In fact, the ablative of separation that completes the participial *renuntians* (*omnibus eius facultatibus*) could only awkwardly refer to the faculties of anyone other than the renouncer. Thus ready to "renounce all his faculties," he renders everything of his own that he, Francis, had. *Pace* Barbero, the sentence is not complicated.[10]

---

[6] *Legenda maior*, chap. II, 4.

[7] Barbero's attempt to explain why Bonaventure changed these words is artificial and unconvincing: "La rinuncia," 846–47.

[8] In the grammatical matter that follows, I have been greatly aided by my colleague Daniel Williman. I heartily thank him for his critical reading of the relevant sources and of this response. Needless to say, however, any mistakes here are my own.

[9] This is different indeed from what Bonaventure does in his rewrite of 1 Celano: he converts Celano's participial phrase into a clause, which he then links to a following clause by a conjunction. Thus the phrase of Celano that is subsumed in the subsequent clause becomes in Bonaventure a clause followed by another clause of equal status.

[10] After trying to show that I am mistaken and that the phrase in 1 Celano is clear, he turns about ("La rinuncia," 848) and calls the latter "ambiguous" and "not suffi-

Barbero is however convinced that the story involves only male goods and tensions, and so now claims that linguistic convention at the time of 1 Celano favors his reading, according to which Francis renounced his father's faculties. As Barbero at first recognizes, the problem is whether *eius* in *omnibus eius facultatibus* refers to the subject of its (dependent) clause, that is, to Francis, or whether for that purpose *suis* would have been required. Barbero refers to Lorenzo Valla to the effect that in dependent clauses classical authors used the reflexive pronoun or adjective *se* or *suus* to refer only to the subject of that clause, and thus the non-reflexive *eius*, according to Barbero, must here refer to some other noun. In fact, however, classical usage is quite ambiguous, as Valla himself reflects in his discourse: *eius, se*, or *suus* are occasionally used in a dependent clause to refer either to the subject of that clause or to that of the independent clause.[11] As Barbero himself recognizes, however, Valla does not insist on what might be his own preferred usage, and in any case, neither classical usage nor the Quattrocentesque Valla is a good witness for the early Duecentesque usage of Tommaso Celano.

To transcend this problem, Barbero proceeds to examine every other use of the word *eius* in 1 Celano — 126 in all — and finds that "this refers to a term other than the subject" in 125 cases. Alas, Barbero does not say which subject, and his calculations obviously forget to take into account the crucial grammatical point in question, which he had himself identified, that is, whether the *eius* occurs in a dependent or an independent clause. At best, the counting needs to be redone.

However, Barbero's subsequent documentation proves that that is not really necessary. The author cites three phrases from 1 Celano which he believes confirm his reading of *eius*, but which in fact affirm my own, namely, that we are speaking of Francis's, and not Pietro's, faculties. In these three phrases, the reflexives (*se, suis*) that are employed refer to the subject of the independent clause and not of the dependent clause in which they occur. Thus grammatically, if Celano had meant to refer to Pietro, he would have said *suis facultatibus* rather than *eius renuntians facul-*

---

ciently clear" when it comes time to explain why then Bonaventure would have changed the phrasing!

[11] Alas, Barbero gives only a general reference to and not a specific place in Valla's work for this alleged view: see "Laurentius Vallae ad Ioannem Tortellium Aretinum cubicularium Apostolicum, de reciprocatione Sui & Suus, libellus plurimum utilis," in *Laurentii Valla opera omnia* (Turin, 1962), 1:235–48 (not 233–49, as in Barbero).

tatibus.[12] As a result, the crucial genitive *eius* in this passage of 1 Celano should refer to the subject of the clause in which it occurs. By Barbero's own evidence, Francis renounced no one else's goods or estate or faculties but his own, and to drive that point home, 1 Celano in his clause subsuming the activity in the preceding phrase follows with the tautological biblical assurance that, like the future apostle, Francis had thus rendered all he had.

Bonaventure's motivations in changing the simple statement of 1 Celano into the litigiously cautious assertion that Francis renounced any rights he had to his father's estate are not clear in the sources at our disposal. It is common knowledge, to be sure, that each decade of the high and late Middle Ages saw the further erosion of women's rights at law, so that the disappearance of Pica from the paintings and the paternalistic aggressiveness of the priestly Bonaventure in his *Legenda* are not hard to understand. This was after all an age whose patriarchy quite normally played as if only male properties and values were at stake in an honorable society, whereas in fact the ownership of a substantial part of any polity's property was in the dowries, if not in the hands, of its women. Much the same can be said regarding the status of property held by the Franciscan order in these crucial decades and in later centuries. Specifically, this was a society whose clergy depended upon mothers for financial support, and vice versa, one in which these mothers relied greatly upon their tonsured sons to support them in old age, and yet that same clergy played as if a polity's compact with God depended only on the relations between male clergy and male laity. But it was not the task of my book to explore such questions, nor can it be here. How can one expect to unravel this complex historical puzzle about Pica when it is still at times a struggle to get the agenda of women's role in history onto the historical table at all?

At this point I hope to have shown that the two key elements of Barbero's critique of my book have proven baseless. I do not claim that Francis was emancipated before he renounced, and *pace* Barbero, Francis renounces his own faculties, and thus eventual rights or gifts that might come his way more from Pica than from his father's estate.[13] It goes with-

---

[12] See the texts in Barbero, "La rinuncia," 844, lines 9, 7, and 6 up: *vota sua, ad sui consensum, viri sui.*

[13] Barbero ("La rinuncia," 845; also 847: "non ai beni paterni, ma ai propri beni") seems to think I claim that Francis gave up only the goods he himself possessed. In fact, my emphasis is always on those he might be assigned by his mother.

out saying that here as in my book I put forward this latter affirmation cautiously, for as with much else regarding Francis and his tradition, the documentation on this matter of renunciation is scarce, and only has force if leavened with the social historian's awareness of context.

If I believe that Barbero's criticism of my understanding of these key passages in 1 Celano and Bonaventure is incorrect, I do take it seriously. Yet now the author's outright misreading of my arguments again raises its ugly head, and reaches an apogee of sorts, when he addresses the evidence I uncovered that the average person in the fourteenth and fifteenth centuries did understood that in the Francis story, the father fought to get his son to renounce any access to his mother's goods. The author proceeds unpleasantly,[14] but more importantly, incorrectly. First, after reporting my finding that "three modern editions of medieval manuscripts of an Italian translation of Bonaventure's Life" all state that Pietro was determined to rescue the mother's estate from any possible control by Francis, Barbero has me claiming that each of these three modern editions was based on separate manuscript traditions. Wrong. As the readers of the above quote can see, I simply mean to show that more than one manuscript lay at the base of these three editions; that is, the three editions do not all go back to a common manuscript. A plurality of Italian manuscripts of this tradition of maternal influence on the story of the renunciation did and probably still do exist.

Next, Barbero has me "surprised" that the language in these three editions as regards Pica's goods is practically identical. Wrong again, and indeed, horrendously so. For as I argue throughout, all these modern Italian texts can obviously be traced back to one Italian translation of Bonaventure's *Legenda* — probably written in the fourteenth century and usually attributed to Domenico Cavalca. How could the author misread so badly?

Now we arrive at a third, truly preposterous, misreading by Barbero. The author actually has me maintaining that the Italian in the 1477 and 1480 incunabula of Bonaventure's *Legenda* represents a brand new translation done at that time! In short, I am supposed to have said that the incunabula of these years were not related to a previous Italian manuscript tradition! Wrong still again!

---

[14] Barbero thinks that "la lettura di questo testo dal Trexler non è così limpida da suscitare un'incondizionata fiducia nella sua interpretazione. Lo studioso americano . . .": "La rinuncia," 848. I am simply a scholar. Barbero's repeated reference to me as an American obviously hints at a lack of confidence in his own argument.

This third misreading is the more startling because the organization of my exposition clearly moves from describing the incunabula's contents backwards to the question of where their translation had come from, and of course I determine that the source was the one and only "Cavalca." Of course! Barbero announces to the world that quite to the contrary of what I have (allegedly) argued, there is a "vast tradition, first manuscript and then in print, of one sole [Italian] translation," and precisely that well-known one and only one before the Cinquecento, the one attributed to Cavalca. It is nothing more than what I unearthed and what I argue in my whole presentation! It is good to have another author's confirmation of my findings, but it is embarrassing to find that this modern Quixote does so by tilting at so many windmills.[15]

Undaunted, Barbero turns finally to the problem of the Italian text itself, for beyond all technical questions, the author cannot escape the fact that from the Trecento Italian translation of Bonaventure forward, Francis is said to have renounced the rights to his mother's estate. How could this happen? At heart simply a student of texts, Barbero avoids all the legal, social, and ecclesiological aspects of inheritance that lie at the root of my argument. The origin of the mother's goods in Bonaventure's Italian version, he says, stems from the Latin manuscript of Bonaventure that was used by "Cavalca" to prepare his translation: it erroneously read "maternis" instead of "paternis."[16]

Wrongheaded again this one last time. As do I, Barbero posits the existence of a Latin manuscript tradition predating "Cavalca" which read "maternis" rather than "paternis." He further recognizes the fact that the first two prints of Bonaventure's *Legenda* in Italian, certainly commissioned by Sixtus IV, also speak of the mother's wealth. Finally, he knows that at least three modern editions of that translation bear the same reference to Pica's property. Yet all these latter-day writers, and their many

---

[15] Like most scholars wanting to avoid new thinking on a conventional topic, Barbero leaves the unmistakable impression that this "vast tradition" of Italian translation of Bonaventure was known to all serious students of Francis, none of whom he cites. Let me assure readers that not until *Naked Before the Father* has this translation, like much other material treated in my study, ever been part of the literature on Francis's renunciation.

[16] "La rinuncia," 849. Barbero imagines that "Cavalca" first transcribed the "erroneous" *maternis* as the Italian "de madre," and then, recognizing the "mistake" of his Latin source, did not just correct his text to "de patre," but rather added to his Italian translation the statement that Francis renounced the inheritance "de patre e de matre": cf. *Naked*, 61.

readers, in their ignorance are supposed to have not noticed the prominence of the mother in this vernacular tradition of Francis's life, which stood in such marked contrast to the official Latin *Legenda*. The medieval Latin scribes who had hypothetically transcribed "maternis" for "paternis," and the poor Italian translator we call "Cavalca" come off worst of all. The former were so simple-minded about the social realities of their own age that they could not tell or did not care about the difference between a mother's and a father's wealth, the latter so indifferent a translator that he was incapable of consulting a better Latin text and then changing "maternis" back to "paternis," "matre" back to "patre."

The image of the renunciation of Francis of Assisi that emerges unscathed from Barbero's critique is one of a conflict between father and son in part over mother's wealth, a battle familiar enough to social historians of this age. This does not mean that Francis had no religious motivation for his renunciation, but simply that, as Jean-Claude Schmitt has emphasized, such motivations are always imbedded in social realities like familial conflicts.[17] It is the task of the historian to provide that social context, and it is clear that in the instant that Francis's renunciation became a template for the policy of a great religious order, that original story of the renunciation diverged. A Latin tradition from now on characterized the battle as purely male in nature; a vernacular tradition — seen first in art but later in words — fashioned a father and son who, true to vernacular experience, fought over the wealth of women.

In a swelling tide, the contemporary historiography of women is everywhere producing a new and complex picture of the role of women in societies that stands in strong contrast to the older patriarchal view. By no means does this new concern with women always result in a revised view of women's societal *power*. Especially in the study of the Italian Middle Ages, the focus has rather been on etching a new image of society functioning through the efforts of both men and women situated in often distinct but always dynamic roles. Hopefully, the story of Francis of Assisi that I tell will prove to have contributed something to this undertaking, despite the scarceness and ambiguity of the sources.

Still, almost everything remains to be done to eliminate the patriarchal character of received historiography. Not much can be expected from the spiritual descendants of those writers who, in a small bow to the female

---

[17] See his thoughtful review of *Naked* in *Archives de sciences sociales des religions* 35 (1990): 303–4.

majority of the population, traditionally insert a woman at the end of a series of male saints' lives.[18] A new effort must come from scholars determined to search out the role of women, or the role of those males gendered female, in the most sacred of seemingly all-male stories.[19] Mother to his brothers and sister to the poor, perhaps Francis can after all still whisper his secrets to us.

---

[18] This mechanical procedure of traditional *Lives of Famous Men*, and of clerical hagiographies, is well known. But cf. also Barbero in 1991 assigning the last of the seven chapters of his *Un santo* to "La santità femminile nel basso medioevo," while concluding four of the previous chapters with bows towards "Mulier virilis," Giona di Bobbio, "la santità femminile," and "La santa moglie e madre." Some things never change.

[19] See in this vein R. Trexler, "Gendering Jesus Crucified," in *Iconography at the Crossroads*, ed. B. Cassidy (Princeton: Index of Christian Art, 1994), 107–19.

The Stigmatized Body of
Francis of Assisi:
Conceived, Processed, Disappeared*

Brother, I would like you to stay near me, because I am afraid to be alone. For the devils beat me a little while ago. . . . The devils are the Lord's officers, sent by him to punish our excesses.[1]

THE PROBLEM WITH CHRISTIANS IMITATING JESUS is that ultimately they can't. They say he died for their sins, and the imitation of the Passion of Jesus has always been at the core of Christian *paideia*. Yet since the early days of Christianity, spiritual directors have cautioned the faithful who could not suffer martyrdom not to kill themselves — as did Jesus die vio-

---

* This essay appears concurrently in *Frömmigkeit im Mittelalter: Politisch-soziale Kontexte, visuelle Praxis, körperliche Ausdrucksformen*, ed. K. Schreiner (Munich, 2001), 463–97.

[1] Thomas of Celano, Vita secunda S. Francisci [2 Cel.], in *Legendae S. Francisci Assisiensis*, in *Analecta Franciscana* [hereafter AF] 10 (Quaracchi, 1926–1942), chap. 84: 119–20. Hereafter I use the conventional abbreviations for the primary sources. The translations are my own, after consulting Marian A. Habig, ed., *St. Francis of Assisi: Writing and Early Biographies: English Omnibus of the Sources for the Life of St. Francis* (Chicago, 1973). I wish to thank Dyan H. Elliott for her help and advice.

lently — for that would be sinful.[2] True, Christians at times did read warnings against ascetic suicide as the work of the devil. In his major *legenda* of Francis of Assisi, Bonaventure of Bagnoregio has a messenger appear before the poor man and say: "Whoever kills himself through harsh penitence will not find mercy in the hereafter." This sounds to us like traditional but sound clerical advice not to kill oneself, as it did to Jean Gerson and a host of other critics of severe asceticism.[3] But Bonaventure says that Francis recognized right away that the bearer of such a message was the devil, who wanted to lead Francis away from the harsh penitential life.[4] Should one really humiliate one's body as the God-Man Jesus is said to have done, and how far can one go? Does such behavior bring you closer to your God, or in fact distance you from him or her? I am interested in the behavioral phenomena by which Christians have dealt with these problems of closeness and distance.

The present paper explores this problem by studying the historical backdrop to and the origins of an historical event in which this distance between lived lives past and persons present was notoriously closed: the stigmatization with the five wounds of the crucified Jesus which fra Elias of Cortona, head of the fledgling Franciscan order, said in 1226 had appeared on that same Francis of Assisi "shortly before his death" in that same year.[5] It was a never before heard-of novelty of a miracle (*miraculi*

---

[2] See e.g., below, at n. 68.

[3] Bonaventure, *Legenda Maior* [hereafter LM], chap. 5; Jean Gerson, *Oeuvres Complètes* 10 (Paris, 1973), 46–51, and below.

[4] LM 5.4.

[5] For future reference, here is the crucial part of the letter: "Et his dictis, annuntio vobis gaudium magnum et miraculi novitatem. A saeculo non est auditum tale signum, praeterquam in filio Dei, qui est Christus dominus. Non diu ante mortem frater et pater noster apparuit crucifixus, quinque plagas quae vere sunt stigmata Christi portans in corpore suo. Nam manus eius et pedes quasi puncturas clavorum habuerunt, ex utraque parte confixas, reservantes cicatrices et clavorum nigredinem ostendentes. Latus vero eius lanceatum apparuit et saepe sanguinem evaporavit. Dum adhuc vivebat spiritus eius in corpore, non erat in eo aspectus sed despectus vultus eius et nullum membrum in eo remansit absque nimia passione. Ex contractione nervorum membra eius rigida erant, sicut solent esse hominis mortui, sed post mortem eius pulcherrimus aspectus est, miro candore rutilans, laetificans videntes. Et membra, quae prius rigida erant, facta sunt mollia nimis, sese vertentia huc atque illuc secundum positionem suam tamquam pueri delicati. Ergo fratres benedicite deum ...": AF 10, 525–28. Unless otherwise specified, as it is in Elias's letter, the term "stigmata" of Jesus, if it was not a metaphor for internal suffering, could refer in this age to any mark or a wound that he suffered (in his Passion); cf. G. Constable, *Three Studies in Medieval Religious and Social Thought* (Cambridge, 1995), 199–200. But the biblical evangelists, if not the medieval imagination, indicate that these

novitatem), Elias seems to claim, but significantly, he does not say that God performed this wonder.[6] However, writing in 1228, Francis's first biographer, Thomas of Celano, introduces the divinity as the agent of the miracle, which he says happened not shortly, but fully two years before Francis's death at the oratory of La Verna, and he was followed in this godly attribution and dating by one fra Leone, Francis's erstwhile confessor, who added that a seraph was God's agent in transmitting the stigmata.[7] Obviously, through this postmortem story that the stigmata had appeared two years before Francis's death, Celano and later Franciscan biographers of the founder through Bonaventure writing in the 1260s created a roomy

---

wounds were limited in kind. Beyond his crucifixion, Jesus was "struck": Mt. 26:67–68, Mk. 14:65, Jn. 19:1; universally, he was scourged or flagellated at the column: Mt. 27:26, Mk. 15:15, Lk. 22:63, Jn. 19:1; he was crowned with thorns: Mt. 27:29, Mk. 15:17, Jn. 19:2; he was struck on the head with a reed: Mt. 27:30, Mk. 15:19; he did fall three times, and once he is said to have been lanced in the side: Jn. 19:24. The gospels do not say that, other than in the crucifixion, any of these latter attacks, or the falls, left stigmata or marks. Thus practically, the term "stigmata Christi" as a physical phenomenon referred most self-evidently to nail marks in hands and feet and to the side wound. They might refer to (biblically unmentioned) welts from the flogging he underwent, to punctures from the crown of thorns, and perhaps to knees scuffed from falling, all marks common in medieval art. For the general meaning of the term, see Josef Merkt, *Die Wundmale des Heiligen Franziskus von Assisi* (Leipzig, 1910), 6.

[6] The universal scholarly and popular presumption is that Elias meant to say that God had performed a miracle on Francis, but that is not what the text says. First of all, Elias carefully and strictly speaking characterizes the phenomenon as a "novelty," not as a miracle, thus staying on one side of the divide between the marvelous and the miraculous; cf. Jacques Le Goff, *The Medieval Imagination* (Chicago, 1985), 30–31. Second, Elias himself hints at self-mutilation by describing the wounds as having been inflicted from outside in and not, as Celano and the later orthodoxy will assert, calculatedly inverting Elias's message, as growing from the inside out; as in Chiara Frugoni, *Francesco e l'invenzione delle stigmate* (Turin, 1993), 154–64, who also reads Elias's statement erroneously (*Francesco*, 53, 56), on which see below, at nn. 85–88.

[7] See Frugoni, *Francesco*, 51–87. While Frugoni avoids dating Leo's message, Merkt long ago showed that it was certainly written after Bonaventure in the 1260s, indeed after Salimbene da Parma still later in the century: Merkt, *Wundmale*, 46; Frugoni, *Francesco*, 52. Further Karl Hampe, "Altes und Neues über die Stigmatisation des hl. Franz von Assisi," *Archiv für Kulturgeschichte* 8 (1910): 280. The best reading of the evidence is that in the wake of Elias's missive, tactically the Franciscans had to come up with some identification of the time and place this happened. Thus La Verna and a vision, or the seraph, or both, occur until Bonaventure: Karl Hampe, "Die frühesten Stigmatisationen und der hl. Franz von Assisi," *Internationale Wochenschrift für Wissenschaft, Kunst und Technik* 4 (1910): 1490; also Hampe, "Die Wundmale des hl. Franz von Assisi," *Historische Zeitschrift* 96 (1906): 395–97. However, I give the strategic reason for the two-year story just below, in the text.

space in time where witnesses to the stigmata might be found to "document" this official story, even if another, less influential group of contemporaries continued to say that they had appeared either shortly before, in the throes of, or simply "in death."[8] The order's need for witnesses who would claim to have seen the stigmata on the living Francis was all the more pressing because many contemporaries, yes even the pope in canonizing him in 1228, chose not to credit the story.[9] Just as predictably, the tale that Francis bore the stigmata for two years before dying, which all subsequent Franciscan biographers adopted, led to preposterous accounts of Francis's activities in that period, the most charming being that of Bonaventure, which has Francis being carried everywhere in these two years because he could not stand upright with the stigmata: nails grew out of his body, making walking impossible.[10]

In an important work that builds on a skeptical and critical tradition regarding the stigmata that goes back to the mid-nineteenth century, a tradition she does not credit, Chiara Frugoni has recently documented this historiographical "invention of the stigmata," by which she means the elaboration to which the original story of Elias was subject; this abuilding historiographical tradition, therefore, need not detain us further.[11] Suffice it to say first that the biographies of Francis, beginning with Celano's first Life, are primarily aesthetic and literary documents of very limited historical value.[12] And second, long before the time of Bonaventure the

---

[8] See Frugoni, *Francesco*, 63.

[9] André Vauchez, "Les stigmates de Saint François et leurs détracteurs dans les derniers siècles du moyen âge," *Mélanges d'archéologie et d'histoire* 80 (1968): 595–625.

[10] LM 14.1.

[11] That tradition contains the works of Hampe and Merkt cited above, but began with the pathfinding biography of Karl Hase, *Franz von Assisi: Ein Heiligenbild* (Leipzig, 1856); also Hase, *Handbuch der protestantischen Polemik* (Leipzig, 1878), 492. Frugoni's apparent unfamiliarity with this century and a half of literature in German causes problems throughout her work. For example, she confuses the date of Leo's witness: see above, n. 7. She does not describe that invention of the stigmata over time in a clear and concise fashion, beginning with her general inattention to the problem of "shortly before his death" vs. "two years before his death." Nor is the author straightforward in her argument. Thus chapter 6 of her synthetic *Vita di un uomo: Francesco d'Assisi* (Turin, 1995), begins by asking: "Le stimmate: Vera scoperta, un pio racconto, o un'audace invenzione?", but never answers that question.

[12] Hampe established this almost a century ago, and subsequent work has only confirmed his insight. Inter alia, see his "Altes und Neues," 262, 271 (Celano as a "phantasievoller Künstler"), 277 ("in ihm der literarische Künstler den Historiker doch stark überwiegt"), etc. To this day, the appallingly uncritical use of these legends by loyal Franciscans is repeatedly evident. See e.g., the case of Gatti below, n. 94.

stigmata of Francis had become a *sine qua non* of the Franciscan Order's legitimacy, with its apologists marvellously embellishing Elias's story, trying to keep ahead of other orders' determination to show the stigmata on their saints. And in fact, in the wake of Francis hundreds of Christians down to the present day have claimed that they, like their great spiritual ancestor, received the stigmata from the same lord God. What does demand our closer attention is the root system, not the branching of the Franciscan stigmata.

In the present paper, I will examine the universal claim of the primary biographers of Francis, from Elias through Bonaventure and beyond, that, to use the former's biblical words, nothing like the stigmata "had ever happened before," or "had ever been heard of earlier," a claim repeated to this day not only by pious apologists, but also by some serious scholars.[13] Perhaps predictably, this paper will show just how wishful such an embellishment of the past really is: the historical roots of the Franciscan stigmata will be seen to have been deep indeed. Secondly, however, this paper will reexamine Elias's original telling of the stigmata story, and determine that despite much research on "the Franciscan question," students of the stigmata have uniformly misunderstood both Elias's words and the context in which he wrote, and they have done so because, in this century at least, they have usually ignored a central document regarding these stigmata. The words of one recent student of the affair were in fact much truer than even he realized. Francis, he said, was "thoroughly a child of the spiritual currents of his time."[14]

---

[13] Thus Chiara Frugoni says just this in a paragraph not free of errors: "Oggi discorrere di stimmate vuol dire riferirsi a un fenomeno noto, anche se fuor del comune; ai tempi di Francisco si trattava invece di un fatto incredibile. Elia in sostanza veniva a sostenere che un essere umano fosse diventato simile a Dio, che la sua carne destinata a corrompersi fosse diventata quella di Cristo. Non esiste alcun santo stimmatizzato prima di Francesco; le rare persone rintracciabili negli atti processuali del XII e degli inizi del XIII secolo che, senza alcuna pretesa di interventi soprannaturali, si erano autoinflitte le ferite della croce erano state punite in maniera estremamente dura dalla Chiesa, che considerò colpa gravissima avere anche solo osato paragonarsi in questo modo a Cristo": *Vita*, 120. See also Constable, who says that "Francis of Assisi, so far as is known, was the first visible stigmatic whose wounds were probably not self-imposed": *Attitudes Toward Self-Inflicted Suffering in the Middle Ages* (Brookline, MA, 1982), 20. Other scholars do not, however, follow the hagiographers: C. Daxelmüller, "Der Untergrund der Frömmigkeit: Zur Geschichte und Pathologie religiöser Bräuche," *Saeculum* 47 (1996): 149; P. Dinzelbacher, "Diesseits der Metapher: Selbstkreuzigung und stigmatisation als konkrete Kreuzesnachfolge," *Revue Mabillon*, n.s. 7 (=68) (1996): 162.

[14] Daxelmüller, "Untergrund," 149.

The first argument of the present paper is that the roots of the stigmata
phenomenon lay in the slow but inexorable growth well before Francis of
a self-mutilative or -mortifying subculture that represented, in a quasi-theatrical fashion, two painful elements of Jesus' Passion or his Way of the
Cross, to wit, his flagellation and his crucifixion. The former potentially
transformed a white body into a black one, in one contemporary's
words;[15] the latter left the body white, but positioned on it black nail
holes on the extremities and a black mark on the side. An *imitatio Christi*
that did not involve physical torture was, of course, as old as Christianity
itself, as was the wish longingly expressed after the Constantinian settlement to die a crucified martyr like Jesus, improbable as that was after the
Christian sect had become a universal church. But I will show that in the
central and high Middle Ages, the practice perhaps first of flagellatory and
then of crucifixional marking became increasingly popular, first in the ecclesiastical and later in the lay world. In what follows, I want to examine
the dual histories of flagellatory and crucifixional marking as they played
off each other, to analyze finally Elias's story of the stigmatized poor man
of Assisi as part of the veneration of tortured bodies so important a part of
the devotional world of the late Middle Ages.

The history of European flagellation begins with involuntary, punitive
flagellation administered by someone whom we may call a corrector. The
merest glance at the record shows that this type of behavior, at least in
Eurasia, has had no beginning nor end; witness the still lively debate even
in post-industrial societies over whether sparing the rod spoils the child.
To go no further back than early Christianity: moralists as early as Paul of
Tarsus, continuing the contemporaneous Roman and Jewish traditions,
drew from a man's "right" to beat his children the implication that in the
(Christian) community at large, artificial kin "fathers" could and should
discipline their spiritual "children." "Can anyone be a son, who is not
disciplined by his father?", Paul asks, and again: "We had earthly fathers
and paid due respect to them; should we not submit even more readily to
our spiritual fathers, and so attain life?" The apostle went so far as to
opine that "if you escape the discipline in which all sons share, you must
be bastards and no true sons."[16]

---

[15] "Aethiopicam contraxisse nigredinem videbatur": Petrus Damianus, "Vita sancti
Rodulphi episcopi eugubini et S. Dominici Loricati," *Patrologia cursus completus . . . latina
. . .* [hereafter *PL*] 144 (Paris, 1853), 1020.

[16] Heb. 12:7–8. Paul meant of course both real and spiritual "sons," and by "dis-

Not surprisingly, early Christian monasticism quickly adopted punitive flagellation as a means of internal discipline, and though radically diminished, it persists till the present day, having even made a modest comeback among conservative Catholics as a protest against modern *luxuria*. Monastic flagellation took two or even three forms. First, there were generic punishments, which abbots meted out on one or more certain penitential days of the year to their "sons." They were not intended as punishment for particular sins, but for the monks' general sinfulness. Second, we encounter confessional floggings, assigned by a priest as a form of restitution for the particular sins that had been admitted during confession. Like generic punishments, flagellation for certain confessed sins was usually carried out by an abbot or equivalent prelate, and some monasteries wrote into their statutes a mandate that forbade an inferior whipping a superior.[17] It must have appeared to most monks that such a practice would have been like beating Lord Jesus himself! Yet in the high Middle Ages, we increasingly encounter cases in which hierarchical rules were subverted so that authority could express humility. Not only might a monastic prelate avoid being complicit by having one of his agents carry out the flogging; the sinner could find himself whipped by another monk of equal status or even by all the other monks. On top of this, it is not unknown, even if unusual, for an abbot to be whipped by one of his monks for that prelate's own sins, thus separating the judge from the executioner and in this way avoiding *passio* while demonstrating humility.[18]

In these early Christian centuries, confessional manuals prescribed the severity of the punishment in terms of a requisite number of strokes, depending on the sin's gravity. Another customary way a confessor punished a penitent was to sentence him to a period of time, usually in years, in which the penitent had to fast and abstain, etc., and so it is not surprising that flagellation — a corporal penalty violent in tone but limited in its time of application — soon joined indulgences or outright money as a

---

cipline" medieval Vulgate readers understood physical punishment. J. Leclercq offers a general overview of "Disciplina" in the *Dictionnaire de spiritualité*, vol. 3 (Paris, 1937), 1291–1302, as does Émile Bertaud of "Discipline," Dictionnaire, 1302–11.

[17] E.g., the order of St. Victor in Paris: "Hoc etiam sciendum est, quod ille qui inferioris gradus est, non debet verberare superiorem, id est, diaconus sacerdotem, sed aequalis aequalem, vel superior inferiorem": cited under "Disciplina," Charles du Fresne Du Cange, *Glossarium mediae et infimae latinitatis*, vol. 3 (Paris, 1938), 130.

[18] See e.g., the case of Stephen of Obazine below, nn. 53–55, or Damian's Life of Rodolfo, bishop of Gubbio, *PL*, 144:1011.

means by which one could shorten, commute, or "redeem" the years of abstinence penances assigned to sinners.[19] A given number of strokes would allow one to expiate so many years of an abstinence penance.

A variant form of punitive flagellation featured not externally imposed flogging for sins, but rather whippings freely decided upon, usually by two monks. This occurred when a single monk, transcending the limits of the confessional or the bank of religious justice within the monastery, would have himself stripped, tried, and sentenced to a whipping as a particular sign of his humility and contrition.[20] Sometimes this was done mutually: the one sinner having been beaten, the flagellator became the flagellated in a turnabout. Such cases are usually found in the high Middle Ages and later. While they occasionally are described as being done in private, being reported on by what I elsewhere have called an illicit witness, more often this form is said to be performative in character, that is, carried out in the presence of the other monks.[21] Early cases of this type are suspicious, because they hint at a commonly theatrical character more often encountered in late medieval flagellation. Needless to say, this mutual, non-confessional or -judicial flagellation easily converted to the type of spontaneous self-flagellation for devotional rather than purely penitential purposes which we shall presently examine.

Monastic penitential flagellation of one monk by another is familiar to scholars. It was rooted in notions of political suzerainty through torture, and is best viewed as a subset of the right of princes to whip their subjects. This makes it all the more remarkable that another type of ecclesiastical flagellation has received little attention: the beating of lay men, but especially women (including nuns) and children, by male religious judges or confessors. A serious study of this practice would not only be important for understanding the high Middle Ages, but for the light it would throw on

---

[19] See Peter Damian's defense of flagellation on this score: if money could buy commutation, how not flagellation?: Owen J. Blum, ed., Peter Damian, Letters, 31–60 (Washington, DC, 1990), 249 (Letter 45); 365 (Letter 56). For the terminus technicus " redemptio," which Christians equated with restitution for theft, see L. Gougaud, Devotional and Ascetic Practices in the Middle Ages (London, 1927), 189.

[20] Imagined by a hagiographer in 1125 penning the Life of the fictional Carolingian Guillelmus Gellone: Gougaud, Devotional and Ascetic Practices, 189.

[21] On the problem of monks ashamed to be seen beaten in public, see the Abbé Boileau, Historia flagellantium de recto et perverso flagrorum usu apud Christianos (Paris, 1700), 222. For the illicit observer, see Trexler, "Legitimizing Prayer Gestures in the Twelfth Century: The De penitentia of Peter the Chanter," in the present collection.

lay confraternal practice from the high Middle Ages to the present day. The penance that the *correctores* of confraternities meted out to their confraters often enough included flagellation, and in this fashion monastic and Mendicant practices made their way into the mainstream of late medieval and early modern religious practice. Let me summarize some of the evidence for flagellation directed against the laity in the earlier period.

The monk Peter Damian (1007–1072), who plays such a large role in the history of Christian flagellation, informs us in a letter of the 1050s that many popes ordered some penitents, presumably including laymen, first to be scourged in their presence, and only then to be sentenced to other, non-violent penances.[22] This was done despite an ancient rule of Pope Hadrian I (772–795) that apparently forbade clerical whipping of the laity.[23] An example from the reign of Innocent III (1198–1216) shows that pontiff ordering the killers of a bishop, whenever they entered a German city, to proceed nude to the cathedral, whips in hand, there to accept a beating from that church's canons.[24] And during the same thirteenth century, several church councils ordered "heretics" suing for reentry into orthodoxy to undergo flagellation from their prelates.[25]

Unsurprisingly, as an earnest of their own authority, clerical writers often told of humble if powerful secular lords who had submitted to beatings by their confessors. So it was with the Duke of Normandy Richard II (996–1026), whose confessor saw to his flogging on the point of death.[26] The high medieval Arthurian cycle describes how this legendary king, tearful, naked, and armed with a whip, came before his confessor in the presence of all the bishops and demanded that the "revenge" of flagellation be exercised upon him. After the confession, so the legend goes, the priest obliged, whipping Arthur "moult doucement."[27] Another story has a Dominican flogging the saintly Louis IX of France (d. 1270) after that

---

[22] Blum, *Peter Damian, Letters*, 365 (Letter 56). Damian adds that this disciplinary norm was common to most holy monasteries, "even though it was not often used." Blum, the editor, provides a reference to Pope Gregory I.

[23] "Episcopus, presbyter, diaconus peccantes fideles verberare non debeant"; cited in Du Cange, *Glossarium*, 3:130.

[24] Cited in Jacob Gretscher, *Agonisticum spirituale* (Ingolstadt, 1609), 158.

[25] John Henderson, "The Flagellant Movement and Flagellant Confraternities in Central Italy, 1260–1400," in Derek Baker, ed., *Religious Motivation: Biographical and Sociological Problems for the Church Historian* (Oxford, 1978), 147.

[26] Gougaud, *Devotional and Ascetic Practices*, 191.

[27] Cited in Boileau, *Historia flagellantium*, 261.

prince's last confession, when he was on the point of death.[28] Tales like this must be taken with a grain of salt, to be sure, but there is little doubt that the ecclesiastical punishment of the laity continued through these centuries. Still in the seventeenth century, Jean-Baptiste Cotelier cites a Byzantine document that notes how Western Christians on releasing someone from excommunication would "strip him down to his loins and beat him on his nude flesh with whips or sticks, to then release him as if forgiving him."[29]

The self-serving tales of clerically flogged rulers should not obscure other indications that confessors did indeed beat more average lay men and women as a routine part of the practice of confession, perhaps especially after 1215, when the sacrament of penance became mandatory during Lent. Thus in a work attributed to Michael the Scot (d. c. 1235) there is a husband-wife joke about the (apparently unexceptional) flogging of a lay-woman by her confessor. On seeing the priest lead his wife behind the altar to that end, the husband cries out to the priest: "O lord, she is so delicate; let me receive the discipline in her place." When he then knelt down, the wife cried: "Hit him hard, lord, for I am a great sinner!"[30] The practice in these centuries was apparently common enough that, in his *Historia flagellantium* of 1700, Boîleau could casually refer consecutively to St. Edmund (d. 1240), Bernardino of Siena (d. 1444), and the Capuchin friar Matteo d'Avignone as having beaten girls (*puellas*) with birch or hemp whips.[31] In conservative Spain, these confessional punishments extended well into the modern period. One of the most notorious of many such cases is that of the adolescent Luisa de Carvajal y Mendoza (1568–1614), who in a wrenching autobiography described at great length how,

---

[28] Cited in Gougaud, *Devotional and Ascetic Practices*, 191; also Jacques Le Goff, *Saint Louis* (Paris, 1996), 758–59. The tale is dubious precisely because it is said that the punishment was carried out in private.

[29] The "latins" "ab excommunicatione aliquem dum solvunt, denudant eum usque ad lumbos et qua parte nudus est flagellantes loris vel virgis, inde tanquam venia donatum dimittunt": Jean-Baptiste Cotelier, *Ecclesiae Graecae Monumenta*, vol. 3 (Paris, 1692), 499; and Boîleau, *Historia flagellantium*, 229. Also, it is said that Henry IV of France was beaten at the time he renounced Protestantism "for a mass": Patrick Vandermeersch, "Du bon usage de la flagellation, et des problèmes posés par son interprétation," *Religiologiques* 12 (1995): 229.

[30] Michael Scot, lib. 4, ch. 17 of his *Mensa philosophica*; cited in Boîleau, *Historia flagellantium*, 229. See also *The Science of Dining (Mensa Philosophica): A Medieval Treatise on the Hygiene of the Table and the Laws of Health*, trans. A. Way (London, 1936), 138.

[31] Boîleau, *Historia flagellantium*, 231.

thankfully, her spiritual director beat her mercilessly.[32]

Needless to say, whipping lay girls and widows — grown men probably much less often — was but the logical extension of the widespread medieval practice of beating nuns. Throughout the Middle Ages and far into the modern age, groups of nuns hired a confessor who often was both judge and sentencer, and then as executioner carried out the flagellative punishment. The late Middle Ages saw some efforts to rectify the resulting temptations. In the sixteenth century, for instance, the Spanish Inquisition viewed flagellation not just as a temptation for the male confessors but as one means of soliciting or seducing nuns. Thus in 1563, friars were told not to live in nunneries, and not themselves to administer the flagellation they assigned the nuns as partial satisfaction for their sins.[33] Clearly, the practice was alive and well at the time.

A serious study of flagellation as a punishment applied by one person to another, even in the narrow sphere of the church courts and confessionals, obviously remains to be done. Our only purpose here has been to establish that by the time of Francis of Assisi, the clerical and religious punishment of sin by whipping the guilty was not uncommon. One may doubt, in fact, that publicly manifested physical punishments actually declined during the Middle Ages, as has so often been argued, if for no other reason than that in the late medieval centuries, flagellation became anchored in lay penitential confraternities, whose clerical *correctores* were often enough responsible for administering flagellant *correctio et disciplina* to the confraters.[34]

There are certain features of penitential flagellation by others that should be distinguished before proceeding to the voluntary type of flagel-

---

[32] Though the modern reader may view these descriptions as pornographic, Carvajal y Mendoza is said to have valued this mistreatment because it taught her perseverance: Luisa de Carvajal y Mendoza, *Escritos autobiograficos* (Barcelona, 1966), 180–85. My thanks to María José del Rio for this reference. A sixteenth-century Spanish view that whipping was reserved to the secular forum, even if Augustinian friars did beat native Americans as fathers did sons, is in Juan de Grijalva, *Crónica de la orden de n. p. s. Agustín en las provincias de la Nueva Espana* (Mexico City, 1985), 158.

[33] Javier Pérez Escohotado, *Sexo e inquisición en España* (Madrid, 1992), 190; Jo A. McNamara, *Sisters in Arms: Catholic Nuns Through Two Millennia* (Cambridge, MA, 1996); Richard C. Trexler, "Celibacy in the Renaissance," in his *The Women of Florence* (Binghamton, 1993), 6–30.

[34] See e.g., my review of T. Tentler, *Sin and Confession on the Eve of the Reformation*, *Speculum* 53 (1978): 862–65. See the phrase in G. Meersseman, *Ordo fraternitatis: Confraternite e Pietà dei laici nel medioevo*, vol. 3 (Rome, 1977), 1299.

lation. First, it is unusual for a source to specify that such flagellation left particular marks or designs on the body, due certainly in part to the prohibition of clerks shedding the blood of others. Penitential flagellation, in short, was not considered a means for re-figuring the body, and thus cannot be viewed as a direct antecedent of the penetrative crucifixional stigmata ascribed to Francis of Assisi. Second, generally speaking, penitential flagellation has historically had a limited narrative or imitative quality. It is certainly true that the week and days before Easter, called Holy Week, and the fifty-two Fridays of the year, formed two occasions on which such punishment was often administered, thus obviously recalling the suffering of Jesus. But other days, such as the Advent cycle and the major and minor Days of Rogation, and later the feast of the Finding of the True Cross (3 May) or its Exaltation (14 September), were also occasions for such punishment, and they did little to evoke directly the passion of Jesus. The limits of imitating the experience of Jesus through such punishment were also drawn by the social reality of the monastery. Whereas Jesus was guiltless when he embarked on his passion, the monks who received such floggings were sinful. The abbot or master of discipline who whipped them was not comparable to a Jew or Roman unjustly whipping Jesus, but was rather an official "good" Christian lord abbot or master of discipline beating institutionalized bad monks for always "keeping Jesus on the cross" or at the pillar, as was so often said. True, if an abbot chose to have himself beaten by a lesser member of the monastic community, he might imagine himself in the role of suffering Jesus, but that scenario involved casting that lesser member as a Jew or Roman. Such humility is not often encountered in this early period.

Finally, let us not be blind to the complexity of another central feature of penitential discipline by others: its often implied sexual content. True, sexual innuendo and explicitness in describing the flagellation of women by men is commonly enough misogynistic in character: it is about power and dominance, and the literature of these centuries is full of anecdotes featuring confessors who practice flagellation on women for the transparent purpose of their own sexual excitement. Yet there is no lack of stories with a different line, telling of confessors and female confessants who conspire at such flagellation, or even mutual whippings, to the end of their dual sexual gratification.[35] It would be centuries before Meibom and then

---

[35] A sixteenth-century case matches a widow and a confessor: Pérez Escohotado, *Sexo e inquisición*, 196.

Boileau would reveal the science of the matter — the role played by flagellation in heightening sexual excitement in either recipient or executor —
but well before then, it was common knowledge that beatings could raise
the fires of sexual desire.[36]

Having sketched the behavior of this ancient penitential culture, where
notions of imitation or narrative were outdone by those of dominance, we
turn to the phenomenon of voluntary self- or mutual flagellation, which
burst upon Europe almost out of nowhere toward the beginning of the second millennium. Properly understood, it is this phenomenon that lies at
the root of the penetrative stigmata of the thirteenth and later centuries,
because self-flagellation, at least, might easily spill over into self-crucifi-
xion, and we shall show the one folding into the other. Self-flagellation
easily escaped the prescribed number of strokes common to the older penitential manuals, ushering in an age in which, in an almost theatrical fashion, one beat oneself without the confessor's externally imposed limits. In
turn, such performance art encouraged the same limitless praxis between
partners as upon oneself, a development all the more natural because monastic and later Mendicant life was usually structured around couples. Rather than being limited in number by a confessor, high and late medieval
whippings sometimes appear as athletic competitions in pursuit of records.[37] Thus the devotional viewing of such increasingly mutilative transformations of the body, that is, the increased association between flagellation and marked or stigmatized bodies, was one of the most important
religious phenomena of the late medieval and early modern periods of
European history. Just as the story of Jesus' passion became marvelously
glossed to aggrandize the violence said to have been visited on his body,
so did those who would imitate him strive after such a record. Our intention here is to show how theatrical flagellation, auto- or bilaterally
applied, provided the audience for such shows.

---

[36] See Pico della Mirandola's description of a friend "che non pratica tuttavia atti
sessuali se non venga battuto; e tanto medita una tale enormità, tanto desidera crudeli
battiture": *Disputationes adversus astrologiam divinatricem libri I–V* (Florence, 1946), 412–13
(bk. 3, chap. 27); also Johannes Meibom, *De flagrorum usu in re veneria et lumborum re-
numque officio* . . . (London, 1770), 13. A search of Boccaccesque literature would surely
turn up repeated links between sex and flagellation.

[37] That tone is nowhere more obvious than in the various writings of Peter Damian.
See especially K. Reindel, ed., *Die Briefe des Petrus Damiani*, vol. 4 (Munich 1988), 135–
44; Blum, *Peter Damian, Letters*, 244–49; 361–68; and especially *PL*, 144:1007–24.

A vivid image may help frame the question of the relation between self-flagellation and the stigmata. Imagine any one of the many high and late medieval representations of Jesus covered from head to foot by wounds.[38] Then try to find the five crucifixional stigmata. So tortured is the God's body that it is sometimes difficult to do so, even if, on closer examination, they do turn up. The marks of the crucifixion tend, so to speak, to be subsumed by the wounds of Jesus's flagellation. This image suggests, therefore, a fundamental inseparability of the two objects of devotion.[39] So it will prove on Francis's body. At present, it is that link between the two corporal images that I seek to mediate in the centuries before Francis.

Peter Damian certainly provided the first theology and psychology for discipline or voluntary self-flagellation, but in effect, his own hagiographical work also provides the earliest datable evidence for its practice. Some scholars have listed earlier holy men whose *vitae* claim they beat themselves, but on examination it transpires that these *legendae* were usually put to paper only after the age of Damian.[40] It was Damian himself, writing mostly of his own contemporary heroes in the early and mid-eleventh century, who gives us our best early information on self-flagellants. We learn the basics of contemporary flagellation at the source: its voluntary nature; the different instruments used for whipping; the physical postures assumed to whip oneself; the intimate link of flagellation to the recitation of the psalter, especially to the "Miserere" or fiftieth psalm; how self-scourging was done both in the presence of others and in private; the supplementation of self-flagellation with other public signs of penance drawn from the passion of Jesus, such as holding one's arms out — as if

---

[38] See e.g., the image in G. Llompart, "Estandartes mallorquines de Pasión," in his: *Religiosidad popular: folklore de Mallorca, folklore de Europa* (Palma de Mallorca, 1982), 70 (fig. 14).

[39] Cf. Damian's suggestive condemnation of a certain monk who resisted flagellation: "Quis te delicatum atque tenellum aggregabit collegio martyrum, in quorum corporibus videbuntur in gloriam verse non modo virgarum vibices, set et innumerabilium vulnerum cicatrices?": Reindel, *Briefe*, 4:141.

[40] This is a point insistently made by Boileau, *Historia*. See e.g., the saints Guillelmus Gellone and Keristan listed by Gougaud, *Devotional and Ascetic Practices*, 187–88; the other early saints cited were whipped by others; and J. Leclercq, "La flagellazione volontaria nella tradizione spirituale dell'Occidente," in *Il movimento dei disciplinati nel settimo centenario dal suo inizio* (Perugia, 1962), 76–77. Though the latter is aware of the problem of dating, he then goes on to assume that these putative saints actually did beat themselves. A good collection of the earliest such references are in Reindel, *Briefe*, 2:35.

crucified[41] — for a long period of time, and so forth. And we see how such monkish behavior, such "a type of purgatory," was imitated by the laity: "not just among men but among noble women."[42] All this information is already in the historiographical record, and so we press on.

Among Damian's several references to scourging holy men and communities, none stands out like the *vita* of the hermit monk Domenico (d. 1060), called Loricatus or the penitential iron breastplate wearer, which Damian enclosed in a letter to Pope Alexander IV, written shortly after the "saint's" death.[43] Here as elsewhere, Damian highlights what for him was the dominant value of flagellation, the ability of individual monastic flagellants on their own to do enough penance for their individual sins so as to save their individual souls — the goal, after all, of the monk's or nun's life. Damian's striking language stating how through self-scourging one might be one's own judge and executioner and thus be serenely prepared to meet one's maker in heaven is well enough known. Somewhat less familiar is his notion that through prowess at flagellation, the monastic devotee could in a relative nonce not only commute or redeem[44] — radically shorten in time — the canonically fixed years of penances (fasting and abstinence) for sins to which non-flagellators, in this period before indulgences were widely developed and inflated, were alas consigned, but also exceed that quotient, thus enabling him to save others through his actions. Though Damian was ultimately no enemy of the priestly confessional power — he ended a cardinal, after all — the thrust of this monk's message was that a flagellating ascetic, at least, could make one's own provisions for his, her's, or others' ascent to heaven by inflicting serious pain on one's own body at certain intervals during one's life.[45] One did not have to live in the enduring penance of fasting and abstinence and the like.

Peter mourned the death of such a unique man as Domenico in keeping with the conventions of his age. To prove Domenico's reputation for holiness, he told how other monks had threatened to rob the cadaver from

---

[41] "Extensis itaque in crucis effigiem brachiis, psalterium coepi": PL, 144:1019, especially emphasized in the Life of Domenico Loricatus.

[42] Damian, in PL, 144:1018.

[43] PL, 144:1012–24.

[44] On the words, see Leclercq, "Disciplina," 1306. For Damian's language, see Reindel, *Briefe*, 4:144; further L. Little, "The Personal Development of Peter Damian," in *Order and Innovation in the Middle Ages: Essays in Honor of Joseph R. Strayer*, ed. William Jordan et al. (Princeton, 1976), 337.

[45] Implicitly leaving the rest of that lifetime outside the penitential state.

the monastery, leading his brothers to bury him in the very cell he died in; how he, Damian, had thereafter had the cadaver removed and placed reverently in chapter; and how, nine days after his "deposition," the body remained uncorrupted. Damian then condemned other sinners at some length, so as to make his hero stand out to the pope.[46] Copying from Paul, Damian says that "our Domenico carried the stigmata of Jesus on his body [in corpore]." He is clearly describing the man's cadaver. "And not only had he painted the sign [vexillum] of the cross on his forehead, but he had impressed [impressit] [it] bilaterally on each and every limb [cunctis etiam undique membris] of his body."[47] All this made good sense, Damian intimated, for Loricatus "had turned his whole life into a Good Friday."[48]

This first substantial description of a self-flagellating Christian holy man may also be the first time a Christian author directly links the practice of flagellation by a holy man, whether mutual or solitary in nature, with the word "stigmata," and so it is important to determine just what Damian meant in his description of these "stigmata," a word which, as we have seen, unless otherwise specified referred to marks or wounds in general. A bit of context: to be sure, Damian meant to relate the state of the cadaver to Loricatus's behavior on Good Friday, when monks particularly remembered the Flagellation and Crucifixion of Jesus, but as well to similar behavior throughout his life. The point is, Domenico had shaped or at least designed a Passion body. But how? Keeping in mind that Damian was a devotee of the cult of the Five Wounds of Christ, a cautious reading of Damian's language at this juncture is likely also the most precise, even if previously this passage has been thought to refer generically to any wounds. Domenico Loricatus bore [portavit] the stigmata on his own body. He had painted "the sign [vexillum] of the cross" on his forehead, a practice common to those in the militia Christi.[49] Then he had "pressed in"

---

[46] PL, 144:1023. See below for Francis of Assisi, whose cadaver is said to have been sealed away.

[47] "Dominicus autem noster stigmata Jesu portavit in corpore, et vexillum crucis non tantum in fronte depinxit, sed cunctis etiam undique membris impressit": PL, 144:1024. The only biblical use of the word "stigmata" is in Gal. 6.17: "Ego enim stigmata Jesu in corpore meo porto." Interestingly, Paul's statement has recently been said to refer to ritual tattooing; see C. Jones, "Stigma: Tattooing and Branding in Graeco-Roman Antiquity," Journal of Roman Studies 77 (1987): 139–55. L. S. B. MacCoull kindly alerted me to this work.

[48] "Tota haec vita facta est sibi parasceve crucis . . .": PL, 144:1024.

[49] That is, similar to the cross of ashes the priest still places on the forehead of Catholics on Ash Wednesday; cf. K. Pennington, "The Rite for Taking the Cross in the

(*impressit*) that same sign on all four limbs.[50] Taken together with Damian's repeated statement that Domenico had often become "an effigy of the
cross" by holding out his arms for long periods (to imitate Jesus hanging
on the cross), this is a powerful indication that with the word "stigmata"
the biographer at least did not mean to exclude the four signs of crucifixion. Thus the monks who mourned the deceased Domenico did not encounter a body simply full of slash wounds from flagellation, thereby com-
memorating Jesus' flagellation. They had, I believe, instead found a body
marked or impressed, perhaps, inter alia, with four of the five marks left
on Jesus' body at the time of his crucifixion and death. The first student
of self-flagellation, Damian may also have been the first to describe holy
men showing on their bodies impressed or penetrative stigmata of Jesus.
This man had not only painted these marks onto the flat surface of the
hands and feet. Obviously seeking to imitate Jesus, he had pressed them
perpendicularly into those surfaces.[51] He had done all this, and Peter
Damian had recorded it all, in the same region where Francis would one
day be said to have borne stigmata.

The next significant hagiographic attention to a particular flagellant
also contains the next mention of "stigmata." In the Vita of Stephen of
Obazine (c. 1085-1159), the anonymous author, writing about 1166, one
century after the death of Domenico Loricatus, describes a French monastic culture that featured mutual, rather than self-flagellation. From the beginning, Stephen was attracted to such behavior, leaving the world along
with a companion and entering into a life of mutual beating "for the sole

---

Twelfth Century," *Traditio* 30 (1974): 432–33, also with the term *vexillum crucis*. God
put the sign of the cross on one crusader: Dinzelbacher, "Diesseits der Metapher," 160.
On Damian's devotion to the Five Wounds, see I. Bonetti, *Le stimmate della passione:
Dottrina e storia della devozione alle Cinque Piaghe* (Rovigo, 1952), 99–105.

[50] This may not mean that Domenico made the same dual mark of the cross on his
limbs that he made on his forehead. Rather, he made some mark (as if from a nail?) into
each part that had been marked in Jesus' crucifixion.

[51] "Impressing" was not limited to the classical wounds. Thus Caesarius of Heisterbach (fl. 1222) says that the Cistercian novice Hartman of Himmerod "crucem fronti
suae imprimi sensit": *Caesarii Heisterbacensis monachi ordinis cisterciensis Dialogus miraculorum* (Cologne, 1851), 2:100 (dist. 8, cap. 23); Constable, *Three Studies*, 215, where also
is a relevant quote of Thomas of Cîteaux. Damian's account gives no hint of a break in
Domenico's skin from this impression. Cf. e.g., the account of the alleged impressed stigmata of the Portuguese nun María de la Visitación. When in 1588 sceptical inquisitors
finally soaked her hands in hot water, covering them with "black soap," then finally
scrubbed them with a rough cloth, the "stigmata" vanished: Luis de Granada, *Historia de
sor María de la Visitación y Sermón de las caídas públicas* (Barcelona, 1962), 54.

desire of suffering."[52] The anonymous first describes how, as the abbot of
the new monastic community of Obazine, Stephen presided over daily chapter "as if over a divine court." It was certainly abbot Stephen himself, who,
as if playing God, meted out punishments for sins, which included flogging. The guilty party presented himself nude in the upper body, and received one stroke for each of the twenty-three verses of the fiftieth psalm
(*Miserere*). If on the other hand the sinner's act was more serious, Stephen
chose lengthier psalms to accompany longer periods of whipping.[53]

Obviously the traditional hierarchical enforcement of penitential
norms was the order of the day in this monastery. Yet our Vita soon makes
clear that the efficacy of such punishment now derived from the abbot's
own willingness to submit himself to flogging, and to an extent even
greater than that merited by his own faults. The author tells how on Holy
Thursday, the eve of Jesus' flagellation and death, the brothers came together for a general confession of all the year's sins and to receive the
special indulgences available to the house on that day. In this setting, the
abbot made it a point to denounce publicly his own sins. Indeed, Stephen
went further. If he beat a sinner more violently than usual, this prelate
would then turn about, strip down to his waist, and then submit himself
to being beaten by one or even all his own subordinates. He did this, our
source explains, first so that he as judge participated in the pain of the sinner. But second, Stephen worried that he might beat one of his subjects to
an extent greater than the sin merited, and to forestall that eventuality,
he would "expiate by taking vengeance on his own body."[54] Following
a rhetoric already established in Peter Damian, Stephen at times had himself beaten not for his own sins, but to even out by his own suffering the
unjust pain he may have caused others.

The anonymous concludes his account of Stephen's penitential rigor
by noting that the latter's public behavior in chapter and in Lent was
only part of the story. Indeed "scarcely a day went by, especially in Lent,
when someone did not secretly beat him in private." "Thus," our author

---

[52] Constable, *Attitudes*, 16.

[53] "Ad judicium veniebat et jam quasi divino examini astans": M. Aubrun, ed., *Vie de Saint Étienne d'Obazine* (Clermont-Ferrand, 1970), 72 (bk. 1, chap. 17).

[54] "Sane cum aliquem exigentibus culpis, gravius solito verberasset, mox se ad perfe-
renda similia preparabat et ab uno vel ab omnibus se flagellari precipiebat, quod faciebat,
ne qui alios judicaret, ipse ab eorum afflictione exsors maneret, ac si quid immoderate
correctionis censura forsitan deliquisset, vendicta proprii corporis expiaret": *Vie de Saint
Étienne*, 72.

concludes, "hit with a whip both privately and publicly, he carried around the stigmata of the passions [sic] of Christ on his body [*in suo corpore*], so that he could say with the apostle [Paul]: 'I castigate my body and render it servile so that I am not unmasked as a reprobate even while I preach to others'."[55]

In its own way, this text is as fruitful for our purpose as that of Damian on Domenico Loricatus. There is no indication, to be sure, that the abbot, like Domenico, had painted or impressed anything on his body, and the text does not refer to a gazer, whereas Domenico's master Damian clearly indicates he was such a witness to Domenico's body. Still, a close reading of Stephen's Life again compromises Giles Constable's suspicion that Stephen's stigmata, like those of Domenico, were perhaps only "symbolically" present.[56] Coming as it does in the same sentence as the Life's description of Stephen's flagellation, the word "stigmata" certainly refers to the (several) *passiones* or welts Jesus bore from being whipped, though again, it does not include by name the presence of the crucifixional stigmata.[57] This passage makes it quite clear that mutual flagellation as much as self-whipping were vehicles through which twelfth-century holy men might imitate Jesus. That is, in the quest to be like Jesus by experiencing the pain of being whipped, subordinate monks or ones of equal status might assume the role of the Jews or Romans who beat Jesus. Finally, in this passage the anonymous clearly pictures our abbot displaying these "stigmata" to his monks — as they might have also displayed similar welts to him — on a quotidian basis as an image of Lord Jesus himself, "as if," Francis's biographers will say, this authority figure "was Christ himself."

The next case of a link between the stigmata and a flagellating holy man is certainly fictitious, but no less important for that. Around 1185, the clerk Jocelin of Furness, certainly inspired by the devotional practices of his own day, wrote the Life of a (fictitious?) early seventh-century Celtic saint named Kentigern. The relevant passage is short and to the point: "On Good Friday," he says, Kentigern "in great pain crucified himself

---

[55] "Sicque privatim et publice virgis cesus stigmata passionum Christi in suo corpore circumferebat ut, cum apostolo dicere posset: 'Castigo corpus meum et in servitutem redigo, ne cum aliis predicaverim, ipse reprobus efficiar'": *Vie de Saint Étienne*, 72–73 (1 Cor. 9.27). Note in this passage that, for the Vulgate reader, Paul refers not to mutual but to self-mortification.

[56] Constable, *Attitudes*, 20.

[57] If however the term *passionum* of Jesus is a mistake, the passage probably refers only to the whip marks.

along with the Crucified. Day and night he continued, nude, with extra-ordinary pain of heart and body, with strokes of the whip and with so many genuflections [read: Jesus' three falls on the *via crucis*] that he scarcely ever sat, carrying around with him on his body the stigmata of the wounds [*vulnera*] of Christ."[58] Again, the image of a holy man made into Jesus on the anniversary of the death of that savior is at the center of this account. As background for describing the saint's stigmata, the author brings the crucifixion into play, saying that Kentigern crucified himself. This was probably a euphemistic metaphor equivalent to "tortured," for in what follows the author describes flagellation and falling or genuflexions as the pains Kentigern suffered, but not actual crucifixion. But in any case, the language of the passional *imitatio Christi* is complete, and especially in light of what we shall soon document for England in the early thirteenth century, we may hypothesize that Jocelin did not mean to exclude the no-tion that holy men might in fact imitate the total passion of Jesus.[59] This is the more likely because by referring to the "wounds" of Jesus, the auth-or certainly did not mean to exclude the crucifixional stigmata, the only certain "wounds" of Jesus indicated in the Bible. In short, the story of Kentigern as well as the previous two cases from Italy and France demon-strate that by the time that Francis of Assisi was born c. 1182, the pres-ence of passion stigmata on the bodies of holy men had long been a hagio-graphic and devotional convention.

It is important to recognize that whether they resulted from the strokes of a whip or as the result of being painted on or pressed into the skin, eleventh- and twelfth-century contemporaries viewed positively the self-infliction of such marks of the divine passion. At this date, that is, no one seems to have attacked them, for example, as a sign of pride or as for-geries. In the words of Damian, they were indications that one wanted to be a martyr, even if, the church now being established, that seemed all but impossible to the great innovator.[60] In Damian's wake, however, the chances of martyrdom did in fact improve. Warriors could "take [up] the

---

[58] "In parasceve vero incredibili cruciatu cum crucifixo semetipsum crucifigebat. Et plagis virgarum et nuditate et crebris genuum flexationibus, vix aliquando sedens, stig-mata vulnerum Christi in corpore suo circumferens, cum nimia cruce cordis et corporis, diem cum nocte continuando ducebat . . .": A. Forbes, *Lives of S. Ninian and S. Kentigern, Compiled in the Twelfth Century* (Edinburgh, 1874), 189; Gougaud, *Devotional and Ascetic Practices*, 201, n. 43.

[59] See the Oxford case of 1222 described below.

[60] See above, n. 39.

cross" and go on crusade, while back home, children appeared who were indeed viewed as martyrs for the faith. I refer to some four Christian males allegedly crucified by the Jews during the twelfth century. The very notoriety of these cases, that is, the fact they were so commonly said to have been generated by the laity, insured that by the end of this century, many European Christians had an image in their minds' eyes not just of monastic ascetics who beat themselves and were said to have the stigmata, but of Christian children actually hanging on the cross like so many other Jesuses.

It is this image, these Christian visions that are important, and not any historical veracity: presumably, the stories of Jews torturing Christians are fictions. The first of the tales concerns *St.* William of Norwich, whom the Jews of Norwich allegedly affixed to a cross so as to mock the passion of Jesus. He was nailed on the left, tied on his right, and lanced in his side. Gloucestershire Jews supposedly murdered a Christian boy in 1168. At his death, the autopsy showed this "glorious martyr of Christ" to have mangled hands (*cruciatus*) among the wounds to his body.[61] Then sometime before 1180, one Richard of Paris is said to have been affixed to a cross and died a martyr; miracles quickly followed at his burial place in the cemetery of the Innocents. Finally and most interesting, during Passiontide 1192 Jews in the French village of Brie-Compte-Robert supposedly seized a Christian they suspected of robbery and murder. Tying his hands behind his back and crowning him with thorns, "they led him through the whole village, flogging him" before hanging him.[62] While the image is not identical to a Christian one — he bore no cross — this tale does yield an early dramatic representation of what, once adopted by late medieval Christians, would be called the Passion Play or the Way of the Cross.

---

[61] "Praemissum puerum immensis suppliciis excruciaverunt. . . . hujuscemodi cruciatus ei illatos fuisse credunt, vel auspicantur. . . . paulo post reperti liquido patuit gloriosum Christo martirem sine crimine necatum effecerunt": W. Hart, ed., *Historia et cartularium monasterii sancti Petri Gloucestriae* (London, 1863), vol. 1:20. For Norwich, A. Jessop and M. James, eds., *The Life and Miracles of St. William of Norwich by Thomas of Monmouth.* . . . (Cambridge, 1896), 20–22 (bk. 1, chap. 5).

[62] "Manibus a tergo ligatis, spinis coronatum, per totam villam fustigantes duxerunt, et postea patibulo suspenderunt . . .": *Oeuvres de Rigord et de Guillaume Le Breton . . .*, vol. 1 (Paris, 1882), respectively 15 (Rigord), 180 (Guillaume), and 119 (Rigord). Daxelmüller's listing of a Richard or Rodbertus of London allegedly punished in 1181 is based on a misunderstanding: "Untergrund," 146. On the other hand, according to one source the deacon who apostatized and was sentenced at Oxford in 1222 had participated in an alleged Jewish murder of a Christian boy, in the midst of Francis's religious life: F. Maitland, "The Deacon and the Jewess," in his *Roman Canon Law in the Church of England* (New York, 1898), 170.

Did contemporary Christians themselves already perform Passion Plays at this early date, thus giving the populace the visual vocabulary with which to describe the "'Jews'" actions? That would be hard to demonstrate, but clearly, they did already *imagine* such a lay, if Jewish, representation. Another way of posing the question would be: Did Christians of this age already have to deal with lay actors "mocking" (read: representing) the sacred mysteries of Jesus' passion? The answer to this question is positive: for in a tale of Caesarius of Heisterbach, redacted by 1222, a wise monk expresses his view that sculptors and painters were not averse to putting the sign of the cross on the forehead of a figure if that would bring in more money.[63] We have here a suspicion, before the death of Francis of Assisi, that those who manipulated images of famous men were not above falsely laying claim to one of the standard stigmata of the time.

Near the turn of the century — during the time of Francis's life in religion — the instances of crucifixional imagery began to accelerate, and sometimes they continue to be linked to flagellants or the practice of flagellation. One of the most important cases is that of the Netherlandish beguine Mary of Oignies (1177–1213), whose Vita Jacques de Vitry (1160–70–c. 1240) penned in all probability shortly after her death.[64] The erstwhile cardinal would also record the stigmata of two other holy men, to be mentioned below. The author, clearly keeping some distance from Mary's "excess," describes her "wondrous torture of the flesh": "As if inebriated ... and in her mistaken fervour, she cut out a large piece of her flesh with a knife, which [flesh], because of her modesty, she buried in the earth." Indeed, Mary had been so inflamed with love, "so invigorated by the wounds of Christ," that she lapsed into ecstasy, "and in this ecstasy of mind, she had seen one of the seraphim standing close by her."[65] Linking as does Vitry the wounds of Jesus with the gouged flesh of Oignies,

---

[63] *Dialogus miraculorum*, 2:100 (dist. 8, cap. 23). See the commentary and text in Vauchez, *Stigmates*, 599.

[64] In Genoa in 1216, Vitry carried with him one of her fingers: Boehmer, *Analekten*, 95.

[65] "Christum imitabatur, seipsam per humilitatem abjiciendo. ... Fervore enim spiritus quasi inebriata, prae dulcedine Agni Paschalis carnes suas fastidiens, frusta non modica cum cultello resecavit, quae prae verecundia in terra abscondit. Et quia nimio amoris incendio inflammata carnis dolorem superavit, unum de seraphin in hoc mentis excessu sibi adstantem aspexit. Loca vero vulnerum, cum corpus ejus in morte lavaretur, mulieres invenerunt, et admiratae sunt: *Acta Sanctorum*, June vol. 5 (Paris 1867), 552 (23 June); also *The Life of Marie d'Oignies by Jacques de Vitry*, trans. M. King (Saskatoon, 1986), 22.

one may imagine the latter wound to correspond to the side wound of Jesus, more fit for carving than the hands or feet.[66] In any case, Mary had been in ecstasy, a state not foreign to Francis, and again like Francis a few years later, a seraph is said to have accompanied her reception of the wound.[67] Needless to say, like Francis in the Celano story, Mary in life concealed her wound, which became evident only when women washed her cadaver; previously, only her confessors had known the story, Vitry says, and vouched for it once she died. After this recounting, Vitry again admonished others not to do these things themselves: "I say this not to commend excess but to show fervor. ... The discreet reader will observe that the privileges of the few do not make a general rule. ... We should therefore admire rather than imitate what we read certain saints to have done at the private instigation of the Holy Spirit."[68]

Thus when Francis was still young in religion, a Netherlandish woman invigorated by the wounds of Jesus had allegedly wounded herself by goug-ing flesh from her body, and the scars from those wounds appeared on her cadaver at death. This pervervid activity of a lay woman in religion is all the more significant because at almost the same time, across the Channel in England, we encounter still another case of self-infliction of Christolog-ic wounds, this time specifically crucifixional, which the sources label "stigmata." Shortly before the ecclesiastical Council of Oxford held in 1222 just two weeks after Easter, thus only nine years after Mary of Oig-nies's death, we have the well-documented case of a young layman playing Jesus, and of a laywoman renamed Mary, who were sentenced either to death or to life in prison by this council. According to several sources, be-fore this council — and thus perhaps during the Holy Week just past — this youth had "caused himself to be crucified" or had himself done so, by "perforating" his hands, feet, side and, in one source, his head as well,

---

[66] But Vitry does not say concisely that Mary "mutilat[ed] herself in the form of Christ's wounds": C. Walker Bynum, *Holy Feast and Holy Fast* (Berkeley, 1987), 119.

[67] The seraph originates in Is. 6.2–6. Note that Vitry does not refer to "stigmata." Some visual evidence of Francis's ecstasy is presented in R. Trexler, *Naked Before the Father: The Renunciation of Francis of Assisi* (New York, 1989), 80–86; see also Trexler, "Francis of Assisi, His Mother's Son," *Studi Medievali*, ser. 3, 36 (1995): 363–74, re-printed in the present collection. Caution is called for in discussing the actual form of Francis's alleged seraphic vision and stigmatization; the elements of what became a to-tality in Bonaventure's Vita of 1266 were in fact juggled in the earlier lives: see Frugoni, *Francesco*.

[68] Cited in Constable, *Attitudes*, 23.

presumably to imitate the crowning with thorns; indeed, he carried the scars of all these wounds.[69] But was this self-mutilation with the stigmatic "signs like those of Christ crucified" the reason for their eventual execution, or were other forces in play?[70] As Merkt and Hampe realized almost a century ago, the latter was surely the case. One source has them executed not because of imitation of the divine but because "Mary" insisted that she could say Mass, while another mentions magic rather than play-acting as the cause. Only Matthew Paris seems to have them put away for their mutilative activity, while still another narrative blames this "pseudo-Christ" for misleading the people, and makes that the reason for their punishment. In fact, this source, not at all friendly to Jesus and Mary, states that Jesus "dared to assert that he had come to emend the errors that had spread among the clergy and people."[71]

All in all, a close reading of these sources suggests that the real crime of these members of the laity was that they were treading on clerical prerogatives. To be sure, they may have known themselves to be shysters making a living off the *populus*. Since all the sources agree, however, that this Jesus had in fact pierced his limbs and side, it is more likely that, as Merkt argues, this savior was a bona fide ascetic trying to influence the laity, even while eking out a living. But intention is not so important here. What this case portrays is nothing less than a dramatic processional representation of Jesus, replete with all that lord's wounds, on the roads and streets of Oxfordshire four years before the death of Francis of Assisi. Before Francis's death, pious laity stigmatized their hands, feet, and side precisely to lead people to conversion.

At this point in time, the attempt to document the forerunners of the alleged stigmata of Francis of Assisi encounters real difficulties, because a hagiographical cluster of such cases of crucifixional stigmata, while chronologically imprecise, definitely surrounds the story of the Franciscan marks, making it difficult to identify their possible relationship to the Francis tale.

---

[69] F. Powicke, ed., *Councils and Synods, with Other Documents Relating to the English Church*, vol. 2, pt. 1 (Oxford, 1964), 104–5 (Walter of Coventry). The latter may refer to the sign of the cross on his forehead. Also Merkt, *Wundmale*, 2. The Oxford Council was also the setting for the trial of a church deacon who had apostatized to marry a Jew. The sources treat the two cases successively: see Maitland, *Roman Canon Law*, 158–79.

[70] "Signa quaedam quasi Christi crucifixi": Merkt, *Wundmale*, 3.

[71] "Qui se Christum, venisseque, ut errores, qui in clero et populo grassarentur, e-mendaret, audebat asserere": Merkt, *Wundmale*, 3, and for Matthew Paris, Merkt, *Wund-male*, 2; further Hampe, "Die frühesten Stigmatisationen," 1486.

Some scholars, defending the position that the stigmata were a behavioral convention before Francis's death in 1226 and fra Elias's account of them immediately thereafter, have unfortunately credited the contents of the Lives of such contemporaries of Francis in order to date their stigmata before 1226. Example: Stephen of Bourbon, narrating about 1260 the story of Robert, marquis of Montferrand, who died in 1234, says that the latter "for many years" bore the "stigmata of the Lord Jesus," and on every Friday pierced his flesh with nails until he bled. To Merkt, these "many years" meant that Robert was perhaps doing this around 1226, when Francis's stigmata were allegedly found.[72] The same has been done with the flagellant Premonstratensian Dodo of Hasha (in Friesia), who before his death in 1231 is said to have concealed "open wounds in his hands, feet, and right side, like Christ," "for many years."[73] But certainly no one today can take so seriously the contents of such lives, which are usually valuable only for the tropes they contain, as to date them in relation to the primal Franciscan document of 1226. The Franciscan Bihl was on the right track when he said that Robert probably imitated Francis,[74] though more exactly, it should be said that Stephen of Bourbon may have mimed the Franciscan story in his tale of Robert. Such copying is less likely to have been the case with the anonymous author of the Vita of Dodo, living as he did in far-off Friesia when he died just five years after Francis. But because his Vita escapes easy dating — the best Merkt could do was to opine that it may have been written in the generation following Dodo's death in 1231 — it is hazardous indeed to see it as contemporary with Francis's death. Bihl could again be right in thinking that this Vita too copied some of the Franciscan story.[75]

While excluding the Lives of these two men from our evidence for the pre-history of the Franciscan stigmata, I will for reasons I shall promptly lay out include one other erstwhile stigmatic, even though his event probably took place before or in the year 1229, three years after Francis expired. The story is quickly told by Jacques de Vitry, who in 1229 was

---

[72] Merkt, *Wundmale*, 4–5.

[73] Merkt, *Wundmale*, 5–6.

[74] Michael Bihl, "De stigmatibus s. Francisci Assisiensis (occasione recentis cuiusdam libri)," *Archivum Franciscanum Historicum* 3 (1910): 396. This *apologia* for the Celano/Bonaventuran stories is directed against the whole German school cited earlier, even if its title refers only to the dissertation of Merkt.

[75] Bihl, "De stigmatibus," 398; Merkt, *Wundmale*, 6.

probably in the small town of Huy near Liège, where he also probably first recorded the story; it is called "Of the Man who Affixed Himself to a Cross." Much like the devil whom we saw tempting Francis at the beginning of this paper, here too the prince of darkness was at work. He admonished an unnamed "simple layman" "that he ought to suffer as much for Christ as Christ had suffered for him." Vitry then describes how this man of Huy managed to nail both his hands and his feet to a cross, a description that became a locus classicus for aspiring Christic imitators in subsequent centuries. Just at the point when the pious layman was about to die, however, God intervened, and some shepherds lowered him from the cross. Vitry concludes his account by saying that within a few days the man had healed so well "that practically no indications of wounds appeared on his [body]."[76]

At this date we are in the midst of Celano's elaboration of the Franciscan story of the stigmata, and so, to repeat, it would be fruitless to speculate whether the "simple layman" of Huy performed before or after the first report of Francis's stigmata, in 1226. What is important about the Huy report are two things. First, as noted by Daxelmüller, Jacques de Vitry's concluding wording in his report on the man of Huy echoes that which the same prelate uses in a sermon to the Franciscans, when describing Francis's stigmata. Thus Vitry has the man of Huy healing so rapidly that within a few days hardly any vestiges of the wounds remained ("paucis diebus ita sanatus est, quo aliqua vestigia vulnerum vix apparuerunt in eo"), while in the sermon referring to the founder, he uses some almost identical wording ("quod in morte eius in pedibus, manibus et latere vestigia vulnerum Christi apparuerunt."[77] In other words, Jacques de Vitry thought of this process of stigmatization as so European in character that, *mutatis mutandis*, he used almost identical language to describe different cases.

A second valuable aspect of this Huy report again links it, indirectly but powerfully, to a variant of the Franciscan story, which in the mouth of Elias in 1226 was simply that stigmata had appeared on Francis "not long before his death" in 1226. Period. The English Benedictine Roger of Wendover, who died in 1236, just ten years after Francis of Assisi, is the only non-Franciscan source for early information on Francis of Assisi,

---

[76] Jacques de Vitry, *Die Exempla aus den Sermones feriales et communes*, ed. Joseph Greven (Heidelberg, 1914), 31–32.

[77] Daxelmüller, "Untergrund," 151.

whom he recognized as an *amicus dei*.[78] Alas, by any critical measure, the report he makes of Francis's alleged stigmata and death is far different from the Franciscan accounts — not surprisingly, given the distance the English monk was from Italy.[79] But among his many errors there may be a kernel of truth, as has long been recognized.[80] Roger says that "when the time arrived for Francis to leave this world and go to Christ," or more exactly "fifteen days before he left his body, there appeared wounds in his hands and feet which constantly shed blood, just as they appeared on the savior of the world as he hung on the wood when he was crucified by the Jews. Also his right side was open so wide, whence a spray of blood appeared, that the secrets of the heart were intimately visible."[81]

From this and another moment of the Wendover report which I shall presently recount, it appears that Roger or his informant had somehow converted Elias's own "not long before" Francis's death statement, or an oral report to that effect, into a fortnight. At a minimum, we can say that Wendover's account is unique in actually concurring with Elias as to the moment when the wounds might have appeared, whereas all other accounts beginning with 1 Celano in 1228 say either that the wounds began to appear two years before his death, or that they appeared upon Francis's death in 1226. True, Roger immediately thereafter loses credibility when he claims that once the stigmata appeared, Francis attracted large crowds (*concursus populorum*), to whom he preached to the effect that these stigmata had been given him so people would know he spoke for God, etc.[82]

---

[78] Carefully distinguished from that of his continuator, Roger's work is contained in his co-Benedictine Matthew Paris's (d. c. 1259) *Chronica majora*, ed. H. Richards Luard, vol. 3 (London, 1876), 134–35.

[79] Cf. Bihl, "De stigmatibus," 422f., who dismisses the whole account. For another of Roger's errors, see Trexler, *Naked Before the Father*, 42. Maitland, however, judges Roger "careful and well-informed": *Roman Canon Law*, 165.

[80] Hampe, "Wundmale," 393.

[81] "Venit hora eius, ut transiret ex hoc mundo ad Christum. . . . Itaque quintadecima die ante exitum suum de corpore, apparuerunt vulnera in manibus eius et pedibus, sanguinem iugiter emittentia, sicut in mundi salvatore in ligno pendente apparuerant, cum crucifigeretur a Iudaeis. Latus quoque eius dextrum adeo apertum et cruore respersum apparuit, ut etiam secreta cordis intima perspicua viderentur": Roger of Wendover, in Matthew Paris, *Chronica majora*, vol. 3:134; Bihl, "De stigmatibus," 422.

[82] "Haec visio in me idcirco ostensa est, quibus misterium crucis praedicavi, ut credatis in eum qui pro mundi salute haec quae videtis vulnera in cruce pertulit, et etiam ut me sciatis eius esse servum": Roger of Wendover, in Matthew Paris, *Chronica majora*, vol. 3:135.

In short, Roger has Francis doing precisely the same world-saving preach-ing carried out by Jesus and Mary in Oxfordshire four years previously. Yet in truth, not one other Franciscan source entertains such a "two-weeks before" scenario, nor is there any report of the alleged stigmata being written before the death of Francis, not to mention any report that he preached about repentance pointing to his own wounds, as had the two members of the English laity.

However, Roger's account has still not exhausted its interest, for in its conclusion, he has Francis fulfilling his own prophecy that the wounds would in fact disappear: "When he died, no stigmata [read: signs] of the said wounds in his side, feet or hands remained."[83] It was this passage which enraged loyal Franciscans like Bihl the most, and it is rarely men-tioned in the literature on the stigmata as a whole. But is it true? Is there any possibility that Roger of Wendover was right that when Francis was buried, he bore no signs or stigmata? We shall soon put forward two pieces of suggestive evidence for this hypothesis, but for the moment, it is the similarity of this account to that of Vitry regarding the simple layman of Huy that demands our attention. Tempted by the devil, we recall, the lat-ter, desirous of matching Jesus' sacrifices for him with his for Jesus, had, in or before 1229, crucified himself but then been saved from death by shep-herds, so that within a few days, "practically no indications of wounds ap-peared on his [body]."[84] It is hard to believe that the identical content of these two sources is meaningless. At the least, these overlapping texts are telling us that at this point in time, the phenomenon of divinely or self-inflicted crucifixional marks was common enough that two separate contem-porary authors, building on that common knowledge, could assure their readers that stigmata might disappear as quickly as they had appeared.

---

[83] " 'Haec vulnera, quae in me ita videtis aperta et sanguine cruentata, statim cum defunctus fuero, adeo sana erunt [sic] et cohaerentia ut carni caeterae similia videantur [sic].' ... Quo defuncto, nulla vulnerum praedictorum in latere, vel pedibus, sive manibus stigmata remanserunt": Paris, Chronica majora; also in Bihl, "De stigmatibus," 422; see H. Thode, Franz von Assisi und die Anfänge der Kunst der Renaissance in Italien (Berlin, 1904), 44; Frugoni, Francesco, 61.

[84] "Quod aliqua vestigia vulnerum vix apparuerunt in eo": Jacques de Vitry, Exempla, 31–32. An eerie echo of similar content pops up in the 1966 account of a young Mexi-can man (of Poza Rica) whose friend nailed him to a cross on Good Friday so that he would feel the suffering of Jesus. The newspaper account states that the friend was not prosecuted because "las lesiones que presenta el primero son consideradas como de las que sanan antes de quince dias y no ponen en peligro la vida": El Universal (Mexico City), 9 April 1966, 1, 13. Could Roger's account possibly refer indirectly to a similar le-gal framework of the fortnight within which such wounds heal?

We have now arrived at a point in time in the immediate wake of the death of Francis of Assisi, and we should summarize our findings to this point. First, I have argued that from the mid-eleventh century forward, Jesus' stigmata, a term I take to include unless otherwise specified all the wounds of or corporal marks on Jesus, are said to appear on one holy man and woman after another as imitations of the passion of Jesus. More often than not the emphasis is upon (non-biblical) whip marks, presumably resulting from Jesus' flagellation before Pontius Pilate, but from that time forward, unless otherwise indicated, a possible role of the crucifixional stigmata in such descriptions cannot be ignored. From that time as well, the universal mode of application of these stigmata is not any type of divine hand, but either self-mortification or their application by a companion, both viewed positively when obtained by Christian holy men and women, if not necessarily recommended to the laity. By the time Francis of Assisi was born c. 1182, the presence of passion stigmata on the bodies of holy men had long been a hagiographic and devotional convention, and Europeans could also imagine public passion processions in which (Jewish) actors allegedly represented the Passion of Jesus and his persecutors of old. From some point shortly after 1213, when Vitry wrote the Vita of Mary of Oignies, gouging into the skin so as to imitate the "invigorating [crucifixional] wounds of Jesus" was clearly established. By 1222, at least one itinerant preacher was piercing his hands, feet and sides so as to bring clergy and laity to conversion. And while Jacques de Vitry's account of the man of Huy and Roger of Wendover's story of Francis's stigmata both would seem to date to a period around or shortly after 1229,[85] well after Elias's announcement of 1226, taken together they show that contemporaries recognized crucifixional stigmata as a devout practice whose wounds would quickly heal if left alone.

With this background, an observation I made at the beginning of this paper comes home to roost. In his report on Francis's stigmata, Elias makes no mention of God as participating in this event; indeed, by describing Francis's wounds as going from the outside in, he rather implied that human agency was involved in making them. All previous readings of this passage have unwarrantedly presupposed that any "miracle," or to be more precise any "novelty of a miracle," involves God.[86] But Elias rather

---

[85] Wendover mentions Francis's 1228 canonization, but not his *translatio* in 1230.

[86] On how to read the term "miraculi novitatem," see the debate of Hampe with Bihl in the former's "Altes und Neues," 289.

meant that when his wounds "appeared," Francis looked identical to Jesus (as he and his wounds were to be seen in the usual contemporary images), or to put it otherwise, he meant that through Francis's action, Jesus had wondrously come to earth in the person of Francis. Thus in mid-century the Franciscan Thomas of Eccleston tells of one friar who saw the cadaver of another Franciscan "which seemed to have been recently taken down [from the cross], for he had five bloody wounds, like the crucified Jesus Christ. So [the friar] approached, thinking that it was sweet Jesus Christ, to find that it was [in fact] Brother Agnellus."[87] Indeed Roger of Wendover referred to the stigmatized Francis precisely as a "vision."[88] What could be more of a novelty than God made man in the person of Francis?

Now, the fact that Elias does not involve God but rather emphasizes Francis in his report of the stigmata is in full keeping with the whole previous history of stigmata, where it is a given that devotees themselves made such marks so as to imitate Jesus.[89] In his other ascetic practices as well, Francis, as noted by previous scholars, had been proactive in torturing his body, so Elias's hint of a self-mutilating ascetic there too conforms to Francis's own self-mutilating past.[90]

---

[87] "Videbatur autem socio suo fratri W. de Maddeley, quod funus quoddam iacuit in choro, quod a cruce videbatur recenter depositum. Nam et quinque vulnera habuit in modum crucifixi Jesu Christi sanguinantia. Cum vero crederet, quod esset ipse dulcis Jesus Christus, appropinquans cominus vidit, quod erat frater Agnellus": cited in Hampe, "Altes und Neues," 263.

[88] See the text above, n. 82.

[89] Some scholars have thought Francis had mutilated himself, but without realizing that Elias in no way belies that reading; see e.g., Hampe, "Altes und Neues," 283, summarizing the influence Merkt's view had had on him. Frugoni does not confront this question: Francesco, 82. Interestingly, Daxelmüller hypothesizes that Francis might have wounded himself for a quasi-theatrical purpose, comparable to his construction of a living creche at Greccio: "Untergrund," 151.

[90] Thus Merkt, Wundmale, 63, cites 2 Cel. 92: "Corpus enim suum, utique innocens flagellis et penuriis subigebat, multiplicans ei vulnera sine causa"; also Hampe, "Frühesten Stigmatisationen," 1492. Further, it is to be presumed that Francis wanted his brothers to copy his devotions, and thus 1 Cel. 15:40, if it can be believed, is probably indicative of his own self-punishment: "Aliqui se instrumentis ferreis circumdabant, aliqui vero ligneis ergastulis se cingebant. Tanta denique maceratione incentiva carnis reprimere satagebant, ut in frigidissima glacie non abhorrerent saepius se nudare, ac totum corpus spinarum aculeis compungentes effusione sanguinis irrigare": Merkt, Wundmale, 63. By the same reasoning, Celano's description of Francis's friend Claire's flagellation is relevant: "Disciplinae flagellis frangit sui corporis alabastrum, ut domus ecclesiae [S. Damiano] repleatur fragrantia unguentorum": Legenda sanctae Clarae virginis (Assisi, 1910), 16.

But if scholars have been wrong to presume that Elias has God applying the stigmata to Francis, their canon proves inadequate in the immediate wake of Francis's death as well. Elias clearly wrote at that point, for,
using the present tense, he told his correspondent that "after his death
[Francis] looks [*sic*] very beautiful, with a marvelous rosy whiteness, looking very happy."[91] Yet in this moment after death, Elias makes no mention of the stigmata! Did Elias only mean to evoke Jesus' revivified and
refreshed condition after his own resurrection, cum stigmata, or did he
have something else in mind by this omission? We shall address this question promptly, but before doing so, let me emphasize again that Elias does
not say anything about the condition of Francis's stigmata in the wake of
his death, nor does he say anything about the burial. Just as it has always
been assumed, erroneously, that one way or the other, Elias proclaimed
that God applied the stigmata to Francis, so it has commonly been assumed that Elias penned his announcement letter after burying the holy
man's stigmatized cadaver, a burial Celano described from his first Vita of
Francis forward, ever elaborating on the account. That is, however, not
the case: Elias's report was, after all, no biography of the poor man of
Assisi, and so he makes no mention of the burial, which took place probably one or two days after Francis's death, thus giving us no hint of the
state of the body.

Let us return now to Elias's intention in saying nothing about the stigmatic state of Francis's cadaver at the moment of burial. We already know
from the contemporaries Jacques de Vitry and Roger of Wendover that
stigmatic wounds may heal quickly. Thus we may be confident that when
Elias says that Francis got his wounds a few days before his death — but
does not say he had them in death, as do the later biographers — he
meant to leave open an understanding that Francis died and was buried
after these stigmata had healed. Indeed, by some unknown route Elias's
own words describing a clean and fresh body with no mention of the stigmata may well be the source of Roger of Wendover's statement that Francis predicted his wounds would disappear in death and that, in fact, in
death he no longer bore them.[92] Once again, the report of the Benedictine Roger of Wendover proves to have more than a kernel of verisimili-

---

[91] "Non erat in eo aspectus, sed despectus vultus. . . . Sed post mortem eius pulcherrimus aspectus est, moro candore rutilans laetificans videntes": cited above, n. 5, and
in Hampe, "Altes und Neues," 266, with analysis.

[92] See the texts above, n. 83.

tude in it. In short, from the beginning there was room for doubt that Francis had any marks on his body when he died.

This insight gains sustenance once, having examined the parts, we now submit the whole crucial text of Elias, given in note 5, to an adequate critical reading, which I alas have not found in any of the enormous literature on the "Francis question," whether apologetic or scholarly.[93] Elias says he will now announce a *miraculi novitatem*, for which there is no precedent "except in the son of God, who is Christ God." He then proclaims the appearance of the stigmata "not long before his death," and what they looked like. Then Elias continues without a break: "As long as his spirit lived in his body, his face was not handsome but rather ugly and no part of him remained without torment. His limbs were rigid because of the contraction of his nerves, just as a dead man's."

"But," Elias continues without a break, "after his death he had a most beautiful mien, with a wonderfully rosy, white skin which brought joy to those who saw it. And the limbs which had previously been rigid, were now so very soft; they had changed such that, *mutatis mutandis*, they appeared those of a delicate boy." Now, there should be little doubt as to what Elias is saying: the *miraculi novitatem* was not primarily the stigmata. The truly wondrous novelty was that Francis's body changed from a mass of torment, *of which the stigmata were one part*, to a beautiful rosy white body. In short, Elias produces a variant on the common announcement coming from an authoritative viewer that a putative saint's body was uncorrupted. This body, Elias clearly understands, was like that of Jesus after his resurrection, when, as Luke and John say, he had already "entered into his glory."[94] Perhaps Elias at this juncture did not mean to say that the

---

[93] The one primary source that refers to this letter is fra Giordano da Giano, in his *Cronaca* of 1262. Giordano says that Elias has Francis absolving others of sins against him, "insuper declarans de stigmatibus et aliis miraculis que post mortem suam ad beatum Franciscum operari dignatus est Altissimus" . . . and ordering the prelates of the order to gather and elect a minister general; text cited in Frugoni, *Francesco*, 93, n. 64. This is a late recollection of limited help: as Frugoni points out, the letter we possess makes no mention of post-mortem miracles.

[94] Lk. 24.26; Jn. 13.31. Elias's emphasis on a soft rosy white body after death hints that before it, the stiff body was an ugly dark. Francis's Christ-like transfiguration in death is one of the thrusts of the introduction to Elias's letter; see *AF* 10:525–26. The only author who reads this passage as a whole is Hase, who says that in his letter Elias "setzt den Wundmalen ganz ebenbürtig ein zweites Wunder," that of the rosy white body: *Franz*, 181. Beyond the limits of credulity, fra Isidoro Gatti, after uncritically referencing Elias and the two lives of Celano on the condition of the body, decides that there was "nessun segno di rigidità e di corruzione cadaverica, dunque, la sera e la notte del 3

stigmata had disappeared along with his other torments, even if Roger of Wendover seems to have understood Elias in precisely this fashion. But what is obvious is that Elias was emphasizing the incredible change in Francis's body once he died. The poor man had been dead in life, but now he was alive in death! The stigmata were *not* the sole focus of the "novelty" Elias announced to the world.

In the light of this reading of Elias's epochal letter, the point to be driven home first is that the elaboration of the Francis story carried out by Thomas of Celano in his first Life of the poor man, not to mention in his radically different second Life of the mid-1240s and Bonaventure's *Legenda* of the 1260s, is even more startling than has heretofore seemed the case.[95] Yes, these two men changed the time Francis's stigmata are said to have appeared on his body from his *extremis* to a point two years earlier. Yes, they along with Leo invented a place where he had received them, and eventually the Isaiahan seraph as their vehicle, perhaps copying Mary of Oignies's *Vita* by Jacques de Vitry. And yes, they changed the appearance of the stigmata so that nails seemed to grow from the inside out. And so forth. But it was Celano as well who first claimed that Francis was buried with stigmata and, still more striking, it was he who, within two years of Elias's original letter, first brought God into the picture, converting the stigmata from a human devotional action to a gift of the divinity, absolutely reserved, be it noted, to Francis and the Franciscans.[96]

To avoid misunderstanding in what follows, let me state my general sense of the evidence. What I have been doing is text analysis, and little more. Though it is plausible that an ascetic like Francis might have stigmatized himself, just as others were doing at the time, I personally do not find Elias's story fully persuasive, for two reasons. First of all, while self-imposed stigmata are plausible, Elias's canonical claim that Francis's body turned a rosy, soft and young white upon his death, and lost rigor mortis,

---

ottobre 1236." He then asks what he obviously considers a scientific question: "Quando, allora, la bellissima carne di s. Francesco morto si disfece e andò in polvere?," to then answer after citing nineteenth-century physicians said to have examined the naked corpse: "dopo la definitiva sepoltura in basilica del 1230": *La tomba di S. Francesco nei secoli* (Assisi, 1983), 58–60.

[95] The radical changes to the first Life Celano made in his second Life of ca. 1246 not only vitiate any claim to veracity the latter may have, but also any such claim for the former. As has long been recognized, Bonaventure's *Legenda* is not a work of history at all.

[96] On the papal prohibition for any other order to claim these stigmata for their saints, see Vauchez, "Stigmates," 611–12, also 603, 606.

is incredible. The formulation is obviously predicated on the fresh and dainty, post mortem, resurrectional body of Jesus. A second reason concerns a suspicious characteristic of his letter that has previously gone unnoticed. Writing probably even before the body was buried, Elias begins not by telling the facts of the stigmata, as would any reporter at first blush, but with a long introductory passage, followed by an advanced statement announcing the significance of what he is about to proclaim. This should certainly have raised eyebrows, especially because the best students of this document long ago noted Elias's highly refined and calculating rhetorical skills.[97] After his long introduction, Elias begins the message per se by saying that he is about to announce a "prodigious novelty" that has never happened before: that is to say, a sign that no one since Jesus had ever carried. Only then does he get down to mentioning the stigmata. This is backwards. It is the common procedure in first recounting a marvelous event that one does it *before* the writer becomes aware of its world-historical significance.

Charged with superintending his order, which now found itself without its hero-founder, Elias recognized his responsibility to ask himself how Francis's death could best be used not to harm but to aid that Franciscan order — just as Bonaventure would later when he crafted the definitive Legend of the same hero-founder. This document provides a finished ideological text and not a narrative. By insisting to the reader that what is important is the institutional meaning of the event — in essence, that the Franciscans have been elected by Jesus to be so many other Jesuses — the letter destroys some of the verisimilitude it perhaps still deserves.

But let us lay aside for a moment this suspicion of Elias, recognize that his letter is far and away superior in its truth claims to any other document, and try to understand what might have been his reaction to the divinification process that set in within two years of Francis's death. If I am right, Elias, though he had followed custom in allowing it to be inferred that Francis mutilated himself, had also sworn that Francis's body in death was like a child's, and so was not above Celano's prompt divinification of the stigmata story, which had such obvious immediate advantages for the order he governed and for the basilica of San Francesco whose funding was

---

[97] Hampe, e.g., characterizes him as a "feingebildeten Stilisten": "Altes und Neues," 268. Contradictorily, however, he had already noted his "ungekunstelte Aussage": "Altes und Neues," 264. See also the insightful assessment by E. Lempp, *Frère Élie de Cortone* (Paris 1901), 72–73. For the text, see above, n. 5.

his responsibility. The pope had canonized Francis in 1228 without mentioning the stigmata (with good reason, because the only relevant text at the time, the letter of Elias, said only that they were a novelty and allowed one to believe that Francis had mutilated himself!). By 1229 Celano's Vita of Francis, with its assertive God-centered description of Francis's stigmatization, and with the story that Francis had died and been buried with the stigmata ornamenting his cadaver, was finding its way into every Franciscan convent. Soon after, the first hints of what became a widespread opposition to the doctrine making Francis another Jesus would become loud across Europe, with many Franciscans themselves joining in. Already, the truth of the stigmata had become the sine qua non of Franciscan legitimacy.

At this juncture, an occasion arose that offered the perfect chance to settle any questions about Francis's skin and stigmata. On 25 May 1230, Assisi hosted a general chapter of the Franciscan order, the highlight of which was to be the triumphal movement (*translatio*) of the body of Francis from the church of San Giorgio, where it had been on deposit in the four years since his death, to the new basilica of San Francesco. The pope had sent gifts and representatives, and the assembled prelates of the order would provide an especially impressive accompaniment for the procession. Such was the plan for honoring Assisi and its favorite son.

Needless to say, as the day approached another expectation was at hand as well, and that was that the coffin would be opened. This was a normal part of the *translatio* of the cadaver of any saint or candidate for sainthood.[98] Not only was nearness to the charismatic body of a holy man or woman a precondition of a certain type of miracle, and thus earnestly to be desired this one last time. Even if they could not seize a primary or secondary relic from such a cadaver, Christians like other religious people throughout the ages have had an intense desire to determine with their own eyes if the body of a holy man or woman had corrupted, indicating whether the erstwhile soul was in heaven or not. In the early seventeenth century, the great Franciscan chronicler Luke Wadding discovered the evidence for the Assisians' desire for Francis's body, and printed the proof that something both expected and yet amazing had happened that 25 May. Two sources were involved, first a commentary of Wadding that

---

[98] See Piero Camporesi, *The Incorruptible Flesh. Bodily Mutation and Mortification in Religion and Folklore* (Cambridge, 1988).

includes some information not otherwise known, but close to the town government, which Wadding paraphrased,[99] and second a papal letter, of 30 June 1230, which Wadding had found in a *Registrum* of Gregory IX.[100] A century later, in 1856, Karl Hase brought this documentation into the modern age, and in 1866 Ernest Renan highlighted it again. Yet from then till now, this documentation has played a distinctly minor role in Franciscan bibliography, and specifically for those seeking to determine the condition of Francis's body at death.[101] Nothing less than a demonstration of *non habeas corpus*, what happened during this festivity is a central fact in the history of the Franciscan stigmata.[102]

The processional *translatio* of Francis's body, enclosed in its rich sarcophagus, had been in the works for some time. The pope had approved the holding of the chapter on the same 25 May obviously to insure plenty of solemn accompaniment. He had offered an indulgence to those who would participate and he had sent his own representatives, armed with many gifts. Further, Pope Gregory had commissioned the minister-general of the Order, Giovanni Parenti, and several of the latter's brothers, to carry out the solemnities and to do so as his vicars or representatives. Thus the movement of Francis's body was to be primarily a Mendicant and papal affair, without serious lay involvement. But obviously, this did not happen. In the pope's words, the podestà, council, and citizens (*populus*) of Assisi "perturbed everything, confounded everything, in danger of their souls, and to [our] dishonor and property loss." More specifically, "incited by a spirit of madness, these [podestà, council, and *popolo*], not taking into account that the sacred mysteries should only be carried out by sacred ministers, seized the said body [of Francis] with outrageous sacrilege and pride, damnably profaning the mystery of the *translatio* [in the midst of] a tumult. They did not allow the friars to exhibit due veneration to the said

---

[99] I use the recent edition of Wadding, *Annales minorum*, vol. 2, (Florence, 1932), 261. Gatti, *Tomba di S. Francesco*, 88, n. 98, corrects the old error that this material came from Gregory's *Registrum*, whereas the only thing emanating from that *Registrum* is the pope's letter cited in the following note. However, Gatti says that this material is only Wadding's summary of the papal letter, whereas it in fact contains material not in that letter.

[100] *Annales minorum*, 2:261f. Readers may determine what documentation I am using by distinguishing between the pagination of n. 99 and that of this note.

[101] Hase, *Franz von Assisi*, 121–202; E. Renan, *Oeuvres complètes*, vol. 7 (Paris, 1955), 933–34. Sabatier and Hampe refer to it casually, not seriously: see below.

[102] It is also a central event in the so-called invention of the stigmata; Frugoni, however, makes no mention of it in her work.

saint."[103] We will see presently what that meant. As punishment, the pope forbade any general chapter to be celebrated from thence forward, and imposed an interdict on the city of Assisi, ordering representatives of the guilty parties, armed with authority for "full satisfaction," to appear before him within a fortnight, and "make restitution for such an insult," or at least to post bond that they would make such restitution.

Obviously, the laity had intruded into the procession and, in the pope's view, created a scandal, which included taking control of the body of Francis. That control was, however, clearly temporary, since in his admonition the pope only required that the laity return some otherwise unspecified papal possessions, surely the gifts he elsewhere says he had given for the celebration. Further details of this tumult, and of the details motivating it, are contained in Wadding's commentary on since-lost, presumably communal documents that spoke of the same event.[104] We hear above many other instruments the clang of multiple trumpets sounding as the wooden casket containing Francis's body was raised up out of the earth at San Giorgio's. The body then being placed upon an ornate wagon pulled by purple-covered cattle because of the huge crowd, the procession proceeded, only to be taken over by the laity. "Through force of arms," writes Wadding, "the citizens of Assisi wanted to be the leading actors in this spectacle. Using many guards and through military means, they took steps to prevent such a distinguished treasure [as Francis's body/casket] from being calculatedly reduced by any of its parts, or removed through any stealth or craftiness."[105] The Mendicants who had been appointed commissioners of this *translatio* were, therefore, not free to act on their own, Wadding continues, "for the rectors of the city took over these duties. When [the procession] arrived at the church, they refused to bend to the common desire of all to view the body. Seizing it pridefully, in the tumult they damnably profaned the mystery of the *translatio*. Not permitting

---

[103] "Sed ipsi vesano spiritu concitati, non attendentes quod sacra mysteria non nisi a sacris sunt tractanda ministris, praedictum corpus ausu sacrilego rapientes in superbia et tumultu translationis mysterium damnabiliter prophanarunt, non passi a fratribus praedicto sancto venerationem debitam exhiberi": *Annales minorum*, 2:262.

[104] It is tempting to think that the original documents are extant, and could be turned up by a thorough search.

[105] "Vi et armis voluerunt esse praecipui actores in hoc spectaculo cives Assisiates, adhibitis multis custodibus, et valida militum manu, caventes ne dolo ullo, aut arte surriperetur, vel praescissis ullis partibus minueretur adeo insignis thesaurus": *Annales minorum*, 2:261.

the friars to perform the veneration due the said body, they disturbed everything, confounded everything," Wadding continues, in part copying the papal bull.[106] This led the pope, he concludes, to issue his letter, even though "some of our [Franciscans] unjustly put all the blame on Elias."[107] Seeking to intuit what might have been Elias's role in this (the former minister general was still in charge of building the basilica), Wadding suggests that Elias may have acted to prevent the body of Francis from being seized by getting it into the church — all our sources assume that it did enter the basilica — and then removing it from the view of all in such a way that no one would know the place where it was hidden nor the spot or door by which one descended to the lower church. A few friars were so agitated by the tumult and their defrauded desire to see the body of Francis that they complained to the pope, who then wrote the afore-mentioned letter to the laity.[108]

The importance of these events is such, their humiliating implications for the story of Francis and his order so palpable, that, as Hase noted, neither the so-called Three Companions in their *legenda* of the mid-1240s, nor Bonaventura, hint of the drama of 25 May 1230. Nor did Celano in

---

[106] "Nam civitatis rectores id sibi muneris assumpserunt, et ut ventum erat ad eccle-siam restiterunt communi omnium desiderio corpus videre volentium. Nam rapientes illud in superbia, et tumultu translationis mysterium damnabiliter prophanarunt, non passi a fratribus praedicto corpori debitam venerationem exhiberi, dum omnia perturbarunt, om-nia confuderunt": cf. the text in n. 103.

[107] "Licet aliqui ex nostris culpam omnem rejiciant in Eliam, cui plura ultra verita-tem imposita": *Annales minorum*, 2:261.

[108] *Annales minorum*, 2:261. If we are to believe the Englishman Thomas of Eccleston writing in the late 1250s, the uproar among the Franciscans stemmed from something quite different. Into this very chapter had stormed supporters of Elias carrying the former general and demanding that he be forthwith reinstalled in that office. In the midst of the uproar the actual general, Giovanni Parenti, stood up from his chair of authority and took off his clothes, which apparently ended the coup attempt. According to Eccleston, the populace, not knowing the facts of the matter, came to believe that the uproar among the friars was due to the fact that Elias had brought the actual cadaver of Francis from San Giorgio to the basilica three whole days before the friars had come together, that is, before the *translatio*. Thus according to Eccleston, the laity thought that the for-mal *translatio* was of an empty casket. The text is in *Fratris Thomae vulgo dicti de Eccleston Tractatus de adventu fratrum minorum in Angliam*, ed. A. G. Little (Manchester, 1951), 65. Varieties of this three-days-before story were then adopted by two fourteenth-century sources, the *Speculum vitae s. Francisci* and the *Chronica XXIIII generalium*: see Lempp, *Frère Élie*, 24–34, 83, 165. But the fundamental primary source for this event — the 1230 letter of Gregory IX — does not entertain this possibility. I am still inclined to be-lieve with Eccleston, however, that some of the laity did harbor this suspicion.

his second Life. Putting these two documents of Wadding together, it is clear that from the beginning the rulers of the city for fear of losing the body were determined to prevent everyone at least outside the church from viewing it, and so changed the ecclesiastical procession into a soldierly march. Probably at the very entrance to the church (*ad ecclesiam*), things slid out of control. Not only could the laity not fulfill its united desire to view Francis; some friars themselves were furious, because they had been unable (even inside the church) to venerate the body, that is, as was the usual procedure in such circumstances, carry out the liturgy for gazing upon a corpse at the so-called second burial, perhaps remove a nail or hair or other relic, and report on their findings. Still more revolting may have been the suspicion that fra Elias had conspired with the rulers to keep Francis removed from view.[109] Perhaps, thought Wadding, Elias had rather only acted alone so as to keep the body from being torn apart and stolen bit by bit.

But this amazing story of the body of Francis of Assisi now becomes still more astonishing. How many pilgrims from around the world who have visited this church, before its recent devastation by an earthquake, have realized that from that day until 1818, for almost six hundred years, no one knew, or was willing to say, where the body of the poor man of Assisi was located? That in that time no miracle was ever claimed for the body of Francis *ad sepulcrum* for the obvious reason that its location was unknown, even if it was generally thought to be somewhere in the lower church of the basilica?[110] That the remains that were uncovered in 1818

---

[109] Recalling the open warfare of the supporters of Elias against the minister general Parenti referred to by Eccleston, one may hypothesize that those denouncing Elias to the pope represented the order establishment. Unaware of the coffin's contents or lack thereof, that establishment may not have favored Elias's action in keeping the body from sight.

[110] Note also that until Bonaventure, none of the miracles attributed to Francis are associated with the stigmata. There is however evidence that in one way or the other, the body of Francis was venerated in the basilica from early on, despite its whereabouts being unclear. Thus in 1260, certain Perugian officials received permission *ire ad asissium pro veneratione corporis beati francischi quando placuerit*: cited in Angela Maria Terruggia, "In quale momento i disciplinati hanno dato origine al loro teatro?," in *Movimento dei Disciplinati*, 434. Still, writing about 1385, fra Bartolomeo da Pisa in his *De conformitate* says that Francis is buried in the Assisian basilica, but that "de cuius corpore ad ostendendum populis nihil invenitur nec habetur; ac in quo ecclesiae loco iaceat, etsi quibusdam sit agnitum, quibus vero, nulli est notum": AF 4:178.

are so nondescript[111] and the few grave goods accompanying the skeleton perhaps so anachronistic[112] as to leave the question open if these remains are those of Francis?[113] In short, the one best hope to document the stigmata, and that body's marvelously soft and roseate white tactility that Elias so admired, before all the world, was to see them on the body during this second burial. That hope vanished on 25 May 1230.

A first hypothesis seeking to explain why this crucial documentation of the stigmata did not occur is that the authorities feared losing the sarcophagus and its contents to some jealous foreign entity, like Perugia,[114] or else that if the casket was opened, Francis's cadaver would be totally torn apart by the crowd. Yet these ideas, self-evident as they must appear to students of medieval religion, are only partly satisfying, for two reasons. First, fear of confiscation does not explain how the rulers could have resisted the desire not just of the laity outside the church, but of many friars also inside it, doubtless in Assisi for the first time, who wanted to see the face and stigmata of their hero founder, especially since many of them had to return home and vouch for the veracity of these marks and for the can-

---

[111] Only a skeleton was found; no cloth, no symbols of the poor man's life: G. Rocchi, *La basilica di San Francesco ad Assisi* (Florence, 1982), 47. There are also no reports of broken bones where any of the five wounds might have penetrated Francis's body.

[112] Weirdly, the tomb contained a ring with the figure of the ancient deity Pallas Nicephora, as well as eleven coins, some of which may date to the end of the thirteenth century and even later: Rocchi, *Basilica*, 47–48, who, given these anomalies, has suggested that on arriving in the basilica, the body may have been deposited in one place before being moved to beneath the main altar of the lower church; the objects are pictured in Gatti, *La tomba*, figs. 24, 26.

[113] As pointed out by Rocchi, *La basilica*, 47, the authoritative papal identification of the remains as those of Francis was based entirely upon their location beneath the high altar of the lower church, which has always been named after the poor man. But the whole history, or rather the non-history of this cadaver, the mystery in which it was wrapped throughout the early modern period, and the badly recorded "rediscovery" of the remains in 1818, will lead all but apologists to reserve their doubts, even after the papal pronunciamento.

[114] In fact, in 1442 Perugia did request the body of Francis from the pope, saying it would be safer in the larger city: Fra Ludovico da Pietralunga, *Descrizione della basilica di S. Francesco e di altri santuari di Assisi* (Treviso, 1982), 262 (commentary of Pietro Scarpellini); see also P. Sabatier, *Vie de S. François d'Assise* (Paris, 1898), 410, who gives similar examples of the time. Note however that when Jacques de Vitry entered Perugia in 1216, he found the cadaver of Pope Innocent III not yet buried: it had been stripped of clothing, "corpus autem eius fere nudum et foetidum in ecclesia reliquerunt": Boehmer, *Analekten*, 96.

did condition of the body.[115] The desire to keep the coffin closed, not just at the time of the chapter but indefinitely, thereby ruling out the usual miracle-fed grave cult to such a body, must have had strong motivations indeed.

Clearly in the beginning Elias as lord of the basilica and later as a repeat minister-general must have cooperated with the civic authorities in the scheme to keep the casket closed, if for different reasons. Sabatier and Hampe have denied such mutual complicity, arguing against Hase that this would have required an improbably large conspiracy. But they ignored the important fact that the body disappeared for almost six hundred years, during which time the friars themselves were the lords of the body inside the basilica.[116] The lay rectors of the city probably insisted on the sarcophagus not being opened at the moment of *translatio* for safety's sake, while Elias, after (perhaps three days earlier) getting the body into the church, insisted on the casket remaining closed and inaccessible for his own reasons. As Hase also recognized, everyone in Assisi wanted the sarcophagus, whatever it might contain in fact, to come into the basilica, where, of course, it would be placed in a central place for veneration world without end.[117] That's the rub! From Elias's point of view, keeping the casket closed and then disappearing it so that the body could not be prayed to must, ultimately, be seen as two parts of one strategy. Fear of the crowd cannot explain that totality.

A second hypothesis is sounder and must suffice until more documentation appears. It begins with the presumption that fear of theft cannot explain all the events I have described. It hesitatingly bypasses Hase's hypothesis that Elias feared opening the casket would reveal that he had himself stigmatized the fresh cadaver of Francis, mainly because such a cadaver could as easily be read to prove that Francis inflicted the stigmata himself, and that reading, as I have shown, is not ruled out by Elias's let-

---

[115] None could or did: there is no documentation showing that anyone present at the chapter did declare his eye-witness of the body.

[116] "Plus j'y réfléchis, plus je deviens incapable d'attribuer une valeur quelconque à cet argment de la disparition du corps; car enfin, s'il y avait eu une fraude pieuse d'Élie, il aurait au contraire étalé ce cadavre": Sabatier, *Vie*, 410. I am baffled by this argument. It never occurred to Sabatier that the sarcophagus could have been empty or could have held a body other than Francis's; Hampe, "Wundmale," 390 sees a large conspiracy as improbable.

[117] Hase, *Franz von Assisi*, 187.

ter.[118] In my view, Elias then, and the Assisian prelates of a later day, perhaps together with an occasional friend in the city leadership, were concerned lest opening the casket would show it to be empty, or filled with a cadaver clearly not that of the advertised Francis, such as one without any sign of stigmata, or of that lovely pinkish white and soft skin that Elias had vouched for four years earlier.[119] The sources leave us nothing to choose among these possibilities. Perhaps Elias knew that while Francis had indeed once stigmatized himself ("fifteen days" or "a few days" before his death), he had died and been buried after these wounds had healed, as Roger of Wendover claimed and as Jacques de Vitry had seen in the case of the simple man of Huy in these very years. Or perhaps Elias had made up the story of the stigmata and the fresh white body so as to raise the money for the basilica to his former master, then been overtaken by the literary fantasy of Thomas of Celano, and now feared being unmasked. In either case the embarrassment to Franciscans of finding a non-stigmatized or crumbled corpse would have been huge, especially since in his first Life, perhaps at just that general chapter being distributed to the representatives of Franciscan houses across Europe, Thomas of Celano the year before had described Francis as having indeed borne these stigmata for two full years before his death![120] One way or the other, however, there is every reason to believe that the potential for an absent or decayed corpse without

---

[118] Something not recognized by Hase: *Franz von Assisi*, 126, 176–80. On the other hand, I do not share Hampe's rejection of Hase's "rationalistisch" view based on the grounds that there were witnesses to the stigmate: "Wundmale," 387–88. That claim comes from the Lives of Celano which, as I have stated, were written for the purpose of generating time and space for witnesses, and are not works of history at all.

[119] Ireneo Affò, *Vita di frate Elia* (Parma, 1783), 54, was the first to suggest that Elias kept the casket closed and buried the corpse sight unseen because he feared he would disappoint the assembled friars and laity if it was shown that the body had turned to dust in the interval. After only dust and a skeleton were found in 1818 — the pope then distributing the dust as relics — that view was again represented, and early in the present century once more: see the bibliography in Gatti, *Tomba*, 93, n. 117.

[120] There is a third, improbable, possibility: that while Francis had been buried with stigmata, Elias feared that the wounds would have healed in the grave. Still a fourth possibility, not so easily dismissed, is that the body had already been broken up and distributed as relics. See Lempp, *Frère Élie*, 87, and H. Boehmer, ed., *Chronica fratris Jordani* (Paris, 1908), 50 for a reference to a list of relics of Francis (such as hair and clothing) given by Celano (!) to a friar who took them to Germany shortly after Francis's death; see further on the saint's relics in E. Ricotti, "Una reliquia del sangue di S. Francesco a Castelvecchio subequo (Abruzzi)," *Miscellanea francescana di storia, di lettere, di arti*, n.s. 34 (1934): 357–58.

stigmata was precisely what had kept the casket closed and caused the body to disappear before, on, or after this fateful day.

It is not too much to say that nothing less than the future of the Franciscan order was at stake as people planned for this day, or put otherwise, nothing less than a devastating blow to its honor and glory — read the tourist economy of little Assisi and its big basilica — if the saint were to be found without any sign of the stigmata. We do not know if Pope Gregory had failed to mention Francis's stigmata in his canonization bull of 1228 because of the fear of just such an eventuality during the *translatio*. But we can be confident that neither a responsible builder and executive like Elias, nor the responsible rulers of Assisi, could take the chance of ruining a city just then emerging to fame. Francis's body, or perhaps only an empty coffin, had to disappear, but disappear within the very building that could, then, continue to chronicle the city's rise to distinction. And so it was.

In the centuries to come, stigmatizations would become common. Repeatedly, many of these claims have proven fraudulent (recently, for example, Theres Neumann), but a few have actually led to an ascetic's canonization (for instance, Gemma Galgani and now Padre Pio), and they remain attractive to a media age always on the lookout for a sanguinary performer. Yet the old dominance of the men and women of the Franciscan order over this category of sacred performance has waned, and surely the Franciscans' *raison d'être* no longer rests squarely, as it once did, on the veracity of the stigmata of the hero founder.

Francis stood within a tradition of stigmata. Elias's proclamation of a "miraculous novelty" "never heard of before" must be understood for what it was, a rhetorical euphemism stemming from the Bible that commonly did not mean what it said.[121] We have shown how thoroughly he stood within this tradition. Yet at another level, through the pen of Thomas of Celano, Francis was indeed made into a new type of saint, one whose body was transformed through divine, and then seraphic, intervention. And as the Franciscan order came to control the whole phenomenon of stigmatization, non-Franciscan self-mutilation, rather than being acceptable, seemed more and more a fraud: devotees imprinted these marks on themselves, it was said, but claimed that they had come from God.[122]

---

[121] Just like the English "unheard of." See Jn. 9.32; 2.18; 4.54.

[122] The earliest post-Francis reference to stigmata as potentially fraudulent appears to be to Elisabeth of Herkenrode, said by the mid- thirteenth-century Cistercian Philip of

In this way, the reservation of the imitation of Jesus to the religious clergy, nominatively the Franciscans, could continue. The notion that only corporately religious persons could approach a perfect imitation of Jesus was safeguarded for the remaining centuries of the Middle Ages.

Clairvaux to have been stigmatized "without simulation or fraud": Constable, *Three Studies*, 220.

Florentine Theatre, 1280-1500:
A Checklist of
Performances and Institutions*

IN THE TRECENTO AND QUATTROCENTO, the Florentine republic's voluntary associations laid the foundations of the theatre of the Grand Duchy. The fruits of this long development, whether in the area of text, stage, or music, are well known to students of theatre, largely because the sources of high and late Renaissance drama are rich and relatively compact. Theatre before the sixteenth century, however, is little known because of sparse and scattered documentation, and the scholarly edifices constructed on these "scarce vestiges" (in De Bartholomaeis's words) seem at times to be built on sand. Although skilled in analyzing the texts of lauds and *sacre rappresentazioni* and solid in reconstructing earlier staging from later descriptions, this scholarship can be merely imaginative when it comes to surveying the early period as a whole. A list of early theatrical performances such as the one appended to this note conflates these virtues and vices: it furnishes an unimaginative yet firm overview not of the texts, but of the performances and institutions of Florentine theatre in the Tre- and Quattrocento.

---

* This essay appeared previously in *Forum Italicum* 14 (1980): 454–75.

The merest glance at this list illustrates what the study of early Florentine theatre requires, and how imperfectly the present writer has met those needs. Despite the rich ethnography of the Italian theatre by Paolo Toschi, most of its students continue to emphasize individual texts and single theatrical personalities instead of studying theatre within its social context. No one in pursuit of theatrical materials has, it seems, undertaken that systematic examination of the rich Florentine documentary tradition which alone can establish that context. While some ethno-historians of the theatre have furnished a valuable overview of the deep social-psychological structures of theatre, the social historians have, in short, failed to provide an analysis of what happened. Students of early Florentine and Tuscan theatre need to develop a systematic research strategy for the investigation and review of Florence's published and unpublished primary sources.[1]

Talk is cheap, of course, all the more for the general historian like myself more concerned with formal behavior as a whole than with theatre in particular. I have not, for example, systematically studied the notarial records of the Florentine archives, certainly the most promising if redoubtable source for information on Florentine theatre, nor have I examined every page of the records of any particular confraternity known for its theatrical activity. Yet in the pursuit of my own research interests I have proceeded systematically through other materials relevant to the history of the city's theatre. It goes without saying, first of all, that to my knowledge I have read all published narrative and documentary primary sources. I have further made my way through all of the archival registers of the laws of Florence (*Provvisioni*), and have extensively studied most of the unpublished narrative histories, chronicles, diaries, and *ricordanze* of that same tradition. Doubtless an enormous amount of material remains hidden in the archival *fondi* I only sampled. Nevertheless, the list which follows does represent the most complete record of theatrical performances and institutions currently available, and its publication may encourage other students to pursue such a systematic approach in other *fondi*.

---

[1] The merits of such an undertaking are now apparent in the excellent work of N. Newbigin, *Feste d'Oltrarno: Plays in Churches in Fifteenth-Century Florence*, 2 vols. (Florence, 1996), which is limited to the study of just three plays, those of the Annunciation, Ascension, and Pentecost, as mentioned repeatedly in the checklist below. Newbigin's Introduction also provides an overview of research on theatre subsequent to the original appearance of the present article.

This list includes that small body of references to the particular theatrical events I encountered, events usually recorded by our sources without reference to a particular text, author, or acting company. Second, it contains early references to public forms which then or later served as vehicles for theatrical performances. Next, it includes significant references to public forms in which participants played someone other than themselves. Finally, it gathers all references to props and apparatuses which can be considered theatrical.

Since by such a content-description I intended to beg the question of what theatre is, it is important to say what sort of performances were *not* included in the list. Doubtless, a substantial part of governmental ritual, all ecclesiastical processions, and all three of the main non-ecclesiastical public entertainments (jousts, dances, *armeggerie*) contained elements of commemoration and thus of imitation or theatrical feigning, yet all these events could not be included. I have only included events of these types whose imitative quality was mentioned by the source. In the one case where I found an ecclesiastical procession consciously organized according to an historical model, I added it to the list; the *armeggeria* was the premium form to which the theatrical apparatus called the *trionfo* was associated, but I list only those *armeggerie* where a triumph was specifically mentioned. The test for inclusion was, therefore, the presence of a recognized theatrical form, the known theatrical intention of the *festaiolo,* or the theatrical perception of such a form by the viewer.

My first goal was a record of performances, although a list of Florentine theatrical institutions was of equal importance, for this would complement the close attention being given to sixteenth-century theatrical groups by Françoise Decroisette and Michel Plaisance.[2] First of all, I recorded the names of those few groups and individuals said to have performed or prepared the staging of specific theatrical pieces. Second, I included all references to confraternities or brigades (*brigate*) which had nicknames or representational names ("the Shell" [*Nichio*], "the Parrot" [*Papagallo*]), for they were all associated with theatrical activities of some type. Students will want to compare my references to those of D'Ancona, many of whose

---

[2] F. Decroisette, "Fêtes religieuses, fêtes princières au XVIe siècle: les Médicis et la fête de l'Annonciation à Florence," in *Culture et Religion en Espagne et en Italie aux XVe et XVIe siècles,* ed. M. Ballestero et al. (Paris, 1980), 11–41; M. Plaisance, "La Politique culturelle de Côme Ier et les fêtes Annuelles à Florence de 1541 à 1550," in *Les Fêtes de la Renaissance,* ed. J. Jacquot and E. Konigson, vol. 3 (Paris, 1975), 133–52.

"companies" (*compagnie*) may have had similar names in the Quattrocento without my being able to verify their usage at that time.

The reader of these names should not assume that any group had institutional continuity unless its name recurs, for many of the groups were ephemeral, created only for a particular performance and thus unincorporated. Nor does the group's name indicate its religious or secular emphasis: "the Magpie" (*Gazza*), for example, might prove to be a religious confraternity in which theatre was only a sidelight, and the Confraternity of the Resurrection, as we shall see, was a primarily theatrical institution with festive rather than pious roots.

The early history of two types of theatrical groups does not emerge clearly from this list, and their general absence calls for a word of explanation. In the sixteenth century the *potenze* of Florence were important parts of the city's theatrical world. These plebeian groups originated as feigned military brigades in the second half of the Quattrocento, but their theatrical element was not unambiguous enough at that time to warrant repeated inclusion in the list. Only at the beginning of the sixteenth century do their institutions and performances become a staple part of historical reportage. For their earlier history, consequently, I must refer interested readers to chapters 11 through 13 of my *Public Life in Renaissance Florence* (New York, 1980, repr. Ithaca, 1990).

The problem with the brigades of youth of "good family" is of a different order. Their names, such as the Squires of Fortune (*Scudieri di Ventura*), do appear in our list, but the ephemeral nature of such groups makes their place in the city's theatrical history uncertain. I would, however, like to emphasize one important aspect of their history which is clear in our list but which I overlookcd when writing the above-mentioned book. A glance at the entry for 27 February 1416 shows that the youth brigade of the Sphere (*Spera*) along with a group of (older) citizens had the official task of welcoming a diplomatic delegation into the city. This standard diplomatic institution involved what the chroniclers called in the Trecento "citizens and companies of *armeggiatori*" and, during the Quattrocento, "citizens and youth." I argued in my book that there was a relation between the task of welcoming distinguished visitors or returning ambassadors and the early history of theatre. The document of 27 February 1416 confirms that hypothesis, since the Brigade of the Sphere clearly showed a sphere and thus possessed some level of theatrical intent: a triumphal ritual — and gate ceremonies were always that — was performed by a group which, through its (*trionfo* [?] of the) sphere, commented on some quality of the entering dignitaries.

We can now trace, therefore, a straight line between the official *compagnie di armeggiatori* of the Trecento, put together on the spot to welcome dignitaries and then dissolved, and the ephemeral, perhaps only proto-theatrical youth brigades of the Quattrocento. Further, since five of the famous theatrical *potenze* of the sixteenth century were originally called *compagnie di armeggiatori,* we now have more information on the process by which brigades of youth "of good family" were transformed into the incorporated plebeian *potenze* of a later period.

I must now clarify my reporting procedures in the accompanying list. As to content, two rules must be kept in mind. First, everything in parentheses is information or opinion not in the texts themselves, and everything not in parentheses is from the sources I list. Second, the primary source material has been rigorously translated in a literal fashion with the exception of time, which I have converted to the proper past tense. Perhaps most disconcerting to the reader intimately acquainted with Italian usage, I have literally translated the word *festa* into "feast," *trionfo* into "triumph," and *edifizio* into "edifice."

The most treacherous of these terms is *festa,* and perhaps a word of elaboration is called for. I have *not* included all references to *feste,* because the word meant holiday and feastday and, in the realm of activities, could also mean no more than a mass or procession participated in by a group. Indeed, in the sixteenth century I have seen the word used to refer to a confraternity which represented something in a celebration. In my list, therefore, I report only *feste* with theatrical content or those which probably had such content. In every case, the literal translation of the texts must guide the reader in determining reality, for I report neither more nor less than the sources.

The same care was taken in reporting topographical information, especially as regards *feste* done in or near churches. In every case, I literally translated indications that performances were done "at" or "in" churches. Not that this eliminates doubts on the place of performance, of course: Italian usage sometimes combines with a lack of specificity on the part of the reporter to leave that uncertain. But again, the precise translation in the list says neither more nor less than the source.

My guidelines for the translation of institutional terms were also rigorously followed. The Italian word *brigata* was always translated "brigade"; the word has no particular legal meaning, but merely indicates a small group. The leaders of these brigades are indifferently referred to in the sources as *signori* or *messeri*; I uniformly report them as "signores," adding any fictive princely title like "king" when that is indicated in the sources.

I adopted a more complex procedure in dealing with the Italian or Latin words *compagnia* and *societas*: they are both rendered with the word "confraternity." With the exception of references to commercial or military companies, Florentines using the Italian word *compagnia* or the Latin word *societas* meant an incorporated lay religious group with episcopally approved statutes, and this is what I intend by the translation "confraternity." In those rare cases where there was any question whether a *compagnia* was actually a confraternity, as there was with the Company of the Star, I preserved the word "company."

The matter of dates requires a final word. Fixed ecclesiastical feasts like Christmas and Epiphany required no dates, but I did add the dates of movable feasts within the year in question. Second, my list distinguishes between Carnival, the day before Ash Wednesday, and the Carnival period, which at the end of the Florentine Quattrocento was said to run for eight days before Lent.[3] Thus when particular dates were furnished in the sources, as for example Berlingaccio, the Thursday before Lent, I so reported them. However, when the sources spoke generally of Carnival activities, the list records them as being in the Carnival period. Third, the reader will want to keep in mind that contemporaries often referred to a feast day but meant its vigil. My dating can therefore be off by one day, for I simply followed the words of the source. Fourth, I took the liberty of assigning to "San Giovanni" all the theatrical events which transpired in the period stretching from 20 June through c. 26 June, even though the feast itself was on the 24th. Finally, the reader will find all dates in the modern style except for source references to Florentine laws passed before 25 March, the later beginning of the new year in that city. In these latter cases for the sake of compatibility with archival dating I included both the Florentine style and the modern style (for example "1421/22").

With these few words of introduction, I leave the following list to the tender mercy of readers. Nothing would serve the study of early Florentine theatre more than further research which would render this list obsolete, not, I hope, because of its errors, but because of its incompleteness:

1283   San Giovanni. Festive courts in the Rossi neighborhood across the Arno. The Company of the Whites was led by the Lord (or God) of Love. Such courts continued throughout the city for two

---

[3] "Mille Quattro Nove et Sette, A di venti di febraio, Carnasciale alzò lo staio. Perse il regno a di venzette": Ben G, 74.

years (MR, 196; VG, VII, 89; PA, IV, 7; DT, 149; SM, 160; TR, P, 217).

1290 May Day. Florentines counterfeit every great baronage (VG, VII, 132; PA, 4:60; TR, P, 217f.).

1304 May Day. The Inferno, represented on boats in the Arno by the youthful Kingdom of San Frediano, which was led by the Signore of the Last Day of April. There is a tradition that Buffalmacco was the *festaiolo*, and that Dante was inspired by it (PP, 78; VG, VIII, 70; PA, IV, 195ff.; V-M, 1:510f.; TR, P, 220).

1333 May Day. A cavalcade of 477 artisans from the Via Ghibellina, called the Company of the Yellows.

——— 11 June (S. Onofrio). A cavalcade of 520 artisans from the Corso dei Tintori (the race track or street of the dyers), called the Company of the Whites. Both these brigades were led by kings (VG, X, 219; PA, VI, 84f.; DT, 165; SM, 495; TR, P, 220).

1343 May Day. Six lower-class brigades. One led by a signore called the Emperor (of the Red City of S. Ambrogio) fought with another led by a signore called Paleologue (from the parish of S. Giorgio) (VG, XII, 8; SM, 566, 575; TR, P, 220f.).

1365 27 Feb. (Carnival). The customary game of rocks or throwing of rocks was scheduled (MD, XXI, 32).

1376 21 Nov. The joust in honor of Madonna Libertà was cancelled (D d'A, 325).

1380 May Day. Customary dances in the churches and squares noted (SM, 217).

c. 1380 1 Jan. Farcical knightings by a king whose realm centered in the Mercato Vecchio (PA, VI, 272ff.).

1384 Epiphany. The formal entry of the new bishop occurred (NM, 67) (noteworthy in relation to the following):

1390 Epiphany. Feast of the Magi and Innocents (the first known for Florence. It was a cavalcade with stations for dramatic action (AP, fol. 157v, text in HR, 144; TR, M, 152ff.).

——— 6 Oct. A large stage was erected in the Piazza della Signoria for relics, singers, clerks, and mass (AP, fol. 160r, diagrammed in TR, P, 49f.).

c. 1391 Ascension. The feast of the Ascension was performed in the church of the Carmine (probably by its Confraternity of S. Maria delle Laudi and of S. Agnese), (SF, lxxii; BG, 320–27).

1391 11 June (S. Onofrio). The Company of the Corso (dei Tintori), centered in the Piazza degli Alberti, cavalcaded through the city, breaking lances (AP, fol. 161r; TR, P, 229).

1393   12–26 Apr. Fistfights occurred between the brigade of La Berta (centered in the parish of S. Maria Maggiore) and I Magroni (centered in the parish of S. Maria Novella) (AP, fol. 172r; ASF, AD, 140, fasc. 7, c. 56; ASF, Pr, 122, fols. 166v–168r; TR, M, 153f.).

1410   San Giovanni. A *caccia* (hunt) in a Guicciardini garden at Ponte a Greve (DC, 248).

c. 1410   San Giovanni. First major description. (1) (Sacred) representations by confraternities within the ecclesiastical procession, each confraternity marching with the clergy of its church. The confreres were dressed as angels. (2) (Profane) games of suitable enjoyment and beautiful representations were done within the offertory procession of the citizens, each game being associated to the citizens of one of the sixteen wards or gonfalons (DC, 84–89; TR, P, 254f.).

1415   10 Feb. (Carnival Sunday), and 16 and 17 March (Lent). Dances and jousts done by the Brigade of the Galley (DC, 254).

——   San Giovanni. A law prohibited pictures or signs of base or undignified words when the gonfalons went in their offertory procession (ASF, Pr, 105, fols. 166v–167v).

1416   27 Feb. (Berlingaccio). Youth Brigade of the Sphere, with a group of citizens, left the city to welcome back Florentine diplomats (DC, 255; TR, P, 306f., 395).

1417   Epiphany. The feast of the Magi was being done every three years on this day by the Confraternity of the Magi, which was meeting in the church of S. Marco (text of law in HR, 145).

1419   24 Feb. (Berlingaccio). Youth Brigade of the (Peach) Flower danced and did the equestrian *armeggeria* (DC, 255f.).

——   29 Dec. (Martyrdom of Thomas Becket). Feast of the same was done in the church of S. Maria Novella, probably at his altar under the screen, where one erected the scaffolding (*palchetto*) for feasts (DC, 265; P, fol. 113r; PL, 107; SMN, 121).

1421   2 and 3 Feb. (Sunday and Monday before Berlingaccio). Youth Brigade of the Parrot danced and did the *armeggeria* (DC, 276; GF, at date; TR, P, 225, 395).

1422   May 21 (Ascension). Its feast was well done in the church of the Carmine, and the writer hopes it will be done again (P, fol. 107r).

1424   9 Apr. (Sunday in Lent). Burning of the Vanities in the Piazza S. Croce held (BS [1424], 2:87).

1425   17 May (Ascension). Its feast was done in the church of the Carmine by its Confraternity of S. Maria delle Laudi and of S. Agnese, using a painting by Masolino (LT, 60).

1428   23 May (Pentecost). Feast of the Holy Spirit was being done each year on this day in the church of S. Spirito by its Confraternity of Lauds, called Of the Dove (*Colomba*) (ASF, Cat, 291, fol. 71v).

———   San Giovanni. The feast of the Magi was done by the Confraternity of the Magi within the ecclesiastical procession (and was thus attached to the friars of S. Marco). The Christ child was shown in a cloud (*nugola*) (P, fol. 122r, text in HR, 146).

1429   Epiphany. The feast of the Magi was performed by its Confraternity. It included the Journey of Joseph and Mary to Bethlehem and, as part of the retinue of the Magi, three giants, a wild man, and a wagon on which David killed Goliath (P, fol. 123v, text in HR, 146).

1430   12 Feb. (Third Sunday before Lent). The Brigade of the Squires of Fortune performed a joust (GF, at date).

1434–1436 or 1439–1443. A representation of the Nativity was done by the homonymous boys' confraternity in the church of S. Pancrazio, in the presence of Pope Eugenius IV (MG, 1:183).

1435   26 May (Ascension). In this year it is said that a figural representation of the mystery (of the Ascension) had been done in the church of the Carmine for many years by its Confraternity of Lauds of S. Maria and S. Agnese. Its members regularly invented new things to increase veneration for the feast (ASF, Pr, 126, fols. 195v–196v).

1439   25 Mar. (Annunciation). The representation of the same was done, it is said, in a friars' church dedicated to the Virgin;

———   14 May (Ascension). A representation of the Ascension was done, it is said, in the church of the Ascension (these churches are respectively the church of S. Felice and the church of the Carmine) (D'A, 1:253; LT, 56f., 60f., 65f.).

———   San Giovanni. Representations, within the ecclesiastical procession, of the Magi, the Nativity (star, shepherds, animals, crib), Crucifixion, Resurrection, and of St. George and the Dragon (GC, 19f.; GP, 104f.).

———   18 Oct. The first *caccia* documented in Florence: bulls and pigs were slaughtered by lions (G d'A, fol. 36v).

1443   Epiphany. Pope Eugenius IV after a cavalcade from S. Maria
        Novella consecrated the church of S. Marco. He departed from
        Florence the following day (G d'A, fol. 48r).

1445   Easter Monday. For many years the feast of the Annunciation
        had been done on this day in the church of S. Felice in Piazza by
        its Confraternity of the Blessed Virgin Mary of the Annuncia-
        tion. This group now received the same governmental subvention
        as did other confraternities for their feasts. In 1497 this group
        had the nickname the Jug (*Orciuolo*) (ASF, Pr, 135, fols. 162v–
        163r; D'A, 1:275).

———   Ascension. The feast of the Ascension was being done annually
        on this day in the church of the Carmine by its Confraternity of
        S. Maria delle Laudi and of S. Agnese, all of whose members
        were poor (ASF, Pr, 136, fols. 212v–213r).

1447   Epiphany. The feast of the Magi was being done on this day
        every five years by long custom, and it was done this day (govern-
        mental deliberations in HR, 113; G d'A, fol. 56v; ML, 173).

———   March and May. The *cero* of the Confraternity of (the Empress)
        S. Maria of the Snow in the parish of S. Ambrogio was shown
        throughout the parish in March of each year to raise funds to fi-
        nance the annual journey of the confraternity to Our Lady of Im-
        pruneta in May, where the *cero* was gifted her (ASF, Cap, 606,
        fols. 40rv; V-M, 3:203; TR, P, 405).

1448 or before. Epiphany. In the feast of the Magi there was a wagon pre-
        pared by one Michelino, who sought out the hapless (fools?) to
        ride in it (B, 228).

1450   Carnival (?). The representation of Abraham and Isaac by Feo
        Belcari was presented for the first time in the church of Cestello
        in 1449 Florentine style (D'A, 1:160). (Since non-calendrical rep-
        resentations were usually done during the Carnival period, this
        play was probably done in 1450 modern style, before 18 Feb.).

1451   Epiphany. Feast of the Magi (text in HR, 136).

———   4 Mar. (Berlingaccio). A contemporary bought a carnival mask
        for his children (G d'A, fol. 64v).

———   San Giovanni. There were many beautiful examples and edifices
        (G d'A, fol. 65r).

———   29 Aug. (Decollation of St. John the Baptist). A representation
        of the same was done in the meadow of the Gate of Justice (i.e.,

the place of public executions), with 5000 or more spectators (G d'A, fol. 65v).

1451-1452. In a writing probably done during Carnival 1452, it is said that the Florentines customarily pull a triumphal wagon full of the insane through the streets during feasts, a most pleasing spectacle. Lorenzo Valla should be elected the Prince of the Fools and Insane (BP, 1:03; TR, P, 255).

1452   2 Feb. (Candlemas). The feast of the Sepulchre or Resurrection was done by the Company of the Armenians of the homonymous church at the cathedral, in the presence of the emperor. Part of the apparatus was known as the Monument or the *Madia* (ASF, CCO, 51, fols. 47v, 48r, 57r; TR, P, 403, 508).

——   San Giovanni. There were many edifices and beautiful processions (G d'A, fol. 67r).

——   24 Aug. (St. Bartholomew). A resemblance of the passion of that saint was done, and was well attended (G d'A, fol. 68r).

1454   San Giovanni. The edifices were severed from the ecclesiastical procession, and a separate parade of the edifices was instituted (PM, 172ff.; TR, P, 255f.).

(The second major description, important because of its complete list of edifices and partial list of confraternities, as well as because it lists cavalcades distinctly):

The Angelic Battle, in which Michael drives Lucifer from heaven; the story of Adam and Eve; Moses Receives the Law, with a cavalcade of the Florentine Jewish community; Sibyls and Prophets, including Hermes Trismegistus; the Annunciation; a cavalcade of Octavian and the Sibyl; the Temple of Peace, an edifice at the base of the edifice of the Nativity, to which the Sibyl points, prophesying Jesus to Octavian; a magnificent and triumphal temple as an edifice for the Magi, within which is another, octagonal temple, decorated with the seven virtues, which is the stage for the representation of Herod; the cavalcade of the Three Kings who come to this edifice to see Herod (and presumably continue to the edifice of the Nativity) and to give gifts to a cavalcade of knights to Pilate guarding Christ's sepulchre; the Sepulchre; the Limbo, from which rise the Old Testament fathers; the Paradise, where the fathers go; (the cavalcade of) the apostles and the Marys; the Ascension; royal cavalcade and retinue pertinent to the Living and the Dead; the Living and the Dead; the Last Judgment.

In addition to the Jewish community, there were four (identifiable) boys' confraternities marching in front and in back of (and thus presumably participating in) the Angelic Battle (PM, 172ff.; TR, P, 256, 376).

The artist Antonio Manetti made a wagon with four bronzes for this feast (*Ricordanze* of Maso di Bartolommeo, reference furnished me by Harriet Caplow).

——— 25 June (S. Lò). The feast of the miracle of (the church of) S. Ambrogio was celebrated by the whole guild of notaries (PM, 174).

1458 4 June (Sunday after Corpus Christi). The feast of the miracle of the Corpus Christi was done at the (residence of the) guild of notaries (G d'A, fol. 73r).

——— San Giovanni. A tightrope walker performed in the Piazza della Signoria (G d'A, fol. 73r).

1459 25 Apr. (Entry of Pope Pius II, probably the occasion of the following processions, edifices, representations, and devotions):

The Zampillo (fountain), i.e., Confraternity of S. Giovanni Gualberto, meeting in the church of S. Trinita; St. Bartholomew; the Holy Ghost (i.e., Pentecost); the Nichio (shell); St. Nicholas of Tolentino; the Angel Raphael (and) the crib (*chapannucia*) (i.e., the boys' confraternity of the Nativity); St. Rossore; the Trinity; Jesus and the Magi; the Crucifix and St. Lawrence; the Gazza (Magpie); St. Sebastian; the Armenians; Camaldoli; the Freccia (arrow); the Living and the Dead; and St. George (DB, fol. 23r).

——— 29 Apr. Joust in Piazza S. Croce, where viewing spaces were for sale;

——— 30 Apr. Dance in the Mercato Nuovo;

——— May Day. *Caccia* held in the Piazza della Signoria, where places were sold; *Armeggeria* done in the Via Larga in front of the Medici Palace, with a Triumph of Wisdom, and a Triumph of the Planet traversing the Third Sphere so as to rule it (G d'A, fol. 76r; CG, 20:369ff., copied from P. fol. 183r; LC, 77; R, lxxxix; LL, 345f.; ML, 177f.; FF; HR, S, with extracts from a ms. whose still-inedited portion (fols. 35r, 74r) contains the references to the Triumphs).

——— 2 May. A feast of the Ascension was done in the church of the Carmine (letter of Galeazzo Maria Sforza made available by HR., dated 3 May).

1460 May. A representation of the Descent of the Holy Spirit was done at (the church of) S. Maria Novella at the behest of the government (D'A, 1: 271).

1461 San Giovanni. Two edifices were made for the feast by Giuliano da Maiano, and three whales or dolphins, and the evangelical symbols, were worked on by Neri di Bicci (NB, 163f.).

1463 Carnival period. A signore of the Corso dei Tintori was appointed for Carnival. The government sent its trumpets to serenade (*sonare*) this signore (ASF, AD, 292, at date).

1464 14 Feb. (Carnival). A courtly snowball fight and an *armeggeria* with a Triumph of the Bleeding Heart Aflame were staged (DL, DO, 200f., 237f.; GP, 40–44).

——— 10 May (Ascension) (or a previous Ascension). A verse by Feo Belcari, written for the *festaioli* of the feast of the Ascension (in the Carmine), urged Cosimo de' Medici, *pater patriae*, to attend (LA, 227).

1465 23 May (Ascension). This feast was being put on by the few poor youths of the Confraternity of the Lauds of S. Maria and S. Agnese in the church of the Carmine (ASF, Pr, 156, fols. 255v–256r).

——— San Giovanni. Pleasure wagons were located between the gonfalons going to their offering (SA, 425f.; TR, P, 255).

1467 A facetious diplomat asks for the umbrella or the Triumph of Aemilius (Paulus) or of Camillus (PL, 64).

——— 25 July (St. James Major). A representation of the martyrdom of St. James was done at (the church of) S. Jacopo tra le Fosse (G d'A, fol. 89r).

1468 19 Apr. (Easter Tuesday). The once-customary mystery of the Annunciation had not been done for some years, and the government had stopped attending. Now this feast of the church of S. Felice was being done again on this day (ASF, Pr, 159, fols. 4v–5v).

1469 Epiphany. The feast of the Magi was performed by the Confraternity of the Magi (the last known representation. A contemporary verse indicates that the confraternity may have stopped receiving communal subventions) (HR, 148–151; LA, 122f.).

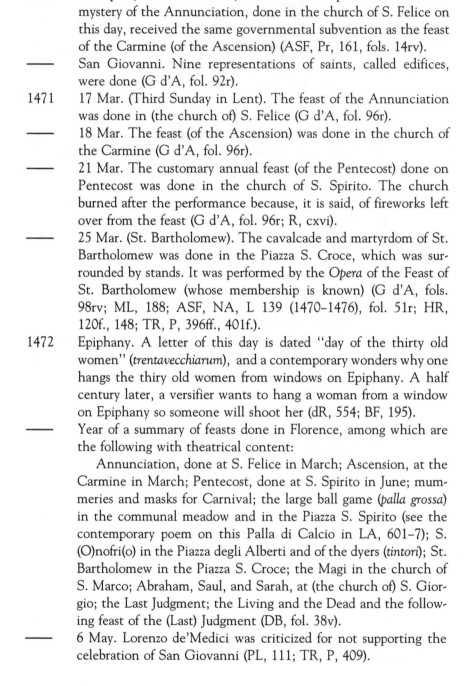

1470   29 Apr. (Octave of Easter). The annual representation of the
        mystery of the Annunciation, done in the church of S. Felice on
        this day, received the same governmental subvention as the feast
        of the Carmine (of the Ascension) (ASF, Pr, 161, fols. 14rv).

——   San Giovanni. Nine representations of saints, called edifices,
        were done (G d'A, fol. 92r).

1471   17 Mar. (Third Sunday in Lent). The feast of the Annunciation
        was done in (the church of) S. Felice (G d'A, fol. 96r).

——   18 Mar. The feast (of the Ascension) was done in the church of
        the Carmine (G d'A, fol. 96r).

——   21 Mar. The customary annual feast (of the Pentecost) done on
        Pentecost was done in the church of S. Spirito. The church
        burned after the performance because, it is said, of fireworks left
        over from the feast (G d'A, fol. 96r; R, cxvi).

——   25 Mar. (St. Bartholomew). The cavalcade and martyrdom of St.
        Bartholomew was done in the Piazza S. Croce, which was sur-
        rounded by stands. It was performed by the *Opera* of the Feast of
        St. Bartholomew (whose membership is known) (G d'A, fols.
        98rv; ML, 188; ASF, NA, L 139 (1470–1476), fol. 51r; HR,
        120f., 148; TR, P, 396ff., 401f.).

1472   Epiphany. A letter of this day is dated "day of the thirty old
        women" (*trentavecchiarum*), and a contemporary wonders why one
        hangs the thiry old women from windows on Epiphany. A half
        century later, a versifier wants to hang a woman from a window
        on Epiphany so someone will shoot her (dR, 554; BF, 195).

——   Year of a summary of feasts done in Florence, among which are
        the following with theatrical content:

        Annunciation, done at S. Felice in March; Ascension, at the
        Carmine in March; Pentecost, done at S. Spirito in June; mum-
        meries and masks for Carnival; the large ball game (*palla grossa*)
        in the communal meadow and in the Piazza S. Spirito (see the
        contemporary poem on this Palla di Calcio in LA, 601-7); S.
        (O)nofri(o) in the Piazza degli Alberti and of the dyers (*tintori*); St.
        Bartholomew in the Piazza S. Croce; the Magi in the church of
        S. Marco; Abraham, Saul, and Sarah, at (the church of) S. Gior-
        gio; the Last Judgment; the Living and the Dead and the follow-
        ing feast of the (Last) Judgment (DB, fol. 38v).

——   6 May. Lorenzo de'Medici was criticized for not supporting the
        celebration of San Giovanni (PL, 111; TR, P, 409).

—— San Giovanni. There were several representations of beautiful edifices (G d'A, fol. 102v).

1473 San Giovanni. There were seven processional triumphs:

Moses receives the Law; the Annunciation; the Nativity; the Baptism of Christ; Limbo, the Liberation of the (Old Testament) Fathers; the Resurrection; Pentecost and the Assumption (text in D'A, 1:273f.; G d'A, fol. 105r).

—— 1 Aug. (Octave of St. James Major). A representation of St. James in front of the church of S. Jacopo tra le Fosse was done by certain youths of the company (of that church) (G d'A, fol. 105v).

1474 17 Feb. (Berlingaccio). A person made a payment to the Signore of Carnival of the Servants of the Signoria (of Florence) (G d'A, fol. 107v).

—— 20 Feb. Some feasts of mummeries were done, which were not as beautiful as past ones (G d'A, fol. 107v).

1475 12 Feb. A German entered Florence with a *tavola* similar to an altar retable, but with weights (*archipendoli*) which made the Magi go to offer, and St. George kill the Dragon, and other miraculous and beautiful things. People paid four quatrins to see it (G d'A, fol. 111r; CA, 62).

—— San Giovanni. Third major description of the feast speaks of the sacred games which included the Annunciation, Limbo, Resurrection, and the (Last) Judgment. It has the best description of the *giganti, spiritelli,* and *fauni* (CP, 224).

—— 22 July. Feast of St. Mary Magdalene was celebrated as usual in the Palace of the Podestà (Bargello). (The only possible indication of a representation is) the foot races of boys, and of girls (G d'A, fol. 113v).

—— 12 Nov. Lorenzo de' Medici held a *caccia* of leopards about seven miles outside Florence on the road to Impruneta, with some 1500 people present (G d'A, fol. 114r).

1476 Carnival period (27 February or before). Terence's *Andria* was performed three times in Florence by adolescent mimers who had been students of Giorgio Antonio Vespucci: first before Vespucci, then in the Medici palace, then before the Signoria of Florence (in the Palazzo della Signoria). Though adolescents, their head, eyes, hands, and feet moved with their voices in time, their faces and gestures fit the words in an elegant performance (MC, xxi-xxii; LT, 72).

——   San Giovanni, Due to the fear of plague, there were no edifices
        and few of the customary ceremonies (G d'A, fol. 115r).

——   19 Aug. The comedy *Licinia* had been prepared by the boys of
        the Scuola Eugeniana, which was directed by Piero Domizi. A po-
        tential site for its performances was the church of Ognissanti.
        Domizi's group was competing with other such groups for pa-
        tronage (LT, 72).

——   31 Aug. (S. Giuliano). The commune of Poggibonsi presented its
        tribute to Florence. Its embassy led an ass loaded with fish up the
        steps of the Palazzo della Signoria to the Hall. There they fed the
        ass from a silver basin, as they do every year (G d'A, fol. 116r).

1477   5 June (Corpus Christi). There was a beautiful feast and proces-
        sions and a representation at (the church of) S. Maria Novella (G
        d'A, fol. 118v).

——   29 June (Sts. Peter and Paul). A representation of the deaths of
        Sts. Peter and Paul was done in the Loggia of the Signoria (of
        Florence), with a great multitude of spectators. This representa-
        tion was a great demonstration of the genius of the person who
        prepared it (G d'A, fols. 119rv).

1478   Carnival. Writing 12 Feb. 1479, Piero Domizi notes that last year
        Lorenzo de' Medici attended a performance of Terence in the
        church of Ognissanti (DL, 172f.).

——   5 July. (The Pazzi Conspiracy had not caused the cancellation of
        the feast of San Giovanni, but) parts of it had been postponed
        until certain foreign dignitaries arrived. On this date certain
        feasts or representations of some saints were done, which were
        called *nuvole* (G d'A, fol. 126r; V–M, 3:200f.).

1479   12 Feb. Piero Domizi asked that the Scuola Eugeniana be per-
        mitted to perform a play of Terence in the Medici Palace (DL,
        DI, 172f.; LT, 72).

1480   14 May (Sunday before Ascension). The first documented As-
        sumption: at the church of the Carmine a representation of the
        Virgin Mary when she went to paradise was done. She gave her
        belt to St. Thomas (G d'A, fol. 136r).

1485   The King of the Millstone incorporated as the Confraternity of
        the Resurrection, meeting in the church of the Armenians. Its
        kings and barons, who were accustomed to making edifices for
        San Giovanni (i.e., the Monument or *Madia* of the Sepulchre,
        Limbo, and Resurrection), agreed to make them only for the prof-

it of this confraternity when, that is, edifices were again used on San Giovanni. Other feasts of the King of the Millstone, such as gifts to (Our Lady of) Impruneta or (Our Lady of) Fiesole (i.e., Primerana), would not be charged to the confraternity (texts in TR, P, 406ff.).

—— Several of the extant Carnival Songs (*canti carnascialeschi*) are referred to in an *incunabulum* of this year (MP, 117).

1488 12 May. The *Menaechmi* of Plautus was performed, probably by the boys' School of (the church of) S. Lorenzo (LT, 72).

—— San Giovanni. Six edifices or triumphs, marvelous and divine works, were done, the first such performance, it is said, for more than ten years (FA, 2:388; RT, 243f.; ML, 197f.; LL, 55, TR, P, 450f.).

1489 May Day. On its vigil, the King of (the neighborhood of) Camaldoli received things in loan from Lorenzo de' Medici for its celebration (ASF, AD, at the date).

—— 24 Aug. (St. Bartholomew). The representation of St. Bartholomew's passion and miracles was scheduled for performance on this day. This first performance of the feast since 1471 was to be done by the mostly youthful citizens of the Confraternity of St. Bartholomew, which met in the living quarters of S. Croce (ASF, Pr, 180, fols. 26v–27r).

c. 1490 The feast of Pentecost was performed in (the church of) the Carmine for the first time (the church of S. Spirito having burned). The *garzonetto* Piero di Lorenzo de' Medici wanted it done. It pleased no one (RT, 276).

1490 21 Feb. (Carnival Sunday). The Company of the Star, headed by one Mariottazio, did a large mummery with seven Triumphs of the Seven Planets, with a thousand beautiful things and inventions from the hand of the master (MM, 39).

—— 22 and 23 Feb. Medici confidants were masked in a house with lovely dames. The writer refers to the songs of the *prima cavalcata* (probably the triumphs of 21 Feb.), written by Lorenzo de' Medici. Though these songs were just Carnival songs, the invention shown in them was new and admirable (MM, 38).

1491 Carnival period. The Judgment of Solomon was performed by young monks of the monastery of S. Maria degli Angeli, in the same. The play was written in Latin by a contemporary priest (SJ, D, 84f.).

——   17 Feb. (Second Day of Lent). Lorenzo de' Medici's representation of Sts. John and Paul was performed by the boys' Confraternity of the Vangelista in their meeting hall (MB, 16f.).

——   San Giovanni. Edifices of the Annunciation and of the Monument were well done. Three or more others were badly done; the
Triumph of Aemilius Paulus, with fifteen wagons and five squad-
rons of riders, was outstandingly beautiful; tightrope walkers in
the Piazza della Signoria amused bystanders (RT, 271f.).

1492   1 Mar. (Berlingaccio). Lorenzo de' Medici was seen at the windows (of the Medici palace) with the hood (*capperuccia*) on his
head, watching the mummers pass by (MM, 39).

——   Carnival period. A *caccia* of lions and bears had not materialized
because of Lorenzo de' Medici's gout. It had been prepared by the
Company of the Star for the Piazza S. Croce (MM, 39).

——   A Latin history of monastic apostasy from the Camaldolan to the
Cistercian order was performed in the monastery of S. Maria
degli Angeli (SJ, D, 85).

——   17 Mar. (Second Sunday in Lent). A procession like that for San
Giovanni celebrated the conquest of Granada (news of which arrived in Florence 5 Jan.; LL, 62). (This is the probable date of) a
cavalcade of feigned ambassadors from Spain who sang of the
conquest (RT, 278; TR, P, 416).

1493   28 May. Burning of the Vanities was done by fra Bernardino of
Feltre at the gate of the friary of S. Salvatore (RT, 282; R, cl;
MB, 18).

——   San Giovanni. In preparation for the feast, its *festaioli* commissioned its apparatus, among which were the *girandole*, charged
to Filippo di ser Giovanni, woodworker, called La Pippa; two *giganti*, charged to Francesco di Benedetto Pacini, called Chazata,
and to Nunziata di Antonio, painter (called Il Nunziata: V-M,
6:535; FS, 508), who was to make a St. Christopher, and to Salimbene, who would carry it; *spiritelli*, charged to Santi, turner; a
wagon or triumph of the buffoons, charged to Francesco di Piero
de' Baldovini; the wagon of the triumph, charged to Biagio; and
the following edifices: (1) the Annunciation, charged to Matteo
di Giovanni, weaver of brocades, (2) the San Giovanni, charged
to Bartolomeo di Olivante, woodworker, (3) the Nativity, charged
to Guglielmo di Carlo, woodworker, and (4) the Resurrection,
charged to Bartolomeo di Antonio, goldsmith, and Jacopo di Antonio, *cimatore* (ASF, MC, 2088).

1494   16 Nov. (Sunday, the day before the entry of Charles VIII of France). The edifice, also called the *nuvola*, of the Annunciation, was pulled through the city (LL, 79).

——   17 Nov. The edifice of the Annunciation was in the Piazza de' Frescobaldi, and Filippino Lippi's Triumph of Peace was in the Piazza della Signoria, as part of the king's itinerary (BE, 111 ff.; MBon, 35ff.).

——   23 Nov. The feast of the Annunciation was done in the church of S. Felice (LL, 83f.).

1495   5 June. A Savonarolan procession was arranged according to the order of David's Translation of the Ark (S, Salmi, 1:289–305).

1496   27 March (Palm Sunday). In procession, the Florentines throw palms and their own clothes before a painting of Christ (entering Jerusalem) on an ass (BenG, 192).

1496–1498 With its additional stands, the cathedral was said to be "like a theatre" by eye-witnesses (references in TR, P, 479f.).

——   Carnivals. The outings to Fiesole and to (the nunnery of) S. Gaggio, where in the past boys did representations and other feasts, were avoided by the Savonarolan boys (PB, 122).

1497   7 Feb. (Carnival Tuesday). Burning of the Vanities (see 1498, 28 Feb.).

1498   Epiphany. A representation of the Magi and the Nativity was done in the church of S. Marco by its friars (TR, P, 189f.).

——   26 Feb. (Carnival Monday). The Brigade of the Compagnacci did masks and farces during its banquet. The Brigade of the Ermellini (Ermines) visited the Compagnacci with a triumph and a gift (SJ, Q, 3:57).

——   28 Feb. (Ash Wednesday). Burning of the Vanities (sources in TR, A, 261f.; diagram of the pyre in BH, 91).

——   May Day. Customarily a Madonna was created to lead the girls of tender age during May. On this day, some thirty pasta-makers, dyers, and purgers between 30 and 35 years of age dressed up like girls and followed their own Madonna, mocking the Savonarolans with songs perhaps written by Il Travaglino or Il Ceo (FS, 495f.).

——   Christmas. The youth Brigade of the Compagnacci desecrated the churches of SS. Annunziata, S. Spirito, S. Maria Novella, and the cathedral. They led a horse into the latter, raced it about, then slaughtered it, in one account on the front steps of the cathedral, in the other in front of the palace of Lorenzo di Pierfrancesco de' Medici. The latter fled the city along with Guido Antonio Vespucci, before whose home the Compagnacci had held a mock trial for lese majesty and burned him in effigy. From a wagon of manure (gathered in the cathedral?), the group walled up the residence of the Milanese ambassador (CG, 21:135f.; SMD, 2:378; DF, 96f.).

1499   12 Feb. (Carnival). Fifteen pyres in as many parts of the city were brought together into two masses, defended with rocks by two lower-class brigades from the Canto alla Coculia and the Ponte alla Carraia. During the day, the pyres were set afire by the government and the rock fight stopped, thus avoiding a disaster that night (CG, 21:136f.).

Abbreviations

AP   *Anon. Panciatichi*, BNF, fondo Panciatichi, ms. 158 (see now *Alle bocche della piazza: Diario di anonimo fiorentino (1382–1401)*, ed. A. Molho and F. Sznura (Florence, 1986).

ASF   *Archivio di Stato, Firenze*
      AD   *Acquisti e Doni*
      Cap   *Capitoli, Compagnie Religiose Soppresse*
      Cat   *Catasto*
      CCO   *Camera del Comune, Onoranze*
      MC   *Monte Comune*
      NA   *Notarile Antecosimiano*
      Pr   *Provvisioni*

ASI   *Archivio Storico Italiano*

B   Burchiello, *I Sonetti* (Milan, 1940)

BE   Borsook, E., "Decor in Florence for the Entry of Charles VIII of France," *Mitteilungen des Kunsthistorischen Institutes in Florenz* 10 (1961)

BenG   Benivieni, Girolamo, *Commento*, in L. Manzoni, ed., *Libro di Carnevale dei secoli XV e XVI* (Bologna, 1881)

BF   Berni, Francesco, *Rime* (Turin, 1969)

BG   Bacchi, G., "La Compagnia di Santa Maria delle Laudi e di Santa Agnese nel Carmine di Firenze," *Rivista Storica Carmelitana* 3 (1931)

BH   Bredekamp, H., "Renaissancekultur als 'Hölle': Savonarolas Verbrennungen der Eitelkeiten," in M. Warnke, ed., *Die Zerstörung des Kunstwerks* (Munich, 1973)

BNF   *Biblioteca Nazionale, Firenze*

BP   Bracciolini, Poggio, *Opera* (Basel, 1538)

BS   Bernardino of Siena, *Le Prediche Volgari* (of Florence, 1424) (Pistoia, 1934)

CA   Chastel, A., *Marsile Ficin et l'Art* (Geneva, 1975)

CG   Cambi, Giovanni, *Istorie,* in DET

CP   Cennini, Piero, in G. Maricini, "Il Bel S. Giovanni e le feste patronali di Firenze descritte nel 1475 da Piero Cennini," *Rivista d'Arte* 6 (1909): 185–227

D'A   D'Ancona, A., *Origini del Teatro Italiano* (Turin, 1891)

DB   Dei, Benedetto, *Cronica,* in ASF, *Manoscritti,* 119 (see now *La Cronica: dall'anno 1400 all'anno 1500,* ed. R. Barducci [Florence, 1984]).

DC   Del Corazza, Bartolomeo, "Diario Fiorentino," *ASI* ser. 5, 14 (1894)

D d'A *Diario d'Anonimo Fiorentino dall'anno 1358 al 1389,* in *Cronache dei secoli XIII e XIV,* ed. A. Gherardi (Florence, 1876)

DET   *Delizie degli Eruditi Toscani* (Florence, 1770–1789)

DF   Dundes, A., and Falassi, A., *La Terra in Piazza. An Interpretation of the Palio of Siena* (Berkeley, 1975)

DG   Dati, Gregorio, *Istorie di Firenze* (Florence, 1735)

DL,Di Del Lungo, I., "Di altre recitazioni di commedie latine in Firenze nel secolo XV," *ASI* 23 (1876)

DL,DO Del Lungo, I., *La Donna Fiorentina del Buon Tempo Antico* (Florence, 1906)

dR   De Robertis, D., "Supplementi all'Epistolario del Pulci," *Giornale Storico della Letteratura Italiana* 134 (1957)

DT   Della Tosa, Simone, *Annali,* in *Cronichette Antiche di Vari Scrittori del Buon Secolo della Lingua Toscana,* ed. D. Manni (Florence, 1733)

FA   Fabroni, A., *Laurentii Medicis Magnifici Vita* (Pisa, 1784)

FF   *Le Feste di Firenze del 1459,* RIS, n.s. 27, pt. I

FS   Filipepi, Simone, *Cronaca,* in P. Villari and E. Casanova, eds., *Scelta di prediche e scritti di fra Girolamo Savonarola con nuovi documenti intorno alla sua vita* (Florence, 1898)

GC   Guasti, C., ed., *Le Feste di S. Giovanni Battista in Firenze descritte in prosa e in rima da contemporanei* (Florence, 1884)

G d'A Giusto d'Anghiari, *Memorie, 1437–1482,* BNF, fondo principale II ii. 127.

GF   Giovanni, Francesco di Tommaso, *Ricordanze,* copied by C. Car-
         nesecchi in ASF, AD, 292

GG   Gori, G., "Prefazione e note a due documenti sull'Eccidio di Ce-
         sena del 1377," *ASI,* n.s. 8, pt. 2 (1858)

GP   Gori, P., *Le Feste Fiorentine attraverso i secoli. Le Feste per San
         Giovanni* (Florence, 1926)

HR   Hatfield, R., "The Compagnia de' Magi," *Journal of the Warburg
         and Courtauld Institutes* 33 (1970)

HR, S   Hatfield, R., "Some Unknown Descriptions of the Medici Palace
         in 1459," *Art Bulletin* 52 (1970)

LA   Lanza, A., ed., *Lirici Toscani del '400,* vol. 1 (Rome, 1973)

LC   *The Libro Cerimoniale of the Florentine Republic by Francesco Fila-
         rete and Angelo Manfidi,* ed. R. Trexler (Geneva, 1978) (from
         ASF, *Carte di Corredo,* 61)

LL   Landucci, Luca, *Diario Fiorentino dal 1450 al 1516* (Florence,
         1969)

LT   *Il Luogo Teatrale a Firenze,* ed. M. Fabri et al. (Milan, 1975)

MB   Masi, Bartolomeo, *Ricordanze di Bartolomeo Masi, calderaio Fioren-
         tino dal 1478 al 1526* (Florence, 1906)

MBon   Mitchell, B., *Italian Civic Pageantry in the High Renaissance. A De-
         scriptive Bibliography* (Florence, 1979)

MC   Marchesi, C., ed., *Documenti inediti sugli Umanisti Fiorentini della
         seconda metà del secolo XV* (Catania, 1899)

MD   Manni, D., *Osservazioni Istoriche sopra i Sigilli Antichi* (Florence,
         1770)

MG   Monti, G., *Le Confraternite Medievali dell'Alta e Media Italia* (Ven-
         ice, 1927)

ML   Morelli, Lionardo, *Cronaca,* in DET, 19

MM   Martelli, M., *Studi Laurenziani* (Florence, 1965)

MP   Minio-Paluello, M., "Firenze, Novembre 1515. Un' occasione in
         cui la storia detta il Canto alla Festa," *Quaderni di Teatro* 2.7
         (1980)

MR   Malaspini, Ricordano, *Storia Fiorentina* (Rome, 1976)

NB   Neri di Bicci, *Le Ricordanze,* ed. B. Santi (Pisa, 1976)

NM   Naddo da Montecatini, *Memorie Storiche,* in DET, 18

NN   Newbigin, Nerida, *Feste d'Oltrarno: Plays in Churches in Fifteenth-
         Century Florence,* 2 vols. (Florence, 1996)

P   Pietrobuoni, Paolo di Matteo, *Priorista,* BNF, *Conventi Religiosi
         Soppressi,* ms. C-4-895

PA   Pucci, Antonio, *Centiloquio,* and "Mercato Vecchio," in DET

PB   Pseudo-Burlamacchi, *La Vita del beato Ieronimo Savonarola, scritta da un Anonimo del secolo XVI e già attribuita a fra Pacifico Burlamacchi,* ed. P. Ginori Conti (Florence, 1937)

PL   Pulci, Luigi, *Lettere* (Lucca, 1886)

PM   Palmieri, Matteo, *Historia Fiorentina,* in RIS, n.s. 26, pt. 1

PP   Pieri, Paolino, *Cronica di Paolino Pieri Fiorentino delle Cose d'Italia dall'anno 1080 all'anno 1305* (Rome, 1755)

R   Rinuccini, *Ricordi Storici,* ed. G. Aiazzi (Florence, 1840)

RIS   *Rerum Italicarum Scriptores* (Città di Castello, 1900–)

RT   Rossi, Tribaldo de', *Ricordanze,* in DET 23

S   Savonarola, Girolamo, *Prediche sopra i Salmi* (Rome, 1969)

SA   Strozzi, Alessandra, *Lettere di una Gentildonna Fiorentina del secolo XV ai figliuoli esuli,* ed. C. Guasti (Florence, 1877)

SF   Sacchetti, Franco, *Il Trecentonovelle* (Florence, 1946)

SJ,D   Schnitzer, J., *Peter Delfin, General des Camaldulenserordens (1444–1525)* (Munich, 1926)

SJ,Q   Schnitzer, J., ed., *Quellen und Forschungen zur Geschichte Savonarolas,* vol. 3 (Munich, 1904) (*Storia* of Bartolomeo Cerretani; see now *Storia Fiorentina,* ed. G. Berti [Florence, 1994])

SM   Stefani, Marchionne di Coppo, *Cronaca Fiorentina,* in RIS, n.s. 30, pt. 1

SMD   Sanuto, Marino, *I Diarii* (Venice, 1879–1903)

SMN   S. Maria Novella, "Chronica," *Analecta Sacri Ordinis Fratrum Praedicatorum* 12 (1915–1916)

TR, A   Trexler, R., "Ritual in Florence: Adolescence and Salvation in the Renaissance," in *The Pursuit of Holiness in Late Medieval and Renaissance Religion,* ed. C. Trinkaus and H. Oberman (Leiden, 1974)

TR, M   Trexler, R., "The Magi Enter Florence. The Ubriachi of Florence and Venice," *Studies in Medieval and Renaissance History,* n.s. 1 (1978)

TR, P   Trexler, R., *Public Life in Renaissance Florence* (New York, 1980; repr. Ithaca, 1991)

VG   Villani, Giovanni, *Cronica di Giovanni, Matteo, e Filippo Villani* (Trieste, 1857)

V-M   Vasari, Giorgio, *Opere,* ed. G. Milanesi (Florence, 1973)

From the Mouths of Babes: Christianization by Children in Sixteenth-Century New Spain*

The Spanish [soldiers] could have ... attained heaven if ... they had killed the old men and women so that those of the new generation lost all knowledge of the old [religion].[1]

In this way the Indians convert to the Catholic faith. Girls learn the first rudiments of the faith from honorable women, and the boys from religious men. Later [the girls and the boys] teach their gentile parents what they have learned. Thus it seems likely that Daniel was speaking of them [when he said:] 'From the mouths of babes ...'[2]

---

* This essay appeared previously in abridged form in *Religious Organization and Religious Experience*, ed. J. Davis, Association of Social Anthropologists Monograph 21 (London and New York, 1982), 115–36, and in R. Trexler, *Church and Community 1200–1600. Studies in the History of Florence and New Spain* (Rome, 1987), 549–73.

[1] D. Duran, O.P., *Historia de las Indias de Nueva España e Islas de la Tierra Firme*, 2 vols. (Mexico City, 1967), 1:79.

[2] Archbishop Zumárraga in 1531, cited in G. Mendieta, *Historia eclesiastica indiana* (Mexico City, 1971), 638.

ANTHROPOLOGISTS AND HISTORIANS HAVE USUALLY considered an Indian tribe of sixteenth-century Mexico as a social and cultural unit, and almost uniformly, that unit's social relations have been viewed as intratribally non-conflictual. Generational and gender divisions within the tribe have been studied even less than economic or class tensions, so that if scholars have occasionally used the established topos of the imperial power seducing certain classes among the colonialized, they have not done the same thing with, for example, the generations. The fashion in which imperial Spain appealed to the boys of the Mexican peninsula has gone largely unstudied because the boys have not been viewed as in conflict with their parents.[3] It is fair to say that scholars still consider the Spanish Conquest as pitting only two social and cultural units against each other, Spain and some particular tribe.

The purpose of this paper is to study the widely-known but usually unevaluated fact that Spanish missionaries indoctrinated the young people of New Spain; the corollary fact necessary to such an evaluation is, we shall show, that the European clergy pitted these boys against their fathers and elders. Departing from Fanon's and Mannoni's studies of the effects of modern imperialism on native people conceived as internally conflictual groups, I want to show that the strategy chosen to impose Christian norms on the Indians had a significant impact on their social structures and important effects as well on the differential experience of Christianity by the elders and the young of native societies.[4]

At one point in his learned if Christophilic work on *The Spiritual Conquest of Mexico*, Robert Ricard off-handedly denounced the "disagreeable" fact that Indian children commonly testified against their fathers in inquisitorial proceedings. Ricard did not go on to explain why that was so; the testimony of even pre-adolescent boys against their elders remained, apparently, an aberration in the otherwise adult struggle between two patronal societies.[5] Not so. In the early Spanish Conquest, the liminal group of the Indian young crossed or were carried over tribal borders and found new

---

[3] See for instance J.-M. Kobayashi, *La educación como conquista (empresa franciscana en México)* (Mexico City, 1974).

[4] F. Fanon, *The Wretched of the Earth* (New York, 1991); O. Mannoni, *Prospero and Caliban: The Psychology of Colonization* (Ann Arbor, 1990).

[5] R. Ricard, *La "Conquête spirituelle" du Mexique* (Paris, 1933), 320–22. Examples are in R. Greenleaf, *Zumárraga and the Mexican Inquisition* (Washington, DC, 1961), 70; *Procesos de Indios idolatras y hechiceros*, ed. L. González Obregón (Mexico City, 1912), 163–64, 210, 225.

fathers among the priests, and the process by which such liminal groups do cross borders is important to the study of imperialism.[6]

In Mexican historiography, such problems have generally been obviated by simply casting the Indian nations as children and the conquerors as adults. Reversing that ideology, Charles Gibson has noted that the Tlaxcalan sources emphasize the youthfulness of Christianity in an Indian Old World of evil.[7] This scientific observation will serve as our point of departure. We shall first examine the European background to the friars' generational strategy during the evangelization, then we shall approach the facts of the utilization of Indian boys in the conversion: their own indoctrination, and their own evangelical activism. Our tasks are twofold: first to understand the Spanish clergy's policies, and then to better comprehend the impact of this youthful Christianization upon the Indian boys, and upon their fathers, in early colonial Mexico. The effects of this children's crusade upon the modern Mexican *mentalité* is another story.[8]

European Children as a New World

> How this Conversion of the Indians was Carried Out by Means of Children, in Keeping with the Talent which God gave them.[9]

Such is a chapter title in the *Histories of New Spain* by the Franciscan friars Mendieta and Torquemada writing at the end of the sixteenth and in the early seventeenth centuries, and we must ask what in their European backgrounds, and in that of their less exuberant mentor fray Toribio Motolinía writing in 1540, explains this paean to child genius.[10] There are two problems. We should first ask the clerical background for such humility in giving Indian children and not only the friars credit for the conversions, since the primary purpose of all three men's *Histories* was to immortalize the clergy's role. Secondly, we wonder whence in European

---

[6] V. Turner, *The Ritual Process* (Chicago, 1969).

[7] C. Gibson, *Tlaxcala in the Sixteenth Century* (Stanford, 1952), 37.

[8] For which, see J. Lafaye, *Quetzalcóatl et Guadalupe: La formation de la conscience nationale au Mexique (1531–1813)* (Paris, 1974).

[9] Mendieta, *Historia*, 221; J. de Torquemada, *Monarquia Indiana*, 3 vols. (Mexico City, 1969), 3:33.

[10] Toribio Motolinía, *Memoriales e Historia de los Indios de la Nueva España* (Madrid, 1970), 16 in the *Memoriales*, and in a different tone in the *Historia*, 320–22.

culture came the conviction that it was proper for a child to change his father. Our quote makes clear that the friars intended to transform the present Indian father, and not merely wait for Indian boys to inherit the future. Since in European culture it was considered natural for the father to instruct the son and not the other way around, and since none of the evangelists openly adopted the stance that the end of Indian conversion justified the means of youthful subversion, a justification for the use of subversive children must be sought partly in European developments.[11]

The first of these questions may be approached through an understanding of the corporate traditions of the European clergy, a type of institutionalized rite-of-passage group which, because of its celibate character, was partially exempt from the biopsychological classifications applied to secular society's age groups. From the earliest church the view that its clergy were like eternal children was in place, so that the Franciscan historians' delight not only that the Indian children had evangelized, but that the early friars themselves had "become as little children" in order to learn the native languages, had a hoary topological past.[12] Ecclesiastical traditions also vaunted the process by which the monastic life was re-invigorated by children. There was the type of the oblate-saint, a young child still bearing the mark of innocent genius when offered to the monastery by willing parents, who legitimized his family by subsequently becoming a saint. And there was the type of the saintly parricide, a pre-sexual or already raucous older boy who defied a bad father often cast as the devil's instrument and entered religion inflamed by God's grace. The Franciscans of Mexico needed look no further than their founder for this inspired child.

Both types of inspired children were rare enough, to be sure. The institution of oblation had largely disappeared in the late middle ages, while the recruitment zeal of the religious orders rarely withstood a father determined to keep his son out of orders and willing to go to Rome to stop it. Yet it is the topos of the inspired child which interests us, and that was alive and well at the time of the Spanish conquest. Charged with the salvation of the *saeculum*, the clergy was born and reborn through children, it *was* in a sense the child of God which worked miracles through its im-

---

[11] Classic missionizing rhetoric is laid out in P. Duviols, *La lutte contre les religions autochtones dans le Pérou colonial: 'L'Extirpation de l'Idolâtrie' entre 1532 et 1660* (Paris, 1971).

[12] Mendieta, *Historia*, 219.

munity from age. And if God is the author and master, friar Torquemada wrote, "a little age is a lot, for through the power of god you have no age, but only will."[13]

In a Renaissance Europe where the legal right of paternity over mothers and children was, if anything, on the increase, this clerical ideology vaunting childish innocence would have fallen on deaf secular ears if a general social and cultural re-evaluation of the young had not been underway. A European adult could excuse Spanish soldiers who pillaged adult Indians, for the laity whether Spanish or native was sinful by definition. But that same layman expected some justification from a clergy which turned Indian children against their parents, for the European clergy was supported by the laity in part because it was expected to show good example. The insistent claim of the Spanish evangelists that they were right to subvert father with children amounted, in short, to recognizing that between *all* human societies, there was a fundamental generational alignment which made considerations of children, for example, more important than the less important category of the tribe.[14] It is this re-thinking and observation of the potential and function of the lay young in Europe which forms the immediate background for the evangelical friars' vaunting of the children of New Spain.

A new religious idea was abroad in fifteenth-century Mediterranean Europe. Organized into age-specific confraternities, the innocent lay sons of worldly fathers could, it was now thought, contribute to the political and eternal salvation of their fathers. Before the appearance of such children's and adolescents' confraternities, the clergy and to some extent the fathers themselves had that responsibility. The product of an Italian patriciate crippled by the rise of one-man rule, this idea was represented in tandem with a thoroughly conservative pedagogic conviction: these innocent children could be so trained in confraternal right action that they would replicate and thus project in time the behavior of their family, even while their childish actions would coerce God's mercy upon their sinful fathers.[15]

---

[13] Torquemada, *Monarquia*, 3:84.

[14] For this shift in classificatory emphasis, see my "Aztec Priests for Christian Altars: The Theory and Practice of Reverence in New Spain," in R. Trexler, *Church and Community, 1200–1600: Studies in the History of Florence and New Spain* (Rome, 1987), 484–89.

[15] The Florentine experience is laid out in R. Trexler, *Public Life in Renaissance Florence* (New York, 1980), chaps. 12, 13.

The extent to which such new ideas and institutions had reached Spain at the time of the Conquest can only be determined by the future student of Spanish Renaissance pedagogy. Doubtless the intellectual influence of the Parisian chancellor Gerson was felt in Spain, and just as surely the Italian humanists who toured Iberia, and the Iberian visitors to Italy at that time, brought such thinking back home. But the most impressive evidence for the power of children was a fact, not an opinion, and must have been known to the Spanish missionary friars even if they never mentioned it in their writings. I refer to the explosion of the Savonarolan boys in Florence, Italy, between 1496 and 1498. Indoctrinated by saintly Dominicans, the young children of the Tuscan metropole developed what some said was a republic of children aimed at supplanting their fathers. These children did more than save their fathers' souls, and more than edify them. The boys of Florence evangelized their elders, through terror and inspiration forcing a tired patriciate to mend its ways. In the midst of the Spanish explorations, and in the lifetime of the early evangelists, it was said that boys had come to rule one of Europe's most influential cities.[16] Children could, and did, teach parents.

The intellectual and historical heritage behind the spiritual conquest of Mexico was, therefore, rich and problematical as it applied to the relation between child and parents. The dominant lay tradition was clearly that of Paul's notion of the natural and legal submission of the child to the father, yet the latent power of organized children was all too evident a part of the recent European past. The Spanish priests would certainly praise pre-Christian Aztec pedagogy to the skies, making no bones of their conviction that both in sophistication and sentiment, the old Aztec father shamed his Spanish counterpart.[17] Yet we shall show that those same friars, inspired by clerical traditions, contemporary pedagogy, and historical models, set out to transform the Indian elders with groups of lay children.

The Internment of the Children

> It is the law among these peoples ..., that the brood follows the mother.[18]

---

[16] Trexler, *Public Life*, 462–90.

[17] G. Höltker, "Die Familie bei den Azteken in Altmexico," *Anthropos* 25 (1930): 513; Mendieta, *Historia*, 503f.; Torquemada, *Monarquia*, 2:476; A. de Zorita, *The Lords of New Spain: The Brief and Summary Relation* (London, 1963), 140.

[18] A. Pérez de Ribas, *Paginas para la Historia de Sinaloa y Sonora: Triunfos de nuestra*

In his masterful work *Tlaxcala in the Sixteenth Century*, Charles Gibson points to the Franciscans' execution of four Tlaxcalan chiefs in 1527 as an event which, only six years after the fall of Tenochtitlán, must have had an extreme effect on the religious life of that province.[19] One of the four, Acxotécatl, was executed because he had killed his Christian son Cristóbal, and the conflict in this case between the younger generation and the indigenous religion recalls an event seven years earlier which must have fundamentally shaped the Indians' perception of a relationship between age and Christianity. I refer to bloody events in the spring of 1520 when, Cortés having left Tenochtitlán to counter Narvaez, the Mexicans celebrated the feast of Toxcatl in honor of the youth's god Tezcatlipoca.[20] The massing of the Mexican youth in and around their *telpochcalli* (the House of Youth or of the Community) led to their massacre by the Spaniards under Alvarado. The death of the Community of the youth while performing its religious duties was like the death of a nation. The fathers and mothers of the young warriors fetched their dead children, took them home, and then returned with the cadavers to the sacred patio of the main temple. Some of the remains were cremated there, while others were torched in the House of Youth.[21] These religious rites by which a generation of youth, "more than two thousand youth, all the children of the nobility,"[22] were cried into the Aztec heaven, announced that this new religion of Christianity, if victorious, would have no room for an armed, virile youth. Las Casas caught what was surely the sentiment of the mourning parents. The world would never forget, he said, "the sad calamity and ruin of the while seminary of their nobility, of which they were wont to boast."[23] At a minimum, we can be sure, this slaughter gave a particularly generational flavor to the Aztecs' experience with Christianity when, in 1523 and 1524, the first evangelists arrived from Europe.

The arrival of the Franciscan lay brother Peter of Ghent and two colleagues in 1523 marked the real beginning of the conversion effort; we

---

santa Fe entre gentes las más bárbaras y fieras del Nuevo Orbe, 3 vols. (Mexico City, 1944), 2:226, describing peoples to the north of Mexico City.

[19] Gibson, *Tlaxcala*, 35.

[20] On whom see J. Soustelle, *Daily Life of the Aztecs on the Eve of the Spanish Conquest* (Stanford, 1961), 246, 42f.

[21] B. Sahagún, cited in M. León-Portilla, *El Reverso de la Conquista* (Mexico City, 1964), 41–43.

[22] B. de Las Casas, *Tears of the Indians* (Oxford, 1972), 23f.

[23] Las Casas, *Tears*, 24.

shall shortly return to his initiatives in the Franciscan missionary strategy. But it was the arrival in Mexico City in mid-1524 of the so-called Twelve Apostles of the Indies which afforded a mythic base for the subsequent generational reception of Christianity by the native peoples. Riding out to meet the friars on his horse (symbolizing his formal superiority over the walking friars), Cortés dismounted to receive them, according to the diplomatic protocol reserved for great lords visiting subject dominions.[24] Endlessly repeated in paintings hung through Mexico for the instruction of the natives, this scene of the captain kneeling and kissing the friars' rags became the model for the triumphal *entrée* accorded the friars whenever they entered a population center.[25] Yet it also helps explain the behavior of the young people of such settlements on these subsequent occasions. The priests were "fathers" to the Spanish soldiers, and the Indians would always be required to address this clergy with that title.[26] By attaching themselves to these friars, the youth and children of early colonial Mexico could themselves be welcomed to the towns of Mexico much as were the friars. They would be the "disciples" of Christ just as the friars were the "twelve apostles."[27] The social and cultural borders which pre-Christian Mexico had set for its young would shatter, and home-town children would go out ..., to come in state. The dynamics of such *entrées* were well known in Europe and in Tenochtitlan;[28] the cross-over of the boys to the friars was even then underway.

In the first sermon delivered to the assembled caciques upon their arrival, the Apostles made a demand which reiterated pedagogic requirements imposed by Cortés and Peter of Ghent the year before. The Twelve told

---

[24] Torquemada, *Monarquia*, 3:21.

[25] In his *Historia*, Motolinía early on documented the centrality of Cortés's act for subsequent native behavior before the friars: *Memoriales*, 284f. Among others, Mendieta and Torquemada considered it the "firm foundation" of the reverences paid the later friars in their entrances: details in R. Trexler, "We Think, They Act: Clerical Readings of Missionary Theatre in 16th Century Mexico," in my *Church and Community*, 576–81. I have found two vestiges of these mandated paintings, in the porches of Tlalmanalco and its dependency Ozumba; for the latter, see F. de la Maza, "Iconografía de Pedro de Gante," in *Fray Pedro de Gante: IV Centenario de su Muerte*, Artes de México 150 (Mexico City, 1972), 17f.

[26] The Nahuatl word for father is *padreme*: B. Sahagún, "Colloquios y doctrina," in *Sterbende Götter und Christliche Heilsbotschaft*, ed. G. Kutscher (Stuttgart, 1949), 107, line 1062; Torquemada, *Monarquia*, 3:21.

[27] See the explicit association in Mendieta, *Historia*, 258; also 211.

[28] On gate rituals in Europe, see Trexler, *Public Life*, 279–330.

the chiefs that they were to turn over their young sons (*hijos pequeños*) for education in Christian doctrine.[29] The chiefs knew the other subjects the boys would be taught, because they were already being taught by Ghent in the city: "good manners," the sciences of reading and writing, singing, and, in certain cases, Spanish crafts unknown in Mexico. The caciques themselves would build the monasteries which would house the friars and the sons of the principals, who would spend day and night with the friars.[30]

The friars did not give the chiefs a firm idea as to how long their sons would be interned, saying only that they would stay until they were indoctrinated.[31] I could find only one source which specified a term for their residence: in Michoacán in the early years, the sons of a chief were told that they would be in school in Mexico City for one year.[32] Yet all this was misleading, for the friars had two other intentions besides indoctrination. First, the indoctrination of the boys would be followed by boys with doctrine teaching those without it. Second, a primary intention of the friars though nowhere stated is everywhere implied: the boys were to be domiciled in the friaries until their fathers converted.[33] A form of extortion was involved, as the Indians of Tenochtitlan well knew. For Peter of Ghent had earlier adopted the policy of, on the one side, sending his boys outside Tenochtitlan to evangelize while, on the other side, "not permitting them to have any contact with their fathers and less with their mothers," obviously because the parents were still not Christians.[34] Thus the boys' indoctrination by the friars was really the least decisive of these important considerations, and Motolinía said as much: the girls of Tenochtitlan, he said, did not need to be educated once their fathers had been baptized.[35] It was the boys' evangelism which would be central to their internment, therefore. Unless perchance a particular father was unques-

---

[29] Sahagún, cited in Mendieta, *Historia*, 214; Torquemada, *Monarquia*, 3:25.

[30] Mendieta, *Historia*, 214, 217, but see also 233, where the boys occasionally return to their fathers' houses.

[31] Mendieta, *Historia*, 258.

[32] *The Chronicles of Michoacán*, ed. and trans. E. Craine and R. Reindorp (Norman, OK, 1970), 86. The number of boys ranged from three hundred to a thousand, according to Motolinía: *Historia*, in *Memoriales*, 270; in 1532, Martin of Valencia spoke of five hundred in one house: cited in Mendieta, *Historia*, 601.

[33] J. Focher, *Itinerario del misionero en America* (Madrid, 1960), 74f.

[34] From a letter of Ghent, cited in M. Cuevas, *Historia de la Iglesia en México*, 2 vols. (Mexico City, 1921), 2:200.

[35] *Historia*, in *Memoriales*, 320f.

tionably loyal to the church, the real time at which the boys would be able to leave the friary was when they married, at about twenty years of age.[36] In the meantime they had to live with the friars, and perhaps die with them. Echoing the sentiments of Ghent almost a century later, the Jesuit Pérez de Ribas would glory in children's death by plague or other illness: if they had lived, they would have been sorely tempted by the heathen world of elders which surrounded them.[37] Better the clergy's schools.

The age of the children the first friars wanted was as little specified as their length of residence, but though they might subsequently accept young men past marriage age who "decided not to marry," the padres definitely aimed to intern all unmarried youth and those children past infancy. In an order issued before the Twelve arrived, Cortés spoke simply of "male children" being sent to such schools, that is, all those still under the authority of their fathers.[38] At the low end of the age pyramid the problem is more complex. When the friars summoned the *hijos pequeños*, for example, did they mean to include the very youngest sons? Since there is no indication of women caring for infants in the schools, we believe that the friars intended to indoctrinate those above the age of reason, perhaps from the age of four years or more upwards. Four was the standard age below which children could be baptized against the will of their parents, but our one relevant source does not suggest that the interned boys received this "baptism of *niños*," but rather that of the (indoctrinated) adults, *after* they entered the friaries.[39] The age range in the monasteries thus went from a low of four to six years to a high of about twenty years of age. We are therefore not surprised to find a division between *niños* and *mozos* within the friaries, one which would play a role in the evangeliza-

---

[36] Mendieta, *Historia*, 136.

[37] Pérez de Ribas, *Paginas*, 3:83f.

[38] *Colección de documentos para la historia de México*, ed. J. García Icazbalceta, 2 vols. (Mexico City, 1858–1866), 1:349f (20 March 1524). According to Mendieta, parents specifically feared to bring their big boys with them to see the friars for fear they would be taken from them. See n. 53 below.

[39] On age differences, see B. de Sahagún, *Florentine Codex*, ed. C. Dibble and A. Anderson, bk. 10 (Santa Fe, 1961), 11–13. On lower ages see Pérez de Ribas, *Paginas*, 2:165; Mendieta, *Historia*, 217; Focher, *Itinerario*, 68. Examples of baptism at c. 12–13 years of age are in Motolinía, *Historia*, in *Memoriales*, 316, 319; Torquemada, *Monarquia*, 3:82–84; Mendieta, *Historia*, 232. There are many others who were ca. 14 and 15 years of age at baptism.

tion itself.[40] Such were the vital statistics of the sons of the principals in the House of God, as the Indians called the "seminaries" of the friars.[41]

Cortés enthusiastically supported the demands of the Twelve Apostles on that day in mid-1524. In fact, if we are to believe the dating of one of his ordinances at 20 March 1524, a date at which the Apostles had still not landed in New Spain and at which the only known school in operation was that of Peter of Ghent in Tenochtitlan, the conqueror had already set the basics of this plan in motion.[42] Cortés commanded all Spaniards having Indian pueblos under their authority to send the male children of the local Indian principals to a nearby city. If there was a monastery in that city, the boys were to be confined in it, but if no monastery existed there, they were to be turned over to the local secular priests or to the person charged with religious instruction. Their needs in food and clothing were to be provided for, the document continues, and it would remain a standard feature of the internments that either their mothers or their family members would bring those needs to the school, or that the boys would send their own servants out to obtain such necessities.[43] These noble children were permitted to bring their servants with them, and in their subsequent evangelical activities, we will find such teams at work in the field.[44]

Two important facts emerge from this ordinance. First, Cortés and all the early missionaries followed the practice of transporting children substantial distances from their homes when that was necessary. Ghent said that in these early years they had come from as far as 60 to 120 miles (20 to 40 leagues) to his school in Mexico City, and Mendieta said simply that the boys there came from "the whole land."[45] While Ghent's school was in some respects unique, it was typical of the friary schools in removing boys from far afield until the establishment of the friaries in distant parts made such transport unnecessary. Thus in these early days the sons of the ruler of Michoacán came to Tenochtitlan's friary of San Francisco, don Carlos of Texcoco received his training in the same capital, and so forth.

---

[40] Torquemada, Monarquia, 3:48.

[41] Mendieta, Historia, 258.

[42] Motolinía, Historia, in Memoriales, 314–16; Mendieta, Historia, 217; Colección de documentos; H. Cortés, Escritos Sueltos (Mexico City, 1871), 32.

[43] Mendieta, Historia, 217; Cuevas, Historia, 2:200.

[44] The team of Antonio and Juan are described further below, at n. 123.

[45] Ghent is cited in Cuevas, Historia, 2:200; Mendieta, Historia, 608.

There was no reticence to move the boys "quite far," in Mendieta's words, to extract them from the influence of their homes.[46]

Secondly, force was employed from the start; there was no paternal choice. In Tlaxcala, the nobles were warned under grave penalties to send their boys to the local monastery.[47] The same threats were made to Spaniards in the ordinance of March 1524, and Ghent tells us that his pre-apostolic school was outfitted with equal admonitions.[48] When the school of Santa Cruz was set up in Tenochtitlan in the 1530s, two or three boys were recruited by force from each governmental unit.[49] It is true that to reassure the boys' fathers that they were not going to end up in slavery, the friars in 1527 neglected to send a group of boys to Spain for their education.[50] Just as surely many fathers gradually lost their fear of the internment and even sought out such schooling for their sons.[51] But many continued to resist, and in the early days almost all seem to have been abducted. Motolinía said that if the boys were surrendered it was because fathers feared for themselves; force was the normal means.[52] The same pattern could be expected any time the evangelists encountered a new tribe, and Mendieta but stated the obvious, if with chilling naiveté, when he told how the Indians of Oztoticpac, six hundred strong, came out to meet the missionary "without the children that they reared. They did not dare to bring the bigger children [*mayorcillos*] to avoid their being taken from them; they knew that the religious collected them and placed them in schools."[53] If it was necessary to place unwilling boys in stocks to punish their fleeing, so be it. It would happen seldom enough, since the Indian often had to choose between the impressments of the Spanish laymen and the prisons of the friars.[54]

---

[46] *Chronicles of Michoacán*, 86; Ricard, "*Conquête*," chap. 16; Mendieta, *Historia*, 258.

[47] Gibson, *Tlaxcala*, 33. However there are cases of chiefs volunteering sons: *Chronicles of Michoacán*, 215; Motolinía, *Historia*, in *Memoriales*, 251.

[48] Cortés, *Escritos Sueltos*, 32–34; A. Trueba, *Fray Pedro de Gante* (Mexico City, 1959), appendix.

[49] Mendieta, *Historia*, 414.

[50] Mendieta, *Historia*, 482.

[51] Motolinía, *Historia*, in *Memoriales*, 314–16; Pérez de Ribas, *Paginas*, 3:320, 322f.

[52] Motolinía, *Historia*, in *Memoriales*, 270; Mendieta, *Historia*, 217.

[53] Mendieta, *Historia*, 750.

[54] *Colección de documentos inéditos relativos al descubrimiento, conquista y colonización de las posesiones españolas en América y Oceanía, sacados en su mayor parte del real Archivo de Indias*, 42 vols. (Madrid, 1864 and seq.), 40:501, 509.

Thus as in Peru, so in Mexico the specific history of the younger generation of Indian nobles was a story of ecclesiastical internment with compulsion.[55] Doubtless there were similarities between the Aztec system of education and the Christian one, as the early friars pointed out, yet the modern attempt to suggest that the friars in central Mexico merely carried on a pre-Christian school system with another dogma is misguided.[56] Perhaps pre-Christian Aztec fathers were compelled to enroll their sons in the House of Youth before the sons were forced into the Christians' schools, as some have suggested. Certainly the question if such Christian force was best for the children or the parents is open, even if it must be left to moralists. The children, we shall see, seem to have by and large welcomed their internment, or at least their subsequent missionary work. But the difference between the schools is simple enough. As this study will make abundantly clear, the Christian clergy compelled the children to attack their fathers, the indigenous schools taught them to obey them. The friars effected a structural scission in the fabric of Indian upper-class society which would have a profound effect on the experience of Christianity. They were interested especially in controlling the heirs of the caciques, it is true. But their schools interned *all* the sons of the nobility, and not just the heirs. It was a brave attempt to sequester the minds and bodies of a whole generation of the leading families of Mexico.

Scarcely in command of the simplest rites and beliefs of Christianity, these interned boys were put into the patios of the friaries to indoctrinate their cohorts among the non-noble families of the area, the second of three important bodies of boys we shall mention. This broad mass of children did not live in the friaries, but merely came there in the morning for instruction, to return home after noon to "help their fathers" and to pass on what they had learned. That did not include reading and writing, and the friars always wanted it that way.[57] Yet in many areas where the monastery was short on resources and the population small, boys from all social

[55] W. Espinoza Soriano, "La Guaranga y la reducción de Huancayo: Tres documentos inéditos de 1571 para la etnohistoria del Peru," *Revista del Museo Nacional* (Lima) 32 (1963): 71.

[56] See e.g., Ricard, "*Conquête*," 120.

[57] These boys were, however, taught to sing and help at mass: Espinoza Soriano, "Guaranga." For the friars' desiderata, see *Nueva Colección de documentos para la historia de México*, ed. J. García Icazbalceta, 5 vols. (Mexico City, 1886–1892), 2:61f.

classes seem to have been interned, leading to the emergence of poor boys in the Indian administrative class of the future.[58]

Since the center of our attention will be the boys who came under the friars' total authority, we may pass from this mass of Indian children who lived at home to another group that also seems to have come partially under the friars' authority. No one reading the primary sources of the evangelization can fail to be impressed with the ample supply of boys the friars had about them in their travels, boys who in several cases, at least, do not seem to have belonged to the two previous groups.[59] Occasionally we get a hint of their backgrounds. There was little Alonsito, a Spanish boy "given" to the Franciscans by his mother because he had picked up Nahuatl from his playmates; Alonso de Molina stayed a lifetime with the friars, and never did want to return to civilian life, Mendieta tells us.[60] We meet Lucas and Sebastian, two Indian *niños* who "offered themselves" to the friars, and subsequently became important missionaries in Michoacán and in the north country.[61] Finally, one Juan of Tuchpa: he was a young man who had many offers of marriage but, with the help of an illness the new God gave him so as to ease his parents' pressure to marry, he "made himself" a Franciscan *donado*. Juan was typical of the oblates because, as Mendieta pointed out, they were males who did not want to marry and who "offered themselves" rather than being given by their parents.[62] Yet the group to which we refer included more than formal oblates. It also comprised those who did not have homes from which they entered the Franciscan friaries. Many of those to whom I refer *could* not marry, or even support themselves.

Without being able to prove the point, I want to suggest that many of these legions of boys in the retinues of friars were essentially orphans, made so by the imposition of the Christian sacrament of marriage. Christian marriage generated large numbers of deracinated children who, I believe, became wards of the friaries. I am hampered in this hypothesis by our very limited knowledge of the Indian family and by the seeming stinginess of early censuses on the subject. So what follows is a mere suggestion.

---

[58] Mendieta, *Historia*, 418f.

[59] Pérez de Ribas refers to "mis muchachos," e.g., *Paginas*, 2:30, 159; see also 1:311f., 2:220f.; also Mendieta, *Historia*, 738, 245, 220, and passim.

[60] Mendieta, *Historia*, 220, 744.

[61] Mendieta, *Historia*, 220, 744.

[62] Mendieta, *Historia*, 444. The Franciscans were the only order to take *donados*.

Simply put, the friars refused to baptize any Indian who had more than
one wife, and in the settled tribes, polygyny was common among the Indian upper classes.[63] The practice had advanced so far, according to
Motolinía, that it had taken on significant demographic dimensions: the
rich men took so many wives that the lesser men could scarcely find
wives. When the friars broke the back of the native resistance to monoga-
my about 1530, however, large numbers of husbands drove all but one of
their wives from the house, and their children with them;[64] rather than
the law of the ancient Texcocan king Nezahualcoyotl being enforced, according to which the sons went to the divorced father and daughters to
the divorced mother, that law in which the "brood followed the mother"
seems to have prevailed in central Mexico then as it did in the north a
century later.[65] The massive baptisms of the chiefs in the 1530s caused
a socio- and cultural-organizational revolution.[66]

It was not only that women and children were regularly used as exchanges in diplomatic agreements.[67] We should also measure the impact
of the caciques' baptisms in terms of the loss of status effected, in Pérez de
Ribas's words, because "the customary superiority and lordship of the principals and caciques" was principally based on having many children, relatives, and descendants, of all of which the Indian deprived himself when
he received the faith.[68] The vivid scenes of wailing women, who cried
out that the Christians had made them widows, and of disheartened husbands who saw their uninterned children for the last time, are part of the
equation.[69] We can take with a grain of salt the assurances of Pérez de
Ribas that some of these abandoned women found new husbands, and it
requires no imagination to believe that the one-time ritual "satisfaction"
which the husbands gave their former wives did not suffice "to feed and
maintain the children who left them."[70]

The early friars and their historiographical heirs have often spoken of
the problem of mestizos in early colonial Mexico, and of the charitable

---

[63] Soustelle, *Daily Life*, 179.

[64] Motolinía, *Memoriales*, 66f.; *Historia*, in *Memoriales*, 262; Mendieta, *Historia*, 301.

[65] Pérez de Ribas, *Paginas*, 2:226; Höltker, "Familie," 506.

[66] See further Motolinía, *Historia*, in *Memoriales*, 263–65; and in the *Memoriales*, 66f.;
also Mendieta, *Historia*, 306.

[67] Soustelle, *Daily Life*, 179; Zorita, *Lords of New Spain*, 90.

[68] Pérez de Ribas, *Paginas*, 2:226.

[69] Pérez de Ribas, *Paginas*, 1:344; 2:101, 226.

[70] Motolinía, *Historia*, in *Memoriales*, 264.

foundations and schools set up to care for them. The fact that Christian marriage polity predictably produced abandoned upper-class children has apparently gone unnoticed. First, all the boys of these now-abandoned mothers found themselves effectively branded as illegitimate by the marriage doctrine of the church.[71] Those who were too young to be interned when the caciques converted en masse in the 1530s must, I think, have ended up as wards and helpers of the friars at a later date. The interned boys, I believe, found themselves shamed by their cast-off mothers and their hopes of paternal inheritance compromised. The fate of the girls abandoned by their fathers leaves little to the imagination.

Teaching Paternity in the Friaries

> If one can stop a father from killing his child, one can certainly stop him from killing the child's soul.[72]

Sequestered in the friaries, the boys of the caciques were exposed to a regimen which both humbled and exalted them. From the beginning they taught the friars the native languages first by signs and then by formal instruction and they also taught the friars a great deal about the local cultures and their meanings. They in turn were taught doctrine, and basic literacy. In the ongoing life of the friary, it was these boys who performed the domestic tasks. Rising in the morning from their always-lit dormitories (like dormitories of nuns, Mendieta said of one of the schools), donning their altar boys' dress which would distinguish them within the monastery and in their later missionary work, they mixed their school duties with the tasks of cooking, sweeping, portering, in one school doing so much grave-digging and begging for the Mendicant friars as to compromise their instruction.[73] Such tasks obviously freed the friars for more important work, but they also helped humble these noble sons, and that was all to the good. Sometimes there were so many noble boys, plus their servants, doing domestic work in the friaries as to whet the appetite of Spanish laymen. In one such case, at least, the civilians so disturbed the friary in search of such human resources as to make schooling almost impossible.[74]

---

[71] Motolinía, *Memoriales*, 143–48.

[72] Focher, *Itinerario*, 68, justifying forced baptism.

[73] Torquemada, *Monarquía*, 3:223; Mendieta, *Historia*, 415, 226, 444, 744, 431; *Nueva Colección*, 2:64.

[74] Mendieta, *Historia*, 380.

The details of the classroom instruction are well known as regards pedagogic method, but little known as regards the comparisons which the friars
used to drive home the distinctions between the boys' native cultures and
Christian beliefs and customs. It is the tone and content of what the friars
said about the religion of these boys' fathers and ancestors which claims
our attention. We shall consider what they taught about the Indian past,
about the boys' fathers, and about those same pupils' relation to the friars.

The teaching of what we shall call the sociology of eternity is of capital
importance to our theme. The Indian past had filled the cauldrons of hell,
the clergy assured the heirs of that past. While one might believe that pre-
evangelic Indian children who died before becoming involved in the native religion had gone to limbo as did all unbaptized innocents, the fact
was that all other Indians had gone to hell because of their worship of
"idols."[75] All the ancestors were thus consigned to the scorching waste-
bin of history; when the boys were taught to pray for the dead in those
early days, they prayed for Europeans alone.[76]

While I found no hint that living Indians might pray or purchase their
ancestors into heaven, the boys were taught that they had a special role to
play in the future sociology of eternity. Simply put, baptized Indian children of both sexes who died innocent would go directly to heaven and begin the work of gathering the rest of the living Indians around them. Children and not adults were the first fruits gathered by the Christian Gods, it
was early pointed out, and the boys learned that if they died on mission,
from plague or from some other illness, it was a cause for rejoicing. For the
Jesuit Pérez de Ribas, the death of the young was evidence of God's favor
for the Indians, and if mourning parents wished to see their children
again, they had only to convert in order to join them in heaven.[77] Thus
three dogmatic points were inculcated. First, there were no ancestors in
heaven; second, the children would be the first there; third, through their
prayers and through the coercion of family sentiment, their parents could
join them. The religious experience of early colonial Mexico structured
the Indian future around its children just as in the material sphere it predicated a social future upon those interned boys.

---

[75] Torquemada, *Monarquia*, 2:119. Pérez de Ribas, however, condemned them all to
hell: *Paginas*, 3:26.

[76] Sahagún, *Florentine Codex*, 1:27ff.; Mendieta, *Historia*, 318; Torquemada, *Monarquia*, 3:23.

[77] Pérez de Ribas, *Paginas*, 2:157; 3:49, 83, 225, 269f. Further Mendieta, *Historia*,
244; Torquemada, *Monarquia*, 3:100 and 1:763.

Given the fate of the ancestors, it made good sense to some of the boys that the whole festive and communal life which revered those ancestors was not only wrong but ridiculous. The time of the tribe's "simplicity," the interns heard, was a "silly" past when men had been so "infantile" as to worship female divinities.[78] Those who carried it on were still more childish, for was it not now evident that "there was but one God and not many, like those their fathers adored"?[79] "The errors, rites, and idolatries of their fathers," in short, were one of the central planks of the friars' pedagogy.[80] It goes without saying that a child's duty to his elders was not a subject in this curriculum, and there is nary a reference to the inculcation of that virtue.[81]

This attack on the boy's cultural roots, the Christian clergy's determination to reduce elders to objects of their children's own ridicule, was accompanied from the start by a rich narrative lore about the "evil fathers" of many of the boys: those who opposed either the imposition of the ritual of Christianity or the abduction of their children.[82] At first the boys learned that their fathers were bad if, instead of turning over all their sons to the friaries, they concealed them at home. In a famous case at Tlaxcala, two such boys confessed soon after they entered the monastery that their father had concealed still another brother at home, and we suppose that such boys were quick to denounce those boys of lower class in their midst whom the fathers had sent there as if their own.[83] Then the boys learned to hate the fathers' daily activities, such as their native religious practices and their fathers' drinking. Finally, these upper-class boys were imbued with a repulsion at the polygamy of their fathers, a denunciation the more problematical, as we have seen, because only a minority of the boys could have been children of what the friars said was the father's one true wife; the boys were in effect told that they were in the majority bastards. We may still hear friar Motolinía thundering the lesson to his young pupils: "each house of the lords of these indigenous peoples," he wrote and doubtless said, "was nothing more than a forest of abominable sins."[84]

---

[78] Sahagún, *Florentine Codex*, 1:27f.

[79] Mendieta, *Historia*, 218.

[80] These were the words of a teacher to his students: Mendieta, *Historia*, 224.

[81] See however Torquemada, *Monarquia*, 1:760 for teaching Japanese children their duty to their elders, and also Pérez de Ribas, *Paginas*, 3:309; 2:190.

[82] Torquemada, *Monarquia*, 3:94.

[83] See the case of Acxotecátl further below.

[84] Motolinía, *Memoriales*, 66.

The fathers thus became akin to Satan for resisting the boys' evangelization. That resistance "was not so much a parent's love as the rabidity of the demon," said Torquemada.[85] In fact, all while recommending to the Spaniards the Aztecs' parental care for their children, the same friars in the moment when those fathers resisted typecast them as fathers who had "lost the natural sentiment of love for sons."[86] At that point the powerful theme emerges that the friars loved the boys more than did their carnal parents. Sometimes this was asserted in indirect, theological terms: if the carnal father killed his son because of the boy's Christian zeal, the celestial father would receive the boy in his arms.[87] More often, however, the touchingly imperialistic conviction was aired that the friars "had more tender love for the converted Indian boys than any father had for his sons."[88] We repeatedly hear about sentiments like those of fray Martin of Valencia, who was said to have treated the boys as if they were his own and who mourned them as his own when they died.[89]

These sentiments were undoubtedly genuine and powerful. But just as surely they must be understood within the context of the material and spiritual power the Spaniards brought to bear on the Indians. Who could forgive an Indian father so cruel as to allow his son's soul to die with his body by refusing to allow his son's baptism?[90] Certainly not "the *niños'* spiritual fathers, who loved these sons more than did their carnal fathers."[91]

We come now to what must be most important for our theme: the boys' love for the friars over that for their fathers, the sentiment ultimately behind the insistence that the Indians address the friars as "father."[92] The boys "loved the friars more than they did their fathers." Like all the missionaries, Mendieta expressed the matter in powerful and convincing language: it was a miracle of the Holy Ghost, he said, "that these friars being so new and so foreign to [the boys], the latter denied the natural affection toward their fathers and mothers and gave all that [affection] heartily to their masters, as if they were the ones who had engendered and

---

[85] Torquemada, *Monarquia*, 1:761; Pérez de Ribas, *Paginas*, 2:160.

[86] Mendieta, *Historia*, 238; Torquemada, *Monarquia*, 3:92.

[87] Torquemada, *Monarquia*, 3:92.

[88] Mendieta, *Historia*, 631.

[89] Mendieta, *Historia*, 241f.; Motolinía, *Historia*, in *Memoriales*, 318–20.

[90] *Procesos de Indios*, ed. González Obregón (Mexico City, 1912), 202.

[91] Pérez de Ribas, *Paginas*, 3:276.

[92] Pérez de Ribas, *Paginas*, 2:178.

reared them."[93] The priests understood that the boys' sentiment was reasonable; did they not owe the priests more than they did their fathers?[94] Yet in the wonder at this transference of sentiment there is, I believe, a genuine social fact of uncertain extent: many boys in New Spain did lose their love for their parents, and did give it wholeheartedly to the European clerics. A story about a dying Indian girl mourned by her parents might have been said of one of these boys. "Why are you crying," she asked her parents. "You are not my parents. . . . A lady came here . . . and told me that she was my mother and that my father was he who was in heaven and that he awaited me there."[95]

The imperial clergy's success at seducing the boys of the friary schools needs emphasis, even if its more profound causes — those beyond the simple fact of Spanish military control — remain matters for future study. Was it something about the harshness of native pedagogy which made such transference possible? The friars give such a view little credence, for they repeatedly praised such native discipline to the boys as much, presumably, as they did to their readers. Was it the fact that Indian children were at times sacrificed to the paternal Gods? With the exception of one indirect contrast between Christian pedagogy and Indian human sacrifice, the friars do not make such a claim.[96] Did the traditional school system of the Aztecs engender loyalties to the masters which could be easily transferred to the Christian clergy? While that idea needs exploration, again, our sources make no such suggestion. These questions thus remain open and important, for the fact of the friars' success with many boys seems indisputable. Every allowance being made for the self-deception of clerical celibates who fantasized about fathering, the competition and confrontation which the padres describe between the Indian fathers and their sons is convincing. "The *niños* were so well off because of their good treatment," the Jesuit Pérez de Ribas said with typical clerical sentiment, "that when some of their fathers tried to extract them from the seminary, they hid themselves and resisted the return to their homes."[97]

---

[93] Mendieta, *Historia*, 222; Torquemada, *Monarquia*, 3:34.

[94] Pérez de Ribas, *Paginas*, 2:225.

[95] Pérez de Ribas, *Paginas*, 3:56. She then encouraged the parents to be baptized so they could join her in heaven.

[96] See the case of Lucas and Sebastian, below.

[97] Pérez de Ribas, *Paginas*, 3:276. In weighing such statements, the Jesuit insistence on only good news being reported must be kept in mind. See e.g., the June 1549 letter of Francis Xavier to his missionaries: Write detailed accounts of the work of conversion,

The boys now made their confessions to their new fathers, and it was in this rite that the latter learned and, through that very sacrament taught, the difference between the boys' individual affections and their inescapable link to their roots. As the boy knelt before his father, he knew the stories of how this Christian God had killed unworthy fathers, but he also knew that neither he nor his fellows could kill their own native names, bestowed by these fathers, derived though they might be from the "filthy Gods" of his ancestors.[98] There was no escape, there could only be restitution for all the past. The boys thus confessed to the friars not only their own wilful sins, but those of a race which had shamed them and made them sinful, and they insisted on that sinfulness despite the friars' admonition to "forget your sins," Motolinía writes:

> They asked their fathers if, when they were *niños*, they were reared in the House of the Demons, and how many times their ear-blood was sacrificed, if it was, and if they had been given human flesh to eat, and other foods dedicated to the demon of idolatries. There were many who accused themselves and said: 'I sinned from the belly of my mother.' And it is true that at first when I heard this I responded: 'Go on telling me your sins, and forget your mother's.' But he said to me: 'Don't be annoyed, for when I was in the womb of my mother, she offered and promised me to the demon.' And others said: 'Beyond my kin offering me to the demon, my mother when she had me in her womb became inebriated and ate human flesh, so that for my part I ate human flesh and sinned. Thus I sinned in that also.'[99]

The insistence of the boys is comprehensible. Apart from the old Aztec practice of death-bed confession, the friars themselves encouraged this scrupulousness about past moral matters: "Tell the Indians ... that they should not fear the confessor, for they know that he is their father." For just as the boys' fathers paid tribute to their sons' new fathers, so the boys with their fathers were required in confession to restitute all those illicit

---

"and let it be of edifying matters; and take care not to write about matters which are unedifying. ... Remember that many people will read these letters, so let them be written in such a way that nobody may be disedified": cited in C. Boxer, *The Church Militant and Iberian Expansion, 1440–1770* (Baltimore, 1978), 94f.

[98] Sahagún, *Florentine Codex*, 1:27f. For the stories, see Motolinía, *Historia*, in *Memoriales*, 208; Pérez de Ribas, *Paginas*, 2:160.

[99] Motolinía, *Memoriales*, 105.

earnings or usury which they had ever taken, "those from the time of their infidelity, as well as thereafter."[100] "Although already Christians," Motolinía noted, "the sons unburden themselves and abandon their patrimony, even though these people love inheritances as much as others. In this way they do not keep [illicit] profits."[101]

The point is not that, as in European usury restitution, much of the restitution certainly went to the clergy as "fathers of the poor" and of the Indians;[102] the enrichment of the church is not at issue here. Rather, such institutions and sentiments help us understand the relation between the young and Indian charity as Christianity was perceived by the first natives exposed to it. If the boys now embarking on their evangelical tasks were to be the "masters of their fathers and of all the other [fathers] in matters of faith," the fathers would pay God for their sequestered sons — encouraged by those very sons — and for the sins of a past without Christianity.[103] In a curious way, the ultimate vindication of Indian society by the mestizo historians of the seventeenth century had its seed in the payments early fathers made for their sons, and those the sons made for their fathers' past.

Into Evil Homes

> The father being old and the son a child, the child manages the elder. Illuminated by God, our child ... admonished the blind and unenlightened elder, his kin.[104]

> For the masters of the evangelists were *niños*. The *niños* were also preachers, and *niños* [were] ministers of the destruction of idolatry.[105]

From the start, Peter of Ghent sent his boys to distant areas on mission, even while keeping them removed from their close relatives who

---

[100] Cuevas, *Historia*, 2:207, citing Motolinía, *Historia*, in *Memoriales*, 238; Mendieta, *Historia*, 289. Also *Nueva Colección*, 2:64, 101.

[101] Motolinía, *Historia*, in *Memoriales*, 238.

[102] For such matters in Europe, see my *Church and Community*, 245–356.

[103] Moles and Daza, cited in Ricard, "Conquête," 121.

[104] Torquemada, *Monarquia*, 3:84.

[105] Mendieta, *Historia*, 221; Torquemada, *Monarquia*, 3:34.

sometimes resided in the town where they were interned.[106] With this radical pre-Apostolic technique in mind, we shall now follow the boys in their ecclesiastical garments out into the suburbs and provinces of their friary towns.

The decision of Ghent to send boys out to the countryside had the explicit purpose of disrupting native festivals — stunning evidence of the revolutionary nature of the earliest Christian clergy's conversion strategy.[107] Yet it is more, for in combination with other information, Ghent's statement allows us to reconstruct the thinking behind the early strategy. The idea was to outflank the fathers (and mothers?) by appealing to the caciques' dependents. Starting with the interns' first appearances in the monastery patios, these boys evoked cohort allegiance by encouraging boys their own ages, but of somewhat lesser social standing, to preach to their own fathers and not to tolerate those elders' "idolatry." The criados y vasillos of the fathers were the targets of the boys preaching in the patios, Torquemada, said, and not so much the fathers themselves.[108] Thus when the Twelve Apostles first sent boys out into the countryside, they chose two young relatives of the fallen Montezuma. The motivation was evident: using the great chief's authority, the boys could undermine the authority of their own fathers.[109] Not surprisingly, rich boys were thus sent to rich dependencies, poorer boys to less endowed villages.[110]

Whether the boys went into the field alone, charged by the friars or indeed with only godly authority, or went with accompanying friars, the ends to which they were used were always the same. They would preach, they would act as information gatherers, and they would be charged with searching out Indian images in public and private places. As to the preaching, we only need to observe that the anti-gerontocratic tone of the friars' preaching now came from the boys' mouths, and then move on to note that the critics of the friars in these early years denounced the practice of sending the boys out unaccompanied. "The boys get into other things than preaching," these laymen observed.[111] But then, they were

---

[106] Mendieta, Historia, 226, 444; Cuevas, Historia, 2:200.

[107] Ghent, cited in Cuevas, Historia, 2:200.

[108] Torquemada, Monarquia, 3:83.

[109] Mendieta, Historia, 259.

[110] That is, there was a distinct strategy for each status, the more powerful within one status working on the less powerful in that same status: Motolinía, Memoriales, 70.

[111] "Espediente promovido por Nuño de Guzman . . . contra Fray Xoan de Zumárraga (1529)," in Colección . . . América y Oceanía, 40:475. See Motolinía, Historia, in Memo-

supposed to. Let us examine their activity in these other areas.

The information-gathering function of the boys was undoubtedly the most socially significant activity they engaged in, and the friars constantly praised their skill. They pictured the younger generation as the key group in native society willing and able, even desirous, to reveal that society's secrets. The information might be a matter of state as when, in 1525, the Indian tribes around Tenochtitlan conspired to revolt against the Spaniards: "Through the Indians whom the friars taught, the [latter] learned about everything that was happening," and the conspiracy collapsed.[112]

Occasionally the friars might learn from the boys of some injustice being done the Indians by the Spanish soldiers,[113] but the annals of the missions are filled with the reverse type of reporting, of "priests' boys"who had protected them by revealing some anti-Christian plot. The boys "revealed everything," said Mendieta, and their willingness to tell the most intimate secrets of their kin's lives would be the friars' definitive proof of how much the boys loved them.[114]

The most important information was certainly the location of Indian images. Sometimes relying on their cohorts in foreign villages, the boys on discovering the whereabouts of these religious objects and encouraged by the friars and apparently by the civil authorities entered the temples and private homes to seize them.[115] The sources in their silence in fact imply that the friars did not participate in such trespassing, but charged the boys — the big boys — exclusively with that task.[116] We have no trouble imagining the scenes, the boys "turning everything in the houses upside down," to quote one critic, seizing the idols and often other property, and then either smashing or burning the images before the residents or in the streets.[117] On the other hand they might, in Bishop Zumárraga's approving words to his superiors, "steal them and faithfully bring them to the religious."[118]

---

riales, 264, for a case of the boys leaving for the field without notifying the friars.

[112] Mendieta, *Historia*, 231; Motolinía, *Historia*, in *Memoriales*, 207.

[113] *Chronicles of Michoacán*, 96.

[114] Mendieta, *Historia*, 318–20, 222, 233; Motolinía, *Historia*, in *Memoriales*, 316; Torquemada, *Monarquia*, 3:34.

[115] See e.g., Motolinía, *Historia*, in *Memoriales*, 318–20.

[116] The "más grandecillos": Mendieta, *Historia*, 234–36; Torquemada, *Monarquia*, 3:48.

[117] "Espediente," 475; *Procesos de Indios*, 11; Mendieta, *Historia*, 657; Motolinía, *Historia*, in *Memoriales*, 318–20.

[118] Mendieta, *Historia*, 638, citing Zumárraga's letter of 1531.

It is in the light of this authorized breaking and entering to "steal" native images that we should consider the so-called "abuses" of the boys, recorded by a Christian historiography as if they were simple perversions of the boys' true tasks. The charges against the boys are serious, to be sure, containing allegations which no friar could have condoned and which, in comparison to those made against the famous boys of Savonarolan Florence a generation before, were heady stuff indeed. Well-founded proofs that certain boys had hung Indians "because they were not good Christians" were laid before civil authorities.[119] In 1529 Indians made two separate claims that boy-preachers had insisted on preaching separately to the women, and had raped some of them.[120] So serious were these allegations, and so fearful were the Indian elders of reporting them to the friars themselves, that in one case a traveling Spanish civil official took matters into his own hands and had the boys whipped in his presence despite the danger that he himself would be punished by the friars.[121] But in view of Bishop Zumárraga's praise for the theft of Indian images, Ricard's characterization of these boys' stealing as the work of "precocious Tartufes and *canailles*" who acted without discernment is questionable indeed.[122] Whether the boys' behavior was right or wrong is, of course, better left to moralists. What is important is that Indian boys were encouraged to spy on elders, invade their homes if they had images (and the normal Indian home did have images), and to remove them and any other cult paraphernalia. Different from Savonarolan Florence, where the boys were ordered to use only words to correct their corrupt fathers, in New Spain the boys were charged with a full-scale search for evidence of the devil, and he, as everyone knew, was to be found in all the homes of the Indian elite.

The violence occasionally visited upon these boys by outraged adults, "so persecuted by the children," must certainly be viewed in the context of the boys' right and duty to enter private homes. The famous "martyrdom" of the Indian boy Antonio, son of the well-known Texcocan cacique Ixtlilxóchitl, and of his servant Juan, resulted from such an entry

---

[119] See the case of Del Pilar in "Espediente," 533.

[120] "Espediente," 475, 510.

[121] "Espediente," 533.

[122] Ricard, "*Conquête*," 122f. Readers will recognize here the ancient adult practice of having children execute their policies because the latter are punished more leniently, if at all.

where the twelve- or thirteen-year-old Antonio smashed some idols in front of horrified elders. Motolinía tells us that these boys had gone on this mission insisting with "the maximum arrogance"that they too had the right to die for Christ.[123] The friar praised their attitude, as did the missionaries in general all "martyrs" of this type. Yet who can doubt that the proud warriors who massacred six boy preachers, for example, were concerned for their people when they did so?[124] The many "other little Indian boys" who died as missionaries were a cause of pride to the friars and perhaps even to some of their fathers, but much of the hatred visited upon the boys was the result of the violation of property and personal rights as even Spanish society would have defined those rights in Spain.[125]

The priests did not quibble about these juvenile actions directed against such strangers, for they were carried out in the name of the One True Faith. What really amazed them, however, was the boys' regular revelation of their fathers' secrets and their often violent action against their parents' culture. The friars' reports on such antipaternal strikes were one long series of heroic tales, to be sure, and yet we have discovered the hidden agenda which must be kept in mind as we consider the behavior of the boys with their fathers. The boys who now entered the paternal lists had for the most part been effectively branded as bastards by their teachers. They contended with fathers who might now pass nothing on to them.

Distinct from the boys of the first missionary Peter of Ghent, the interns of the Twelve Apostles were not cloistered from their parents. Once they had mastered the basic prayers and rituals of the church, they were apparently permitted to attend a family gathering staged by their father.[126] The friars encouraged the boys to use such opportunities to evangelize their fathers, and the conflicts which unfolded among the generations in such meetings make some of the most revealing and interesting reading of the spiritual conquest. In what follows, we shall first examine what the boys said to their fathers, and secondly the range of responses of the fathers to the sons. It goes without saying that since our sources are

---

[123] Motolinía, *Historia*, in *Memoriales*, 318–20; Motolinía, *Traducción de las vidas y martirios que padecieron Tres Niños Principales de la Ciudad de Tlaxcala*, in *Documentos para la historia de Méjico*, ser. 3, vol. 1 (Mexico City, 1856), 20; For persecuted adults, see D. Muñoz Camargo, *Historia de Tlaxcala* (Mexico City, 1892), 245–46.

[124] Mendieta, *Historia*, 751.

[125] Mendiete, *Historia*, 245.

[126] Mendiete, *Historia*, 233; Torquemada, *Monarquia*, 3:61.

almost exclusively ecclesiastical, the results are colored. Yet because the friars certainly taught their boys with such examples, they reflect an attitude which the boys were expected to take toward their own recalcitrant fathers, and that which could be expected from the latter.

If we are to judge by the famous story of the thirteen-year old Cristóbal and his father Acxotécatl, and by other such conflicts, the friars instructed the boys to go beyond the mere subtraction of native images from their native domiciles, and to proceed to attack directly the life-style of their parents. In sum, although the theft of images was regularly recorded, the boys' attacks on paternal inebriation, domestic religious rites, and, improbably as it might seem, on the fathers' polygamy, were the bread and butter of these battles. As had been the case from the earliest days of Peter of Ghent, therefore, the boys were sent out not only to preach, but to "disrupt," this time in the home in which they had been reared.

The groundwork having been laid by flanking their fathers through appeals to the latters' subjects, the boys seem to have first appealed verbally to their father to end his sins, to then threaten him with a series of reprisals, that being followed by actual attacks on the property of the patron.[127] Among the Spanish ecclesiastical historians of New Spain, none of the Indian boys' admonitions to their fathers includes a recognition of filial duty, leaving the modern reader stupefied when he then reads these same historians' high praise for the humble fashion in which pre-Christian Aztec children visited their fathers. For from beginning to end, these Mexican stories picture a brash saint who pitied his father's ignorance, and desired only to save him from himself through aggression.

In the case of Cristóbal, we find the boy first threatening to reveal the father's sins to the friars. Next the boy warned Acxotécatl, "grown old in evil and sin," that if the father did not reform, he would "forfeit the obedience and respect that he had for him as his father," an interesting addition to the basic story not by a priest, but by a late sixteenth-century lay mestizo historian.[128] All this pleading, said the earliest teller of the tale, the friar Motolinía, "went in one and out the other" paternal ear, moving the boy to then say he would "lose all sense of decorum" and himself burn the images, break the pulque vats, and generally defame his

---

[127] Torquemada, *Monarquía*, 3:93.
[128] The nod to filial devotion is in Muñoz Camargo, *Historia*, 245f.; on evil and sin, Motolinía, *Historia*, in *Memoriales*, 316.

father before the Christian community of Tlaxcala if something were not done.[129] Perhaps the most interesting argument which the son offered his father is found only in our Tlaxcalan mestizo, and though it is consistent in tone with the narration of Motolinía, must, because of its lateness, be handled with care. Cristóbalito told his father that he lived "reproached and shamed" in the monastery because of the paternal life-style, indeed was so shamed that he "did not dare appear before his masters the religious."[130] This addition to the basic story by a mestizo suggests a pattern of competition within the friary, in which boys were granted greater or lesser hearings by the friars and their cohorts depending on how successful they had been in reforming their fathers.

When Cristóbal carried through on his threat and took to rupturing pulque vats, first Acxotécatl's vassals complained that the son's actions were impoverishing them, and then one of Cristóbal's stepmothers, Xuchipapalotzin, with her obvious interest in having her son and not Cristóbal inherit the father's wealth, confronted her husband. She asked why Acxotécatl tolerated the impudence of the boy, who threw everyone and everything into confusion. "Flay and kill him," she is said to have demanded, "for why do you want a son who spits in your beard and puts himself above everyone else?"[131] Almost certainly, Cristóbal had in fact been involved in the most indecorous public defamation of his father. For when the boy's own mother then appeared before her husband to defend him, she had to explain away defamatory drawings which Cristóbal had apparently done in public. According to our Motolinía, our primary source, the mother asked her husband if he aimed to punish Cristóbal because of the boy's preaching, or rather "because he had thoughtlessly committed some misdemeanor with the pen, smut, or picture? Didn't you commit the same misdemeanors when you were young?"[132] The father was unpersuaded, and set about the murder of his son. The friar-historians spun it out into an interminable affair, near the end of which the boy cried out with all the spite he had imbibed:

Oh father, don't think that you've made me angry with you for the things you've done to me. I'm not anything but happy. Know that

---

[129] Motolinía, *Traducción*, 7; Muñoz Camargo, *Historia*, 245f.
[130] Muñoz Camargo, *Historia*, 245f.
[131] Mendieta, *Historia*, 237.
[132] Motolinía, *Traducción*, 10f.

you've done me a great favor, and that you've given me more honor than if I had inherited your lordship.[133]

The story of Cristóbal is valuable not only for the insight it gives into the tenor of relations between some fathers and their interned sons, however. Within the context of this story and others we may also gauge the attitude of the fathers toward a new religion being brought to them by their born-again sons. The friars not only paint for us a justified "divine ire" of the sons against the fathers, Motolinía heatedly disputing the suggestion that the boy had perhaps not acted with due reason;[134] they show us as well fathers who have written off their sons, and just want to be left alone.

Perhaps the best sense of the attitude of upper-class Indian adults in these early days comes from a statement attributed to Chichimecatecutli (Carlos of Texcoco) by his nephew Francisco de Chiconautla in 1539, when Carlos was tried and executed for heresy by Bishop Zumárraga. Francisco was teaching doctrine, but Carlos criticized him less because he believed Francisco's Christian doctrine wrong than because the boy had stepped out of the role which the natives believed a noble wise man had to assume. Carlos asked:

> Why do you travel about to say what you have to say? For it is not our [priestly] custom to do what you are doing. Our ancestors say and teach thus: that it is not good to know the active life. Rather, [the wise man] should stay [in one place] as did [our ancestors], withdrawn and grave, and not associate with the lower class.[135]

In this impassioned plea, therefore, Chichimecatecutli demanded not only that the Indians be allowed to follow their ancestors' path in general. He also insisted that the evangelical type of truth-saying special to the Mendicant friars not be adopted by Indian nobles: it subverted the dynamics of Indian life and especially class structure, Francisco obviously having attempted to outflank the authority of the chiefs by appealing to the lower-class *macehuales*. The message was clear: the Indians should be left alone, especially by traveling boy preachers from their own midst: "Each

---

[133] Motolinía, *Historia*, in *Memoriales*, 318; Mendieta, *Historia*, 239. The reader surely intuits that these are accounts meant to defend the friars from ongoing criticism about the outcome of these boys' actions.

[134] Motolinía, *Traducción*, 17; also Torquemada, *Monarquia*, 3:21.

[135] Text in Cuevas, *Historia*, 1:372.

person," said Chichimecateculti, "should follow the law, customs, and ceremonies that he wants to."[136] While this case of Carlos of Texcoco does not involve a father and son relation, therefore, it does point to an upper-class resentment against young, mobile truth-squads. The experience of Christianity through the friary boys' social organization had generational, class, and spatial-dynamic aspects.

We find the Indian father's desire to be spared this youthful evangelism directly documented in the trial of Xpobal (Cristóbal) in 1539. Testifying against his father and his uncle Martin, Xpobal's son Gabriel told the inquisitors that he resided "in the church, learning the things touching on our holy Catholic faith," but that in his visits home, he had condemned the men's rites to the sun and moon, their loud ritual singing, and also their inebriation.[137] Gabriel was convinced that his father and uncle set the *macehuales* a bad example, "because if they did not become inebriated, [the *macehuales*] would fear them and would not dare to inebriate themselves." He must have also criticized his elders to their faces in that which regarded their knowledge of Christian prayers, for he told the inquisitors that his father did not know the Hail Mary, Credo, or Our Father.

We have here then another case of an insistent intern, attempting to transform his elders' life patterns. Yet the reaction of Xpobal holds our particular interest. In fact, Gabriel admitted that he had not seen all the times that his father and uncle had been inebriated because "they had fought to keep him away [from the house] so that they would have more room for their rites, [and] so that the son would not reveal them."[138] Xpobal's parental decision to ban his son from the ancestral home could not have been rare. Rather, it must have been a common decision for fathers who not only wanted to be spared their sons' evangelism, but also the humiliation, documented in this case, of having their sons sent home by the civil authority to stop their customary religious chanting.[139]

Yet there was no stopping the boys, and in many cases exasperated fathers must have poured out their resentment to their sons as did Acxotécatl to Cristóbal after the latter had subverted the father's subjects, stolen his images, and turned his own mother against her husband:

---

[136] Cuevas, *Historia*, 1:372.

[137] This case is in *Procesos de Indios*, 163–66.

[138] *Procesos de Indios*, 163–66.

[139] *Procesos de Indios*, 163–66.

How can it be, my son! Did I beget you so that you would per-
secute me and go against my will? What difference does it make to
you that I live according to the law I like and that which suits me?
Is this the payment you make to me for my having reared you?[140]

Again we observe the desire to be left alone, and yet in these words
put into the mouth of the father by the mestizo historian Muñoz Camargo
there is something else, a paternal feeling that Cristóbal is not really a
son, and for this reason should have no concern for his father's life. Acxotécatl did regret that his son did not follow the paternal will, but more
insistently asks why, once Cristóbal had decided not to obey his father, he
should have any filial impulse to change his father into his son, so to
speak. Acxotécatl mourned the passing of a native law which Carlos of
Texcoco could yet conceive as a *ius gentium* but which the father of Cristóbal clung to only as a law of elders ridiculed by severed sons. Evangelical
Christianity had destroyed this native family.

Into the Streets

[My students and I] travel roundabout destroying idols and
temples, and raising churches to the true God. In such a fashion we pass our time ..., so that this faithless people will
come to know the faith of Jesus Christ.[141]

Even as the boys evangelized their fathers in their homes, they set
about the decisive task of modifying the ritual public spaces of the towns
and villages where the monasteries were located. We can isolate three
points of this complex process. First, the boys were encouraged to attack
images during the public activities of their home-town elders, an extension
of the disruption of native celebrations which the boys of Peter of Ghent
on mission had undertaken from the earliest days of Christianity. Second,
the boys attacked the sacred *spaces* of the native religions, the fundamental architecture of sacred and profane inherent in all urban life. Finally, the boys were important in taking command of the streets through
Christian processions, a process which began the creation of new ritual
geographies.[142]

---

[140] Muñoz Camargo, *Historia*, 246.
[141] Peter of Ghent letter of 27 June 1529, cited in Trueba, *Fray Pedro de Gante*, 22.
[142] For these constructs, see my *Public Life*.

The attack of the Tlaxcalan boys upon a native priest during the festivities of the god of sociability Omacatl during the friars' first year in that town (1524) was archetypal. Passing through the main marketplace on their way to fetch water, a group of friary boys was first taunted, Motolinía insisted, by a native priest who criticized them for "leaving [Omacatl's] house and going to that of St. Mary."[143] Undaunted, the bigger boys in the group retorted that *they* were not afraid of the priest and, doubtless after ripping off his festive "symbols of the devil," they stoned the man to death. Critical at first of their minions' actions, the friars were soon ready to believe that the victim was not merely a priest, but the demon Asmodeus in person, so that the boys were heroes rather than homicides.[144] Anyway, the friars insisted, the ostentatious presence of a dancing Omacatl in the marketplace was a clear provocation, since normally Indian priests rarely left their temples, and when they did they presented themselves in such an immobile, godlike, posture that those who witnessed them did not dare raise their eyes.[145] Thus the act was not only virtuous, according to Motolinía, but it had been a decisive step in immobilizing the religious activity of the natives, especially the *macehuales*, who were the objects of both Omacatl's and the boys' eyes.[146] These humble natives stood there and watched how another of their noble priests did not dare come to the aid of his colleague. Everyone was stunned, this contemporary said, "like people frightened out of their wits at seeing such great daring among boys."[147]

It was only a year later when a second aspect of the boys' transformation of public life got underway, their destruction of the temples. In a series of lightning attacks, the great temples of Texcoco (1 January 1525) and then those of Tenochtitlan, Tlaxcala, and Huejotzingo were destroyed by the boys in the presence of friars, with the assistance, says Mendieta, of some convert-*macehuales*. Always more hesitant to play up the *niños*, Motolinía does not mention them, but Mendieta followed by Torquemada knew that the "children and youth had taken part.[148] In fact the friars

---

[143] Motolinía, *Historia*, in *Memoriales*, 314–16.

[144] Motolinía, *Historia*, in *Memoriales*, 314–16; Mendieta, *Historia*, 234f.

[145] Mendieta, *Historia*, 234f.

[146] Motolinía, *Historia*, in *Memoriales*, 314–16.

[147] Motolinía, *Historia*, in *Memoriales*, 314–16; Torquemada, *Monarquia*, 3:63–65, who compared them to Gideon and other heroes.

[148] Motolinía, *Historia*, in *Memoriales*, 209; Mendieta, *Historia*, 226f; Torquemada, *Monarquia*, 3:48.

had specifically selected for the task "the sons of the same Indian lords and principals" of the different towns, and had done so for a highly suggestive reason. It was because the boys attacked the heritage of their own fathers, Mendieta clearly indicates, that "God gave them the strength of giants."[149]

One can visualize these scenes, the boys "lifting their voices in praise [to the Christian God]," "the loyal children ecstatically happy" at destroying the temples.[150] The friars well understood that as long as the Indian priests retained their positions in the cues, the sacred geography of these towns could not be jarred loose; the ridicule of the children for their fathers' sacra ringing in the night air, the friars could be sure of the destructions' impact on the elders: "those who were not happy were terrorized and stupefied, it breaking the auricles of the heart, as they say, to see their temples and gods in the dirt."[151] Yet the most important result of this action from our point of view is that here, as in the previous murder of the devil, the natives viewed this world-historical religious event in relation to the aggressiveness of their boys:

> For the most part the Indians showed themselves vanquished. They did not try to resist the lesser [actions which followed], when the friars went, or sent their disciples to search out the idols [the Indians] kept [outside the temples] and take them from them, [nor when] they destroyed the lesser temples which remained. Rather such was the cowardice and fear provoked by this [burning of the main temples] that [afterwards], the friars only had to send some of the boys with the rosary or some other sign. Finding [adults] in some idolatry or wizardry or inebriation, [the boys simply] told them to stop it, [and that] the father wanted to see them. This incredible subjection was necessary to the conversion.[152]

Torquemada's words could not be more to the point: the subjection of the adults to their own young was a key to their subjection to the friars. The symbol of authority through which the boys exercised their will was the rosary, serving as a symbol of coercive authority before it became a

---

[149] Mendieta, *Historia*, 227.
[150] Mendieta, *Historia*, 227.
[151] Mendieta, *Historia*, 227f.; Torquemada, *Monarquia*, 3:63.
[152] Torquemada, *Monarquia*, 3:51; Mendieta, *Historia*, 230, with almost the same report.

standard prayer talisman of Mexican religion.[153] That object which in the future would give the Indians a hearing before the Christian God was like a herald's mace in these early days and insured the obedience of the Indian elders to their young. As the innocent Indian children who died were said to help get their elders to heaven, so through the rosary-bearing children, the adults of the early conquest might gain a hearing with the friars.

Once the religious figures and ceremonies of the elders had been driven from the streets and their temples destroyed, the friars instituted the third aspect of their strategy for reorienting ritual space, the Christian procession. Elsewhere I have argued that the friars used the European panoply of the Journey of the Magi as a social-organizational icon by which to reorient the real caciques or kings of New Spain's traditional processions toward the new altar of Bethlehem in the friary churches.[154] In fact, in the first documentable gatherings of Indians in a quasi-processional act, during the Christmas season of 1526 when Peter of Ghent attracted a mass of visitors to the great Franciscan patio in Mexico City, "each province made a tent where its principals gathered," as in the European Magi festivals.[155] Yet this was not a civic procession, as far as we can tell, and the boys were not specifically mentioned. We must wait until the two following years 1527 and 1528, when the friars' boys were certainly involved.

According to Motolinía, the first Christian procession in New Spain was held in 1528 in Texcoco. The problem was too much rain, and the friar tells us that after "the Indians" marched behind a simple cross, the rain stopped. This source again does not say that boys participated in the procession, yet Motolinía does assert that after that first success many processions were held, and that to make them more joyful the *niños* were brought to dance in them.[156] Now in almost the same words Peter of Ghent recounts that he only became successful in attracting the *macehuales* to his mission church when he learned the importance of singing and dancing to the Indian religious rites. The Christmas celebration of late 1526 was, he said, a success because of the attraction of song and dance

---

[153] Mendieta, *Historia*, 429. The children's specific cult of the rosary is noted in Pérez de Ribas, *Paginas*, 2:171.

[154] See "Ludic Life" elsewhere in this volume.

[155] On this gathering, see Ghent cited in Cuevas, *Historia*, 2:202. Further R. Trexler, *The Journey of the Magi: Meanings in History of a Christian Story* (Princeton, 1997), 146.

[156] Motolinía, *Historia*, in *Memoriales*, 252.

offered to the new God.[157] Thus from an early point in the mission experience, a central purpose of the singing and dancing which was taught
not only to the interned boys, but to the boys of lower social class in the
patios, was, as Pérez de Ribas would take for granted, "so that [these boys]
could serve in ecclesiastical festivals."[158] We must conclude, it seems to
me, that the first Christian processions in Mexico emphasized the spiritual
force of the children.

That appears quite probable when we examine another procession,
probably held in Tlaxcala in 1527 and aimed this time against too little
rain. The background to this procession is important, because it contextualizes the boys' fundamental role of ritual spatial reorientation in Tlaxcala.
As Charles Gibson has shown, Cortés had bestowed a Virgin Mary upon
the noble Acxotécatl in the earlier days of the Conquest, and this later
filicide had installed the image in his house, surrounding it with all the
paraphernalia of sacrality. The fascination of Cortés being what it was, the
Virgin quickly became a pilgrimage center for the local population, and it
was carried from Acxotécatl's home and back in public dances and ceremonies long before the friars arrived there in 1524.[159] Only shortly after
they arrived, however, the friars seized the image and placed it in their
monastery.

Thus when around 1527 the image was carried out from the monastery
to induce rain, it symbolized the shift of proto-Christian Tlaxcalan Christianity from a ritual geography which had the home of Acxotécatl as its
hub to one where the friary was at center.[160] This procession had the
further significance that, different from the Texcocan procession of the
following year, which had a "miserable cross" as its centerpiece, this one
had a sacred image with a past civic history and a future. Since ritual
spaces are always organized around holy objects, the Tlaxcalan procession
is fundamental in the transformation of Tlaxcalan ritual space.

Thus it is all the more crucial that in this procession, an Indian boy
from the friary carried the object; our source says an Indian sacristan did
so, but that was one normal function of such boys.[161] Behind this boy
and, perhaps, the other children of the friary, came the exemplary fray

---

[157] Cuevas, *Historia*, 2:202.
[158] Pérez de Ribas, *Paginas*, 3:318; Motolinía, *Historia*, in *Memoriales*, 234.
[159] Gibson, *Tlaxcala*, 35f.
[160] Gibson, *Tlaxcala*, 35f.
[161] Gibson, *Tlaxcala*, 35f.; Mendieta, *Historia*, 431.

Martin of Valencia flagellating, now showing "the Indians" who followed how to punish themselves just as he and his colleagues had taught the friary boys as part of their introduction to Christian life. The procession concluded at a chapel with a cross, and the rain started. The violent masochism of the friar had worked; his blood had saved the community.[162]

Did the boys of the friary flagellate with him, as they had been taught? We may only suspect so. All that can be said with certainty about this procession is that our sources speak of the whole Christian community of friars, boys, and Indians being that which took control of the streets and thus affirmed a new ritual geography which the boys in particular had done so much to prepare. The classical Mexican propitiative procession of innocent children alone marching for their parents cannot, perhaps, be documented before 1544, when the young are said to have marched to Guadalupe to combat an epidemic.[163] Certainly by then, their flagellation, the "*niños* doing a procession of blood to a chapel of Our Lady" to induce rain or stop it or epidemics, was established.[164] As the children had buried their fathers' religion, so they would now play a central role in public penitential activities to save the new, Christian, nations. Adults would offer them a banquet on the feast of the Holy Innocents, a symbolic final meal before their sacrifice for their elders.

The Marriages of the Innocents

> It pleased not only the spiritual fathers, but [the boys'] carnal ones ..., [this office of] the *niño fiscal*. To increase this cult of children, which is the principal harvest of these new Christianities, the *padres* initiated a feast made just for them, which was celebrated the day of the Holy Innocents. ... [The priests] served the little barbarians their meals ..., there being a trumpet blare at each course, [the boys] being [thus] saluted as if they were adults. ... The carnal fathers stood there in wonder, and the boys learned the doctrine of Christ well.[165]

---

[162] Perhaps this was the original cross of Acxotécatl: Mendieta, *Historia*, 599.

[163] Ricard, "*Conquête*," 228.

[164] As in Pérez de Ribas, *Paginas*, 2:116, also 124, 184.

[165] Pérez de Ribas, *Paginas*, 3:261, also 320.

From such feasts of the Innocents to the boys' marriage feasts of Cana was a short time in the early history of Mexican Christianity as, in each region, the Spanish clerics first interned the boys and then soon were faced with the task of marrying them. The *Wunderkinder* of the conversion had soon enough to become the respectable young husbands of a new Christian society which, theoretically, would educate *its* children in the home.

Could the friars pull it off? Could they find wives for the young *convertidos* of the lower class in a situation in which the polygynous upper class helped itself to so many potential spouses? Until about 1530 it seemed to Motolinía that the demon of lechery, Asmodeus, mocked the friars by his success in preventing such marriages.[166] Could they find wives for their upper-class interns, given the fact that a majority of them had effectively been branded bastards by the marriage practices of the church? After 1530, as we have seen, polygamy in central Mexico began to weaken, freeing a pool of wives for the converted non-nobles. The archangel Raphael defeated Asmodeus, said Motolinía, and thus solved an inter-class conflict between the rich old and the poor young.[167] Yet the fate of the interns is our more particular interest — they too had often been unable to marry because their fathers monopolized eligible women — and their marriages and settlement deserve closer attention.

The Christian clergy had three perceptible goals in marrying these boys, the first being to monopolize the ceremony of bestowing wives on young Indian nobles. Thus in the years between 1524 and 1530 when, according to Motolinía, almost the only Christian marriages performed in New Spain were those of interned boys, the friars adopted a highly ceremonial marriage procedure intended to emphasize the honor which they alone could bestow on their alumni.[168] Motolinía describes the fanfare at the marriage in 1526 of the alumnus don Hernando Pimentel of Texcoco and seven of his fellow graduates in just such terms, calling the first marriage in New Spain what his successor Mendieta said was only the first celebrated with great pomp.[169] It was a public reward bestowed on good students, in short, Mendieta explaining the marriage of one don Calixto from that point of view. Even though he was already a big boy, Calixto

---

[166] That devil was even rendering some women sterile: Motolinía, *Memoriales*, 66f.

[167] Motolinía, *Memoriales*, 66f.

[168] Motolinía, *Memoriales*, 66–68.

[169] Motolinía, *Memoriales*, 66f.; *Historia*, in *Memoriales*, 262f.; Mendieta, *Historia*, 296; also Torquemada, *Monarquia*, 3:190.

had entered the friary as an intern along with the *niños,* so when it came time for him to marry, the friars, said Mendieta, "wanted to send him off from the church with that honor of marrying him."[170]

Bestowing property and status upon their alumni, the second goal of the friars, was more difficult. Because of their noble status it might be easier to find wives for these boys than for non-nobles, to be sure, but problems as well as potential were created by the fact that many of the boys were considered bastards by the Christians, that is, by the fact that much of the property rights of the Indian elite had been compromised by the Spanish laymen *and* the church. From the beginning the clergy intended to prepare their minions "for the regiment of their pueblos."[171] Which pueblos, and with what honor?

We do not mean to imply, of course, that no Indian lands passed to their rightful upper-class heirs in the friaries. First, the Christian God killed some of the caciques to hasten such a legal passage.[172] Then we must keep in mind Jacques Soustelle's observation that though primogeniture might be the rule in central Mexico, dividing property among more than one son was not unknown even before the Conquest, so that boys branded as bastards by their spiritual mentors might inherit goods through their father's will even if there was no such requirement in Spanish law.[173] Finally, Indian laws of inheritance could at times be applied in favor of the Christian interns against the father's will but through his own ruse. The early Franciscans noted with glee that the lower-class boys whom the fathers sent to the monasteries as their sons, though they were not, sometimes ended by inheriting those chiefs' property, God thus mocking the Indian elders' duplicity.[174] If we add to these types of cases those inheritances which passed from Christianized fathers to their Christian sons, therefore, it is evident that Indian law helped some of the interns to acquire status and property.

Yet who can doubt that the Christian institution of marriage as often confounded those laws, relieving soon-monogamous caciques of the necessity of leaving property and status to the sons of their former "concubines," as the friars called them? It is improbable that the friars passed up

---

[170] Mendieta, *Historia,* 296.

[171] *Nueva Colección,* 2:62; Pérez de Ribas, *Paginas,* 3:42f.

[172] See above, at n. 98.

[173] Soustelle, *Daily Life,* 179f.

[174] On these *burlados,* see Mendieta, *Historia,* 217.

any opportunity to insure that their alumni were preferred, for as Motolinía emphasized, the fundamental credibility of the friars and of their God
was at stake. Thus it was the Franciscans' fundamental policy to obtain
property and status for these boys. "In dividing the land," they insisted as
early as 1526,

> . . . One should pay great attention to the *niños* and *señoritas* who
> are in the monasteries. Where possible, the division should sooner
> fall to them than to others. For these boys are central to the con-
> version of all the other [Indians].[175]

The results of this policy cannot be stated with certainty; our knowledge of the land transfers to the sons of the friaries is simply too limited.
Yet we do know what Indian elders thought had happened, and their assessment, understood in our context, adds up to something more than the
"minor social upheaval" Benjamin Keen thought the chiefs' testimony
witnessed.[176] In 1554 some thirteen principals from the northern half of
Mexico City (Tlaltelolco), from Cuautitlán, Atzcapotzalco, and Huitzilo-
pochco were restrained, almost impassive when they were queried by the
Spaniards on the treatment their peoples had received from the Europeans.
But they came alive when asked who were now being made caciques in
the towns and villages of the Valley. They were "persons of low birth, or
boys reared in the churches and monasteries," they retorted, and not the
lawful heirs.[177]

Some of these "persons of low birth" achieved their position by virtue
of being educated in the friaries, as we have seen; we may presume that
boys of noble ancestry as well acceded to property and titles which were
not theirs by Indian law. Some, we suspect, achieved such positions after
having established themselves in the area as resident missionaries, like
medieval German *Vögte* or *ministeriales*. Others certainly advanced by direct assignments to them of land left to the individual friaries by charitable Indians. And so forth. As we have stressed, the documentation of this
complex of property transference remains to be studied.[178] But the In-

---

[175] García Icazbalceta, *Colección de documentos*, 2:551.

[176] In the notes to Zorita, *Lords of New Spain*, 286.

[177] Zorita, *Lords of New Spain*, 286.

[178] Alas, J. Lockhart's important *The Nahuas After the Conquest* (Stanford, 1992) does
not address, indeed does not mention, such early colonial property dynamics involving
the friary schools and native property.

dian elders' conviction that Christian religious institutions were associated with the confounding of property rights for Indian young people is established.

If the friar Motolinía writing in 1540 could already vaunt the number of his interns who had settled into married life and were rearing Christian children, he did not mention the destruction of tribal structures which those innocents had wrought.[179] When the friars arrived in New Spain in the 1520s, they were quick to praise the authoritarian paternalism of the cultures of central Mexico and, in the generations to come, the Christian clergy would imagine no greater glory for the Christian God than a Christian republic of lay Indian fathers. Yet in these early decades of the evangelization a peculiar association between the paternal authoritarianism of the clergy and a recognition of juvenile genius was maintained which it has been the purpose of this paper to document. We realize as we begin to summarize this paper that between the European *and* indigenous paternalisms of pre-Conquest days, and the new paternalism of post-Conquest colonial Mexican society, stood the imperial padres, and their indigenous boys.

Summary

During the early Conquest of Mexico, a peculiar ecclesiastical organization consisting of a handful of Christian clergy and a large number of young Indian interns attacked several native structures. The ritual structures were the most evidently and quickly modified, fundamental divisions between sacred and profane times and spaces being destroyed by the burning or movement of sacred things. Along with Spanish civilians, the new church also attacked property structures. Exchange structures felt the brunt of the new religion, the medium of exchange through wives and children being radically modified when Christianity branded most of the nobles among them as concubines and bastards. The cohort solidarity of Indian youth against elders rather than against foreigners is, after all, an important structural fact, as is that age group's association with the class of the *macehuales*. Elders' fear of cross-marginal conspiracies between "the young and the plebs" is too well documented in the Old World for us to mistake its relevance to the New.[180]

---

[179] Motolinía, *Memoriales*, 67.

[180] This is a major theme in Trexler, *Public Life in Renaissance Florence*.

Finally, native legal or normative structures suffered heavily at the hands of the new religious organization, because the missionaries legitimized breaking and entering for, and the theft of, any culturally significant property by Indian boys who had themselves been taken by force. Then and now, European and Amerindian law abhorred the violation of sacred objects more than of profane ones, yet in New Spain, such actions were good not bad, saved their perpetrators rather than damned them. If the early historians were right that the Indians stole more after the Conquest than they had before it,[181] the legitimation of the theft of their sacra must be part of any explanation.[182]

Caution is called for as we thus move from structures to experience. With the few exceptions noted in this article, it is difficult to document the Indians' reaction to the Christian religious organization in their own alleged words, and, since we have generally avoided the natives' pre-Christian religious organization and experience, we compare the old to the new at some risk. Instead, we have described the religious experience the friars and their interned boys made available to the natives, and that which they themselves largely recorded.

The friars and their boys offered the Indian adults what can be best described as a new dynamics of moral space which worked horizontally and vertically. At one pole was the charismatic or spiritual center of the friars in their monastery, which performed miracles. At the opposite end was adult Indian society, the receptors of the benefits of that charisma. In the middle were the young Indian interns as exchange agents. Their power was peculiar, for within the monastery they were servile to the friars, and were not said to exercise any force upon the outside from the inside, as did the friars. Yet on entering tribal adult society they exercised an effective *plenitudo potestatis*, carrying with them the sacred objects (rosaries, images, and the like), coercive symbols for that adult world just as, within the monastery, the friars coerced their God with them.

It is important to emphasize what the Mexican interns were not. Generally speaking, their cohort solidarity in action was shown by pairs rather than in large groups of boys; usually, adults only felt rather than saw the force of the corporation of the young. Second, neither in groups, pairs, nor individually did the boys work miracles, nor did they have visions. In

---

[181] Motolinía, *Memoriales*, 136; Mendieta, *Historia*, 503f.
[182] Duviols, *La Lutte*, 48–50.

Brazil, by way of comparison, a group of seminary boys prayed over a dying child who then got well, and from then on, our source says,

> [the parents] offered their own *niños* ... to be instructed in that doctrine of the padres which taught miracle working. ... The reputation of these *niños* ... [became] excessive, [the adults] revering them as though sacred objects. No one dared do anything against their will. They believed what [the interns] said, and acted as if some divinity was hidden in them. They bowered the roads where [the boys] passed.[183]

None of this *fascinans tremendum* in New Spain. To the extent we can determine the matter, the Indians were stunned by the boys' daring, not their sacrality, by their very human spite rather than the "divine ire" of which the friars spoke. In the early seventeenth century there was a clerical move afoot to have the "martyr" Cristóbal canonized, but it has still not happened.[184] From the earliest days, the Mexicans were forced to celebrate their defeat on the feast of St. Hippolytus; they never, it seems, celebrated their children's victory.

Properly understood, this moral force of the boys had an enormous impact on the adult world not only through their aggressiveness but by the very fact that they were evangelical. The Indians experienced their young carrying symbols and sermons to them *and* to the *macehuales*, whereas, as Carlos of Texcoco noted, their world was one in which wisdom and symbols tended to be unmovably embedded in the *viejos* of the temples.[185] This horizontal moral space was complemented by a vertical evangelism of the boys. The past was dead, and the only ancestors who could be prayed into heaven were the living elders, whose cultural destruction was their salvation. The story of the "martyr" boys Antonio and Juan epitomizes the religion the friars urged upon the Indians. Ruthlessly murdering them while they were ransacking houses, the adult perpetrators nonetheless

---

[183] S. Vasconcellos, *Chronica da Companhia de Jesu do estado do Brasil* (Lisbon, 1865), 71.

[184] Pope John Paul II has now, however, beatified these Tlaxcalan boys who, as we have seen, abused, attacked, and otherwise humiliated their elders, just as he has Junipero Serra, the Californian flagellator of native Americans. For the earlier moves in that direction, see Torquemada, *Monarquia*, 3:93; also Motolinía, *Traducción*; Gibson, *Tlaxcala*, 246f.

[185] See above, at n. 135.

asked to be baptized before they were executed for their act. Mendieta explains this improbable request:

> It appears that the prayers, blood, and merits of these blessed inno-
> cents had had their effect on [the men]. For [otherwise], they had
> only received the preaching and instruction which those they had
> killed [showed] in dying.[186]

In short, the killers had been converted through the actions of the boys in heaven. Martyrdom at the hands of elders saved the innocents, who in turn could save elders.

Back on earth, the *viejos* of the tribes slowly came to grips with the enormous resentment which the Indian interns had shown their elders in the early years of the conquest. For from the midst of the nations came a new generation of boys, who would lead the old in the Mixton uprising of 1541. From the hills of Juchipila (Zacatecas) came sermons of resurrection:

> Tecocoli ... comes and brings your resurrected ancestors. ...
> Those who believe and follow, and who abandon the teachings of
> the friars, will never die or feel want. The old men and women
> will become young, and they will give birth though they are very
> old.[187]

---

[186] Mendieta, *Historia*, 244; Motolinía, *Historia*, in *Memoriales*, 320.

[187] A. Aiton, *Antonio de Mendoza: First Viceroy of New Spain* (Durham, 1927), 140; *Rebeliones indígenas de la época colonial*, ed. M.-T. Huerta and P. Palacios (Mexico City, 1976), 199ff.

At the Right Hand of God:
Organization of Life
by the Holy Dead in New Spain*

To bury the dead is no less important than to sustain the living.[1]

DURING THE SPANISH CONQUEST OF MEXICO, wealth- and salvation-seeking Iberians broke open thousands of Amerindian graves and destroyed hundreds of temples, through such profanations calculatedly destroying the systems of sacred and profane spaces in which the natives had traditionally formed and expressed their social identities.[2] In turn, these very acts of destruction began the creation of significant new spatial coordinates around

---

* This essay appeared previously in *Quaderni Storici* 50 (1982): 112–46.
[1] Baldus, cited in Juan de Torquemada, *Monarquia Indiana*, 3 vols. (Mexico City, 1969–1975), 2:504. I would like to thank Randall Kritkausky, Michael Rocke, and Hugo Rossi for their help with this article.
[2] Z. Nutall, ed., *Documentos referentes a la destrucción de templos de idolos: Violación de sepulcros y las remociones de Indios e idolos en Nueva España durante el siglo XVII* (Mexico City, 1933). For Peru, see the excellent study of P. Duviols, *La lutte contre les religions autochtones dans le Pérou colonial: 'L'Extirpation de l'idolatrie' entre 1532 et 1660* (Lima, 1971).

the tombs of the Christian dead in new temples, and no group of the new
dead was more significant than the keepers of these temples, the Christian
clergy. The Christian treatment of dead holy men during the military and
spiritual conquest was one important part of a cluster of thanatic activities
establishing the borders of social life in colonial Mexico. It offers a case
study of the way conquerors shape new spaces to live in through the disposition of their heroes.[3]

How did the Spaniards and the Christianized Indians organize themselves around their holy dead, and what does the activity around dead
clergy tell us about the relation between Spanish and Indian social units
in this early period? Our organization follows from these questions. We
first examine the creation of saints in sixteenth- and early seventeenth-
century Mexico, that is, of a corpus of clergy indubitably in the Christian
heaven. Then our attention turns to their place of burial, and thus to
questions of devotional and political geography created by the dead. Finally, we shall examine the livings' commerce around the dead, the sociology
of thanatic activity and its exchange structures.

Creating Saints

> One pays much reverence to one's saints, especially to [their]
> holy bodies.[4]

The authors of early colonial ecclesiastical histories reserve the concluding sections of their works for information about saintly clergy's lives
and deaths. Though the contents of these lives are often exotic, the format is thus traditional European: first come the lives of those who died
"in the odor of sanctity" though without martyrdom, and then the lives
of the martyrs of the Indies. Throughout the Franciscan writings of Motolinía (c. 1539–1542), of Mendieta (c. 1590–1596), and of Torquemada (c.
1610–1613), and in the *Triumph of Our Faith* of the missionary Jesuit Pérez

---

[3] I use the word "clergy" to refer to both secular and religious branches, and the
words "friaries" and "monasteries" interchangeably. Generally speaking, the Spaniards
avoided building their monasteries, churches and, as far as one can judge, their cemeteries directly over Indian temples. J. McAndrew, *The Open-Air Churches of Sixteenth-
Century Mexico* (Cambridge, MA, 1965), 183, shows they commonly used materials from
the old temples, but devalued setting and structure. See the keen remarks of G. Kubler,
Mexican Architecture of the Sixteenth Century (New Haven, 1948), 163f.

[4] Torquemada, *Monarquia*, 3:416.

de Ribas (c. 1644), our main sources for this paper, the martyrs and non-martyrs described in these pages are referred to as "saints."[5]

Torquemada followed Mendieta in putting the best face he could on such unorthodox usage, protesting at the beginning of the lives that, of course, only the Roman pope could actually canonize a person a saint, that is, guarantee the faithful that a holy man was in heaven. Mendieta said that he would use the term "saint" in the sense that Paul had employed it, so as to refer to those "who had left the opinion and fame of sanctity behind."[6] The friars in their hagiography protested too much. No one can read these histories without being overwhelmed by the writers' propagandized certitude that their saints were in heaven, and there is as little doubt that the same historians presented live clerks as saints waiting to happen.[7] This was an age of heroes, when priests did constant battle with the Indians' "demons" and the latter's spaces could be filled only by the bones and bodies of Christian holy men.[8] Speaking of the Aztecs having "canonized" their Gods, the contemporary saint Sahagún[9] understood from his own experience that every society made its saints, and that his clerical corporation was no exception. The Spaniards' creation of saints was no mere "popular canonization," but the work of the leaders of clerical society, before all its historians.

There were three types of saints made in New Spain, the first of which, the martyrs, held unequivocal proof to the title in Rome as well as in

---

[5] Toribio Motolinía, *Memoriales e Historia de los Indios de la Nueva España* (Madrid, 1970), the former 1–190, the latter 191–333. The non-martyr information is on 277–93, that on martyrs on 354–422. Gerónimo Mendieta, *Historia eclesiástica Indiana* (Mexico City, 1971), bk. 5, pt. 1 has the non-martyrs' lives, pt. 2 those of martyrs. Torquemada reserves bk. 20 for the former, bk. 21 for the latter. Andrés Pérez de Ribas, *Historia de los triunfos de N. S. Fe entre gentes las mas barbaras y fieras del Nuevo Orbe*, 3 vols. (Mexico City, 1944) places the lives first of non-martyrs, then of martyrs at the end of each of his books.

[6] Both bowed toward orthodoxy in their sections on non-martyrs, not martyrs: Mendieta, *Historia*, 568; Torquemada, *Monarquia*, 3:390. Motolinía wrote his surviving works before there were actual martyrdoms, and was more reserved: Motolinía, *Historia*, 278.

[7] The chapter titles in Mendieta's *Historia*, for example, distinguish "St. X" from "the blessed Y." The reason people came to these persons' funerals was that they were "already considered saints." Among many examples: Mendieta, *Historia*, 695, 707, 724, 771f.; Torquemada, *Monarquia*, 3:592, 579. Some were referred to in life as "Saint Friar X"; the above examples, also Torquemada, *Monarquia*, 3:504.

[8] For heroes and giants, see Torquemada, *Monarquia*, 3:506, 556.

[9] E.g., Bernardino de Sahagún, *Historia general de las cosas de Nueva España*, 4 vols. (Mexico City, 1969), 1:49.

Mexico. One prayed to and not for a martyr, Pope Innocent III had said, for to do the latter insults him or her, as if to say that one doubted that the martyr was in heaven.[10] No martyr needed help "along the road that all flesh travels," for the passage from earth to heaven was instantaneous.[11] In Mexico there was no doubt that anyone killed by the Indians in the process of evangelizing went right to heaven, to receive there the crown of martyrdom and other crowns that were due even as, at the funeral, those were crowned who were surely in heaven.[12] Repeatedly martyrs left behind clear proof that they were defending the cross at the time they died, usually through rigor mortis miracles of "action and posture": they crossed their hands or feet so the faithful would know, covered their privates to show their virginity, reached up to heaven, and so on.[13] But such poses were unnecessary; none of our sources questions the view that clerical victims of Indians were in heaven.

A second formal proof of sanctity was as unquestioned in the New World as it was at times doubted in the Old. This was the incorruption of cadavers, a growth industry in the clergy's intellectual struggle with the atomistic kineticism of cremating Indian society. Christianity's epidermal spirituality knew few bounds. In Europe it might be said that incorruption proved damnation rather than glory and vampirism rather than saintliness, but no Mexican church authority I could find entertained such doubts in these years.[14] The resurrection of Jesus was miraculous after all as much because he stayed immaculate the third day after burial as because he had risen. Torquemada intimated this even as he composed a prayer which Jesus addressed to his father:

> Lord, you will not allow your saint to see corruption. My body will not convert to powder or ashes after I die. For through [your] spe-

---

[10] *New Catholic Encyclopedia*, vol. 9 (New York, 1967), 315.

[11] The Psalm cited by Torquemada, *Monarquia*, 3:517, who pointed out elsewhere that the word "pasqua" meant "journey."

[12] The biblical basis of the crown is mentioned by R. Charles, *Eschatology* (New York, 1963), 434. Two of many references to that of martyrdom are in Mendieta, *Historia*, 741, 594.

[13] Because of lactic acid buildup in stress, such postures could have been real. See Pérez de Ribas, *Paginas*, 1:179f.; 3:181f., 235.

[14] On the European question, see J. de Pina-Cabral, "Cults of Death in Northwestern Portugal," *Journal of the Anthropological Society of Oxford* 11 (1980): 7; also P. Camporesi, *The Incorruptible Flesh. Bodily Mutation and Mortification in Religion and Folklore* (Cambridge, 1983).

cial privilege and grace, it will be preserved entire until the third day of my resurrection.[15]

In keeping with this example, therefore, the clergy in Mexico preached that the bodies of many martyrs and some other holy men remained perfectly "entire and without corruption" for long periods after death. A corrupt body did not mean that one was damned, to be sure, but an incorrupt body guaranteed that its soul was in heaven. "Who will not admit that this is a great wonder of God," Torquemada exuberated like a man who could not afford to have the materiality of the Christian afterlife doubted:

> Thus when a defunct body entirely preserves itself for some period of time without corruption and without human intervention, one must hold for certain that this happens with the particular providence of God. For this is a gift of grace and not of nature. . . . Thus this phenomenon of bodies preserving themselves entire and without corruption is proof of great sanctity . . . , God in this way making it understood that just as [the incorrupt] exceeded others in life, so they will have the advantage in death.[16]

Pérez de Ribas used much the same well-chosen language, assuring the reader of the incorrupt's saintly status without actually preempting the pope's right to proclaim it formally.[17] Mendieta shared the same convictions as the others, and actually rewrote Motolinía's first-hand account of one holy man's death so as to perfect the relation between incorruptibility and heaven. In the 1540 writing of his master, the Franciscan read of the death and unceremonial burial in 1534 of the leader of the Twelve Apostles of the Indies, Martin of Valencia. Then Mendieta read that four days after burial, Valencia's replacement had the casket-less body exhumed and honored by a solemn mass before being "decently" interred. From the start of the Gloria until its conclusion, Motolinía said, a participant saw Valencia standing in front of his casket, his eyes lowered and his hands joined in prayer. For this contemporary, there could be but one reading of this miracle: Valencia was in purgatory when the Gloria began, and had

---

[15] An inspired gloss of Ps. 16:11: Torquemada, *Monarquia*, 3:416.

[16] Torquemada, *Monarquia*, 3:416.

[17] This author notes that while some virgins stay incorrupt, many martyrs do: Pérez de Ribas, *Paginas*, 3:196, with an extensive discussion. On the link of terrestrial virginity to incorruptibility, see Pina-Cabral, "Cults of Death," 8. Virginity on earth, like incorruption itself, presumes a particular potency in heaven.

gained heaven when that prayer had ended.[18] Yet this account posed a serious problem for Mendieta. Writing six years after Valencia's death, Motolinía gave not the least hint of cult or incorruptibility, for the perfectly sound reason that a soul in purgatory suffering material fire could not preserve an immaculate body in its terrestrial grave. That must be why Mendieta, who had a long story to tell about Martin of Valencia's thirty-three years of incorruption and death cult, told the story of the vision but omitted Motolinía's explanation that showed Valencia in purgatory. He lifted these very interpretive words of the master out of the narrative and added them to the life of another person who was not said to be incorrupt![19] Torquemada embellished other parts of Valencia's life, but he textually copied Mendieta's account of the second funeral.[20]

In addition to these two compelling proofs, there was a third type through which one should "piously"but not necessarily believe in sanctity. Such pious belief stemmed from various facts which I will list in increasing order of importance. First there was the fact that the clergy's charges were Indians, children as far as their ability to understand the "deeper mysteries of the church" and parricides when they revolted.[21] One could piously believe that God would not withhold the crown of martyrdom from a religious who faithfully ministered to such a flock over a long period of time, even if he died naturally.[22] So superhumanly did these men perform their

---

[18] "Y que de esta manera le vió desde que se comenzó la Gloria hasta que hubo consumido. No es maravilla que este buen varón haya tenido necesidad de algunos sufragios, porque varones de gran santidad leemos haber tenido necesidad y ser detenidos en purgatorio": Motolinía, *Historia*, 284f.

[19] The lines were added to the life of fray Juan de San Francisco, a merely moral interpretation taking their place: Mendieta, *Historia*, 596, 660f. Just as important, Mendieta added a story of Valencia grumbling in his grave to protest rich accoutrements around it: *Historia*, 596. He could do that, since an incorrupt could noise about. Motolinía did not, since he knew nothing of this father's incorruptibility.

[20] Torquemada added, for example, that those who exhumed Valencia's body could hardly believe how fresh and spotless it was: Torquemada, *Monarquia*, 3:415f.

[21] On Indians as parricides and "apostates and parricides," see Mendieta, *Historia*, 740, 766; Torquemada, *Monarquia*, 3:609. Indians as children was still the view of R. Ricard, *La "Conquête spirituelle" du Mexique* (Paris, 1933).

[22] "Many suffer martyrdom without death": Torquemada, *Monarquia*, 3:601. One non-martyr receiving the martyr's crown is in Mendieta, *Historia*, 623. A martyrdom of continued penance is *Historia*, 641. A brother who got the martyr's crown only because he desired it is in Torquemada, *Monarquia*, 3:443. A person killed by Indians though not evangelizing gets the martyr's crown because being a religious person was "reason enough": Pérez de Ribas, *Paginas*, 3:201.

tasks of baptizing and confessing that God had surely sanctified them, and the Franciscans jokingly but significantly referred to one of their number who had heard countless Indian confessions as "the martyr of the Indians."[23]

Much more tenable as a proof of sanctity was evidence that a religious person had led a morally excellent life, and such assertions were commonplace. Yet the proof of that goodness was in the cadaver. A good man, first of all, left expectations that he would remain incorrupt in death.[24] Just as important, a good man would surely show that quality in the devotion rendered his body before, during, and after a funeral by mourners who did not need to be there. Together, the actions of the body and the mourners were the "grand demonstrations of sanctity," the "opinion and fame" to which our writers referred.[25] Either uncontrolled fervor or awful reverence in the presence of the deceased, or both, might prove that the dead needed no prayers. But since this behavior around the tomb is our best means of viewing thanatic social organization, we shall postpone its study until we know where the bodies were buried.

Placing the Dead

> And they marked the place so one would know it, for he had died while considered a saint.[26]

Where did holy men find burial in early New Spain? This is an important question in such a hegemonic bi-racial society, for its answer reveals something about the devotional and political geography of social exchange. Many religious persons died and were buried with little fanfare, and their location as well as that of the laity are questions to which this

---

[23] Mendieta, *Historia*, 643, and note the interpretation of Torquemada, *Monarquia*, 3:468. Mendieta himself wanted to suffer enough in this world, and did, so that he would go directly to heaven: *Historia*, 562.

[24] Those who exhumed Zumárraga expected incorruption, "pareciendole que tan singular vida como la suia debia de estar galordonada con algun particular don concedido à su bendito cuerpo": Torquemada, *Monarquia*, 3:457. At a funeral: "Oltro padre grave, que tenía mucha noticia de la santidad del padre Hernán Gómez . . . dijo: Que se persuadía que N. Señor había de hacer alguna manifestación de santidad tan humilde y escondida": Pérez de Ribas, *Paginas*, 3:301.

[25] For demonstrations, see Torquemada, *Monarquia*, 3:531.

[26] Torquemada, *Monarquia*, 3:598. This was a case of a friar who died on the road, too far from a town to be transported.

paper does not address itself.[27] But with vast spaces to be devotionally signified, epic holiness was rampant. When martyrdom or a devotional outbreak occurred on death, or when sometime after death incorruptibility reared its odoriferous head, where were the bodies put?

The answer to this question begins with a necessary division between the settled areas of the Valley of Mexico on the one side, and the frontiers on the other. In the former, Indians who requested that such holy men be buried in their own native bailiwicks sometimes obtained their wish, but on the frontiers similar requests were always denied. On the frontiers, therefore, the European religious in their struggle to establish monastic and diocesan boundaries around prelatial and political centers fought the development of alternate centers through the placement of the dead. From the Indian viewpoint, the natives sought protection through cadavers which the clergy might or might not concede.

In three known cases Indian communities successfully requested the remains of clerical dead for churches other than those originally decided upon by the authorities. When fray Francisco Gomez died in the Franciscan friary of San Andrès of Cholula in 1611, the friars of that town's *convento grande* promptly sent for his body "to give it honored burial" in the latter church. But when the friars of San Andrès "and the Indians of that *cabecera*" firmly opposed the loss "of such an estimable treasure," the Conventuals of the main friary acceded and Gomez was buried in San Andrès with "great solemnity and applause."[28] When Pedro Oròz died in 1597 at the Franciscan friary of Santiago Tlaltelolco in northern Mexico City, the friars of San Francisco de México to the south tried unsuccessfully to move the body to their place, but "the concourse of the natives and the clamor that such a holy prize not be taken from them" was so great, according to Torquemada, that the friars of San Francisco, moved by the Indians' devotion and faith, decided to leave it in the old church of Tlaltelolco. Writing about 1610, Torquemada added that the Indians' devotion to Oròz's body remained so great that it was not moved to the friary's new church when that was finished. Instead, all the natives came to the site every All Souls to lay flowers and other gifts before the grave.[29]

In both these cases in which cadavers stayed where they died, the in-

---

[27] The burial places of many such average saints are given at the end of the Franciscan lives in Mendieta and Torquemada. For the hospitals, see below.

[28] Torquemada, *Monarquia*, 3:554f. The *cabecera* is defined in C. Gibson, *The Aztecs under Spanish Rule* (Stanford, 1964), 33.

[29] Torquemada, *Monarquia*, 3:576f.

tervention of the Indians seems to have been the decisive element in a dispute which may also, *sotto voce*, have involved competition between two friaries of the Franciscan order. A third case involving the movement of a body takes us out of the realm of urban geography even while preserving the suggestion of complicity between friars and Indians. Francisco de Lintorne was the guardian of the Franciscan monastery of Tlaxcala when he died in his order's friary at Puebla, the nearby Spanish city. Torquemada describes what happened:

> Because he was the guardian of [the friary of] Tlaxcala, the Indians of the said city asked for him and, because of their devotion, [the friars of Puebla] gave him to them. . . . When they took him out of the first sepulchre after he had been buried for two days and two nights, he gave off no bad odor from himself. With great solemnity they translated him to the said friary of Tlaxcala. And such were the crowds which came [to Puebla] from the said province of Tlaxcala that, there being five leagues between the one and the other, the men and women held a procession. From the one city to the other, no one moved from his place until the body passed, and after it had passed, those followed it who had stood along the route.[30]

Although the typical ecclesiastical practice of ascribing devotion to the faithful so as to fortify clerical interests certainly underlies all these cases, it is just as evident that the native Americans did participate in building up the charisma around their own local friaries, both at the neighborhood and at the civic level. In the case of the burial of the famous Peter of Ghent, there was no need nor thought to oppose the wishes of the Indians that he be buried in the great Indian Chapel of San José which he had built in the patio of Tenochtitlan's friary of San Francisco:

> His death made the natives feel great sadness and pain, and they showed it in public. . . . The natives requested his body from the prelates of the order so as to bury it in their solemn chapel of San José. [The prelates] conceded it.[31]

---

[30] Torquemada, *Monarquia*, 3:598. The interesting evidence of civism at Tlaxcala is superbly discussed by C. Gibson, *Tlaxcala in the Sixteenth Century* (New Haven, 1952), 28–41.

[31] Mendieta, *Historia*, 611; Torquemada, *Monarquia*, 3:431.

In the central area, therefore, the clergy allowed the Indians the protection of holy men, but only as long as such prizes remained under ecclesiastical supervision. When in 1584 the Dominican friars of Amecameca discovered that without informing the authorities, local Indians had preserved secondary relics of the eponymous Franciscan Martin of Valencia for a half century, they were impressed by such chthonic devotion, but they quickly took them from the Indians and put them in their friary.[32] In the midst of the tumultuous burial of Francisco de Gamboa in 1604, a mass of excited Indians raided the remains of Domingo de Areizaga (d. 1582) when they were exposed, but it was a religious person who carried off his head and toured the countryside showing it, and religious hands which finally reinterred it in the friary of Tecamachalco (Puebla) where Areizaga had worked. Torquemada explained that, in essence, it belonged near the Indians whom he had evangelized but also among the brothers missionary:

> God did not want that head to remain away from where in life it had occupied itself so much in the glory of his service. Rather, he wanted it to be in the company of others whom he had sent to heaven because of their teaching and saintly sermons. This is why he wanted [the head] to return to be buried where [Areizaga] had also sung his divine praises.[33]

The fate of Indian requests for holy bodies was as negative on the frontier as those requests were capable of being fulfilled at the center. The Jesuit Gerónimo Ramírez died a natural death in 1621 while ministering in a village some twenty leagues distant from the Tarascan town of Pátzcuaro. Pérez de Ribas tells how his body was deposited in that village, leading the locals to want to keep it, "considering themselves lucky by his presence, to hold in their church the body of him whom they considered a saint." But despite the Indians' "great reluctance," the body was moved to the Jesuit college of Pátzcuaro.[34] The authorities reacted strongly

---

[32] Mendieta, *Historia*, 603. The relics were taken first to Mexico City to be authenticated, and then returned to the Dominican friary. Their subsequent fate is discussed below.

[33] Torquemada, *Monarquia*, 3:557f., 582f. Further on Areizaga in Mendieta, *Historia*, 543. Areizaga's corrupted corpse was exposed because Gamboa was to be buried in the same casket.

[34] "Se tenían con su beneficiado por dicosos": Pérez de Ribas, *Paginas*, 2:203.

when it was a question of martyrs, the pattern being set as early as the death of the Franciscan Antonio de Cuellar in 1541:

> Those of the pueblo of Ameca very much wanted the body to be left and buried there. But the friars in no way wanted to consent to this, but rather [wanted] to take it, as they did, to be buried in the monastery of Ezatlán, together with his companion fray Juan Calero.[35]

Such rejections continued as long as did the frontier. When in 1616 during the revolt of the Tepeguanes four Jesuits were killed in the town of Zape, the Indians of nearby Guanaceví where the priests were headquartered pleaded for their bodies, "because of the devotion they had to them and the instruction they had received from them, reason[s] they alleged as giving them a right to [the bodies]." But the Spanish official who recovered the bodies refused, the contemporary Pérez de Ribas tells us, "for he was very devoted to our Society [of Jesus] and wanted to take them with him . . . , to deposit them in our collegiate church of Durango, to which they belonged."[36]

The religious certainly refused such burials in the pueblos for reasons of their safety, for they greatly feared the insults heaped on clerical bodies when they were taken by Indians. Some of these pueblos which wanted bodies were, furthermore, mere "chapels of visit" without a residential clergy to care for the bodies. Thus while such translations evidently functioned to keep sacred bodies away from Indian communities, the stated reasons for taking them were more pragmatic. And among these, none was more practical than that the bodies "belonged" to the order of the martyrs. Let us examine how these orders disposed of their own.

One important fact at the very beginning: the disposition of the martyred or indeed non-martyred religious did not depend on suitable social status within the order. As far as I can determine, lay brothers and fully professed religious were treated equally in this respect even if, as we shall see, the title of "martyr" might be reserved for the latter and denied to the former lay brother member of an evangelical team. So preponderant was the sense of order over the sense of status among the Franciscans, in fact, that incorruptibility could be found in lay brothers, Torquemada

---

[35] "por ninguna via quisieron consentir en ello": Mendieta, *Historia*, 741.
[36] "Razón que alegaban para tener derecho a ellos": Pérez de Ribas, *Paginas*, 3:194f.

explaining to dubious readers that even in King David's army the baggage train got as much of the spoils as the warriors.[37] Throughout the annals the need for bodies proved superior to intra-order status divisions. In disposing of martyrs, their corporeal condition, and the interests of Spanish social and political groups, were decisive.

First of all, the bodies of those religious that were found mixed with the remains of the laity received no particular attention at all. In the Tepeguanes revolt, for example, two martyrs were found in the cemetery of the scorched church of Santiago Papasquiaro, their corrupted remains mixed with those of Indian Christians who had died with them. All the remains were promptly interred together in the ruined church.[38] If the bodies were separate and identifiable, on the other hand, they received "more decent" fates. Thus when after these 1616 massacres the Spanish governor of Nueva Vizcaya found the body of the Dominican Sebastián Montaño, he gathered it up and buried it later in the unsoiled church in the mining town of Guancevi which, though far from the friar's monastery in Zacatecas, was a more fitting place than where the body had been found.[39] The fate of Antonio de Cuellar in 1541 was more predictable. He returned to his monastery of Ezatlán, not far distant from the village where his body had been deposited.[40] It clearly belonged there, among the friars living and dead with whom he had associated. Every religious house had its collection of brothers buried together so as to ascend together on the last day. Alonso de Urbano's body being buried in his Franciscan monastery of Tula about 1589, Torquemada spoke of that body "making company with other holy bodies which from [the friary of Tula] will be raised to glory with their holy and blessed souls on the Day of Judgment."[41]

Yet it would be wrong to assume that, once the Indian requests were answered, the only thought of those who decided the placing of bodies was to unite them with their missionary associates. Civil and ecclesiastical

---

[37] "Y non ai que maravillar. . . . Mereciò con ellos parte de este dichoso premio, como sucediò en el exercito de David . . .": Torquemada, *Monarquia*, 3:502. Motolinía found it promising that Calero, the first martyr, was a lay brother: text from a lost work cited in Mendieta, *Historia*, 735f.

[38] Pérez de Ribas, *Paginas*, 3:196, also 174.

[39] Pérez de Ribas, *Paginas*, 3:192f., 201.

[40] Mendieta, *Historia*, 741.

[41] "Haciendo compañia à otros santos cuerpos, que de allí se han de levantar à ser gloriosos con sus santas y benditas animas el dia del juicio": Torquemada, *Monarquia*, 3:573.

factors had to be weighed. Thus the first bishop of Mexico City and the second of Tlaxcala found repose not among their order brothers, as they had wished, but in their cathedral churches.[42] This is no more surprising than that partial relics of saints traveled outside the world of their brother missionaries: the head of Domingo de Areizaga might go home, a bone from the otherwise scattered remains of the Tepeguanes martyr Santarén went all the way back to his Jesuit college in Huete, Spain, but the head of the Jesuit Tapia (d. 1594) traveled to Mexico City from the far north where he had missionized.[43] What is noteworthy is that whole bodies, especially those of martyrs, played a political role which transcended the confines of a particular monastery or order.

Thus the pile of bodies in the Franciscan friary of Ezatlán near Guadalajara grew up not by planning but through the force of events; the house ended up as an important devotional center. During the Mixton revolt of 1540–1541, first the lay brother Juan Calero suffered martyrdom, his body being returned to that monastery after being found miraculously preserved five days after death.[44] Shortly afterwards it was the turn of Antonio de Cuellar, whose body returned to Ezatlán to be buried, Mendieta added, "together with his companion fray Juan Calero."[45] The stock increased a decade later on the deaths of the "saintly guardian and martyr fray Francisco Lorenzo and his companion fray Juan," the former already a contributor to Ezatlán's building cult by having obtained the lost habit of Calero from hostile Indians and brought it back to the monastery.[46] Francisco and Juan were returned, "where they are buried jointly with the other martyrs."[47] When Mendieta considered that one of the Twelve

---

[42] "No consintió la clerecía de ella [iglesia] carecer de tan santa reliquia" of Zumárraga: Torquemada, *Monarquia*, 3:455; Mendieta, *Historia*, 636. The "second bishop" of Tlaxcala (actually the third: Gibson, *Tlaxcala*, 56) is mentioned in Torquemada, *Monarquia*, 3:520; he died c. 1557. The bishop of Puebla was also buried in his cathedral church, in 1607, against his wishes: Gil Gonzales Davila, *Teatro eclesiastico de la primitiva iglesia de la Nueva España en las Indias Occidentales* vol. 1 (Madrid, 1959), 138f.

[43] Pérez de Ribas, *Paginas*, 1:273; 3:71 (Tapia); 3:68 (Santarén). Another case of a head moved and venerated separately is in Torquemada, *Monarquia*, 3:444. Partial relics were in short supply in New Spain until the 1570s: Davila, *Teatro*, 1:54, 59–61; McAndrew, *Open-Air Churches*, 352f.

[44] Mendieta, *Historia*, 738f. Ezatlán had only been founded in 1539 and Cuellar was its first guardian: *Historia*, 736.

[45] "Juntamente con su compañero Fr. Juan Calero": Mendieta, *Historia*, 741.

[46] Note that Mendieta calls the professed friar a martyr but not the lay brother: *Historia*, 756–58, also 739. The pair died c. 1555: Kubler, *Architecture*, 494.

[47] "Donde juntamente con otros mártires están sepultados": Mendieta, *Historia*, 758.

Apostles of the Indies was also buried in this church "with the other four saintly friars killed by infidel Indians in defense of the faith," he could not resist explaining the occult significance of the place. Ezatlá meant "place of the waters or the rivers of blood," he noted, so that God had obviously picked this place for the martyrs' bodies with forethought:

> He settled upon it as the place where not only the first blood was spilled by martyrs of this new church, but also as the place where the bodies of other martyrs would be deposited and guarded, more than in any other part of the land.[48]

Thus a group of friars who had lived together on earth would stay together in death in a place intended to be the first-fruits cemetery of clerical saints of New Spain. Indeed they would be buried together in the same casket so as to rise as one on the Last Day. Cuellar had been the traveling companion of Calero, Juan of Francisco de Lorenzo; all shared together in death not only their mutual affection but their joint participation in that historical series of revolts.[49] History did not, on the other hand, obtain for the Indians who had also participated. Calero had died with two Indian boys and one adult clinging to him, and, as would Pérez de Ribas in a similar circumstance of 1616, Mendieta thought this physical contact made it "piously credible" that the "saintly martyr . . . took [their souls] with him to heaven." But the bodies of the Indians had been eaten by the birds and ants, while in the midst of this carnage Calero's body had survived integrally.[50] In itself that ruled out the unimaginable idea of burying Indian bones with the bodies of the corporately holy men.

The sequence to the Jesuit martyrdoms during the Tepeguanes revolt of 1616 affords our best example of bodies removed to cultic centers far from their missionizing for mainly political reasons. In all five bodies, all of which were said to be incorrupt, went substantial distances. We left the body of the Dominican Montaño at Guanaceví, where he had been buried

---

[48] The Apostle was Palos, one of only two of the Twelve said to be buried in a casket: Mendieta, *Historia*, 628, 741.

[49] "Como fueron compañeros en la peregrinacion y muerte, es de creer lo son tambien en la gloria": Mendieta, *Historia*, 628. For further traces of history binding together in heaven, see further below.

[50] This was of course a miracle: Mendieta, *Historia*, 738f, an identical corporate differential being *Historia*, 761. The Indians who died and were buried indistinctly with the Tepeguanes martyrs probably went to heaven with the latter because they had just been confessed and received communion: Pérez de Ribas, *Paginas*, 3:174.

by the governor of Nueva Vizcaya. Wonders were told of his body. Though it had lain two months in the open field, it had a remarkable fragrance, while the blood on the head, feet, and on the Eucharist fingers was as fresh on being found as if it had just come from the body. Reported in the chronicles of Montaño's native Madrid, these marvels proved irresistible to the Dominican mother house in distant Mexico City. Though Zacatecas had been Montaño's residence, the mother house had the whole body brought from Guanacevi, past Zacatecas, to the capital.[51]

The four other bodies proved even more important once they were recovered incorrupt from the village of Zape and, we recall, refused to the dwellers of Guanacevi. For it was the provincial governor himself, and not religious persons, who made the decision to transport them with pomp. And it was certainly more for political reasons than through piety that the governor decided to house them in his relatively new and still sacrally undistinguished provincial capital of Durango.[52] In this colorful and portentous event, a lay official created sacred spaces with holy bodies. Let us recount their translation, and then pass to analyzing this powerful funeral scene.

The governor had determined that a diplomatic triumph or *entrada* should be accorded to the bodies when they arrived in his capital, and every step of the way back to Durango matched that epiphanic ritual. Pérez de Ribas first describes the precedence of the governor's army, and then notes that "for decency," this lord had placed each of the four incorrupts on one of his mules, all of them draped with the governor's own coat of arms.[53] Two Jesuits from Durango joined the entourage still some leagues from the city, and a quarter league away a royal carriage came out to accommodate the saints.[54] Then came "the triumph of the governor and of those ministers of God and his gospel" into the city. We are told

---

[51] A breviary which Montaño had also remained like new despite rain and snow: Pérez de Ribas, *Paginas*, 3:193, 201. Further on fresh blood in Mendieta, *Historia*, 738; note that none of the incorruptibles was said to bleed after death.

[52] Founded in 1563 as capital of the new province of Nueva Vizcaya, in 1616 Guadiana (Durango) was still not a cathedral city: Pérez de Ribas, *Paginas*, 3:198.

[53] "Cubiertos con reposteros de sus armas": Pérez de Ribas, *Paginas*, 3:197. For comparable diplomatic receptions, see my *Public Life in Renaissance Florence* (New York, 1980), chap. 9, and my edition of *The Libro Cerimoniale of the Florentine Republic. . . .* (Geneva, 1978).

[54] Reception outside was standard practice. The carriage was not actually used, because it being late, the burial was postponed and the bodies brought only inside the gate: Pérez de Ribas, *Paginas*, 3:197.

that the whole population jammed around the gate and the streets at the nearby Franciscan church to see this "celebrated entrée," each resident grasping lit tapers which a rich merchant had provided for all.[55] Church bells rang and firearms exploded as the bodies were carried into the Franciscan church for deposit. After solemn vespers a military guard of honor flanked the holy remains throughout this and the following night. The morning after the entrance the Franciscan provincial had to restrain himself from saying the mass of a saintly martyr rather than that of the dead, so sure was he and his colleagues "that they were already in heaven much crowned with glory."[56]

On the next morning a delegation of Jesuits left their church and headed for San Francisco, surrounded by a great procession whose precedential order Pérez de Ribas gives, and whose noise of chant and gunfire he vividly recounts. There the Franciscan friars joined the progress with their sacred prizes, and the parade then returned to the Jesuit church. During the solemn funeral services that followed, eulogies of prose and verse "celebrated the triumph of these valorous soldiers of Christ, who fought till they died."[57] Finally the four incorrupts were placed in one capacious wooden casket and buried. Pérez de Ribas concluded his long account by calling to mind four other Jesuit martyrs who lay in distant mass graves because "they could not be recognized or differentiated from the other faithful [lay] Catholics." They too deserved their earthly triumph, the author implied, even if their bodies could not participate in the political legitimations of sainthood we have described. Pérez de Ribas gave a historian's

---

[55] "Y llegando a la ciudad se recibió el triunfo del governador y de aquellos ministros de Dios y de su evangelio": Pérez de Ribas, *Paginas*, 3:197. The "célebre recibimiento" is *Paginas*, 3:198.

[56] At vespers the previous night: "Quiso honrar este recibimiento con capa de coro para hacer el oficio. Bien quisiera su muy reverenda persona (que se mostraba aquí con los ojos arrasados con devotas lágrimas) celebrar unas vísperas de mártires de Cristo; pero como esa calificación es sólo del vicario de Cristo . . . se contentó con que hubiese un rato de buena música, como la hubo al tiempo de celebrarlas." At mass the next morning: "Hicieron el oficio de difuntos y de cuerpo presente los padres de San Francisco . . . y aunque de difuntos por la razón dicha, pero muy acompañada de solemne música, porque aquellos difuntos los miraban y consideraban ya en el cielo muy coronados de gloria": Pérez de Ribas, *Paginas*, 3:198. Note the Franciscan's tears, evidence of the holiness of the bodies as shown below. Saying not a requiem mass but the mass of a martyr was not in fact uncommon: see e.g., Mendieta, *Historia*, 621; Torquemada, *Monarquia*, 3:578 (funeral of Motolinía). On the belief in the power of a requiem mass to kill a living person, see Trexler, *Public Life*, 287. The opposite effect is implied in our case.

[57] See the extensive details in Pérez de Ribas, 3:198f.

triumph: their "signal virtues and well-derived memory [would] be extensively related at the end of this book."[58]

Thanatic Commerce

> And I witnessed everyone exalting him as a saint. They took his clothing and the very flowers from the litter, because these had touched his body. They took them as relics.[59]

A triumph is no common phenomenon. On the one hand it expresses an established set of social relations, while on the other it probes and challenges, and thus finally modifies those relations. A ceremony involving gates is the rite of passage par excellence.[60] On a theological plane, the diplomatic entry of our martyrs expressed the definite state of relations between their heavenly bodies and those of the mortal sinners who venerated them, but at the imminent level it forged and signified a set of new and future relations with those cadavers, the funeral celebration in this view being the essence of such relations. Since the martyrs entered Durango stamped with the arms and associated with the person of the provincial governor, the structures and lines of meaning became still more complex, for the set of relations between him and his subjects now was informed and modified by the set of relations between him and his martyrs.[61]

A triumph is therefore an ongoing process by which social groups identify by ordering themselves in relation to all others. This formative quality was certainly the case in the fledgling town of Durango, where the procession or parade helped assign original significances to the city's spatial, social, and moral objects. Yet it was no less true that the martyrs were

---

[58] Pérez de Ribas, *Paginas*, 3:199. The incorruptibles endured: "Afirmó un religioso muy siervo de Dios ... que años después, abriéndose el sepulcro, fueron hallados los cuerpos tan enteros, que parando en pie el del padre Luis de Alavés, se tenía, poniéndole solo un dedo en el hombro, y que salía de los santos cuerpos un olor suavísimo": Pérez de Ribas, *Paginas*, 3:235.

[59] A typical example of sworn testimony to establish the saintliness of the deceased: Torquemada, *Monarquia*, 3:548.

[60] See Trexler, *Public Life*, 118–28, 299–306, and passim. Interments as triumphs in Europe are mentioned by L. Rothkrug, "Religious Practices and Collective Perceptions: Hidden Homologies in the Renaissance and Reformation,'" *Historical Reflections* 7 (1980): 32f.

[61] Those relations were also informed by the story that the governor had gotten a secondary relic, a necklace, from the body of one incorrupt: Pérez de Ribas, *Paginas*, 3:231f.

sanctified, and thus reshaped heaven and the relations between heaven and Durangan social groups, through the terrestrial procession. More than merely expressing ideas about the afterlife, worship incessantly created and transformed not only purgatory, as Christianity taught, but heaven and hell.

A cursory examination of the Christian defense of funereal honors shows that the triumphs accorded recently dead saints involved more complex exchanges than those purgatorial ones envisioned in that defense. Such honors were justified in the traditional view because the dead went to purgatory, so that those who honored their last rites helped the dead achieve heaven. It was for this reason that people said that the rich gained heaven so much more easily than the poor: the deceased and his family could insure the prayers of the poor, which the poor on their death could not afford to obtain from the rich.[62] This peripatetic theology of the maculate dead, the primary defense of funeral honors, gave rise to a second rooted in it. These pomps effected a redistribution of property from the rich dead to the poor living, the latter being paid for joining the procession to pray and wail for the body and soul of the dead.[63]

Since the holy men who are the subject of our paper were already in heaven, the honors paid them involved an at least consciously different set of relations altogether. "St. Gamboa, pray for us!" was a prayer for the living and not for the grateful dead,[64] the offerings to the rich clergy a redistribution of property upwards and not the reverse. To paraphrase an Italian wit, these were pomps where the mourners paid the dead rather than vice versa.[65] Those seas of tapers which the pious merchant of Durango provided for the processants were doubtless bought from the church, which had itself obtained them from the faithful in offering; they reverted to it on the conclusion of such rites.[66]

From this summit, a rich colonial clergy recycled some of this wealth to poor laity so that, in the classical missionary view, the clergy of this period was a personally abstemious redistributor of wealth.[67] That was of course true in terms of individual property-holding and, in general, the

---

[62] The standard defense is in Torquemada, *Monarquia*, 2:512f., also 518.

[63] Torquemada, *Monarquia*, 2:512f. On such rich-poor relations in formal acts, see Trexler, *Public Life*, 276, 476, 522.

[64] Torquemada, *Monarquia*, 3:582.

[65] Franco Sacchetti, *Il Trecentonovelle* (Florence, 1946), 234 (CIV).

[66] Wax candle offerings are mentioned below, and their return after use was normal procedure in Europe.

[67] Ideal types in Torquemada, *Monarquia*, 3:462, 584f.

clerical creation of important eleemosynary institutions is a matter of fact,[68] the physically uncoerced nature of much Indian giving evident, the clerical defense of Indian property against Spanish laity in no need of comment. Our point is rather the nature of the authority at that summit that allowed it to so modify the exchange structures of society: the set of relations of the living clergy with its dead brothers. Some time after the death of Peter of Ghent an Indian woman brought six habits to a friar, and named those who were to receive them. Along with five living friars, Ghent was included. Telling the story, Mendieta praised the woman's faith even as he recalled her naiveté. When the friar asked the woman if she did not know that Ghent was dead, she replied: "Father, I give the habit to fray Peter of Ghent as an offering; you give it to whomever you want."[69]

The Aztec matron's imperious words showed greater comprehension of the immanent and transcendental structures in which she lived than the paternalism of Mendieta was ready to admit. The very physical concentrations of dead holy men with living ones indicated that the two together directed divine commerce. The very universe of discourse, in which living religious represented each other to the Indians as saints and showed how generations of saints began by worshipping at graves and ended by becoming miracles themselves, drove home the point.[70] The funeral triumphs of these saints were thus more than mere immanent exchanges between the living just as they were more than expressions of belief about honoring the dead. Like the hair of the bishop growing in the grave, these rituals established and modified the social identities and spaces of the clergy, of Spanish lay society, of Indian society, and of all their distinct dead.[71] First the clergy.

---

[68] Ricard, "*Conquête*," chap. 2.

[69] "Padre, io doi en ofrenda un habito à Fr. Pedro de Gante, dalo tu a quien quisieres": Mendieta, *Historia*, 610; Torquemada, *Monarquia*, 3:431.

[70] The best case of the latter is Miguel de Estibaliz, "among those Spaniards who were present at the interments of . . . Calero and . . . Cuellar." On his conversion, subsequent visions and miracles, involving *inter alia* Cuellar, and on the great concourse at his funeral with "demonstrations of sanctity" including several habits cut up as relics, see Mendieta, *Historia*, 459, 466, 741, 758; Torquemada, *Monarquia*, 3:59–61. Cf. the Peruvian belief that the Franciscans *were* living dead: L. Milliones, "Introducción al estudio de las idolatrías," *Aportes: Revista de Estudios Latinoamericanos* 4 (1967): 78.

[71] On Zumárraga's body, see Torquemada, *Monarquia*, 3:457. Reaffirming the life-giving quality of what Torquemada decided was Zumárraga's incorrupt body, the author showed how a ring taken from the bishop later saved the life of a fetus: *Monarquia*, 3:459.

The most reverend and religious [Franciscan] fathers wanted those blessed [Jesuit] remains in their church, so that from it [the remains] could go with honor to our [church] of the Society of Jesus.[72]

The Durangan triumph manifests the predominant social fact about clerical participation with the dead in early colonial Mexico: the cooperation between different orders in the funeral honors paid individual religious. Yet behind that social fact there lies an important quality of behavior cited by our sources whose understanding first reveals how this cooperation confirmed saintliness: the disorder of the religious around the body at the four different stages of the immediate aftermath of death, burial, first exhumation, and successive ones.

The immediate clerical family or order of the deceased formed the exclusive social unit right after death, whether the demise took place in a small provincial house or in the hospital of a large institution like San Francisco de México, to which many Franciscans came for care when they were ill. In the latter we see the nurse leading the way. At times himself a "devout and saintly religious ... curing more by miracle than by science," on whose own death miracles would occur,[73] the nurse knew the whole saga of the saint's last days: how one had entered the hospital knowing the day and hour of his impending death and how another had passed his marvelous final hours; he could even authoritatively inform his brothers as they now gathered around the bed that the deceased's looks had improved since the wasting process of death had passed.[74] When such a man cut a finger from a just-dead brother, the increasing audience knew that an extraordinary event was brewing. When such a nurse put a palm in Alonso de Escalona's hand right after death, others soon crowded around to crown the saint with fresh flowers.[75] The infirmary large or small often began the miracle of sacrality, and the nurse was its handmaiden.

---

[72] Pérez de Ribas, *Paginas*, 3:197.

[73] For these characterizations of Lucas de Almodóvar (d. c. 1550), see Mendieta, *Historia*, 626f; Torquemada, *Monarquia*, 3:523f.

[74] Hour of death knowledge was commonplace, the very fact that a person who died in a hospital had come to it already having a significance: Torquemada, *Monarquia*, 3:497. Better looks are common, e.g., *Monarquia*, 3:585. The revived freshness of a corpse, as well as the absence of rigor mortis, were themes of the death story of Francis of Assisi; see elsewhere in this collection, "The Stigmatized Body."

[75] See the eye-witness report in Torquemada, *Monarquia*, 3:497f. Almodóvar cutting the finger off is in Mendieta, *Historia*, 626f.

Then the other brothers joined in, in 1584 they being the ones who flexed Escalona's joints and determined that, as the hours passed, rigor mortis did not set in. Gathered as if in chapter, they began to pare the nails from the cadaver's feet and hands and to clip off the hair. All of his brothers, the participant Torquemada remembered, wanted "a relic of the saint."[76] This household scene also dominated events at the first exhumation, which for different reasons might take place about three Christ-like days after the burial. It happened with Escalona. When his body on excavation proved incorrupt and sweet-smelling, and his joints flexible, the friars of the house again gathered around and began to kiss the hands and feet of the corpse, according to our witness passing half the night serenely communing with their dead brother. The mood at both these stages may in fact have been less than serene, for Torquemada remembered that while at the exhumation the prelates forbade the brothers from taking anything from the body of the corpse, only "some" obeyed.[77]

Evidently these reserved activities solidified the immediate community, especially because they encouraged its members subsequently to defend their group action by maintaining, and elaborating upon, the marvelousness of the corpse. The value of the relics they had obtained, whether traded or treasured, also depended upon their own excited brotherly state. Only such a unified state could justify the fact of exhumation, for example, which except for translation and other extraordinary causes was prohibited by custom. Exhumations tempted God, who might think that the clergy did not believe that the divinity could maintain bodies incorrupt.[78]

---

[76] "Con mucha devocion le cortaron los cabellos de la corona, y las uñas de las manos, y pies, y cada uno procuraba tener en su poder alguna cosa, que fuese reliquia de esto santo": Mendieta, *Historia*, 673; Torquemada, *Monarquia*, 3:498. No rigor mortis among nonmartyrs was a "señal de la puridad y limpieza que en su alma y cuerpo había guardado": Pérez de Ribas, *Paginas*, 3:301. Virginity is a body "soft like a child's": Mendieta, *Historia*, 616.

[77] "Tanto el contento . . . que se estuvieron en este acto hasta la media noche": Torquemada, *Monarquia*, 3:498. The contentment at Zumárraga's exhumation is described in *Monarquia*, 3:457–59. Both these accounts have detailed epidermal information, but the most extensive regards the exhumation of García de Salvatierra: Mendieta, *Historia*, 725. See a similar scene at a Franciscan hospital in Torquemada, *Monarquia*, 3:585.

[78] Mendieta, *Historia*, 596f.; Torquemada, *Monarquia*, 3:459. Torquemada asked how God could on the one hand show his power by having bodies exhumed incorrupt, yet that act could be considered wrong: *Monarquia*, 417, also 499. Mendieta considered such exhumations from curiosity irreverent, through which one bore guilt: *Historia*, 597. In a burst of reality, Torquemada recognized that only after Valencia was exhumed and casketed did "God begin to esteem [his] sanctity . . . and make it known to men": Torquemada, *Monarquia*, 3:415.

The evidence for cooperation between the orders emerges from the funeral itself and from subsequent exhumations, that is, those disinterments which were repeated as public acts. As to the funeral, we are less interested in those cases where bishops of one order were attended by retinues from the others, for such accompaniment was a function of episcopal authority.[79] Our attention is rather drawn by several cases in which the Franciscan chroniclers found marshaled ranks from other orders attending their own brothers' exequies. Thus Mendieta noted that the priors and other brothers of the Dominican and Augustinian orders bore the body of Escalona from the Franciscan chapter to the church, and that "all the orders" came to the funeral of the Franciscan Domingo de Areizaga in 1592 so as to accompany the body to the grave.[80] Torquemada attended the latter funeral, and brought out a standard element of such narratives: the Augustinians and Dominicans came to honor Areizaga on their own and without constraint.[81] Five years later the same witness saw a similar case at the burial of the Franciscan Pedro Oròz, when the other orders came "without being called. For they followed only the calling of God," Torquemada explained, "who calls upon the heart to accompany and honor the bodies of his servants."[82] The Franciscans' honor for the Jesuit saints of Durango was obviously no novelty in New Spain.

Nor was that cooperation limited to the funeral itself. In the case of Martin of Valencia's body and possessions we see a type of exchange system at work between Dominicans and Franciscans. First of all, Mendieta assures the reader that for thirty-three years after Valencia's first reinterment, the Franciscans repeatedly exhumed the eponymous father's incorrupt body so that not only their brothers, but the Dominicans, could view it.[83] Then when the body disappeared and the Dominican friary of Amecameca gained control of secondary relics of Valencia, it ultimately had to share the prize with the Franciscans. That seems to be the point of the latter history of these relics as told by Mendieta, certainly no uninterested witness to the Dominican possession of his Franciscan order's relics. He recounts how the Dominicans started to alienate pieces of these relics

---

[79] See for example Torquemada, *Monarquia*, 3:520; Mendieta, *Historia*, 636.

[80] Mendieta, *Historia*, 673, 713.

[81] Torquemada, *Monarquia*, 3:557, 498, and 583, where the author found the finger of God at the funeral of his mentor St. Gamboa "pues esta mocion fue hecha sin ser llamados."

[82] Torquemada, *Monarquia*, 3:576, also 498 for a similar formulation.

[83] Mendieta, *Historia*, 596.

He recounts how the Dominicans started to alienate pieces of these relics from their sacristy until their vicar saw "that if the business continued all [the relics] would be carried off."[84] At that point he converted Valencia's cave, where the Indians had kept the relics hidden and which was in effect a Mexican La Verna, into a chapel, moved the relics out of the monastery back to this now-Dominican chapel, furnished it with door, lock, and key, and placed an Indian guard before the cave so the relics could be seen but not taken. Mendieta tells us with evident gratification that this chapel was right on the road from Tenochtitlan to Puebla and thus became an important pilgrimage site for Spanish and Indian laity,[85] but certainly also for Franciscans, who may have preferred this Cave of their Fray Martin for venerating that father to a Dominican friary. Perhaps the Franciscans played a role in this whole affair; Mendieta says nothing on that score. What he does emphasize is the Dominican devotion to Franciscan relics.[86]

We come now to the actual behavior of this foreign clergy at the celebration of the body. At such funerals and exhumations, it was first of all the very presence of "the devout ones" of Spanish society which witness the deceased's sanctity.[87] The clergy was after all the grave division of labor in this society, charged with identifying sacred spaces and acts by their rigid behavior. Thus their formal appearance together at the burial of someone from another order counted just as much as their word that the deceased was "a holy man and a resident of heaven."[88] The institutional certification of holiness by other religious specialists was partially behavioral: starting with gravity, it ended in disorder. The very inversion

---

[84] "Si el negocio iba adelante se las llevarian todas": Mendieta, *Historia*, 604.

[85] Interesting details on the cave are in Mendieta, *Historia*, 604f.

[86] There is an earlier record of competition between the two orders at Amecameca: Kubler, *Architecture*, 89.

[87] Sahagún thus characterized the priests of the Aztecs: *General History of the Things of New Spain, Florentine Codex*, ed. A. Anderson and C. Dibble, vol. 9 (Santa Fe, 1950), 81. See my analysis of priestly function in *Public Life*, 39 and passim, but especially my "Aztec Priests for Christian Altars. The Theory and Practice of Reverence in New Spain," in R. Trexler, *Church and Community, 1200–1600: Studies in the History of Florence and New Spain* (Rome, 1987), 469–92.

[88] Said of Areizaga by the foreign friars who kissed his feet: Mendieta, *Historia*, 713. Motolinía was "grave and exemplary": Mendieta, *Historia*, 619. For grave religious at Escalona's funeral, see Torquemada, *Monarquia*, 3:498. A grave man looked like someone dead to the world. One friar was "mui compuesto en su persona . . . , y asi andaba en la mortificacion de su persona, como si fuera fraile amortajado, para hecharlo en la sepultura": Torquemada, *Monarquia*, 585.

of the clergy's gravity in the midst of the funeral, the mad scramble for relics at the moment of greatest pomp, that made a difference to our quasi-notarial, quasi-legal accounts of clerical funeral behavior.

Clerical frenzy is not mentioned in Pérez de Ribas's account of the Durango triumph, and it may have been absent for two reasons. First, the Franciscans held the body for two nights, and may have had every opportunity to obtain relics from it; second, in both processions the soldiers shot off their weapons to the very end of keeping people away from the bodies.[89] But such clerical disorders were present at other funerals, and especially marked at that of Alonso de Escalona. His own brothers had excitedly taken their relics from the body before the funeral when, the Dominican and Augustinian pallbearers transporting the body to the church, all their brothers crushed in around the litter to get close. When the body then slid from the bier as if alive, still free of rigor mortis, the excitement exploded. The very foreign friars charged with the solemn task of bearing the body now instantly led the assault on the miraculous corpse, going from ritual rigidity to sacred madness in a nonce.[90] First the habit or shroud on the corpse, and then other clothes no sooner than they had touched the electric hearse were shredded to pieces by the crowd, an attack so fierce that the Franciscans in this and other cases threw the body naked into the ground and covered it up.[91]

The excitement was not limited to the clergy. Thus if at the services for (the Franciscan) archbishop Zumárraga "the tears and sobs of the religious and clergy" became such as to prevent those services "from being able to be done according to custom," at the exequies for Antonio de Cuellar it was crowds of laymen "announcing and acclaiming him a martyr of Jesus Christ" that got so out of control that "the friars could not perform the [divine services], nor could anyone contain himself without

---

[89] "Mucha salva de arcabuería de los soldados, que hicieron calle entre la gente que se había juntado": Pérez de Ribas, *Paginas*, 3:198.

[90] "Se desliçaba de las manos y braços como si estuviera vivo, estando sus miembros mui tractables y blandos. Y atribuiendolo todos à mui grande milagro, llegaron los religiosos de las otras ordenes à cortar": Torquemada, *Monarquia*, 3:498. At a funeral mass, the key moment was after the body, placed high out of reach, was lowered for burial in the ground: see e.g., Torquemada, *Monarquia*, 3:582.

[91] Torquemada, *Monarquia*, 3:498f., 582, 592 are cases of such nude burials after disorders. The "disrespect" shown Escalona's body explains why it was then exhumed *and* why it then was put in a casket "como à cuerpo, que creian ser de santo, segun la larga experiencia, que tenian de su santidad": Torquemada, *Monarquia*, 3:499.

shedding many tears."[92] Sometimes our sources remembered that "everyone" had simultaneously ecstasized, and doubtless that universal legitimation was what the writers sought.[93] But the excited behavior of the clergy was especially significant. Cast as a type of saintly competition within the controlled environment of the clerical body, where the guardians of their ex-brother were unequal to the thirst of other orders for relics, such activity sacralized the space which contained such behavior and was a compelling evidence of sanctity.[94]

The student of European religious practice may have trouble at first comprehending the exotic clerical cooperation which spans such excitement, for in the Old World religious orders were jealous of their saintly bodies at funerals. Given the fact that the ultimate prize, attracting devotees, was the same in America as in Europe, why such a difference? While it is evident that our historians highlighted such inter-order burials because they implicated outsiders in the legitimation of one's own saints, that does not explain the fact of that cooperation. The answer must, I think, be sought in the different physical and human ecologies of Europe and America. Europe was dense with holy places. In early colonial Mexico, on the contrary, there were relatively few holy places and even fewer religious to go around; we have seen the clergy limiting the places by removing bodies from the hustings, and they limited the religious body by not allowing Indians to enter holy orders, in which they too might have won sainthood.[95] Such an ecology must have encouraged the clergy to band together to first establish through action the principle of the sacrality of Christian places and bodies. In this environment, clerical bodies were rich for all:

Divine disposition[s] following this mortal [one] we live in, pertaining to the immortal life where bodies will stay entire and glorious.

---

[92] Mendieta, *Historia*, 636, 741.

[93] E.g., Mendieta, *Historia*, 741.

[94] Note the formulation that the brothers unsuccessfully tried to defend the body from (inspired) relic seekers, e.g., Mendieta, *Historia*, 725, and in Torquemada, *Monarquia*, 3:582.

[95] The only Indian candidates were children killed by elders while preaching Christianity, one of whom was an incorrupt: see my "From the Mouths of Babes: Christianization by Children in Sixteenth-Century New Spain," in *Religious Organization and Religious Experience*, ed. J. Davis (London, 1982), 115–35, and in enlarged form earlier in the present volume.

To see an incorruption was to see heaven.[96] The laity agreed.

§

> The principal people of the [Spanish] city wanted to accompany [the bodies], and 150 soldiers from the secular militia made salvoes with their arquebuses.[97]

Clerical ecstasy kept holiness in churches, and drew the laity to them. As a reading of long-term behavior, that statement is true, for it is no more than to say that the solemn division of labor in society, enthusiastic in its veneration of sacra, attracts the jaded. Yet the same statement would not be a valid reading of the funeral services themselves, for not only the clergy but the Spanish and Indian laity participated in the common devotional cycle of original solemnity and subsequent excitement. What distinguished the clerical frenzy, we have said, was the physical rigidity expected of that division of labor. What distinguished the Spanish laity in the funeral context was their presumably disinterested, occult acclamation of saintliness through their individual sworn word.

The role of the Spanish laity in affirming sanctity began none the less at the superstructural level, in a marshaling of the total lay society by the secular lord at its apex which demonstrated to the satisfaction of the clerical scribes that only the funeral of a saint could so perfectly reproduce heavenly society. Torquemada told how on hearing of the death of Domingo de Areizaga in 1592, the viceroy ordered that the funeral be postponed until he could be present, already evidence of the repute in which the man was held.[98] In the royal presence great things might be expected, and so they occurred: so many secular officials followed, such a pompous number of religious graced the viceroy and the saint by their presence. Though no one required attendance, "so many people [came] as if

---

[96] "Conservando en aquella forma . . . por disposicion divina, que pertenece a la vida inmortal, que se consigue despues de esta mortal, que vivimos, donde los cuerpos han de permanecer enteros y gloriosos. Y siendo esta vision ia milagrosa, no es maravilla . . . que causase temor reverencial. . . . Asi le sucediò al. . . . Ecechiel . . . y à San Juan . . . acerca de las revelaciones . . . , y à otros santos varones que han merecido los aparecimientos divinos": Torquemada, *Monarquia*, 3:458.

[97] Pérez de Ribas, *Paginas*, 3:198.

[98] Torquemada, *Monarquia*, 3:557; also Mendieta, *Historia*, 713f.

for a public act which prescribed presence."[99] In these and similar appearances of the highest secular authorities the legitimacy of the saints was established as surely as the governor of Nueva Vizcaya would legitimate the Durangan martyrs through his coats of arms. It was with such structural visions of terrestrial and celestial overlappings in mind that Torquemada could speak of a friar who "finishing with congregations on earth, went to be a participant, one believes, in that [congregation] of the fortunate in heaven."[100] Describing still another funeral attended by high secular officials, the same writer explicitly compared heaven and earth: the funeral procession of the Indians was like the Last Judgment.[101] The "public act" of total congregation led by high civil authority was a portent of holiness.

When we move from superstructure to actual lay behavior, the record at first seems little different from the alternating solemnity and enthusiasm noticed in the clergy. The Spanish laity too might rip funeral shrouds to pieces, as they did at the Ezatlán interment of Juan Calero in 1541 after discovering that though it had lain in the field five days, his body smelled fragrant at that burial. Lay frenzy *and* rigidity at the funeral were precisely what Mendieta meant when he spoke of the "great devotion *and* solemnity" which left Calero "with the reputation of a saint."[102] But beneath the similarities lay a difference. The Spanish laity "acclaimed" miracles and visions relative to the state of the dead, announcements which were decisive in a way the interested word of a religious person could not be, and which had a force no Indian's words could possess. The Spanish sinner's word was the saint's bond.

Sinners' sex mattered. The woman Leonor Marín obtained a speck of the habit of Alonso de Escalona even before his hectic burial. On promptly being released from a long-term fever, this "devout woman" proclaimed that possession to the friars.[103] Another Spanish laywoman was fully credible when she told how fray Juan de San Francisco had appeared to

---

[99] "Como si para un acto publico, y mui forçoso, se huviera llamado": Torquemada, *Monarquia*, 3:557; also Mendieta, *Historia*, 714. See other lists of officials in Torquemada, *Monarquia*, 3:548, 582f., and Mendieta, *Historia*, 636.

[100] Torquemada, *Monarquia*, 3:576.

[101] Torquemada, *Monarquia*, 3:582. See also further below.

[102] Mendieta, *Historia*, 739. "Devotion" is in many cases a synonym for "excitement."

[103] Mendieta, *Historia*, 673.

her and told her that he was in heaven after two hours in purgatory.[104]
Just as important, however, are such avowals involving not devout women
but sinful men. The setting is the funeral or later exhumations, when the
clergy's incessant desire to know whether a body was still incorrupt, one
very essence of the long-term authority of the Mexican clergy in these
centuries, conflicted with the evident necessity of that same clergy to
accept God's dispositions, and not tempt or doubt his power. To be sure
a dead man was in heaven, in short, a sinner was required. That role could
occasionally be filled by the Spanish laity, as witness the funeral services
for García de Salvatierra:

> Without being called, the whole pueblo arrived to see dead him
> whom they had always considered a saint. And they saw him in-
> comparably more handsome than when he was alive, and his body
> more tractable and soft than before. . . . [It was] not only tractable
> but even warm, as many Spaniards affirmed who, the friars unable
> to stop them, got their hands on his chest and back after breaking
> through his habit, whose pieces they took as relics.[105]

The Spanish laity had a certain marginal but important role to play in
the creation of worshipful space and objects: soiled by the *saeculum*, its
word was yet reliable where the Indians' was not. When therefore Andrès
de Olmos died in 1571, it was "the religious and the lay Spaniards"
around the body at the funeral who noticed that the ornaments of the altar and those with which "the saint" had said mass "left such an odoriferous fragrance," the laity too who "praised God for it and declared that
sweetness and odor overpowered the odors of the earth."[106] The Spanish
laity was part of that group which held this a manifest miracle, and it was
a Spanish lay friend of Olmos who was the beneficiary of the saint's first
miracle when, at the time of the body's translation, he "reverenced the
earth" where Olmos had lain and was thus cured of an illness.[107]

But those who convinced the historians that Olmos was in heaven
were hopeless condemned sinners rather than venial ones, Olmos's ene-

---

[104] Mendieta, *Historia*, 660. Here was the place for the passage lifted from Motolinía's
Life of Martin of Valencia.

[105] "Segun lo afirmaron muchos españoles": Mendieta, *Historia*, 725.

[106] Especially important when one had stank during the last illness: Mendieta, *Historia*, 650f.; Torquemada, *Monarquia*, 3:474f.

[107] Mendieta, *Historia*, 650.

mies and not his friends. One of these "sinful men," Torquemada says, chose the funeral itself to testify to his evil and Olmos's sanctity:

> [He was so] taken aback by the many marvels seen at the death of the servant of God [that he] went to the place where they kept [Olmos's] dead body and, throwing himself at its feet, cried out with a great flow of tears and sighs, saying: 'This was a saintly man. And he told me the truth, but, an evil man, I did not want to believe him.'[108]

Such testimony was the more decisive, Torquemada knew, because it came "at the time of death, [which is the time] of truth." It involved "the shame of having to say the contrary to what they had previously affirmed," he continued in reference to both sinners, and that could not be ignored.[109] As if that were not convincing enough, Torquemada made a third point. Even as the sinners testified to Olmos's glory, they were aware of the saint's oncoming "revenge" for their lifetime of opposition to him. The one died of cancer of the mouth and the other of contagion.[110] The Indians knew all about divine ire.

§

> To transport [the holy bodies] decently, the governor ... [had] the Spanish soldiers go ... in ... front ..., with friendly Indian soldiers ... at their side. ...[111]

One of the most significant aspects of the Spanish lay response in our accounts is what is missing. Our historians rarely describe large ordered processions of the Spanish laity as part of their evidence; for now, the peculiar military triumph of Durango stands alone. Thus though the secular prince might trigger the assembly of the people, the actual role of the

---

[108] Mendieta, *Historia*, 650. Inadvertently the author makes it sound like the "truth" Olmos told was that he was a saint.

[109] Torquemada, *Monarquia*, 3:475. Another guideline of a "caso ... sin raspa de duda" was a reading of Matt. 18:16: "that from the mouth of two, or of three, comes all truth": *Monarquia*, 3:458.

[110] "Dios no se olvida de tomar venganza," etc.: Mendieta, *Historia*, 650; Torquemada, *Monarquia*, 3:475. On that fundamental activity of martyrs in heaven, see Charles, *Eschatology*, 411.

[111] Pérez de Ribas, *Paginas*, 3:197.

average Spaniard in proving holiness seems more individual than social. While social formations of the clergy were important, it was their subsequent disorder which cinched sanctity. Processional order itself belonged to the Indians. That was their contribution to canonization.

Witness again the death of Andrès de Olmos, where Spanish sinners gave their word but the Indians, intensely watched by all Spaniards at such times, responded as to a great ceremonial representation and organization. Mendieta remembered:

> In the moment that [Olmos] expired, the Indians heard a music from heaven, coming from diverse instruments such as trumpets, flutes, and clarinets. And they all came streaming to the church, from whence it seemed to them to be coming. There they asked [the friars] who was the important person who arrived from abroad, to be welcomed with such [triumphant] solemnity.[112]

We have chosen this mere tale to introduce our study of Indian responses for two reasons. First, in the context of Mendieta's narration this alleged Indian response was one of the "many marvels at the death" of Olmos which made Olmos's Spanish enemy repent; the social organization of the Indians in thanatic procession provoked conversion among individual Spaniards.[113] As we then attempt to pin down that native funeral response, the same tale accesses the three particular qualities emphasized by the historians in reporting such obsequies.

Like the occult vox populi familiar to the European historian, the Indians' mysterious knowledge of death points up the intense interest shown by our sources in their collective psychology, their "sentiment." It is "great," "odd," "notable," and so on.[114] More important, this sentiment belongs almost exclusively to them alone; only the rarest mention is made of the "great sentiment" of the collective Spanish clergy or laity at a funeral.[115] Next, our sources document this sentiment largely if not exclusively in terms of the Indians' organizational response to a death. Thus

---

[112] "Todos corriendo . . . , preguntando si habia venido de fuera alguna persona de cuenta, á quien con tanta fiesta recebian": Mendieta, *Historia*, 650; also Torquemada, *Monarquia*, 3:474, for diplomatic terminology, and *Monarquia*, 3:591f., for other "uncalled" Indians.

[113] See the striking case of *social* transformation at the end of this article.

[114] Mendieta, *Historia*, 644, 650, 684; Torquemada, *Monarquia*, 3:510, 582, all separate cases.

[115] Torquemada, *Monarquia*, 3:582.

the dreamy triumph of Olmos occurred to Mendieta as a social form appropriate to these native Christians. The outspokenly social and organizational character which the sources register as the Indian response to the death of holy men, so different from what they had to say about the Spanish laity, is evidently central to our theme. It proved the triumph of the saints in heaven by showing the victory the Spanish had achieved in socializing the inhabitants of this earth.

The natives came dressed, and they came in order. When Sahagún died in the friary of San Francisco de México in 1590, his students processed from Tlaltelolco to attend his interment "[dressed] in cassocks and surplices [and] showing their sentiment at his death."[116] We recall the enormous impression which the Indians' translation of the body of Francisco de Lintorne from Puebla to Tlaxcala made on Torquemada at about this time, and how minutely he described their processional order and technique. But perhaps the most revealing example of such intense attention to Indian organization is the same historian's account of what followed the death of Francisco de Gamboa in 1604:

> Then the Indians throughout the whole city knew of his death, [and] they stirred, congregating themselves so as to bury him. It was miraculous that, the interment being scheduled for late on the same day [of death], the cantors from all four cabeceras of Tenochtitlan ... came with their black crosses, and those [Indians] from Tlaltelolco, where [Gamboa] was guardian, also [came] with their cross. All the lords and principals of the [Indian] community accompanied [the crosses], as well from the area of Tenochtitlan as from that of Tlaltelolco, [followed] by an infinite number of women all with lit wax candles in their hands, and almost all dressed in mourning.[117]

Here was "the act which appeared a representation of the Day of Judgment":

> This whole accompaniment entered into the friary, to fetch the body of their beloved father, showing very great sentiment at having lost him. ... [It was like the] Day of Judgment, because on the

---

[116] After repeated urging, Sahagún had gone to San Francisco to die among the "old saints": *Monarquia*, 3:488.

[117] "Los Indios ... se movieron para venir à enterrarle": *Monarquia*, 3:582.

one side so many lit candles and six crosses went in front, while on
the other [were] the clamor and sobs of the people. They made
their act so unique, and so much more imposing than ordinary
ones. Some went saying: 'St. Gamboa, pray for us sinners.'[118]

This dramatic if structured description of Indian behavior includes information on the forms, clothes, crosses, and geography of the procession,
and of course on its sheer size, the same writer here and elsewhere measuring the extent to which the Aztecs filled up their great patio during such
services.[119] A further part of the description of Gamboa's funeral records
the Indians' subsequent disordered zeal to obtain for themselves his habits
and Areizaga's bones, but mention of such Indian lack of control is infre-
quent.[120] It was rather the almost insentient fashion in which the Spaniards perceived the Indians organizing themselves which delighted them,
even made them weep. Torquemada tells us that after witnessing the incredible totality of the funeral of St. Gamboa, a young relative of the deceased started to cry tenderly:

He said that he did not weep because he felt the absence of the de-
funct, but rather because of contentment on seeing that a single
relative whom he knew on earth had found such a death, [one] so
honored and enriched by conjectures of his predestination and
glory. And that even if he had not loved him as a blood [relative],
he would have held him in much reverence and treasured [him af-
ter] seeing what happened at his interment.[121]

The strong organizational content which is the hallmark of our sources'
descriptions of Indian responses to the death of a Spanish holy man does
not cease with the burial. To the contrary, and distinct from Spanish lay
reactions as described by the same historians, the Indian response long
after the death is very significant, and its structural character remains pro-

---

[118] "Hacian el acto mas particular, y de mas consideracion que los ordinarios. Iban
diciendo algunos: 'Santo Gamboa, ruega por nosotros pecadores'": Torquemada, *Monarquia*, 3:582. Other infinite Indians in somber order in *Monarquia*, 3:548.

[119] Torquemada, *Monarquia*, 3:468, 582. Significantly, Torquemada also noted that
the four barrios of Tenochtitlan which came included two that no longer were under
Franciscan *cura*: *Monarquia*, 3:582, and on the dispute with the secular clergy, see Gibson, *Aztecs*, 373.

[120] Torquemada, *Monarquia*, 3:557, 582.

[121] "Tan enriquecida de conjeturas de su predestinacion y gloria": Torquemada, *Monarquia*, 3:582f., also 558.

nounced.[122] The last quality of Indian behavior before dead holy men is that the natives' social units bring offerings to the saint over time.

Attention to those geographical structures led the way, Mendieta emphasizing them at the death of Peter of Ghent, when he often pointed to Indian processions as a sign of sentiment:

> His death was much felt by the natives in sadness and pain, and they showed it in public. For after a most copious number of them had taken part in his interment with shedding of tears, many of them took on mourning [clothes] for him, as for a true father who had left them. And after having made very solemn exequies all together in common, they made them separately, each confraternity for itself, and each village of the region, and other individual persons, [all] with generous and abundant offerings.[123]

Torquemada noted the same structures at the death of Alonso de Urbano at Tula, when after the burial the Indians requested their own mass for the deceased. . . .

> and offered [the body] bread and wine and many other things. And the pueblos of visit did the same, each for itself, and they said: 'What will become of us now that this saint whom we held a saint has left us.'[124]

Once these funerary structures had been mentioned, our sources pass over to emphasize the wealth Indians continued to bring to the grave of the dead. On the anniversary of Ghent's death, for example, they offered so much "for the servant of God fray Pedro that the friary of San Francisco de México was jammed in that year with provisions and victuals."[125] On the novena and then the anniversary of Gamboa's death the

---

[122] Cases of Spaniards long remembering dead religious are in Mendieta, *Historia*, 677, also Torquemada, *Monarquia*, 3:502. A case of long Indian memory is in Torquemada, *Monarquia*, 3:576f.

[123] "Cada cofradía por sí, y cada pueblo y aldea de la comarca": Mendieta, *Historia*, 611, and 609, showing that these confraternities were Ghent's own creations. How the Franciscans structured Indian processions by representing the Magi and Shepherds is shown in my "Ludic Life in New Spain: the Emperor and His Three Kings," elsewhere in this volume.

[124] "Pidieron los Indios del pueblo una misa . . . y lo mismo hicieron los pueblos de visita, cada uno por sì": Torquemada, *Monarquia*, 3:573.

[125] Mendieta, *Historia*, 611. See below for other evidence that perishables were kept in stockpiles; this measure was a standard device.

Indians celebrated with masses in exchange for "much bread, wine, and fruit," which they poured not only upon the friary of San Francisco, Torquemada carefully noted, but upon that of Tlaltelolco as well.[126]

Our survey of the sources has shown a special interest in the occult collective sentiment of the natives (*movimiento*), here miraculously channeled into support for clerical bodies and spaces instead of into insurrectionary "apostasy and parricide";[127] interest in their processional and thus organizational modes, a curiosity rarely bestowed on Spanish lay units at such exequies; and finally an almost exclusive concern with Indian tribute or charity in the long-term funerary context.[128] Dead Christian holy men, these pedagogues and masters of ceremony saw, permitted a new communal life through ritual which was doctrinally less dubious for the natives than the natives' veneration of All their Souls.[129] From a more practical viewpoint, the clergy which so often criticized the Spanish laity for stealing from the Indians could prove through such rites that the natives could be brought to yield their wealth voluntarily, in the best diocesan, confraternal, and civil order.

It was all a matter of loving the Indians so they would love you: that was the constant message these sources sent. The natives would respond to the death of a holy man who had "treated them like a father" with disciplined enthusiasm and charity, just as the body of a martyr might respond by incorruption to false claims of his assassins that he had harmed them.[130] There is something touching if ultimately irrelevant in these often personally persuasive clerical assurances that they "loved the Indians as if they were sons born of their entrails."[131] Our writers saw the funer-

---

[126] Torquemada, *Monarquia*, 3:583.

[127] Torquemada, *Monarquia*, 3:609; also above, n. 21.

[128] I could find no evidence of attention to Spanish geography and little to Spanish charity. See below for one case of Spanish organization.

[129] Diego Durán was horrified to find that the Indians honored their children and adults separately on that feast: *Book of the Gods and Rites, and the Ancient Calendar* (Norman, OK, 1971), 441. On All Souls in Mexico, individuals (Torquemada, *Monarquia*, 3:576f.) and the particular pueblo's dead were honored (Pérez de Ribas, *Paginas*, 3:80; Motolinía, *Memoriales*, 51).

[130] "Halláronlos todos comidos de los adives hasta los huesos. . . . Solo el cuerpo del sierve de Dios fray Pablo de Acevedo hallaron entero . . . , mas tan revenido y encogido que parecía cuerpo de algun niño. . . . Quiso Nuestro Señor mostrar en esto, que habia guardado ileso el cuerpo de su siervo por su inocentia . . . , los indios . . . creyendo les era contrario": Mendieta, *Historia*, 760f.

[131] Torquemada, *Monarquia*, 3:553.

al as the proof of the matter, and indeed, Indian funeral behavior made the saintliness of a merely moral corpse. It also was part of the ideal "public act" of a just, paternalistic society. That society would not die, the friars and priests intimated, which began around a community of incorruptibles who, from both the tomb and the counting table, created, maintained, and modified values, and exchanged wealth. Kings might have two bodies; the clerical corporation was one.[132]

From the apex of that exchanging social system, Motolinía assayed the celebration of Easter Eve, 1536. The incredible wealth the Indians brought in serialed ranks — the cloth, food, copal, gold, and "enough [candles] for a whole year" which they laid at the feet of Jesus and friar — challenged the imagination.[133] It was "enough to wake the dead," Motolinía significantly hyperbolized about that night when his lord prepared to emerge incorrupt from the grave after his death. The Indians brought this wealth in such good and solemn order to their savior "with such simplicity and bashfulness, as if the lord of the earth stood there visibly."[134]

Images of Triumph

> Putting his head into the casket, he saw that entire holy image.[135]

The saint had been buried, exhumed, and now reinterred in a casket, steps now being taken to place the virile incorrupt "where [his body] could be expected to remain entire."[136] The priests scramble, the Spanish sinner gives his word, the Indians march in order to make their saint. In a curious carnivalesque dance of death, each order inverts its expected behavior, and that inversion saves the social identity of the individual

---

[132] Questions of the perishability and immortality of the clerical estate have not been studied as have those regarding kings, by E. Kantorowicz, *The King's Two Bodies* (Princeton, 1957).

[133] See the long descriptions in Motolinía, *Memoriales*, 52f., *Historia*, 233f.

[134] "Para poner espíritu a los muertos ... como si allí estuviese visible el Señor de la tierra": Motolinía, *Historia*, 233f. See the Spaniards' visible Christ and Virgin further below.

[135] "Y metió dentro [la caxa] la cabeça ..., y metiendo la cabeça en el atud, vido aquella santa imagen entera": Torquemada, *Monarquia*, 3:457 (Zumárraga).

[136] "Lo bolvieron à enterrar donde debe permanecer entero": Torquemada, *Monarquia*, 3:499 (Escalona). This is the one direct statement of intention to preserve entire, and Torquemada follows with assurances that God can do it anyway, whatever the condition of the ground and water.

soul: now the body social lived around the spotless dead, the dead among the living saints.[137] The incorrupt saint's body is like the Virgin's assumed one. Both guarantee life to the living from their evident heavenly domicile, even while both live on earth through their images: the saint's his own body,[138] the Virgin her likeness who suffers and enjoys. The Virgin makes relics for earth though her body is assumed, the living dead send their souls, and Martin of Valencia perhaps even his body, to heaven.[139] Like the Virgin's so delicate cadaver, so the body of this eponymous father of the Indies disappeared, and after a diligent search Mendieta was convinced that no mortal hands had stolen Martin of Valencia. God had acted.[140] In fact, Valencia may have had his own type of Assumption or Resurrection.[141]

The devotional and moral geography around these living saints was distinct according to the groups involved. The clergy clearly lived in communion with the faithful immortals, to join them on their own demise. Where was the laity put to rest? Though a separate study of this topic is called for, there is some evidence that the Spanish laity did indeed often obtain burial in churches near saintly religious, in keeping with the custom, applauded by our missionaries, of profiting from saints' charisma through burial near them.[142] The Indians, it seems, remained at a distance. Although little is known about their cemeteries, there is no evidence in our sources that they were encouraged to, or did in fact, seek burial in churches.[143] In some cities and pueblos they seem to have been

---

[137] The Italian version of the article ended at this point. What follows appears in print for the first time.

[138] See n. 135, for one example of a topos in which incorruptibles are images. See the cases of standing bodies upright (obviously to be alive like an image) in Pérez de Ribas, *Paginas*, 3:235; Torquemada, *Monarquia*, 3:457.

[139] See above.

[140] It was "impossible" for the body to have been stolen without the Indian guards knowing of it, and Mendieta was satisfied that they had not been involved. "Mas desde el año de 1567 á esta parte no ha parecido, aunque el sepulcro se abierto algunas veces. . . . Quitó Nuestro Señor tan santa prenda de aquel convento . . .": Mendieta, *Historia*, 596f.; Torquemada, *Monarquia*, 3:418.

[141] Thus having been the first Apostle of the Indies, Valencia's body disappeared after thirty-three Christ-like years incorruptible, etc.

[142] Torquemada, *Monarquia*, 3:518, citing Augustine.

[143] No Indian is said to have been buried in the ground in churches, as were all clergy. On Indians wanting to be buried together and not with others, see Gibson, *Aztecs*, 128. In general, native Americans considered churches to be the place where Spaniards were buried.

buried in the patios of churches;[144] on the frontiers, we recall, they were excluded from any association with the saints' remains.[145] The stage for an Indian religion of martyred images was set.

As the bodies of the saints flowed toward centers, the Spaniards developed another type of thanatic geography in the sacrally barren interstices of native pueblos: imaged records of the places of native defeats and Spanish triumphs. Just as the friars, always carrying an ample supply of images, bestowed them on friendly villages, where they became the property holders of their church's land,[146] so in the wake of the Tepeguanes revolt the Jesuits and the Spanish laity would impose them for and in places and times which would not be forgotten.

Four Jesuits had died at Santiago Papazquiaro, Pérez de Ribas relates, but Jesus himself had "suffered in his sacrament that which he had suffered in his person and mortal flesh" at the Crucifixion. At Zape four more Jesuits had died, but also Mary:

> Even if here our savior did not suffer in his divine sacrament ..., he suffered the more in the image of his most sacred mother, [and] he suffered in four priests, that is, [anointed of] Christ the lord.[147]

A festival at Zape to collocate a new image of the Virgin was, in fact, the occasion that had brought on the slaughter. In this moment of triumph she had been desecrated in her body, in time, and in the social frame of her image which the Spanish festivities had provided. The Spaniards assessed the situation:

> [The Indians] showed their greatest rabidity and destruction against the sacred images of our lord Christ and his saints, who in this persecution suffered in [their images] as did the blessed [Jesuit] fathers. [They were rabid] especially [against] some of the sacred Virgins.[148]

---

[144] Kubler's suggestion that an engraving of c. 1579 shows grave sites is probably right. An overlooked passage in Torquemada (*Monarquia*, 2:519) demonstrates conclusively that the patio was a traditional Indian burial ground. For "the cemetery outside" where Indians are buried, see Pérez de Ribas, *Paginas*, 3:160, 174.

[145] See above, at n. 34, and following.

[146] Mendieta, *Historia*, 753; Gibson, *Aztecs*, 130.

[147] "Cuatro sacerdotes y cristos del Señor": Pérez de Ribas, *Paginas*, 3:178, and 175.

[148] Pérez de Ribas, *Paginas*, 3:214.

The Spaniards of Guanaceví were particularly outraged, Pérez de Ribas continues, because of the special devotion they had assumed to the destroyed Lady, and one of their number who after a vow had escaped the slaughter at Zape now decided to replace the Virgin, "who had suffered so much ignominy in this pueblo." To "renew her," he had a new image made in Mexico City and then surrounded it with jewels; it would later become famous as the Virgin of the Martyrs.[149] He had it brought first to Guanaceví because he wanted "to collocate her in the church of Zape where she had been outraged and destroyed." This transpired on the feast of the Assumption (15 August), one year to the day from when she had been defamed.[150] As the Assumption approached, the Indians prepared a triumph ... over themselves. They would worship the face they had disfigured and bloodied. These native Americans on the frontier would worship the places they themselves had defiled. And the Spaniards, dazzled by the fervor yet domesticity, in short by the ordered sentiment of their subjects, would themselves be converted to socialized discipline and sacralize the place:

> When [the Assumption] arrived, many Indians gathered from three pueblos into this one. With the Spaniards, they spared no effort to adorn and celebrate this *entrada* of the Queen of Heaven, who returned triumphant over the devil and his [Indian] allies to her tabernacle and dwelling, from whence she had been torn with greater outrage than when she fled to Egypt because of the persecution of her son. At spaces of half a league on the road from Guanaceví to Zape, they raised a great number of triumphal arches of flowers from their mountains and fields, raising a bower adorned with flowers in the place where they had taken the life of the two blessed padres Fonte and Moranta when they went to celebrate the feast. There they collocated the Virgin at the beginning. ...
>
> It appears that this lady wanted by her triumph to celebrate that [triumph] of her devout and loving [Jesuit] servants, who had shed their blood to honor her and her most blessed son. A very

---

[149] Pérez de Ribas, *Paginas*, 3:214f. On the sensate nature of European images, see my "Florentine Religious Experience: the Sacred Image," in Trexler, *Church and Community*, 37–74.

[150] Note the conflation of two images into one Virgin: "hasta que llegase sazón para colocarla en la iglesia del Zape, donde había sido ultrajada y destruida": Pérez de Ribas, *Paginas*, 3:214.

singular circumstance of this feast augmented it and [added to the Spaniards'] joy, noticed at the time and celebrated thereafter: the sight of the fervor shown by the converted Tepeguanes toward [the feast] which amazed the Spaniards who were present. ... The Spaniards' awe was such that for almost half a league, from this station [where the Indians had killed two Jesuits] up to the church [next to which they had killed the two others] where the holy image was collocated, they all went on foot, [indeed] many [Spanish] persons of note went shoeless in procession, with [Indian] dances and clarinets and trumpets.[151]

The long-suffering, now triumphant image of the Virgin had insured that these paths and this pueblo would remember. Even as the scattered pieces of the previous Virgin now started to work miracles, the "resurrection of the Christianity of the Tepeguanes" from its corrupt past was patent:

... not only in the spiritual [sphere], but also in the temporal, so that in both [Mary] is the mother of mercy. For once the uprising and rebellion had passed, one of the richest mines in this land of New Spain was discovered and populated. It is called Parral. ...[152]

Pérez de Ribas concludes his account of the fiesta:

At the time that the Virgin entered the pueblo, it seemed to [the Spaniards] that she entered triumphing over her enemies, a celestial thing which caused such respect and reverence among [the Spaniards] that they could not put their finger on it.[153]

---

[151] "En el lugar donde habían quitado la vida a los dos benditos padres": Pérez de Ribas, *Paginas*, 3:214f. In this land "fertilized with the blood of martyrs," (*Paginas*, 3:213), the converted Tepeguanes had "fervor de la piedad": *Paginas*, 3:215. They were "más domesticados que antes": *Paginas*, 3:215. They "acuden a la doctrina con puntualidad," all being a miracle owed to the new (and thus old) image, according to the Spaniards: *Paginas*, 3:215.

[152] Pérez de Ribas, *Paginas*, 3:215f.

[153] "Como una cosa celestial que les causaba tal respeto y reverencia que no acertaban a significarlo": Pérez de Ribas, *Paginas*, 3:215.

RELIGIOUS

STRUCTURES

Legitimating Prayer Gestures
in the Twelfth Century:
The *De Penitentia* of Peter the Chanter*

For the Kingdom of God does not consist in talk, but in power (1 Cor. 4.21).

Different from his predecessors and successors, Peter the Chanter (d. 1197) justified prayer gestures by their presence in a sacred book rather than by their use by successful historical figures. From the Bible he derived a canon of seven de-individuated body postures, described each in words and, unique at the time, provided for pictures of each mode. An examination of the nine extant manuscripts of his work and their fifty-nine pictures shows, however, that pictures could never be mere translations of texts. In each manuscript the postures vary with the age and status of the "mannequins" represented. The Chanter's failure to recognize this points to his, and his readers', clerical status. Clerks were the defenders of the Word, yet they were here called upon to learn how to image themselves in ritual through images, which they corporately scorned.

---

* This essay appeared previously in *Gestures*, ed. J.-C. Schmitt, History and Anthropology 1 (Paris, 1984), 97–126.

*Peter's attempt at a technologization of submission postures remains sig-
nificant, however. It is congruent with the general technical direction of
high medieval thinking.*

IF THERE IS A NORM WHICH NO COMMUNITY denies without threatening
its foundations, it is that body's systems of physical comportments, and
especially those actions which communicate sovereignty and submission.
How are these forms legitimated? Societies avoid the question, indeed they
sooner debate their supreme beings than the unquestionable rightness of
these acts. How does one teach them? Rarely formally, for their pedagogical formalization itself casts doubt on their assertedly "natural" character.

The student approaches this area of faith and asks whence in fact come
these gestures of sovereignty and submission, for example those abject
movements Christians use when praying to their Gods and rulers. Surely
evolutionary biology provides a necessary part of the answer. Several of
these submission gestures are in place among our primate ancestors, and
must be interpreted as adaptive behaviors in part genetically transmitted.[1]
Yet if anything is clear from the bibliography on the subject of human gestures, it is that humans prefer to seek origins within the species and not
outside, and that they emphasize the evolution of such gestures within human history.[2] The fiction of a segregated human culture, therefore, is the
paradigm for studying the normalization of gestures within human history.

In this paper I propose to examine a medieval liturgical actor and
writer who attempted to defend a system of submission gestures and tried
to teach them systematically — an exception, that is, to the human tendency to avoid the topic. Before the twelfth century, if I am right, the

---

[1] See I. Eibl-Eibesfeldt, *Love and Hate* (New York, 1972); M. von Cranach and
I. Vine, eds., *Social Communication and Movement: Studies of Interaction and Expression in
Man and Chimpanzee* (London, 1973). Peter the Chanter himself links the gesture of prostration to animal behavior: ms. Klosterneuburg Monastery 572 (hereafter KN), fol. 12rb,
also 12vb. I want to thank John Baldwin, Penelope Mayo, and Daniel Williman for invaluable discussions and for reading a draft. My thanks are also due to Julian Plante and
the Monastic Microfilm Project for the Klosteneuburg and Zwettl manuscripts, and to
Susan McChesney Dupont for certain illustrations.

[2] See D. Morris et al., *Gestures. Their Origins and Distribution* (New York, 1979), and
J. Bremmer and H. Roodenburg, eds., *A Cultural History of Gesture* (Ithaca, 1991). In
general on prayer modes see T. Ohm, *Die Gebetsgebärden der Völker und das Christentum*
(Leiden, 1948); L. Gougaud, "Attitudes of Prayer," in his *Devotional and Ascetic Practices
in the Middle Ages* (London, 1927); and G. Ladner, "The Gestures of Prayer in Papal Iconography of the Thirteenth and Early Fourteenth Centuries," in *Didascaliae. Studies in
Honor of A. M. Albareda*, ed. S. Prete (New York, 1961), 245–75.

primary means of legitimating gestures was by casual reference in text or image to the examples of individual living or dead persons who had effected marvels through particular gestures. Such behavioral exemplars are still used as models for the young, and the pedagogical principal of miming the physical comportments of successful adults was still in place at least as late as the European Renaissance.[3] In that age and earlier, the lives of famous men and women were the sources for historically efficacious actions, and the figurative programs of the churches of Europe showed useful actions of such heroes for all to see. Both living and dead exemplars were and are considered legitimate sources of imitation because the efficacity of their lives (miracles, wealth, etc.) led to their being considered immortal.

The attempt at legitimation and teaching I want to examine first appeared in the late twelfth century; I shall call it abstract figured literalism. The doll-like mannequins of the pre-photographic age are a modern example of the figures I refer to. These technical works characteristically deindividuate their figures in the interest of universalizing the legitimacy of the various postures of greeting and contact behaviors they teach. In the medieval sacred realm with which we will be concerned, however, a literal legitimizing base for these images was provided by sacred books. To be sure, these books not only provided normative statements about how one should pray, but also offered many behavioral exempla of the type mentioned above, for example: "Look, Christ did this, and his buried body remained incorrupt, so you should do the same." But what happened in the late twelfth century went beyond this traditional utilitarian legitimation. In his work *De Penitentia*, the Parisian moral theologian Peter the Chanter (d. 1197), assertedly drawing on the authority of the sacred scriptures, presented a series of technical, written descriptions of seven "authentic" modes of prayer and, what was unexampled at the time, provided for the depersonalized, nonnarrative figuration of each mode after the verbal description.

The result of this technologization of prayer was a group of manuscripts which have almost the same words describing each mode of prayer, but significantly varied prayer figures. After a short analysis of the manuscripts, this paper studies how Peter the Chanter thought to teach prayer gestures by abstracting technical verbal descriptions of such gestures from sacred

---

[3] R. Trexler, *Public Life in Renaissance Florence* (New York, 1980), 171. A classical case of a behavioral example are the postures assumed by the Three Wise Men when they visited the infant Jesus in his crib, a scene figured in thousands of European paintings; see my *Journey of the Magi: Meanings in History of a Christian Story* (Princeton, 1997), and the articles on the magi or Three Kings in the present volume.

writings, and then producing abstract figures to copy his verbal descriptions. The project failed. Historically, the next treatise on prayer gestures with illustrations returned to the authority of a hero (St. Dominic) for legitimation, and pictured that hero in the drawings.[4] But the attempt of Peter the Chanter is intensely interesting. This article will show that preexisting behavioral models in the Chanter's society and the paucity of his sources forced him to misrepresent the consistency and explicitness of his sacred authorities, and it will demonstrate how the accompanying pictures further modified Peter's own written canon. At the conclusion of this paper, I will describe how reverential systems were in fact maintained by studying what Peter the Chanter suggests about the border between reverence and insult.

De Penitentia

The best-known work of Peter the Chanter is the so-called *Verbum Abbreviatum*, written in the early 1190s, extant in an inedited long version and in a published short version.[5] The manuscript tradition of these versions has been carefully studied by John Baldwin, who also identified several variants on the basic work, including seven complete manuscripts which he called a "reorganized abridgement."[6] Baldwin cautioned that he had not studied this "abridgement" carefully and he urged further work on the manuscripts, but like Artur Landgraf, he did consider this "reorganized abridgement" a variant on the published *Verbum Abbreviatum*.[7] The work is however essentially independent, as I have now demonstrated in a

---

[4] "Secundum quod modum sepe Dominicus orabat, hic aliquid est dicendum": the Latin text and pictures of this later thirteenth-century work are in I. Taurisano, ed., "Quomodo Sanctus Patriarcha Dominicus orabat," *Analecta Sacri Ordinis Fratrum Praedicatorum* 30 (1922): 93–106; a Castilian text with pictures of the same work is in G. Alonso-Getino, ed., "Los nueve modos de orar de señor Santo Domingo," *La Ciencia Tomista* 24 (1921): 5–19. See now J.-C Schmitt's study of the Dominican prayer modes, "Entre le texte et l'image: les gestes de la prière de Saint Dominique," in *Persons in Groups: Social Behavior as Identity Formation in Medieval and Renaissance Europe*, ed. R. Trexler (Binghamton, 1985), 195–220, and the same author's *La Raison des Gestes dans l'Occident médiéval* (Paris, 1990).

[5] J. Baldwin, *Masters, Princes, and Merchants. The Social Views of Peter the Chanter and his Circle*, 2 vols. (Princeton, 1970), 2:246ff. My thanks to John Baldwin for his orientation and encouragement. The short version is in Migne, *PL*, 205 (Turnhout, 1968).

[6] Baldwin, *Masters*, 2:254.

[7] Baldwin, *Masters*, 2:255. A. Landgraf, "Werke aus der engeren Schule des Petrus Cantor," *Gregorianum* 21 (1940): 54.

monograph and partial edition. Most important, the author himself said so. Writing it after the edited *Verbum Abbreviatum*, he referred to the earlier work at three different points by the name of *De Vitiis et Virtutibus*.[8]

There is every reason to believe that he named the later work *De Penitentia*, even if he did not call it that within its text; some of the nine manuscripts I have examined in fact bear that title.[9] Thus both this work and the earlier one begin with the words *Verbum Abbreviatum*, but Peter the Chanter referred to neither by that name. For convenience and accuracy, then, I shall refer to the published work by its correct title, *De Vitiis et Virtutibus*, and to the subject of this paper as *De Penitentia*. Researchers can easily identify the latter work by the uniform explicit *premium perfectorum* and by the presence of or provision for illustrated prayer modes, neither of which is found in the *De Vitiis et Virtutibus*.[10]

Verbal and corporal prayer seem to have furnished the original inspiration for the work, and it is even probable that its early sections were written after the prayer section was done. Different from the chapter organization of the *De Vitiis et Virtutibus*, the *De Penitentia* is organized into books: one group of manuscripts has ten, the other seven books.[11] Most of the manuscripts of this latter subdivision begin their fifth book as follows: "Incipit quintus liber cantoris parisiensis de oratione et partibus

---

[8] "Haec omnia dicta sunt supraplenarie in alio nostro opere quod preintitulatur de vitiis et virtutibus": KN, fol. 8vb, also fols. 15va, 29ra. Thus an old authority's hunch was right that the author actually named his treatise not *Verbum Abbreviatum*, but by the nature of its subject matter: *Histoire littéraire de la France*, 2nd ed., 15 (1869), 288. For the text and pictures of the section *de oratione* of the *de penitentia*, see now R. Trexler, *The Christian at Prayer: An Illustrated Prayer Manual Attributed to Peter the Chanter (d. 1197)* (Binghamton, 1987). The attribution to the Chanter is all but certain, especially since the determination of Nicole Bériou that our *de oratione* has much in common with the Chanter's *Distinctiones*; see her review of my edition in *Le Moyen Age* 96 (1990): 584f.

[9] KN does, as does its ancestor ms. Zwettl Monastery 71 (hereafter ZW), as well as the later ms. Prague University Library 1518 (hereafter PR), which I have not yet personally examined. Mss. Leipzig University Library 432 (prov. Leipzig Thomaskloster?: LE-TK) and 433 (prov. Altzell: LE-AZ), also derived from Zwettl, lack proper titles. The Italian manuscripts have the title *De penitentia*: ms. Venice State Archives, S. Maria della Misericordia in Valverde, b 1 (V), and ms. Padua Antonian Library 532 (PA). Ms. London British Library, add. ms. 19767 (prov. Ottobeuren: LO-OT) and its copy ms. Munich State Library 17458 (M) are entitled *Viaticum tendentis Iherusalem*.

[10] All the identified manuscripts have pictures except M, where empty spaces with the instruction "figura" remain.

[11] Mss. to the west and south have ten: LO-OT, M, V, PA (the latter two calling a "treatise" what is bk. 10 in the former). Mss. to the east have seven books: LE-TK, LE-AZ, ZW, KN.

eius,"[12] and it is this book *de oratione* that I have now published. Added
to the fact that one manuscript of the ten-book version has no book number in the introduction to its book 8, while another bears an erroneous
number, this unusual naming of the author in an introduction mid-way
through the treatise suggests that *de oratione* was written first.[13] Thus
manuscript students will look for the first words of this section, *Conforta
me rex sanctorum*, in their search for the work's hypothetically oldest
manuscripts.

Apparently alone among the tracts *De Penitentia* known from this age
in having non-narrative pedagogic behavioral illustrations, this work is
also unique because the text calls for and refers to the pictures: they are
neither an afterthought nor at times even a distinct undertaking. For
whom, then, did the author intend this integrated picture book? The text
accompanying the figures does not say, but the work speaks generally to
the clergy, and specifically to a *dilectissimus lector* who wants to incorporate
other prayers into his canonical hours.[14] One would think, therefore,
that the Chanter had ecclesiastics in mind as those who could learn from
texts and pictures. Yet the author apologized to his clerical audience for
the pictures only "idiots" needed.[15] At whom then were the illustrations
aimed by the patrons of the several copies? Apparently mostly the laity, as
we shall see, yet Peter assumed they could not read his textual legitimation of the figures.[16] Clearly, Peter the Chanter's decision to fuse words
and pictures had to reveal the deep clerical ambivalence toward pictures.
This is a work which has not resolved the problem of representing personal norms, even as it moves into the brave new world of abstract corporeal
technology.

Creating the Text

Peter the Chanter associated with the Cistercians, and probably
watched their silent monks signal each other in the order's sign language,
one they learned, it seems, through words and mime rather than through

---

[12] KN, fol. 17va; ZW, fol. 4r; LE-TK, fol. 63r.

[13] For the mistakes: M, fol. 146va; LO-OT, fol. 193r.

[14] The Chanter names the seven hours, and then says: "Quicunque ergo velit
iamdictas horas cantare vel etiam alias preces privatas confundere, ad hoc. . . .": KN, fol.
17vb. See the text continuation at n. 19.

[15] See below.

[16] See below.

pictures.[17] How unproblematical such communications must have seemed to him. Mis-signaling the sign for "pass the cheese" did not insult anyone, as would a bad sign to God; custom was the only needed legitimation for these signs whose main purpose was general communication and not, it seems, the expression of submission. Prayers were something else, and Peter wanted to go beyond custom in defending their execution. Nor did he consider the similar reverences paid secular lords as in themselves justifying their use in divine discourse, which required a divine legitimation. The Chanter did not ignore such evidence, to be sure, but he did not view it as legitimating his modes of prayer.[18]

Peter legitimated his seven prayer modes by telling his readers that they were scripturally documented. Here as throughout the work playing the role of the scholar who returns to basics and deserts the glosses of sophisticates, he remarks:

> So that it please [the supplicant] and is useful to him and others, he ought to pray in any of these modes which will promptly be named. There are seven regular and authentic and meritorious modes of praying, which is proved by the authority of the sacred scriptures. For as the wise man says: 'Unless something which is asserted is justified and proved by suitable and legitimate witnesses, it should be denied with the same facility with which it is asserted.'[19]

The Chanter's prayer modes were, therefore, said to be derived from the book through which the Christian God is said to speak to us, and praying in these fashions was, inversely, viewed as speaking authentically to God.[20] Evidently, one faced east to correctly direct that speech.[21] And as the Chanter said in discussing the verbal prayers he mandated, the whole pro-

---

[17] Figural representations of these signs in this age are unknown; see G. Van Rijnberk, *Le langage par signes chez les moines* (Amsterdam, 1954), with an inventory of Latin descriptions. Peter died in the Cistercian house of Longpont: Baldwin, *Masters*, 1:ii.

[18] See below.

[19] "Ad hoc ut ei placeat et sibi et aliis prosit, debet orare aliquo istorum modorum qui statim dicentur. Sunt autem septem modi regulares et auctentici et meritorii orandi quod probatur auctoritate sanctarum scripturarum. Porro ut ait sapiens: 'Quicquid asseritur, nisi idoneis et legitimis testibus convincatur et probetur, eadem namque facillitate repellitur qua astruitur' ": KN, fol. 18ra.

[20] KN, fol. 17rb.

[21] KN, fols. 19ra, 19vb, and at the beginning of this book (fol. 17vb), "faciei tendentis in Ierusalin," the title of LO-OT and M.

cess of prayer was a type of restitution to God of what God had given us in the Bible.[22]

Peter's claims in this regard are first of all conditioned when we note that Peter does not derive his seventh and last mode of prayer from the Bible but from Gregory the Great. The physical posture by which, *more camelorum*, Gregory's aunt prayed with her elbows and knees on the ground, had no parallel in the Bible whatever, and Peter did not conceal the fact.[23]

But a more important question is how Peter the Chanter uses the biblical authorities he does cite, and we can answer it by comparing his technical descriptions of each mode to his sources. He says that in body prayer, as distinct from heart or mouth prayer, there are three fundamentally "devout postures": standing, kneeling, and lying flat on one's stomach (prostration), and on examination we find that the Chanter's seven modes incorporate four standing postures, one kneeling one, and one prostration; the "camel type" (proskynesis) fits between these latter two.[24] Certain of these modes, such as kneeling and standing with arms outstretched are so simply described that they are amply documented by his biblical sources.[25] But others are not, as for example modes one and six, whose texts are:

The first mode of praying is this, namely the arms and both hands joined and extended over your head toward heaven as far as you

---

[22] A faithful supplicant is one who renders back the prayers he owes, and one who omits prayers is a thief: KN, fols. 20vb–21ra, and further fol. 18vb.

[23] "Item nota Gregorius papa docet difficilem modum orandi et alium a predictis sex . . . 'Cumque corpus eius de more mortuorum ad lavandum esset nudatum, longe orationis usu in cubitis eius et genibus, camelorum more, inventa est cutis obdurata excrevisse, et quod vivens eius spiritus semper gesserit vel caro mortua testabatur.' Et ita habes septem utiles modos intercedendi": KN, fol. 19rb. The ancient practice of validating postures through cadavers is also used in describing Anthony the hermit: KN, fol. 18rb. V (s.p.) says at the beginning of its descriptions that there are *six* authentic modes, not seven, and I suspect this represents the oldest wording, the Chanter adding the *mos camelorum* later so as to equal the seven canonical hours.

[24] Heart, mouth, and body prayers are the *forme orandi*. The "devota corporis positio" is "tripliciter: stando, et flexigenibus, [et] toto corpore ad terram prostrato": KN, fol. 19vb. The four standing modes are: with hands over head (no. 1); with hands outstretched (2); with hands placed in front of the eyes (3); with body bowed or inclined (6).

[25] "Secundus modus orandi debet fieri manibus et ulnis expansis ad modum ad quedam similitudinem crucis": KN, fol. 18ra. "Quartus modus deprecandi deum fit positis genibus in terra": KN, fol. 18vb.

can extend them. Thus I say not sitting nor lying nor supported, but erect, the whole body raised. . . .[26]

You should further know that beyond the already mentioned modes of praying there is another one which should be done thus: also in an erect stance, the supplicant with the whole body bows his head before the sacred and holy altar.[27]

An examination of the one source for mode six (Ps. 37.7–9) finds David "inclinatus . . . usque quaquam rugiebam a gemitu cordis mei," which as quoted by the Chanter does indicate both bowing and standing. In fact, however, David was not praying at all, but describing how God's punishment had bent his spirit. Even more questionable is that the Chanter constructed his text by taking one part of his quote from the Vulgate and the other from the *Vetus latina* version of the psalm.[28] Mode one proves even more revealing on examination. Peter cites Isaiah (1.15) and Paul (1 Tim. 2.1–2.8) as his biblical authorities. Isaiah actually has God say that the mode will *not* be efficacious, while both the prophet and Paul speak only of raising the hands, no mention being made of the arms or other parts of the body, and nothing being said as to how far the hands should be raised or that they should be joined. Among his non-biblical authorities, finally, only the *vita* of Martin of Tours adds anything, namely that this saint turned his eyes toward heaven.[29]

For all his fundamentalist insistence on biblical simplicity, therefore, the Chanter often found precious little biblical authority for his modes of prayer, which had obviously been developed by a scholar and no mere reader. We see his intellectual bent at work when, in the context of mode three, he attempts to clarify the difference between modes one and two (arms out as if on a cross) on the one hand, and mode three on the other:

The third mode of interceding with God is done standing, the supplicant being positioned with the whole body erect, as the two pre-

---

[26] "Primus orandi modus est talis, videlicet brachia et ambas manus coniunctas et extensas supra caput tuum versus celum, inquantum prevales extendere. Ita dico non sedens neque iacens nec appodiatus, sed erectus, sursum toto corpore": KN, fol. 18ra.

[27] "Insuper sciendum est quod preter modos iamdictos orandi est alius qui sic habet fieri: cum orans, stans etiam erectus, toto corpore inclinat caput suum ante sacrum et sanctum altare": KN, fol. 19rb.

[28] Cf. in A. Colunga and L. Turrado, eds., *Biblia Sacra iuxta Vulgatam Clementinam* (Madrid, 1977), 481.

[29] KN, fol. 18ra.

vious modes are to be done. Nevertheless this mode differs from the others as follows: In this third [mode] the supplicant is required to stand erect on his feet so that he is not supported nor does he adhere to anything — as in the aforesaid. [But here] he has his hands stricken together and contiguous, extended and directed before his eyes.[30]

The author cites three biblical sources for this mode. Luke says that Christ stood up to *read* in the synagogue (4.16), David has Phinehas staying a plague by standing up and successfully interceding (Ps. 106.30), and the prophet Esdras says he stood on a step, opened the *book* in public, and blessed God (1 Esd. 9.42–46). The Chanter's interest in postures for reading bears emphasis, but note our context that in describing the third mode, he actually further defines the first: While the third mode has the arms and hands extended directly before the eyes — the supplicant implicitly if not expressly looking straight ahead —, Peter indirectly says that the first mode has the eyes turned toward heaven, which was not part of his original definition. The author apparently assumed that aspect into his subsequent definition while unconsciously recalling that Martin of Tours had prayed with his eyes skyward, and we shall see that such tergiversations confused the illustrators of this text. But once again, Peter does not successfully document this third mode of prayer. The Bible, and often his patristic sources and *vitae*, did not conform to the neat series of modes the scholar constructed. The eminent theologian must have understood that his reader would espy this meager harvest, but could be persuaded to follow the modes by the force, if not the argument, of custom.

At two points in the work, the Chanter hints at the role which church practice played in his own understanding of legitimacy. The first concerns

---

[30] "Tertius autem modus intercedendi ad deum fit stando, orante existente directo toto corpore, utpote in duobus est agendis superioribus. Tamen in hoc differt iste modus ab aliis, quoniam in hoc tertio tenetur orator esse erectus super pedes suos, ita quod non sit adpodiatus neque inherens alicui rei, sicut in iamdictis, habens manus complosas et contiguas, extensas ac directas coram oculis suis": KN, fol. 18rb. At another point the Chanter refers to the same position with "manibus iunctis": KN, fol. 19va. Peter's instructions for modes 1 and 3 (*manibus iunctis*, etc.) predate most of the evidence for joined hands gathered by Ladner, "Gestures," 258ff. Ladner's argument of a eucharistic inspiration for the spread of "hands joined" prayer is compromised by Chanter's work: Peter does not relate modes 1 or 3 to eucharistic devotion, and in modes 5 and 6, which he does relate to transubstantiation, he does not enjoin joined hands. Almost all the *figures* in these thirteenth-century manuscripts, on the other hand, show the hands joined, with the obvious exception of mode 2 (arms outstretched as on a cross).

the practice of males removing their hats in church which, together with the three "devout postures" mentioned above, are the "body prayers" Peter distinguishes from prayers of the heart and mouth. He cites Paul (1 Cor. 11.3—4) as his biblical authority, but then proceeds:

> From the said words of the apostle a very durable tradition of the monks of Clairvaux has emanated. At all times, even in the greatest cold, they are required to pray with their head bare, their whole hood dropped. All those who are up to it should follow this [practice].[31]

Thus while mentioning Paul, it is the long tradition of the Cistercians which ultimately counts for the author, who wants all able-bodied male supplicants to be bareheaded whether they are in church or not.

Much more illustrative of Peter's actual reliance on the reader's respect for practice is a passage which concerns an unaccustomed style rather than a habit time out of mind. In the explication of mode six (bowing), the Chanter continues the passage after that at note 27 as follows:

> ... holy altar. Catholic and faithful men ought always to do the same when the *Gloria patri et filio et spiritui sancto* is said, and when during the celebration of mass there is the transubstantiation of the bread into flesh and wine into blood. The French however, among whom religion is alive [and] where studies flourish, who have schools of the arts and virtues, the faith of whom still burns somewhat (for the charity of many has cooled), these godfearing men, I say, not only bend their head and kidneys but also remove all their hoods and caps from their heads, [and] prostrate themselves and fall on their face during the making and taking of the flesh and blood of Christ. . . .[32]

---

[31] "Ex verbis denique apostoli prelibatis emanavit satis dura traditio Claravallensium monachorum qui omni tempore, etiam in maximo frigore, debent orare detecto capite, deponito velamine universo. Et hoc siquidem omnibus est agendum qui ad hoc sufficiunt": KN, fol. 19vb.

[32] ". . . sanctum altare. Ita debent viri catholici et fideles semper facere quando dicitur 'Gloria patri et filio et spiritui sancto,' et cum sit transsubstantiatio panis in carnem et vini in sanguinem in misse celebratione. Galli vero, apud quos viget religio ubi floret stadium, qui habent scolas artium et virtutum, quorum fides adhuc fervet aliquantulum (quoniam refriguit caritas multorum), illi autem viri dei et timorati, non solum flectunt caput et renes, immo remotis capuceis et pilleis omnibus a capitibus, prosternunt se et cadunt in faciem suam in confectione et perceptione carnis et sanguinis Christi": KN, fol. 19rb. Note that Peter does not mention gazing at the host, implying the contrary, while

This passage is confusing at first because the prostration mode five had already been described and because the author here goes from bowing to prostration by latching on to the importance of a certain gesture at a certain moment. Once we get past this, however, the importance of a reference to the behavior of stylish French schoolmen is clear, all the more so because the Chanter may be addressing non-Frenchmen, probably Germans or Italians in the areas where the manuscripts of the work are found. This new practice is recommended to these readers not on the basis of hallowed texts, but because good scholastic ecclesiastics of Paris (where else?), like Peter himself, had taken to it, and elsewhere in the work the Chanter insists on the crucial role of these intellectuals in Christian life.[33] It will not surprise anyone that in fact if not in Peter's stated conviction, the role of live images as models for his modes is quite as important as his textual documentation. They fused art and virtue. What then could mere pictures represent to their viewers?

Making the Pictures

> Neither God nor man is [here] present other than as an image of flesh. But God and man are present as the image signifies.[34]

What the author had actually done with his modal descriptions was to limit a relatively sparse and thus free biblical model. The figures he planned were thought of as nothing more than exact translations of his verbal descriptions. "The following figure will demonstrate what has been said," he states at one point.[35] "The figure declares how this [described mode] is done,"[36] and "this seventh figure teaches in a nutshell what was said by Gregory above."[37] Thus the figures would reproduce the word, even as the Chanter's words were said to reproduce sacred texts. The exercise would be purely technical in nature, and the one clear instruction the Chanter gave the illustrator represents personal emotion as a function of

---

a famous Parisian statute of the early thirteenth century provided for gazing: Ladner, "Gestures," 267, n. 69.

[33] KN, fol. 30rb, glossing *Corpus Iuris Canonici* (CIC), d. xxvii, c. 12.

[34] "Nec deus est nec homo presens quam carnis imago. Sed deus est et homo presens quam signat imago": KN, fol. 18ra, introducing the mode 1 figure.

[35] "Quod autem est dictum, qualiter illud fiat, imago presens ostendit": KN, fol. 18rb.

[36] "Quo hoc fit, figura declarat": KN, fol. 18rb.

[37] "Hec figura septima quam habes antea; hic preoculis docet enucleatus quod dictum est a Gregorio superius": KN, fol. 19rb.

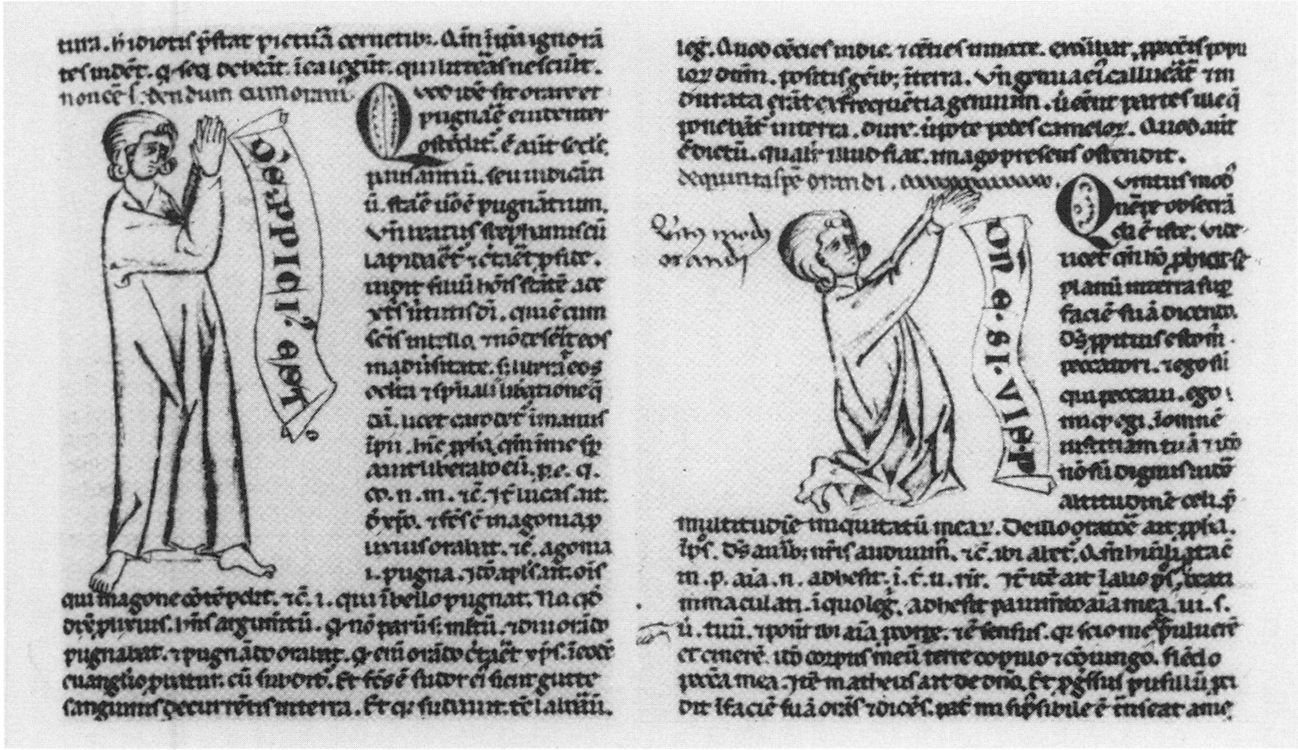

Figure 21.
Modes 3 and 4.
Klosterneuburg, fol. 18v.

physical stance, not of expression. In mode five the author begins by defining "a man throwing himself flat on the ground on his face," then toward the end of the modal section, he says: "This mode is painted, and is
supposed to show the supplicator lying on the ground on his chest, and his
face kissing the ground, fearing to raise his eyes to heaven."[38] What then
is the actual relation between the texts and the pictures?

Limits of space force me to merely assert that the fifty-nine illustrations
presently at my disposal show remarkable differences among one another,
and thus from the text of the Chanter. At the simplest level that seems
less true: the text of mode four, for example, is always followed by kneeling figures. Even here, however, there are significant variances, the Klosterneuburg figure kneeling more comfortably uphill, neither his feet nor
his knees shown as touching the ground (fig. 21). And the moment one
moves away from these simple modes, the differences multiply. The drawings by various artists and by single ones proved incapable of reproducing
either the text or the moral quality intended by the writer.

One demonstrable reason this was so was because different illustrators
misunderstood the text.[39] Take the Ottobeuren manuscript, where such
misreadings in part explain why this manuscript has ten instead of the
standard seven illustrations, including three of mode one, and two of mode
two (figs. 22 and 23). First the reader will note that in preparing the
manuscript, illustrators worked in tandem with the copyist: the mode two
drawing within the text (arms as on a cross) was drawn before the copyist
wrote around it, and the same happened in later figures. Second, the read-

---

[38] "Quintus modus nempe obsecrandi est iste, videlicet quando homo prohicit se
planum in terra super faciem suam, dicendo . . .": KN, fol. 18vb. "Sed quia ut ait Oratius, 'Segnius irritant animum dismissa per aures, quam que sunt oculis subiecta fidelibus,'
idcirco species ista depingitur que orantem habet significare iacentem in terra super
pectus suum, et facie sua osculando terram, timentem oculos ad celum levare. Est autem
gestus sic prostrati et iacentis hominis significatio, et cum iactura, humilitate compuncte,
concerte, devote atque intente ad deum mentis": KN, fol. 19ra. Nowhere does the author hold forth on "excessive gesture" or the *via media*, as had Hugh of St. Victor in his
influential *De institutione noviciorum*: J.-C. Schmitt, "Le geste, la cathédrale, et le roi,"
L'Arc 72 (1978): 9–12. The Chanter does not refer to this or any other work on novice
instruction.

[39] Purely for the purpose of this article, I assume that the illustrators were literate.
Further, I do not here study the implications of the (originally oral) scholastic *responsiones*
in the texts. One such implication is that these prayer instructions could have originally
been sermons, Peter as preacher hypothetically having the modes illustrated *vivo corpore*.
There is no such evidence in the book *de oratione*, however. A study of the whole work
might reveal more on this subject.

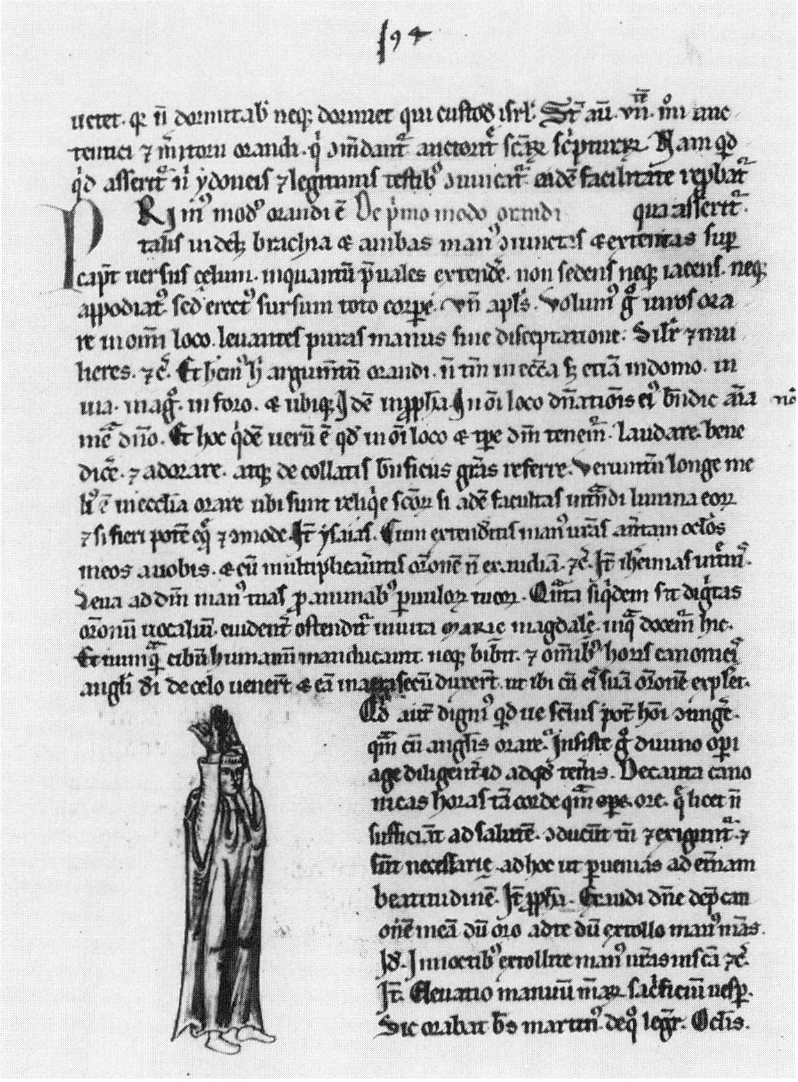

uetet. qz ñ dormitab neqz dormiet qui custos isrł. Sr̄ au uñ in ui̇e
remei 7 mt̄om orandi q ostdant auct̄ori sc̄ē sc̄ptur̄e. Nam qd
qd asserit ñ ydoneis 7 legitimus testib' inuenit ea de facilitate repbat̄
P r̄ in mod' orandi ē De p̄mo modo orandi   qua asserit
taliß inde't brachia & ambas man' inuenies & extenias sup
capr̄ uersus celum. inquantu p̄uales extende. non sedens neqz iacens. neqz
appodiat sed erect' sursum toto corpe. un apłs. uolum' g̅ uiros ora
re in oūi loco. leuantes puras manus sine disceptatione. Silr̄ 7 mu
lieres. 7c̄. Et b̄en hi argumtū orandi. ñ tm̄ in ecc̄a sz etia indomo. in
uia. mag̅. in foro. & ubiqz ī de mystka si n̄ ōi loco ōrarōis ei' biudie aña ñ
me dño. Et hoc qd' ueru ē qd in ōi loco & tpe dm̄ tenem. Laudare bene
dice. 7 adorare. atqz de collatis bisicus g̅as referre. uerumtu longe me
li ē in ecc̄ta orare ubi sunt reliqe sc̄o̅r̄ si ade facultas undi lumina eo̅r̄
7 si fieri pot eō 7 amode sr̄ ysaias. Cu̅m extendr̄is man' uras auta̅m oc̄los
meos a uobis. & cu̅ multiplicauitis orone ñ exaudia̅. 7c̄. sr̄ ibi emas untū
deua ad dm̄ man' uias p̄ numab' p̄uulo̅r̄ meo̅r̄. Qia si qdem sr̄ digtas
orōnū uocaliū euidens ostendu̅ iuxta orarie magdale. iuq doce̅m inc.
&ruiuq̅ cibu̅ humanū manducant. neqz bibu̅t. 7 ōmib' horis canonieū
angli di decelo uenerit & ea ma̅ca secū duxerit. ut ibi cu ei siu̅ orone expser.

Ad aut digni qd ue scius por hoi uinge-
qin cu anglis orare. Iuhste g̅ diuino opi
age diligentia adq̅s reins. Decaña cano
meas horas tā corde qin ope. ore. g̅ ticet ñ
sufficiu̅. it ad salut̄e. oduciu̅ tñ 7 exigunt 7
su̅t necessarie. adhoc ut puenias ad etiam
beatitudine. sr̄ zphs. &audi dñe dep̅ea̅m
one mea̅ dū oro. adte dū extollo man' i̅as.
sd. In noctib' extollite man' uras insc̄a 7c̄.
sr̄. Eleuatio manuū ma̅r̄ sacficiu̅ uesp.
sic orabat bs martin' deq̅ leg̅r̄. &c̄tis.

Figure 22.
Mode 1.
London-Ottobeuren, fol. 194r.

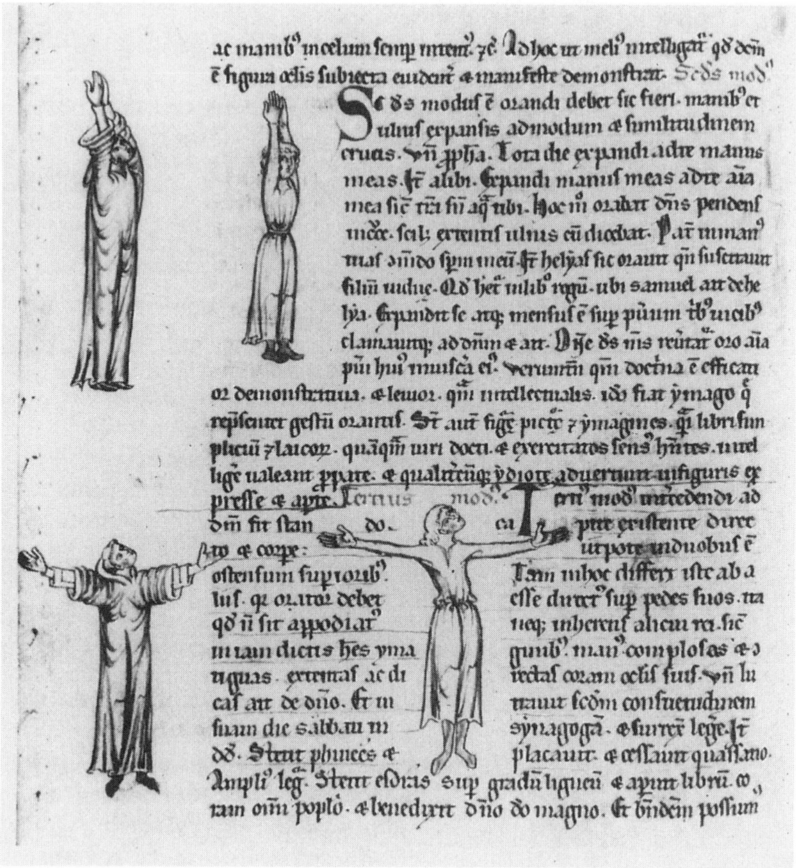

Figure 23.
Modes 1 and 2.
London-Ottobeuren, fol. 194v.

er should know that the figures for modes three through seven all picture monks within the margins of the text. The monkish figures the reader sees in the illustrations of modes one and two on the second reproduced folio, however, show monks in the margin but *conversi* or oblates in the body of the text. Finally, the hand of figures three through seven is the same as that which drew the marginal figures of modes one and two, and possibly also the same which drew the mode one figure in the oversized space on the first folio pictured here. The hand that drew the two oblates drew none of the others.

It is far from inconsequential that the patron of this manuscript, the abbot Bertholdus (1229–1248), chose to represent monks in the prayer figures after an illustrator had already drawn two figures of oblates.[40] Yet from our present vantage point a still more significant fact may be noted from figure 23. The bodies of mode two are copies, but those of mode one are different in one important respect: the earlier oblate figure shows the eyes and head pointed straight ahead while the later marginal monk has his head and eyes turned toward heaven.

The explanation seems to lie in a misread text. Recall that the directions for mode one do not mention the head being turned toward heaven, a particular the Chanter only mentioned later in speaking of Martin of Tours. What probably happened here is that the artist (or his associated copyist) read the description of mode one and drew the figure with the face outward, there being no instructions to the contrary. When the preparations were being made to draw mode three, however, it became clear that the Chanter had actually wanted mode one's figure to have its eyes toward heaven, and that fact, combined with what might have previously been thought the unimportant indication that Martin of Tours had prayed with his eyes up, led to the decision to redo mode one and, since the patron had determined to have monastic figures, mode two as well. Still later, according to this hypothesis, an original plan to fill in the large space on the first folio (fig. 22) with a double figure of Christ and supplicant, as had been done in the Ottobeuren source (see below), was abandoned, and still another figure of a mode one supplicant was added.

Here then is an outright attempt to bring the figures into agreement not with holy writ, but with the text of Peter the Chanter. The intention

---

[40] Bertholdus's patronage of the manuscript is documented in LO-OT, and noted by P. Lehmann, "Mitteilungen aus Handschriften II," *Sitzungsberichte der bayerischen Akademie der Wissenschaften, phil. -hist. Abteilung* (1930), no. 2, 5f.

is the more impressive because the original drawing of mode one showing the hands over the head, but the eyes straight ahead, probably did not represent any accepted liturgical practice of the time. The original draftsman was ready to defy convention so as to be true to the text as he originally read it, just as the second draftsman accepted the conventional raising of the head, but also in the interest of text fidelity. There are other cases where the draftsman left errors, of course. In the one manuscript where the artist through scrolls over the figures tried to match some figures to the prayers the Chanter wanted said while in some such postures, the Klosterneuburg illustrator got the prayers mixed up.[41] But more importantly, all the drawings reveal how easily the Chanter's text lent itself to misreading, and this corpus suggests that even with his invariable text, the resulting figures tended to expand into freedom and variation from the physical rigidity which the author recommended to his readers.

A second reason the figures do not agree with the physical features described in the text is that the artist or his patron consciously violated the author's intention. First, local custom seems to have influenced certain artists. We recall that mode six calls for the supplicant to bow while standing erect, yet the Paduan manuscript crosses that intention and shows a kneeling figure bending forward (fig. 24). The author had especially recommended the bow at the moment of transubstantiation, and later in his section on this mode he adds: "We hold that one ought to pray thus bowed and humiliated in every place where there is an image or cross of Christ or any holy figure, *sicut docet haec imago.*"[42] The draftsman picked up this statement, showing the supplicant before an altar. Why then is that figure kneeling? Perhaps this is so because in the area in which this manuscript was produced people knelt at the consecration or the Gloria, and the artists felt compelled to preserve that local custom.[43]

But artists consciously violated the author's instructions for another reason, which is evident in the manuscripts. We may label this reason aesthetic, and an examination of the prostration figures of mode five (fig. 25), and the hands-over-head figures of mode one, are the prime exhibits. If

---

[41] See e.g., KN, fol. 18vb, mode 5, with a prayer-incipit enscrolled which belongs to another mode.

[42] KN, fol. 19rb. My italics.

[43] On the practices at this crucial time in the development of eucharistic practice, see J. Jungmann, *The Mass of the Roman Rite*, 2 vols. (New York, 1950), 1:240. An alternate reading is that the figure shows the supplicant moving into the position of prostration, as the author describes the French scholars doing for the consecration.

one surveys the prostration figures, one immediately determines that some artists simply turned mode one at a 90° angle to show mode five, while the Klosterneuburg artist did the same with his mode two figure. The viewer quickly reasons that the technical limitations of the artists caused them to do that, for they feared they could not show a prostrate figure well. This may in fact have been those artists' reason, and such technical limitations tell us something more about the distance between text and picture. Our ultimate concern is, after all, the function rather than the intent of these pictures, and to the extent that pictures were mimed by the faithful, technical limits of this sort enriched rather than constrained the limited body of gestures listed by the writer.

Yet do technical limitations fully explain why not one of the prostration figures shows the face and mouth to the ground, as Peter had ordained in his original description of the mode and in his instructions to the artist? I think not; at some cost, the artist could have hidden the head between the arms outstretched on the floor. But in my reading this was a cost he or his patron was unwilling to pay. Perhaps the heads are turned to the side or kept from the ground by the forearms because of considerations of status, it being thought unseemly in the Ottobeuren drawing, for example, to show such prestigious choir monks grovelling in the dirt, even if the writer had sought that very effect.[44] The metaphorical formulation of the same status consideration, namely that the clerk was head to the laical body as Christ was head to the body of the church, may also have entered into the patrons' thinking.[45] Whatever the actual reason, it seems clear that non-technical considerations of a broadly aesthetic nature forbade the representation of a faceless praying figure even if monks did in liturgy actually kiss the ground — unseen by the laity.

This aesthetic consideration is still more evident in the figure of mode one (fig. 26). Probably in the interest of a stately beginning, the Zwettl draftsman in this mode showed not only the supplicant but, to his left, a figure of Christ in Majesty. This formulation was then followed by the Leipzig-Thomaskloster illustrator. We have already seen that the Ottobeuren first prayer mode folio left a large space for such a double figure, and it is probable it did so because the Zwettl manuscript was its source.

---

[44] On "copulating with the earth," KN, fol. 18vb, and for "kissing the earth," above, n. 38.

[45] See e.g., KN, fols. 23ra–b; Schmitt, "Geste," 12.

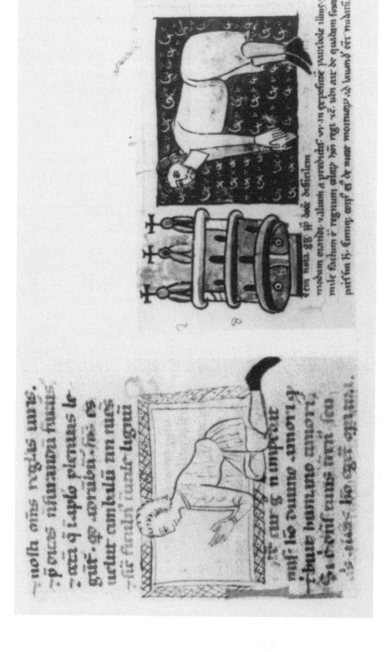

Figure 24.
Mode 6.
Padua, fol. 47v and Leipzig-Thomaskloster, fol. 70v.

Figure 25.
Mode 5.
Leipzig-Altzell, fol. 57v; Klosterneuburg, fol. 19r; Venice, s.n.

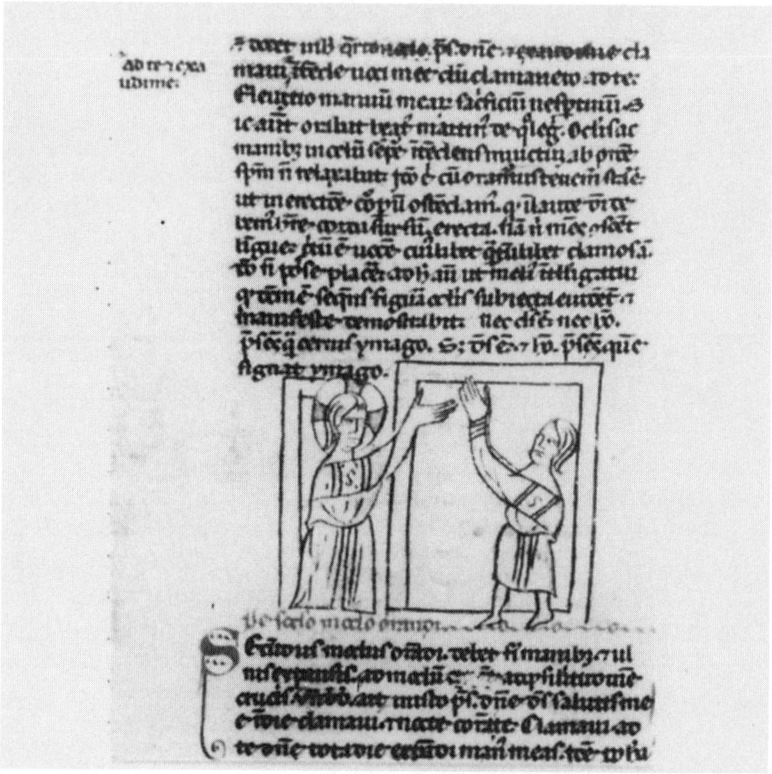

Figure 26.
Mode 1.
Zwettl, fol. 26v.

The aesthetic motivation of these illustrators and patrons had direct implications for text fidelity, however. Artists showing a standing suppliant opposite to but on the same horizontal plane with a seated Christ could not reasonably raise the arms of the supplicant above his head, but rather had to show them stretched out toward the God-figure, raised at most 45° above the horizontal plane, and that is just what the Zwettl and the Leipzig figures represent, in clear violation of the definitive description of the mode by the author. And it is probably this discrepancy between the Zwettl manuscript and the text which caused the Ottobeuren authorities, who had left a large space for a double figure, to give up the idea and instead fill half that space with a single figure correctly represented.

In these several ways, then, the figures did not reproduce the literal instructions of the author and, most suggestive, perhaps they could not. For on the continuum from technical limitations through the calculated formulation of the pictorial program of mode one to the gothic elegance of the Klosterneuburg figures, the figural intention of Peter the Chanter was violated at every turn. If technical limits made some figures look different from what the author intended, at the other extreme the elegance of the Klosterneuburg drawings voided the author's intent just as much. Having noted that technical limits opened up the imitable figural vocabulary, we will now show how new styles and greater technical fluency did likewise. For the corpus of figures definitely suggests a relation between style and morality.

The author's moral intention was as little effectuated as was his text. He had wanted representations of abject humility, but the patrons and artists seem to have begun with the assumption that no one would learn from gauche sinners. First they clothed their figures, deserting the abstract impersonal quality the author reveals in his text; Peter the Chanter had made no mention of clothes, with their inevitable association with status. Second, the artists introduced decorative and stylistic innovations which heightened elegance. We shall examine each of these elements singly.

The moral quality of these drawings was inevitably affected by the status and age of the figures, and these are fairly clear from their hair and clothing. Most evidently, of all the manuscripts only that from Ottobeuren pictures monks, and no manuscript unequivocally shows secular clerks. Four of the manuscripts on the other hand quite certainly represent lay figures.[46] In a work written for an ecclesiastical audience this is in itself sig-

---

[46] That is, ZW, V, PA, LE-TK.

nificant, for it shows that most of the manuscripts were intended for secular eyes, it being quite improbable that secular figures would have been used to instruct monastic audiences. Secondly, this fact suggests that the patrons of these secular figures felt that the laity would pay more attention to lay figures than to pictures of clerical paragons of correct reverence. Most important in our context, however, the richness of the clothing in some manuscripts shows that their artists counted on attracting attention, and thus mimicry of the figures, through stressing economic status. The Ottobeuren figures do not lag behind in this respect: for all their humble demeanor and monastic threads, they are clearly *potentes*.[47]

The age profile of the figures is quite as significant as the status represented. Again, clothing and hair style tell most of the story. While the figures of Leipzig-Altzell seem to show children (fig. 25), all the other manuscripts (including the two oblate figures of Ottobeuren) show adolescents — their long flowing hair remarkably seductive — and youths. In picturing young rakes (Padua) and youth with stylish jaw beards (Venice), the artists represented that one age group which medieval society thought had no religious profile at all, but rather an irreligious one![48] Just as interesting, it is quite probable that one would not have normally encountered such youthful images at prayer in the real world. It may well be true that the explanation for these young figures was that they were meant by their patrons to instruct youth, the idea being that cohorts would copy one another. Yet that has nothing to do with legitimacy. If showing the rich and powerful might do so, showing innocent children and seductive adolescents certainly could not mirror the grave demeanor the Chanter associated with prayer. There are no sinners in these drawings!

The figural prominence of youth, not to mention the veridical female figures in some mode seven illustrations (fig. 27), made it inevitable that the corpus at large would breathe a courtly rather than a penitential air; in Leipzig-Thomaskloster, that image of youthful elegance is further heightened by rich multi-colored geometric backgrounds (fig. 28). Yet at this point the relationship between style and moral posture becomes irresistible. In the same Leipzig manuscript, the figures' garments are swirled

---

[47] Notable among the lay figures are LE-TK and PA, but also in the rich simplicity of KN.

[48] Trexler, *Public Life*, 388ff. The negative attitude toward youth is reversed in the hagiographic convention that a youth is the one to break with his father and enter religion. That was truly remarkable.

Figure 27.
Mode 7.
Leipzig-Thomaskloster, fol. 70v and Venice, s.n.

Exaudi voce deprecatiois mee dum oro ad te. dum extollo manus mee ad templum sctm tuu. Hoc exemplum habet in ps. qui sic incipit. Ad te dne clamaui de meus. ne sileas a me. Jte id ad. aur me ps. Ecce nuc bndicite dnm. Jnoctibz. extollite man ues i sctm. abnd dominu. Jte id id docet Thau. ps. dne clamaui ad te exaudi me intende uoci mee dum clamauero ad te. Eleuatio manuu mearu. et tcuu uesptm. Jt Sic aut orabat beat martin. de quo legmus Oculis ac manibz in celum sp intendens. inuictum ad orationem spm ū relaxabat. Jdo eni cum orani tenem fare. ut in erectione corpum ostendam q in laude di debemus habere corda sursum erecta. Illā n mens conform lingue. certum e uoce cuxibz xpicitbz clamoram. do ū posse place. Ad ħ aut ut melius intelligat q dictum e. seqns figa oculis subiecta eundit et manifeste demonstrabit. Nec dc est ħ homo ipene quis eni imago. S. dc e. homo ipiens quem signat imago

Figure 28.
Mode 1.
Leipzig-Thomaskloster, fol. 65v.

and angled so that the very pride the Chanter condemned in prayer stamps the folios. Even more problematical: the Klosterneuburg figures are in the gothic style, with a delicate sway informing the shoulder position and bursting through the elegant gowns at the legs. This style dictated that its figures *not* stand erect, but that the figures rest one leg by placing weight on the other. In these figures, style itself required a type of leaning, which for the Chanter was close to depravity.[49] Just as in that age critics might have asked if the increasing command of human corporeal fluidity associated with gothic figures was as destructive of "devout posture" as resting one's weight on one foot was in real life, so today the Catholic might wonder if, beneath that opaque gown, his priest is not resting as he elevates the host, and if he is, if he truly effects the eucharistic miracles.[50] Anxiety on that score encourages us all to seek refuge in the charisma and the authority of the figure itself.

The very idea of a set of "right" rhetorical stances, verbal or corporeal, I have elsewhere argued, includes in it principles of elegance and formal dignity, whether the postures are to "capture the benevolence" of God or of man. A clerical Florentine who lived a century after the Chanter, Francesco da Barberino made just that point. After citing an Augustinian commentary on Matthew, he glossed it:

'The uncultured come and seize heaven, and we with our books descend to hell. ...' We cannot believe that God is more drawn to the illiterate and uncultured ... than to men of learning and those more lettered. ... Otherwise absurdity and illegality would follow, the foolish being of better condition than the experts, the uncultured [of better condition] than the judicious.[51]

We have come to the idea of legitimation through power, that of the word, that of the clerical scholar. The figures of Peter the Chanter's work are rooted in this idea. Now we shall examine the social force the Chanter used to get his reader's attention for the images in his text, and for the images of the living clergy.

---

[49] See below.

[50] See below. Cf. Schmitt's view ("Geste") that Hugh of St. Victor preferred gothic prayer representations to romanesque ones, to my view that increasing technical ability enabled later artists to represent natural "irreverences" like leaning.

[51] Trexler, *Public Life*, 107f.

Readers and Viewers

"Is it not written? Why must it be shown?"[52]

Peter the Chanter is not unusual in the identity he establishes between prayer and clergy on the one hand, and the clergy and moral science on the other. Adopting the tripartite model common to the age, he distinguishes workers and artisans from warriors, and warriors from supplicants (*orantes*), "for example ecclesiastical persons and everyone devoted to God, namely hospitalers, templars, and clerks, and all monks, canons, priests, and *conversi*."[53] Throughout the work, the supplicant is a clerk, and the clerk is assumed to have the *scientia litterarum*. While the laity was of course required to pray, praying was a type of profession, and professions required knowledge: body prayer had as much need of study as military action.[54] Peter ridiculed those who did not know what they were saying while praying, and that de facto had to include most laity, who said their prayers in Latin.[55] The Chanter's own credentials for addressing his reading clerical audience were his profound knowledge and its source, his ability to read.

How then could he defend his use of pictures, since he does not say that they were meant for non-readers lay or ecclesiastical? Examining that defense will reveal his fundamental ambivalence on the subject of pictures, and a tension between his goal of a legitimized depersonalized prayer code in text and pictures and the traditional legitimation of prayer through the *vitae* of clerks and saints.

We do not have to go looking for Peter's ambivalence about pictures; he openly represents two different views as to their nature. The first is

---

[52] A complaint against biblical floats in sixteenth-century Venice: E. Muir, *Civic Ritual in Renaissance Venice* (Princeton, 1981), 227, n. 37.

[53] KN, fol. 23ra. See Baldwin, *Masters*, 1:56–59, for the more complex social analysis this author found in Peter's other works.

[54] Consideration of prayer as an occupational skill is in KN, fol. 17va. Also: "Sane si materiale sive usuale bellum quod sit gestu corporis minime potest fieri graviter et prudenter nisi actor totis viribus dimicet contrarium, et resistendo atque repellendo eum et renitendo, multo ergo minus spiritualis lucta seu pugna habet exerceri vel poterit fieri sapienter, meritorie, atque utiliter et competenter atque maxima et habundanti cautela, sine supremo et diligenti studio": KN, fol. 23vb.

[55] "Cave igitur ne sequaris illos qui nesciunt quod dicant cum orant" (KN, fol. 31rb, also fol. 22vb) refers to those whose minds are elsewhere, but evidently includes as well those non-Latinists saying Latin prayers, a problem to which the Chanter did not direct his attention.

epistemological in nature. Never doubting that a sentence and a figure were interchangeable, he nonetheless argues first that pictures were "evident and manifest," "express and open" in a way which words evidently were not, even for those who read.[56] Citing Horace, he says this greater immediacy of pictures comes from perceptive differences between the senses, but then avers that this immediacy is due to a fundamental difference between word and picture. A doctrine or practice which is demonstrated visually, he says, is more efficaciously and easily grasped than one which is "intellectually" transmitted, the Chanter here identifying intellect with words.[57] At one point, therefore, Chanter is of the sound opinion that everyone grasps some things, including prayer modes, better through pictures.

More repetitively, however, Peter defends his gestural pictures through class and status divisions rather than by general theory of knowledge. Without ever saying so, he often implies that the illustrations are for those who cannot read. The curious nature of this stance seems particularly inappropriate in this book written for readers, though the defense itself is standard. Citing Gregory, he says that pictures are the books of the simple and of laymen. "In this picture," he says at another point, "the ignorant see what they ought to follow, [and] in it they read who do not know how to read."[58] For all the conventionality of this defense, how can it be taken seriously in a treatise meant for readers, with non-narrative figures meant to technologize prayer, not render edification?[59] It would be like taking seriously the same Gregorian motivation when applied to the rich cathedral sculptures of Western Europe.

The ambivalence between epistemological and social defenses of his pictures fairly explodes to view when Peter lays aside the scientific trappings and comes to grips with the fact that many of his readers will resent

---

[56] "Ad hoc autem ut melius intelligitur quod dictum est, sequens figura oculis subiecta evidenter ac manifeste demonstrabit": KN, fol. 18ra.

[57] "Doctrina demonstrata est efficacior et levior quam intellectualis": KN, fol. 18rb. The author seems to use the word "doctrina" here in the sense of a systemic behavior, just as "religio" could be used for the whole system of such behaviors. The Horace citation is above, n. 38.

[58] "Nam ut ait Gregorius: 'Quod legem tibi scriptura, hoc idiotis prestat figura cernentibus. Quoniam in ipsa ignorantes vident quod sequi debeant, in ea legunt qui litteras nesciunt' ": KN, fols. 18rb–va.

[59] The surmise that the author intended the pictures for oblates or young monks, *conversi* or young canons finds no support in the mss.; if that had been his intention, the Chanter would probably have consulted the literature on the education of novices.

the pictures. Concluding his description of the first six modes with one final biblical reference, he assures his fellow literates that

> ... many other even more valid authorities and live prayers and
> witnesses could without fail be adduced from the new and old
> testament to prove the said six modes, which will have to be omit-
> ted. For as the wise man understands much from little, inversely
> the idiot understands little from a lot.[60]

Hinting as scholars often do at a vast hidden storehouse of secret documentation, the Chanter then fairly apologizes to the same audience for the
pictures. "Even if scholars with a developed mind's eye [*exercitatos sensus
habentes*] understand through writings," he flatters his readers, idiots learn
through seeing.[61] The people learn their obligations through seeing, he
cites Gregory again, we learn ours by reading.[62] Thus just as Peter hinted
at his concealed knowledge, he played on the group solidarity of his clerical readership whose very identity, it seems, was bound to their possession
of a secret, non-visual "intellect."

Thus the greatest problem of legitimation Peter the Chanter faced, if
we are to understand his confused defense, was the legitimacy of his pictures for those who read. Yet how simple the matter seems to us, whose
corporate identity is not linked as was our clerical ancestors' to the simple
ability to read and to the mistaken idea that only readers had an exercised
mind's eye. Peter the Chanter knew that the most sophisticated reader
would learn body motions more quickly through pictures, and he wanted
clerks to then act out his seven modes of prayer in a fashion which would
edify spectators. Depersonalized figures would teach clerks, whose ritual
life would then be the "book of the simple."[63]

It is a singularly complex idea, this view that clerical images were types
of books. The Chanter had thought by abstract designs to inspire the simple through the implementation of these modes of prayer by live clerks.

---

[60] "Possent longe plures valide autoritates et vive orationes atque testes omni excep-
tione maiores adduci de novo et veteri testamento ad probationem predictorum sex modorum, que sunt omittende. Nam sapiens paucis multa conprehendit, e contrario idiota
multis pauca intelligit": KN, fol. 19rb.

[61] "Sunt autem figure, picture, et imagines quasi libri simplicium atque laicorum,
quiaque viri scholastici et exercitatos sensus habentes intelligunt per scripturas, pro parte
et qualitercunque idiote animadvertunt in figuris expresse et aperte": KN, fol. 18rb.

[62] See text above, n. 58.

[63] "Nota quod vita clericorum est liber vulgi quos imitare volunt, et maxime in
malo": KN, fol. 18rb.

He cannot refrain from citing clerks he has known who perfectly enacted those modes, and inspired the writer himself.[64] In his repeated exhortations to the clergy to behave well, there is a fundamental tension between a world of norms and one of examples, between the abstract law of his definitions and the visceral reality of mimicry. Could verbal and figural technology inspire? The manuscript illustrators said "no," even if the author had been inspired by the idea in teaching his clerks. As a theologian and scholar, Peter the Chanter had sought to rely on documented words and their figurative translation to inculcate laws of motion. Yet when he doffed his pastoral threads and weighed the impact of these gestures on the laity and on the Christian Gods of the acting clergy, he recognized that his mere elaboration of legitimate signs of reverence was not enough. Such signs, he understood, could only be legitimated if they were received by their objects as reverences, not insults. Could insults be proved such by biblical authority, or were they actually called so because the living accepted them as such? The borders between prayer and insult informed the definition of each.

Reverence and Insult

> It should sooner and more truly be called an execration and sin than a prayer.[65]

The essence of traditional legitimation of reverential behavior was that its practitioners had effected marvels, and now as we watch the performance of the clerk in real life through the Chanter's eyes, we note how central that legitimation was to elementary Christian teaching. The commonest priest, it was said, no matter what his intention or the quality of his life, changed bread to body and wine to blood of Christ if he said certain words in the context of the mass sacrifice. In modern language: in a cultural performance, the environment is transformed through the verbal gesture of an official actor.

In the dogmatic approach of his age, then, the priest's verbal gestures were right because they made miracles, yet Peter was not ready to push his own approach to legitimation into this area; he did not provide for figures of the correct physical comportment of the celebrant at the consecration

---

[64] See the end of this article.

[65] KN, fol. 21rb, referring to a supplicant who ruminates on a prostitute while praying.

of the mass. He could not, on the other hand, resist probing questions of *verbal* comportment at that juncture and their implied impact on the performance of marvels. What if, for example, the celebrant failed to clearly enunciate the first word or syllable of the eucharistic formula, or slurred the last? What if, the consecration past, he could not remember having said the formula? Should he repeat the performance, even if it angered the faithful who wanted to be on their way? He did go so far as to answer this latter question affirmatively, but otherwise pulled back from the fundamental question of whether there was a miracle with syntactical sloppiness![66] Nor did he even address the question of whether corporeal sloppiness could effect the eucharistic action. The Chanter found the eucharistic action, for all its centrality to his own approach to legitimation, an uncomfortable setting in which to place his supplicant actors.

For all his reticence, however, Peter the Chanter did make one central association between words and actions in what regards their efficacity before God which shows that he considered legitimate behavior as defined in relation to illegitimate behavior. Slurring a word of reverence was in the same category as half a genuflection or other imperfectly executed forms, he intimated; they were both "depraved prayers" relevant to the *forma orandi*.[67] In addition to imperfectly executed prayers (note that an imperfect genuflection is halfway between the two correct postures of standing and kneeling), there were also postures which were the antithesis of prayer, which the Chanter might have but did not compare to verbal curses. Finally, there were certain modes of liturgical behavior for certain times and places, just as certain verbal prayers were more fit than others for some times and places.[68] We shall examine what the Chanter has to say about the first two of these complexes, and then examine why he thought them right and wrong.

The one repeatedly denounced posture for praying is sitting; the author mentions lying on one's back only in passing, and omits all the other con-

---

[66] The whole *responsio* is in KN, fol. 21va.

[67] See *de pravo oratore* in KN, fol. 21ra; further KN, fols. 19ra, 20vb, 22rb.

[68] I must neglect this context, but note that the author was much less scrupulous about the sequences of prayers and his recommended integration of bodily and oral prayers than he was with the correct form of each prayer. He tempered his sequences and integrations at one point by saying "non ideo diximus ut legem sapientibus prescriberemus, sed ut simplicibus formam bene agendi offeremus": KN, fol. 23rb. Though sacrally documented, the body prayers are also akin to athletic exercises which one changes about as one tires: KN, fols. 18vb, 19va. Further on the Chanter's integrated program and sequences in KN, fols. 19rb, 20ra, and especially 23rb.

ceivable postures which he apparently thought his readers would ipso facto consign to the arsenal of postural insults.[69] Sitting, he said, was for judges and pausers, not for supplicants of healthy body,[70] and the Chanter conventionally denounces slackers such as those who sit down in church no sooner than having risen from sleep.[71] But what of those who consider sitting at prayer legitimate? Inflexible, Peter denounced as false those cloistered monks, religious only in name, who insisted that it was the custom of their house to sit during the office of the dead and the gradual canticles. "Such a defect" in an *opus dei* was just bad custom, the theologian said, and the moralist added that the resulting verbal prayers were frivolous, vain, and as much as useless, for they did not penetrate to God.[72]

Peter next condemned leaning, which we might characterize as crossing the border toward insult. This was a "depraved" and, significantly, "damnable" thing to do; it was also inefficacious.[73] The Chanter mocked the use of what he called "artificial feet," and also spelled out what it communicated to God and man. Such persons are adjudged by mortals to reprehend God, he said, as if they were telling him that since he had made man imperfect — not having given man enough support —, they did not have to bother how they stood.[74] In describing this sin of leaning, then, the Chanter supplements the idea that certain physical comportments do not "penetrate" to God (as if he did not see and hear everything), with the more acceptable idea that certain actions insult, and others reverence God. . . . and man.[75]

---

[69] It was good to fall forward, bad to lie backwards: KN, fol. 18vb; further fols. 22rb, 23vb.

[70] KN, fol. 18va, with the exemption for the ill on fol. 21ra; further fol. 20ra. On the association of sitting with judging, see H. Martin, "Les enseignements des miniatures. Attitude royale," *Gazette des Beaux Arts*, ser. 4, 9 (1913): 173–88.

[71] KN, fols. 19vb–20ra; further fol. 18va.

[72] "Allegant enim falso claustrales predicti pro se talem esse domus sue consuetudinem non stare erectos toto corpore neque genua flectere in decantione cantici gradus et officii defunctorum": KN, fol. 20ra. On prayers not penetrating to God, which are "neither answered nor heard," fol. 23vb.

[73] KN, fol. 23vb.

[74] "Porro tales qui in tempore et hora orandi appodiantur, substentantur, seu inherent baculo vel arche aut scanno sive muro, iudentur contempnere atque reprehendere deum, ac si dicant: 'Non sufficiunt, o domine, nobis duo pedes quos dedisti et cum quibus creasti et fecisti nos. Idcirco opus tuum, id est orationem tuam, non curamus prudenter ac diligenter et bene agere, quoniam inpotentes minus perfectos et inbecilles et informos nos condidisti et fecisti. Hinc est quod orando tertium aut quartum aut etiam plures nobis adquirimus, construimus, et facimus artificiales pedes' ": KN, fol. 23vb.

[75] Perhaps characteristically, Peter does not take the next step and warn the reader

The third physical posture our author excoriates is partial genuflection, which we can characterize as an insult area between two legitimate prayer modes; notably, the Chanter does not include genuflection among his prayer modes, but only kneeling and standing.[76] Those who do not bring their knee down to where it is level with the foot are performing a "fraudulent genuflection," as are all those sinners who genuflect onto kneelers or other objects which prevent the knee reaching the level of the foot. The only "true genuflection" is when the knee touches the ground, and the Chanter continues in this valuative vein. Bringing down the other knee into a full kneeling position is a proper mode of bodily prayer. Now, if the kneeler leans forward so that his mouth is on the ground at the same level with knees and feet, that gesture becomes "especially sincere and optimal,"[77] while only seeming to bring the face to where it would "strike" or "kiss" the ground would certainly have been dissimulative and hypocritical.[78]

Thus if we go from standing to prostration, we can piece together the following valuation scheme: standing, and bowing forward from a standing position, are "authentic" modes of prayer. Continuing only into a partial genuflection is fraudulent. A knee touching the ground is a proper peni-tential act, as kneeling on both knees is another authentic mode of prayer. Bowing forward from that position is not mentioned by the Chanter, but we have seen that the Paduan illustrator thought it acceptable. Leaning forward from a kneeling position as if to kiss the ground, but without doing so, was wrong, but when the mouth did touch, that was especially sincere. Finally, lying down, the stomach and chest on the ground, was "among all modes of praying . . . as much as the best and most useful."[79]

---

of the catastrophes which befall those who insult God, just as he does not fill his pages with the miracles which happened to those who reverenced him. He did of course as-sume both would occur; he did not, that is, believe man was safe because God did not hear and see insults.

[76] Genuflection, the "potissima et principalis pars . . . penitentie exterioris," is exam-ined in bk. III, de modis peccandi: KN, fols. 12rb–13rb. Kneeling, the fourth mode of prayer, is at fol. 18vb.

[77] "Fit autem fraus genuflexio sive peccatur in ea, quotiens genua imponuntur et apo-diantur super aliquam lapidem vel aliquod lignum ita quod sit magis remota a terra quam digiti pedum. . . . Illa enim et sola est vera genuum inflectio quando sunt in eadem equa-litate. . . . Tunc precipue genuflexio est sincera et optima cum os et genua et digiti pe-dum pariter inherent terre": KN, fol. 12rb.

[78] The Chanter does not directly brand it such, but see KN, fol. 21va.

[79] KN, fol. 12rb.

How does the Chanter *know* all this, what is his authority for these confident moral judgments? Evidently the intent of the supplicant, or more exactly the communication the supplicant intends to make to God, is an important factor for the author; that much the foregoing formulations make clear. "A body gesture argues and proves mental devotion," he says, "[and] man's exterior state instructs us on his interior humility and affect."[80] It is perfectly true that Peter the Chanter was second to none in insisting that without true intent, actions were inefficacious no matter how perfectly enunciated words or bodily actions might be.[81]

Yet quite to the contrary, the same person accepts the orthodox view that the eucharistic words were miraculous apart from intent, and just as significant, he brands certain physical postures as depraved quite apart from questions of intent. Furthermore, he specifically states that good intentions do *not* obviate the bad effects of bad prayer performances.[82] For while he could brand standing an authentic prayer and genuflection truly penitential, and thus call half a genuflection "fraud" because God and man presumably ascribed a foundation of good intent to standing and full genuflection, so that partial genuflection had to be viewed as fraudulent of the divine command, he could not do the same with sitting. Sitting was not located between two acceptable modes, and we recall the monks who protested Peter's condemnation of their sitting during certain prayers.[83]

The interesting point about this protest is that in his condemnation Peter never questioned the "mental devotion" of the monks, never confronted what must have been their rejoinder: that because they were sitting did not mean that they did not have a proper internal reverence for God.[84] In fact, when we probe further and ask about Peter's authority for condemning a sitting position, we find that he cites none.[85] In the

---

[80] "Gestus vero corporis est argumentum et probatio mentalis devotionis. Status autem exterioris hominis instruit nos de humilitate et affectu interioris": KN, fol. 21ra. Also: "Nempe oculo corporis videt cor exteriora, qui est nuntius et instrumentum quo homo interior scit exteriora. Cor enim sequitur oculis": KN, fol. 22ra.

[81] This sentiment is constantly repeated. On the Chanter and intent, see Baldwin, *Masters*, 1:49f.

[82] "Non excusatur vitium orationis per intentionem sive affectum orantis": KN, fol. 23ra, responding to an interpretation of Augustine by an *emulus*.

[83] See above.

[84] See n. 82 for the reason. He does say they do not live "caste, iuste, ac pie" because they do not follow their order's rule: KN, fol. 20ra.

[85] Instead, he notes often that a source does *not* say one did sit: e.g., KN, fols. 22rb, 22vb.

Chanter's view apparently, sitting was a physical posture which *ipso facto* marked off the world of reverence from that of insult apart from questions of intent. The point is not to document the author's negligence, of course. Many authors pick and choose, and if the Chanter neglected to mention actual biblical authority for praying while sitting,[86] he did not hesitate to mention Moses having his arms held up by colleagues while praying, even though that obviously weakened his admonitions against leaning.[87] Rather, it was my intention to show that while any position might be insincere internally, there are in the Chanter's view certain positions such as sitting which are, irrespective of intent, *objectively* insincere. The very cultural weight of the word "sincere" goes to the heart of how something can be objectively insincere, and thus something else objectively sincere (such as transubstantiation), for "sincere" was an adjective used almost exclusively to refer to young nobles, those who might in the Chanter's language fight for Christ with the sword as the supplicant-clerk fought spiritually in prayer.[88] We see the epitome of the sincere if not warrior youths in the Klosterneuburg drawings, kneeling elegantly on an incline so that those knees are above his feet (fig. 25), nay the whole body floating above the mean soil. That was whom the illustrator had to show, and how he had to picture them, if the viewer was to consider the mode of prayer legitimate.

Peter the Chanter might view sitting as objectively insincere (apart from questions of intent) because its opposite numbers, those abasing acts of supplicants not judges, would only be done for God in public by those who were truly ashamed of their lives. That is the clear implication of what the Chanter has to say about these gestures of subjection in the presence of others. Conventionally but significantly, he notes without criticism that in civil society the various modes of subjection are performed without objection. People speak distinctly before judges so as to capture their benevolence, he says, and they prostrate themselves before tyrants just to avoid punishment.[89] Citing Benedict, he says that no one presumes to approach powerful men for something without humility and reverence, and notes that "artisans, furriers, farmers, vintners and all other people of whatever profession" when before powerful humans, if not clerks when before

---

[86] Beginning of course with Jesus himself sitting during the Last Supper. See also 2 Sam. 7.18. On sitting during services in practice, see Jungmann, *Mass*, 1:241f.

[87] KN, fol. 29ra.

[88] On them see KN, fols. 18va, 23ra, 30ra.

[89] KN, fols. 21ra, 19va.

God, "faithfully, diligently and carefully prepare how they plan to act, so as to achieve it." The vile women weave better than clerks pray![90]

This was because of the shame inherent in groveling in the presence of men. It was the act of supplication, and less the object of the act, which was at issue. Thus the Chanter might speak of those who "disdain to kneel before God," but it is actually humble Christian witness he wants from the clergy, as is clear from his citation of Christ's warning that the latter will be ashamed before the father of those who are ashamed of him before humans.[91] The plain fact was that many clerks considered it shameful to prostrate themselves, and we recall that none of the figures shows the mouth on the ground.[92] There were others who maintained that one should not kneel or genuflect on feastdays[93] ... when the faithful would see those acts. Others said it was shameful to pray with the arms extended as on the cross even during the celebration of the mass (crucifixion was the execution reserved for the lowest criminals), and still other clerks thought it shameful to raise one's hands over one's head in public (as in an act of surrender).[94]

Throughout the work, Peter the Chanter had maintained that prayers in solitude were better than ones in society because public prayer led to hypocrisy.[95] Yet he also recognized that clerical prayer in public was essential because it charitably instructed others in correct prayer.[96] The Chanter faced a quandary, for there was evidently strong resistance among his readers to the public manifestation of submissive acts. The clerks insisted on acting like judges. Comparable to nobles who fornicated in the presence of villains, they taught insults instead of reverences.[97] The figures we have studied breathe much of that elegant pride and haughtiness.

---

[90] "Si cerdones, pelliparii, agricole, vinitores, et omnes alii homines cuiuscunque sunt professionis elaborant fideliter et diligenter ea que acturi sunt perficere, multo itaque fortius clerici et omnes religiosi debent. . . . Inbecilis quoque sexus mulierum . . . procutat agere telas suas diligenter. . . . Econtra clerici. . . .": KN, fols. 21ra–b.

[91] KN, fol. 19vb, and on disdain, fol. 18vb.

[92] "Fortasse autem dicit aliquis cervicosus insolens et superbus: 'Verecundor orare manibus extensis supra caput vel ulnis extensis sive in terra prostratus' ": KN, fol. 19vb.

[93] "Contra eos qui dicunt genua non esse flectenda in diebus festis": KN, fol. 19ra. It had been traditional to pray standing on feasts like Easter: Jungmann, *Mass*, 1:240.

[94] In the rubic *Quomodo sacerdos teneatur assistere altari*, one reads: "Nec verecunderis expandere manus tuas ad modum crucis": KN, fol. 29ra. See also fols. 19vb, 22rb.

[95] Especially KN, fols. 22ra–b, but also fols. 20rb, 21va.

[96] KN, fol. 13rb.

[97] KN, fol. 19ra.

In a crucial statement, the author bent to recognize the social coercion which actually legitimated prayer gestures, and discovered a new benefit of praying in private: "Thus those supplicators will not be able to excuse themselves, [saying] they are ashamed. . . ."[98]

A work which began by constructing modes of prayer in reference to the communal performance of the canonical hours consigns us ultimately to the private sphere of prayer, where the image of the clerk praying might be seen by God, but not judged by man.

Conclusion

Peter the Chanter's attempt at a technology of prayer failed, in keeping though it was with the technological thrust of the age.[99] He had abstracted seven modes of prayer from what he said were authoritative written sources, but he could not in fact document all those modes. He had charged artists to translate perfectly into figures what was in fact an intellectually creative instructional code, yet those artists could not translate non-edifying words into non-edifying pictures, so they clothed them in a status and age, and posed them in moral configurations that might draw attention. The Chanter had not called for saintly figures, which might have encouraged miming, and the artists did not draw persons. Instead they illustrated the rich, the young, and the innocent, the only living non-persons who could ensure miming, in styles which were not oblivious to history, status, or school. A later treatise on modes of prayer, we noted, actually opted for the heroic person of St. Dominic as an exemplary legitimator.[100] Evidently, the legitimacy of modes of subjection actually derived from their practice, either by privileged statuses or ages, or by the marvellous hero.

The Chanter's failure certainly does not invalidate the remarkable nature of what he attempted, for it is a fundamental property of humans in

---

[98] In the rubric *de furtivis orationibus*: "Ibi vero non potest se excusare orator quod verecundetur se erigere brachia super caput vel orare ulnis extensis ad modum crucis aut aliquo aliorum modorum septem": KN, fol. 22rb.

[99] On which see L. White, Jr., *Medieval Technology and Social Change* (Oxford, 1963).

[100] It is most significant that that author used the Chanter's words at times. Cf. "toto corpore directus super pedes suos, non appodiatus, neque herens alicui rei" (Taurisano, "Quomodo," 100) to n. 30 above, and "manibus et ulnis expansis ad similitudinem crucis" ("Quomodo," 101) to n. 25. Also cf. "hoc modo oravit dominus pendens in cruce, scilicet extensis manibus et ulnis" ("Quomodo," 101) to the identical language in KN, fol. 18ra. The link between the two works is presently unknown.

groups to *know* what is sacrilegious without daring to ask why. Peter admittedly placed limits on his daring, for example leaving unmentioned many imaginable postures which he could not conceive anyone thinking decorous. Yet moving from a world which legitimated actions or gestures mostly in terms of their efficaciousness, he derived an abstract canon of physical comportment from narrations whose elements of miraculous efficacity he did not stress, and thought to provide equally abstract and depersonalized figures which would be law, not history.

We have seen that the styles of the powerful were allegedly the enemy of the Chanter and his law of comportment. And yet. . . . Today the viewer immediately sees these pictures as statements of subjection — for we are still subject —, and is ready to follow the efficacious behavior of today's men or women of power. It would be wrong to exempt Peter the Chanter from this observation, misleading to believe that in these elegant pictures he did not get the simplicity he wanted. Was it not the author who spoke of sincerity, with all that word's status connotations for the medieval reader? Did not Peter himself recommend to rude foreigners the dramatic new style of the internationally famous French schoolmen? The Chanter was not exempt from the human readiness to associate law with power, and to consider the submission of the powerful a miracle. Telling his reader of a holy man he had personally known, master Peter awakened his reader's wonder at the saint's perpetual fasting, endurance, and ragged clothing by noting that the man of god suffered all this *although*

> . . . he was erudite in the science of letters and known for the decency of his mores, and he was titled and instituted in the cathedral church, as well as born of noble race and well adorned with the goods of nature and grace.[101]

---

[101] "Ille fuerat scientia litterarum eruditus atque honestate morum preditus, et in cathedrali ecclesia intitulatus et institutus, necnon nobili genere ortus, plurimum bonis naturalibus et gratuitis adornatus": KN, fol. 18rb.

Dressing and Undressing Images:
An Analytic Sketch[*]

THE PRACTICE OF DRESSING SCULPTED — and at times even painted — images of the human form is certainly one of the most neglected subjects in the history of the visual arts. One can read whole books on sculpture without encountering any reference to the phenomenon.[1] Yet who can

[*] This essay appeared previously in *Gepeinigt, begehrt, vergessen: Symbolik und Sozialbezug des Körpers im Spätmittelalter und der frühen Neuzeit*, ed. K. Schreiner and N. Schnitzler (Munich, 1992), 365–402; and in *L'image et la production du sacré*, ed. F. Dunand (Paris, 1991), 195–231.

[1] For example, the works of K. Clark, *The Nude* (Garden City, 1956), J. Pope-Hennessy, *An Introduction to Italian Sculpture*, 3 vols. (London, 1970), and A. Hollander, *Seeing Through Clothes* (New York, 1975), say nothing on our subject. Nor does Thomas Carlyle's brilliant *Sartor Resartus* (New York, 1970). An article by P. Fehl ("The Naked Christ in Santa Maria Novella in Florence: Reflections on an Exhibition and the Consequences," *Storia dell'arte* 45 [1982]: 161–64) is an exception. Fehl explores what happens when a crucifix sculpted to bear a real loincloth is exhibited without one. See also the useful pages on "indumentaria postiza" of M. Trens, *María. Iconografía de la Virgen en el arte español* (Madrid, 1946), 640–49, esp. 640f. on clothes finding their way onto Byzantine icons, but not Spanish paintings. Also J. Cassador, "Une questión iconologica: Les imatges vestides," *Revista de la Asociacion Artistica Arqueológica Barcelonesa* 3 (1901–1902): 445–58; U. Mayerhofer, "Bekleidete Prozessionsfiguren in Tirol. Ein Beitrag zur Kult-Funktion von Bildern," *Jahrbuch für Volkskunde*, n.f. 8 (1985): 107–20. Veiling images to limit their revelation to the faithful is a closely related practice which cannot be studied here; see my *Public Life in Renaissance Florence* (New York 1980, repr. 1990), 117–18, 354–56; and the article of H. Dünninger, "Gnad und Ablaß — Glück und Segen. Das

doubt its importance to an understanding of human behavior and artistic objects? With his usual insight, Gerardus van der Meer speculated that indeed, sculpture may have begun with clothes thrown over mere stumps of wood, rather than, as is sometimes imagined, clothing having originally been added to statues in early modern times to heighten realism.[2]

Not that dressing has ever functioned merely to make objects visually more convincing. True, some critics at least since the sixteenth century have encouraged sculptors to produce realistic, "beautiful" and "worshipful" works of divinities shown clothed in the hope of discouraging the clothing of images.[3] But this has been in vain, as shown by the many protests not only against the tendency to leave unfinished those sculptures intended in advance to be covered by real clothes (in today's Spanish: *imágenes de vestir*),[4] but against those who dress quite realistic sculptures

---

Verhüllen und Enthüllen heiliger Bilder," *Jahrbuch für Volkskunde*, n.f. 10 (1987): esp. 142 for an 1870s report about a Franciscan preacher in Naples who cries to Mary: "Zeige dich deinen Kindern!" "Der Vorhang fällt, und man erblickt die Statue der Jungfrau, über und über in Seide, Sammet, Gold und Spitzen gehüllt, eine immense Krone auf dem Kopf."

[2] G. van der Meer, *Sacred and Profane Beauty: The Holy in Art* (Nashville, 1963), 165.

[3] "Muy mal uso hay en los vestidos de las imágenes que se ponen en las iglesias, porque las atavían con toda la profanidad que las mugeres mas profanas se atavían; de lo cual se siguen tales males. ... Parece cosa conveniente que ninguna imagen hubiese vestida, y las que hubiese de bulto fuesen tan bien hechas, que provocasen a devocíon y no a lo que ahora provocan, especialmente las que hay en lugares pequeños y de mucho tiempo hechas. Lo que mejor me parece [es] que no las hubiese sino de pincel, salvo el crucifijo, y en algunas partes alguna imagen de Nuestra Señora, como las hay en algunas y iglesias, de mucha decencia y devoción muy antigua": *Memorial primero para Trento* (1551), in *Obras completas del santo maestro Juan de Avila*, vol. 6 (Madrid, 1971), 74. This and several other Spanish references come from my friend William A. Christian, Jr., to whom I am very grateful. An alternate justification for clothing — that it was used to cover bare flesh represented in a sculpture — is rarely encountered in fact, even if one can still find it said that Christians first put clothes on statues to cover the bare flesh of works from antiquity, that of Christ shown naked on the cross, and that flesh shown on certain "indecent" works of the Renaissance: R. Ros Ráfales, "Razones de estética y de sentido común que aconsejan desnudar las imágenes de la santísima Virgen de sus inconvenientes vestidos, volviéndolas a su primitivo estado," no. 8 in *Certamen Público celebrado por la Academia Bibliográfico-Mariana de Lérida, para solemnizar el Aniversario LIV de su instalación en la Tarde del 15 de Octubre de 1916* (Lérida: Imprenta Mariana, 1917), part 2, 206.

[4] F. Solá Moreta, "Las Imágenes marianas de talla y los vestidos postizos," no. 7, *Certamen Público*, part 2, 199. Perhaps life-sized wax ex-votos have been made this way as long as the genre has existed; for late medieval Florence, see Trexler, *Public Life*, 114–15, and the fundamental monograph of J. von Schlosser, "Geschichte der Porträtbildnerei in Wachs," *Jahrbuch der kunsthistorischen Sammlungen des allerhöchsten Kaiserhauses* 29 (1910–1911): 171–258.

already "decently" attired by the sculptors. Still today, of course, statues are said at times to be dressed to cover their "barbaric style."[5] But people do dress beautiful statues as well, including those that as carved feign all manner of clothes and drapery. Indeed people also dress vacuous scaffolds. The motivations of the practice of dressing objects go beyond a desire for visual realism.[6]

For millennia, then, "dressing images," which for the purposes of this article includes the practice of covering with cloth as well as fitting clothing over various substantial forms, in both private or public formats, has been a standard part of the ludic, but central to this article, the spiritual and cultic life of many peoples.[7] For as many years, those who made that cloth — in the West, almost always women — have been part of the identity of the finished product. This was true in ancient Greece.[8] It was the case in more recent times, as stressed by a modern believer who vaunted with telling words the "cloaks and veils that blind with their brilliance the pious generations of those who wove them."[9] And the future identity of cloth can still be borne through such persons. In the Maya province of Chiapas, Mexico, at the end of the nineteenth century, for instance, an important craft revival is said to have started when Mary Magdalene appeared to three women of a village named after her and ordered them to

---

[5] As in Tirlemont (Belgium): G. Schnürer and J. Ritz, *Sankt Kümmernis und Volto Santo. Studien und Bilder* (Düsseldorf, 1934), 244.

[6] As is evident even now in the Iberian peninsula; see the debates on whether to undress standing, or redress recently refurbished statues, e.g., in Solá Moreta, "Las Imágenes marianas," 183–201; Ros Ráfales, "Razones," 203–9. As William Christian brought to my attention, the problem confronted the town of Moya (Las Palmas de Gran Canaria) very recently: see the story and picture in *La Provincia* (Las Palmas), 14 January 1988, 16.

[7] Among plenty of extra-European examples, see the guardian statues on Bali recently dressed in protective checkered black and white: M. Gittinger, *Splendid Symbols. Textiles and Tradition in Indonesia* (Washington, DC, 1979), 43–44, and figs. 17, 32.

[8] On the role of Greek women making gowns for goddesses like Athena, and their processions to clothe them, see J. Pollard, *Seers, Shrines and Sirens* (London, 1965), 44–46; M. Nilsson, *Greek Piety* (Oxford, 1948), 11, and by the same author, *Griechische Feste von religiöser Bedeutung, mit Ausschluss der Attischen* (Leipzig, 1906), 62, 130; Pausanias, *Description of Greece*, trans. W. H. S. Jones, vol. 2 (Cambridge, MA, 1926), 97 (bk. III, xvi, 2); 471–72 (V, xvi, 2). Interestingly, in neither of Pausanias's accounts is it said that a robe was actually put on the statue.

[9] "Los mantos y velos que cegaron con su brillo las piadosas generaciones que los tejieran": Solá Moreta, "Imágenes marianas," 183.

make her a new *huipil*, the classic Maya female garment, with the local cosmology woven into it.[10]

Second, the identity of anyone who perchance had worn that clothing before it was put on a statue became part of the identity of that statue. These too seem usually to have been women. Certainly late medieval and early modern male courtiers and citizens did lend, if not give, their clothes for dramatic performances, and churchmen, at least, did lend, if not give, their liturgical clothing for religious theatre.[11] Also in the early modern period, the official clothing once worn by famous men began to be used to cover their life-sized wax votive statues in parts of Europe, and indeed there are cases where the clothing they had worn during famous events was displayed in this way.[12] But in their testaments, men of this age seem to have donated their clothing to cover poor living males rather than to cover statues of holy men or women, perhaps due in part to a preponderance of female statues.[13]

Women were different, if perhaps only because of the same statuarial predominance: "Si donne men boin tissut pour caindre le ymagène Nostre-Dame de Tournay," wrote one not atypical northern European testatrix in 1325.[14] Thus to capture the full identity of a statue as of the cloth that

---

[10] W. Morris, Jr., *Living Maya* (New York, 1987), 113–16.

[11] For the former, see S. Orgel, *The Illusion of Power: Political Theatre in the English Renaissance* (Berkeley, 1975), 5–6, and P. Meredith and J. Tailby, ed., *The Staging of Religious Drama in Europe in the Later Middle Ages: Texts and Documents in English Translation* (Kalamazoo, 1983), 130–46 ("Costume"), esp. 144. For the latter, E. Mâle, *Religious Art from the Twelfth to the Eighteenth Century* (New York, 1949), 107.

[12] Referring in his Life of Verrocchio to a wax figure of Lorenzo de' Medici made after the Pazzi Conspiracy of 1478, G. Vasari says: "E questa figura è con quell'abito appunto che aveva Lorenzo, quando ferito nella gola e fasciato, si fece alle finestre di casa sua per essere veduto dal popolo": *Le Opere di Giorgio Vasari*, ed. G. Milanesi, vol. 1 (Florence, 1906), 374. See also Buchellius's description of SS. Annunziata in Florence, where among the life-size votive statues "spectabantur illic Leonis, Clementisque pontificis habitu regumque ac principum nonnullorum suspensa simulachra": cited in A. Warburg, *Gesammelte Schriften*, vol. 1 (Leipzig, 1932), 348–49.

[13] Dressed statues of male adult saints — e.g., Santiago — are found in the Spanish colonies of the Americas, but are unusual in the old world; see St. James in the anonymous painting of the sixteenth-century Procesión del Corpus: J. De Mesa and T. Gisbert, *Historia de la Pintura Cuzqueña*, vol. 2 (Lima, 1982), fig. 237; and the many modern dressed male saints in E. Porter and E. Auerbach, *Mexican Churches* (Albuquerque, 1987).

[14] J. Dumoulin, "Le Culte de Notre-Dame à la Cathédrale de Tournai," *Revue diocésain de Tournai* 18 (1963): 279, kindly brought to my attention by Sharon Farmer. For women's clothes on the male Christ crucified, see below, at n. 64.

moves from place to place, it is important to establish if the clothing put on a statue was new or had been worn before.

Just as certainly, the sex and social status of those who usually preserved the statues (for example, by bathing them annually),[15] and of those who applied clothing to, and then displayed the objects, is a third important point in the identity of such products. The general guideline as regards such preservation and demonstration seems to have been that the smaller the community, and the less public and formal the act of changing clothes, the more likely women were to fill this role. In modern Spain, such women still have a group name: *camareras*. They have occasionally been said to be virgins but have always been assumed to be "moral women" of "decent" ancestry. A mere half century ago, the honorary *camarera* of one shrine with a dressed Mary was no less than Carmen Polo, the wife of the dictator, Francisco Franco.[16]

As one moves toward formal urban contexts containing clerical and lay corporations, males are seen to play an increasing role, though with obvious complications because of the shame European males might be said to feel at dressing "undressed" women. Thus in the eighteenth century at the Spanish shrine of Palencia, a priest changed the Virgin's clothes, but he did this in the presence of the principal women of the village, who pointed out with poles the places where the clothes were to be fastened.[17]

Significantly, this priest was forbidden to remove the statue's underclothes, which therefore became as it were an unalterable part of the Virgin in question. Here it is important to know whether these underclothes were actual fitted clothes like those worn in reality beneath an outer garment — beginning with or immediately under a tunic — or an

---

[15] On the women's ritual of bathing the goddesses in ancient Greece, see Pollard, *Seers*, 45; in the Middle Ages: W. F. Volbach, "Il Cristo di Sutri e la venerazione del SS. Salvatore nel Lazio," *Rendiconti della pontificia accademia romana di archeologia* 27 (1940–1941), 97–126. On the same practice in Chiapas, where the clothes are laid out to dry and for veneration during the washing, see Morris, *Living Maya*, 113.

[16] M. Barbero Moreno, *La Imagen de la Virgen del Carmen Coronada de Jerez y su Basilica* (Jerez de la Frontera, 1970), 185 (1943).

[17] "Quando se viste à su Magestad, jamàs se le quita el vestido interior, perseverando hasta el dia de oy con el que apareciò y sólo la mudan los vestidos exteriores, y sobrepuestos; y el vestirla, y adornarla de joyas, y cintas, siempre es por mano de sacerdote, aunque assisten à tan piadosa accion alguna de las señoras mas principales de la Villa, que con una caña señalan el lugar en que se ha de prender la cinta, o la joya, para que luzcan mas, y quede mas vistoso el ropage": Juan de Villafañe, *Compendio historico en que se da noticia de las milagrosas, y devotas imagenes de reyna de cielos, y tierra, Maria Santissima, que se veneran en los mas celebres santuarios de España. . . .* (Madrid, 1740), 5.

outer garment like a cape or *manto*. As we shall see, the practice of dressing statues up in fitted underclothes grew in the Iberian peninsula in modern times, whereas elsewhere, further research may show that the latter
practice of confining dress to outer garments remained more common.
Thus in Chiapas, statues still wear layers of the outer *huipiles*, the oldest
one of which is next to the saint's body. In the former situation involving
layers of different types of clothing, shame at intrusion might be a consideration, whereas in the latter, a sense of communal history might also provoke awe. For Walter Morris, the Chiapas practice of piling outer *huipil*
upon *huipil* means that "in a place without libraries or museums, the saints'
wardrobes are the sacred repositories of [women's] traditional designs."[18]

Doubtless awe at age, and shame at intrusion, were in the event often
experienced as fear of the substantial image itself. In a town near Bamberg
about 1470, locals claimed that pictures or representations became powerful once they had attained an age of sixty years. That age, it was said, explained why a certain crucifix was performing many miracles, and why the
locals had dressed it with no less than nine tunics, six of silk and the
other three of fine linen. People said it was very dangerous to remove any
of these tunics from the crucifix.[19] Thus in certain venues, only the older
statues were dressed, apparently beginning at some ceremonial, fixed point
in time. In others, from early on in a statue's life, cloth was used to draw
attention to what was usually women's work.[20]

------

[18] Morris, *Living Maya*, 113. The *huipiles* apparently last about a century; when they
become too ragged, they are removed, and put into the saint's coffer.

[19] Here is Hertel's paraphrase of Johannes Wuschilburgk's ca. 1470 treatise on superstitions: in a city in the Bamberg diocese was seen "ein an einer Bildsäule hängendes
Kreuz, welches die Bewohner der Stadt und Umgegend wegen seines Alters allgemein
'den heiligen Geist' nannten, denn sie glauben, dass mehr Göttliches (*plus numinis*) in
alten, als in neuen Bildern sei. Darum sagen alte Weiber, dass Bilder erst sechzig Jahre
nach ihrer Herstellung Kraft erhielten. Darum wurden jenem alten Holzkreuz wegen
seines hohen Alters viele Wunder zugeschrieben, andererseits stand das Sakrament des
Abendmahls nur in geringer Ehre. Sie hatten es mit neun Überzügen (Röcken, *tunicis*)
bekleidet, von denen sechs aus Seide und drei aus feinem Leinen (*byssus*) waren; diese
konnten nur unter grosser Gefahr weggenommen werden": G. Hertel, "Abergläubige Ge-
bräuche aus dem Mittelalter," *Zeitschrift des Vereins für Volkskunde* 11 (1901): 277, kindly
passed on to me by Jean Wirth. Though the object itself is only called a cross, Hertel's
added discourse about pictures makes me think this was in fact a crucifix.

[20] But not necessarily. In certain parts of America, native women's weaving production units seem to have been led by men dressed as women, the so-called berdaches;
see H. Whitehead, "The Bow and the Burden Strap: A New Look at Institutionalized
Homosexuality in Native North America," in S. Ortner, ed., *Sexual Meanings* (Cambridge, 1981), 80–115, and R. Trexler, *Sex and Conquest: Gendered Violence, Political*

Since women of many types dressed statues in European history, whereas I still lack certain cases of Christian lay males actually dressing and undressing statues,[21] the institutional androgyny of the celibate sacerdotal clergy who did and at times still do dress statues must be a factor in the equation, especially because this clergy was involved in what will be the next stage of identity, the wearing of clothes that had already been worn by statues.[22] Take for instance those cases where the cloak of Mary was changed not every century or so, when it wore out, but annually. In such cases, the action was often the occasion for males to manifest political loyalties between themselves, as was done annually in medieval and early modern Tournai. Once the cathedral clergy of this city received the annual gift of a cloak for their Virgin from the Count of Flanders, they removed the old cloak — which they might soon put on themselves when they did not use it for altar cloths — and then redressed Mary.[23]

The fourth and final stage of the cycle we are sketching is the human wearing of clothing once removed from statues. The fact that living clergy might wear a cloak once removed from a statue is particularly significant because, according to the liturgical scholar Durandus writing in the thirteenth century, all occupational groups other than certain ecclesiastics wore only a shroud to the grave: clergy in holy orders wore their sacerdotal gowns to eternity.[24] Thus certainly at times their funereal getup came

---

Order, and the European Conquest of the Americas (Ithaca, 1995), 134–37.

[21] Since writing this article, I have discovered the *maricas* of Andalucia, presumed male homosexuals who still today do in fact dress images: E. Aguilar Criado, *Las hermandades de Castilleja de la Cuesto* (Seville, 1983). Porter and Auerbach, *Mexican Churches*, 19 describe modern confraternity members dressing and undressing statues used in dramas on a weekly basis and for special occasions, manipulating their movable arms while doing so. But it is not specified if men as well as women members are involved. See further below on activity at Eastertime. See also the information of Llompart below, n. 70.

[22] Recently on clerical androgyny, R. Zapperi, *L'Uomo Incinto: La Donna, l'uomo e il potere* (Cosenza, 1979).

[23] Dumoulin, "Culte," esp. 279, 295f., 333. Of course in many other venues cloth offered to the Virgin "for her mantle," when not indeed gifts made to paintings that could not wear capes, then made superabundantly to statues, was routinely converted into clothes for priests or auctioned; see the case of Or San Michele in Florence, below, at n. 92.

[24] Among laypersons, perhaps only Italians wore their regular clothing to the grave, according to the same authority: "Debent quoque fideles christiani sepeliri induti sudariis prout provinciales observant, que sumunt ex evangelio in quo legis de sudario & syndone Christi. Quidam vero cilicio insuuntur ut hac veste insignia penitentie representent. Nam cinis & cilicium arma sunt penitentium. Nec debent indui vestibus comunis, prout in Italia fit, & ut quidam dicunt debent habere caligas circa tibias & sotulares in pedibus ut

from cult statues, an association between the clothes of priests and statues that will be encountered again.

The laity, on the other hand, wore or were covered with clothes previously worn by important cult statues apparently only when they were sick to death, and then perhaps less to cure their illness than to allow them to die in contact with such cloth. Prohibited no later than the sixteenth century,[25] this activity is still practiced in Spain, where, as at the Aragonese shrine of Pilar, mantles are especially made for that purpose, then sacralized by being placed on the cult image, to be kept in deposit for those in the area around Zaragoza who are near death. "Falleció bajo el manto de Nuestra Senora del Pilar" is indeed an honorable record of one's death.[26] Nothing new, to be sure. According to Gabriel Llompart, confraternities were formed in the early modern period whose purpose was to assure that brothers had the *manto* of that group's cult image placed over them in death. This author claims indeed that in Italy and Majorca, the design of the *manto* on the figure at times became that of the habit of the confraternity itself.[27]

The range of such practices involving cloth used on statues, and their implication for identity formation, are doubtless enormously varied. Here I wanted only to introduce the subject of dressing images by showing that both the dressing itself, and the static dressed image, incorporated social meanings, not the least important of which were those referring to the

---

per hoc ipsos esse paratos ad iudicium representes. Cleri vero si sunt ordinati, illis indumentis induti fit que requirunt ordines quos habent. Si vero non habent ordines sacros, more laicorum sepeliantur": Gulielmus Durantis, . . . *Rationale divinorum officiorum* (n.p., 1479), bk. 7 (in modern eds.: chap. 35, § 39).

[25] In 1565 the ordinary authorized veneration of the Virgin covered with a mantle at the shrine of Lluch (Majorca), "pero prohíbe el que sea llevado a los enfermos y el que los fieles se cubran con él": G. Llompart, *Entre la historia del arte y el folklore. Folklore de Mallorca, Folklore de Europa. Miscelanea de Estudios II* (Palma de Mallorca, 1984), 318. Note the similarity between this practice and that of *ad succurandum*, where a layman is buried in the habit of a religious order, which he in effect joins in death.

[26] W. Christian, "The Spanish Shrine," *Numen* 24 (1977): 77. The custom is found widely in Castile as well. The Pilar practice may be compared to one in Washington, DC. All day long, an employee runs one, then another and still another American flag up and down a flagpole at the Capitol. These consecrated flags, "that have flown over the Capitol," are then given to constituents by congresspersons.

[27] Alas, he presents little evidence: Llompart, *Entre la historia*, 319.

gender and sex of those who made, themselves wore, and arranged the clothes of a divine statue.

At this point, however, the matter of gender identity through clothing is complicated by that of the object itself. The sex of the object onto which the cloth is put — when indeed the object without any cloth added to the sculpture has or is understood to have sex signs — forms a part of the notion of the totality.[28] Next, the age of the represented object onto which clothes are put, whether that is ascertainable through the image's size or its design, complicates because it compromises gender identity. For Infant Jesuses of Prague, whose regal clothing is still sold with the statues of the Infant in some churches in New York City, are dainty though male, as are the nineteenth-century Iberian images of little soldier Jesuses, though they may playfully hint at adult macho violence.[29] "Structurally," Barthes wrote, "the *junior* is presented as the complex degree of the *feminine/masculine*; it tends toward androgyny."[30]

Finally, the gender identity of the clothes put on the image — if indeed gendrically-signed *clothing* rather than genderless *cloth* was used — adds to the meaning of the clothed image. Thus it seems to me that of the myriad of questions one can raise about this ancient social practice of clothing images, given a yawning bibliographical void, none are more important than those touching the gender of both the makers of these images and of the images themselves.

I want to explore this problem of gender using one type of image: those whose male or female sex in their sculpted state can be identified in the

---

[28] On interchangeable body parts and commercial mannequins, see recently S. Culver, "What Manikins Want: *The Wonderful World of OZ* and *The Art of Decorating Dry Goods Windows*," *Representations* 21 (1988): 97–116. On scaffolds for clothing, see further below.

[29] Crowned Infant Jesuses of Prague in plaster (dated 1966 and labeled Made in Italy) with seven different colors of clothing for the liturgical seasons, are still on sale at the Paulist bookstore at Grand Central Station, and in the church of Our Lady of Mt. Carmel, on E. 116th Street, New York City; on which see R. Orsi, *The Madonna of 115th Street. Faith and Community in Italian Harlem, 1880–1950* (New Haven, 1985). The Infant Jesus of Prague was originally (ca. 1628) a small wax figurine: C. Van Hulst, "La storia della divozione a Gesù Bambino nelle immagini plastiche isolate," *Antonianum* 19 (1944): 50–51. On the little soldier Christs, see F. Gonçalves, "O Vestuário mundano de algunas Imagens de Menino Jesus," *Revista de Etnografia* 9.1 (1967): 5–34. Such military Jesuses were outlawed by the synodal constitutions of Vich (Spain) in 1748: Solá Moreta, "Imágenes marianas," 200.

[30] R. Barthes, *The Fashion System* (New York, 1983), 258.

historical records of late medieval and early modern Europe, including the European colonies. The images beneath the added clothing in this study are, therefore, substantial, and not a scaffolded void: devotees needed have no doubt that there *was* a sexed reality.[31] Nor are our images originally hermaphroditic, like the Aphroditos/Aphrodite whom men in antiquity worshipped while dressed as women and women while dressed as men.[32] In cases involving our single-sexed images, the placement of clothing would, therefore, either confirm sexual identity, invert that identity, add the sexually-opposite identity to the one indicated by the image, or, finally, deceive viewers about that identity.

In this paper, I will examine only inert images, excluding those called "mannequins" that have multiple movable parts, conscious though I am that from early times, such automatons form an important chapter in the history of clothed images.[33] My images are studied as if, in their sculpted state at least, they stopped changing identity when they died, so to speak, and thus I also exclude from this study all those Christian images which, like the famous crucifix at Burgos, were said to be uncopiable because they themselves were never the same at any two moments.[34]

So must I also exclude humans acting as images, as for example the

---

[31] See the end of this article for more on the deception.

[32] H. Usener, *Legenden der Pelagia* (Bonn, 1879), xxiii. Of course remember that in medieval European religious theatre, women were usually represented by male clergy.

[33] Maspero believed that already in ancient Egypt, images that prophesied were expected, as a class, to gesture in certain ways, for instance waving arms and moving the head: cited in E. Bevan, *Holy Images* (London, 1940), 25. I will however touch on Crucifieds whose arms alone moved. For the middle ages, see G. and J. Taubert, "Mittelalterliche Kruzifixe mit schwenkbaren Armen," *Zeitschrift des deutschen Vereins für Kunstwissenschaft* 23 (1969), 79–121, and a shorter version in J. Taubert, *Farbige Skulpturen. Bedeutung, Fassung, Restaurierung* (Munich, 1978), 38–50. My thanks to Hans Belting for these references. Such statues were used in judicial contexts. Peter Arnade tells me that the Spanish Inquisition used a statue of Mary whose movable arms, when they hugged a condemned person seeking solace, proved to be full of nails and knives that decimated the victim: J. Plaidy, *The Spanish Inquisition* (New York, 1967), 144.

[34] See such a description in the seventeenth-century work of Antonio de la Calancha, *Cronica moralizada*, 6 vols. continuing pagination (Lima, 1974–1981), 589; further in von Schlosser, "Geschichte," 223f. Owning a copy of an important pilgrimage image might involve trying to keep up with certain changes in the original. As originals became darkened by burning candles, polychromatic copies were blackened to show the changed state, even though the originals had long been covered with clothing that did not permit the "skin" to be seen by devotees; according to H. Hahnloser, "Du culte de l'image au moyen age," in *Cristianesimo e ragioni di stato* (*Congresso internazionale di studi umanistici*), vol. 2 (Rome, 1952), 229.

Spanish tertiary María de Santo Domingo who, said an admirer in the
early sixteenth century, donned clothes that devotees gave her to wear
while in a trance "as an image might wear them."[35] Among human
images, Joan of Arc is the historical personage in this age perhaps most
relevant to our inquiry. Whereas she herself suppressed all hints of her female sex in her dress, artists from the beginning have endlessly manipulated not just hair and breasts, but that dress as well so as to show her to
be a woman transvested as a man.[36] My problem is similar: what happens
gendrically when real clothes are added to sculpted and painted images
whose sex is pre-established?

My remarks will center around figures of Jesus and Mary. Although
these two persons are peculiar among Christian numens, in that they both
are said to have ascended to heaven, the treatment of their figures will be
seen to be relevant to general social history.[37] To begin at the end, the
evidence I have on images of Jesus and Mary allows the following hypothesis: in some periods of Western history and in certain areas, images of
Mary — a woman and thus thought dependent at whatever age — in some
sense existed to be dressed and undressed *over* the clothes the sculptor usually represented her in. On the other hand, the Jesuses whom we know to
have been clothed and unclothed are usually Jesuses at a dependent age
and status rather than independent male adults.

This circumstance may be compared to practices in social behavior. In
European society generally, actual women of whatever age have been customarily dressed and undressed ceremoniously, sometimes publicly, for the
delectation of audiences, whereas until the seventeenth century, it is my
impression this happened less often to living males, especially mature and

---

[35] My thanks to Jodi Bilinkoff for allowing me to read her "Charisma and Controversy: The Case of María de Santo Domingo," *Archivo dominicano* 10 (1989): 55–66 before
publication. Note that despite admonitions, people for luck did therefore put clothes on
images — at least living ones — and not just for dying.

[36] A. Harmand, *Jeanne d'Arc, ses costumes, son armure. Essai de réconstitution* (Paris,
1929), 5–19. Having established that Joan always concealed her femaleness, Harmand demands that modern artists not show her as a female. On a similar problem, see Fehl,
"Naked Christ," above, n. 1.

[37] Jesus but not necessarily Mary had been buried and exposed to corruption before
ascension, to be sure. But the mother left behind plenty of relics (often kept in images!),
so Mary's assumption did not remove her from the world of social interaction, as indicated by L. Rothkrug, "Religious Practices and Collective Perceptions: Hidden Homologies in the Renaissance and Reformation," *Historical Reflections* 7 (1980): 10.

independent ones.[38] Conclusion: social dependency may be as important a factor as biological sex in interpreting the dress of Christian images whose sex is clear beneath the added clothes.

Let us begin with Jesus. As far as I can determine, images of him were dressed and undressed that showed him as a baby, as the Crucified, and as a corpse, all states of dependency.[39] First the infant. I do not refer to the infant shown with his mother. That subject clearly requires study as well, but the combination with Mary makes it too complicated a subject to be handled here: it appears, generally, that in late medieval sculpture, there was a tendency to keep such infants nude even while the Mary who held him was increasingly being subjected to ever more sumptuous dressing.[40] Rather, our subject is the free-standing baby Jesus.

From a recent study by Christiane Klapisch-Zuber we know a good deal about the *bambini* produced en masse in early modern Tuscany.[41] According to Klapisch, these objects, passed from woman to woman, were used in part to encourage the birth of male babies. They perhaps also permitted ersatz maternalism for nuns.[42] Such *bambini* originally were meant to stand

---

[38] The public dressing of princes in absolutistic Europe requires separate consideration. A Maya fresco at Bonampak shows its lord being dressed by male servants: Morris, *Living Maya*, 13. Females were usually those punished by being undressed in European public judicial proceedings: see R. Trexler, "*Correre la Terra.* Collective Insults in the Late Middle Ages," *Mélanges de l'École française de Rome. Moyen Age-Temps Modernes 96* (1984): 845–902. For males voluntarily undressing for public penance, see G. Llompart, "Penitencias y penitentes en la pintura y en la piedad catalanas bajomedievales," in his *Religiosidad popular. Folklore de Mallorca, Folklore de Europa* (Palma de Mallorca, 1982), 145–55.

[39] It goes without saying that Jesus' imaged factual dependency was often interpreted as the church's triumph, but I am interested in the physical states. The charivari character of this re-interpretation is most evident in the so-called triumphant entry into Jerusalem, where in medieval recreations Jesus was dressed and undressed with the so-called red *Spottmantel*, as was the ass on which he rode and the ground before them: K. Young, *The Drama of the Medieval Church*, 2 vols. (Oxford, 1933), 1:93–98.

[40] On the turn to the nude infant in the high middle ages, see L. Steinberg, *The Sexuality of Christ in Renaissance Art and in Modern Oblivion* (New York, 1983), 28. For Catalonia, see Solá Moreta, "Imágenes marianas," 189. On the increasingly visible Christic penis in late medieval painting, see Steinberg, *Sexuality*, passim.

[41] "Les saintes poupées: Jeu et dévotion dans la Florence du Quattrocento,"in J.-C. Margolin and P. Ariès, eds., *Les Jeux à la Renaissance* (Paris, 1983), 65–79; I cite from the English translation in the author's *Women, Family, and Ritual in Renaissance Italy* (Chicago, 1985), 310–29. On the Luccan industry of *bambini*, which started in mid-Cinquecento, see Van Hulst, "Storia," 44.

[42] Klapisch-Zuber, *Women*, 317, 326–27.

up in triumph, but from the fourteenth century onward they were made to lie down — on domestic altars for example — where they were swaddled, dressed, and redressed by *female* devotees.[43]

Klapisch found that the dolls which formed part of the trousseaus of such brides and nuns were listed "not nude but generally richly dressed," often with two or more sets of clothes.[44] Still, the dolls themselves are listed as *male,* and in fact, several such *bambini* which have survived show the infant's male parts. They were not sexless mannequins.[45] Devotees might use a relic of mother Mary to bring forth a healthy baby of presumably male sex: the blouse or tunic that she was said to have worn at the Nativity, reputedly preserved at Chartres, was such an object.[46] But apparently, if the sculpted *bambini* in question were intended to help produce male children, their male sex had to be shown. Certainly young girls played with girl dolls then as they do now, but presumably they did not use them in prayer for female offspring.[47]

Though misleadingly referring to Jesus' visible penis as evidence of his "humanity" instead of his masculinity, Leo Steinberg does document how insistently this age drew attention to such masculinity, whose covering and uncovering in the social life of the period was a matter of more significance than Steinberg imagined.[48] Margery Kempe told how, passing through Umbria in 1414, a woman in her company would take out an

---

[43] Klapisch-Zuber, *Women*, 314.

[44] Klapisch-Zuber, *Women*, 312. Calendrically liturgical clothes on sale today are documented above, n. 29.

[45] Klapisch-Zuber, *Women*, 312, and the several photographs.

[46] Helpful presumably because worn at the time Jesus was born; described in S. Sharbrough, "The Cult of the Mother in Europe: the Transformation of the Symbolism of Woman," (Ph.D. diss., University of California Los Angeles, 1977), 74. Interestingly, this cloth was also used as a type of flag to ward off threatening armies: Sharbrough, "Cult of the Mother," 120. On female deities covered with enemy flags, or with a cloth Palio which, at the goal line, was the prize for a race, see below, n. 112.

[47] See however a Mantuan synod of 1585 on nuns making dolls: "De ecclesiis: . . . nec etiam parvulae illae puellarum statuae adiungantur [to altars] quas moniales inutili studio, ac nonnumquam indecoris ornamentis comunt et ornant": C. Corrain and P. Zampini, *Documenti etnografici e folkloristici nei sinodi diocesani italiani* (Bologna, 1970), 85.

[48] Since it was infantile it was only potentially macho, of course. Steinberg explained Mary's revelation of Jesus' penis in so many paintings as a figuration of a theological doctrine. But with little sense of generational or social differences, the author considers a child's and an adult's, a common man's and a noble's penis signs of one and the same "humanation," at one point conflating humanness with "manhood": Steinberg, *Sexuality*, 9, 78. These are taken into account by S. Brandes, *Metaphors of Masculinity. Sex and Status in Andalusian Folklore* (Philadelphia, 1980).

image, certainly of the Christ child, "and set it in worshipful wives' laps. And [these local women] would put shirts thereon and kiss it as though it had been God himself."[49]

An instance in an organized nunnery drama again emphasizes the corporate character of dressing these little Jesuses, even as it refers to the clear importance of women as clothiers. In Mary's marvelous appearance to Caterina de' Ricci on Christmas 1540, the divine mother loaned the infant Jesus to Caterina, who was astonished to find that the infant was clothed. Mary as quickly explained that Caterina and her sisters were the ones who had clothed the infant . . . through their Advent prayers.[50] The following Christmas in a repeat vision, Mary again loaned the Infant to Caterina, but this time it was naked. Once Caterina returned it, however, mother Mary diapered the infant with clothes that had been made, she again explained to the ecstatic Caterina, by the prayers of the same nuns.[51] Until comparable devotional traditions regarding the swaddling of saintly female figures are found, the emphasis on the sex of these male figures, lovingly manipulated always by women with non-gendered diapers, deserves our attention.

In the second and third instances where Jesus is often found to be clothed, he is an adult, but definitely a humiliated and dependent one, and thus in a position analogous to his childhood status. First Jesus crucified. According to the evangelists, Jesus was thrice stripped of clothing during his passion, the last time being after he had been hung on the cross, at which point, according to John, his tunic was definitively removed.[52] Thus the best bet is that Jesus was quite naked as he hung dying. So while the earliest mode of representing the Crucified in art — shown in a tunic and sometimes a cloak, eyes open and hanging at right angles — might portray him before his final humiliation, the far more common mode — wearing just a loincloth — has no canonical authority, but only late legend to sustain it: Bridget of Sweden learned in a vision that

---

[49] The image was probably the infant Jesus because the author relates what Kempe saw to her previous meditations on the infancy of Jesus: S. Brown Meech, ed., *The Book of Margery Kempe* (London, 1940), 77.

[50] Cited in Klapisch-Zuber, *Women*, 326.

[51] Klapisch-Zuber, *Women*, 326.

[52] Mt. 27.27–31, 35; Mk. 15.17–20, 24; Lk. 23.11, 34; Jn. 19.3, 23–24. Stripping criminals of their distinctive male clothing was, in fact, a traditional if uncommon punishment for males still in our period: cf. H. P. Duerr, *Nacktheit und Scham* (Frankfurt am Main, 1988), 270–72.

Jesus covered up his own nakedness, whereas the fourteenth-century Pseudo-Bonaventure knew that it was Mary, upset by Jesus' nakedness, who used her own veil to cover him.[53] Still, it is my impression that many high- and late medieval Christians knew Jesus was naked on the cross, and viewed the loincloth as a mere convention to avoid shocking "decent people." Certainly when Francis of Assisi stripped himself even of his underpants at the time of his renunciation of worldly goods, he thought he was copying Jesus.[54]

But while the old way for a sculptor to show Jesus — in a sleeved tunic that covered his body — disappeared in most of Europe in the high and late middle ages, it remained fairly common in certain parts of Catalonia, as shown by Manuel Trens in his work on these so-called *majestats*.[55] The very commonality and continuity in Catalonia of sculpturally dressed Jesuses on the cross, according to this author, assured that there, few would mistake this Jesus in the long gown . . . for a woman. In most of the rest of Europe, however, sculptors or others since the tenth century covered the sculpted and increasingly diagonally-hanging Jesus only with a loincloth.

The stage was set, so it seems, for a major misunderstanding, and Gustav Schnürer and Joseph Ritz are the scholars who have most comprehensively studied the result. Their story is so richly complicated, however, that we can do no more here than touch on those elements of their story that regard the clothing of crucifixes. According to these authors, when in

---

[53] Bridget's fourth Revelation, involving a small piece of cloth, is described in Fehl, "Naked Christ," 163. The latter story, which has a tradition in pictures, is in Steinberg, *Sexuality*, 32–33. A dramatic rendering of Mary covering Jesus, who is imagined to be naked but is not, is in Meredith and Tailby, *Staging*, 146, also 112 on how an actor feigned nakedness, e.g., with skin-colored shorts. It goes without saying that when Jesus was first seen after his resurrection, he was thought by the late middle ages to be already out of the shroud and clothed in a gown: Meredith and Tailby, *Staging*, 143–44. Durandus faced several questions of this type, including whether Jesus was dressed at the Resurrection: *Rationale*, bk. 7 (in modern eds: chap. 35, § 39).

[54] See R. Trexler, *Naked Before the Father. The Renunciation of Francis of Assisi* (New York, 1989), 3, 43; cf. the disrobing of Francis attributed to Jan Provost (Trexler, *Naked Before the Father*, fig. 29) with the Westphalian disrobing of Jesus, in Steinberg, *Sexuality*, 33, fig. 39. Paintings I encountered in Munich's Old Pinakothek (Van Dyck's *Mourning*, Rembrandt's *Deposition*, etc.) and some scenes in the Krippen collection of the Bavarian National Museum show Jesus naked on being removed from the cross. Finally, the French stage required that people act as if Jesus was naked: Meredith and Tailley, *Staging*, 146.

[55] M. Trens, *Les Majestats Catalanes* (Barcelona, 1966). Deriving the *majestats* from Byzantine art, Trens casts his Catalan ones as triumphant images. I am interested in the experience of Christians: that crucifixion was humiliating in fact, however they might be symbolized.

the late fourteenth century a Lucchese merchant colony in northwestern Europe made the home city's famous *volto santo* — an old-style crucifix carved with a tunic — widely known through one or more copies, the locals in this northern ambience of barechested Jesuses mistook the man Jesus in the *volto santo* for a woman. As Schnürer reconstructs the events, Flemings soon manufactured the story of a clothed female saint who, on developing a beard to avoid marriage, had been crucified by her father.[56]

As Schnürer read the documents, verbal misunderstanding now compounded the visual mistake. The new saint got her name Wilgefortis when the Flemings misunderstood the words *virgo fortis* the Lucchese applied to the statue, another name Ontkommer from the Lucchese saying that the statue "gave peace" (cf. the Germanic *entkümmern*), and in the sixteenth century her name Liberata through association to a long-established, characterologically similar Iberian worthy. In the very years of Joan of Arc, then, and in the same general area, figures of a clothed, bearded woman on a cross made their appearance who looked for all the world like a man. In later centuries the cult achieved widespread popularity in some parts of Europe. Old romanesque crucifixes were prominent among the many media used for figuring Wilgefortis, Schnürer notes. In several cases, Jesus became Wilgefortis when some old romanesque crucifixes carved with tunics and some carved with just a loincloth, were dressed with real women's clothing.[57]

Here I want only to call attention to the extent to which Schnürer's reconstruction privileges intellect and imagination over social fact. For example, this author does not really assign the sex change from Jesus to Wilgefortis great importance in his description of the phenomenon. He

---

[56] Schnürer and Ritz, *Sankt Kümmernis und Volto Santo*; G. Schnürer, "Die Kümmernis- und Volto santo-Bilder in der Schweitz," *Freiburger Geschichtsblatt* 10 (1903): 110–81; A. Lütolf, "Sanct Kümmerniss und die Kümmernisse der Schweizer," *Geschichtsfreund* 19 (1863): 183–205; Trens, *Majestats*, 42–45.

[57] Schnürer and Ritz, *Sankt Kümmernis*, 181; see further Schnürer, "Kümmernis- und Volto santo-Bilder," 112 (Naters), 125 (Schönbrunn), 126 (Schwyz). Schnürer says the cult of Wilgefortis did not extend to Italy. However, elsewhere I hope (a) to show how important the ancient *literary* tradition of the transvestite female saint was to the emergence of St. Wilgefortis — a link Schnürer downplays; and (b) to investigate the claim that the Spanish transvestite saint Liberata or Librada, whose relics at Sigüenza are supposed to have come from Florence, Italy, around 1300, is related to the Florentine patroness Reparata, earlier known equally as Liberata ("Liberated"). The Florentine patron saint may have been the ancient transvestite St. Reparata ("Repaired"). On the ultramontane Liberata, see R. Castex, *Sainte Livrade. Étude critique et historique sur la vie, le martyre et les reliques du culte* (Lille, 1890).

does not, for instance, elaborate on the evidence he presents that long before Wilgefortis, the famous Volto Santo crucifix of Lucca, through cloths
placed over its male loins, was said to be world-famous at protecting child-
bearing *women*.[58] Once this is mulled over, things look different. It is
possible, for instance, that the northern Europeans may have seen a truly
dressed Volto Santo in the Lucchese colony, and that they may have preferred a (dressed) woman saving women's lives rather than a male's genitals doing so. In any case, the fact that the "mistake" involved a sex
change is not immaterial.

Moreover, Schnürer leaves unmentioned the probability that women
and not men were the sacristans who redressed Jesus as a woman, over and
over again, in the many small towns and villages where the cult became
especially popular. In Naters, Switzerland, for example, the story in
Schnürer's time still was that the female Wilgefortis — really a wooden
male Jesus dressed up in a colorful cloth dress and cloak — insisted that
the people "have a new dress made for *her*"every seven years, and threatened to leave the town when they once failed to do so.[59] A more serious
reexamination of this important tradition of a man consciously being made
into and maintained as a woman than is possible here will emphasize precisely such social facts.

Still, the conventional fashion of representing the Crucified in most of
Western Europe was without any distinguishable article of male clothing:
naked except for a loincloth, or diaper if one wishes to draw the traditional comparison to Jesus' birth.[60] Perhaps sculptors usually carved veils
— called *mantillas* in Spain — to cover such Jesuses, that commonly give
no indication of male genitalia beneath. Indeed, some images show such
veiled Jesuses sexless.[61] The work of the Counter-Reformation in cover-

---

[58] Buoncompagno da Signa in the early thirteenth century wrote that "fama per or-
bem exivit, quod linea quibus imago illa praecingitur, parturienti conferat mulieri
sanitatem": Schnürer, "Über Alter und Herkunft des Volto Santo von Lucca," *Römische
Quartalschrift für christliche Altertumskunde und Kirchengeschichte* 34 (1926): 273.

[59] My italics; Schnürer, "Kümmernis- und Volto santo-Bilder," 112.

[60] Choreographers in medieval European drama might specifically call for sex-neutral
clothes, at least for males. In the Castilian "Trial in Heaven," Man, who was to "look
very old, have a white beard and a headdress," was to wear "clothes which are neither
typically those of a man or a woman": Meredith and Tailby, *Staging*, 143, where "The
Eternal Word" also dressed in sex-neutral clothes.

[61] J. Wirth, *L'image médiévale. Naissance et développements (VIe–XVe siècles)* (Paris,
1989), 322–41; also his "Sur l'évolution du crucifix à la fin du Moyen Age," *Les ateliers
des interprets. Revue européenne pour étudiants en histoire de l'art* 2 (1989): 166–84.

ing up Christic penises, scrotums, and buttocks still needs much study. Yet it is known that the Crucified was often carved naked and then given a loincloth of a distinct material, as can still be suspected about many road-side crucifixes in Europe today. That was once the practice in Spain,[62] while in Italy in 1399, those sectarians called the Bianchi employed car-vers to clothe wood crucifixes with loincloths of cloth soaked in plas-ter.[63] The question whether the placement of this cloth over Jesus' geni-talia ever formed part of the *group* or confraternal activity or experience of traditional European laymen will be better addressed when his deposition from the cross is confronted.

Yet the question of women's role in the representation of the all-but-naked Jesus on the cross does deserve attention, since this sex so seldom had a formal consororal identity, and because we already are confident that women were important in the transvesting of male Jesuses into female Wilgefortises. The query about women's role is no sooner put than a posi-tive response emerges in the form of a remarkable contemporary practice which certainly has ancient roots that remain to be unearthed and de-scribed. In a series of photographs from Mexican pilgrimage churches made during the 1950s, the traditional genderless loincloths on sculpted cruci-fied Jesuses of the seventeenth-century have been replaced by a *female* arti-cle of clothing![64] And what a revealing article of clothing it is: frilly, shiny women's slips!

Here I think is important evidence both for the tendency to convert the humiliated crucified Jesus into a woman, and for the prominent role of women in doing so. In the pilgrimage villages in question, after all, cer-tainly it was the women and not the men who maintained the crucifixes and other liturgical things. They were the ones who put slips on male Je-suses. Even if these slips do not necessarily reflect women's production ac-tivities since they are not of woven cloth — as often *are* the souvenir cloths also common in contemporary Latin America as coverings for the Crucified[65] — they do help us to grasp these women's statements, espe-

---

[62] Real Spanish *mantillas* were originally used to cover naked crucifixes: Ros Ráfales, "Razones de estétic," 206.

[63] M. Lisner, *Holzkruzifixe in Florenz und in der Toskana* (Munich, 1970), 56. It cannot be excluded, however, that the Bianchi were pretending to cover already "decent" Crucifieds, as in contemporary plays; see above, nn. 53, 54.

[64] Porter and Auerbach, *Mexican Churches*. This book contains many valuable pictures of dressed images of recent times.

[65] An example in Porter and Auerbach, *Mexican Churches*, pl. 84; such medallions

cially if we keep in mind the distinction already made between covering up a human representation with cloth, and dressing it up underneath with layers of clothing. Here, if I am right, local females, covering up the humiliated Jesus as one might any humiliated dependent, but desiring to participate themselves in Jesus's agony, employed the glossy yet normally hidden undergarment of young girls, and thus rendered such "shameful" clothing public.[66] That these village choreographers intended to reverse clothing, and *bring what normally is closest to the skin out*, is evidenced by one such slip, which is decorated with a striking large red rose, symbol of fertility, which, I suspect, would not be found on an actual, quotidian slip.[67]

I read these marvelous images in which man Jesus is covered by a woman's slip to mean at least in part that village women thought of Jesus as having suffered the way women do. Indeed the blood shown on some of these slips, though it does not stem usually from the area of the genitalia, may still be thought of in relation to the menstrual blood of women. In the end, from the end of the middle ages till the present, clothing this humiliated man made him a woman, if I may be permitted this verbal shorthand. The question arises how often in history *independent* humans have ever been "dressed up" as positive cultural images. Put differently: how is gender related to being dressed up?

The third Jesus who was clothed and reclothed is the cadaver in the Pietà, the non-biblical image of the expired Jesus held by a seated Mary. As with the clothing in the two earlier emblems, here too it is a sex-neutral piece of cloth that covers the genitalia. Leo Steinberg may be right that just as paintings of the crucifixion with "banner loincloths" trumpet Jesus' masculinity,[68] so in some pietàs or related men of sorrows, especially by Maerten van Heemskerck, Jesus' masculinity is emphasized by an Osirian erection surmisable beneath the cloth.[69]

More germane to my interests, however, is the liturgical social action which occurred at the moment at which the dead Jesus was covered over

---

are also used in Peru, for instance in the procession of the "Lord of the Earthquakes"in Cuzco, shown on a postcard sent me by Caroline Dean.

[66] Porter and Auerbach, *Mexican Churches*, pls. 9, 10, 39, 41 (pink), 73, and 74.

[67] Porter and Auerbach, *Mexican Churches*, pl. 67 (former church of S. Domingo, Yanhuitlán, Oaxaca). A contemporary Chilean woman who has just finished dressing the Crucified (with movable arms) in a church in Chíuchíu, Chile, is pictured in *National Geographic* 174.1 (July 1988): 58–59.

[68] Steinberg, *Sexuality*, 91–95.

[69] Steinberg, *Sexuality*, 82–108.

with a shroud: in traditional Christianity, after about 3 P.M. on Good Friday. In this period, statues were covered with dark cloth (to be stripped in favor of white clothing on Easter morning).[70] And at this time in the convent of S. Vincenzo, Prato (Tuscany), late sixteenth-century nuns "dressed up" their colleague Caterina de' Ricci to play the widowed Mary, and then "placed the dead Jesus in her arms to represent the day's mystery."[71] Whether, as was fairly common in Europe and especially in Tuscany, that Jesus of S. Vincenzo was none other than the image actually taken down from the cross by devotees is unclear.[72]

There is much evidence for the activity of monks at this liturgical juncture, but one may easily imagine other nunneries and certainly lay confraternities arranging for a loincloth or a shroud to cover quickly Jesus' "shame." In Vienna in 1512, the brotherhood of the Body of God is found purchasing not only a Good Friday dress for "Mary Magdalene" but a shroud for Jesus.[73] In Wittenberg in 1517, one finds the authorities joining to fund a group of fourteen men to pray at the drama of the deposition, which was carried out by four chaplains in "Jews' clothes."[74] There was, after all, a seventeenth-century Italian confraternity charged with washing, swaddling, and cradling the dependent infant at the begin-

---

[70] From no later than the sixteenth century, the dramatization of the Easter *encuentro* or encounter of Jesus and Mary in some places in Spain included the "descubrimiento del manto blanco de la Virgen, al despojarla del negro": Llompart, *Religiosidad popular*, 174.

[71] See the text in Trexler, *Public Life*, 191.

[72] An instance in Louvain of a statue stapled to a cross with an iron belt because no longer taken down is in Schnürer and Ritz, *Sankt Kümmernis und Volto Santo*, 244. See also on this activity K. Gschwend, *Die Depositio und Elevatio Crucis im Raum der alten Diözese Brixen* (Bolzano, 1965); P. Sheingorn, *The Easter Sepulchre in England* (Kalamazoo, 1987). A list of Tuscan crucifixes with movable arms is in Taubert, *Farbige Skulpturen*, 43.

[73] See the ledger entries in G. Taubert, "Spätmittelalterliche Kreuzabnahmespiele in Wels, Wien und Tirol," *Jahrbuch des oberösterreichischen Musealvereines* 119 (1974): 84.

[74] "Und in des die vier Caplan die leyttern aufsteygen, und bildnus ordenlich abnehmen, Und das bildnus in die par legen, Und mit seydn also bedecken, das das bildnus angesicht bloß und unbedeckt bleybe, Und so bald das bildnus auf die bar gelegt sollen ...": G. and J. Taubert, "Mittelalterliche Kruzifixe," 99; see also 97, where English priests c. 1370 "vulnera Crucifixi vino abluant et aqua" right after the deposition and before the shroud envelopment prior to burial. See further Taubert, *Farbige Skulpturen*, 46–47, where are also several early sixteenth-century examples of cloth shrouds put over sculpted Jesuses. Taubert and Young before him noted how important in this age was the placement of the shroud and sweat-cloth in the sepulchre: *Farbige Skulpturen*, 46–47, and Young, *Drama*, 1: 134–35. In Brixen in 1550, the "shroud" was made up of priests' vestments: G. and J. Taubert, "Mittelalterliche Kruzifixe," 107–8.

ning of life.[75] The lay confraternities charged with dressing and undressing Jesus during his Passion largely remain, however, to be identified and described.[76]

The performance of Caterina de' Ricci in playing mother Mary holding a plastic Jesus is conventional enough, but in other dramatic moments this visionary imitated Jesus himself. At one point we find her in the biblical red gown of Jesus as she bore the cross through the nunnery of S. Vincenzo,[77] while on another occasion Caterina is the twelve-year old Jesus teaching in the temple. These cases in the dramatic if not sculptural sphere are significant because they show a dependent Jesus played by a dependent woman. In his record of the latter play, the confessor of the nunnery, fra Serafino Razzi, lapses confusingly into calling Caterina "he," then "she," then "he" again. His/her garment of red satin reached halfway down his/her legs. She/he wore a wig of real curly hair, topped by a "make-believe light royal crown." She/he bore a scepter, and on her feet she wore low leather sandals decorated with gold and silver.[78]

In ecstasy, Ricci — that is, Christ Teaching in the Temple — then went about the nunnery teaching his/her colleagues how to behave. One nun remembered that "the mother sister Caterina while she was being dressed as Jesus went into ecstasy for a little while, so that it was easy to dress and arrange her as [the nun] wanted. For [while in ecstasy] she did not object to anything, as she did at other times."[79] One remembers the earlier Spanish case in which lay women took to dressing up the visionary tertiary María in their clothes before she entered ecstasy, to retrieve them

---

[75] Klapisch-Zuber, *Women*, 324. The evangelists have Jesus' cadaver placed in a linen shroud: Mt. 27.59; Mk. 15.46; Lk. 23.53. Jn. 19.38–40 says his body was also preserved with myrrh and aloes. See the simple covering over almost the whole "body" in Porter and Auerbach, *Mexican Churches*, pl. 59.

[76] A prominent candidate for study is the Confraternity of the Resurrection at Florence, charged with its representation: Trexler, *Public Life*, 403, 508. Note however that women (in this case the Three Marys with their myrrh and aloes) were those who traditionally washed bodies; it would be interesting to determine if the corporations of (female) professional mourners at funerals were employed here.

[77] This was done in Carnival, on the Sunday before Lent, to placate God: text in Trexler, *Public Life* 191–92.

[78] See the text in Trexler, *Public Life*, 194–96.

[79] Trexler, *Public Life*, 194–95. According to Razzi, the nuns initially had trouble with Caterina, "la quale sempre fuggiva di comparire così vestita in pubblico. Imponendole nondimeno l'ubbidienza ...": S. Razzi, *Vita di Santa Caterina de' Ricci* (Florence, 1965), 172.

afterwards.[80] It is as if the very nature of being dressed up by someone else, in which one becomes someone or something else, is related to obedience and suppliance, just as the dressing of statues, from time immemorial, has been part and parcel of bringing their spirits under control.[81]

In truth, this review of the three major moments in Jesus' life when we find his statues dressed and undressed with real cloth is a meager harvest, especially when compared to the dressing and undressing of Mary. I hope only to have sketched out areas for future research.[82] But before discussing Mary, let me suggest that this paucity is precisely the point. Perhaps Jesus emblematizes the powerless majority of males: they are "dressed" by powerful adult males who, at least until the seventeenth century, do not render themselves passive so as to be themselves dressed. In any case, a better understanding of the ages and statuses of men who have been dressed at different points in history is a precondition to understanding the dressing of the humiliated Christian savior.[83] Females, on the other hand, of whatever status, seem to be capable of being dressed throughout their lives.

My interest in this problem of the relation between sex identification or gendering and being "dressed up" in traditional Europe was stimulated by a naively telling description of Spanish adult males given by the famous collector of travel accounts, Peter Martyr of Anghera.[84] Spanish men are

---

[80] See above, at n. 35.

[81] For a Christian example of this standard ethnographic notion, see below, n. 101, for the statue which, "así vestida, era tan miraculosa."

[82] A comparable beginning needs to be made regarding the behavior of dressing Byzantine images of Jesus; in a personal communication, Hans Belting informs me that that culture made a fundamental distinction between plain and "dressed or ornamented" icons.

[83] Certainly one thinks of the dressing of matadors and samurai, which would reward study; see also the marvelous scene in the movie *Cat Ballou* (Harold Hecht 1965), where a servant makes available to cowboy Lee Marvin each piece of warrior clothing, but the hero himself puts it in place. The whole phenomenon of uniforms worn by subordinate males is germane of course, but perhaps especially the "feminine" styles and colors in which, comparable to Peter Martyr's nobles cited below, uniformed military officers still fit themselves out. See the enlightening summation in N. Joseph, *Uniforms and Nonuniforms. Communication Through Clothing* (New York, 1986), 195. Such ironies are often shown in the cinema work of Federigo Fellini.

[84] The following analysis is based on this text of ca. 1516: "Maior preterea Hispaniorum pars annullatos aut gemmatos derident & probra ascribunt gemmarum gestamina, populares precipue. Nobiles autem si quando nuptiales vel alias regiae parentur pompae celebres, tot quibus aureis gemmis consutis gaudent & vestibus margaritas gemmis admixtas intertexunt. Alias minime, effoeminatorum esse huiuscemodi ornatus atque Arabi-

generally very masculine, this early sixteenth-century Italian intimated, and they make fun of males who wear rings and gems and don "the perfumes of Arabia." Getting down to class and status specifics, Peter writes that Spanish burgers avoided "effeminacies" because of their humble station, whereas the nobility avoided the same "effeminacies" because "effeminized" persons are suspected of complicity in *obscoena Venere*, by which he seems to mean offering one's self as a passive for a homosexual liaison.

Yet there was an exception to this general rule, and Peter described it even at the risk that soft and sweet words about such matters "make for effeminacy more than for good morals." In one context, Spanish males do dress up as women. At marriages or at regal pomps, he admitted, Spanish nobles did after all enjoy wearing the very types of objects Peter elsewhere categorized as "feminine." Peter Martyr, therefore, certainly recognized that in public representations, noblemen so to speak seduced other noblemen with effeminacies.[85]

Like Peter, European males in general classified as female a group of objects that were in fact not worn only by women. They therefore implicitly accepted, while vehemently denouncing, transvestism as a standard part of representational intercourse between male personas. Certainly this is a topic that deserves serious attention from students of cultural images, and for no period does this seem more pressing than in the seventeenth and eighteenth centuries, when some fashions and clothing — like wigs, short pants, heavy cosmetics, and so on — that had previously been labeled as effeminate came to be adopted by males of the political classes.[86]

---

corum odorum spiritus & suffumigationes continuas diiudicant. Obscoena Venere obvolutum putant si cui castoreum vel muscum olenti occurrant": *De orbe novo decades octo,* in his *Opera* (Graz, 1966), 121 (III, 4). "De suffumigiis, & odoribus harum terrarum, dulcia, molliaque verba dici quirent, quae pretermittimus, quia magis ad effoeminandos animos, quam ad bonos mores faciunt": *Opera,* 150 (IV, 4).

[85] One historian of clothing has remarked without comment that women wore jewels daily, men on particularly grand occasions: J. Herald, *Renaissance Dress in Italy 1400–1500* (London, 1981), 175–76.

[86] This whole perceived effeminization of behavior — or rather, the question of the perceived gender of "fine" manners — has not yet been forthrightly studied by cultural historians as far as I can see; for example, the various works of Norbert Elias seem to positively avoid such questions. A beginning might be made by studying sumptuary laws that forbade transvestism, and the cultural criticism of the age; see e.g., R. Levi Pisetzky, *Storia del Costume in Italia,* vol. 3 (Milan, 1966), 127. Machiavelli was outspoken; see Trexler, *Public Life,* 314–16.

Let me turn now to images of Mary, emblematic of her sex as was Jesus of his. Recall that I am talking about images of her that, for whatever reasons, were recognizably female even without cloth clothes. As indicated earlier, there may be no bambine Marys with defined genitalia; in general, representations of Mary are not biographical unless they relate to Jesus' birth and death, and they almost all show her as a mature woman. But certainly most Marys were sculpted if not with female clothes, then either with raised breasts or distended stomachs, and even where the bodies of statues have been replaced with mere scaffolding to accommodate clothing, femaleness is often made at least ephemerally clear in a head or mask that is beardless, coiffed, etc.[87]

Certainly, the dressing of such sculpted Marys commonly heightened feminine identity. Yet what of changing gender identity? In actual civil society it was customary enough for women prostitutes, for example, to dress as men to attract them.[88] Are sculpted Marys ever dressed so as to assert independence and masculinity, as male Crucifieds can show femininity?[89] What is the gender thrust of the dressing of Mary in late medieval and early modern Europe?

The first thing to be said is that figures of Mary and perhaps female numina in general were incomparably more often dressed and redressed than were male divinities. So taken for granted was this supremacy, for example, that in 1576 the Third Council of Lima, after referring to the Tridentine legislation on the matter, did not even mention images of males as it ordered that "the image of Our Lady or of any other female saint is not to be adorned with women's clothes and dresses, nor are cosmetics or colors of the type used by women to be put on [such a female image]."[90]

---

[87] See such scaffolding in Trens, *María*, 641; Porter and Auerbach, *Mexican Churches*, pl. 55.

[88] R. Trexler, "La prostitution florentine au XVe siècle: patronages et clientèles," *Annales E. S. C.* 36 (1981): 995.

[89] Barthes notes that at least today, there is a social prohibition against the feminization of men, but almost none against the masculinization of women: *Fashion System*, 257.

[90] "La imagen de nuestra señora o de otra qualquiera santa no se adorne con bestidos y trages de mugeres, ni le pongan afeites o colores de que usan mugeres." The official Spanish translation continues: "Podrá empero ponerse algún manto rrico que tenga consigo la imagen." The Latin text: "Caput 53. *Quod sanctorum imagines sint omni decentia ac reverentia tractandi*. Quia quod legentibus scriptura hoc idiotis cernentibus praestat pictura, utile et necessarium judicamus, quod per ordinarios et locorum rectores sanctorum imagines visitentur, et si aliquae inventae fuerint adeo deformes et indecentes, quod a

Secondly, a distinction should be made between two different types of cloth and clothing presented to Marys. First, there was the cloth or cloth-ing placed at her feet or on her altar but without being put on her. Cer-tainly the bulk of cloth offered to Marian paintings, but perhaps also most of that given to sculptures, even when they are labeled "cloaks," was of this type.[91] Such gifts were more singularly identified with their giver than their receiver. A 1333 statute of the Florentine confraternity of Or San Michele, for instance, ordered that *mantelli* placed as gifts before the altarpiece painting of Mary had to be left there a minimum of eight days before being removed for sale.[92] Propaganda for the bestower or, put otherwise, testimony that an individual's vow had been fulfilled, was obvi-ously a moving force in such a gift. I can find no clerical objection to be-stowals of *mantos* at the feet of images.

But the same can be said regarding capes that were actually put on

---

veritate gestae rei devientur, et propter earum deformitatem indevotionis materiam praes-tent, statim reformentur, adeo ut populorum crescat devotio, et per eas ad gestorum cog-nitionem homines excitentur, et, ut sanctum Tridentinum concilium dicit, per salutaria exempla quae oculis fidelium subjiciuntur, Deo gratias agant, et ad sanctorum imitatio-nem vitam et mores suos componant.

Et cum idem generale Concilium [of Trent] dicat, quod imagines non procaci venus-tate pingantur aut ornentur; praecipit haec sancta synodus, ne deinceps ulla imago Dei-parae Virginis seu aliarum sanctarum, muliebribus vestibus ornentur, aut earum facies fucis et adulterinis coloribus exterminentur; nec propter hoc haec sancta synodus prohi-bet, mantellum super imaginem Virginis aut alicujus sanctae poni": *Concilios Limenses (1551–1772)*, ed. R. Vargas Ugarte, 3 vols. (Lima, 1951), 1:125. See the full Tridentine text (session 25, 1563) in *Conciliorum Oecumenicorum Decreta* (Bologna, 1973), 776, 776 (*de invocatione, veneratione et reliquiis sanctorum et de sacris imaginibus*). The description of the Lima constitution by Antonio de la Calancha is correct to this point: *Cronica morali-zada*, 571, but see further below. Note well that the constitution assumes that only a stat-ue representing a female would be dressed with female clothes. A later European prohibi-tion against dressing male "imagines domini nostri Iesu Christi et sanctorum" is in Solá Moret, "Las Imágenes marianas," 200 (Vich in Catalonia, 1748). Whether adult repre-sentations were being referred to, or merely ones of of male infants, is unclear.

[91] On the habit of confraternities offering *mantos* to paintings of their patroness Our Lady of Grace (beginning at Faenza) or of Mercy, see G. Llompart, "La Virgen del Manto en Mallorca: Apuntes de iconografía mariana bajomedieval y moderna," in his *Entre la historia*, 287–335.

[92] S. La Sorsa, *La compagnia d'Or San Michele* (Trani, 1902), 203. Florentines of the late fifteenth century record *mantelli*, some of gold brocade, as well as "molte pianete e paliotti e cose di drappi," gifted not to a sculpture, but to the *tavola* of Our Lady of Impruneta: Luca Landucci, *Diario fiorentino* (Florence, 1969), 308, 337; see also 199 for a 1499 procession in Florence bearing Mary with a cloak. According to Trens, gifting *mantos* to Catalan paintings, but not for dressing them, was practiced by the thirteenth century: *María*, 641–42.

statues. Indeed, after it prohibited "women's clothes," the Lima constitution mentioned earlier specifically permits female statues to be covered with capes.[93] Thus the legislators leave no doubt they aimed only at forbidding "dressing," as against covering, female images. What are we to make of this clerical prohibition of dressing Marys with women's clothes, but tolerance of covering the same Marys with more sex-neutral *mantos*? The answer is not the clothes' differential potential for family honor. For not only did the outer capes offer every opportunity to manifest that honor.[94] So too did the specifically female items of dress: if Mary was to have rich clothes, says a recent Spanish confraternal disposition whose sentiments speak for the ages, the *camareras* who dressed her had to be rich,[95] and thus the presence of rich clothing beneath the cloak manifested the family honor of the women known to dress the images. The explanation rather seems to lie in the area of the cloak's less sex-specific character. While clothes next to the skin may recapture a self which seems betrayed by those worn outside,[96] especially since women themselves changed them, the *manto* or cloak verily pointed toward a self other than Mary. As Father Trens with insightful naiveté recognized, the Virgin's *manto*, especially when free of the "disagreeable" tunic next to the female skin, gives off a very male "sacerdotal air."[97]

Thus what on the surface appears a simple clerical attempt to suppress women's "play" in dressing dolls, in effect challenged the right of lay

---

[93] "Podrá empero ponerse algún manto rrico que tenga consigo la imagen." See the Latin text in n. 90, which specifies women's figures: "imaginem Virginis aut alicujus sanctae." On the distinction between coverings and clothing, see Solá Moreta, "Imágenes marianas," 186, 188; Trens, *María*, 648–49.

[94] For the family honor of the Counts of Flanders shown on their capes, see Dumoulins, "Culte."

[95] "Por estas razones ha sido siempre desempeñado por damas principales, en las que se ha unido a una gran devoción y un fervor extremado a la Virgen una posición social en consonancia con las necesidades que el cargo le demandaba. Para guardar y disponer las alhajas y vestidos son necesarios muebles y salas, de que no todas disponen, casa que ofrezca la conveniente seguridad y servidumbre que pueda prestar servicios que en determinadas ocasiones se requiere": N. Montalbo, *Resumen historico de Nuestra Señora Maria Stma. de 'Setefilla', patrona de la villa de Lora del Rio Sevilla* (Seville, 1960), 52 ("De la Camarera — Su Mision": post-1926 confraternal constitution).

[96] See Joseph, *Uniforms*, 54–58.

[97] "Los mantos primitivos, sin la desabradable concomitancia de la túnica . . . , colocados como capas pluviales, dieron a sus imágenes un aire sacerdotal, semejante al del preste teniendo en sus manos el ostensorio": Trens, *María*, 648–49. Thus certain objects of clothing I have called non-sex specific might be better called unisexual.

women to manipulate sacred images. A 1575 synodal constitution from Burgos (Spain) clearly addresses this situation. It insisted that any statues that were dressed wear dedicated clothing: they were not to be adorned with outfits that might at the same time be used by women.[98] But how did such statues gain status to begin with? Explaining the origins of the first miraculous image in Peru, Calancha provides an excellent example of the competition lay women offered the priests. In Lima, he wrote, it was the custom to dress up images of the Virgin in the style rich noblewomen dressed in. So one doña Juana, fulfilling a vow, determined that the image which subsequently became miraculous should be dressed with the clothes and jewels of that social class.[99]

In effect, Calancha has prepared us to understand how this image then performed wonders. He began simply: beautiful materials help move us to spiritual fervor.[100] But what actually moved the faithful in this specific instance were the marvelous petticoats, the embroidery and brocades, "a uso Español,"[101] that the laywoman doña Juana had added. Miracles followed.[102] So marvelous was the result, Calancha said, that the Council of Lima specifically exempted this particular image, and it alone, from the prohibition against dress I mentioned above: "they left unaffected only this image, seeing that it was so miraculous when dressed in this way."[103]

What is significant here is that Calancha describes this lay woman's dressing of an image as part of the construction of a miraculous female

---

[98] "Otrosi, ordenamos, y mandamos, que las imagines de bulto, ansi las que estuvieren en altares, como otras que ay para sacar en procession, se aderecen de proprias vestiduras para aquel effecto si las tuvieren, y no con vestiduras profanas, que sirven a mugeres": *Constituciones synodales del arçobispado de Burgos . . . año de M. D. LXXV* (Burgos, 1577), 262 (lib. III, *de reliquiis, & veneratione sanctorum*, chap. 8).

[99] "Usávase entonces vestir a las imágenes de la Virgen con ropas, sayas i tocas al modo que se visten las mugeres nobles . . . que los vestidos de la [subsequently miraculous] Virgen fuesen de ricos bordados de oro, seda i plata, i de brocados i telas costosas de plata, seda i oro, adornándola con ricas joyas de perlas, i piedras preciosas": Calancha, *Cronica*, 569–70.

[100] "Lo rico si se llevava los ojos de la curiosidad, la belleça de la imagen ganava la común devoción, que importa mucho, según se descaece nuestra naturaleza en las cosas espirituales que sean las imágenes deleytables, con que los ojos suelen negociar coraçones": Calancha, *Cronica*, 569–70.

[101] Calancha, *Cronica*, 336.

[102] "La república tenía en esta Imagen su devoción, i repetíanse continuos milagros": Calancha, *Cronica*, 570.

[103] "Dejaron solá esta imagen, *viendo que así vestida era tan miraculosa*": Calancha, *Cronica*, 571, my emphasis. Alas, I can find no such exemption in the texts from the Lima Council.

object in early colonial Lima. The noble dress of noble women proved the very condition of the (female) statue's subsequent wonders. With the soundest causality, the noble beauty of the whole image attracted devotees, and that popularity was followed by miracles.[104]

I have now mentioned *mantos* offered to the Virgin but not worn, *mantos* that were worn, and then items of specifically women's attire. A fourth important type of "clothing" has its own special place in contemporary accounts: precious stones and metals and coins, often woven into capes and feminine attire. Calancha's account of the miraculous image of doña Juana, for example, shows him writing as if he sought to legitimate the image by moving in his description from doña Juana's cloth to the benefactor's *gold* and *silver* embroidery with costly brocades of *silver* and *gold*, all adorned with "rich jewels of pearls" and "precious stones." Even today, chroniclers are inclined to privilege the glitter of "rings, watches and earrings" over the bestowal of mere cloth.[105]

This prejudice may reflect more than the value of permanence over perdurable cloth. It seems that hard more than soft objects were associated to notions of idolatry. In the early sixteenth century, the Spanish *alumbrados* did, it is true, denounce as idolatrous the mere "dressing up an image of Our Lady and taking it out in the streets in procession."[106] But more often, moralists of the time tended to think of metals and stones rather than cloth as the clothing that was idolatrous. In a revealing statement, the early Quattrocento Dominican Giovanni Dominici wrote that parents should use paintings and sculptures at home to encourage their children to good deeds. Neither paintings nor sculptures, however, should contain gold or jewels, he said, lest the young be made more idolatrous than believing, revering gold and precious stones instead of the "figures or the reality represented by the figures." Dominici seems to have assumed that clothing, but not metals and stones, was part of the "reality represented by the figures."[107]

---

[104] See R. Trexler, "Ritual Behavior in Renaissance Florence: The Setting," and "Florentine Religious Experience: The Sacred Image," in my *Church and Community, 1200–1600. Studies in the History of Florence and New Spain* (Rome, 1987), 11–74.

[105] Orsi, *Madonna of 115th Street*, 12, describing an image in a New York City church.

[106] W. Christian, *Local Religion in Sixteenth-Century Spain* (Princeton, 1981), 159–60.

[107] Dominici does not, however, specifically refer to the clothes worn by the figures; cited in S. Ringbom, *Icon to Narrative: The Rise of the Dramatic Close-up in Fifteenth-Century Devotional Painting* (Doornspuk, 1984), 32–33. A more modern problem of this

It may be assumed that the notion of idolatry is affected by gender, although as so often with gender, how it is remains to be studied. But here, I believe that our metals and stones bring us back forcefully to the question of how gender was created or affected by the dressing of Marys. We recall the assessment of Peter Martyr to the effect that perfumes, rings, and gems were effeminate by definition. My reading, on the other hand, is that while odors might be quickly lost,[108] precious metals and stones have a durable quality ideologically associated with men, and not with the women on whom they might be displayed. In her work on the Australian Walbiri, for example, Nancy Munn shows how a distinction between perishable and durable media informed the division of artistic labor among the sexes in that tribe.[109]

Let me come to the point through a slight diversion. It was a commonplace to say that Mary's (or other women's) bravery made her more a man than a woman. Well then, is there evidence of Virgin Marys pictured as having allegedly masculine traits added to or replacing their female image? Although my answer appears to shortchange human potentiality, the answer at this date must be a firm no. While St. Wilgefortis is not the only case of man Jesus made woman, and while in real life the woman Joan of Arc made herself man through metal armor, I have not yet found an instance of a Mary rendered macho through actual cloth clothing. Dependent men were turned into women through cloth in images, but in traditional Christianity, women were not imaged into men.

Precious metals and stones were durable signs of masculinity, I have suggested. It was men who de facto put them on women, and they could rip them off. Similarly, they might be put on Marys, but were taken off if they were needed to finance wars.[110] Clothing itself, however, never was used to show a male Mary.

---

type is the use of paper money to clothe Virgins: quickly perdurable as paper, such money until recently stood for precious metal.

[108] Except, significantly, when the tomb of a saint was opened, in which case the sweet odor of a female or male corpse lasted; see recently L. Rothkrug, "The 'Odour of Sanctity,' and the Hebrew Origins of Christian Relic Veneration," *Historical Reflections* 8 (1981): 95–142.

[109] N. Munn, *Walbiri Iconography* (Ithaca, 1973).

[110] The procedure with statues was a topos of Mediterranean wit: Dionysius the Younger of Syracuse stripped Zeus of his gold mantle and replaced it with a woolen one. He remarked that the God would find the woolen one both lighter and warmer in winter: Bevan, *Holy Images*, 22.

There was, it is true, one important piece of plain cloth used to cover Marys which, if not an object of men's clothing per se, was identified with male activity. I refer to flags, and to reliquary cloths used as flags, like Mary's famous Nativity blouse that was waved about to protect Chartres from besiegers.[111] Yet on examination, Our Lady covered over or dressed with banners, easily encountered in the middle ages, really remained a dependent, like the servile heralds of any European noble, who also dressed up in the blazons of their lords. For in fact, the flags that we sometimes find covering cultic figures of Mary — or live prostitutes, for that matter — were at times those enemy banners that had been captured during battles, as is the case in an image at Tournai. Further, the famous cloth Palios toward which Italians raced were akin to enemy flags, pursued in these mock battles by ardent competitors mounted or on foot. In short, Mary wears the clothes of the defeated, and thus, humiliated though she is shown off, further humiliates the enemy, that sees its macho symbols worn by a woman.[112]

§

Throughout this paper, I have attempted to trace a tension between the sex of an image beneath all real cloth adornment, and the gendering accomplished by the clothing of the image. Because of the corruptibility of cloth, and the absence of previous work on dressing Christian images, I have of necessity ranged widely in an attempt to establish guidelines for further work. Now nearing the completion of my probe, I want to raise the question of deception, and to show, first of all, that the "true" sex of images was often duplicitously or purposely concealed by dressing them, rather than the cross-over being open, as presumably was the case with the figures of St. Wilgefortis. Indeed the Protestant Reformation, marked as it was by a professed joy in the "naked Christ" and the "naked Bible," was the first epoch since the Iconoclastic Struggle to positively revel in the discovery of such deception. The Catholic missionaries of that time, com-

---

[111] Sharbrough, "Cult of the Mother," 120.

[112] See further at n. 46 above; for ancient documentation of this practice, note that the robe made for Athena to wear in the Panathenaea was woven with battle scenes: Pollard, *Seers*, 44. For the Sienese Palio, see A. Dundes and A. Falassi, *La Terra in Piazza. An Interpretation of the Palio of Siena* (Berkeley, 1975); and Trexler, "*Correre la terra.*"

batting the "idols" of the native American gentiles, did not drag their feet in this regard.[113]

In this age as always, men were turned into women to insult an enemy. Thus in 1538 a painting of Thomas Becket, the sainted archbishop of Canterbury whom Henry VIII now disgraced, might with new painted clothes be converted into a female figure — one more example of how a great male saint might be emasculated but no Christian female saint could be masculinized.[114] But the discovery that earlier Catholics had deceptively inverted a sexual identification was still more exciting to the reformers, and this matter concerns our problem precisely.

A particularly suggestive case of this nature involved the statue of Our Lady of Worcester, who by order of the Anglican bishop Hugh Latimer was stripped of her garments in 1537.[115] Once Our Lady was naked, alas, she proved not to be a Madonna but a male, otherwise anonymous bishop of Worcester. That is, Mary, her "coat and her jewels ... taken from her," to use the words of the official report, was a man who at an earlier point had been turned into a woman. At this juncture one Thomas Emans entered the picture. He realized, he said, that "the lucre and profit of this town is decayed through" the decline in devotion caused by the discovery that underneath, Mary was a man. He acted, he said, "with the intent that the people should resort to her ... as they had done before." Emans's insistence on identifying the now-male statue as a female stands out immediately.

On the vigil of Mary's feast of the Assumption, Emans entered the chapel where the statue was kept, said some prayers, kissed the image's feet, and then turned to address the people. Accounts differ. According to one, Emans said that Mary had been stripped of her clothes as cleanly as are men at the gallows. But another source has him say: "This lady is now

---

[113] Thus John Milton insisted on a "naked Christ": "He that will clothe the gospel now, intimates plainly that the gospel is naked, uncomely, that I may not say reproachful. Do not, ye church maskers, while Christ is clothing upon our barrenness with his righteous garment to make us acceptable in his Father's sight; do not, as ye do, cover and hide his righteous verity with the polluted clothing of your ceremonies, to make it seem more decent in your own eyes": cited in J. Phillips, *The Reformation of Images: Destruction of Art in England, 1535–1660* (Berkeley, 1973), 189.

[114] T. Borenius, "Some Further Aspects of the Iconography of St. Thomas of Canterbury," *Archaeologia* 83 (1933): 182, and pl. L, fig. 3.

[115] The following is based on Phillips, *Reformation of Images*, 75; *Letters and Papers, Foreign and Domestic of the Reign of Henry VIII, 1509–47*, 21 vols. (London, 1862–1910), 12, pt. ii, 218, reg. no. 587 (27 August 1537).

stripped. I trust to see the day that they who stripped her shall be stripped as naked."

Quite as interesting as this association of statuary with judicial disrobing before execution is that Emans, by all accounts, continued to address the image as "Lady" though she had been revealed a man, and that he called on "her" devotees to continue to make offerings to her. "Ye that be disposed to offer," he cried, "the figure is no worse than it was before, and the lucre and profit of this town is decayed through this discovery." In another version, Emans is supposed to have identified as "her" clothes and jewels those worn by an image people now knew were "his": "Though Our Lady's coat and her jewels be taken away from her," one source has Emans say, "the similitude of this is no worse to pray unto, having a remors unto her above, then it was before." A formidable notion, indeed! Here too Emans's goal was the same: that the devotion to "her" might continue. Thus it appears that Emans expected people to pray to a female who stood there sculpted as a prelatial male. This is presumably because the faithful had given the jewels and the cloak to what was assumed to be a woman. This case of conscious deception unmasked forces us to confront the implications of the fact that it is one thing for a given sex to pray to a man, and another to pray to a woman.

One further story of deception from this time will allow me to conclude by positioning the images we have studied in a larger context of dressed images. It concerns the oft-cited Brown Virgin of Tournai, or rather, what in the sixteenth century was thought to be her. This woman, of such hoary age and reputation, was in all truth destroyed during the Time of Troubles (1566). And yet the ecclesiastical authorities made her live! They simply covered a mere block with clothes so thoroughly that only a small piece of a face appeared. The latter being suitably colored brown, this Virgin, it is said, fooled the faithful.[116] The notion that a "living statue" could transcend death and go on living through clothes alone proves not only the authorities' joke on us, but on our own ability to fictionalize.

This paper has studied the dressing of objects whose sexual identities were established, exploring some of the ways in which that underlying sexual identity was gendered by added cloth. As a general rule, it seems that images of a dependent Jesus and the eternal woman Mary were either feminized or androgynized, through intimate inner clothings (though as

---

[116] Dumoulins, "Culte," 333.

with the Mexican slips, they could be externalized) or through overlaid garments reminiscent of the celibate priesthood. A type of indulgent and knowing self-deception was the result, one that did not lose sight of the actual sexual identity of the figure beneath.

Thus we are surprised that Emans, though disabused of his illusion that Our Lady of Worchester was a female, still calls him "she." The trouble lies in our arbitrary definition of the images we have dealt with. We began with the notion that there was a "true identity." In fact that was a trick as well, as Emans realized: In fact, the thing was what one said or acted as if one prayed to, and no more. And in any case, from before Emans's time and since, the category of statues whose sexual identity was a given does not begin to encompass the world of images. Let me conclude by referring to just two other worlds of "images," the Iberian *imágenes de vestir* and the Italian stuffed dolls.

For the victims of the hoax of Tournai, the age of the famous *imágenes de vestir* had arrived. Here the ecclesiastical authorities re-made the Brown Virgin out of a block of material whose face alone was finished — as were the wax statues we mentioned earlier — and was thus made to be dressed. They might, however, have chosen another type of *imágen de vestir*, a mere scaffold of sticks with no body and thus no place for figures of sex. Precisely such vacuous "images" seem to have become more and more popular in seventeenth-century Iberia. Here are substances which have none, though their learned students have difficulty comprehending that. Explaining that these *imágenes de vestir* began as romanesque statues that through mutilations were made ever smaller in relation to the sea of gothic and baroque cloth that made them many times greater in size, these modern scholars talk of the "true martyrdom" such "materially quartered" statues have undergone.[117] These "statues" have truly no sex, no identity, and thus by definition, no deception. It is a "laughable solution," says Father Trens: even as they obtain an obsessive reality, "they are mannequins more than they are images."[118]

In Italy, a similar phenomenon is found, and better than most, the Italians learned how perfectly the right clothes literally made the man — in

---

[117] Trens, *María*, 644.

[118] Trens, *María*, 646. On 641, Trens has a good double picture of a mutilated thirteenth-century statue whose body is wood scaffolding on the left, and on the right the Virgin dressed. See further denunciations in Solá Moreta, "Imágenes marianas," 194–99. A good collection of pictures of such Virgins is in De Mesa and Gisbert, *Historia de la Pintura Cuzqueña*, vol. 2.

this case men and women of straw not vacuum. Put into their niches in the great gallery of the church of Santa Maria delle Grazie in Mantua in 1517, at the height of Italian Signorial culture, were rows of marvelously dressed dolls packed with papier mâché — no sexed images these! They stayed. Even in the twentieth century in the wake of the Risorgimento, they remained in place as pompous representations of grand national saints and heroes. Despite continued protests, the statues remained, an infamy because apparently certain better materials were thought to be used to make "images" or "statues," while other, less costly, materials were said to be proper for "dolls." In 1902 a patriot spoke out against a government that would not remove them: "The dummies remain guarding . . . the national monument!"[119]

Cultural critics imagined and imagine that the past was more solid. The sculptures should be freed of cloth, Spanish moralists insist even today, but they do not know what to make of the "statues" that have no body and *only* clothes, but still make miracles. Where then is the root of this seemingly willed deception?

In ways that I but dimly understand, I believe that these cultural fictions about the nature of reality are related to the conditions of real women, and especially to the practice of clothing them. I have always been taken aback, for example, by the repeated statement that precisely the dolls, wax figures, and scaffold images are expressive of "obsessive Baroque realism." That would appear to make sense only if the total dressing up of the woman, by her men, which is the common referent in experience, is a similarly impressive and unquestioned "realism." Again: what passes for gendering in the dressing up of statues is also a commentary about social *dependency*.

For ages, the most enlightened of males have put hundreds of florins "on their women's backs," as Bernardino of Siena once said.[120] Men still do, and when they do not, then their women themselves take up the task. It seems clear that cloth then as now was used to heighten feminine dependency, even if, as the ethologists teach us, many a female uses cloth-

---

[119] "I fantocci rimasero a guardia . . . del monumento nazionale": Vittorio Matteucci, cited by Warburg, *Gesammelte Schriften*, 349. Two good early photographs of the images in S. Maria are in von Schlosser, "Geschichte," 208–9.

[120] Bernardino da Siena, *Le prediche volgari, vol. 4 (Quadresimale del 1425)*, ed. C. Cannarozzi (Florence, 1940), 227.

ing to identify herself, or even when, under the yoke of "civilization," woman, pure marble beneath, still clothes herself to stoop to conquer.

Or seems to conquer. For I have argued that men may indeed put on the things said to be of women to seduce other men. But they do not try to seduce women in that way.[121] We have seen that to take the mantle off the local Mary to place it upon a person sick to death, either a female *or a male*, is still common practice in some places. That is, once sick, and thus again a dependent, a man may indeed wear the coat of a woman. Say not: "Yes, but no longer that of a man." As Father Trens has said, the Virgin's mantle gives off "a sacerdotal air."[122]

---

[121] See above, n. 85.
[122] See above, n. 97.

The Construction of Regional
Solidarities in Traditional Europe[*]

C'est un des traits fondamentaux des sociétés occidentales que
les rapports de force qui longtemps avaient trouvé dans la
guerre, dans toutes les formes de guerre, leur expression principale se sont petit à petit investis dans l'ordre du pouvoir
politique.[1]

AT LEAST IN LATE MEDIEVAL ITALY space proved much less liable to carry
a charge of sacrality than did objects. Nonetheless, in the present paper,
I ask how neighboring peoples in traditional Europe created common behavioral patterns across space, so that they could communicate among
themselves with less danger of miscomprehension. The nature of the question itself assumes a distinction between a region, whose inhabitants already shared commonalities of markets, language, rulers and the like, and
transregional spaces, entering which our inhabitants sensed themselves in
a qualitatively different space through which, as in pilgrimages, they

---

[*] This essay appeared previously in Riti e rituali nelle società medievali, ed. J. Chiffoleau
et al. (Spoleto, 1994), 263–83.
[1] M. Foucault, Histoire de la sexualité, vol. 1 (Paris, 1976), 135.

passed in danger.[2] The lines between region and beyond are fluid, to be sure, and, quite as certainly, just how common behavioral patterns are constructed depends greatly on specifics of time and place. Nevertheless on this occasion, in the search for the spatiality of behavioral structure, I wish to describe some recurring behaviors in traditional European society that are related to the formation of solidarities.

A series of assumptions underlies this undertaking. The first is that solidarity is basically not a psychological but a behavioral phenomenon: participants assign functional meanings to processions after they decide that such actions have been successful in creating solidarities. Second, in becoming customary over time, both the places and the objects of such processions do come to be associated with certain emotional states, and on becoming aware of this, political authorities try to impose such collective emotions on the base through instituting such processions, just as later from the bottom, those wishing to subvert emotions of solidarity make use of the same insights.

A third assumption explains this article's organization. In describing actions performed outside, historians usually privilege static inside institutions. As an example, they usually explain military institutions as deriving from and postdating civil institutions. To the contrary, I think that civic forms are sometimes developed from military ones. By extension, then, the rituals of war are found at work in peacetime or within a seemingly stable political universe; they are utilized to build the polis. Rather than to argue that civility decays in short half-lives, I argue that, at least in the patriarchal societies we study, forms of civil society have their roots and their inspiration in the engagements of the field.[3]

---

[2] Cf. L. Rothkrug, "Religious Practices and Collective Perceptions: Hidden Homologies in the Renaissance and Reformation," *Historical Reflections* 7.1 (1980): chap. 2: "Transregional Pilgrimage." See also my *Public Life in Renaissance Florence* (New York, 1980), 47ff. In early modern Europe, the regional trip or pilgrimage (*Nahwallfahrt*) won out over the longer ones: K.-S. Kramer, "Typologie und Entwicklungsbedingungen nachmittelalterlicher Nahwallfahrten," *Rheinisches Jahrbuch für Volkskunde* 11 (1960): 195. On the regional Flemish *ommegangen*, see J. Toussaert, *Le sentiment religieux en Flandres au moyen age* (Paris, 1963), 245–46. On the general topic in this paper, see V. Turner, "The Center Out There: Pilgrim's Goal," *History of Religions* 12 (1972): 191–230.

[3] The model is developed in R. Trexler, "*Correre la Terra*. Collective Insults in Late Medieval and Renaissance Europe," *Mélanges de l'École française de Rome. Moyen Age, Temps Modernes* 96 (1984): 845–902. Cf. R. Girard, *Violence and the Sacred* (Baltimore, 1972) and W. Burkert, *Homo Necans* (Berlin, 1972).

SOLIDARITIES THROUGH VIOLENCE

Warfare

Perhaps the most fundamental form of extending territory in traditional European warfare was to march or ride behind a flag, and to fight to the death to defend its posting. At the extremity of the military polity, the flag not only allowed warriors to locate their units easily; it was also this now "sacred" object that in the heat of battle marked off the geometry of expanded territorial claims. In ways that have yet to be the topic of a serious monograph, this perdurable object also provided courage for those in its train to protect "her." Interestingly, *Bannenträger* were often children or young adolescents, protected or cocooned, like mascots, by older, armed soldiers or knights. Now just as the victors' flags expanded their geography, so the humiliation of the losers' captured flags, first dragged through the dirt of the field and then later insulted in the triumphal reentry of the victors, to still later be hung in humiliation in their churches, also initiated the process of realigning solidarities.[4]

Thus the display of flags seems to have been a usual way for victors in the field to mark locative expansions, thereby setting the stage for the transfer of allegiances within that new space; at this stage, the space might be physically under the control of a victor but still morally at best a no-man's-land. Now, one first formal step to begin the process of moral resolidarization was often to put the victor's altar in place in the conquered area and to maintain it undefiled until more permanent structures might be erected. This was aided by introducing the vanquished to the rites and manners of the victors as they were performed around such altars.

In the Spanish conquest of America, one finds that it was less important to furnish these altars with Christian priests as celebrants than it was to prove that those altars, and the images that were placed atop or within them, remained undamaged.[5] One would expect, therefore, that in Old World wars, such as in the Reconquista or Crusades or in wars between Christians, the victors performed variants on this theme, a new or purified

---

[4] H. Zug Tucci, "Il Carroccio nella vita comunale italiana," *Quellen und Forschungen aus Italienischen Archiven und Bibliotheken* 65 (1985): 1–104, esp. 48 for the age of those defending these symbols in England. Further in R. Trexler, "Follow the Flag. The Ciompi Revolt Seen from the Streets," *Bibliothèque d'Humanisme et Renaissance* 46 (1984): 357–92, and Trexler, "*Correre la Terra.*"

[5] R. Trexler, "Aztec Priests for Christian Altars. The Theory and Practice of Reverence in New Spain," in *Scienze, Credenze e Livelli di Cultura* (Florence, 1982), 175–96.

altar being armed with copies of a miracle-working home-town image.[6] In any case, a type of moral behavioral conversion began *in the field* around new altars and images.

Evocatio and Invocatio

The next step in this process of extending common behavioral territory was outrightly spiritual: to summon sacred objects or to evoke them from the conquered polity — including those objects that commemorated *its* past victories — and to incorporate or invoke those objects into the polity of the victor. This may be thought of as the first annual tribute losers paid victors. That phenomenon of "deflating" and "inflating" political spirits, of drawing from one center to another — rather than across the military front — may, however, be seen already to have been implied in battle formations. Military formations in traditional Europe seem in fact to have had two focuses, two vortices: the expansive area around the forward flags, and the area at the center of the military force with the polity's own sacred image: the general or holy of holies or true cross or war wagon.[7]

Thus already during the conflict, but perhaps especially in its wake, an exchange of spirits took place through ritual acts. During the late middle ages in Italy, one encounters the ancient phenomenon of *evocatio*: priests of one army who were devotees of one group of saints or of particular images of the general superterrestrials of Christianity had those patrons *call* upon their opposite numbers in the enemy land or city to abandon that enemy.[8] What Christians evoked were only the spirits of the opposing deities, but at its base, evocation implied actual transfers of wealth, sacred and material. This is clearly seen in the fact that establishing the new area of solidarity sometimes involved the material transfer to the victor's churches of the relics of victims' protector saints. The transfer might be permanent — the victims thus losing a main prayer object of their earlier polity — or it might be temporary. After a saint was triumphantly brought

---

[6] The "true cross" the soldiers in the Third Crusade "tried to defend" certainly rested in or on such an altar: F. Gabrieli, ed., *Arab Historians of the Crusades* (New York, 1957), 136–37. It would be interesting to know if in the sixteenth century, as one might expect, victorious Protestants replaced "gaudy" Catholic altars with simple ones, and vice versa.

[7] See for example the position of the war wagon in Zug Tucci, "Carroccio," 43–45, 49–50, and the information in Gabrieli, *Arab Historians*, 136–37.

[8] Trexler, *Public Life*, 4–5, with bibliography.

to the victor's city and, so to speak, placed under the authority of the patron saint of the victor, he or she, seriously denuded of charisma and authority, might be returned to his or her "native" town.[9] It was only to be expected that in some cases, the saint in question might be required to make annual visits in the future to pay tribute to the conquering city and its patron. We therefore encounter the broad phenomenon, to be addressed further below, that many polities did not have the required or sufficient power objects or resources to meet threats to themselves, and therefore had customarily to march to other towns, and behave as did such towns, to access such power. Power consisted in marshaling objects across spaces.

Next, triumphal entries provide a focus for studying this deflation and inflation of spirit, especially since they commonly served as models for the future annual commemoration of victories or defeats.[10] Quite as germane to our topic, triumphal entries also provided the prisoners and hostages among the victims at the gates an education in the formal behavior of the victors. Thus the losing youth who first learned in the field that victors humiliated such losers by gendering them "women," for instance by stripping them naked and raping them, were now brought into the conquering polity to attend schools and become "civilized" — that is, learn correct manners — so that they could one day return home as interpreters and allies.[11] It was at the gates of triumph that they began to learn that in this new polity, one kissed the buttocks of a lion as a sign of humiliation, or that one walked by kneeling in approaching certain of the victors' sacra, or that one ate in certain fashions, and a myriad of other rules of this

---

[9] Trexler, *Public Life*, 4–5.

[10] The vanquished often had to carry and offer annually a cloth of submission (*palio* in Italian) to the city which had earlier conquered them, thus repeating their original humiliation: Trexler, *Public Life*, 4–5. On triumphs and *adventus*, see further S. MacCormack, *Art and Ceremony in Late Antiquity* (Berkeley, 1981) and M. McCormick, *Eternal Victory. Triumphal Rulership in Late Antiquity, Byzantium and the Early Medieval West* (Cambridge, MA, 1986). How a loss "takes the air out," so that the vanquished lose their sense of solidarity and thus the behaviors that go with it, is well-described in Gabrieli, *Arab Historians*, 137.

[11] See e.g., Gabrieli, *Arab Historians*, 82. A Spanish application of these ancient Mediterranean procedures is studied in R. Trexler, "We Think, They Act. Clerical Readings of Missionary Theatre in Sixteenth-Century Mexico," in *Understanding Popular Culture: Europe from the Middle Ages to the Nineteenth Century*, ed. S. Kaplan (Berlin, 1984), 189–227, and Trexler, "From the Mouths of Babes. Christianization by Children in Sixteenth-Century New Spain," elsewhere in the present volume.

type.[12] Even as the breath went out of them, the victims breathed in the new spirit of the conquerors.

However, we should be wary of seeing in the triumphal entry the quintessential polarization of matched "losers" from matched "winners," of one nation polarized from another nation, one patriarchy set over against its equal in the other polity. In such entries of victorious armies, the particular roles and tensions of distinct social units within the polities appear at the surface. For instance, adults said to be too old to fight cheered their combat youth on while the latter were defending the polity abroad, but once the battle was over, that support for violence abated: within the polity they now reentered, the young men did not have a right of political participation or the right of violence that they were encouraged to exercise in the field.[13] Again: when victors marched into the urban territory of a losing polity, an infame group like the winner's prostitutes might themselves enter victoriously, thus humiliating the adult male losers who could not resist that insult.[14] Finally, if the rape of losers' women often fostered solidarities between their patrons in the field, the winners' women at the triumphal gates also played a specific role. It was often the women and girls of the victorious polity who most viciously humiliated the losing males who were forced to march in the triumphal entry.[15]

Though it might seem, therefore, that the patriarchal polity was the sole matrix for these evolving regionalisms, in fact each polity contained different social groups with their own behavioral solidarities, which were by no means always the same as those with other social groups, and not even always different from those of their cohorts in other polities.[16] Regional solidarities might, therefore, first be constructed through the alliance of such dependent groups in the conquering and conquered groups, united in that dependency.

---

[12] See the many examples in Trexler, "*Correre la Terra*," especially 894–99.

[13] Trexler, "*Correre la Terra*," 864–66, 892.

[14] Trexler, "*Correre la Terra*," 870.

[15] See the general information in G. Friederici, *Skalpieren und ähnliche Kriegsgebräuche in Amerika* (Braunschweig, 1906), and the European information in his "Über die Behandlung der Kriegsgefangenen durch die Indianer Amerikas," in the *Festschrift Eduard Seler*, ed. W. Lehmann (Stuttgart, 1922), 71, 81–82.

[16] Access to such problems is in R. Numelin, *The Beginnings of Diplomacy. A Sociological Study of Intertribal and International Relations* (Oxford, 1950); P. Farb, *Word Play* (Toronto, 1975), 52–56; and M. Van Gennep's fundamental "Essai d'une théorie des langues spéciales," *Revue des Études ethnographiques et sociologiques* 1 (1908): 327–37.

Maintenance

Its lost lands marked out by flags and altars, the losers' shrines and relics disempowered on the field of battle and at the gates of the victors, the new formal order was maintained and a moral solidarity with the victors was put in place by certain procedures one finds across Europe and in the European dependencies of the early modern period. Perhaps the most customary usage was to disestablish the old feastdays of the conquered and to establish in the subject area the behavioral calendar of the victors. A comparable phenomenon in expanding European monarchies was the supplantation of civic feasts with dynasts' own princely ones.[17] The roots of such practices, I again suspect, lay in the military sphere.

There were other, less concrete means for integrating the conquered area into the world of the victors. In Italy one finds political authorities ordering the bells of the conquered to ring either after those in the conqueror's area, or at the same time so as to celebrate the victorious polity. Similarly, legislators attempted to synchronize in time the celebrations of the capital with those of their subjects, as if there could be one unified paean to the (victor's) divinity.[18]

But clearly the most important way to maintain solidarities was to constrain the victims to worship the divinities responsible for their defeat, thus reconstructing victims' history, so to speak, to begin once they lost independence, that is, in their humiliation. One finds this procedure at work in European urban contexts where, as in Italy, former revolutionaries had to honor the saint who had defeated them, and one sees it as well in the Spanish dependencies. In Mexico, for instance, the conquerors ordered the celebration of the feast of Santiago and St. Hippolytus so that once each year millions of indigenous people effectively swore renewed fealty — with their new-found gestures of prayer — to the divine captains who had defeated them.[19] This had the significant effect of integrating many dif-

---

[17] Y-M. Bercé, *Fête et révolte* (Paris, 1976), 93ff.; on the notion of the official festive world M. Bakhtin, *Rabelais and His World* (Cambridge, MA, 1968); on supplanting royal festivals, M. Vovelle, *Les Métamorphoses de la fête en Provence de 1750 à 1820* (Paris, 1976), 102ff.; Trexler, *Public Life*, 423ff.

[18] Trexler, *Public Life*, 82–83 for a flagrant case of the same.

[19] The post-revolutionary case is in Trexler, *Public Life*, 222. The humiliation of native Americans in festivities is in Trexler, "We Think, They Act," 194. Hidden resistance within the songs and plays of such celebrations are being studied by L. Burkhart. See her "The Amanuenses Have Appropriated the Text: Interpreting a Nahuatl Song of Santiago," in *On the Translation of Native American Literatures*, ed. B. Swann (Wash-

ferent peoples into the useful notion of "Indians."

An important variant on this theme of integration through humiliation was the Spanish introduction of annual theatrical recreations of their victories, in which the children of the defeated played their parents' everrenewed roles. The inspiration for these New World spectacles was none other than the *Moros y Cristianos* dramas and dances of the Iberian Peninsula.[20] Further afield, annual tributary processions and obeisances recreated the triumph of defeat — the original triumphant entry — across much of Europe, and it may indeed be that the famous decorated *ceri* that Italian losers had to offer each year graphically represented that loss, just as did the victors' war wagon (*carroccio*) when it was wheeled about on such anniversaries as it had been at the time of the victory.[21] Thus it was perhaps nothing new in kind, but only in the level of exoticism, for the Spaniards to force native American losers to dress up in the now-archaic clothes of their fathers to recreate in a play the actual ceremonies of the original defeat.[22] I do not wish to suggest that such recreations, which still take place in many parts of Latin America, have identical meanings for today's participants as the humiliation (mixed with some exotic new pride) they highlighted in these early days. I only suggest that these modern plays and parades definitely show us that a technology for spreading behavioral solidarity that was military to the core was in place within the Christian realms of Europe half a millennium ago.

DYNAMIC SOLIDARITIES WITHIN

Turning now to some of the processes at work within civil society that maintained and modified regional solidarities, I hope to show more clearly the similarity those forms of solidarity that are practiced in towns and villages have to those already encountered in the field.

---

ington, DC, 1992), and *The Slippery Earth: Nahua-Christian Moral Dialogue in Sixteenth-Century Mexico* (Tempe, AZ, 1989).

[20] Trexler, "We Think, They Act," nn. 5, 40. I have not determined if Moors were forced to dance and play in Spain, as natives were in Mexico.

[21] Zug Tucci, "Carroccio," 84ff.

[22] Trexler, "We Think, They Act," 204.

Behavioral Solidarity through Replication

One of the standard means by which communities established a behavioral identity and iconography for themselves was to replicate by communal choice, rather than by orders from abroad of the type just mentioned, the processional procedures of some great nearby center. Certainly elements of social and cultural constraint other than military ones were in fact at work in such seeming choices, but they need not be analyzed here. What is central is that a weak part of a region hoped that by copying the behavioral vocabulary of the regional center its significant objects would become as sacred for it as the originals were to that center.

An impressive example of this phenomenon of replication is provided by the cult of the Christian Savior across Lazio, admirably described by Volbach.[23] By the seventh century, the painting of Jesus in the chapel of the *Sancta Sanctorum* in Rome, allegedly painted by the evangelist Luke, was carried along a fixed processional route in the Eternal City on 14 August, the eve of Mary's Assumption. At the site of the present Santa Francesca Romana, clerks washed Jesus' feet situated on the lower part of the painting. Then Jesus proceeded to the church of Santa Maria Maggiore, where his mother Mary — that is, her venerated image — came forward to encounter him, doubtless the one bowing or kneeling before the other.[24]

At the center of Volbach's study is his argument that the Lazians' original intention and inspiration was to copy the Roman *procession*, the copies they made of the Roman *image* being a necessary consequence of the behavior they had determined to replicate.[25] Volbach begins by describing the type of such cult images: common in Lazio from the twelfth century forward, they show a frontally seated Jesus whose feet are often damaged because they have been washed and kissed over hundreds of years on the same feast of the Assumption. The author then shows that these images were essentially copies of the Roman original. Thus in the high middle ages, in a great theatrical act in Sutri and several other Lazian towns, "Jesus" marched along a fixed route, had his feet washed, and met his mother in a major "encounter," as he had long done in Rome.[26]

---

[23] W. Volbach, "Il Cristo di Sutri e la venerazione del SS. Salvatore nel Lazio," *Rendiconti della pontificia accademia romana di archeologia* 27 (1940–1941): 97–126.

[24] Volbach, "Cristo," 117.

[25] Volbach, "Cristo," 117–18, and further below.

[26] In turn, Volbach convincingly derives this procedure from the Roman and Byzantine practice of parading the image of the emperor: "Cristo," 125.

The dramatized *encuentro* of Mary with her resurrected son has long been standard usage for Spanish images, and in 1982 the present writer witnessed one in Seville, where during a festivity, one processing Virgin entered a church and (its litter) bowed deeply to another Mary standing on the high altar.[27] Writing in 1940, Volbach himself noted that in Tivoli at that time, the one painting genuflected before the other before both went into church together to attend divine services.[28] Our contemporary etiquette of lowering certain flags to and below others, especially on "greeting," is certainly a variation on this same phenomenon of one statue bowing to another.

By fleshing out these medieval rites with modern observation, therefore, we can verify two phenomena. First, behavior replication or miming, whether it be forced upon conquered peoples as I documented earlier, or, as Volbach believes to have been the case here in Lazio, freely entered into by the replicators so as to legitimate their behavior by an appeal to the cultural authority of Rome, is a common means of expanding behavioral solidarities. The voluntary replication documented here results in the "colony" falling in behind the behavioral authority of that center.

Second, the phenomenon of encounter between personified objects teaches greeting behavior outright. While within the processions of, say, Jesus and Mary, or even of two Marys or two Jesuses, it seems to be the supernaturals themselves who teach divinely legitimated manners to this region, in fact, of course, the figures of "Jesus" or "Mary" — or for that matter those of the evangelical Magi bowing and scraping before the Child on the feast of Epiphany — carry out the manners of the clergy or the confraternity, the authoritative group of men who own the figures, and it is they who teach us to act in unison.

Established Order

What then was the shape of classical behaviors within a region, once basic behavioral commonalities had been established? I will first present such an order, and then dynamize it as I think the actual evidence demands. Following up on the views of Berlière, Nicholas Kyll has the story begin at the center. Bishops in early medieval Europe, he claims, obliged

---

[27] A modern Extremaduran *Quem quaeritis* meeting (*encuentro*) is documented in J. Ramón y Fernandez, "Costumbres cacereñas," *Revista de Dialectología y tradiciónes populares* 6 (1950): 101–3.

[28] Ramón y Fernandez, "Costumbres cacereñas," 119.

their subject clergy and their leading men (*homines viriles*) or heads of households to visit him and his cathedral church annually in procession. Only later did such obligatory processions become less centralized in character.[29]

What is not arguable in Kyll's model is that when these obligatory processions of subordinates to superiors did occur, they did have a generally similar morphology. A parish or other subordinate unit about to execute such a procession took with it some combination of its own unit's flags, relics, and images, that is, those objects around which the community customarily ordered itself, that endowed its own territory with sacrality, and marked it off from other units. Upon arrival the bearers of these objects deposited them with the authority they were visiting.[30] Soon an exchange followed, in which the visitors paid an obligatory tribute in exchange for the hosts providing hospitality.[31] Finally, when ready to depart, the visitor "redeemed" his flag and other regalia to transport home. As a general rule, the return home was less processional than the trip to the center.[32]

This ritual, so well documented in German cultural areas, is not foreign to very different climes. On processing into the center of Florence, for example, late medieval gilds first deposited their flags in city hall, from whence they were publicly hung for the length of the event.[33] Nor is the inspiration and significance of this widespread rite far to seek. It strongly resembles the procedure for claiming and displaying the regalia of conquered enemies, except that here the symbols are not held permanently. This basic rite of the deposit of regalia demonstrates, finally, the fragile character of so-called established orders. As the depositing of *sacra* indicates, the definition of a region as revealed in its processional order was always subject to change.

---

[29] N. Kyll, *Pflichtprozessionen und Bannfahrten im westlichen Teil des alten Erzbistums Trier* (Bonn, 1962), 17, 23; U. Berlière argues that the episcopal calling of synods gave rise to these processions: "Les processions des croix banales," *Bulletin de la Classe des Lettres et des Sciences morales et politiques* 8 (1922): 419–46, esp. 442.

[30] Kyll, *Pflichtprozessionen*, 17, 70, 114 (*signum debite subiectionis*), 118. Further Berlière, "Processions," esp. 442, and P. Paquay, "Les antiques processions des croix banales à Tongres," *Bulletin Limburgs Geschieden Oudkundig Genootschap te Tongeren* 21 (1903): 127–96.

[31] Note that of the works noted above, only Kyll (esp. *Pflichtprozessionen*, 17) insists upon the deposit and exchange character of the visit.

[32] Kyll, *Pflichtprozessionen*, 70, 118.

[33] Trexler, "Follow the Flag," 380, 386.

Mistaking episcopal prescriptions in the area of Trier for reality, Kyll may have been wrong, therefore, in assuming that a centralized order preceded a decentralized one. In fact the first obligatory processions that Kyll could actually document were ones of the twelfth century that headed not for the cathedral, but for places outside the city of Trier. In the relevant documentation, the Trier bishop permitted sub-diocesan units to execute their legal duty to the bishop by processing to certain outlying churches or monasteries nearer to them than was Trier.[34] The fact was that such monasteries usually had the relics, and thus drew crowds. As events in the Peace Movement in Aquitaine in the eleventh century clearly show, the trick for a bishop (who alone could summon the populace to synod) or for any prelate was to successfully advertise the great saintly body he possessed so that other prelates, in acts of subordination, would bring theirs in procession to visit it, thus honoring the great saint while advertising themselves. In Aquitaine, this competition contributed, in fact, to the establishment of a regional church.[35] Seeming obligations, then, often conceal competitive, switching, allegiances.

Switching Allegiances

Traditional Europe offers much evidence of shifting allegiances and solidarities, of course, and in this setting I wish only to highlight two particular forms that such switching took.

A first ritual pattern is associated with caves and wells, and has recently been studied by William Christian in districts of rural early modern Spain: a divine prediction that a holy image or relic or some other awesome object will be found in such unfrequented places proves to be true,

---

[34] The author cleverly suggests, however, that at times the bishop may have authorized some of his dependent units to make obligatory processions to other, more distant units within the diocese as a means of *extending* his own authority. That is, once such processions leading away from the see were overtly ordered by the bishop, their execution would be seen as performed under his authority: Kyll, *Pflichtprozessionen*, 42. But Kyll also found cases in which obligatory processions were established outside the city of Trier against the bishop's will or without him playing any role: *Pflichtprozessionen*, 38.

[35] D. Callahan, "The Peace of God and the Cult of the Saints in Aquitaine in the Tenth and Eleventh Centuries," *Historical Reflections* 14 (1987): 448–50; and B. Töpfer's fundamental *Volk und Kirche zur Zeit der beginnenden Gottesfriedensbewegung in Frankreich* (Berlin, 1957), 95ff., and esp. 100. An early (949) example of regional cooperation to establish common processions to a single monastery is in Berlière, "Processions," 432.

leading to the establishment of new devotional centers at those points and to processions and other devotional practices leading to them.[36] This resolves the problem of how to extend processional patterns to include new areas that had grown up at the edge of villages, or how to legitimate already effected social and economic changes in communal traffic patterns, including the demise of earlier routings and significant places. Thus fraternal solidarities are built up where previously, despite close economic and social patterns, only relations between strangers had existed.

Another pattern of switching allegiance concerns towns and villages involved in regional pilgrimage networks. To this point, two fundamental assumptions have underlain our inquiry. I have assumed first that, taken as a whole, processional routes to the extent they became traditional increased the emotional solidarity linking different points on those routes. Second, I have assumed that political and ecclesiastical authorities sought to impose such emotional ties institutionally, from the top down. My second example illustrates these forces at work in a particular historical case. In his recent work on Westphalian pilgrimages in the early modern period, Werner Freitag reveals a dynamic world in which pilgrimage geography and, I assume, the solidarities that went with it might change rapidly.

The bulk of Freitag's work documents the process by which the bishops of Münster successfully converted the pilgrimage to Telgte, just east of Münster, into what Freitag calls "an episcopal pilgrimage."[37] But Freitag was also able to document the fact that allegiances might shift within this dominant Telgte/Münster regional axis. Thus in the later seventeenth century the ambitious rectors of the village of Eggerode, some distance to the west of Münster, succeeded in reviving the worship of an old image of Mary. Armed with a papal indulgence, they first began to attract individual outsiders to this miraculous statue, which was enough to bring Mendicant friars to the village for confessions on procession days.

An interested spectator to this increase in visitation was the pastor of the church of nearby Schöppingen, which happened to be Eggerode's mother church. The latter had traditionally led his parishioners to Telgte on pilgrimage, but in 1708 certain "excesses" in the fees Telgte imposed on pilgrims led him to bring them to Eggerode. Then in 1712 the nearby village of Horstmar also headed for Eggerode instead of Telgte, and before

---

[36] W. Christian, *Apparitions in Late Medieval and Renaissance Spain* (Princeton, 1981).

[37] W. Freitag, *Volks- und Elitenfrömmigkeit in der Frühen Neuzeit. Marienfahrten im Fürstbistum Münster* (Paderborn, 1991). For what follows, see 180–97.

the new fashion had run its course, at least three other village churches had joined the procession to Eggerode. One reason for this switch was that Eggerode was nearer to these parishes than Telgte — the range of the Eggerode pilgrimage procession was never greater than about 15 kilometers.[38] But the point to be made here is that processional routes, and thus solidarities, were always in the process of change.

Certainly the prelates in Münster recognized that without asserting their authority, spatial routings would inevitably depend on other considerations, like the distances involved, the economic utility of particular processions, the interests of other politicians who profited from such pilgrimages, and the like. And they had a procedure to resist centrifugality, which, the record suggests, was sparingly enforced. As long as rural processions remained within their own walls, it seems, the diocesan authorities raised no objection, but once other villages, as distinct from individuals from them, started to go there and not to Telgte, they then took steps to resist.

Thus the year after the first extramural parish, that of Schöppingen, joined the Eggerode procession, the pastor of Telgte complained to the episcopal general vicar in Münster that another village, that of Ahaus, was considering leaving the Telgte procession and joining the pilgrimage to Eggerode.[39] The Eggerode cult was unauthorized and contravened diocesan rules, the Telgte pastor wrote in protest, and he was also dubious about the miracles that Eggerode's Mary was said to have performed; the vicar should look into the events at Eggerode and, if possible, the community of Ahaus should be forbidden to go on pilgrimage there. This was in fact the established way to end such challenges.[40] For if Ahaus went to Eggerode, the Telgte pastor warned, a shift of other processions away from Telgte was sure to follow. The bishop never did foster the cult of Eggerode, and its popularity expired even before the cult in Telgte crumbled in post-revolutionary times.

---

[38] Freitag, *Volks- und Elitenfrömmigkeit*, 192.

[39] Freitag, *Volks- und Elitenfrömmigkeit*, 194–95.

[40] In 1701, for instance, the bishop of Münster is found ordering the pastor of Bocholter to lead his people not to the town of Kevelaer but to Telgte: Freitag, *Volks- und Elitenfrömmigkeit*, 127–28.

TRANSMITTED BEHAVIOR

A fundamental assumption of this paper is that when collectivities traverse particular routes or areas to encounter strangers, they come to associate certain behavioral forms with those routes and tend to cement common behavioral forms with the collectivities they encounter. This assumption is difficult to demonstrate because contemporaries, but also many modern historians of traditional societies, have had different analytical interests. This concluding section presents evidence that such processes were indeed at work.

Resources

In the middle ages, there seems to have been a fundamental division between those (usually large) communities that possessed sacred resources adequate to their defense and those (usually small ones) that did not. Thus whenever there was a crisis, some late-medieval Alsatians left their own villages and processed to a nearby town in order to appeal to its holy objects for the salvation of their villages.[41] This suggests that because they could not gather around sacred objects within their own space and despite the presence of the sacred host, such villages may have assumed the devotional behaviors common to the town or towns they relied on for a sacred charge.

And yet as we have seen it was customary for parishes and other subgroups in obligatory processions to regional centers to carry their most important relics with them to that center and deposit them, seemingly depriving their villages of these protective forces.[42] Townspeople might at times physically oppose such removal precisely because they feared losing that protection,[43] but inversely, at a council in Limoges for the Peace of

---

[41] F. Rapp, "Zwischen Spätmittelalter und Neuzeit: Wallfahrten der ländlichen Bevölkerung in Elsass," in *Laienfrömmigkeit in sozialen und politischen Zusammenhängen des späten Mittelalters*, ed. K. Schreiner (Munich, 1991), 127–36. Rapp's article deals with an important allied matter that cannot be examined here: how early modern Alsatian occupational fraternities developed regional behaviors through trips to regional shrines.

[42] See further W. Brückner, "Zur Phänomenologie und Nomenklatur des Wallfahrtswesens und seiner Erforschung," in *Volkskultur und Geschichte. Festgabe für Josef Dünninger*, ed. Dieter Harmening et al. (Berlin, 1970), 415–16.

[43] Cf. the occasional uproars in different eleventh- and twelfth century towns whose churches, wishing to rebuild, sent professional beggars abroad with their relics to raise money: P. Héliot and M.-L. Chastang, "Quêtes et voyages de reliques au profit des

God, one finds it said that St. Leonard, brought from a subordinate unit, was necessary for the protection of those in Limoges.[44] Finally, there can be no doubt that villagers were often told by prelates that while they were on deposit in a more powerful regional center, their relics were being recharged, for instance by being near the bones of superior regional supernaturals.[45] The whole question of the spatial character of supernatural resources, especially in light of the increasing claim that the eucharist had a charge unrelated to space, requires more serious study.

Processional Forms

a) Participants. Obviously, how residents participated in processions to regional places depended on whether they did so voluntarily or under obligation. Still, as a historiographic category, that distinction so often proves chimerical — imagine finding people paid to take part in an allegedly voluntary procession! — that it commonly confounds analysis rather than fostering it. In any case, as Freitag has noted regarding Westphalia, regional processions have historically tended to replicate the social order rather than to counter it, and that implies underlying constraints fostered by governors.[46]

So rather than to develop different behavioral models based on whether actions were "really" obligatory or "truly" voluntary, it is more helpful to distinguish ideal from reality. The ideal in the obligatory processions of the diocese of Trier, for example, was for *everyone* in any given subunit to process, in order, to the center to absolve their obligation, but the reality was that villages sent an "ambassador" or one member from each family.[47]

églises françaises du moyen âge," *Revue d'Histoire Ecclésiastique* 59 (1964): 803. Such exporting was called a *delatio* in Flanders: G. Koziol, "Monks, Feuds, and the Making of Peace in Eleventh-Century Flanders," *Historical Reflections* 14 (1987): 535.

[44] Callahan, "Peace of God," 451.

[45] Callahan, "Peace of God," 450–51.

[46] Freitag, *Volks- und Elitenfrömmigkeit*, 257ff. For paid processants, see Toussaert, *Sentiment*, 202. The attempt to base analysis on a distinction between obligatory and voluntary processions weakens Brückner's "Zur Phänomenologie," as well as Kyll's *Pflichtprozessionen*, with its fundamental distinction between obligatory processions and the *Bannprozessionen* which derived from them.

[47] Kyll, *Pflichtprozessionen*, 49, 132. Whether the family representative was male or female, and an older or younger member, is an obviously important consideration in determining if and how behavioral solidarities were passed on through such processions. To be sure, the notion that a successful procession mixed everyone together *sine distinctione personarum* was an ecclesiastical figure of speech; yet no one, least of all the ecclesiastics,

Relics might the more easily be taken along, incidentally, if it was thought that rather than being a fixed locus, the village was there where this representative procession was. It might seem that processions would be capable of building behavioral commonalities only to the extent that members of a collectivity actually participated in them, and certainly, medieval and modern urban prelates' tactic of taking relics to the villagers if the latter would not process to them resulted in individual villages retaining their own distinct behavioral forms rather than learning common regional ones.[48] Still, if, as was often the case, processions first wound through their communes of origin before moving out, residents might have mimed them as they passed and thus built behavioral commonalities through such representational means.

b) On the Road. In traditional Europe there were different ways to process from the departure to the arrival point of a regional procession. Certainly song and prayer were common and one presumes that they were quickly standardized. Still, Kyll was unable to show that was the case with the songs and prayers within the single archdiocese of Trier.[49]

One important question regarding behavior on the road is the relative formality with which processors moved toward their goal. It is in fact not uncommon to find medieval groups processing in quite loose formations until they arrived at the gates of the magnet town, where they formed themselves into strict processional order, before or behind other arriving towns' processions.[50] But there are also cases where the processions to the goal were formal, while those returning home were either loose or indeed nonexistent. It was usual enough to dissolve the procession at the goal so that individuals went home on their own.[51] All of these options played their role in the construction of behavioral solidarities.

Our particular attention, however, is drawn to those incoming processions or parts thereof where participants used theatrical forms and objects to represent themselves. It was through such representations, after all, that

---

actually wanted such a *scandalum*: cf. P. Brown, *The Cult of the Saints* (Chicago, 1981), 42–43.

[48] The just-mentioned *queteurs* who moved from village to village with relics are the best example of such nonparticipatory practices. An example of what in modern church parlance is called the *Grand Retour* — prelates processing to their constituencies — is given by Toussaert, *Sentiment*, 250–51.

[49] Kyll, *Pflichtprozessionen*, 139.

[50] Kyll, *Pflichtprozessionen*, 138.

[51] Kyll, *Pflichtprozessionen*, 145.

processants showed off their identity, while it was upon such processants that the hosts hoped to impose their own communities' formal behaviors.[52] Seen from this angle, the first interesting moment was when a procession approached another village on the road to the processional goal. It was apparently a fairly common procedure for such "passage villages" to send delegations out a certain distance to welcome incoming processions.[53] A refinement of this standard diplomatic procedure, through which states as well as neighbors assessed the warmth of their relations with each other, was to imagine that the object being welcomed was actually a relic of the incoming town. This common conceit helps explain in part why the next step was to accompany the arriving procession triumphantly into the village and to its church for common prayers. As the procession passed from town to town toward the center, encounters of the type mentioned earlier in this paper were imagined to take place between saints as well as between villages, a common comportment being the ideal result.[54]

Whether such welcoming villages in turn joined to the existing procession so as to proceed together toward the center obviously depended on their obligations. Thus in the early modern period Kyll found actual written agreements in the Moselle area in which as many as four parishes promised to join one at a time a procession toward their obligatory goal, whereas Freitag found no such *Anschlüße* in his study of Westphalian pilgrimages during the same period.[55]

There can be little doubt that such collegial performances had the effect of standardizing villages' behaviors, as did another form of encounter, which took place at the intersections of roads rather than within villages. That rural encounter might, however, have been itself intended by the goal-city. Since objects become sacred much more readily than do spaces, it is not surprising that cities often put relics in open fields outside their town walls so they could be worshipped by a mass of people; inversely, those trying to settle a feud with relics would plump them down right in

---

[52] One means was for the goal-city to sponsor a total biblical theatre, and invite other cities to present different parts of that totality: see e.g., Toussaert, *Sentiment*, 256.

[53] Héliot and Chastang, "Quêtes," 60 (1965), 12; Freitag, *Volks- und Elitenfrömmigkeit*, 263–64.

[54] Héliot and Chastang, "Quêtes," 60 (1965), 12. In Florentine receptions, one finds the city's different ages, sexes, and statuses marching with their matches among the visitors: Trexler, *Public Life*, 312–13; see 308 for measuring the distances hosts went outside town.

[55] Kyll, *Pflichtprozessionen*, 92–93; Freitag, *Volks- und Elitenfrömmigkeit*, 263f.

the midst of the contendants, wherever that might be.[56] The sacralization of crossroads often followed; that is, the greeters erected statues or
other markers to serve as objects for their consensualized behavior at those
spots.[57] These new focusses of consensus behaviors might, in turn, run
counter to the sacrality of the town or other place that was the pilgrimage
goal and to the profit of its merchants.

Of course one of the great attractions that the pilgrimage goal offered
those processing toward it was its large population and the thespo-religious
clergy found at such places. Such a clergy could honor the visitors, such a
city gave visitors a chance to convert that center. Usually, therefore, visitors saved their collective performances for their goal place, and we have
a good deal of evidence showing how small communities competed with
larger ones in the competitions to create solidarities. In the western part
of the diocese of Trier, for instance, Kyll found three different processional
performances associated with particular areas as they marched into Trier
for their obligatory rites. There were certain villages whose processions featured dances; others performed so-called standing processions like so many
tableaux vivants; while kneeling processions were the property of still
other villages and towns.[58]

In this processional world, the behavioral patterns that resulted of
course functioned to exchange simultaneously spiritual and material values. Some modern scholars still have difficulty reconciling this simultan-
eity, Wolfgang Brückner, for instance, ruefully documenting what he de-
claims as the "deals" (*Geschäfte*) through which lay authorities and
churchmen split the take from pilgrimages.[59] In fact the mutual profita-
bility of such regional processions to several sectors of a community was a
central point of any effort put into establishing such routes. Markets and
fairs must indeed have been fairly predictable once the populace in such
goal-areas reached a number that made such a fair profitable; commercial
and spiritual and collective exchanges were, and are, inseparably

---

[56] The twelfth-century source for this act continues: "Everyone was astonished and
humbly lowered his eyes. And their restraint showed clearly enough that they recognized
[the saint] who lay in their midst, even they who had not known him. Tears flowed from
the eyes of all. Piety and wrath vied in their hearts. At last, piety won out": Koziol,
"Monks," 538. For the open fields, see Töpfer, *Volk und Kirche*, 95ff., 103.

[57] Freitag, *Volks- und Elitenfrömmigkeit*, 264f.

[58] Kyll, *Pflichtprozessionen*, 143–46; Berlière, "Processions," 434–35; Paquay, "Les antiques processions," 171.

[59] Brückner, "Zur Phänomenologie," 413.

linked.[60] What needs study is the experience those visiting such markets had of different *market* behaviors, and how that experience compared to that of processions in constructing solidarities between the towns and villages of a region. One thinks, for instance, of the market in indulgences and relics.

The last element of the regional procession — if indeed the marchers came home in procession — was the solemn reentry back into the home village or town. As documented by Freitag in seventeenth-century Westphalia, it might resemble a triumphant diplomatic or military reentry, and in fact, the seventeenth-century German erudite Aventinus compared a return from pilgrimage precisely to a Roman imperial reentry.[61] And the processors might solemnly hang up the souvenirs of their pilgrimage in their native church just as did a returning victorious army.[62] Thus villagers on revisiting these memorials might relive their past processional behaviors, just as they took their male children on procession to teach them the stories, as well as the boundaries, of the polity.[63]

Conclusion

In a fundamental article on the history of pilgrimages, Wolfgang Brückner uses the variegated dresses worn by visitors to the lower Rhenish pilgrimage site of Xanten to warn students of collective behavior. The variety of such dress might seem to hint at free choice, but in fact, Brückner pointed out, processions to Xanten were actually obligatory in nature and those who did not attend were excommunicated. Thus variegated behavior is not the enemy of control. To the contrary, in early modern Europe there is increasing evidence of behavioral particularism at the base even as the absolute states of Europe concentrated power in their hands.[64]

The present paper has not, therefore, argued that behavior was increasingly standardized in this period. Rather, I have only claimed that by the means we have described, authorities tried to construct regional solidarities by establishing common behaviors in traditional Europe. Without any

---

[60] See Trexler, *Public Life*, 3.

[61] Brückner, "Zur Phänomenologie," 395; Freitag, *Volks- und Elitenfrömmigkeit*, 272.

[62] Freitag, *Volks- und Elitenfrömmigkeit*, 272.

[63] E. Schubert, "Erspielte Ordnung. Beobachtungen zur bäuerlichen Rechtswelt des späteren Mittelalters,"*Jahrbuch für fränkische Landesforschung* 38 (1978): 58; further Kyll, *Pflichtprozessionen*, 96.

[64] See my *Public Life*, chap. 11; Brückner, "Zur Phänomenologie," 413.

doubt, revolutionaries and reformers used other strategies than those sketched here to subvert such common communication networks, but that is another paper. The two manipulators of behaviors, the authorities and the revolutionaries, were and are, however, related, for the world of forms that both sought and seek to seduce or impose upon others, themselves emerge from problems of diplomacy fundamental to all complex societies — the fact of competition, the ubiquity of exchange, the need to greet or encounter — problems that reach across borders and are the beginnings of understanding, love, and conquest.

Thus it is indeed possible for a variegated procession of many identities to construct solidarities and to impose order. One Benedictine was profoundly moved in 1615 by the procession of many surrounding villages to the Spanish shrine (and market) of Sopetrán (Guadalajara) on Ascension Day, and by the positions they assumed on arriving:

> It is very pleasing to see them eating in family groups. Each village separately spreads out very large tablecloths in the meadow. ... To see in one meadow thirty or forty entire towns, some with two hundred, others three hundred men all together around their food, is very pleasing to the eye.[65]

Obviously, there was great unity of behavior in such diversity.

---

[65] W. Christian, *Local Religion in Sixteenth-Century Spain* (Princeton, 1981), 118.

Bending Over Backwards:
Prayer Posture and Sexual Posture in
Traditional Europe and America[*]

> The patriarchs came into the world to repair the senses and
> this they did to four of them. Then came Sabbatai Zevi and
> repaired the fifth, the sense of touch, which according to
> Aristotle and Maimonides is a source of shame to us, but
> which now has been raised by him to a place of honor and
> glory.[1]

AFTER THE SPANIARDS CONQUERED THE ANDEAN INCA IN 1534, an important number of missionary-ethnographers began to record the religious customs of the indigenous peoples, just as their colleagues had begun to do a few years before in the Valley of Mexico. At the great shrine of Pachacamac, just south of Lima, some of them encountered a particular mode

---

[*] This essay appeared previously in *Verletzte Ehre: Formen, Funktionen und Bedeutungen in Gesellschaften des Mittelalters und der frühen Neuzeit*, ed. K. Schreiner and G. Schwerhoff (Cologne, 1995), 235–51.

[1] Nathan of Gaza, cited in D. Biale, *Eros and the Jews: From Biblical Israel to Contemporary America* (New York, 1992), 119.

of prayer. This practice marks the departure point of this study, which explores the sexual roots of reverence.

According to the Jesuit Joseph Acosta (ca. 1575–1576), the devotee at Pachacamac approached the image of the God as follows. He:

> ... stepp[ed] backwards, [with] his back turned to the idol. Then he bent his body and inclined his head, putting himself in an ugly position. They consulted [with the God] in this fashion.[2]

Later authors elaborated on this basic information. By 1653, Bernabé Cobo wrote that:

> They proceeded with their backs turned to the said idol, with their eyes lowered, full of consternation and fear. Making repeated bows, they set about awaiting the oracle with an indecent and ugly posture.[3]

From the earliest sources, therefore, the Spaniards associated this posture with reverence toward a specific type of native image, or "devil," in the Iberians' words. Pachacamac was one of the limited number of shrines where an oracular devil "gave responses to questioners." For future reference, it should be added that according to the authoritative Cieza de León (1545), the temples that harbored such talking images were those in which the devil wanted berdaches installed, that is, the biological males who acted in every way, including sexually, like women. In a now published book, I have argued that the priests who approached the deity in this way were in actuality such berdaches, who were, we know, penetrated from behind by big men on such temple mounts.[4]

Further primary and early secondary sources confirm Acosta's original reading. Thus about 1601, the royal historiographer Antonio de Herrera paraphrased Acosta by highlighting the phenomenon of consultation:

---

[2] "Las espaldas vueltas al idolo, andando hacia atras, y doblando el cuerpo y inclinando la cabeza, ponianse en una postura fea, y asi consultaban": J. De Acosta, *Obras*, Biblioteca de Autores Españoles [hereafter *BAE*] 92 (Madrid, 1954), 153 (*Historia*, V, 12).

[3] "Iban las espaldas vueltas al dicho idolo, con los ojos bajos, llenos de turbacion y temblor, y haciendo muchas humillaciones, se ponian a esperar el oraculo en una postura indecente y fea": B. Cobo, *Obras*, 2 vols., *BAE* 92 (Madrid, 1964), 188 (*Historia del Nuevo Mundo*, XIII, 17).

[4] R. Trexler, *Sex and Conquest: Gendered Violence, Political Order, and the European Conquest of the Americas* (Ithaca, 1995). For details on such devils, see "The Talking Image," elsewhere in the present collection.

The consultation consisted in the priests entering face backwards during the night. And making a great bow or inclination, they asked for what they wanted.[5]

Then about 1638, the Augustinian Antonio de Calancha added our last original observation on this score:

The means priests used to resolve doubts or ask for answers about future events or present graces were to enter early in the night with their backs turned to the idol, bending the body.[6]

The interpreter will not be far wrong if he or she begins to explore this prayer posture by studying the meaning attached to it by the Spaniards themselves. First, the Spaniards considered supernatural predictions by these "devils" to require the most difficult form of prayer (did they not practice it themselves?!),[7] and thus this prayer posture, the most extreme. Secondly, the same Iberians clearly viewed this prayer posture as extremely self-debasing in relation to a general Amerindian reverential rule, which was never to reverence a God or lord face to face. Not for nothing did the Iberians recommend the obviously more profound reverences of the Americans to the so-called Old World! Indeed, the earliest source we have that describes backwards approaches to authority figures mentions the hiding of the face. Describing the way inhabitants approach their rulers in the Tierra Firme, Gonzalez Fernández de Oviedo by 1535 writes:

They enter where he is with their backs turned to him and bowing deeply. And if they enter face to face, they lower their faces deeply, such that it appears they are walking like cats. And when he comes up to his lord to talk with him, he turns his back to him, for in no manner can they talk face to face.[8]

---

[5] "La consulta era que entraban de noche los sacerdotes, andando la cara atrás, y haciendo una gran dobladura o inclinación pedían lo que querían": Antonio de Herrera, *Historia general de los hechos de los castellanos en las islas y tierrafirme del mar Océano*, 17 vols. (Madrid, 1934–1957), 10:290f. (V, iv, 5).

[6] "El modo de consultar dudas, o pedir respuestas los sacerdotes en casos futuros o mercedes presentes, era entrar a prima noche bueltas las espaldas al idolo, agoviando el cuerpo": A. de la Calancha, *Crónica moralizada* (Lima, 1974), 838f.

[7] See Trexler, *Sex and Conquest*.

[8] "Entran donde está, vueltas asimesmo las espaldas, a recular; e sí entran cara a cara, es bajando mucho las cabezas, tanto que paresce que van a gatas, e cuando llega cerca para hablar a su señor, vuélvele las espaldas, porque en ninguna manera ha de hablar cara a cara": G. Fernández de Oviedo, *Historia general y natural de las Indias*, 5 vols., BAE

Herrera says much the same:

> The reverence that subjects have toward their lords is very great.
> For they never look them in the eyes, even when they are in
> everyday conversation. And they approach the point where their
> lord is with their back turned.[9]

The Spaniards interpreted this gesture at a third level, however, and it
is the one that we want to explore in this paper. Cobo provided the clue
to this meaning: While he and his colleagues were not permitted to mention the "unmentionable sin," it is enough that he stated with emphasis
that this prayer posture was not just ugly, as Acosta had already opined,
but downright "indecent." Now, like all our sources, it was known since
the Andean kenner Domingo de San Tomas in mid-sixteenth century that
in the Andean temples one could find big men who mounted and had intercourse with berdaches; being mounted by such men was in fact one of
the fundamental tasks of the berdaches in this region.[10] Thus in claiming
that the devotee at Pachacamac assumed an "indecent" posture, Cobo
certainly suspected that the priests of Pachacamac, either really or symbolically, offered themselves to the "idol."

As unwilling as the Spaniards were to talk about sexual behavior, Calancha comes as close as one could hope for in the following description:

> In the pueblo of Tauca they adore the goblins that we call succu-
> buses, but they call Huaraclla. ... And this adoration was much
> desired. ... And those goblins had seduced all the [village] men's
> desire, *their adoration increasing through this sensuality.*[11]

117–21, (Madrid, 1959), 3:126 (XXVI, 31). Still earlier, during Columbus's fourth voyage,
it was observed that "the population of Veragua and thereabout turned their back when
they talked to each other": *Journals and Other Documents on the Life and Voyages of
Christopher Columbus*, ed. S. Eliot Morison (New York, 1963), 345.

[9] "La reverencia que tienen los súbditos a los señores es muy grande, porque jamás
los miran a la cara, aunque estén en doméstica conversación, y entran con las espaldas
vueltas adonde está el señor": Herrera, *Historia*, 12:394 (VI, v, 6).

[10] Parallels can be established with the Mexican seed festival of Ochpaniztli. In it,
priests dressed up with women's garb and playing the Goddess Toci laid down before the
God Huitzilopochtli with their arms and hands outstretched": see G. Olivier, "Conqué-
rants et missionnaires face au 'péché abominable': Un essai sur l'homosexualité en Méso-
amerique au moment de la conquête espagnole," *C.M.H.L.B. Caravelle* 55 (1990): 36.

[11] My italics. "En el pueblo de Tauca adoravan a los duendes, que nosotros llamos
sucubos, i ellos llaman Huaraclla, i era el umilladero i ordinario adoratio en unos alisos
que estavan junto al pueblo adonde se aparecían, i sus adoradores oían sus voces, i era

Precisely this link between adoration and sensuality, obviously a notion current among early modern Europeans like Calancha, is what we shall now pursue into the European and Mediterranean past. For obviously, all these writers were aware that they were describing "presentation," the submissive position of the (in the first place, male) sexual recipient. In Yucatan as elsewhere in the Americas, the Spaniards found, passives were indeed referred to as "those who are used to showing their buttocks" in submission.[12] But not just there and not just in lasciviousness. This posture was a recognized posture of reverence in the so-called Old World, as we shall see.

The Faces of Down

In Desmond Morris' ethological scheme, among the higher animals the essence of only a very few gestures are genetically rather than culturally determined. One of these is making oneself lower than the party with whom one interacts, and it is safe to say that one animal's mounting of another, with or without penetration, is one particularly expressive manifestation of this up-down, higher-lower organization of dominance and submission among mammals. It is true that among non-human primates, and within a complex game of deceit initiated by factual dominants, mounting in this way can occasionally express submission rather than domination.[13] This is comparable to certain Roman rulers who assumed the passive role in homosexual relations. But the underlying, all but universal presumption that up is "superior" and low "inferior," to use two common, revelatory, Latin words, certainly holds. Being down is dishonorable, and the act of presentation, as the ethologist Eibl-Eibesfeldt has shown in sur-

---

tan apetecida esta adoración, i tan venerados estos alisos, que las ojas eran reliquias i casi adoradas ... i toda el ánima tenían en aquellas duendas los varones, acrecentándose la adoración por la sensualidad": *Crónica moralizada*, 1065.

[12] "Ah wawa tulupoob" or "los que suelen mostrar su dorso," the sin of Nacxit Xuchit: J. Imbelloni, "La 'Essaltatione delle Rose,' del Codice Vatican Mexicano 3738, el 'Nictekatun' de las fuentes Maya y el 'pecado nefando' de la tradición peruana más remota," *Anales de Arqueología y Etnología* 4 (1943): 198, analysing the Book of Chilam Balam of Chumayel. R. Roys, *The Book of Chilam Balam* (Princeton, 1933), 169, mistranslates the key phrase as "backsliders."

[13] F. de Waal, "The Relation between Power and Sex in the Simians: Socio-Sexual Appeasement Gestures," in *Gender Rhetorics: Postures of Dominance and Submission in History*, ed. R. Trexler (Binghamton, NY, 1994), 15–32.

feit, is a sexually-represented act of social submission that is found among all primates.[14]

One of the fundamental problems confronting the student of submissive and thus reverential gestures is the possibility that different meanings may be attached to him who faces down toward, and down away from, the object of reverence. In other words, what is the relative importance of or relation between avoiding the face of a ruler and presenting to him? Clearly, what is considered reverential in one culture may be an insult in another, especially in those many cultures in which the buttocks, as well as the visage, is termed a "face," or at a minimum, is said to have "cheeks," so that the problem may be construed as *which face or cheeks* face the object of reverence.

The matter can, perhaps, be further simplified. In the view of Detlev Fehling, for example, whose pathfinding study of ancient gestures in the light of recent animal ethological scholarship deserves the highest praise, both positions — that is, on the one hand kneeling, proskynesis, or prostration, in which the face proper faces the reverenced object but is lowered, and on the other hand that of presentation, in which the buttocks are presented to the object — *both* are *sexually* meaningful.[15] Each, that is, presents different genitalia to the reverenced object, and that commonality may be more significant than the obviously gestural variance.

Thus what I am suggesting is that, like Priapus, we be open to various interpretations of the most ancient acts of reverence. Take the story of Mordecai. In it (Est. 3.2), Haman, on being made Grand Vizier by King Ahasuerus of Persia, found that all the king's servants except the Jew Mordecai "bowed down and did obeisance to him." Still today, Mordecai is at the root of a living Jewish rule of thumb that prohibits the orthodox from bowing down to anyone except Jahweh. It might appear that in these and similar cases, the message was simply one of refusing a subordinate repre-

---

[14] On the sexual meaning of this greeting, I. Eibl-Eibesfeldt, *Love and Hate* (New York, 1971), 177f., 195, and especially the illustration on p. 178; and the section on the buttocks in D. Morris, *Body Watching* (New York, 1985), esp. 205–7. The human gesture has been studied by M. Müller-Jabusch, *Götzens Grober Gruss* (Munich, 1936). Needless to say, being down was more dishonorable for a man than for a woman. Indeed, women on top was the reason that God sent the biblical flood: J. Brundage, "Let me Count the Ways: Canonists and Theologians Contemplate Coital Positions," *Journal of Medieval History* 10 (1984): 87.

[15] D. Fehling, *Ethologische Überlegungen auf dem Gebiet der Altertumskunde. Phallische Demonstration–Fernsicht–Steinigung* (Munich, 1974).

sentation toward others, the bow being no more than a "symbolic" expression for such subordination. Yet the fear of bowing down may conceal another fear, that of being raped.

Even at this early date of our research, a closer look dispels the notion that no more was involved than a "mere ritual." I will no more than mention the Attic bowl that shows a Greek running behind a Persian and ready to thrust his penis into the latter, for there is no evidence of reverence in this scene.[16] But another Attic black-figure bowl shows a Dionysian procession in which submissive males assumed a female role and appearance, in part by presenting their buttocks, as the great phallus rides by in triumph.[17]

Then among the writings of the Hellenistic dream interpreter Artemidoros, John Winkler found this association to the word "penis": "the penis is ... like the respect of being held in honor, since it is called 'reverence' (aidos) and 'respect'."[18] Thus in Priapian fashion, Artemidoros locked together prayer and sex: in his view, the very notion of reverence stemmed from the appearance of the erect penis. Indeed in the ancient Near East, we can find subjects sacrificing to the Gods by either presenting themselves to the latter, that is, his priest, or alternately servicing that God/priest as he presents himself to the devotee.[19]

Fellation

I have already noted that an object of worship, like a God or lord, may not only play the active role of insertor but that of the recipient. Again, that fact has been impressed upon me forcefully by an American description of sacred fellation which raises, and begins to resolve, the problem seemingly associated with that act. In the medieval European vocabulary, in anal intercourse the insertor was called the "active," while the insertee

---

[16] Reproduced in Trexler, Sex and Conquest, 15.

[17] W. Burkert, Homo Necans (Berkeley, 1983), 69f., Müller-Jabusch, Götzens, 259. J. G. Wood reports in The Natural History of Man. Africa (London, 1868), 234, that an African mountain spirit demands the dropping of one's drawers as a reverencing from those passing by. If one neglects to, he won't be able to sit down for the rest of his life.

[18] J. Winkler, The Constraints of Desire (New York, 1990), 42. Cf. the Greco-Roman word kinaidos, that is, the ancient Romans and Greeks who, transvested, were sexually penetrated by others.

[19] Herodotus, The Persian Wars, ed. G. Rawlinson (New York, 1964), 107, where Babylonian women had to have intercourse with a stranger once in life at the shrine of Venus.

was called a "passive" or "pathic." Honor and dishonor have followed in lockstep: the active partner might be considered honorable in that he penetrated (from on top!), the passive without honor because he had been penetrated.

But who was honored or dishonored by fellation? Overwhelmingly, the fellatee now, and apparently in one part of traditional Europe as well, was the younger and desired party, while the fellator was the older of the two and the one who purchased the services of the junior. Michael J. Rocke discovered to his surprise that in late medieval Florence, this fellator was considered the "active" (because his mouth is, after all, the active party) and the fellatee the passive.[20] The American document, which I now paraphrase, shows that in the world of human culture, the Gods themselves might suck.

The *Popol Vuh* is the cosmogonic book of the Quiché Maya of highland Guatemala. It was presumably written down in the sixteenth century; the only surviving manuscript copy — in Quiché with a Spanish translation — dates from about 1701.[21] In it, one of the four Quiché "motherfathers," or heads of patrilines, obtains a God/image named Tohil, and from that God comes fire for the four groups. These four tribes were, however, forbidden to give other tribes fire, "until [the latter] give something to Tohil," that is, until they sacrificed to him.

It soon becomes clear enough that the desired sacrifice was sexual in character. When the freezing tribes beseech the four stem groups for fire, Tohil tells the latter to address those seeking fire as follows:

"Don't they want to be suckled on their sides and under their arms? Isn't it their heart's desire to embrace me? I, who am Tohil? But if there is no desire, then I'll not give them their fire. When the time comes, not right now, they'll be suckled on their sides, under their arms."

"Very well, let him suckle," the freezing tribes responded to this message. "And very well, we shall embrace him. ...."

---

[20] M. Rocke, *Forbidden Friendships: Homosexuality and Male Culture in Renaissance Florence* (New York, 1996), 92–94. Eugene Rice, who is preparing a work on the language of same-sex behavior in traditional Europe, informs me that the Florentine situation was an anomaly as regards Europe as a whole.

[21] All the following citations come from *Popol Vuh: The Mayan Book of the Dawn of Life*, trans. and ed. D. Tedlock (New York, 1985), 28–30.

According to the *Popol Vuh*, all but one of the other tribes "received their fire" in this way. That tribe was the Cakchiquels, who stole fire from Tohil. Our text continues: "The Cakchiquels didn't ask for their fire. They didn't give themselves up in defeat. But all the other tribes were defeated when they gave themselves up to being suckled on their sides, under their arms."

The tale concludes: "And this is what Tohil meant by being 'suckled': that all the tribes be cut open before him, and that their hearts be removed 'through their sides, under their arms.' "

Three important facts emerge from this account, which should, I think, be related to the Maya practice of penile blood-letting.[22] First, the God is represented as needing the semen, or some fluid, of others. That is, different from the all-powerful "active" divinity who only penetrates (and different from certain tribal elders of New Guinea who until recently contributed to the growth of their young by ejaculating into them), Tikul is a "passive" God who, perhaps older than his subjects, can only generate fire if he is allowed to partake of the semen or fluids of devotees. God though he is, he depends for his existence on the devotee.

Second, the *Popol Vuh* casts this whole activity as sacrificial in nature, both in the fact that the tribes offer or "give something to Tohil," and in the sense that in the end, those who offer their semen or fluid will be sacrificed by losing their hearts. Third and as a consequence, this whole sexual/religious activity or prayer is viewed as a process by which the tribes, in being seduced, suffer defeat, subordination, humiliation.

I doubt that the student of this admittedly difficult narrative will emerge from reading this account without a nuanced sense of the range of meanings that can be assigned to different sexual positions and prayers, and especially, a grasp of the power that may be involved when even the Gods "stoop to conquer." In truth, this text recalls to mind one of the earliest commentaries about the prayer modes of Christianity, one which explicitly linked sexuality and prayer posture. I refer of course to the second- or third-century Christian, Minucius Felix, who in his *Octavius* has the so-called pagans accuse Christians of worshipping, or really fellating, the genitals of their priests, obviously extrapolating from the fact that the faithful knelt before their standing priests.[23] We miss the point if we only

---

[22] On which see L. Schele and M. Miller, *The Blood of Kings* (New York, 1992).

[23] "Etiam ille, qui de adoratis sacerdotis virilibus adversum nos fabulatur, temptat in nos conferre quae sua sunt. Ista enim impudicitiae eorum forsitan sacra sint, apud quos

insist that the charge was untrue and scurrilous. As Minucius Felix himself intimated, an association between reverential kneeling and fellation only made sense in a world where that association was plausible, or at least problematic. As we have seen, associating sexual posture and prayer posture was not unknown in antiquity.

If we are to judge by certain remarks of the Parisian theologian Peter the Chanter (d. 1197), that association never faltered in Christianity, despite the notorious sense of shame proper to this religion. First of all, the Chanter, the first author of a manual on modes of prayer, considered humans to be different from animals in standing "naturally erect," and he states that by standing erect, humans expressed equality to other humans. Still, to express our fallen state and to do penance, we fall down to the position of the quadrupeds.[24] At this point, the return to our animal state of sexuality is made explicit: Just as in human fornication we lie down meanly *like animals*, so also do we so justly so as to repent our sins. We copulate with and join ourselves to the earth so as to copulate ultimately with heaven.[25]

Peter's analysis is worth examining at closer range. First, Peter introduces a link not only between prayer and sexuality, but between prayer and animality, in part by linking sexual behavior with animal behavior (One is reminded of Martial, who on the basis of the instinctive "piety"

---

sexus omnis membris omnibus prostat, apud quos tota inpudicitia vocatur urbanitas, qui scortorum licentiae invident, qui medios viros lambunt, libidinoso ore inguinibus inhaerescunt, homines malae linguae etiam si tacerent, quos prius taedescit impudicitiae suae quam pudescit. Pro nefas! id in se mali facinoris admittunt, quod nec actas potest pati mollior nec cogi servitus durior": in Tertullian, *Apologia de Spectaculis*, and Minucius Felix, *Octavius*, ed. and trans. T. R. Glover and G. H. Rendall (Cambridge, MA, 1984), 402–5 (*Octavius*, chap. 28).

[24] See my *The Christian at Prayer: An Illustrated Prayer Manual Attributed to Peter the Chanter (d. 1197)* (Binghamton, NY, 1987), 36 for full references. Citing Paul ("Qui enim fornicatur, in corpus suum peccat" [1 Cor. 6.18]), Peter explains that "hanc faciem et erectionem naturae, maxime deturpat fornicatio. . . . ut facies hominis quasi in faciem quadrupedum convertatur. Unde et libidinosus, sui vel parco comparatur, vel 'qui fornicatur in corpus suum peccat,' quia contra venustatem et erectionem corporis sui, incurvans illud ad lutum": *Verbum Abbreviatum* (*De vitiis et virtutibus*), in PL 205:265.

[25] "Et ponitur corpus meum terre copulo et coniungo, flendo peccata mea": Trexler, *Christian at Prayer*, 188, further 193. Cf. Peter's point of view with that of Encratites in early Christianity. He thought that humans' sexual behavior in and of itself was a fundamental indication of man's relation to the world of animals: P. Brown, *The Body and Society: Men, Women, and Sexual Renunciation in Early Christianity* (New York, 1988), 95.

of lesser animals before human sovereigns argued that his emperor was divine and should also be venerated with proskynesis).[26] This linkage became still more specific when one posture in human sexual intercourse, the dominant mounting the submissive, becomes known as the *mos canis* or *canino more*. A second point is that the Chanter mystifies the reverential dynamic by introducing the earth as that object with which the orant "copulates," whereas in fact that object was, and always continued to be, a God/image or a lord. Nevertheless, Peter the Chanter's linkage of prayer to that which is sub-human, whether sexual activity or animality, is significant. Peter does no less than to image the human in the act of prayer as animal, fornicating. We look like a human when we converse, erect, but like a beast when we pray.

Jean-Claude Schmitt has shown that at just this point in time, there was a strong movement, spearheaded by the likes of the Chanter, to emphasize such animal-like fornication postures as fitting and proper for the adoration of the host. Doubtless, much of the inspiration for this increasingly profound prostration before the host stemmed from contemporary practices of humiliations before secular rulers, of which Geoffrey Koziol has written.[27] The Chanter mocked opponents of such profound kneelings as being the first to assume precisely such positions in front of their secular lords.

Yet in the process of fostering such sexualized *and* bestialized imagery of devotion, Peter the Chanter left no doubt as to the true enemy of such "proper" devotion. It was the sentiment of shame, which obviously was not limited to those aristocrats who so notoriously resisted the deep prostrations increasingly required by their lords and inspired by the Byzantine East. Proud canons and monks too were not ready to allow themselves to be seen publicly assuming postures that were so clearly associated with subordination, not lastly, as we have seen, because of their association with "bestial" sexual submission. They preferred to sit — the posture of judges — while praying.[28]

---

[26] Cf. O. Weinreich, *Studien zu Martial* (Stuttgart, 1928), 74–85: without being taught, an elephant behaves *pius et supplex* before rulers, performing proskynesis (Epigram 17). For Martial this position was obviously "natural": cited in A. Alföldi, *Die monarchische Repräsentation im römischen Kaiserreiche* (Darmstadt, 1970), 55.

[27] G. Koziol, *Begging Pardon and Favor: Ritual and Political Order in Early Medieval France* (Ithaca, 1992); J.-C. Schmitt, *La raison des gestes dans l'Occident médiéval* (Paris, 1990), 307ff.

[28] Trexler, *Christian at Prayer*, 41, 48. As late as the tenth century Byzantine orants

Further Study

A serious study of this topic, which on the one hand recognizes the link between "bestiality" and prayer and on the other that between sexual behavior and prayer, would obviously begin by tracking down the scholarly tradition that must lie behind Peter the Chanter's insights, something that is lacking in today's discourse about ritual, including the shame aspect of public rituals. For instance, Geoffrey Koziol has written a learned book on early French rituals of supplication not only without working out their morphology, but without mentioning either animality or sex.[29] And while Jean-Claude Schmitt's work on gesture does an excellent job of studying gestural morphology, neither does he broach these apparently frightening links of human gestures to animals or to sexuality.

Alas, such *pudeur* gets in the way of understanding some of the foundational categories which ground our sense of honor and our sense of seduction across borders. Our hesitation to include animal formalisms in the search for the foundations of human behavioral patterns, as in the case of Koziol and Schmitt, is particularly costly, especially given the obvious: that medieval commoners and confessors so easily linked what they called "sodomy" with what they called "bestiality." It is almost as if a conspiracy still exists among what Bernardino Sahagún called "the solemn class" of the clerics or intelligentsia to conceal the fact that what is solemn is at the same time what is raucously seductive.

The peoples of traditional Europe and the Mediterranean knew that well. They knew, for instance, that prostration was commonly equated with animality in the world of practice; that is, the prostrator created an image of himself or herself as animal to make the prostration "work." Thus in early medieval liturgies we find monks (often "naked") being beaten while they lie prostrate before their abbot. To obtain forgiveness, they were then forced to crawl to and grovel at the feet of each member of the chapter. The matter was not much different in the secular realm. The count of Hiémois sought peace from a duke of Normandy by "groaning and rolling on the ground at his feet ..."[30] A close study of such

---

neither knelt nor did proskynesis on Sundays, perhaps because of that day's non-penitential character, or because they would be seen by the public on such feast days: Alföldi, *Monarchische Repräsentation*, 61; O. Treitinger, *Die oströmische Kaiser- und Reichs-idee nach ihrer Gestaltung im höfischen Zeremoniell* (Darmstadt, 1956), 89.

[29] Cf. Koziol, *Begging Pardon*, 301 for one sentence on the matter.

[30] "Novissime deliberavit apud se equius illi fore cum vitae discrimine fratris [ducis]

prostrations would reveal a great deal about the imagic conversion of humans into animals.

No less can be said about a study that would concentrate on sources linking prayer postures to sexual positions. The tale begins on the field of battle, where, in heroic poetry as a whole, it is thought disgraceful to turn one's back to an enemy not only because that represents cowardice, but because it images sexual submission.[31] The story extends to prayer rites in the city temple. It can hardly be an accident, for instance, that among the eight modes of prayer that accompany the prayer treatise of Peter the Chanter, the one mode which illustrates a woman, that is, the "naturally" subordinate sexual partner, as the orant in these illustrations is what I call proskynesis, but which the text refers to as *mos camelorum,* in which the orant, leaning forward on her knees, thrusts her buttocks outward, much like a camel raising itself. Since the time of the penitentials, this *sexual* position had been "incorrect," to be sure, but was doubtless widely used, both by women and by passive partners in homosexual acts.[32] Linkages of this type will certainly appear in Christian literature to those who look. Thus Edwardes found a ninth-century sacramentary which admonished "pro Judaeis non flectant," a double entendre which obviously includes the understanding that Jews were homophilic, and would penetrate anyone who bent over.[33]

At this point, however, that linkage is more easily documented in the world of Islam (the word means "submission," the word "Muslim" in turn meaning one who surrenders to God) where, different from Christianity,

---

clementiam attentare. . . . Cujus vestigiis illico solo tenus provolutus, veniam commissi ab eo expetebat lugubris": Koziol, *Begging Pardon,* 185–87, 386 no. 23.

[31] P. Meulengracht Sorensen, *The Unmanly Man. Concepts of Sexual Defamation in Early Northern Society* (Odense, 1983), 68, with examples.

[32] Alexander of Hales (1185–1245) said *coitus retro* sex — "the fashion of brutes" — was always a mortal sin. Aquinas was of the opinion that any deviation from the natural [missionary] position in marital intercourse was a bestial act and violated the role assignments of the sexes: cited in Brundage, "Let Me Count the Ways," 86f. Some early modern Mexican penitential examples are in S. Marcos, "Indigenous Eroticism and Colonial Morality in Mexico: The Confession Manuals of New Spain," *Numen* 39 (1992): "Did you lie with your wife making use of the proper entry? Or did you take her by the back way thus committing the nefarious sin?" (157) (1565); "Have you sinned with a woman while she took the position of an animal on all fours, or did you put her like that, desiring to commit sin with her?" (164) (1697). See further P. Payer, *Sex and the Penitentials: The Development of a Sexual Code, 550–1150* (Toronto, 1984), 29f.

[33] A. Edwardes, *Erotica Judaica: A Sexual History of the Jews* (New York, 1967), 179. Unfortunately, the author does not give a specific reference.

profound public proskynesis was a daily matter. Rowson, for instance, has recently turned up an early Islamic rule regarding the *mukhannath* or effeminate, to the effect "that one should pray behind a *mukhannath* only in cases of necessity"; that is, the danger was that the latter would attempt to seduce another orant by extending his buttocks.[34] Certainly the deep, public, prostrations of the Islamic *salaat* lent themselves to comments of this type. Muhammad Ibn Malik, secretary to the king of Murcia (1124–1172) says so in one of his poems:

> I saw a shapely youth in the mosque. . . .
> Those who see him bending to pray say:
> 'All my desires are that he prostrate himself.'[35]

But *mutatis mutandis*, the same associations of sex and prayer postures must have been quite as widespread in Christendom, for example in the Western opposition to adopting the suggestive Byzantine rites of subordination. It remains for scholars to explore this area.

In the West, there was one interesting result of the conviction that while rulers had to represent their humility (for example, to a divinity), at the same time they had to show their equality to opposite numbers. This was the development of a welcoming ritual between rulers which involved their kneeling on both knees directly facing each other, perhaps each with his hands joined in prayer.[36]

However, clearly the most striking, or more available evidence of the link between sexuality and reverence comes from neither the Islamic nor the Christian canon, but from the world of medieval and early modern European Jewry. In the middle ages, a shifting war of ambivalences and anxieties already pitted asceticism and sensuality against each other, and in that war, the analogy between prayer postures and intercourse was taken for granted, a discourse that had apparently not yet been developed in

---

[34] E. Rowson, "The Effeminates of Early Medina," *Journal of the American Oriental Society* 111 (1991): 675.

[35] Cited in N. Roth, " 'Deal Gently with the Young Man': Love of Boys in Medieval Hebrew Poetry in Spain," *Speculum* 57 (1982): 28.

[36] In addition to an illustration in the *Nueva Coronica* of Guaman Poma de Ayala (1609), note the description of a picture, "het eikenhouten beeld in de Sint-Amanduskerk te Geel, dat het Doopsel in de Jordaan voorstelt, Christus en Sint Jan den Doper voor elkander knielen": S. Axters, *Geschiedenis van de Vroomheid*, vol. 4 (Antwerp, 1950), 264, with reference to L. Réau, *Iconographie de l'art chrétien*, vol. 2 (Paris, 1957), fasc. 2, 304, and to a reproduction in B. Knipping, *De iconografie van de Contra-Reformatie in de Nederlanden*, vol. 1 (Hilversum, 1939), 261, Abb. 181.

Christianity. Then in the eighteenth century, a critique of the pietistic Jewish sect of the Chasidim by David of Makov, active in Vilna, argues for a direct physical equivalence between sexuality and prayer among the Chasidim, and not just analogy. According to David:

> The Chasidim commit the sin of involuntary ejaculation at all times during their prayer, for they deliberately give themselves erections during prayer according to the commandment of Rabbi Israel Baal Shem [the founder of Chasidism], who said to them that just as one who engages in intercourse with an impotent organ cannot give birth, so one should be potent at the time of prayer and, in prayer, it is necessary to [unite] sexually with the Shekhina [the female emanation of God]. It is therefore necessary to move back and forth as in the act of intercourse.[37]

That this denunciation was not merely scurrilous is evident from a passage in the writings of the same Baal Shem Tov, founder of Chasidism:

> Prayer is a form of intercourse with the Shekhina and just as in the beginning of intercourse one moves one's body, so it is necessary to move one's body at first in prayer, but afterwards one can stand still without any movement when one unites with the Shekhina. The power of his movement causes a great arousal, for it causes him to think: "Why am I moving myself?" [And he answers himself:] "Because perhaps the Shekhina is actually standing in front of me." And from this great power, he comes to a great passion.[38]

Now, not for a moment should the substantial differences between Judaic and Christian traditions be overlooked; the reference to the Shekhina, the female emanation of God, as the object of desire, makes those differences evident enough: she is *not* the full equivalent of the Virgin Mary. It is just as important to note that, according to David Biale, in the medieval Kabbalistic tradition, the sexual relation of a (male) orant to his wife was distinct from the all-encompassing sexual relation to the godhead that emerges in the Chasidim texts.

---

[37] D. Biale, "Ejaculatory Prayer: The Displacement of Sexuality in Chasidism," *Tikkun* (July/August 1991): 21. See the same author's important *Eros and the Jews*, chap. 6. Bending regularly during public and private prayer is, of course, a standard behavior in orthodox Jewry to this day, and its link to sexual posturing is widely commented on, and indeed considered unexceptionable.

[38] Biale, "Ejaculatory Prayer," 88.

On the other hand, our analysis of performances should not give way to any presumed primacy of such theological considerations. For example, through much of the Christian and Jewish tradition under review, the question of whether a man should take pleasure in intercourse with his wife is at the center of theological discourse, and yet, as Biale concedes, such theological demands can have had little bearing on the quotidian joys of sexuality.[39]

What is to be stressed here is the fact that in this Judaic tradition stretching from the eleventh to the nineteenth century, while the problem of the linkage between prayer and bestial behavior may have been muted, a link between sexual performance and prayer was largely taken for granted. How could much the same constellation of concerns, and specifically, the same linkage between prayer on the one hand, bestiality and sexuality on the other, *not* have been present in mainstream Christianity?

Summary

In the previous pages, I have sought simply to lay the groundwork for a serious discussion of the common roots of solemnity and sexuality. To do that, it has been necessary to gloss over many of the fundamental problems that an analytically solid examination would address. I have made no distinction between male and female, for example, perhaps because I think that determining the spatiality of up-down in the worlds of sexuality and reverence is in some sense a task that takes us to something even more fundamental than sexual differentiation. Still, any consideration of such matters must have sexual differences as a focus, if for no other reason than that a woman — or a man — is *not* in fact dishonored by being sexually on bottom. Further, no account has been taken of age, which clearly must be a focus, for we have much information suggesting that in the European middle ages, only with a certain age did being gone down on become dishonorable.[40] Indeed, in the case of both women and young boys, their legal and customary dependent status enormously complicates a consideration of the linkage between religion and sexuality.

The utility of this paper lies not in such admittedly central details, but in the fact that it raises general questions about the meanings, many and single, of a common gesture, that of presentation or proskynesis. Three

---

[39] Biale, *Eros and the Jews*, 108f.
[40] Rocke, *Forbidden Friendships*.

theses for future research have emerged. First, it seems that revulsion for this posture can be traced back to the fact of low vertical position, that is, to a spatial fault rather than to notions of morality, sex differentiation, and so on. Second, observers have long noted that when we reproduce ourselves we look like (low) animals, a problem mirrored in the historic legal equation of sodomy and bestiality. Third, acts of reverence, prayer, and submission upon which all human order is based, have their roots in animal postures that long predate us. The mix of power and seduction, which is prayer and sex, we do to survive. Or, if we are optimistic, we may say: we practice them as if stooping to conquer.

The Talking Image:
An Attempt at Typology, Using Spanish
Sources of the Sixteenth Century*

Figure 29. Amerindian Priests Speaking with the Devil.
Woodcut from P. Cieza de León,
Parte primera de la crónica del Perú (Seville: M. de Montesdoca, 1553).

* This essay appeared previously in *Laienfrömmigkeit im späten Mittelalter*, ed. K. Schreiner (Munich, 1992), 283–308.

*The devil spoke with the priests, with the lords and with other people,
but not with everyone. [The natives] offered the devil all their property,
if he would appear to them. He appeared to them in a thousand ways,
and in the end he associated with everyone, very often and very intimately. And the simpletons became very dependent on the Gods speaking with man. And since they did not know that these [Gods] were demons, and from them they heard about things before they happened, they
all believe what was told them. And since [the devil] wished it, they offered up many men. And they carried a painted figure with them, [which
showed] how [the devil] showed himself to them for the first time. They
painted him on the gates, on tables, and in every part of the house. And
since he showed himself to them in a thousand vestments and forms, so
they painted him in the most different ways, and some [were] so ugly
and frightful, that our Spaniards were astonished. [The natives] on the
other hand did not consider them ugly. Thus because they believed in the
devil, [the natives], who thought of themselves as religious and faithful,
had arrived at the pinnacle of cruelty.*[1]

WHEN EUROPEANS BEGAN TO SETTLE IN AMERICA in the early sixteenth
century, they had to categorize the different societies so as to understand
them and, to a certain extent, so as to create a right of conquest. For
example, many explorers, settlers and writers undertook to distinguish
each people according to whether they practiced or did not engage in
homosexual behavior. Obviously, such categories in part sought to explain
how the Aztecs to the north and the Incas in South America, but also the
Maya in Central America, had developed the rich and complex cultures
that they possessed. Normally to label a culture "sodomitic" was equivalent to saying that it lacked polarity and hierarchy, principles, one assumed, that were central to a developed culture. Nevertheless, these three
obviously very powerful cultures actually built same-sex behavior right into
their ritual practices, and even tolerated the practice among their subjects.
Cieza in Peru noted that the devil approved of male homosexual behavior
so as to be sure that there would always be young men to take part in

---

[1] "Hablando el diablo con los sacerdotes, con los señores y con otros, pero no á
todos": Francisco López de Gómara, *Historia general de las Indias*, Biblioteca de autores
españoles [hereafter *BAE*] 22 (Madrid, 1946), 444. My thanks to Sabine MacCormack
and Jeffrey Russell for reading and commenting upon an early version of this chapter.

those rites that required "sodomy."[2] Obviously, it was difficult for the Spaniards to understand how these peoples had achieved what they had.

However in the present paper I want to describe a second such category, which deals precisely with this devil. Different from the previous one, this categorization did not give the Iberians any right to conquest at all. When I read the Spanish chroniclers, historians, and correspondents at those points where they introduce the different tribes, I have often been impressed with how often these authors categorize by saying that this or that tribe "speak [hablar] with the devil," (not vice versa!), or that it did so before the Spanish conquest. It is not said that other tribes did *not* speak with the devil, but the impression is always left that certain people had, but others had not regularly spoken with the devil. I want to say immediately that this is a Spanish and not a native classification. The Spaniards prayed to God and the saints; one did not say that they spoke with God. But certain Americans spoke with the devil, the word "prayed" seldom being used.[3]

I have not yet found such a classification in Europe, although the idea that the Romans and other early gentiles had spoken with the devil is not at all absent from the sources.[4] Here I would simply like to describe and organize what Spaniards had to say in their sixteenth- and seventeenth-century writings about Americans speaking with the devil. In concluding, I will make some observations linking this classification to certain ideas

---

[2] Pedro de Cieza de León, *Crónica del Perú*, 3 parts in 3 vols. (Lima, 1984–1987), 1:198–200 (part 1, chap. 64).

[3] Acosta's observation that the Incas were accustomed to "hacer oración a Viracocha" is an exception: José de Acosta, *Historia natural y moral de las Indias*, in *Obras*, BAE 73 (Madrid, 1954), 144 (V, 4). No source says that speaking with the devil was "le trait caractéristique de toutes les sociétés indigènes," as claimed by C. Bernand and S. Gruzinski, *De l'idolâtrie. Une archéologie des sciences religieuses* (Paris, 1988), 34. S. MacCormack also picked up on devils speaking to the indigenous peoples: *Religion in the Andes: Vision and Imagination in Early Colonial Peru* (Princeton, 1991), 56–58, 92ff. For possible aboriginal backgrounds to this colonial phenomenon, see J. Paz, "The Vicissitude of the Alter Ego Animal in Mesoamerica: An Ethnohistorical Reconstruction of Tonalism," *Anthropos* 90 (1995): 445–65.

[4] In the important chapter "Maneras de comunicación de los espiritus con los hombres," Las Casas cites Valerius Maximus's description of the talking statue of Fortuna in Rome: Bartolomé de Las Casas, *Apologética historia sumaria*, 2 vols. (Mexico City, 1967), 1:518–22 (III, 99). The apologia of Justin Martyr and Plutarch's *Lib. de Trac. re.* (cap. "cur cessaverit Pithias fundere oracula") are similarly cited by Acosta, *Historia*, 153 (V, 12). See also Gonzalo Fernández de Oviedo, *Historia general y natural de las Indias*, 5 vols., BAE 117–121 (Madrid, 1959), 4:221 (XXXIII, 47).

about cultural development. In the body of the paper I intend to determine if the representations themselves, to which the natives talked, seemed to the Spaniards to be of any particular type.

I begin by commenting on certain expressions, and especially on the term "the devil." The seventeenth-century Jesuit José Acosta says that the devil had left the old world once Christianity had emerged triumphant, just as idolatry itself was annihilated "in the largest and most noble part of the world." Then it moved to America, as did the devil. He came to America and became its absolute master.[5] As Las Casas once determined by a process of elimination, this and no other is the devil or the demon of our sources.[6] For such authors it is this one and only enemy of the human race who had settled in America and become its monarch. Thus he appears to be a Manichean if not fully equal competitor of the divine ruler of Europe. Obviously such a single and personalized Prince of Darkness, and thus the European devil, was unknown to the natives. They rather spoke with Gods, who could bring them good *and* bad, and as Calancha says, only the wizards among them knew that their helper was actually Satan.[7]

How then did the Spaniards discover this devil in the New World? European Christians imagined the devil as a God that deceived and hurt people. So in the New World they "discovered" a God or Gods that, according to the natives, tricked them. The Aztecs named this God Tlacatecolotl[8] and the Maya named him Xibilba.[9] The Incas named him Zupay and spat before they addressed him,[10] while the Tupinamba called him Ingange.[11] These then were the different names of the one and only Christian "devil."

Naturally one could link certain other native Gods with specific demons in the Christian tradition. Normally the Spaniards considered the many named native Gods as such demons rather than as a plural number

---

[5] Acosta, *Historia*, 140 (V, 1). See also Pierre Duviols, *La lutte contre les religions autochtones dans le Pérou colonial. 'L'extirpation de l'idolâtrie' entre 1532 et 1660* (Lima, 1971), 29.

[6] "Necesario es decir o temer que no habite allí ni responda otro alguno que sólo el diablo": Las Casas, *Apologética*, 1:527 (III, 100).

[7] Antonio de la Calancha, *Crónica moralizada*, 6 vols., continuing numeration (Lima, 1974–1981), 848 (II, 11).

[8] Juan de Torquemada, *Monarquia Indiana*, 3 vol. (Mexico City, 1969), 2:81.

[9] Pedro Sánchez de Aguilar, *Informe contra idolorum cultores* (Merida, 1937), 143.

[10] Duviols, *Lutte*, 37.

[11] Hans Staden, *Wahrhaftige Historia* (1557) (Kassel, 1978), pt. 2, chap. 7.

of devils.[12] The Nicaraguans were told that their different "idols" were images of the demons who had been expelled from heaven, and thereafter wandered about in the night.[13] But it was the Prince of Evil who spoke with the Americans and misled them, rather than some such specific member of that empire. In the early seventeenth century the Jesuit Bernabé Cobo wrote: "Once one has carefully examined the rites and ideas of these Indians, I believe that most of them have the same customs and notions as those of the Romans. And this is not surprising, because the ones and the others have the same master."[14]

A second point can only be mentioned here. There are certain indications that some Spaniards believed that the New World possessed a group of native demons different from those of the Old World, that is, a distinct group of servants of the one devil. Thus it looked not only as if the old Roman Gods had moved here just as had the devil himself; there were American demons, for example, those of the sun and moon living at Lake Titicaca, who spoke with each other through embassies of their priesthoods.[15] According to the title of a chapter in the *Commentaries* of Garcilaso de la Vega, it was actually "the demons *of Peru*" whose fate it was to be forced into silence by the missionaries.[16] In Mexico there are even signs of a competition not only between God and Satan, but between European and native demons. Yet in this northern cultural world as well, the European demons were victorious over the American ones.[17]

---

[12] E.g., Tezcatlipoca and Jupiter "es un mismo Demonio": Torquemada, *Monarquia*, 2:40.

[13] "Et simulachra illa, quibus ipsi humano sanguine litant, praestigiatorum daemonum imagines esse, qui ob superbiam e sedibus aethereis disiecti, ad antra sunt tartarea detrusi. Unde noctu exeuntes . . .": Petrus Martyr de Anghera, *De orbe novo decades octo*, in *Opera* (Graz, 1966), 209 (VI, 4). The nocturnal spirits (Staden: Teufelsgespenste) are often named *duendes* and tied to the idea of a fleeting vision. In one case a *duende* is equated to a *demonio* (Sánchez de Aguilar, *Informe*, 114), in another to a succubus ("i toda el ánima tenían en aquellas duendas los varones, acrecentándose la adoración por la sensualidad": Calancha, *Crónica*, 1065).

[14] "Pues los unos y los otros tuvieron un mismo maestro": Bernabé Cobo, *Historia del Nuevo Mundo*, in *Obras*, BAE 91–92 (Madrid, 1964), 2:147 (XIII, 1).

[15] Cobo, *Historia*, 2:193. Such conversations are seldom mentioned; obviously they may be compared to the European rite of *encuentro* between different statues of the Christian numina.

[16] "Enmudecieron los demonios del Perú con los Sacramentos de la Santa Madre Iglesia Romana": Garcilaso de la Vega, *Comentarios reales de los Incas*, in *Obras completas*, 3 vols. BAE 133–135 (Madrid, 1960–1963), 3:59 (pt. II, bk. i, chap. 30).

[17] The tension between native and European demons is pointed to in R. Trexler, "We Think, They Act: Clerical Readings of Missionary Theatre in 16th Century Mexi-

To summarize, according to the Spanish authors, the evil one to whom the natives spoke was *the* devil or his servants. Second, the natives said openly that the Gods with whom they discoursed were friendly and not always deceptive Gods. The Spaniards on the other hand considered all these divinities as local demons, who were perhaps native subjects of the one, originally European devil.

Let it be said up front that at the time of the conquests individuals may actually have talked to such local "demons," even if this paper does not intend to pursue this still-debated question. It is my own impression that in several parts of the Americas at the time of contact, a figure later called a nagual or a guardian spirit was present in native consciousnesses, an animal or astral alter ego natives used to protect themselves, and in some very early sources, that figure is identified with the devils who converse with natives, the actual subjects of this paper.[18] While this chapter limits itself strictly to the devils who talk, its content will surely contribute as well to the nettlesome problem of whether the nagual, so well documented in the later colonial period, was in fact in place before the conquest.

Now we should put in place the historical framework of our discussion of the discussions with the devil, as it emerges from the narrative sources for the New World. Let us begin with the end of the fifteenth century. In the descriptions of the voyages of Columbus, the Spanish view is clear that some of the island and coastal peoples had no true relations with the devil, and that was so because they were in a pre-image stage of development: "At the beginning of the world there were no idols," Acosta said.[19] The very early authors Ramon Pané and Bartolomé de Las Casas,

---

co," in my *Church and Community, 1200–1600: Studies in the History of Florence and New Spain* (Rome, 1987), 592, n. 61.

[18] See e.g., Petrus Martyr, *De orbe novo*. Herrera (c. 1600), Vetancourt (c. 1594), Nicolaus de León (1611), and Alarcón (1629) all link talking devils to these native spirits: cited in D. Brinton, *Nagualism: A Study in Native American Folk-lore and History* (Philadelphia, 1894), 4–6. Most recently on this problem, see J. Paz, "The Vicissitude of the Alter Ego Animal in Mesoamerical: An Ethnohistorical Reconstruction of Tonalism," *Anthropos* 90 (1985): 445–65.

[19] Acosta, *Historia*, 146 (V, 6). Abstractly, Acosta also names the Peruvian worship of the sun, thunder, rivers, etc. as "idolatry," but concedes that one cannot properly talk about idolatry without idols. And he mentions first off the voice of the devil, when he discusses representations or "idols": *Historia*, 140–52 (V, "On Idolatry"). Further Felipe Guaman Poma de Ayala, *El Primer Nueva Corónica y Buen Gobierno*, 3 vols. (Mexico City, 1980), 1:70, where it is explained how the demons first came to the area of Titicaca: the second Inca — Sinchi Rocha — ordered the people to make idols and give them offerings. The devil then immediately took them over and spoke.

as well as later ones, thought that although the devil could *always* express himself, if only through natural objects, humans on the other hand could only speak with the devil, which is to say that true discourse or a *platica de conversación* with the devil only began once men made anthropomorphic figures, into which the devil could insert himself.[20] Second, priestly fraud was greater in a pre-image state than it was later. About 1557 the German Hans Staden told how the priests of the Brazilian Tupinamba tribe claimed that they could inject the speaking God into a rattle. Once he himself knew better, he wrote:

> Wie ich nu das erste mal unter sie kam, und sie mir darvon [den Rasseln], sagten, meynte ich es were ettwan eyn Teuffels gespenste, dann sie sagten mir offtmals wie die dinger sprechen. Wie ich nun in die hütten kam, da die Weissager inne waren, welche die dinger solten sprechen machen, musten sie sich alle nider setzen. Aber wie ich den betrüg sahe, gieng ich zur hütten hinaus, gedachte, wie eyn armes verblentes volck ist das.[21]

Images could begin to talk in the following ways. Someone might notice that a tree swayed differently from the others, and therefore had a spirit. This tree would be cut down and then sculpted into the form of a

---

[20] The devil "hablava y tenía platica de conversación": Sánchez de Aguilar, *Informe*, 114. Naturally, my hypothesis is not expressed so sharply, but on the other hand, no source speaks of a conversation of these peoples with a God without anthropomorphic, even if ugly, pictures. Cf. the words of the English explorer Samuel Purchas: "These people wholly worshippe the Devill, and oftentimes have conference with him [!], which appeareth unto them in most ugly and monstrous shape": cited in James A. Boon, *Other Tribes, Other Scribes* (Cambridge, 1982), 165. The practical definition of idolatry communicated by Christopher Columbus to the Spanish monarchs in 1496 is in Ramón Pané, *Antigüedades de los Indios* (Mexico City, 1974), 89; further on Cuba, where "ni idolo, ni estatua" was found, see Las Casas, *Apologética* 2:178 (III, 167).

[21] The priests (Paygi) travel about once each year "und geben für, wie das eyn geyst sei bei jnen gewesen, welcher weit her von frembden örtern kommen were, hette jnen maacht geben, das alle die rasselen Tammaraka, welche sie wollen, sollen sprechen und macht bekommen wo sie es umb bitten solle er gewehret sein." Naturally everyone wants his Maraka to have this power, and at a great feast, after gifts have been presented, a priest wants "jnen die gewalt uberlifferen das si sprechen sollen." The *piache* takes each Maraka and says: "Nee kora, nun rede, und laß dich hören, bistu darinne. Dann redet er kleynlich, und gerad eyn wort das man nicht wol mercken kan ob es die rassel thu, oder ob er es thue. Und das ander volck meynet, die rassel thu es. Aber der warsage thuts selbs. ... Wenn nun der warsager Paygi auß allen rasseln götter gemacht hat ..., begert von jme alles was jme von nöten ist, gleich wie wir den warhafftigen Gott bitten. Das sein nu jre götter. ... Wie ich nu ...": Staden, *Wahrhafte Historia*, pt. 2, chap. xxiii.

man, in order to keep this spirit and to maintain its utterances.[22] Second, images might be the result of dreams. An early student of things Hispaniolan said that the natives made figures in cotton of the figures in their dreams, which were then converted into wood or stone.[23] Finally, at the time of a death, a desire to maintain family or political memories might be fulfilled by funeral statues of relatives or leaders. Such likenesses would then be possessed by the devil, who slyly hoped to win for himself in perpetuity those honors and presents which were given to the just-dead person.[24]

These gentiles really had no way to talk with the devil other than through making such likenesses. There are exceptions in our sources, but in general it is assumed that humans could talk with the devil, or he could make himself understood to them, only after the devil, who had no body, as the Franciscan Torquemada noted,[25] entered into a human figure made by humans. It is doubtless interesting that the Jesuit Acosta saw a great difference in this regard between the Incas and the Aztecs. The Mexicans were "worse idolaters," because they were completely dependent on images in their devotions, whereas the Incas honored not only images, but also natural objects, from the sun down to the smallest river.[26] What remains decisive for our purposes, however, is that Acosta finds the talking devil in the image and not in nature. The Spaniards thought that the embodiment or visualization of the divinities was the precondition for discussion with them. To judge from their descriptions of their contacts with the Carib, the Iberians believed that mutual discourse with the devil began with this so-called idolatry.[27]

Now we should explain how, according to the Spaniards and other than through their own iconoclasm, this phenomenon came to an end in

---

[22] Pané, *Relación*, 41 (19); cf. Las Casas, *Apologética*, 1: 634–35 (III, 120).

[23] Petrus Martyr, *De orbe novo*, 72, 74 (dec. I, chap. 9).

[24] Acosta, *Historia*, 152 (V, 11).

[25] Torquemada, *Monarquia*, 2:67–68.

[26] "La idolatría de los Mejicanos fué más errada y perniciosa que la de los Ingas ... porque la mayor parte de su adoración e idolatria se ocupaba en idolos y no en las mismas cosas naturales": Acosta, *Historia*, 143, also 141, 145, 149.

[27] I continue to refer to statues: it is often said that visionaries have their imaginings painted afterwards, but not that these paintings talk. A true exception is that more than once it is said that the devil spoke from a snake, "as in paradise to Adam and Eve": Calancha, *Crónica*, 839. Julio Caro Baroja, *Las formas complejas de la vida religiosa* (Madrid, 1978), 51–76 has much of interest on how the devil actualizes himself in forms, but alas does not relate that to speech.

the New World, and when the devil and the natives stopped talking with each other. In the very first sources it is claimed that the native divinities in their statues were forced into silence merely by the presence of a cross or by a picture of the Virgin.[28] But after a while a more spiritual or ecclesiastical idea made itself felt, whose classical expression is given by the famous historian of the Inca, the clerk Garcilaso de la Vega (1609). Complete silence was brought about with the entrance and distribution of the Christian sacraments. Garcilaso said that perhaps the devil had talked with the natives before the sacraments, but that thereafter he was disempowered, and no longer spoke. I cite El Inca:

> The demons who had once associated with the pagans so easily ... lost the power of public speech. ... The idols lost the power of public speech and from then on could only speak in secret, and then only seldom with the great witches who were their ongoing servants. ... The difficulty [for the natives] was general. ... [The natives] feared and respected the Spaniards more and more from day to day. They were the people who had the power to silence their oracles.[29]

After that, Garcilaso continues elsewhere, the native authorities read entrails, watched birds and sun positions, etc. But "they did not ask the devil because, as we have seen, all over the empire he had lost the power of speech in that moment when the sacraments of our holy mother church of Rome appeared."[30] (As will be seen later, in the meantime Christian pictures or numina had gained the power of speech in America.)

Thus in general, Christian authors though that people could talk with the devil from the time that they spoke idolatrously or with human figures, and until the time in the Conquest when the sacramental rites, or still earlier figures like a cross or a picture of the Virgin that spoke, became parts of the moral or physical landscape. Then the devil became quiet, and after that the priests stopped putting questions to the devil. It

---

[28] "Y que los dichos del demonio son falsos y sin fundamento: cuyas engañosas respuestas han cessado. Y por todas partes donde el sancto evangelio se predica, y se pone la cruz, se espanta, y huye: y en público no osa hablar, ni hazer más que los salteadores que hazen a hurto y en oculto sus faltos": Cieza, Crónica, 1:160 (I, 49). In 1611, it is said, thirty-seven crosses were put in thirty-seven American adoratorios: Calancha, Crónica, 741. Holy water and hosts were also used to this end: Gómara, Historia, 450–51.

[29] Garcilaso, Comentarios, 3:59 (pt. II, bk. i, chap. 30).

[30] Garcilaso, Comentarios, 4:143 (II, viii, 10).

is as if Old World Christians before their images spoke with God or the saints, whereas natives of the New World before their images spoke with the devil.[31]

Garcilaso de la Vega, however, tries to prove that within this age of talking to the devil, and thus before the triumph of the cross and without silencing heaven, the Incas had taken a huge cultural and social step forwards. First of all, according to Garcilaso, all adoration of earthy or unclean things such as animals, vegetables, and minerals had been forbidden to the conquered within the Inca empire.[32] For instance, the Inca Pachacuti destroyed the "idol" of the Huancas because the idol was a dog. But the same Pachacuti allowed a tribe to keep an idol of a man, through which, he said, a talking devil gave out his commands and answered the questions of the tribe. This figure was "a talking oracle," Garcilaso said, and "that was not at all in conflict with the idolatry of the Inca."[33]

The Inca had taken a second forward step, according to Garcilaso. Even if they still honored the noble sun and the mummies of their dead rulers (huacas), they were already in a position to give up all that "idolatry." Garcilaso maintained that the Inca aristocrats, the orejones, were already aware of the true, invisible God. Without the gospel they obviously did not know him, and thus if already corporeally, they could not talk with this "unknown God"[34] verbally:

> They made emotive signs of reverence: the shoulders held high,
> head and whole body deeply inclined, eyes directed first high
> toward heaven and then low toward earth, the open hands lift-
> ed up above the shoulders, kissing the air . . .[35]

---

[31] Certain "heretical" inhabitants of Peru made this comparison: "que como los Cristianos tienen imágenes, i las adoran, así se pueden adorar sus guacas, o idolos, o piedras que ellos tienen, i que las imágenes son los idolos de los Cristianos . . .": Calancha, Crónica, 857–58 (II, 12).

[32] Garcilaso, Comentarios, 3:59 (pt. II, bk. i, chap. 30). Garcilaso calls reverence toward "unnatural" but also not anthropomorphic forms "the first idolatry": Comentarios, 2:19 (I, i, 9).

[33] "Era oráculo hablador, y no contradecía la idolatría de los Incas, y desecharon el perro, porque no consintieron adorar figuras de animales": Garcilaso, Comentarios, 2: 206–7 (I, vi, 10).

[34] "Dios no conocido," in the sense of the unseen opposite to the visible sun: Garcilaso, Comentarios, 2:43–45 (I, vi, 2), 232–37 (I, vi, 30–32), 2:337 (I, ix, 4). But this also means that they did not know any of this God's Christian figures.

[35] ". . . que entre los Incas y sus vasallos eran ostentaciones de suma adoración y reverencia, con las cuales demonstraciones nombraban al Pachacamac, y adoraban al sol,

There is therefore a level of development before Christianity in which one perhaps still talks verbally with the devil but already also speaks bodily with the true God.[36] Garcilaso, who did not know our modern ideas of "body language," described these movements instead as a "spiritual reverence" to the true God.[37] Without the Christian message, this upper class (which like the Spanish upper class left handwork to others) had renounced the worst type of idolatry, but had also discovered, obviously with the help of their priests, one type of true divine conversation — the corporeal. The basic argument of his monumental *Royal Commentaries of the Indies* (1609) was that before the Spaniards, less a people than a class had brought culture to the peoples of the Andes.

Garcilaso claimed that the Inca emperors had actually already begun to destroy other images as they began to localize the true God. Pachacamac, as the true God was called in the Quechua language, then came to be worshipped in a temple of this name south of Lima.[38] It was to be expected, of course, that the devil shamelessly seeped into the corners of this temple so as to win this reverence for himself. But how he did this, according to Garcilaso, reflects the class-informed thought of the author. The devil at the site of Pachacama began to converse only with the Inca and his court; he referred all other conversations to his subject-demon Rimac. And in fact an image-God of this name Rimac (=Lima), whose statue had human

---

y reverenciaban al rey y no más": Garcilaso, *Comentarios*, 2:43 (I, ii, 2); a similar description in *Comentarios*, 2:232 (I, vi, 30).

[36] Other mestizo historians of Garcilaso's time discovered this ideal type. For instance, the Texcoco author Ixtlilxóchitl maintains that even before 1521 the Texcoco philosopher king Nezahualcoyotzin had begun to worship the "Dios no conocido," because he was repelled by the "idolatry" of the Aztecs, whose Gods in fact did not talk: Fernando de Alva Ixlilxóchitl, *Historia de la nación Chichimeca*, in *Obras Históricas*, 2 vols. (Mexico City, 1975–1977), 2:125 (45), and further 136–37 (49).

[37] "Adoración mental": Garcilaso, *Comentarios*, 2:236 (I, vi, 32). "El verdadero sumo Dios y Señor que crió el cielo y la tierra": *Comentarios*, 2:43 (I, ii, 2).

[38] Garcilaso's development theory is significant; if this sacred place was truly without an image, which Calancha also says ("No tenía este Dios Idolo ni estatua": *Crónica*, 924), is debated. E.g., already in 1534 it is said that "the Indians have this Pachacama as their God and they offer him much gold and silver. And it is generally known, that the demon is in this idol and talks to those who go there to ask him a question": Pedro Sancho, *An Account of the Conquest of Peru* (New York, 1917), 97. Cf. also Francisco de Xerez, *Verdadera relación de la conquista del Perú* (1534) (Madrid, 1985), 124: Near to Pachacama there was "un gran sabio, el cual los indios creían que sabía las cosas por venir, porque hablaba con aquel ídolo y se las decia," and *Verdadera relación*, 136–37, the description of the image by Miguel de Estete.

form, was called: "he who speaks."[39] Here Garcilaso clearly indicates
that both Gods spoke, but that the cult shrine of Pachacamac was reserved
for aristocratic "spiritual reverence," while the cultic shrine of Rimac was
for the ritual prayers of the lower classes, who received in exchange from
the God what Garcilaso scornfully dismissed as "flattering rigamarole."[40]
On the other hand, what the unseen Pachacamac imparted to the Inca
leaders was obvious. The empire itself was the gift of knowing him. In Calancha's simile, the place was "the Athens of this monarchy, and the
synagogue of these pagans."[41]

Thus for Garcilaso there was no success if all Gods fell silent, but the
greatest success if an aristocracy, even before the Christian gospel, understood that one could speak with and receive from a God without his simultaneous presence in a figure. Naturally an Inca *could* speak with the figures
of the devil; each Inca had the ability *ex officio* to discourse with the main
God (or *huaca*) of each region in the empire.[42] But according to Garcilaso, this better class knew that *the unseeable divinity saw and answered.*

Yet it appears that space was also central for the true, still unseen God:
the space of Pachacamac, where the unseeable God was honored, as well
as those spaces, where the devil received adoration. Garcilaso took it for
granted that "the places where the devil spoke to the wizards and priests
and to his other worshippers . . . were decorated with gold and silver, because they were considered holy places."[43] The Augustinian Antonio de
Calancha also understood how central sacral space was. At one point, as
he was about to describe the installation of a new statue of Mary in the
neighborhood of Lima, he wrote:

> It is worthwhile to consider, that all miracle images of the Virgin,
> which heaven and the church have given us, are in places and lo-
> cations, where the devil was obviously heard, seen and adored.[44]

---

[39] "El que habla": Garcilaso, *Comentarios*, 2:233 (I, vi, 30). "Porque a su grandeza y
señorío no era decente hablar con hombres bajos y viles, sino con reyes y grandes señores, y que al ídolo Rimac, que era su criado, mandaría que hablase a la gente común, y
respondiese a todo lo que le preguntasen": *Comentarios*, 2:235 (31).

[40] "El famoso ídolo hablador . . . de muchas bachillerías y grandes lisonjas": Garcilaso, *Comentarios*, 2:337 (I, ix, 4).

[41] Calancha, *Crónica*, 924–25.

[42] Guaman Poma, *Nueva Corónica*, 91, 234–35.

[43] Garcilaso, *Comentarios*, 3:66 (II, i, 35).

[44] Calancha, *Crónica*, 1259 (III, 4). Another comparison: "Los Indios . . . traian un
Idolo en su egército a quien ofrecian el despojo de sus enemigos. . . . Entraron . . . nues-

It was of course necessary for noble Christian priests to discover where and how nobles were to speak with divinities, just as the noble gentile priests had to. It appears that once the Christian priests had discovered such places, they could bring their own statues to speech. The conversation with heaven, therefore, continued at this newest level.

After we identified the devil, we gave some historical perspective for the talking devils and their devotees. Now we are at a point where some fundamental information about the phenomenon itself of talking with the devil can be imparted. Note to begin that a partial answer has already been found for a first fundamental question — where these conversations actually took place. Fundamentally, the devil could speak in all possible forms and places. As a ghost in the night, "there in one moment, vanished the next," one could hear him speak in the countryside. He could live in a tree, a brook, at the foot of a cross, like the Spanish cult figures that people the work of William Christian.[45] Cieza de León said that in the countryside, even Spaniards had seen the devil dressed as an Indian.[46] And it was almost common there to see natives talking with the devil. Cieza wrote: "I myself have heard the Indians when they talked with the demon."[47] Perhaps the most notable case with such Spanish evidence comes from the time of the Inca uprising of Manco Capac in 1536. "Just look at how my God speaks with me," Manco raved to the Spanish prisoner Francisco Martin. Then on being freed, Martin later told his conationals that he had himself actually heard the voice of the demon, when the devil answered a question that Manco Capac had put to him.[48]

But the utterances of the devil that were of social importance, and especially the mutual discussions at this level, did not take place in the countryside independently, outside all context. All of them were at least brought into relation to the ceremonial centers or "holy places," in Garcilaso's words, where the priests of the devil also lived.[49] It should be said

---

tros religiosos, i la Madre de Dios . . . , i aniquilando el falso idolo . . . , i dedicando las dádivas a la Virgen se vido sin tributos de sangre umana la infernal tiranía": *Crónica*, 1250.

[45] William A. Christian, Jr., *Apparitions in Late Medieval and Renaissance Spain* (Princeton, 1981); Cieza, *Crónica*, 2:85 (II, 28).

[46] Cieza, *Crónica*, 2:85 (II, 28).

[47] Cieza, *Crónica*, 2:122–23 (II, 41).

[48] Cobo, *Historia*, 2:199 (XIII, 20); cf. Pedro Pizarro, *Relación del descubrimiento y conquista del Peru* (Lima, 1978), 81–83.

[49] See however Blas Valera, who describes certain hermit priests who more often

right off that it was an Inca custom to bring the main cult image of each conquered people to Cuzco as a hostage.[50] But a highly significant example of decentralization is the Cuzcenian custom on the feast of Citua of sending certain priests out "to all the places where the devil speaks." They brought gifts to the different Gods of the locales, and then after listening to the oracles' utterances, they brought its substance back to Cuzco.[51] Thus even if the Gods themselves might not have been brought to the capital, their messages were delivered. I found precisely such a dynamic between the local divinities and empire in Italian "evocations" of the fifteenth century.[52]

The second question — what was said to "the devil" and how he responded — is perhaps the easiest to answer. According to the Iberian sources, the natives' "talking with the devil" was not so much a liturgical performance of self-abasement and praise, and also not really dominated by requests for favor, "gleich wie wir den warhafftigen Gott bitten," to cite the confident words of a German in Brazil.[53] "Talking with the devil" really referred to the opening of a mutual conversation, the essence of which was fate: what was the future, and how could the orant exploit fate?[54] It must be said, however, that the Spaniards did not think the natives showed much curiosity about cosmological matters, and that what the devil did tell them, he had from God. Cieza remembered: "I very often asked the natives if they understood that the world would come to an end. They laughed. They know little about such matters, and what they do know is only that which God allowed the devil to tell them."[55]

However in truth, the Christians did not at all hesitate to express their respect for the devil's knowledge. He knew all about the stars and everything about Rome and Jerusalem, the sources not seldom and quite freely admitted. After all, the well-known predictions that are supposed to have

---

spoke with the devil in isolated places "que no en poblado"; *Relación de las costubres antiguas de los naturales del Pirú*, BAE 209 (Madrid, 1968), 164.

[50] Garcilaso, *Comentarios*, 2:163 (V, 12).

[51] Garcilaso, *Comentarios*, 2:253 (I, vii, 6).

[52] R. Trexler, *Public Life in Renaissance Florence* (New York, 1980), 4.

[53] Staden, *Wahrhaftige Historia*, pt. 2, chap. 23.

[54] See Las Casas' classic indications above, n. 4: also Hernando Ruiz de Alarcón, *Aztec Sorcerers in Seventeenth Century Mexico. The Treatise on Superstitions by H. R. A.*, ed. M. Coe and G. Whittaker (Albany, 1982), 81: "children, riches, long life, family and health."

[55] Cieza, *Crónica*, 2:78 (II, 26).

been made in North and South America, according to which white men from across the ocean would conquer the natives, derived from such devilish knowledge.[56] These were the questions of "the devil's" faithful. Like the Christians, native Americans wanted to know the future which would directly affect them. Rulers sought information that would allow them to deal with political and military crises, those who worked the land on the other hand sought information about children and maize, continued life, and death.

According to the Spaniards, the devil's answers had in general served the indigenous people well; I will later show that certain Spanish authors sought to explain that by reference to contracts they had with the devil. But how were the Americans served by the devil? What should first be emphasized is that the Spaniards always imagined the relations between the natives and the devil to be an intellectual and not an emotional tie.

The difference from the European experience in this regard was very great. Perhaps it can best be expressed by comparison. What always marked a miraculous Christian image was motion. Just as they do today, so then as well Christian images cried, laughed or grimaced, spoke, turned their heads, raised up their arms in welcome, etc. This motion in turn triggered feelings, and it was these sentiments that actually gave legitimacy to Christian figures.[57] According to the Spaniards, here in America our devil was active only with his voice. He neither physically moved, nor were his orants emotionally moved.[58] In short, the sources leave the impression that the legitimation of this devil had nothing to do with the emotional conversion of an individual, but rather only with the socially successful fulfillment of a prophecy through intellection.

The third question about the structure of this phenomenon of talking with the devil is who, according to the Spaniards, talked with the Gods or devil. It should be said at once that the discourse is almost always about

---

[56] Gómara, *Historia*, 338; Petrus Martyr, *De orbe*, 74–75 (I, 9); Calancha, *Crónica*, 233–34; see also Guaman Poma, *Nueva Corónica*, 91. One person familiar with the matter explained that it was because the devil had long been an astrologer that he knew the future so well: Gonzalo Hernandez de Oviedo y Valdés, *Sumario de la natural historia de las Indias*, BAE 22 (Madrid, 1946), 482 (10).

[57] On the dynamics of Christian miracles, see e.g., Peter Brown, *Society and the Holy in Late Antiquity* (Berkeley, 1982), 103–52; on their legitimation, further in Trexler, *Church and Community*, 11–36.

[58] Thereagainst, the native priests changed their own faces to imitate the faces of the Gods; see the text below, at n. 72.

residents who "were called" to the task of talking with the devil. One can find sources in which old men and women had this charge,[59] which seems especially appropriate for talking with household divinities like Zemis or certain Huacas. In other cases it is said that certain "wise men" (Quechua: *amautas*) were so intimate with the devil that they themselves could tell the future.[60]

Such references to personal attributes remain exceptions, however. Normally the *consultores* and *consultoras*, as the Spaniards in the Andes named them,[61] are presented to us as if they were a type of corporation. What Gómara says about the Mexicans — "the devil spoke with the priests, with the lords and others, but not with everyone" — is universally applicable.[62] Let us begin with the lords. The Aztec emperors, all males, spoke regularly with the great Gods Huitzilopochtli and Tezcatlipoca in their temples in the capital.[63] In Peru the relation of rulers with the Gods was still closer. According to Gutierrez de Santa Clara it was actually an Inca, Topa Inga Yupangue, "who taught the Indians how one can speak with the demon,"[64] while Guaman Poma maintains that the wife of the first Inca, the "great witch" Mama Uaco, was just as important in this respect.[65] We have already seen how important the Incas were as conversational partners at the shrine of Pachacamac, but usually the Spaniards saw and heard the less lordly caciques talk with other images. Finally, the lords exercised the right to destroy statues that did not fulfill their promise, something not unknown in Europe.[66]

---

[59] Cieza, *Crónica*, 1:141–42, 147, 219 (I, 43, 44, 74); Rodrigo Hernández Principe, "Mitología Andina [1621]," *Inca* 1 (1923): 33, 39.

[60] Garcilaso, *Comentarios*, 2:354 (I, ix, 15).

[61] Hernández Principe, "Mitología," 27–39 et passim. The concept of the *sacerdotisa* was not unknown: Calancha, *Crónica*, 869, 1062, 1067.

[62] See the citation at the beginning of this paper.

[63] Bernal Díaz del Castillo, *Historia verdadera de la conquista de la Nueva España*, 2 vols. (Mexico City, 1968), 1:134–35, 331 (41, 108).

[64] "Fué el que enseñó a hablar a los indios con el demonio": Pedro Gutierrez de Santa Clara, *Historia de las guerras civiles del Perú*, BAE 166 (Madrid, 1963), 215.

[65] "Hablaua con los demonios. Esta dicha señora hacía hablar a las piedras y peñas": Guaman Poma, *Nueva Corónica*, 99. Irene Silverblatt adds much to our knowledge of the role of women in Inca religion. The translation of Acosta with which she introduces her book ("it is usually old women who speak with the devil") is, however, mistaken. Acosta refers only to men speaking with the devil: *Moon, Sun, and Witches. Gender Ideologies and Class in Inca and Colonial Peru* (Princeton, 1987), xvii; cf. Acosta, *Historia*, 172 (V, 26).

[66] Guaman Poma, *Nueva Corónica*, 93.

The other groups that spoke with the devil, according to Gómara, and far and away the largest, were the "organized priesthoods." The Spanish writers, who were mostly also priests, normally described the qualifications, liturgies, and abilities of these American priesthoods as if they were not really that different from their own. I have already hypothesized that the missionaries made such brotherly assumptions in Mexico as well.[67]

A case of common comportment by Christian priests and Venezuelan piaches, the most famous priests of Central America, which directly addresses the problem of talking with the devil, strengthens this hypothesis. Indeed, in the midst of describing these priests, our sources uniformly tell how the Dominican Pedro de Córdoba himself began to "talk with the devil." In the first years of the sixteenth century, the Dominican brother Tomas Ortiz gave witness to events. In great need, his colleague Pedro de Córdoba asked a *piache* if a Spanish ship would arrive soon. The piache immediately spoke with the devil, who promptly responded that a ship would soon enter the harbor. The *piache* passed the answer on to the friar, and the ship soon arrived. Thus the Christian priests tried to find out the future from the mouth of the devil. Indeed in a second case, Córdoba himself forced the devil to speak out through a *piache*. He directly struggled with the exorcised devil in Latin and Spanish until the *piache*, who was in a trance, as a mouthpiece of the devil proclaimed the Christian dogma of heaven without a mistake.[68] There was thus no doubt that the devil was very smart, and that the Christian priests, just like the native ones, could "speak with the devil."

It is clear by now that those who spoke with and those who spoke for the devil could be different persons. And with that distinction, the similarity between European and native priesthoods ends. It is true that in Christianity as well priests speak for the divinity, in that they repeat the words of Jesus. In the same religion as well, certain groups of religious people are not uncommonly looked upon as prophetic or as mouthpieces of the numina. But here in America the Gods often spoke through the mouths of ecstatic priests, who in the Spanish sources are presented to us as drunken or as hallucinating with coca (Peru) or the cabbage *cohoba* (His-

---

[67] Cf. R. Trexler, "Aztec Priests for Christian Altars. The Theory and Practice of Reverence in New Spain," in my *Church and Community*, 469–92.

[68] The report of Ortiz on both cases has apparently not survived, but it was copied by Peter Martyr, *De orbe novo*, 255–61 (VIII, 8–9); see further Gómara, *Historia*, 209; Las Casas, *Apologética*, 2:547 (III, 245); 1:520–21 (III, 99).

paniola).[69] That was not normative in Christendom, and here in America these "thousand types of false prophets"[70] presented a serious challenge to the intellectual authority of the European priests.

Thus a fourth question needs to be put to the material. Who actually spoke *for* the devil? An important chapter in the chronicle of Pedro de Cieza de León gives us context. At least in cases involving the main Gods, the priests who posed question to the images — elsewhere called *consultores* — were different from the priests who spoke for the single images. These latter were responsible for the defense and maintenance of such images, indeed they actually owned them.[71]

The Spaniards in Peru said that these spokespersons were "incorporated" in the image whose utterances they passed on,[72] and perhaps that was said because, as was often noted, as part of their reverence these priests sought to imitate the face of the images of their "devil," whom they had become.[73] It is not known if masks were used to accomplish that.[74]

Now comes the question as to when these conversations took place, and here again, the answer is rather certain. Normally the devil spoke only on holidays; exceptionally he spoke continually. In his list of the six main shrines of the Inca empire, for example, Cieza singled out the fifth,

---

[69] "Todos los que comen coca son hicheseros que hablan con los demonios, estando borracho o no lo estando": Guaman Poma, *Nueva Corónica*, 251; Pané, *Relación*, 35. J. Brown has described the ecstasies of the contemporary Italian nun Benedetta Carlini, who was a mouthpiece, with appropriately different voices, for various divinities: *Immodest Acts. The Life of a Lesbian Nun in Renaissance Italy* (New York, 1986), 59, 67, 111.

[70] Acosta, *Historia*, 152 (V, 11).

[71] Cieza, *Crónica*, 2:87–89 (II, 29); on the *consultores*, see Hernández Principe, "Mitología," 27–39 et passim.

[72] E.g., "Inés *Huaylla Jámoc* incorporada en la huaca *Collquillano*, y que daba sus respuestas": Hernández Principe, "Mitología," 28; see "Mitología," where such an *incorporada* is already dead; also 33: "consultora y soñadora," thus a distinction between one who puts a question and one who answers it, though in this case both united in the same person.

[73] "Encojendo sus onbros, meten las barbas en los pechos, haziendo grandes papos, quellos mismos pareçen fieros diablos comiençan a hablar con boz alta y entonada": Cieza, *Crónica*, 2:122 (II, 41). The Spaniards saw a link with the fact that the Americans painted their own persons "very ugly": Oviedo y Valdés, *Sumario*, 482 (10); the Franciscan Landa on the other hand said that certain Maya reshaped the skulls of their honored dead until they looked like the living: cited by C. Klein, "Masking Empire: The Material Effects of Masks in Aztec Mexico," *Art History* 9 (1986): 66.

[74] One is reminded of the medieval clerics who used masks in liturgical dramas — but not to pass on the utterances of the divinity. See further the emphasis placed on remembering the historic past, in Klein, "Masking."

Coropuna, because, he said, "the devil has spoken here much more freely than in the previously named shrines, because he has given a thousand answers continuously and not periodically, like the others."[75] Naturally it was otherwise with the conversations that the devil of the great images of state entered into. In Mexico City, for example, Moctezuma told the Spaniards that he and his priests had spoken almost daily with Huitzilopochtli and Tezcatlipoca, primary Gods of the city.[76]

These Mexicans, the so-called *Relazione* of 1525 had already proclaimed, see the devil in the figures that they made; so much was notorious.[77] What then did the talking devil look like? Almost always ugly, the Spaniards said, even if the natives themselves may have thought of them as beautiful.[78] Certain writers like Torquemada explained that happened because beauty was not the purpose of their creation. In his words, the natives simply made no effort to represent their Gods as beautiful.[79] Today we recognize that these cultures obeyed other norms, but the Europeans of that time had known for a long time, through their own pictures and visionaries, that the devil was in fact ugly.[80] And just as at home the Europeans tested for the devil in dreams and visions according to how he looked in paintings in the local church — at the feet of Sts. Michael and Bartholomew, Oviedo specified[81] — so in America they could recognize him.

---

[75] Cieza, *Crónica*, 2:85 (II, 28). Other places with continuing repetitions are in Calancha, *Crónica*, 738 and 1249 (Pacasmayo, where the devil also "visibly took part in the dances").

[76] See above, n. 62.

[77] "E cosa molto notoria che quelle genti vedeano il diavolo in quelle figure che essi facevano, e que tengono i loro idoli, e che il demonio si metteva dentro à quelli idoli e di lì parlava con esso loro": in José García Icazbalceta, ed., *Colección de Documentos para la Historia de México*, 2 vols. (Mexico City, 1858–1866), 1:387.

[78] In the sources the repulsion is constant, but I only found the comparison once: "Algun tan feas y espantosas, que se maravillaban nuestros españoles; pero ellos no lo tenia por feo": Gómara, *Historia*, 444. In his biography, Gómara has Cortés link the ugliness of the image to the lower class: "No os dan . . . estas cosas, no las duras piedras, no los maderos secos, no los frios metales ni las menudas semillas de que vuestros mozos y esclavos hacen con sus manos sucias estas imágines y estatuas feas y espantosas. . . . Adorais lo que hacen manos que no comeréis lo que quisan ó tocan": *Historia*, 353.

[79] Torquemada, *Monarquia*, 2:69 (VI, 36). In that way he answered the question of Columbus, if the Caribs kept certain sculptures "because of their beauty or to pray to them": cited in Pané, *Relación*, 89.

[80] The Revelations of Bridget of Sweden seem to have been the main source for this notion of the devil's ugliness; see S. Brigida di Svezia, *Le celesti rivelazioni* (Milan, 1960), 176, 178 (Rev. 2).

[81] Oviedo, *Sumario*, 484 (10).

They knew that the devils they saw in pictures were copies of those images which the natives had seen in their dreams, rivers and trees.[82] The face of the devil was "ugly," and therefore his figure was the same. And the uglier the image, Cobo even said, the readier was its devil to speak.[83]

The absence among the Iberians of a notion that the devil could in fact have taken a beautiful form, if only to the end of deceiving or seducing the natives, is striking, especially when one considers that the form that the devil took in ancient Rome had remained the basis of the European idea of beauty. The devil, that is, the pictures the natives prayed to, who obviously had responded very well to the questions and requests of the individual and collective faithful, was ugly. The Spaniards could not believe that the devil furnished any aesthetic satisfaction for the natives. But they saw that this ugliness had produced some truly powerful commonweals!

A second physical characteristic was that talking devils perhaps never assumed a flat form, but rather always a volumetric one, whether that of a monolith, a human, or a statue. So far I know of no histories of talking devils in the famous frescoes of the Maya, for instance. I think this is an important fact for this inquiry. After the Roman period, in which speech had been thoroughly identified with sculptures,[84] almost all talking or otherwise moving artificial figures of the European high and late middle ages were paintings and not sculptures. In the New World as in the pre-Christian era of the Old World, the devil always in fact took up room, even if he allegedly had no body.[85]

---

[82] For such tests in Spain, see Christian, *Apparitions*, 64–67; for Mexican visions, see Serge Gruzinski, "Délires et visions chez les Indiens du Mexique," *Mélanges de l'École française de Rome, Moyen Age, Temps modernes* 86 (1974): 445–80. For copies of dreams, see Petrus Martyr, *De orbe novo*, 74 (I, 9).

[83] "He notado una cosa particular, y es que los que tenían forma de animales y legumbres eran comúnmente más bien abrados e imitaban con más propiedad lo que significaban; per los de figura human tenían de ordinario tan feos y disformes gestos, que mostraban bien en su mala catadúra ser retratosa de aquel en cuya honra los hacían, que era el demonio; el qual debía de gustar de hacerse adorar en figuras mal agestadas, pues en las que éstas solía dar respuestas, eran las más fieras y espantosas": Cobo, *Historia*, 2:167 (XIII, 11).

[84] See the references above, n. 4. In the medieval Iconoclastic Controversy, sculptures were considered much more dangerous than paintings: D. Freedberg, "The Structure of Byzantine and European Iconoclasm," in *Iconoclasm*, ed. A. Bryer and J. Herrin (Birmingham, 1976), 170. See also Las Casas, *Apologética*, 1:529 (III, 100), for the rumor that Albertus Magnus "hobiese fabricado él la cabeza [del demonio] que dicen que respondía. . . ."

[85] That is why he used images: Torquemada, *Monarquia*, 2:67 (VI, 36).

According to the sources, the talking figures appeared in different media. The earliest sources, those from the Caribbean, already mention wood and stone figures, including kidney and gall stones.[86] The Peruvian sources add to the list the famous *huacas* or mummies of the Incas. And naturally hollow bones were found, and in them figures of humans were carved in black wax; these were kept by certain South American religious specialists (*homo*), who spoke with the devil.[87] Of course these talking images could be monumental, but also "not bigger than the fingers of a hand."[88] To this inventory come the few but famous statues of gold and silver. They were the goal of the conquerors' greed, but the Spaniards do not say that any single medium like gold or silver was more likely to trigger divine aurality.

Another question touches on the relative thickness of the materials. Because it is said so often that the devil seeped into holes so as to speak, one might think that the dictum of Las Casas — "Whatever the material, the statue or idol must necessarily be hollow" — has to be true.[89] Certainly it was easiest to discover deception in an image of this nature. From the most varied corners of the Iberian empire come stories of trick statues of the devil, first in Hispaniola. Columbus himself told how Christians having once broken into the house of a protesting cacique, the zemi that was kept there began to scream:

Then it was discovered that it had been made by artisans. It being hollow, a blowpipe or trumpet was slipped in underneath, which extended all the way to the other side of the house, camouflaged with leaves and branches. [On this corner] there was a person who uttered whatever the cacique wished when he wanted to speak through the blowpipe.[90]

---

[86] Pané, *Relación*, 34–35 (15).

[87] "Hablan con el demonio, y traen consigo su figura hecha de un huesso hueco, y encima un bulto de cera negra que acá ay": Cieza, *Crónica*, 1:307 (I, 117); Cobo, *Historia*, 2:225 (XIII, 34).

[88] Cobo, *Historia*, 2:167 (XIII, 11).

[89] "Cualquiera madera" is a variant on "cualquiera materia": Las Casas, *Apologética*, 1:523 (III, 100). Naturally the Spaniards often spoke of the devil found in corners, holes, etc.

[90] Cited in Pané, *Relación*, 89–90. Deception of the talking sculpture in Cozumel: Gómara, *Historia*, 305; in Peru: Duviols, *Lutte*, 31; in Brazil: Staden, *Wahrhaftige Historia*, chap. 23.

We recognize immediately a rhetoric akin to that of the Protestant reformers in Europe, who in the coming years would also brag that they had
discovered the priestly and confraternal deceits of the Catholic figures.
Here in America the Catholics had the same complaints about the gentiles, which in Europe the Protestants raised against the Old Christians,
and often with the very same economic and political motivations. In the
case at hand the cacique insistently begged the Spaniards not to tell his
subjects the truth, for the talking zemi was, after all, the basis of their
obedience.[91]

But the devil was not found only in such hollowed figures. There is, for
example, the case of the talking monoliths which were supposed to replicate Mexican ruler portraits. In two extensive descriptions of the late sixteenth century it is told how the emperor Moctezuma II (d. 1521) and a
colleague had ordered two huge statues with their true images to be placed
in the center of Tenochtitlan. But neither the one nor the other stone figure would allow itself to be brought into the city. "Speaking from inside
the statue," the devil protested loudly and repeatedly, until the emperor
himself gave up his plan to have his portrait done outside the city.[92]
Thus here and elsewhere the devil spoke from a stone which had no cavity.

In the materials used up till now, there is much that contributes to an
explanation of the classification "talk with the devil." Already on the
table are two apparently contradictory Spanish claims. On the one side
the conversations with the devil, quite intellectively, are supposed to have
contributed to planning life, but on the other side these religions are supposed to have been of a quite domestic, intimate type. We might therefore
conclude that this type of devotion was proper for the so-called "private
idols," which Motolinía, an early missionary in Mexico, had contrasted
with "public idols."[93] And we recall the Peruvian, who very intimately
"spoke with his demon" to ask forgiveness: Only force made him go to

---

[91] "Porque con aquella astucia a todos los tenía en obediencia": cited in Pané, Relación, 89.

[92] Hernando Alvarado Tezozomoc, Cronica Mexicana (Mexico City, 1975), 662–67
(102); Diego Duran, Historia de las Indias de Nueva España e Islas de la Tierra Firme, 2
vols. (Mexico City, 1967), 2:485–90 (66); 245–46 (31); 275–80 (36); Acosta, Historia, 236
(VII, 23). Another case of a large boulder on an island in Lake Titicaca, which the people held in great honor, perhaps because "the devil conceals himself in it and talks with
them": Pedro Sancho, Account, 163.

[93] Toribio Motolinía, Memoriales e Historia de los Indios de la Nueva España, BAE 240
(Madrid, 1970), 213.

the catechism classes of the Christian priest.[94] These must be the "private idols."

But the Spaniards actually did not describe different levels of affect in the relations between the natives and their Gods; the claims made above are only apparently contradictory. In truth the Spaniards found this Indian intimacy rooted directly in the institution of a charismatic priesthood, which spoke for the devil. The sources thus leave the impression that through direct revelation from their talking priests, certain tribes had been able to construct astounding or at least functional world orders. Thus no routinization of charisma. These intimate official cultures, to use Bakhtin's term,[95] had made enormous intellectual strides without the printing press, and mostly without writing. But further: without a sacred book, the devil had constructed great empires through intimate conversations. Thus beneath the bravura of the conquerors lay an incomprehension of the successes of the conquered. At the end of this paper, I wish to pursue this idea somewhat further.

The Europeans' sense that the natives had an intimate familiarity with the devil makes itself felt in our sources, and most notably in those few which use the language of the European witch hunt to understand these American religions.[96] Rarest of all that language of witchcraft is any sexual content. In the very early reports of Peter Martyr,[97] and in the great chronicle of Calancha, one of the last of the Spanish conquest sources in America,[98] it is claimed that in *certain* areas incubi (Hispaniola) or succubi (among the Peruvian Huaraclla) could be found. Just as seldom do we encounter the idea of possession. One would have thought that priesthoods which in so many areas spoke for the devil would have been labeled possessed. But in fact only the Central American *piaches* were so described, and then only in the early text of Peter Martyr.[99]

Finally, contracts with the devil are mentioned in an occasional source

---

[94] Calancha, *Crónica*, 821.

[95] Naturally following Max Weber's concept; Mikhail Bakhtin, *Rabelais and His World* (Cambridge, MA, 1968).

[96] Although, as emphasized earlier, the sources for *European* witchcraft do not use the expression "talk with the devil."

[97] Petrus Martyr, *De orbe novo*, 73 (I, 9); Gómara, *Historia*, 172–73.

[98] Calancha, *Crónica*, 743, 1065, 1427.

[99] Peter Martyr, *De orbe novo*, 257, 259 (VIII, 8–9). In fact they are called possessed because, being physicians as well, they could extract the devil from other possessed persons.

at the beginning and at the end of the discoveries. However very differently from European witchcraft sources, which commonly describe poor
women, the intimate contract here in America is meant to explain how
political and cultural power is created. Surely the case of the simple *consultora* who is said to have had a contract with the devil is not unique.[100]
Calancha once opined that in one Peruvian area almost all Indians had
such contracts,[101] and elsewhere the same chronicler suspected that an
individual woman had a pact with the devil because she had successfully
deceived her people.[102] Indeed the contemporary ethnologist Michael
Taussig has written a book about certain twentieth-century tribes whose
workers are said to have made contracts with the devil allowing them to
raise their production and to become rich.[103]

But the devil's pact is more often and characteristically met with as
one between the devil and actual rulers. Acosta says that the great Texcocan philosopher-king Nezahualpilli, "a great magus," made such a
pact.[104] And according to Blas Valera, in the Andes all Inca rulers made
such treaties.[105] What is decisive is that for the Spaniards, such ruler
contracts explain political and cultural achievements. That is expressed
simply and incisively by Pedro de Cieza de León. He suspects that the
founder Inca Ayar Cachi and his associates "were enchanters, who could
accomplish what they had through the art of the devil."[106] Thus on
those unusual occasions when the vocabulary of witchcraft is used, it is to
explain the cultural achievements of the inhabitants.

In those cases where contracts with the devil, which are essentially intimate, are regarded by the Spaniards almost as state treaties, it becomes
clear that the essence of the Spanish concept of the native talking with
the devil was not an opposition, but rather a fusion of intimacy and pub-

---

[100] Hernández Principe, "Mitología," 31. Such exceptions are almost made the rule
in Silverblatt, *Moon, Sun, and Witches*, 159–96.

[101] La Barranca; Calancha, *Crónica*, 1412–13, where in this way the author tries to
explain some native success. See here as well the attempt to link these women to the
striges and *lamias* of the Romans.

[102] Calancha, *Crónica*, 1424.

[103] M. Taussig, *The Devil and Commodity Fetishism in South America* (Chapel Hill,
1980), 95ff.

[104] Acosta, *Historia*, 236 (VII, 23).

[105] Valera, *Relación*, 164. The devil gave his contractual answers in the *más señalados
templos*.

[106] "Encantadores, que sería causa de por arte del demonio hazer lo que hazían":
Cieza, *Crónica*, 2:15 (II, 6).

licity. Indeed we have already encountered this essential character once, in the idea of Garcilaso de la Vega regarding an intimate relation of an Inca class with the very public shrine of Pachacamac. At that time I said that Garcilaso saw that intimacy of the upper class with its God as a cultural progression. Now we turn fundamentally to these formal development theories of the Spaniards, in the hope of rounding off our explanation of the idea of talking with the devil.

Two specific theories of how "barbaric" peoples develop will be considered here, theories which — it must be said at once — do not directly address the phenomenon of talking with the devil.[107] The Jesuit José Acosta's theory of barbarism (1577) does not even mention the devil, but that does not make it less relevant. Barbarism has three stages. The first and highest, says this _Schriftgelehrte_, includes those like the Chinese, Japanese, and Indians who have writing, obviously because "wherever there are books and written monuments, the people are more humane and courteous" (_política_).[108] The second stage does not have writing, but indeed does possess "some reverent form of religious cult." To this stage belong the Inca and the Mexicans, as awful as their rites, customs, and laws may have been. The last and most primitive form of barbarism, according to Acosta, are those groups without political order. People in them wear little or no clothes, eat human flesh, practice incest and sodomy. In short, they are like animals in their behavior. The best among this third and worst group have perhaps some development, but their institutions remain infantile. Most American tribes were in this group. For Acosta what is important is the intellectual process of reason, which the different life styles of the stages are supposed to possess or lack. At the top, so to speak, one sees the intellectual, under him the priest, while at the base are people living apart without a body politic.

At first, Bernabé Cobo's theory of barbarism (1653), which is con-

---

[107] Las Casas' consideration of "barbarism" is a polemic rather than a theory of development. For example, he demonstrates how the Americans considered the Spaniards barbarians, and that Europeans, for example in the Spanish War of the Communes, had comported themselves as barbarians. Absolutely pragmatically, he defines the Americans before 1492 as "passive" barbarians because they did not know the gospel: Las Casas, _Apologética_, 2:637–54 (Epílogo, chaps. 264–67).

[108] This and what follows in Acosta, _De procuranda indorum salute_, in _Obras_, 391–93. See in general on the question of the so-called barbarism of the Americans, J. Elliott, "The Discovery of America and the Discovery of Man," _Proceedings of the British Academy_ 68 (1972): 101–25.

cerned only with the Americans, sounds quite similar to that of Acosta, just reversed: divided according to the type of government, this theory climbs from the lowest stage upwards. Peoples of the first class, therefore, have no government broader than those in their families, and obedience is foreign to them; the peoples of the third class — the Mexicans and Incas — live under caciques and kings, are courteous, and know how to obey.[109]

But when one looks closer, it becomes clear that Cobo is much more interested in religion than in Acosta's linear reason. And Cobo's stages are in fact decidedly less geared to cultural criteria than are Acosta's:

> The difference that one saw between the peoples of these three classes of barbarism were very few. For when one overviews their rudeness, inhumanity and wildness, one finds these [qualities] sufficiently in each of the three classes. Indeed within the noblest and most courteous [class], nations of Caribs [cannibals] are found, eaters of human flesh who make human offerings to the demon.[110]

Thus Cobo recognized that the most developed form of governance among the so-called barbarians could incorporate wildness and inhumanity, just as the least developed might do something praiseworthy. So-called reason did not automatically increase with a "higher" form of life. How he then built religion into this development theory is especially interesting.

Let us begin at that point where Cobo hears from citizens of Cuzco that before the Incas, the peoples of the Andes were wild, without leadership, and lived in villages at best. They ate human flesh and practiced incest, "just like those whom we placed in the first order of barbarism."[111] At this point, in Cobo's view, the devil was doubtless already active. All pre-Inca peoples "were very involved with the demon," they "honored him and served him assiduously." This was proved by the fact that despite their bestiality, certain of these pre-Inca peoples had many temples, and thus were very religious. Almost the same thing had been said by Cieza de León a century earlier. In pre-Inca times, this historian thought, people prayed to the demon, "and the demon was seen and honored by

---

[109] This and the following in Cobo, *Historia*, 2:29–31 (XI, 10).

[110] Cobo, *Historia*, 2:29–31 (XI, 10).

[111] Cobo, *Historia*, 2:58 (XII, 1). The following was very much influenced by Cieza, *Crónica*, 1:123–24 (I, 38).

them.''[112] Cieza's basic text could indicate that, according to Cobo, the devil could somehow be seen among the people before he appeared as an "idol," and thus before the Inca were taught by their leader how to hold a conversation with the devil.[113]

This reconstruction appears to be documented in the remainder of Cobo's development theory. For much more fundamentally than Acosta, Cobo relates cult development and the appearance of statues to the steps of barbarism:

> The more they depart from the first [thus lowest, class of barbarism], the more religious and superstitious they become. And since almost all Indians of the first class and order of barbarism surpass the other [classes in their barbarism], they also remain backwards in their idolatry. Indeed almost all [of the first class] use not one single type of reverence. Those of the second class recognize some false Gods, and do reverence to them, but with very few ceremonies and sacrifices. Those who worship the greatest number of Gods, with the greater order, cult and celebrity of temples, priests and offerings, were those of the third [and highest class of barbarism].[114]

Thus according to Cobo there is a definite link on the one hand between divine services and courtesy — "the less religion a nation has, the more rudeness and barbarism it has"[115] — and on the other hand between these two and the creation of images. We saw the same thing in the early reports from Cuba and Hispaniola, where it was assumed people were in a pre-image stage: although the devil perhaps spoke with the residents, for lack of anthropomorphic images these peoples did not talk with him. That means, therefore, that they could not ask about the future, and therefore could not control the world. I maintain, with a certain convic-

---

[112] Cieza, *Crónica*, 1:123 (I, 38).

[113] See above, the text at n. 58. But certainly that was not Cieza's opinion. He, but not Cobo, continues that the pre-Inca peoples also had "idols": "haziendo delante de los ydolos grandes sacrificios y supersticiones": Cieza, *Crónica*, 1:123–24 (I, 38).

[114] "Item, cuanto más se apartan de la primera, tanto más tienen de religión y supersticiones; porque casi todos los indios del primer grado y orden de barbaridad, así como en serlo se adelantan a los demás, así se les quedan atrás en idolatrías, porque casí todos ellos no usan de ningún género de adoración. Los de la segunda clase reconocen y hacen reverencia a algunos dioses falsos, mas con muy pocas ceremonias y ofrendas. Los que más dioses adoraban y con mayor orden, culto y celebridad de templos, sacerdotes y sacrificios, eran los de la tercera": Cobo, *Historia*, 2:30 (XI, 10).

[115] Cobo, *Historia*, 2:147 (XIII, 1).

tion, that "talking with the devil" is implicitly linked to ideals about development.

Before I begin to draw the balance of this study, I must again warn the reader against trivializing this expression, "talking with the devil." Because of the implicit assertion of the Spaniards that certain but not other tribes talked with the devil, one cannot maintain that the Spaniards wanted to say no more than that they talked with God, the Americans with the devil.

On the other hand, we should not equate a conversation with the Christian lord and the content of the conception of talking with the devil. Certainly it is evident that the Spaniards described American image customs that were in fact similar to European ones. The German Staden, we recall, directly compared a Brazilian tribe talking with its Gods with Europeans doing the same with theirs.[116]

And in truth, the way to understand this notion does lie through two insights, the first of which is that perhaps worldwide, there are indeed certain common characteristics in the religious comportment of classes or social orders. The mestizo Garcilaso may be compared to other ethnologists who at that time found *European* peasants to be the same across the continent, and who compared and contrasted them to the best classes of the whole Old World.[117] Through his aristocratic, Europeanized eyes, he saw the practical religious differences between the *orejones* and the other residents of Peru as expressions of different religious principles: monotheism against polytheism, but also a religion of possible communication with an unseen God versus a religion of the lower classes that spoke only with visible images. And just as Garcilaso the aristocrat spoke in the interest of his own class, so did the university professor Acosta speak in his group or class interest when he labeled non-Christian written cultures as the highest stage of barbarism because they were "more humane and courteous."[118] Universalistic Spanish notions of class and group covered over the ethnic differences of the Americans, which the Spaniards elsewhere had wanted to emphasize.

Second, the Spaniards experienced a certain Christian feeling of loss with reference to those they had subjected. This sentiment had different levels. First, it was clear, as Las Casas but also other missionaries

---

[116] See the text above, n. 18.
[117] See Trexler, "Aztec Priests for Christian Altars."
[118] See above, n. 108.

emphasized, that in many areas of life the great cultures of the New World were far in advance of Spanish culture.[119] So the conquerors had to explain how that was possible, and obviously, the idea of talking with the devil helped. In part it explained how these decentralized agrarian peoples had such success: their states had remained intimate with their figures and their devil, whereas the Christians encased in their institutions were perhaps less intimate. It explained also the enormous power of the great empires of the Aztecs and Inca: their rulers, their ecstatic priests, could develop these empires according to a plan. On the other hand, Christians normally did not expect their God to tell them the future. This is what is most impressive about the natives "talking to the devil." The prince of darkness, and he alone, was willing to foretell the future to those who would worship him, whether they were native or Spanish.[120]

Everywhere in this idea of talking with the devil, therefore, there remains the notion of the intellectual, or should I say prophetic, superiority of the devil and his empires. That was another loss, and the Christians were convinced that to suppress the devil's knowledge and therewith force obedience from the Americans, they had to exterminate every space and thing to which reverence was paid, even if one knew that, among the Aztecs for example, replacing or remaking their images was part of the reverence residents had for their Gods.[121] There was always the possibility of a revolt by the conquered, the Viceroy Toledo knew. So when he described to King Philip II the statue of Punchao, which the Spaniards had captured in 1572, he emphasized its functional power in the society. It "is the best piece found in this land," Toledo wrote, a representation of the sun that

---

[119] Las Casas, *Apologética*, 2:646 (Epílogo, 266).

[120] See Calancha, *Crónica*, 233–34, an explanation of why pagans so often make predictions, Christians seldom. In the contemporary penitential literature, it is assumed that not God but the devil is asked about the future: Johannes Friburgensis, *Summa confessorum* (s.l. 1476), *De sortilegiis et divinationibus* (tit. xi, quaes. ii). But already in the eighth century it was "non Christianus, sed paganus," to want to know the future *from God*: C. P. Caspari, *Eine Augustin fälschlich beilegt Homilia de sacrilegiis* (Christiania, 1896), 7. My thanks to Klaus Schreiner for these references. Augustine, Aquinas, and Jacopo Passavanti also knew that the devil was the *only* numen from whom the future could be learned. See *The Malleus Maleficarum of Heinrich Kramer and James Sprenger*, ed. M. Summers (New York, 1971), 103, 110 (II.i.2) and A. Kors and E. Peters (eds.), *Witchcraft in Europe, 1300–1700. A Documentary History* (Philadelphia, 2001), 46, 89, 106–11.

[121] Which was obviously the case with the famous Gods made of seeds: Gómara, *Historia*, 350.

... gave the rules of cult and the laws of idolatry to these non-believers extending over 1500 places. It is thanks to its lies and the falsehood of its answers [!], thanks to its protection, that the Inca were able to bring this poor people under their control. Since we captured it, we understand better the arrangements and conspiracies that this demon had with this people. [This statue] is the source and the basis of all deceptions. ... [122]

In his *relación* of the conquest of Mexico, the one-time conquistador and now priest Francisco de Aguilar bemoaned the decline of reverence which accompanied the conquest. Before the Spaniards arrived, he said, the temples were marvelously quiet, so great was the respect for the Gods. Since the conquest, he found in the new Christian churches a babel of noises without respect. [123] Thus the now dead images of the native past, as rich with speech as they may or may not have been, had been accompanied by a tangible reverence, whereas the Christian images had obviously provided little of that.

In the categories that the Iberians made of the native cultures, the assertion that a tribe had spoken with the devil was definitely meant to be positive. Indeed, in the sense of a mutual conversation with positive material consequences, perhaps the Christians had forgotten how that was done with their God.

---

[122] Duviols, *Lutte*, 131–32.

[123] Francisco de Aguilar, *Relación breve de la conquista de la Nueva España* (Mexico City, 1977), 103.

Historiography Sacred or Profane?
Reverence and Profanity in the
Study of Early Modern Religion*

> There are limits that one cannot
> cross even if there is no barrier.
> *Sovetskaya Rossiya*[1]

SOCIAL HISTORIANS' FASCINATION WITH THE IDEA of popular culture and popular religion is surprising in the light of folk ideology's destructive role in recent history. The concepts of *Volk* and *peuple* had come to a bad end in Europe, not least because of their evocative rather than actual content. The people was a chimera, we learned. Yet from the 1960s until today, a profusion of scholarly conferences and writings has raised this alleged culture and its religion to new heights.[2] Not without criticism, to be sure.

---

* This essay appeared previously in *Religion and Society in Early Modern Europe, 1500–1800*, ed. K. von Greyerz (London, 1984), 243–69.

[1] Criticizing C. Vermorelle's "Lenin, Stalin and Trotsky," as performed in Belgrade; cited in the *New York Times*, 30 May 1982. I thank Roger Chartier and especially Robert Seaberg for reading two different versions of this paper. The views and errors are mine; some comparative English materials were furnished by Professor Seaberg.

[2] F.-A. Isambert lists several conferences in his "Religion populaire, sociologie, histoire et folklore," *Archives de sciences sociales des religions* 43 (1977): 162–63.

Various scholars have convincingly argued that to this day neither cultural forms nor social groups have been isolated which can exclusively be identified as popular.[3]

For this reason, the title of the volume for which this paper was originally prepared, *Religion and Society in Early Modern Europe*, represents a hopeful sign for a future social history of religion. In the last generation great storehouses of the religious artefacts of the past have been retrieved and studied with a seriousness and ingenuity few would have thought possible a generation ago, and no one would doubt the fruitfulness of that work or that it has enriched our understanding of humanity's material and spiritual heritage. Yet rich as the quality and quantity of religious studies inspired by the focus on popularity has been, that very concept has perpetuated serious biases, and not the least of these has been the focus on defining popularity rather than religion. The search can have a Grail-like intensity: "I was born of the people," Jacques Le Goff cites Michelet; "I have the people in my heart. But its language is inaccessible to me, and I have not been able to speak it."[4]

The insatiable search for popular essence has meant two things for the study of religion before the French Revolution. First, religion usually remains undefined by historians. Secondly, the emphasis on "popular" rather than on "religion" has led us to think of "popular religion" as essentially different from what is variously called high, elite, or learned religion. Indeed, elite religion is more likely to be called something else, like "spir-

---

[3] Most recently R. Chartier in his "La 'culture populaire': un découpage questionné," in *Understanding Popular Culture: Europe from the Middle Ages to the Nineteenth Century*, ed. S. Kaplan (The Hague, 1984). The absence of social specificity has been a criticism of the important work of P. Burke, *Popular Culture in Early Modern Europe* (London, 1978). See also D. Rei, "Note sul concetto di 'religione popolare,'" *Lares* 40 (1974): 264–80; J. C. Schmitt, "Les traditions folkloriques dans la culture médiévale. Quelques réflexions de méthode," *Archives de sciences sociales des religions* 52 (1981): 5–8, with accompanying bibliography; N. Zemon Davis, "Some Tasks and Themes in the Study of Popular Religion," in *The Pursuit of Holiness in Late Medieval and Renaissance Religion*, ed. C. Trinkaus and H. Oberman (Leiden, 1974), 307–36; W. Christian, Jr., *Local Religion in Sixteenth Century Spain* (Princeton, 1981). The range of objects and patrons labeled popular is wide in *Religion et traditions populaires (Musée national des arts et traditions populaires, 4 déc. 1979–3 mars 1980)* (Paris, 1979).

[4] Michelet is cited in J. Le Goff, *Pour un autre Moyen Age* (Paris, 1977), 8. See the round table allegedly on "les interprétations de la notion de 'religion populaire,' " but actually only on the word "popular," in the volume *La Religion populaire (Paris 17–19 oct. 1977)*, CNRS Colloque 576 (Paris, 1979), 394ff. In his intervention, C. Ginzburg recommended putting the word "popular" in prolonged hibernation: *Religion populaire*, 399.

ituality," and books on spirituality exclude "the people" almost by definition. The absence of a book, conference, or field called "high" or "elite
religion," or even "clerical religion," if it does not document an older
view that "religion" is by definition a possession of the elite (where the
populars have only "religiosity"), might suggest that religion has become
by definition popular. It will be worthwhile, I think, to go back to the
question of what religion is.

This study has three purposes. First, I want to relate our understanding
of religion to the development of the modern European intelligentsia.
Arguing that conventional definitions have crippling disadvantages for its
study, I will suggest a definition of religion which, I think, proves particularly appropriate for the social historian of early modern Europe. Finally,
I want to explore the relation between religion and historical writing and
discourse, and argue their procedural and affective similarity. In the course
of this contribution I will suggest tactics and strategies for the historian
wishing to write a profane rather than a reverential history of religion. Before plunging into early modern history — taking for granted what religion
is — we should re-examine what we are doing when we talk and write
about religion.

Our Religion and Their Religion

A survey of what Western historians mean by religion reveals one per-
vasive assumption: religion in the West was either identical with or the reverse of meaningful activities of formal ecclesiastical or state institutions.
Whatever practitioners have said religion was, their historians have defined it *with reference to* the real and idealized behavior and reflections of
a corporate division of labor, the clergy. Perhaps this is most evident in
the German academic tradition, where a discrete confessional approach to
the discipline of religious and theological studies remains in place to this
day. What religions have in common, that is, religion, is discovered in the
relation of each to its clergy.

Yet the institutionally focused study of religion is but part of a larger
propensity of the West's complex societies. If in medieval Europe the idea
of religion was limited by reference to the exemplary actions and reflections of an institutionalized clergy, reduced into norms, so today the pursuit of knowledge is associated with the university, and power is usually
described with exclusive reference to the state. Now if it is true that in
Western practice such fundamental human activities or states are normally
referred to institutions, it is reasonable to ask if this corporate thrust is

related to the institutional character of those who formally define what religions were and were not. The social historian more than any other must
begin the study of past religions by examining the corporate paradigms of
intellectual, moral, and fideistic constructs.[5]

The sacramental and lay clerical groups that have normatively defined
and limited religion have clashed since the Renaissance in defining religion, its social location, and who the "people" are who practiced it. Before
a corporate lay intelligentsia appeared in the Renaissance, the sacramental
clergy said that religion consisted of lay and clerical liturgical behavior as
well as in clerical reflection on the divine, that is, on order and disorder
and their meaning. Pointing to itself as that social body which behaved in
a graced or particularly efficacious form and which contemplated, the
sacramental clergy defined all non-ordained or non-ecclesiastical persons
as the *populus*, even if the clergy in the interest of its finances co-opted its
patrons out of those very "people" by ambivalently associating them with
itself, for example by clothing the merchant or king in religious habit for
burial, allowing their presence in the choir, and so on. As Roger Chartier
recently noted, the people was not a social group but a status;[6] in the
view of the clergy, that *populus* did not reflect, but its liturgical behavior,
however inadequate, was "religious." The people had religion in certain
of its activities.

The lay (non-sacerdotal or -ministerial) intelligentsia of the early modern period increasingly rejected this concept of religion and of the people.
Generally not wealthy or powerful patrons, who might be co-opted into
grace by the clergy, they rejected a concept of the people which embraced
them and, competing for patronage with the sacramental clergy before
their princes, they increasingly disputed the centrality of graced behavior
to a definition of religion.[7] Beginning with conventional attacks on par-

---

[5] T. Kuhn has suggested that intellectual historians must do the same thing: *The
Structure of Scientific Revolutions* (Chicago, 1962). Opposition to a social history of the
hard sciences is lively at this time; a social history of humanist historians does not seem
to exist.

[6] See his paper cited n. 3. J. Le Goff finds status implying domination whatever the
actual wealth or power relations: the "people" or laity was "subordinate to the clerks in
religious matters": *Religion populaire*, 403.

[7] In northern Europe, I am thinking of certain strands of the Common Life, and thus
of the pre-Reformation. Though Erasmus insisted on the value of acts in the free-will
debate with Luther, his *philosophia Christi*, already reflected in the *Praise of Folly*, is built
on criticism of clerical action; the neo-Platonists of Florence had earlier carved out an
area for their own "magic" by similar criticisms.

ticipatory acts like processions, pilgrimages, and the like, which for the laity at large were observably the most significant liturgical acts, some of these lay intellectuals ended by questioning what some called clerical magic, that is, sacramental activities in which the clergy's intervention was said to be decisive.[8] The essence of religion for the *Schriftgelehrten* or humanists became contemplation or reflection on a single world or cosmic order. Behavior was relatively unimportant to religion, and the simpler the behavior, the better.[9]

Thus in this view the sacramental clergy was religious mainly to the extent that it was reflective; depending on the power of the local clergy, the cosmic efficacy of its liturgy was thrown into question more or less radically. More important, this emphasis on reflection excluded "the people" from religion, for everyone agreed that they did not reflect. One has only to read Erasmus or Pico della Mirandola among a host of writers of the age to see that lay scholars were even more determined to separate themselves from the vulgar than they were to attack clerical pretensions.[10] On the one side this intelligentsia attacked the religious activism of the "people," while on the other it questioned the liturgical activities of the clergy. Its socially passive definition of religions was ready-made for its patrons, the territorializing princes of early modern Europe.

In the courts, these laymen now turned their attention to the assertedly non-liturgical behavior called courtesy, and gave it a religious aura. In the Middle Ages "good manners and religion" had been two sides of the same behavioral coin, and bad manners were a type of sin. One and the same system of bodily comportment, for example, was considered appropriate and efficacious in dealing with princes and Gods, actions towards the latter being legitimated through biblical authority and actions towards the

---

[8] D. P. Walker, *Spiritual and Demonic Magic from Ficino to Campanella* (London, 1958).

[9] The attack on behavior in religion was part of a larger distancing of this new intelligentsia from manual activities at large; F. Yates's brilliant attempt to relate a neo-Platonic "magic" — essentially a mental operation or reflection — to the artistic work of the Italian Renaissance was ultimately undemonstrable: *Giordano Bruno and the Hermetic Tradition* (London, 1964).

[10] The pages of such writers are full of admonitions for the "vulgar" to better themselves, to be sure, but such sentiments are perfectly congruous with despising the "brutes" who did not hire a teacher. "Man" in Pico della Mirandola's *Dignity* did not include such "beasts." For a different reading, see M. Venard, "Dans l'affrontement des réformes du XVIe siécle: regard et jugements portés sur la religion populaire," in *Religion populaire*, 115ff.

former by custom and by natural law transference from divine to human princes.[11] This symbiosis was muted in the Renaissance, especially by those lay intellectuals like Von Hutten and Pomponazzi, Montaigne and More, Vivés and Guazzo, who increasingly doubted the efficacy of liturgical behavior. A group of terms like courtesy, regality, urbanity, and civility, classicized later in the term *civilisation*, came to the fore, and the princes became their mirror. Challenging the liturgical efficacy of the sacramental clergy, the lay intelligentsia offered the prince their services in creating a system of princely behavior which would guide and legitimate, and render efficacious, *human* communications. Though sometimes viewed as thaumaturgic in those actions, the prince of early modern Europe became the predominant model for a binding *social* behavior developed by his intellectual masters of ceremonies and emanating from his court.[12] The "religion" of gentlemen was spawned in a "sacred" ambience. Irreverence remained outlawed and profane, only now, decorum went by different names and was defined by different clergies.

This early corporate history of definitions of religion helps us to understand how the social history of religion has been written in modern times, and what have been the focuses of its various practitioners. In the modern age and in most liberal states, the ordained clergy's monopoly of the historiography of European religion has been broken, and clerical historians have almost everywhere been supplemented by lay scholars still committed to clerical leadership who share with the sacramental clergy the view of religion as a reflective and a behavioral phenomenon. This body of committed historians studies historically conditioned behavior; their writing chronicles changing lay behaviors and beliefs in terms of how closely they approach or depart from ideal clerical states or norms. Secondly, historians

---

[11] R. Trexler, *Public Life in Renaissance Florence* (New York, 1980), chap. 3; and his "Aztec Priests for Christian Altars. The Theory and Practice of Reverence in New Spain," in *Scienze. Credenze occulte. Livelli di cultura. Convegno internazionale di Studi (Firenze, 26–30 giugno 1980)* (Florence, 1982), 175–96 (another valuable conference on the "relation between popular culture and elite culture": *Scienze*, p. v); R. C. Trexler, "Legitimating Prayer Gestures in the Twelfth Century: The *De Penitentia* of Peter the Chanter," elsewhere in the present volume.

[12] Castiglione's *Courtier* and Della Casa's *Galateo* are innocent of such structural considerations of manners; the neglected Stefano Guazzo's *De civili conversatione* is a masterpiece along these lines. N. Elias, *Die höfische Gesellschaft* (Darmstadt, 1979), chap. 6, notes the gradual limitations placed on kings through such courtesy systems. It is significant that Elias's book on court etiquette scarcely mentions the thaumaturgic powers associated to some of these kings, and M. Bloch's *Les Rois thaumaturges* (Paris, 1961) hardly mentions etiquette, though the two are deeply related.

following Gabriel Le Bras, himself a "religious sociologist," are comfortable with sociological categories in studying the people of the Gods. Indices of class, residence, age, occupation and sex have been used not only by pastors to discover how to get today's people to church, but by historians studying ages as far removed as that of the Merovingians.[13] This clerical approach remains remorselessly moralistic, to be sure, yet that attitude makes it critical of past and present political authority; the behavior of "the people" can still be the *vox dei* for committed historians. The immutable Gods of Christianity, surprisingly, allow a history, sociology, and critical philosophy to their historiographic devotees.

If infinitely more complex, the assertedly secular intelligentsia's study of lay religion, descended from the Renaissance, also betrays a corporate character. Generally speaking, this historiographical tradition in the study of Western religion has proven less concerned with change than the church tradition, in part because it privileges static models derived from social anthropologists studying distant tribal societies. Secondly, the anthropologists' emphasis on overarching tribal unity has discouraged the historiographic application of trans-tribal sociological indices like age, sex, status, and class to European societies, resulting in a model of social operation that is non-conflictual with regard to the relation between "tribes" and which identifies the "tribe" with its mature males. Finally, modern secular historians' criticisms of the biases of the committed intelligentsia and their own commitment to value-free scholarship notwithstanding, they tend to conceptualize the study of religion in such a way as to accept and perpetuate rather than to view critically both the states whose religions they study and those they themselves live in, not unlike some of the anthropologists who inspired them.[14] Applying tribal models to the Euro-

---

[13] This type of work is encountered in the series *Histoire et sociologie de l'église* (Sirey), which was edited by Le Bras. See also the pioneering work of J. Toussaert, *Le Sentiment religieux en Flandre à la fin du Moyen-Age* (Paris, 1963), with *nihil obstat*. Especially characteristic is Le Bras, "Le clergé dans les derniers siècles du Moyen Age," *Unam Sanctam* 28 (Paris, 1954): 153–81, in an issue on "Priests of yesterday and today" edited by J.-F. Lemarignier. Criticism of this tradition is in F. Isambert, "Autour du catholicisme populaire: Reflexions sociologiques sur un debat," *Social Compass* 22 (1975): 193–210. On "historical religious sociology" as against sociology of religion, see C. Langlois' contribution to *Religion Populaire*, 325ff.

[14] For the ongoing anthropological debate, see the articles in "Towards an Ethics for Anthropologists," in *Current Anthropology* 12 (1971): 321ff., and the debate over C. Turnbull's *The Mountain People*, *Current Anthropology*, 16 (1975): 343ff. Similarly, see B. Lewis, "The Attack on Orientalism," *The New York Review of Books* (24 June 1982), 49ff. Evidently, historians are as variegated as anthropologists, and the striking absence

pean "popular" world, they have converted the old clergy-*populus* distinction into a sociologically amorphous, quasi-cosmic Manicheanism pitting
mental light against mental darkness, a religious world in which the state
does not figure as a religious structure and thus cannot undergo a critical
review in religious terms. The state has become power, not religion. The
problem is rooted in this intelligentsia's group-interested definition of religion as reflection.

Since the nineteenth century, this secular intelligentsia has had three
stances towards Western religion. The most remarkable has been to ignore
it. Just as many anthropologists turned towards Africa and Asia and thus
avoided studying Western religion in the same fashion used in distant
parts, so historians of the "secular" Renaissance long ignored its religion,
which presumably could not be studied in the same way as its "modern"
political and artistic institutions could be.[15] The other two stances have
examined the subject, but diverged from each other in their attitudes towards non-reflective or "false religion," identified, as we have seen, with
"the people." The first group of historians are the linear descendants of
the Renaissance intellectuals I have mentioned, and they have viewed this
false religion as dangerous to "true religion" but even more to "civilization," that is, to that paraliturgical theatre of manners earlier mirrored
in the prince, but in post-revolutionary Europe hypostatised in the bureaucratic structures of the modern state and in the "businesslike" behavior of
its employees.[16]

---

of political considerations in the literature on popular religion at large is merely more impressive than the presence of historians of "plebeian culture." Still, the latter historians
accept their states, since they describe relations between the latter and "popular culture"
in terms of resistance not revolt; see further below. A structured exclusion of the state
from "popular religion" is available in E. Le Roy Ladurie's *Montaillou, village occitan de
1294 à 1324* (Paris, 1975). Religion and politics are reintegrated in R. Firth's important
"Spiritual Aroma: Religion and Politics," *American Anthropologist* 83 (1981): 582–601.

[15] Not until C. Trinkaus's *In Our Image and Likeness. Humanity and Divinity in Italian
Humanist Thought*, 2 vols. (Chicago, 1970), was the Burckhardtian "secularization" of
thought fundamentally put into doubt. Until recently, religion has played no significant
role in explaining Renaissance politics. N. Elias's works, including *Über den Prozess der
Zivilisation* (Bern, 1969), have remarkably little to say about religion.

[16] The link between a "civilization" of unquestioned manners and bureaucratic structures is best understood by S. Freud in his *Civilization and its Discontents* (New York,
1962), and by R. Sennett, *The Fall of Public Man* (New York, 1977). Elias, *Prozess*, does
not mention it; see his chap. 1 on the specifically French and English emphasis on behavior as *civilisation*.

The most recent stance towards non-reflective religion has been positive, its adherents' ancestral opposition to the sacramental clergy often being supplemented by an opposition to the modern bourgeois state, that is, to their patrons. Such historians generally agree with their civilizational colleagues that the beliefs of the people are false, and that actions based on them are "irrational." But behavior like industrialization which the civilizationalists ridicule, the populists praise as a spiritual and social force which gave "the people" identity and solidarity against the modernizing state from which these intellectuals themselves are alienated.[17] Impressed by the wealth of behavioral information gathered by folklorists like Van Gennep and by committed historians like Delaruelle, these secular historians, thinking they were secularly reflecting instead of religiously acting on the past, believed that they could recover from a functionally useful behavior an actual intellectual coherence inaccessible to the unreflective people. Mental darkness became for scholars like Bakhtin a type of liturgical inner light, and "popular religion" became a good reversal of the meaningful if baneful behavior of the clergy and state.[18]

Thus among secular social historians of religion, the behavior of the "people" has steadily come to the fore as a matter of serious intellectual inquiry. To historians like Mandrou and Laslett, popular religion is basically a rural behavioral world lost through some cosmic event like industrialization, whose reflective meaning persists only as a mental light among the historians of those religions. To others like Edward Thompson, this active "plebeian religion" can lose all chronological or locative reference and so live on despite social change, a force ready to resist the modern state especially if "the people" heed the ideal role and essence the historians assign them.[19] Both approaches are acts of faith. With little clear ref-

---

[17] Such a crude typology does not justly describe any one historian, of course, nor is it meant to; I found myself in all the categories I describe. But it is fair to suggest that Michelet was a type of godfather to this latter group and in its most brilliant form that spiritual cognation is evident in the work of E. P. Thompson. Thompson's own reading of his progeny is in an interview in *Radical History Review* 4 (1976): 4–25. Such historians, including myself, tend to replace class considerations with emphases on age and sex; see the interview with N. Zemon Davis, *Radical History Review* 24 (1980): 115–39. A critique of this approach is provided by E. Fox-Genovese and E. Genovese, "The Political Crisis of Social History: A Marxian Perspective," *Journal of Social History* 10 (1976): 205–21.

[18] *Rabelais and his World* (Cambridge, MA, 1968).

[19] For the equation rural-collective, see R. Mandrou, *Introduction à la France moderne; essai de psychologie historique 1500–1640* (Paris, 1974), chap. 16; P. Laslett, *The World We*

erence in group sociology, "the people" easily become a victimized fancy produced by pop-psychological characterizations among historians who, even as they defend or attack "the people," do not consider themselves behaving towards the religions they study. Paradoxically, the result has often been a gulf between past peoples and their elites, between the same social groups and their historians, between the study of religion and the study of power.

From the earliest days of cultural classifications, apologists have distinguished between irrational and rational, external and internal, collective and individual, routine and spontaneous religions, and until recently such conceptual territorializations passed unchallenged for science. Romans used the former quality of each set to brand Christians, Christians to label Jews, Protestants to dismiss Catholics, and Westerners to characterize natives. Then the same irrationality, externality, collectivism, and routine were applied first by sixteenth-century internal missionaries "Christianizing" "our [European] Indians," and last by secular intellectuals to condemn and then to praise "the people." In my analysis, secular historians could apply these marginalizing conventions even less ambivalently than committed ones. If committed historians condemned religious externality, for example, they did so only because the behavior they observed seemed to them to lack interiority, or what Savonarola once called "enamorative virtù."[20] External, collective and routine, yes even irrational behavior ("holy madness"), remained in itself an essential part of religion. For the secular historians, however, religion was essentially reflective and its terminology psychological, so their use of such labels was the more fatal. We shall see that, paradoxically, the use of these categories lends the secular historiography of religion its own particular religious character.

These categories are distinctly ideological rather than intellectual in quality. Distinguishing between inside and outside in this fashion bestows an a priori unity upon "popular religion" which contrasts sharply with the diffuseness of contemporary life experienced by the working historian. These categories certainly do help the historian to assemble a persuasive portrait of past religions. Yet when rooted in such categories, these por-

---

Have Lost (New York, 1965). The observation on Thompson could also fairly be made of my Public Life, cited n. 11 above.

[20] Trexler, Public Life, 471. The comparison of Europeans to Indians is studied by A. Prosperi, " 'Otras Indias': missionari della contrariforma tra contadini e selvaggi," in Scienze, 205–34.

traits can be so devoid of scholarly rigor as to make the reader wince. Keith Thomas's by now well-known retort that historians do not have the time to get straight what it is they are doing has just such an effect. Thus Stuart Clark has noted that Jean Delumeau, for example, argues that the irrationality of "the people" causes their acts, but does not notice that such an aetiology is tautological.[21] The ideological component in such an approach becomes particularly glaring when the spell is considered irrational and pre-religious, but prayer, at least private prayer, is reckoned as good common sense, eminently rational.[22]

The ideological content of the other standard polarizations is no less evident. Without asking if it is theoretically sound to oppose externality and internality, recent students have argued that Martin Luther more or less discovered internal religion, that Protestantism appealed to merchants because it avoided the time consumed by "external apparatus," that "magic" has been in decline since then and that the history of religion records the slow victory of internality over externality, that is, of reflection over action.[23] Before questioning whether individual identity is describable or observable apart from collective frames of reference like societal rites *and* the historian's language, sympathetic historians of "the people" conspire in the deindividuation of their subjects by rooting their behavior in timeless ritual or mythic structures. Instead of recognizing that under the rubric of "routine ceremony" lie legions of individual lives changed decisively by participation in ceremonies, historians like Le Roy Ladurie speak of villages "without a state and without politics," where the dynamic conflicts and contracts of "routine," which produce memory and identity for individuals and groups, find no constitutive significance.[24]

---

[21] S. Clark, "French Historians and Early Modern Popular Culture," *Past and Present* 100 (1983): 62–99. See K. Thomas citing A. Dyce in "An Anthropology of Religion and Magic, II," *Journal of Interdisciplinary History* 6 (1975): 91.

[22] As in Thomas's epochal *Religion and the Decline of Magic* (London, 1971), 41. When prayer alone of human actions toward the Gods is considered efficacious, the results are curious: see my review of R. Manselli, *La Religion populaire au moyen âge* (Montreal, 1975), in *Speculum* 52 (1977): 1019–22.

[23] Respectively M. Ruel, "Christians as believers," in *Religious Organisation and Religious Experience*, ed. J. Davis (London, 1982), 9–31; H. Trevor-Roper, *The Crisis of the Seventeenth Century* (New York, 1956), 24; K. Thomas, *Religion*; N. Belmont, "Superstition et religion populaire dans les sociétiés occidentales," in *La Fonction symbolique. Essais d'anthropologie*, ed. M. Izard and P. Smith (Paris, 1979), 53–70.

[24] Le Roy Ladurie, *Montaillou*, chap. 22. This deindividuation is particularly marked in R. Muchembled, *Culture populaire et culture des élites* (Paris, 1978), esp. 127ff. I have

Historians' unwillingness to deal with such conceptual problems is not new, of course, but their persistent use of such psychological categorizations, themselves functions of the scholars' own ambivalent social position, ensures that history remains in part what it was for our clerical and humanistic ancestors, an edifying science. Reverence lives, whether it be one of respect or rancor. Beneath the asserted secularity of much of the profession resides a structural reverence for the past and present functionally quite as forceful as that which others bestow on personal Gods. The cosmic dualism between psychologically but not sociologically defined high and low cultures, and between the subject and object of the historical discourse, is what produces that reverence. Reverence lives through the very absence of exchange, that is of politics, between these worlds.

Thus the problems associated with the concept of popular religion are not soluble by the editorial elimination of words like "superstition," "gläubiges Volk," "magic," and the like. These marginalizing characterizations of religions are in part the result of a particular historically developed corporate identity, and they will persist in other guises until a behavioral and reflective strategy of negation challenges the established image of the historical scholar.[25] To counter either respectful or rancorous reverence for "the people," therefore, one should directly attack the source of the problem in those who "are not of the people." Short of redefining religion itself, the most negating or profane approach to the study of religion would be to examine the high culture with which historians identify themselves with the same methods and modes of discourse used now to study "popular culture."

If historians of religion were to take seriously those unsettling similes which compare scientists to priests, academic departments to tribes, scholarly conferences to collective rituals, and professional journals to folklore, the results might be not only therapeutic and amusing but of significant methodological and epistemological value. I have noted that there are no books called "elite religion" to match the many on popular religion, so

---

examined contract and competition combined in ritual in my *Public Life*, chap. 8. The classic treatment of social identity is the papers of the 1974–1975 seminar conducted by C. Lévi-Strauss, *L'Identité* (Paris, 1977).

[25] The process of interpreting the past as "not us" must, I believe, include an understanding of the interpreters as simultaneously negating the present as "not us." Assessments of this "critical philosophy" are in *The Critical Spirit. Essays in Honor of Herbert Marcuse*, ed. K. Wolff and B. Moore, Jr. (Boston, 1967).

with a methodology in place and the elite certainly a more specific or determinable social entity than "the people," the abundant sources for such a study are inviting. The profanity of studying the behavior of the elite, its externality, collectivism, and routines, when the intellectuals within that elite fundamentally identify themselves as a rational reflective division of labor, would have three important results. Erstwhile students of popular religion would soon discover that, for evident reasons of corporate interest, historians know almost nothing about past elite religious behavior.[26] Secondly, they would quickly understand that in comparing non-elite to elite religions, one must compare behavior to behavior and not to ideas. Finally, this approach would have the great benefit of ultimately ascribing to the non-elite the same measure of internality, individualism, and spontaneity as the inside has always reserved for itself.[27]

Doubtless, scarcity of sources will always complicate historians' ability to study reflection among non-elites, impressive as has been the progress of the Menocchios of that world in recent years.[28] This is but one more reason why the social history of religion must be founded upon the study of behavior if that study hopes to examine all social groups without a priori psychological assumptions. The task is not to dismiss ideas, but to gain the behavioral foundation to begin to understand them. The following definition of religion could not only decrease the evident ideological functions of an association of the intelligentsia with reflection and of reflection with religion. It may also prove useful in conceptualizing the history of early modern Europe.

---

[26] This is despite the fact that church attendance today, and probably in the past, is directly related to wealth and status. Academics go to church more often than workers or rural peoples: see, for example, M. Argyle, *Religious Behavior* (London, 1958).

[27] The absence of mediation when such psychological characterizations are used is epitomized in the title of H. Dedieu, "Quelques traces de religion populaire autour des frères mineurs de la province d'Aquitaine," in *La Religion populaire en Languedoc du XIIIe à la moitié du XIVe siècle* (Toulouse, 1976), 227–49, where the behavior of friars becomes vestigial "popular religion."

[28] C. Ginzburg, *Il formaggio e i vermi* (Turin, 1976). In *Religion populaire*, 399, Ginzburg insists historians place religion within social contexts; this essentially corrects his handling of Menocchio, whose mental gymnastics are excellently described but whose occupation as a miller takes on no significance until the last part of the book. See also Giovanni Morelli's experiences edited by R. Trexler, "In Search of Father: The Experience of Abandonment in the Recollections of Giovanni di Pagolo Morelli," *History of Childhood Quarterly* 3 (1975): 225–52.

Religion Reformed

Reverence or decorum, *pietas*, is, I would argue, the foundation of social life.[29] Many incorporated or fleeting groups in society are persuaded
to swear to systems of bodily and verbal behaviors labeled appropriate by
statutes or customs, and these systems are said to be efficacious in internal
bonding and in distinguishing one group from another. Such a group is
called a religion when it practises this sworn behavior in the context of
operational and nominal classifications of sacrality and profanity. A religion's sacred activity is that rigid or formalized motion around certain
times, places, and objects named sacred during that activity, while that
same religion's profane activity consists of insults toward the *sacra* of outsiders done with non-rigid and sometimes unprescribed behaviors.[30] The
memory of such behaviors is called religious experience, and is distinguished from ordinary social exchange.[31] A religion's profane activity
also includes similar activities directed towards its own *sacra*, but these activities, though described as religious experience at the time, are rarely remembered and then labeled sacrilege or irreverence.[32]

Isolated tribal entities already possess several such religions for their
different sexes, ages, and clans, and such tribes commonly have masters of
ceremony who are also masters of the meanings of the various groups' sacred and profane activities, which may or may not be ceremonially integrated. Contacts with other tribes produce the conditions of religions in
societies. The sacred and profane times, places, and objects of different
tribes are increasingly irreconcilable. The enforcement by the tribal mas-

---

[29] Besides Elias's *Prozess*, cited n. 15, see E. Shils, *The Constitution of Society* (Chicago, 1972), 143–75, on deference.

[30] C. Geertz warns against associating gravity with reverence: *The Interpretation of
Cultures* (New York, 1973), 97. I am not aware of a definition of religious behavior which
attempts to integrate profanation. See F.-A. Isambert, "L'élaboration de la notion du
sacré dans l'école durkheimienne," *Archives de sciences sociales des religions* 26 (1976): 35–
76. On the problem of reconciling the socially defined state of rigid reverence with ecstasy or "excessive gestures" viewed as an instrumentalization of humans by the Gods, see
my *Public Life*, 104ff.

[31] The process of memorizing affect through a mental architecture that profanes the
outside is studied by F. Yates, *The Art of Memory* (Chicago, 1966).

[32] More on these different descriptions of religious experience below. This approach
tries to exorcise an inadequate interpretation of carnival as inversion and anti-religious
behavior, or as *intervallum mundi*: J. Caro Baroja, *El carnaval* (Madrid, 1979), introduction. By my definition, carnival is religious; see R. Scribner's richly documented attempt
to link carnival as inversion to Protestant propagandization of beliefs in "Reformation,
Carnival and the World Turned Upside-Down," *Social History* 3 (1978): 303–29.

ters of ceremony of the behavioral patterns of their religions' living and dead members fails, in part because of the development of voluntary associations that can unite sexes, occupations, and even cohorts across tribal lines.[33]

To regulate religions within complex societies, rulers, through their public activities as precedence-setters, propagate an overarching classification of sacred and profane times, places, and objects, which it is the duty of their masters of ceremony to actualize and justify. Rulers and their clerks call reverence within this classification "religion" in the singular, and they identify its practice with authenticity. In complex societies, religion and an absence of deceit become normatively identical. Yet deceit and authenticity only being determinable through behavior, contending groups *testify* so as to prove their own religion or piety.[34] Beliefs, in short, exist only in performance. Groups and individuals perform bodily and verbal imitations of their codified past before the masters. They claim these testimonies are authentic within the classification of sacred and profane established by the precedence- and thus precedent-setting ruler.

Understanding religions primarily as plural communities of behavior seems at first particularly inappropriate for early modern European history, which is renowned for its doctrinal disputes. These disputes are of undeniable importance for social historians of this period, who rightly view the debates as glossing fundamental questions of social organization. Let us realize, however, that the verbal articulation of such doctrines can be studied as behavioral systems of aural and visual semiotics uttered within specific social and political contexts, and that the most pressing task of new religions was not the articulation of clear intellectual differences from Catholicism and among one another, but the establishment of new sacred times, spaces, and objects for meaningful behavior.[35] Once the imperativeness of these needs is recognized, our approach permits the social historian to understand the religious strife of the period partially in terms of its general behavioral history. I refer, of course, to the intense process of cast-

---

[33] This irreconcilability, I suggest, arises first in the area of behavioral diplomacy, only much later as a question of meaning or theology.

[34] Imposed behaviors, a precondition of order and affect, complicate the discovery of transparently "true sentiment." See W. Christian, Jr.'s important study on using tears as such an indicator, even though a technology for inducing them and thus the presence of deceit had long existed: "Provoked Religious Weeping in Early Modern Spain," in Davis, *Religious Organisation*, 97–114.

[35] As is shown by N. Zemon Davis, "The Sacred and the Body Social in Sixteenth-Century Lyon," *Past and Present* 90 (1981): 40–70.

ing social behavior into a framework of norms, which took place between
the fifteenth and seventeenth centuries.

Long ignored as "mere externality" or dismissed as pathologic, the attention early modern Europeans gave to questions of precedence, manners,
and social rituals has recently become a focus of historical research. We
are far from fully understanding why Burgundian and Italian rulers of the
late fourteenth and fifteenth centuries, guided by their new masters of
ceremony, increasingly turned their public and private actions into dis-
plays of meticulously arranged precedence and extraordinarily detailed
bodily and verbal language.[36] The movement seems to have started in
the monarchical and republican courts, and especially in the context of
diplomatic receptions, where the new ceremonialism emphasized the majesty of princes in relation to their noble retinues as well as in their status
relations with visitors.[37] From the courts, this enormous attention to organized public display spread downwards into society, producing in the end
hundreds of tracts enjoining specific behaviors for men, youth, adolescents, boys, women, girls, widows, distinct occupations, and so on. The
post-Schism papacy joined the parade, and churchmen at large recognized
the trend before the Reformation, and later significantly entitled some of
their works on prayer modes and preaching "Christian rhetoric."[38] The
Renaissance was a ceremonial age *par excellence,* and it is particularly interesting that contemporaries charged official historiographers with the responsibility of organizing and recording such "externalities." The rhetoric
of modern historical writing and discourse has its deep roots in the organizing and the recording of public representations by historian-masters of
ceremony.[39]

---

[36] See R. Trexler, introduction to *The Libro Cerimoniale of the Florentine Republic by
Francesco Filarete and Angelo Manfidi* (Geneva, 1978). To date there is no modern work
on Burgundy to supplant O. Cartellieri, *The Court of Burgundy* (New York, 1929), but see
P. Arnade, *Realms of Ritual: Burgundian Ceremony and Civic Life in Late Medieval Ghent*
(Ithaca, 1996). Also see E. Muir, *Civic Ritual in Renaissance Venice* (Princeton, 1981);
links between diplomacy and everyday rituals are in the three volumes of *Les Fêtes de la
Renaissance,* ed. J. Jacquot and E. Konigson, esp. vol. 3 (Paris, 1975). On confraternal
rituals, R. Weissman, *Ritual Brotherhood in Renaissance Florence* (New York, 1982). My
view is not that there was more "external behavior" in this age, but rather greater attention to more organized behavior.

[37] See my *Public Life,* chap. 9.

[38] See for example Diego Valvades, *Rhetorica christiana ad concionandi et orandi usum
accommodata* (Perugia, 1579). Earlier churchmen had been known to scorn rhetoric: Trexler, "Legitimating Prayer Gestures."

[39] Trexler, *Libro Cerimoniale,* 20–31.

This new liturgical fervor, antedating the Reformation, helps explain what happened after its outbreak. Beforehand, Savonarola protested against excessive ceremonialism, while after 1517 Luther, unable to do the ceremonies right, wished he could pass one day without thus communicating with his God.[40] The Ferrarese friar wanted to replace many short masses with one affective ceremony lasting three hours! The German friar and the Protestants, beginning precisely with attacks on excessive ceremonialism, structured new devotional worlds. There could be no direction without expression. At Münster the Anabaptists at first forbade flags as idolatrous, but once surrounded by the enemy they received illumination through the visions of a minister and quickly hoisted standards. Defense of their community imposed the organization of space, and organizing units in space required figured banners.[41] Comparable in this respect to the French Revolution as studied by Soboul, Ozouf, and Vovelle, the revolutionary struggles of the early modern period occurred in a hypertense world of anxiety in which different behavioral systems competed with each other so as to define binding organizations of time, space, and objects.

Where to meet? Various reformers chose rural hedges and had them sanctified before moving to closed quarters, which were either purified Catholic churches or new divine houses reverentially sealed off from profanity. The process of establishing new sacred places proceeded with protests against the very idea of doing so, with the tension and uncertainty presumably being the more pressing in those border areas of repeatedly changing testimonial commitments studied by Trevor-Roper.[42] Sacred time too was not eliminated but transformed, old festive calendars being challenged by new ones through calculated profanities on old sacred days. Protestants as well as Catholics quickly incorporated the celebrations of princely births, victories, marriages, and deaths, a calendrical integration which was the major innovation in the sacred time of the early modern period.[43]

---

[40] Trexler, *Public Life*, 474; J. Wirth, *Luther. Étude d'histoire religieuse* (Geneva, 1981).

[41] M. Rocke, "Ritual, Identity and Social Order in the New Jerusalem: Münster, 1534–1535," read at the conference "Persons in Groups. Social Behavior as Identity Formation" (Binghamton, New York: 14–16 October 1982).

[42] Trevor-Roper, *Crisis*, 90ff.

[43] Elizabeth I of England, as an example, had the *Acts and Monuments* of John Foxe, a work incorporating all these new sacred times, places, and objects, put up in every church in England: W. Haller, *Foxe's Book of Martyrs and the Elect Nation* (London, 1963), 13.

Objects were modified and remodeled by the turmoil, and it is not surprising that in these religions of the book, the printed word would first be stripped of its rich authenticating bindings and then rebound with new jewels and relics. If Luther burned the books of the law, he did so to bring men and women to their knees before the Bible. Yet the object of worship was not just any Bible, but the Word in the national language, and reverence to the one was commonly engendered by profanation of the other language. Nor would just any Bible in the national language engender the awe reserved for the locally revered volume of the particular church, square, meeting house, or for the Bible revered precisely because it came from a distant court or had been touched by a fabulous preacher. The Bible, the soon-refurbished law, and the polemical tracts of this period were in the first place privileged objects used to restructure behavior.

The elites of the new religions quickly produced a mass of printed norms to regulate distinct behaviors, and the Catholics followed suit. The myriad Confessions, Books of Discipline, Prayer and Ritual of the early modern Christian world first must be understood as behavioral phenomena, means through which, in public contexts, the actions of the faithful could be compared to the inspiring lives of their leaders to determine election or salvation, damnation or purgatorial status. Weapons in the battle for religious primacy, these tracts stimulated literacy because in them one could learn the verbal and behavioral codes which would pass the Christian through the fire of testimony.[44] Beginning with the engravings in these books, which furnished new devotional images — for example, the icons of reformation heroes — and then instruction in bodily behavior, one moved to the captions and then to the text to learn the way.

Testimony was a condition of the time. If I found "memorization" a feature of the humanistic education of adolescents in pre-Reformation Florence, a learning meant for public performance, Gerald Strauss has studied a strife-torn Germany in which children learned by heart formulas of "good manners and religion" while their parents also prepared themselves for testimonial performances in the public visitations of the time. After centuries of decline, public confessions rose to renewed prominence.[45]

---

[44] The primarily religious causes of increasing literacy are emphasized in F. Furet and J. Ozouf, *Lire et écrire*, 2 vols. (Paris, 1977).

[45] R. Trexler, "Ritual in Florence: Adolescence and Salvation in the Renaissance," in *The Pursuit of Holiness*, ed. Trinkaus and Oberman, 200–64; G. Strauss, *Luther's House of Learning. Indoctrination of the Young in the German Reformation* (Baltimore, 1978). Public confessing was, of course, a feature of certain Protestant confessions. It was fostered by

Similar patterns of testimonial public behavior are found in the New World, the missionaries being quite as determined to uncover through public performances the deceits of the Antichrist and "Lutherans" as were the ministers and lords in Europe.[46] The new worlds, times, and objects of awe and profanation were central contexts for these meaningful performances and thus creation of individual and group identities. The Americans who suffered the violence of these radically new contexts and, as Natalie Davis has shrewdly noted, the Protestants who denied their relevance regarding salvation had no less a decorum or behavioral reverence for such things than did Catholics.[47]

Thus a series of behavioral facts conventionally defined as being within the religious sphere take on a new life once they are placed alongside the ceremonial facts of the court, which are not so defined even though they have all the earmarks of religious activities as we have defined them above. Is this definition of religion too broad? I do not think so. Our definition is in fact close to the terminology used in traditional Europe, where religions as plural were defined as sets of social behaviors rather than as communities of doctrine, while religion in the singular meant something akin to the behavioral piety of a group as found in the affected individual.[48] If the modern usage of religion as reflection (see for example the type of books stacked under "religion" in any bookstore) represented an epistemological advance over the traditional one, that definition would, of course, be preferable. But such is not the case. Putatively, "religion" is the result of reflection as well as its essence, but in modern usage

---

the late medieval confraternity system. The use of public punishment was on the upswing, the punishment identifying the crime. The medieval decline of public confession did not lead up to "internal" Lutheranism: see my review of T. Tentler, *Sin and Confession on the Eve of the Reformation* (Princeton, 1977), in *Speculum* 53 (1978): 862–65.

[46] See, for example, R. Padden, *The Hummingbird and the Hawk* (New York, 1967), esp. chap. 13.

[47] N. Z. Davis, *Society and Culture in Early Modern France* (Stanford, 1975), 174.

[48] Thus the hospitallers were a religion or a *doctrina*, both words referring to sets of behaviors, clothing, and so on, summarized in statutes. A person who "had religion," in Geertz's excellent formulation, had "liabilities to perform particular classes of acts or have particular classes of feelings": see Geertz, *Interpretation*, 97. On the other hand, those like Geertz who view religion as a system of interpretative symbols are at odds with those many interpreters of traditional Europe who argued that the less one knew the holier one might be (*sancta rusticitas*). Note that, with no special word for religion, the Chinese language speaks of doctrine — of the literati — and rites. Like me it does not distinguish a priori between church and secular rites: M. Weber, *The Religion of China*, ed. H. Gerth (New York, 1951), 144.

it actually has ideological institutional foci. The modern definition's victory over the traditional one is linked more to the victory of the state, which controls the ritual stage and says faith is private but behavior a public matter. It is also linked to the supremacy of an intelligentsia which has celebrated a mind-body dualism in which symbols are made to seem factual rather than facts being made to seem symbolic. That modern definition's victory is much less due to historical observation.[49] Instead of greater methodological or conceptual clarity, the modern approach features ideological convenience.

Sharing in that fatal disciplinary tendency to cauterize human experience so as to conform to academic departments of knowledge, the modern idea of religion permits the historian as the apostle of conceptual progress to decide what was religious and what not, and allows her or him to root "real religion" in, when it is not derived from, elite institutions. The concept of Christianization is exemplary in this regard. At its least occult, the term designates the clerical effort during the early modern period to cast lay behavior into a normative framework. Many historians try to measure the success of such campaigns by studying lay performances in institutionally authenticated "Christian" contexts. For confessional historians, the approach presents no problems: either a Catholic or a particular Protestant practice *is* Christian. For less engaged historians, the concept is problematical, since these scholars are increasingly realizing that what they call Christianization, but what I see as a ceaseless search for group-identifying sets of behavior permitting religious experience, was common to all Christian religions of early modern Europe.[50] Those who call this ubiquitous process "Christianization" become enmeshed in the passions of their sources, for each group labeled its behavior Christian and others devilish; those despised practices which moderns may label non-Christian, pagan, or traditional vestiges, their sources commonly recognize as satanic performances by their so-called Christian adversaries. Recognizing therefore that two committed historians studying two different religions may find both being successfully Christianized, even though the practices of the groups are quite incomparable, these historians rely upon internalization to bridge

---

[49] See Geertz's interpretive definition of religion in *Interpretation*, 90ff.

[50] J. Delumeau, *Le Catholicisme entre Luther et Voltaire* (Paris, 1971); and the same author's *La Mort des pays de Cocagne* (Paris, 1976), chaps. 6–7. Vovelle's thesis of modern de-Christianization has predictably raised hackles among the faithful: see *La Religion populaire dans l'occident chrétien*, ed. B. Plongeron (Paris, 1976), 17.

the behavioral problems and to discover the reality beneath the mask. This process can also be found in their sources, where the thought dominates that transparency, authenticity, or internality are Christian, and deceit or "mere externality" non-Christian.

Those historians who descend directly from the Renaissance view of religion as reflection have meanwhile reached the same point by more direct means. For them no behavior but only internality is *really* religious in the first place, and since internality is by definition unobservable if describable, these historians simply intuit which Christianization was successful and which not, which ages were Christian and which not.[51] This fatal link between institutions and internality, epitomized in the idea of Christianization but linked to the broader modern link between power and virtue, ends by requiring or allowing the historian to uncover the deceit of others, and thus leads her or him implicitly to denounce that deceit as an irreverent profanation. In this process, sincerity is recognizably modern and actualized in the words of the historian, the past is deceptive to the extent it varies from the written word of its resurrector.

Instead of opting for this approach with its blissful ignorance of current deceit theory, we should imagine the early modern village as synonymous with procession, the court as associated with the parade, the city blending the two.[52] Contemporaries called both processions and parades sacred, and the groups in them religions. Both marched beneath crosses and flags with similar figures, and processions and parades could be occasions for violence, even if the stated purpose of both was to display the community of behavior at certain times around certain objects. A behavioral approach warns us not to define the one as religious, the other as secular, not to tell the reader that instead of having a religious intent, Richelieu, for example, "used religion as a pretext." The authority for such censorial assurances is often nothing more solid than our own association of procession with religion more than with parade. The denunciations of Richelieu by contemporaries for using religion as a pretext tell us something about their

---

[51] See the review of Manselli cited above, n. 22. See also S. Kierkegaard, *Fear and Trembling* (Princeton, 1974), 81–82, and esp. 89 for the "Knight of Faith" whose internality was not recognizable, even to another such knight.

[52] An issue of *Daedalus* (Summer 1979) on "Hypocrisy, Illusion and Evasion" completely avoided the scientific literature on animal deceit and its implications for the human question: see R. Dawkins, *The Selfish Gene* (Oxford, 1976), 171ff.

strategy for constructing their own sacred co-ordinates, but not necessarily anything about the cardinal; our judgment requires other supporting evidence. The historian's presumptive judgment on what was a religious and political strategy of his subjects only raises the suspicion that that presumption is part of an historiographical strategy with the comparable end of establishing sacred co-ordinates in historical writing.

If we watch what happens instead of plumbing the internality of our elite, we may determine that the procession and parade were certainly not identical: the procession was linked to established sacred places, while the parade in the same places augured the defilement of the sacred places of the internal or external enemy. Then, once carried abroad out of sacrally defined spaces, the two forms remain associated but distinct. Parading besiegers staged processions as if the land were already theirs, as if the spaces to be conquered already were redefined within the sacred–profane structures of the conquerors.[53] Whether those contested spaces were neighborhoods or kingdoms, the historical observer notes that before the combatants forgot, they had used deceit not only as a military but as a processional strategy to produce victory through various types of conjurations, exorcisms, threats, prayers, and insults stimulating through tricking themselves and their Gods. The victor remembers smashing the images of others but suppresses the memory of his sly challenge to his own Gods, parading them as if their identity had never been doubted by deceitful offerants. A behavioral approach to religion recognizes deceit as essential to religious experience in both the parade and the procession. The social history of sacralization through profanation, and profanation through sacralization, is a key to understanding the politics of religion.

The institutional biases of our contemporary understanding of religion is nowhere more evident than in the study of early modern iconoclasm, that phenomenon which, while beckoning us to admit the relation between the profane and the sacred, most powerfully seduces historians into imposing their modern concepts of the sacred as non-violent, non-political, non-dynamic, and non-deceitful. Sure that "true religion" is reflective and immaterial, historians sometimes consider iconoclasm either a vestigial phenomenon of Christian animism or as a necessary recurrent attack on fetishism.[54] Defining religious representations as those which churches

---

[53] See examples in my Public Life, 3–6 and "insults and ridicule" in the index.

[54] See the critique of this position in P. Geary, "La coercition des saints dans la pratique religieuse médiévale," in La Culture populaire au moyen âge, ed. P. Boglioni

say they are, many historians emphasize the ecclesiastical impact of iconoclasm to the exclusion of the impact such destruction had on the honor
and property rights of the objects' lay as well as ecclesiastical owners. But
it is perhaps the most telling reflection of the historians' own depoliticized
understanding of religion that iconoclasm is regarded as pre-eminently a
crisis phenomenon and not as a secular one, the result of parade violence,
so to speak, rather than of processional stability.

A behavioral study proceeds differently, beginning by laying aside the
presumption that there has been a decline in conceptual animism and
leaving the question open whether such an eventual decline has been
accompanied by a secular decline in iconoclasm itself. It notes first that
the verbal and bodily behavior used against the most varied material objects is remarkably similar in past and present, and it would appear that
the common element in these attacks is the inimical status of the objects,
which are "in the way." Iconoclasm is a general historical phenomenon.

Secondly, the observer will conclude that to distinguish between images which are religious and those which are not is abstract, for in practice, iconoclasm against figures conventionally defined as religious, like
Virgins, has been regularly approved by those who worship "the Virgin"
when a particular Virgin was said to be but a shape of the Devil. Con-
versely, colors (for example, the Levellers'), shapes (such as eucharistic
hosts), and images which are not representations of divinities (like coats of
arms) have commonly been viewed by the authorities as Godly or devilish
or, more precisely, they have claimed for such objects the same behavioral
reverence or profanation as that accorded to divine figures.

Thus, thirdly, to insist on the relation between the behavior and belief
of iconoclasts is to miss the fundamental nature of the behavior itself.
When a Jesuit missionary forced Indians publicly to smash a particular
image, the belief of the missionary might be as complex (the image as devil *and* as mere matter) as that of the natives, but the significance of the

---

(Quebec, 1979), 145–60. On English iconoclasm as "lamentable . . . but not without its
compensations," see G. Elton, *England under the Tudors* (London, 1960), 149. Thomas,
Religion, 75ff., sees Protestant iconoclasm as part of an attempt to take magic out of religion. The tendency to empty iconoclasm of iconoclasts is particularly marked in England,
where the state had an important hand in it: see J. Phillips, *The Reformation of Images:
Destruction of Art in England, 1535–1660* (Berkeley, 1973), where the actual actor when
unguided by the state becomes irrational. P. Mack Crew's *Calvinist Preaching and Iconoclasm in the Netherlands 1544–1569* (Cambridge, 1978) identifies the iconoclasts and judic-
iously evaluates their motivations.

event was behavioral.[55] There is in fact no reason to believe that icono-clasm necessarily presupposes beliefs about animism at all, but only inter-personal associations extended through objects.

Historians' emphasis upon iconoclasm against pictures of Gods is com-parable to the verbal manner with which the iconologists among art histo-rians have traditionally examined art for its meaning: both assume a cer-tain canonical meaning of a picture and fail to consider the questions of who owned the picture, in whose chapel it resided and, most important perhaps, whose occupational or noble or confraternal coat of arms was painted on or otherwise associated with it. Yet if anything is characteristic of early modern iconoclasm in Europe or in the European dependencies, it is that the iconoclasts attacked particular property rights, and that the massive assaults on those conventionally sacred objects during the period in question were attempts to redistribute property.[56] Property was and is secured within and in part through the sacred and profane behavioral clas-sifications in a society, and iconoclasm is an historically widespread be-havior when societies redistribute property. No more than iconologists can historians understand this other image of the image when they isolate the picture from its context.

A close behavioral emphasis in studies of iconoclasm, finally, shows that breaking, reshaping, or ignoring previously venerated representations are central parts of ongoing religious behavior, and are in no way limited to the political crises which draw such actions to our attention. Religions continually test the utility of their objects, and then apologize to the fig-ure or relic; they change divine representations to increase their utility; they discard or store away those proved useless and, since objects harm as well as heal, these various modes of ongoing group iconoclasms are prac-

---

[55] Notoriously, the statement that an object is lifeless is a means of making it so: R. Trexler, "Florentine Religious Experience: The Sacred Image," in his *Church and Com-munity 1200–1600: Studies in the History of Florence and New Spain* (Rome, 1987), 37–74. W. Brückner's important *Bildnis und Brauch* (Berlin, 1966) spends inordinate time show-ing that belief in *Bildmagie* was less widespread than art historians assume, and not enough on the behavior towards the "shame-effigies" he richly documents. The distinc-tion between planned and unpremeditated iconoclasm, between conscious and unconsci-ous behavior (see Phillips, *Destruction*, 4), between belief and non-belief in animism (Brückner) should not divert one from recognizing the fundamentally antagonous nature of the behavior and of the object attacked.

[56] As brought out in M. Warnke, ed., *Bildersturm. Die Zerstörung der Kunstwerke* (Munich, 1973); see also Phillips, *Destruction*, 201ff., and 90–94 for some telling contem-porary sources.

tised against both Gods and devils to prevent harm as well as cause good. Precious metal objects of worship may be melted when fiscal needs require, and contrarily, icons may be put back together, like Osiris or St. Bartholomew, a scattered polyptych or a flooded pastiche of fresco flecks, a fragmented ancient scroll.

This little-studied phenomenon is evidently not limited to hosts, relics, and icons, but is a procedure of any group dealing with the objects around which it organizes its behavior. Just as certainly, there is a difference in scale and publicity between the iconoclasm of politically stable and revolutionary times. But once this complex topic receives the attention it deserves, iconoclasm in both times will be found to rest on the same fundamental principles of group and individual identity formation and transformation. The competition within a particular religion changes its images, and the competition within a given body politic for images such as flags accomplishes similar ends. Iconoclasm in the great revolts of the early modern period was part of a fundamental, ongoing social process involving the modification and transformation of existing religious order.

The turmoil of behavioral order in early modern Europe involves profanations that, when directed against "false Gods," are called religious experiences.[57] Far from being an understanding of order, the sacred is often not even its experience, but rather an exhilaration in disorder resolved through action. When one reads diaries and letters rather than official group histories, where forgetfulness edifies memory,[58] one uncovers religious experience in an iconoclasm towards one's own *sacra* which reflects the inherent disorder of the changing identities of religions. The historian's willingness to accept at face value a group memory which invariably emphasizes group solidarity amounts to a depoliticization of social processes going on inside a group and to a deindividuation of the persons involved in this competitive face-to-face behavior towards each other and towards their changing Gods.

Across early modern Europe and its dependencies, peasants and Indians, monarchs and missionaries experienced the sacred in the act of profaning their own and others' Gods by attacking properties. These were sacred times, to be sure, remembered and relived as an age of aweful, efficacious behavior, in which, in Hegel's formulation, heaven came to earth.

---

[57] I have only to call attention to the searing religious convictions in N. Z. Davis, "Rites of Violence," in her *Society*, 152–87.

[58] On the differences in these sources, see my *Public Life*, chap. 2.

Call its widespread testimonial iconoclasms a world-historical event if one likes, yet understand it not as the reverse but as the mirror of "routine" times. When watching not just the parade but also the procession, profanation appears as a condition of sacrality.

Historiographical Rhetoric and Religious Experience

To the sound of Brahms, historians still annually march in uniform beneath the truncheon, as did their ancestors in cities and courts. A mere tradition, even historians might argue, but the social historian of religion knows by now that the *survivances vivent*. In the academic procession of commencement, the historian who wants to study "popular religion" will begin by studying this elite. Colleagues' rigidity increases as the procession, including one's self, comes into view of the audience. At this moment, scholars in cap and gown use bodily and vocal persuasion — the more sculptured the more powerful — upon parents and students in a sacral setting. Beneath those grave academic robes one may wear levis and read articles and exams as the commencement speaker drones on. Yet who can dismiss the rhetoric? The rhetoric of academics at commencement mirrors the persuasions they use to communicate at a conference, in a classroom, in writing. Reverential forms are no mere sacrament of simple folk; on the contrary, the elites have historically been categorized as "the solemn persons." In concluding, I want to examine the relation between historiographical rhetoric and religion, and suggest elements of a behavioral strategy for combating the deceit that there is none.

Societies record religious experience in two different fashions, we have said. In his diary, the individual includes his profanation of his own Gods, and thus of his living associates; in the history, on the other hand, the group forgets its self-profanations, and religious experience becomes our memory of individuation as we revere our group and its Gods while profaning some other group.[59] Historical writing is not dissimilar. Beginning with insight, during which the images are subject to iconoclasm, we proceed to written communications, a type of open social behavior in which the imperatives of linguistic convention and the corporate intellective paradigms of the historian's colleagues make their reverential influences

---

[59] This distinction does not apply where, as in the Puritan diaries, they were written for future testimony or printing: see W. Haller, *The Rise of Puritanism* (New York, 1947), 97, 101ff.

felt. Charles Tilly has found that most historians of the United States express their findings in terms of a limited number of recognizable questions.[60] The study of early modern religion is no exception to such behavior. Like Françoise Zonabend's peasant woman, the religious experience of the "old days" flattens out into predictable patterns.[61] Recalling idols which did not change and creating ones that did not exist can become the condition of identity for the historian and the peasant.

All historians evoke ancestors, as do most religions. Once stated, this simile highlights the difference between the historian of religion and other historians, and the difference between past religions and historiographical evocation. It is a question of exchange and its objects in present and past. In the present, all historians exchange with colleagues and patrons recognizable formations of past behaviors and ideas, but the student of a past religion deals with social formations which created affective, meaningful solidarities in the past, and those solidarities are on their face quite as imperious as those the patronized historians themselves obey in their present world.

When that historian of religion looks to the object of his or her study, the nature of these conflicting exchanges becomes clear. The historical religion had as a condition of its solidarity making *its* ancestors its own; its legitimacy was rooted in giving the behavioral ghosts of its past an "aura of factuality."[62] Separated from that religion by time and usually place, the historian of that religion tries to raise up for present colleagues a religion part of whose essence was the ongoing resurrection of its specific dead. This difficult task calls for the historian to successively affect his or her religion, so as to evoke its specific dead, and it requires that he or she be affected by those individual generations of a past religion. At such distances from the objects, the historian's results, achieved under the pressure of his or her own colleagues and patrons, are not shocking. Concepts like "popular religion" eliminate the line between past life and death and the specifics of time and place, while psychological characterizations distance the past from the present. The fact that the historian evokes the past for a decorous exchange with the living, while the historical religion evoked a specific past that was behaviorally exchanged with its living, amounts to a fundamental obstacle in the study of religion. It explains in part why the

---

[60] C. Tilly, *As Sociology Meets History* (New York, 1981), 18–21.

[61] F. Zonabend, *La Mémoire longue: temps et histoires au village* (Paris, 1980); cf. Le Roy Ladurie, *Montaillou*, 419–31.

[62] For C. Geertz, ritual clothes conceptions with this aura: *Interpretation*, 109–19.

religious actors of early modern Europe, though dead, often are made to behave without thinking, while their historians, though alive, seem at times
to breathe only thoughts.

Awareness of the ideological dangers this complex exchange system
poses for the study of religions cannot in itself dissolve them; the fact that
the language through which we communicate has inherent structures of
sacrality and profanity alone negates that possibility. Yet exactly this insight does, I believe, offer a way of alleviating the danger. Language as
used by the historian *is* a political behavior, and if the language of reverence makes it seem that it is not, the language of profanation allows us to
maintain awareness of deceit and to constantly subvert an instrument of communication that is essentially sacred in its significations for the present.

The ongoing profanations I recommend for the study of past religions,
that is, for the affective exchanges the historian seeks with the past and
present, might take many different forms, of which I want to single out
four. The first approach profanes the present, and involves avoiding all
distancing and marginalizing linguistic conventions which are demonstrably modern and violations of past linguistic usages. I shall limit myself to
the phenomenon of capitalization, almost unknown until adopted with a
vengeance in the sixteenth century in evident relation to an explosion of
authoritarian ideology. Today's scholars use an admittedly narrowed range
of capitalization with a certain flexibility. If it is not unusual to encounter
"King," "Church," "Pontiff," "Him" (*sic!*), and so on, perhaps most historians no longer capitalize such words. But a non-scientific survey of my
library shows that all historians preserve the capitalization of the Judeo-
Christian "God," though many of the same writers speak of "god" or "the
god" when referring to non-Christian deities, and almost all these writers
render references to more than one God in the lower-case "the gods." It
is unnecessary to spell out the conceptual assumptions such usages preserve,
or to insist that explaining this as "mere convention" only makes the point
that conventions are powerful and that writers, not editors, are the ones who
exercise that power. In capitalization the concept of ideal conceptual and political unity is encapsulated, while the plural gods on the margins are rendered small. The rational Western present is preserved for exchange among
the living, but the quality of the exchanges past religions made with their
living, and especially with their dead, is unavoidably contorted.

The second usage would profane the religion we study by refusing to
adopt those past characterizations of the objects of religious exchange
which at the time had self-evident marginalizing or exclusionary functions.

I refer only to the use of the terms "image" and "idol." We know that in the immediate context of religious experience, one group of Christian contemporaries opposed to another group did call the latter's images, such as a certain Virgin or Bible, "idols," but the historian recognizes that passion as marginalizing, so he or she refers to any Christian image as just that, even if it is not unusual to find Protestant historians still verbally smashing Catholic images. Yet how are we to explain that when either committed or uncommitted historians deal with images of non-Christian religions, they regularly refer to them as "idols," as in "the idol of Huitzilopochtli"? In the past this and similar distinctions were evidently signs by which devotees testified as to those objects one exchanged with and those which one avoided. For the historian wishing to analyze instead of judging the ubiquitous social phenomenon of religion, the injunction is apparent: refer to such objects as images, and drop the word idol with all its ideological baggage. The alternative is historiographical idolatry.

A third usage returns to the profanation of the present, and involves adopting all those linguistic usages of past religions which characterized religious exchange without the evident function of marginalizing the persons and objects of those exchanges. I refer to exchange terminologies historians of religion are familiar with but usually do not use. Consciously or unconsciously, such terms are now considered irreverent as characterizations of the exchanges most historians understand to underlie the phenomenon of religion; religion as reciprocity is one thing to say but, as we noted regarding the use of the words "spell" and "prayer," another to communicate. Thus contemporaries called a secular priest who sold exchanges between heaven and earth without benefice a mercenary; we mention the fact but do not integrate the word. In their account books if not in their histories, members of religions kept what they called "accounts of God"; what was a matter-of-fact usage for them is a curiosity to us.[63] Contemporaries expected to be "paid" by their Gods, to receive "interest," and so on; we avoid integrating such business terminology into our analysis. A painting of the Adoration of the Magi which shows the infant with his hand in the jar of gold pieces is taken as evidence of the famous "mixing of the sacred and profane" of those ages, often with the clear implication that we moderns have got them straightened out, especially by not using

---

[63] Trexler, *Public Life*, chap. 3, on exchange. On Puritans who "posted [their] account with God" and spoke of "incomes and profits received in spiritual traffic," see Haller, *The Rise of Puritanism*, 100.

the language of *do ut des* in our analysis.[64] Precisely because of our embarrassment with past exchange language, the result not of a better but of
a more controlled practice of religion, incorporating such language into
analysis would be not only true to the primary sources of religious life, but
disruptive of the segregation of the decommercialized holy the present ex-
pects of its historians.

My last suggestion profanes both the past and present, and involves applying the systematic language of economics to the portrayal of past religious behavior. The practice might be dangerously anachronistic if it were
not for the fact that the late Middle Ages came so close to a systematic
mathematization of the business of salvation. The phenomenon is not unknown. Contemporaries moved from investments based on calculations of
life expectancies to calculating the solidarity they could expect from their
living friends and relatives once they had died; armed with the church's
estimations of the value of different indulgences, they then proceeded to
calculate the length of purgatory and to arrange their testaments on that
basis. Rarely mentioned except in the context of Protestant attacks on
Catholic "superstition," pride, and rationalism, the phenomenon has now
been studied by Jacques Chiffoleau in a book on Avignonese testaments
significantly titled *La Comptabilité de l'au-delà.*[65]

Chiffoleau has drawn the systematic consequences from his sources'
common but unsystematized use of the economic terminology referred to
above, and casts these usages into an economic framework. Thus the
author speaks of the "economy of salvation" and of its "mathematics"; his
contemporaries are made to reckon the "price of passage," the laws of
"spiritual supply and demand" in constructing a "budget of the beyond."
The author presumably chose this terminology to drive home what he
took to be the essence of the religious behavior he was studying.

But the procedure has other benefits. It provides the type of affective
aesthetic unity moderns rightly expect from their historians without doing
irreparable violence to the images of the past, since that systematic terminology is implied in the sources. Incompatible though it might seem
with my insistence on the specificity of each community of behavior I
have called a religion, such terminology yet evokes that behavioral process

---

[64] See, for example, Muchembled, *Culture*, 129. On the Adoration, E. Gombrich,
"The Evidence of Images," in *Interpretation*, ed. C. Singleton (Baltimore, 1969), 90–91.

[65] *La Comptabilité de l'au-delà: les hommes, la mort et la religion dans la région d'Avignon
à la fin du moyen âge* (Rome, 1980), esp. pt. ii.

of individuation within social codes which is religion itself. By material-izing past affects, it may also challenge historians of religion to consider their own tenaciously defended identity-in-reflection as a strategy for ren-dering the body of their work incorrupt in death.

Less preachily and more to the point, systematizing the language of re-ligious exchange, and the other linguistic procedures I have suggested, drives home the point that the historian does behave towards the past. Chiffoleau's judgments, for example, are the more apparent because of the systemic language of exchange he chose to describe the religious experi-ence of composing a testament.[66] Historians too testify. Like our religious ancestors, and like the operators of today's computers, experimenting with body and verbal language can produce facts, new insights and concepts.

§

This essay has tried to critique the language and concepts we use to study past religion by relating them to our own corporate identity, for I be-lieve that this is a precondition for an improved approach to the religions of early modern Europe. I pointed to an association of historians with re-flection and of "the people" with behavior as a sound reason for emphasiz-ing religious behavior in our studies.

It would be counterproductive, I argued, to create a new marginaliza-tion between ideas and behavior to replace those psychological marginal-izations I faulted. Emphasizing the behavior of elites would, I thought, lead historians of religion to recognize the behavioral aspects of their own work, but becoming familiar with the ethology and semiotics of verbaliza-tion would help us understand the nature of ideas better, including their deceit. To that end I offered a behavioral definition of religion.

Such an approach seems on examination to be particularly appropriate to the study of religion in early modern Europe. It allows us to study its parades and processions as intimately related and intimately religious. It is clear that the religions of the time all faced the common task of classifying times, spaces and objects into systems of sacrality and profanity, though the solutions were individual, indeed the very identity of each religion.[67]

---

[66] He repeatedly judges whether testators were "sincere" or not, whether they clothed themselves in friars' habits for burial because of "magic," or because of "true piety," and so on.

[67] N. Z. Davis, "Sacred," and "Rites" in her *Society*, attempts to distinguish between Reformed and Catholic solutions on the basis of what she occasionally calls "style"; I am

That process was not, finally, limited to the institutions conventionally defined as religions. One result of a behavioral approach to religion was to note the fundamentally similar formal and affective characteristics of the contemporary mass *and* court, and I suggested that to ignore these similarities was to calcify the study of religion and of the religious experience of past individuals and groups.

Early modern Europe began and ended in great waves of iconoclasm, and surely the historian inevitably recreates a more or less reverential, more or less profane picture of those times. It is therefore not a question of historians being objective or dropping their beliefs and prejudices, but of interminably profaning the past and themselves in the face of ever-new linguistic authoritarianism and corporate orthodoxies. Reverence is the enemy as it is the condition of social life and historical writing. Loath to consider St Anne as a witch, as Jean Wirth has profanely done,[68] we prefer our sacred-profane organization to that of the past. We have been understandably slow, therefore, to study that most Christian, most iconoclastic of all activities and ideas of European religion, the eating of the God ... then, and now.

---

suggesting that to the extent that one religion identifies another, it is done on the basis of observed behavioral characteristics, whether the observations are right or wrong.

[68] J. Wirth, "Sainte Anne est une sorcière," *Bibliothèque d'Humanisme et Renaissance* 40 (1978): 449–80.

RELIGIOUS DYNAMICS:

THE GENDER

COMPONENT

Gendering Jesus Crucified[*]

We are more moved by seeing Christ hanging on the cross
than by reading that he was crucified.[1]

UNLIKE THE REPRODUCTIVE ORGANS of many other divinities, the penis
and testicles of Jesus Christ have only recently been suspected of having
much meaning. That is true even in the context of the Crucifixion, where
the very fact that Jesus hung naked before the crowd capped his humiliation. Perhaps there's the rub. Whereas historically the actual importance
of the divine genitalia lay in their perception by those who gazed upon or
thought about them, in our time penile significance is looked for, if at all,
away from that madding crowd of devotees and ridiculers. Repeated calls
in the last generation to pay attention to historical peoples' responses to
devotional images have largely fallen on deaf ears.[2] I believe that the

[*] This essay appeared previously in *Iconography at the Crossroads*, ed. B. Cassidy
(Princeton, 1993), 107–20.

[1] Johannes Molanus, cited in D. Freedberg, "Johannes Molanus on Provocative
Paintings. *De Historia Sanctarum imaginum et picturarum*, Book II, Chapter 42," *Journal of
the Warburg and Courtauld Institutes* 31 (1971): 234. My thanks to Caroline Bynum Walker, James A. Boon, William A. Christian, Jr., Klaus Schreiner, and Jean Wirth for their
input on this subject, and Lyn Blanchfield for reading a draft.

[2] D. Freedberg, *The Power of Images. Studies in the History and Theory of Response*
(Chicago, 1989) and M. Camille, *The Gothic Idol: Ideology and Image-making in Medieval
Art* (Cambridge, 1989), are recent exceptions. See also R. Trexler, "Florentine Religious

primary meanings of devotional objects, whether of flesh and blood or artificial, are those that move people to devotion and, in the contemplative regimes of traditional Christianity, to tears.[3]

Historians of religion are of course often ready to tell us what "people" thought (not did), but on examination, these thoughts often turn out to be little more than the historians' own, projected back onto past intellectuals and thence, according to trickle-down theory, onto simple folk. Thus in his pathfinding *Sexuality of Christ*, Leo Steinberg laudably unveiled Jesus' penis for serious study, only to then indicate that these genitalia did not *affect* medieval and Renaissance painters: the latter *only thought* of them as a sign of Jesus' humanity.[4] In her equally important *Holy Feast and Holy Fast*, and especially in her review of Steinberg's *Sexuality*, Caroline Bynum, in this at one with Steinberg, warned that medieval people did not assign sexual meanings to things as do we moderns. The Christic penis, for example, referred to Jesus' circumcision rather than being a sexual object.[5] Jean Wirth capped off this assignment of potential genital sensualities to the fleshless spheres by claiming that the Middle Ages considered (male *and* female?) generative organs to be "ridiculous and ugly."[6] So away with those legions of Boccaccesque men and women who, on reaching their erotic goal, are known to have cried *Che bella!* Obviously, historians are

---

Experience: The Sacred Image," in his *Church and Community, 1200–1600. Studies in the History of Florence and New Spain* (Rome, 1987), 37–74; and W. Christian, Jr., *Moving Crucifixes in Modern Spain* (Princeton, 1992).

[3] It follows that a "devotional object" is one to which we pray, at the time we do, irrespective of the artist's original intent. On contemplative regimes, see J. H. Marrow, *Passion Iconography in Northern European Art of the Late Middle Ages and Early Renaissance. A Study of the Transformation of Sacred Metaphor into Descriptive Narrative* (Kortrijk, 1979); W. Christian, Jr., "Provoked Religious Weeping in Early Modern Spain," in *Religious Organization and Religious Experience*, ed. J. Davis (London, 1982), 97–114. One man's contemplation of Jesus' body parts, though not including his genitalia, is in R. Trexler, "In Search of Father. The Experience of Abandonment in the Recollections of Giovanni di Pagolo Morelli," *History of Childhood Quarterly* 2 (1975): 225–52.

[4] L. Steinberg, *The Sexuality of Christ in Renaissance Art and in Modern Oblivion* (New York, 1983).

[5] C. Walker Bynum, *Holy Feast and Holy Fast* (Berkeley, 1987), and especially the concluding section of "The Body of Christ in the Later Middle Ages: A Reply to Leo Steinberg," *Renaissance Quarterly* 39 (1986): 399–439.

[6] J. Wirth, "Sur l'évolution du crucifix à la fin du Moyen Age," *Les ateliers des interprètes. Revue européene pour étudiants en histoire de l'art* 2 (1989): 177; see also his *L'Image médiévale* (Paris, 1989).

still far from considering audience reactions to cultural artifacts as an integral part of their meaning. And as regards the Christian divinities' sexuality, the task of integrating viewers has scarcely begun.

In this paper I shall concentrate on how certain thinkers assumed that devotees, in the *imitatio* of Christ's Passion, responded to seeing or sensing his genitalia. I shall argue that not completely unlike other Gods, Jesus, whether in his image or in the vision made of him in imitation, might physically seduce his devotees and even those who ridiculed him. The goal of maintaining decorum in the presence of such representations was, therefore, important to moralists and, I shall argue, their opposition to representing Jesus naked had broad political and social roots.

On the basis of contemporary moralists' evidence, how *did* people in traditional Europe react to Jesus on the Cross? And how did they imagine people would act if they saw him naked, as the Bible said he had been — to the discomfort of all those who wished to cover him? Let it first be said that Jesus' whole crucified body was conventionally perceived by medieval people as a volume to be penetrated by audience. Thus in a dream Rupert von Deutz (d. 1129/30) envisioned himself French-kissing the crucified Jesus,[7] while Peter of Blois (d. 1200) opined that Jesus' side wound, or "corporal opening," allowed one to peer in at the divine entrails, and Battista Varani (1458–1527) actually wanted to "enter the vase itself" so as to locate the Christic heart.[8] The women did not lag behind. They in fact led in the development of the cult of the externalized (fetched from the inside) Sacred Heart and the devotional theme of exchanging hearts with Jesus through such corporal intrusiveness.[9] Long before modern psychoanalytic insights, the genital implications of such penetrations were

---

[7] "Quod cum festinus introissem, apprehendi quem diligit anima mea, tenui illum, amplexatus sum eum, diutius exosculatus sum eum. Sensi quam gratanter hunc gestum dilectionis admitteret, cum inter osculandum suum ipse os aperiret, ut profundius oscularer": Rupert von Deutz, *De gloria et honore filii hominis super Mattheum*, ed. H. Haacke, Corpus Christianorum. Continuatio Mediaevalis 29 (Turnhout, 1979), 383.

[8] Cited in Wirth, *Image*, 323; see also Wirth's "La naissance de Jésus dans le coeur: étude iconographique," *Publications du Centre européen d'études bourguignonnes* (XIVᵉ–XVIᵉ s.) 29 (1989): 149–58.

[9] M. Carroll has studied the erotic roots of the cult of the Sacred Heart: *Catholic Cults and Devotions. A Psychological Inquiry* (Kingston, 1989), 138–43; also A. Vauchez, *La sainteté en occident aux derniers siécles du Moyen Age d'après les procès de canonisation et les documents hagiographiques* (Rome, 1981), 517–18.

clear among late fifteenth-century German printmakers, who might, for instance, provocatively place the crucified Jesus' pierced, externalized heart over the space where his genitals belonged.[10]

Few can ignore the massive evidence of medieval and early modern women's erotic involvement with the body of Christ — medieval Swabian women claimed they had had sex with Jesus or had brought themselves to orgasm with his body;[11] the Englishwoman Margery Kempe (1373–ca. 1439) saw dangling genitals before her when faced with the Host;[12] Alexander Pope's Heloise (ca. 1715) had an orgasm on seeing the erect Abelard in place of the Jesus hanging before her.[13] Yet the crucifix was not always merely male, nor was its manipulation purely imaginary. A second fundamental element of late medieval and early modern interaction with crucifixes is evidence that devotees might manipulate the male gender of crucifixes — the opposite, say, of women taking on the male bodily features of Jesus through contemplating him on the Cross.[14]

One sign of this process of gender manipulation, which appears interesting enough in itself, was that the wound in Jesus' side sometimes came to look more and more like a vagina.[15] But more important to this paper is evidence that to devotional ends, male images were rendered effeminate, or even female. It is well known that Sebastian and John the Evangelist took on strongly androgynous features in the late Middle Ages, but it is less familiar that certainly by the fifteenth century, and as cult required, Jesus Crucified in parts of northern Europe was changed into and clothed as the female transvestite Saint Wilgeforte (also called Kümmernis) and

---

[10] Wirth, *Image*, 323.

[11] H. Grundmann, *Religiöse Bewegungen im Mittelalter* (Berlin, 1935), 412–14.

[12] *The Book of Margery Kempe* (London, 1985), chaps. 35, 59, 79; see the suggestive article by S. Beckwith, "A Very Material Mysticism: The Medieval Mysticism of Margery Kempe," in *Medieval Literature. Criticism, Ideology and History*, ed. D. Aers (Brighton, 1986), 34–57.

[13] Although he had been castrated! See the marvelous verse cited by G. Wills, "The Phallic Pulpit," *New York Review of Books* (21 December 1989), 21–22.

[14] As suggested by Beckwith, "*Material Mysticism*"; her evidence is from Vauchez, *Sainteté*, 517–18. See also C. Bynum's documentation of twelfth-century abbots calling themselves mothers, which she traces to larger gender conventions in the period's social relations: *Jesus as Mother* (Berkeley, 1982), 135–46.

[15] Most striking in the breviary of Bonne of Luxemburg, reproduced in Wirth, *Image*, 329.

then changed back again to Jesus.[16] By the end of the sixteenth century, and continuing until the present day, Spaniards and Latin Americans have sometimes adorned the male Jesus on the Cross with what we today call slips. This regendering deserves our attention.[17]

Jesus' body was therefore more than a vehicle for expressing female as well as male gender qualities, as Bynum rightly insisted in her critique of Steinberg's exclusive emphasis on the salvific penis.[18] Crucifixes might be manipulated to represent the one or the other sex. In her study of certain Hindu devotions, Wendy Doniger showed that the object of prayer always has to be heterosexually gendered in relation to the sex of the orant, at times switching gender to facilitate that relation.[19] Here is something to examine for the comprehension of Christian devotion as well. At the very least, the gender relation between orant and object needs to be considered as a fundamental factor of worship, rather than ignored, as if to say that the Crucified, this fetish of a decisively patriarchal ecclesiastical structure, stands in no such gender relation to his supplicant.

These two facts — that Jesus was experienced as a volume to be penetrated, and that his crucifix could be physically manipulated to change gender or even sex — attain their full meaning only when we know something about the devotees and, perhaps most fundamentally, about their sex. If we wish to evaluate the change in the Crucified from clothed to barechested,[20] or in the late Middle Ages toward transparent loincloths

---

[16] G. Schnürer documented three eighteenth- and nineteenth-century cases in small Swiss villages where statues went from male to female: "Die Kummernis- und Volto santo-Bilder in der Schweiz," *Freiburger Geschichtsblätter* 10 (1903): 112f., 125f., 149; and the standard work of G. Schnürer and J. Ritz, *Sankt Kümmernis und Volto Santo* (Düsseldorf, 1934), with excellent illustrations. But the practice was doubtless common in the late Middle Ages for Wilgeforte, as it was for other worthies, for which see R. Trexler, "Dressing and Undressing Images," elsewhere in the present volume.

[17] The role of the different sexes in fashioning Jesus in this way remains to be determined. One of the oldest such loincloths or "slip-perizoniums," from late sixteenth- or seventeenth-century Mallorca, is shown in G. Llompart, *Religiosidad popular. Folklore de Mallorca, Folklore de Europa* (Palma de Mallorca, 1982), 190. In a personal communication, William Christian suggested that post-Tridentine insistence on Crucifix-worship to the detriment of Mary-worship may help explain the Crucified's taking on such female characteristics. See further below, n. 68.

[18] Bynum, "Body of Christ."

[19] W. Doniger O'Flaherty, *Women, Androgynes, and Other Mythical Beasts* (Chicago, 1980), 87–93.

[20] Best traced by P. Thoby, *Le Crucifix des origines au Concile de Trente* (Nantes, 1959).

or perizoniums with no signs of male genitalia (hardly a genderless representation!),[21] or in the Italian Renaissance to the increasingly creamy flesh of the crucified Jesus, we must know what role devotees of each sex played in them. The same applies, finally, to our particular interest here — to the genitalia of the man/god.

Around the year 1500, scholars, even from the pulpit, raised the question whether Jesus' penis had been visible while he hung on the cross. The counterreaction was predictable: moralists asserted that such things should not be discussed, especially in the presence of women, whose so-called shame was pleaded.[22] This leads me to ask if women's reactions were also used *to justify* opposition to *pictures* of Jesus crucified. My evidence encourages me to answer in the negative. Over the course of Christian history, mostly only males' reactions to an eventually palpable Christic penis are found to be worthy of analysis. In male discourse, the male's fear of the sight of a naked Jesus explains why, in all of Christian art, Jesus was rarely shown naked.[23] I now wish to describe this fear, but I also wish to defend the hypothesis that, in fact, the authorities were concerned about both male and female reactions to the naked Christic penis, worrying that, at its sight, certain women and men would be tempted to escape the control of their masters.

One of the earliest and most influential studies of nakedness in the Christian era was undertaken by Augustine of Hippo in his *City of God* where he explained the corporeal impact upon Adam (not Eve) of the Fall. On viewing Eve, Augustine indicated, Adam had an involuntary erection. To Augustine's mind, we have here a fundamental characteristic of post-lapsarian males: on being stimulated by desirable objects of either sex,

---

[21] This is the subject of Wirth's "Sur l'évolution." The author argues that Jesus without genitalia was understood by average people as a statement about an ideal, virginal clergy.

[22] In 1499 this was Wimpfeling's and Nicholas Besler's opinion: G. Knod, "Jacob Wimpfeling und Daniel Zanckenried. Ein Streit über die Passion Christi," *Archiv für Literaturgeschichte* 17 (1886): 5–8. It was also Johannes von Paltz's view in his 1502 *Coelifodina* (Erfurt) as it had been that of his teacher Johannes von Dorsten; see Paltz, *Werke*, vol. 1 (Berlin, 1983), 51–53. My thanks to Craig Harbison and Klaus Schreiner for help in this area.

[23] The only medieval Crucifixion I have found with a penis clearly visible (through a transparent perizonium) is part of the *Sendlinger Altarpiece* (1407), once in the Frauenkirche in Munich. The painting is today in the diocesan museum in Freising. Clement of Alexandria early objected to showing erections in paintings: cited in Freedberg, "Molanus," 245.

their penises become erect, or remain flaccid, independent of their wishes. The penis does not obey reason, will, or the collective sense of propriety. Moreover, because males are ashamed that the penis disobeys, even the most barbaric among them put on clothes to conceal involuntary erections or flaccidity.[24] Thus shame comes after and not before penile behavior; it is an effect and not a cause. It need hardly be pointed out that Augustine failed to praise women for not showing corporeal signs of sensate disobedience. It is as if, missing an apposite, visible body part, women do not respond to sensual stimuli.

Generally speaking, traditional Europeans followed the Bible in assuming that Jesus was hung naked on the Cross — "that horrific nakedness of the shamed," Jacob Wimpfeling called it — so as to humiliate decisively a male too weak to resist such treatment.[25] Why then was he practically never represented in that state? This question is the more important for any Christian theory of devotion because a covered Jesus, not being fully humiliated, obviously derailed devotees' *imitatio Christi*. No encyclopedic survey of medieval tractates' discussions of sexual matters exists, as painfully as it is needed, but on the evidence of Augustine, one hypothesis explaining Christianity's historic unwillingness to show not only naked females, but naked adult males, especially Jesus on the Cross, is that male viewers might have had an erection, as Pope's Heloise had an orgasm, if they saw the salvific genitalia. A loincloth reduced the likelihood of this happening. A church based on that icon did not wish to have its faithful interacting sexually, if necrophilically, with a naked image, a danger represented by the Rohan Master (ca. 1420–1430), who showed the Crucified ejaculating blood, while opposite, two lovers engage (fig. 30). In short, a

---

[24] On "illa qua obscenae partes corporis excitantur" and "quidam barbari," see Augustine of Hippo, *The City of God Against the Pagans*, vol. 4 (Cambridge, MA, 1966), bk. XIV, chaps. 16, 17. See also P. Brown, *The Body and Society* (New York, 1988), 416–17; G. Wills, Phallic Pulpit"; and U. Ranke-Heinemann, *Eunuchs for the Kingdom of Heaven. Women, Sexuality and the Catholic Church* (New York, 1990), 90–93.

[25] The fourteenth-century Ps.-Bonaventure was especially graphic in making this point. Thus on the way to crucifixion, among a whole list of humiliations, "gli hanno tolto il mantello e legata alta la tunica ai fianchi, senza alcun rispetto,"*Anonimo francescano del '300. Meditazioni sulla vita di Cristo* (Rome, 1982), 127–28 (chap. 75). For "illa horrenda nuditas verendorum," see Knod, "Wimpfeling," 5. To the Crucifixion may be added the story of the naked Jesus' flagellation. Significantly, its Old Testament complement or type was Job being ridiculed and beaten up by his wife; see, for example, the complementary pictures in *Heilsspiegel. Die Bilder des mittelalterlichen Erbauungsbuches Speculum humanae salvationis*, ed. H. Appuhn (Dortmund, 1981), 42–43.

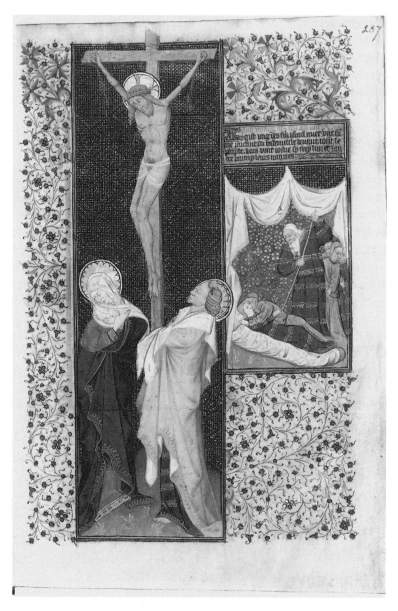

Figure 30.
The Master of Rohan, *Crucifixion*, and *Phinehas Punishing the Lovers*,
from Book of Hours, 1420–1430.
Paris, Bibl. Nat., Ms. lat. 9471 fol. 237.
Photo courtesy of the Bibliothèque Nationale.

Jesus covered at the crotch might help prevent the seduction of the faithful.[26]

There were other ways to mitigate the threat of seduction. One way to prevent images from arousing viewers during the Middle Ages — those of the androgyne Saint Sebastian, for example — was to show their flesh mutilated.[27] That was a tall order, since Jesus, still in the prime of life, had a "beau corps bien formé," as one Roman soldier in a sixteenth-century play observed on seeing Jesus in the buff. Though little is known in particular about medieval imaginings regarding the condition of Jesus' genitals, the body as a whole was considered perfect in every respect, white and lithe, in short, ultimately seductive.[28]

Representing the bare-chested Jesus in the mutilated state of the Passion, while rendering him sensually undesirable to the hardened contemplative, could not hide what could be expected of any male on the point of expiring on a cross: an erection, followed by an ejaculation. This embarrassingly public and uncontrollable *motus corporis* might be anticipated

---

[26] The Rohan Master presumably meant to refer to Jesus' circumcision, but, in fact, the painting looks like the result of a castration, which is what the Israelite Phinehas, after having speared the pair's genitalia, inflicts on the lovers: *The Rohan Master. A Book of Hours*, ed. M. Thomas (New York, 1973), pl. 127; and A. Edwardes, *Erotica Judaica. A Sexual History of the Jews* (New York, 1967), 17f.

[27] For a case where a St. Sebastian by Fra Bartolomeo was removed because it excited nuns, see Freedberg, *Power of Images*, 346; and *Le opere di Giorgio Vasari*, ed. G. Milanesi (Florence, 1906), 4:188. Ordered to create a Virgin Mary that would not be alluring, Toto del Nunziata, in good Wilgefortian manner, put a beard on her: Vasari-Milanesi, *Opere*, 6:536 and Freedberg, *Power of Images*, 322, and, in general, his chap. 14; also Wills, "Phallic Pulpit," 22.

[28] The play line is from J.-C. Bologne, *Histoire de la Pudeur* (Paris, 1986), 224. Statements about the quality of Jesus' body occur regularly in devotional literature. The Ps.-Anselm called it "delicata enim et naturalis ingenuitas et formosa membrorum principalium": *Dialogus beatae Mariae et Anselmi de passione domini*, PL 159:279–80. A medieval English nun spoke of "his beauty, loving face, and white flesh beneath his clothes": cited in H. P. Duerr, *Traumzeit. Über die Grenze zwischen Wildnis und Zivilisation* (Frankfurt am Main, 1985), 312–13. Margery Kempe: "the handsomest man that ever might be seen or imagined": *Book*, 249 (chap. 85). Ps.-Bonaventure: "nudo di fronte a tutti, giovane dal corpor armonioso e riservato, lui, il più bello degli uomini": *Anonimo francescano*, 132 (chap. 78). Brunelleschi is said to have criticized Donatello's crucifix: "che egli avesse messo in croce un contadino, e non un corpore simile a Gesù Cristo, il quale fu delicatissimo [!] ed in tutte le parti il più perfetto uomo che nascesse giammai": Vasari-Milanesi, *Opere*, 2:398. Wirth brought together some hints in literature and art that Jesus' penis was thought of as modest in size: Wirth, "Sur l'évolution," 169, 170, 173. But the whole subject of Jesus' body needs much more study.

to stimulate male viewers to an erection.[29] Neither was the power of Jesus' agonized ejaculation totally ignored in the Middle Ages. According to Duerr, the first crop of henbane, the poisonous herb favored for medieval witches' ointment, was held to have sprung up where the divine semen had fallen.[30] Again, a loincloth concealed such activity.

The fear of such a thanatologic erection may explain why medieval stories recounted that on the Cross, Jesus covered his genitals with his right hand until it was nailed to the wood, then with his left hand, so it may explain why in many *pietàs* his corpse is shown with his rigid hands over his genitalia.[31] Fear of a visible erection — and no vague reference to an otherwise ill-defined "shame" — may also lie behind at least three different legends — the Ps.-Anselm, a Revelation of Bridget of Sweden, and the *Meditations* of the so-called Ps.-Bonaventure — to the effect that either Jesus covered his genitalia himself, or Mary or the Magdalen did so with a veil after seeing him hanging naked.[32]

In Augustine's age, as now, people presumably used images for sexual gratification. Demonstrable evidence remains to be discovered that medieval males had intercourse with representations of Jesus, but it will probably turn up in judicial sentences of those who insulted Jesus on the Cross.[33] The conviction that males can seduce other males — and this political formulation inevitably becomes part of our discourse — remains

---

[29] Steinberg, *Sexuality*, illustrates dead Jesuses or Men of Sorrows with erections. Describing the phenomenon, H. P. Duerr said the shame of long erections (up to seventeen hours!) was the reason men were "never" hung naked. He cited a German case of 1547 in which a hangman castrated a corpse so no one would see his genitalia: *Nacktheit und Scham* (Frankfurt am Main, 1988), 270–72.

[30] On this *Bilsenkraut*, see Duerr, *Nacktheit*, 271, who does not document his statement.

[31] S. Axters, *Geschiedenis van de Vroomheid in de Nederlanden* (Antwerp, 1960), 4:264–65. Note that such actions presume a naked Crucifixion, not one with a perizonium. On Julius Caesar doing the same before falling from Brutus's thrust, see J. Döpler, *Theatri poenarum suppliciorum et executionum criminalium, oder Schauplatzes der Leibes- und Lebenstrafen* (Sondershausen, 1693), 1047, kindly brought to my attention by Klaus Schreiner.

[32] For Ps.-Anselm, see the *Dialogus beatae Mariae, PL* 159:282; and Bologne, *Histoire*, 282; for Bridget, see P. Fehl, "The Naked Christ in Santa Maria Novella in Florence: Reflections on an Exhibition and the Consequences," *Storia dell'arte* 45 (1982): 163; and M. Brisson, "An Unpublished Detail of the Iconography of the Passion in *Le Chastel Perrileux*," *Journal of the Warburg and Courtauld Institutes* 30 (1967): 398; for Ps.-Bonaventure, see the *Anonimo francescano*, 135 (chap. 79), and Steinberg, *Sexuality*, 31–32.

[33] For the Testard accusation against the marquis de Sade to this effect, see *Der Spiegel* (4 June 1990): 199.

strong a thousand years after the church father. Directing himself exactly to the problem of the *imitatio Christi,* Jacob Wimpfeling in the first years of the sixteenth century blared: "In order to stimulate feelings, it is not necessary that hanging on the Cross, Christ naked all over without a cov-ering exposes the most abstruse and secret parts of his body for human eyes to see."[34] A half century later, alarm that the tortured adult Jesus might actually face Christians "as naked as the day he was born"emerges in Gio-vanni Andrea Gilio da Fabriano's *Degli errori de' pittori circa l'istorie* (1563).

Gilio maintained, in part because Christians needed to gaze upon and contemplate holy persons so as to imitate their lives, that sacred figures should as a rule be shown in their physical condition at the time of the events represented.[35] That is, the viewing of actual history, including the brutality of Jesus' Passion, would produce pious sentiment. Thus Gilio would have approved of Grünewald's *Isenheim Altarpiece's* Crucifixion, its body replete with wounds and scars. From scenes of extreme cruelty could be "learned just how acerbic was the pain, the jokes, the afflictions" suf-fered by the martyrs.[36]

Gilio's general rule did not, however, extend to showing male genital-ia. He limited his previous generalization by stating: "But I will say that some fictions have been invented for reasons of decency which are praise-worthy, and they ought not in any way be abandoned. These are to cover the shamed part of sacred figures with some nice cloth."[37] Now, as an in-terlocutor in Gilio's dialogue points out, while the Bible says that on the last day everyone will arise *tutti nudi,* this does not mean that artists should represent people in this way. Gilio was not bothered: "I praise the fic-tion," he proclaimed;[38] historical accuracy extends to everything but na-kedness, he insisted. In their imitations of Christ, therefore, people like Margery Kempe would have to do without visual aids and "use the imagi-

---

[34] Knod, "Wimpfeling," 9.

[35] Giovanni Andrea Gilio da Fabriano, *Degli errori de' pittori circa l'istorie,* in *Trattati d'arte del cinquecento,* vol. 2 (Bari, 1961), 31–32.

[36] Gilio, *Errori,* 40. I am not suggesting that Grünewald's terribly mutilated Jesus could not itself provide a sadomasochistic pleasure. Thus Netherlandish accounts feature Christ being burned in the loins and private parts, while people delight in bursting the blisters that form there: Marrow, *Passion Iconography,* 118.

[37] "Ma ben dirò che sono state trovate alcune finzioni per cagione de l'onestà le quali sono lodevoli, e queste lasciare in verun modo non si deono. E queste sono il celare con qualche bel garbo le parti vergognose de le sacre figure": Gilio, *Errori,* 77.

[38] Gilio, *Errori,* 78.

nation," as the Ps.-Bonaventure recommended. They would have to summon up the naked Jesus on their own, which, Gilio assured us indirectly,
would take little enough imagination: "It seems to me that there is no
great secret of nature or art in those few shameful parts."[39]

The reasons Gilio gave for his antinakedness rule are varied. Of course,
shame and decency forbid nakedness: "Rather than deriving pleasure from
[Michelangelo's naked works, for example] the majority of viewers are outraged."[40] But being aware of Augustine's psychology — that male shame
originates in a body motion, and not vice versa — we may suspect that
such cries of shame are used to neutralize references to such a *motus corporis*, of which more below. Gilio also protested that the persons represented, who might be too ashamed even to look at their own genitalia,
would be offended by others looking at them. "If we bear that reverence
for saints whose sanctity stems from thus abhorring," why then would
painters violate those saints' own wishes, Gilio asks.[41]

Gilio further argued that nakedness is in conflict with Church power.
Thus figures of Jesus should never be naked, "whether they be of his childhood, baptism, flagellation, crucifixion, resurrection or whatever";[42] if
holy figures are shown naked, the "purity, chastity, and reverence" of
religion, which make up the force that engenders decorum and devotion
among the people, would be lost. Not surprisingly, Gilio equated "religion" with the Christian Church, and the covered Christ as standing for
it.[43] He implied that a naked Christ would indicate that the Church was
impure, and encourage people to be indecorous toward it. The inherent
conflict between history — Jesus' nakedness — and Christian order comes
to the fore, and the latter wins. The fear that devotees might be moved to
individual "indecent" acts by the state of the image is supplanted by the

---

[39] See this Gilio text at n. 46. "Metti in moto l'immaginazione, e puoi vedere . . .
chi spoglia Gesú": *Anonimo francescano*, 135 (chap. 79).

[40] "La maggior parte de'riguardanti se ne scandelezzino anzi che diletto ne piglino":
Gilio, *Errori*, 77.

[41] "Se dunque portiamo quella riverenza ai santi per la santità loro che ciò aborrisce
. . .": Gilio, *Errori*, 78.

[42] "Da la fanciullezza, dal battesimo, da la flagellazione e crucifissione e resurrezzione
in poi, non mai": Gilio, *Errori*, 79.

[43] "E questo per onestà la quale deve tenere il primo luogo nè le figure sacre. Per
mostrare l'istorico la purità la castità e la riverenza de la religione, deve fare con la penna
e con le parole l'orecchie caste de chi legge, et i pittori col pennello e coi colori gli occhi
casti di chi mira: dal che ne nasce il decoro de la pittura, la lode de l'artefice e la devozione de' popoli": Gilio, *Errori*.

fear that social groups might attack an undressed Church. Again, the question of Christ's nakedness reveals itself to be in part a discourse about political power, this time the Church's.

Political fears of this type reached their natural conclusion in the thought of the northerner Johannes Molanus, a contemporary of Gilio. "Christ *was* crucified naked," he volunteered, "but I think it is pious to *believe* that his shameful organs were [then] veiled for decency."[44] Here the plot thickens: Christians are inhibited from the *imitatio* and *contemplatio Christi* not because their faces redden at nakedness but because that redness appears epiphenomenal, and related to a more fundamental concern for social order. Christians are actually in a better state of grace if they believe the inverse of biblical fact: that Jesus' humiliation was not, after all, as complete as it might seem to have been.

A final reason Gilio gave for covering Jesus takes us back to Augustine, to the danger of an audience *motus corporis* in reaction to such nakedness. For instance, by suppressing saints' nakedness, the painter removes "occasions for laughter, ridicule, *and scandal*."[45] The artist who uses "such diligence to thrust these parts before viewers' eyes" does so "for no other reason than to provoke a few poorly educated youths to laughter by a thousand indecent and vain discourses."[46] Perhaps Gilio had some contemporary Passion play in mind. "Ho, villains,"cried the barker advertising one such play in France, "come to the festival. Neither ass nor head will there be that will remain concealed from you."[47]

Even if we reject Gilio's questioning of the motives of contemporary artists, his reading, as opposed to those that deduce art only from formal intellectual inspirations, has the distinct merit of deriving the image of Jesus on the Cross from artists' desire to affect viewers — and a particular group of viewers to boot, young males. Youths more than mature men respond to such nakedness, he assumed, and they ridicule it. Such youths included Canaan, the son of Noah, Gilio suggested. Before the other two

---

[44] My italics; cited in Bologne, *Histoire*, 281; see the further text in Freedberg, "Molanus," 238–45.

[45] My italics; Gilio, *Errori*, 78.

[46] "Perché non mi pare che in quelle poche parti vergognose sia tal secreto di natura nascosto ... Tanta diligenza à metterle avanti agli occhi de' riguardanti. ..." That is really done "non per altro che per far ridere, con mille discorsi disonesti e vani, i poco accorti giovini": Gilio, *Errori*, 80.

[47] "ça vilains, venez à la fête. / Il n'y aura ni cul ni tête / Qui vous demeure ja couvert": cited in Bologne, *Histoire*, 222.

sons covered their naked father while avoiding looking at his genitals,
Canaan laughingly made fun of him. But was ridicule all "that his younger
son had done to [Noah]" (Genesis 9.24)? Surely not. The "sexual perver-
sion" to which the Revised Standard Version of the Bible refers seems to
indicate that the excited young Canaan had an erection, then fellated the
stuporous father's bulging penis.[48] As Europeans traditionally identified
sexual roles, the helpless father Noah was the negative passive agent (patiens) and his son the relatively positive active sodomite. A serious matter,
something both generationally and canonically contra naturam. It remains
to be pointed out that the image of the drunken Noah was the primary
Old Testament complement or type of the Crucifixion of Christ.[49]

Thus for Gilio, youth, the most sexually licentious part of the male
population, would react most — if with calculated ridicule — to a naked
Jesus. We are on the brink of reencountering Augustine's justification for
covering the Savior, now linked to a particular male age group. Gilio's
wariness was not otherwise unknown in his own time — as in earlier centuries, the term "idol" could still refer to any naked statue, such as one of
a Roman emperor. In the 1420s the Rohan Master showed two Israelites
embracing passionately and uncontrollably after they both had gazed upon
such a "decently" fig-leafed "idol."[50]

It is not surprising, therefore, that Gilio, in defending clothing for holy
images, also referred to the pre-Christian experience of nakedness. He
cited Pliny's story of Pheidias's Venus, which was so beautiful that certain
sexually aroused "lussuriosissimi giovini" ejaculated their sperm onto the

[48] Gilio, Errori, 79. See Thomas, Rohan Master, pl. 28. For Noah and Canaan on
same-sex behavior, begin with The Interpreter's Bible, vol. 1 (New York, 1952), 556. In his
summary of possible interpretations of this passage, Pierre Bayle omitted fellation, but included castration: The Dictionary History and Critical, vol. 2 (London, 1735), 431–32 (s.v.
"Cham"). See the Jewish commentaries in Edwardes, Erotica Judaica, 45.

[49] Besides the many "type books" showing both scenes, see Knod, "Wimpfeling," 8,
11, and 15, where Augustine's association of the two stories is referred to, in part to
shore up the view that Mary did cover Jesus on the Cross; also Johannes von Paltz,
Werke, 1:51. In his De doctrina christiana, Augustine made Noah's uncovering and recov-
ering the prefiguration or type of the treatment of Jesus on the Cross: Wimpfeling, cited
in Knod, "Wimpfeling," 15. See also above, n. 25, where Jesus is imagined as a man as-
saulted by women.

[50] See Thomas, Rohan Master, pl. 123. P. Brown said that early Roman emperors
showed their unchallenged power by posing in the nude: Body and Society, 438. Note that
Wimpfeling denounced the idea of a naked Jesus because that would have made him
comparable to Priapus, in whose rites "pudenda gentiles populo denudabant": Knod,
"Wimpfeling," 14. See further Camille, Gothic Idol, 87–101.

statue. No wonder, Gilio intimated in commenting on this heterosexual image, that Mary had never been represented naked in art.[51] Switching to a homosexual paradigm, he cited the story of Noah, mentioned above, to drive home the evil of fathers, living or dead, appearing naked before their issue.

Recent art-historical work has begun to evaluate the fact that European paintings of females often sought to accommodate the male gaze and emotions — and those of males, the female gaze. But few scholars have raised the problem of the male gazing sensually at the male form.[52] Jesus is especially interesting in this regard. In art only the *infant* Jesus is often shown with uncovered genitalia, and Gilio had no serious objection to such *piccioli fanciulletti* being painted naked. Why? Because given the infants' innocence, male devotees are not scandalized on seeing them naked, and thus "will not fall [into sin with them] by natural instinct" ("non potendoci per naturale istinto cadere").[53] I take this to mean that male adults who gaze on very young boys will not have an erection.[54]

In short, though these sources speak far from frankly, it appears that from early Christianity onward a powerful reason for keeping the crucified Jesus covered at the crotch was the danger that he would seduce other males, yea even in death — if not with his *beau corps bien formé*, then with his dying penis.[55] Making no pretense at accounting for the historical

---

[51] Clearly, he assumed Mary, too, had a beautiful body. "Lussuriosissimi giovini, de la cui libidine restò macchiata. I pittori che furono avanti Michelagnolo non fecero mai la figura de la gloriosa Vergine nuda . . .": Gilio, *Errori*, 79. Significantly, contemporaries labeled such a male loss of penile control as "effeminization of the soul": "Quod si gentiles ipsi philosophi . . . picturas nudarum mulierum prohibuere, quod earum aspectu animi effeminarentur, prava foverentur desideria et ad scelera proniores redderentur . . .": (the theologian Antonio Possevino, cited by Gilio, *Errori*, 602).

[52] In a book on responses, Freedberg, *Power of Images*, seems to avoid all references to one such type of response, namely homoeroticism. See, however, J. Saslow, *Ganymede in the Renaissance. Homosexuality in Art and Society* (New Haven, 1986); and in general N. Bryson, *Vision and Painting: The Logic of the Gaze* (London, 1983).

[53] Gilio, *Errori*, 78. Erasmus and other writers, however, felt that children might be corrupted by naked infant Jesuses: Freedberg, "Molanus," 240.

[54] This may concur with Florentine practice. Michael J. Rocke found that male passives were rarely below the age of puberty: *Forbidden Friendships: Homosexuality and Male Culture in Renaissance Florence* (New York, 1996).

[55] One early text may even imply a homoerotic relation between Jesus and his apostles: S. Levin, "The Early History of Christianity, in Light of the 'Secret Gospel' of Mark," in *Aufstieg und Niedergang der römischen Welt*, ed. W. Haase and H. Temporini, part 2: Principate, 25.6 (Berlin, 1988), 4270–92; further in J. Boswell, *Christianity, Social Tolerance, and Homosexuality* (Chicago, 1980), 225.

specificities of such seduction, I aim only to open up the possibility that
seduction was part of this nonhistorical God's armor across the ages. Perhaps it was, therefore, not completely fortuitous that Panurge was in
Christ's Passion cortège when he had his enormous erection, which led to
such disorder that the audience and actors fell into a sexual frenzy seeking
to fellate him.[56] Before the advent of modern communications, sacred
images, like today's holy cards, were probably the most available for erotic
ends. Just as importantly, the passive male's seduction of other males is
not devoid of political meaning.

Seduction by the Gods, whether in medieval times or in antiquity,
could not be excluded simply by covering the genitalia. As Steinberg has
noted, the perizonium itself could draw attention to the genitalia, suggesting that activity continued beneath it, as in the flying bannerlike perizoniums of Lucas Cranach. Other parts of the body of the Savior might be
rendered corporeally erotic, even strikingly unmutilated. As mentioned
earlier, the social context for the Crucified's being regularly bare-chested
by the twelfth century, and the social and psychological effects of that undressing, remain to be determined. But the growing eroticism of the Christic torso in some Renaissance art, with its understatement of Jesus' suffering,[57] appears to have had important effects on devotion — and this was
the thrust of Gilio's treatise. Although this is not the place to enter into
the matter, it should be said that several Jesuses of this new age, whether
from their shiny skin surface or from their exposed, if not erect penises,
seem almost to be pathics, dutifully prepared to receive sexual service. Perhaps these motifs are best combined in the supremely seductive hanging
Jesus of Laurent de La Hyre, where the Magdalen appears to dwell not just
on the Savior's pearly skin, but also on his active erogenous zone, which
threatens to cast off the veil (fig. 31). Besides the penis remaining a part
of the dynamic between Jesus and the orant, therefore, the skins of the

---

[56] "Tant joueurs que spectateurs, entrer en tentation si terrificque qu'il ne y eut
ange, homme, diable ne diablesse qui ne voulust biscoter": cited in N. Zemon Davis, *Fiction in the Archives* (Stanford, 1987), 31 (*Tiers Livre*, chap. 27).

[57] Among many others, I am thinking of Francesco di Giorgio Martini's *Jesus Stripped
at Calvary*, Borgognone's *Cristo Risorto*, and many paintings of Pontormo and Rosso Fiorentino. Among the sculptures are Michelangelo's wooden Crucifix and his *Cristo Risorto*,
Cellini's marble Crucifix, etc. Included in this phenomenon should be the increasingly
effeminate representations of John the Evangelist, the "friend of Christ," often at the
side of the Cross.

Figure 31.
Laurent de La Hyre, *Mary Magdalen at the Foot of the Cross*,
ca. 1630, oil on canvas.
Saint-Denis, Musée d'Art et d'Histoire.
Photo courtesy of the Musée d'Art et d'Histoire.

figures as well help to transmit conventional gender relations between object and orants.

The demand that young men and, even more, women not hear about or see penises worked to preserve adult males' property rights and influence over these dependents. If such *lussuriosissimi* types knew the joys of seeing male genitalia, the patriarchs might be cuckolded and lose their property rights. This was the social and political foundation of the oft-described "shame" of dependents. Although I cannot develop this train of thought fully here, I do not wish to end this paper with the idea that a so-called covered, suffering Christ, like that of the *Isenheim Altarpiece,* obviates the danger of eroticism and the intrusion of gender ambiguities. It does not. Gender is there; only it emerges later, on Jesus' road to heaven.

There is literary authority for this view. The Bible says that we will all be bodily resurrected in a naked state, and Augustine determined, against those who claimed that women would be resurrected in more perfect male bodies, that we would reassume the sex we had on earth.[58] Heaven *does* have gender, and as for age — with all *its* indirect gender implications — everyone, including Jesus himself, would have the Savior's corporeally perfect, and thus endlessly seductive, thirty-three years.[59]

Thus in heaven, body is back. And such ruminations left a visual track behind them. I can only mention in passing the topos of a newly beauteous Jesus releasing souls from hell,[60] before going on to discuss the Resurrected Jesus, where gender mutations abound. In the *Isenheim Altarpiece* (fig. 32), Jesus' awful wounds have healed in the very earth. If saying that the body has been regendered is problematic, I shall use the word rejuvenated. Now it is soft and creamy, and Jesus' hair, no longer its earlier Mediterranean black, has turned a remarkably northern, or, may I say, feminine, blond. *Che bella!*

---

[58] See the discussion in Gilio, *Errori,* 66, and the references, 597–98. The apocryphal Gospel of Thomas had said that "every woman who will make herself male will enter the kingdom of heaven": see W. Thompson, *The Time Falling Bodies Take to Light. Mythology, Sexuality, and the Origins of Culture* (New York, 1981), 252.

[59] Gilio, *Errori,* 66. There seems to be no modern literature on sex and gender in the Christian beyond.

[60] A particularly striking painting is in the Landesgalerie, Hannover, a *Jesus in der Vorhölle* of ca. 1420 that once belonged to the Cistercian nuns of Osterode. Jesus is tall and of magnificent bearing. His hair is blond, right down to his upper-class goatee. His skin is very white, while his wounds are indicated only by mere circles. This is a good *Fürst der Welt!*

Figure 32.
Matthias Grünewald, *Resurrection*, from the *Isenheim Altarpiece*,
ca. 1512–1516, oil on wood.
Colmar, Unterlinden Museum.
Photo courtesy of Giraudon/Art Resource.

In an earlier work I noted that Florentines habitually categorized certain figures according to their use or emotional impact. Some figures, for instance, were said to "give peace." I also showed that once a painting had performed a miracle, its owners retrofitted it with objects known to "maintain devotion": a sky full of stars, or *cielo*, a crown, etc. I urged historians to try to discover or reconstruct the iconography of this "technology of devotion" that contemporaries used to manipulate our sentiments.[61]

I do not expect tomorrow to fall upon a case in which Jesus' exciting genitalia performed miracles. But in the spirit of Augustine, Margery Kempe, and Ganymede himself, I would argue that Jesus' very gender, no mere symbol of some ideologically sexless "humanity," is part of a technology of seduction. Keeping in mind that in the Middle Ages patriarchy permitted women much sooner than men to be humiliated in their bodies,[62] I believe that we should look at the impact that the effeminized — or dependent — masculinity of the humiliated Jesus Crucified had, and still has, on Christians' actions. Devotees' deep-rooted practice of affixing real loincloths to crucifixes already fitted with artificial ones is a place to start.

Torturing the helpless Jesus did not render him genderless. Rather, as Simone de Beauvoir and many Christian women know — this paper does not pretend to do justice to the subject of the Crucified Jesus' impact on women — torture rendered Jesus like unto a suffering woman (for example, Wilgeforte), to be worshipped by women,[63] or like unto a powerless man, to be venerated by other powerless males in early modern Europe: "I see the god on earth," yelled a sixteenth-century French burgher on encountering the man who had played Christ in his sarcophagus in a Passion play

---

[61] R. Trexler, *Public Life in Renaissance Florence* (New York, 1980), 113–15.

[62] See my "*Correre la Terra*. Collective Insults in Late Medieval and Renaissance Europe," *Mélanges de l'École française de Rome. Moyen Age, Temps Modernes* 96 (1984): 845–902.

[63] Beckwith, "Material Mysticism," 476f., cites de Beauvoir, *The Second Sex* (New York, 1976), 686: "In the humiliation of God, she sees the dethronement of man, inert, passive, covered with wounds, the crucified is the reverse image of the white, blood-stained martyr exposed to wild beasts, to daggers, to males, with whom the girl has so often identified herself; she is overwhelmed to see that man, man-God has assumed her role. She it is who is hanging on the tree, promised the splendour of the resurrection." If I understand rightly, Beckwith, with great insight, saw female mystics transforming the Crucified into female gender by a process of "feminization." Jesus is "passive, and his body becomes the site onto which desire is projected."

the previous day. "Did you keep your shameful member stiff while playing God?"[64]

It remains to be proved, of course, that young men in medieval Europe were, in fact, sexually aroused by Jesuses. Indeed, it remains an open question if even the patriarchs of medieval culture revered a male like Jesus, who proved to be not a man, but a worm, to cite the usual simile.[65] In a profound remark addressing the threat of imitating Jesus, Johannes von Paltz mused: "I do not know how a preacher can say [that Jesus was naked] without being ashamed. For it seems such a preacher is undressing the lord in front of the whole audience."[66] For a preacher to bruit it about that Jesus was naked, said Jacob Wimpfeling, "doesn't move one to devotion, but rather to a certain *vilitas* or disrespect for our lord Jesus."[67]

And, in fact, confraternal male devotion to Christ in passion appears to be largely an early modern, non-elite avocation.[68] But whatever may result from a serious study of the relationship between the different sexes and people of various ages and this humiliated half-man/God, we can be sure that the meaning of those Jesuses on the Cross lies less in the intentions of the image-makers than in the sense of self with which male, and female, devotees and ridiculers felt themselves attached to the figure, and who thus, so to speak, refused his application for godhood.

---

[64] Davis, *Fiction* 31 (1530).

[65] And a circumcised one at that. "Ego autem sum vermis, et non homo; opprobrium hominum, et abiectio plebis. Omnes videntes me deriserunt me" (Ps. 21.7–8). This simile is regularly encountered in the sources: see Marrow, *Passion Iconography*.

[66] What follows is still more impressive: "Et nescio, quomodo praedicator hoc posset dicere absque verecundia. Videtur talis praedicator denudare et dominum coram multitudine populi, quae vix illam denudationem videre potest. Et si dicitur: Si praedicator propter hoc, quod refert denudationem, dicitur denudare Christum, tunc similiter si refert passionem Christi, dicetur eum crucifigere, respondetur concedendo: Sed hoc non offendit, cum hoc certum sit et dominus iusserit celebrationem fieri in sui memoriam dicens: Hoc facite in meam commemorationem sic et hic praedicationem. Sed quia denudatio incerta est et non omnes hoc dicunt, igitur etc.": Johannes von Paltz, *Werke*, 1:52.

[67] "Et profecto moleste tuli quod Christo fuit tributa illa horrenda nuditas verendorum coram virginibus et matronis et quidem multis, quod non michi ad devocionem sed pocius ad quandam vilitatem aut despectum domini Jhesu (ni fallor) deservire visum fuit": Knod, "Wimpfeling," 5, and similar text, 7.

[68] William Christian noted the increasing devotion to the Crucified in early modern male confraternities; *Local Religion in Sixteenth-Century Spain* (Princeton, 1981), chap. 6.

An Early Printed Text Against
Homosexual Behavior (c. 1485)

AROUND 1481, THE PRESS OF SIXTUS RIESSINGER brought out a folio, and
then about 1485 Eusebius Silber a quarto edition of a contemporary tract
dedicated to the "crime" of sodomy.[1] The author addresses it "to a sodomitic sinner, so that he recognizes how much more detestable the crime of
sodomy is than other sins." To judge from the contents of the work, the
author was a canon lawyer and perhaps also a civilist, or a student on his
way to becoming such. He is identified only as "R. D. G. M.," presumably
referring to *Reverendus dominus* G. M. I have been unsuccessful in identifying "G. M."[2]

Perhaps the first printed text dealing with a discretely sexual theme,
the work has been mentioned by an occasional student interested in past
sexual practices,[3] but on the whole, it remains practically unknown. For
this reason it deserves reediting as a useful primary source for understand-

---

[1] Both were printed in Rome. My references are to the more commonly extant Silber
edition.

[2] The date of the treatise is roughly comparable to that of the publication. The latest
canonist it mentions is Giovanni di Anagni (d. c. 1457). There is no reference to contemporary events.

[3] Such as P. Ragon, *Les amours indiennes ou l'imaginaire du conquistador* (Paris, 1992),
20.

ing legal thinking regarding mostly male homosexual behavior in the later fifteenth century.[4]

Those familiar with medieval legal texts of the type edited here know that because of their complex references to authorities they do not easily lend themselves to translation. I have decided that in any case the non-Latin reader will be quite as well served by the running summary of the contents I provide, which also refer the reader to specific lines in the Latin text. What is in this text for the Latinist, on the other hand, is clear. It is no great product of the jurisprudent's craft, to be sure. Cribbing liberally from Thomas Aquinas, the text sometimes reads more like a student's paper than a smooth scholarly production. Still, the text points the serious student to most of the customary references in the canon and civil law regarding male homosexual behavior, references I have completed in today's citation form to provide easy access to the laws in question.[5] As well, the text refers the reader to many of the authoritative legal glosses on these laws.

The author begins by reminding his reader(s) that they should know how bad this (not directly defined) sodomy is because they will one day have to answer for their sins (1-11). From Genesis he lists the five or six Old Testament cities his authorities said were famous for sodomy, including of course Sodom and Gomorrah, and then adds to that list the Dead Sea town of Aspala or Asphalt as an example of the wages of similar sins (12-28). The Genesis story of Lot and his daughters turned prostitutes to avoid male homosexuality is inserted, and then Jerome's notion that all sodomites died the night Jesus was born, so that Jesus would not have to take on that "ignominious" male trait in his own person (35-49). For two crimes cry out their horror to God, homicide and sodomy, but the latter is worse because it prevents humans from being born, whereas homicide merely separates the soul from the body (51-57). Sodomy's well-known ability to cause natural disasters is mentioned, as is the notion, attributed

---

[4] Some important works on this subject are J. Boswell, *Christianity, Social Tolerance, and Homosexuality* (Chicago, 1980); M. Rocke, *Forbidden Friendships: Homosexuality and Male Culture in Renaissance Florence* (New York, 1996); G. Ruggiero, *The Boundaries of Eros: Sex Crime and Sexuality in Renaissance Venice* (New York, 1985). See also R. Trexler, *Sex and Conquest: Gendered Violence, Political Order, and the European Conquest of the Americas* (Cambridge and Ithaca, 1995).

[5] In the edition, I use parentheses to enclose references provided by the text, and brackets to enclose standard reference material not in the text. Bracketed folio numbers are to the so-called Silber edition. The introduction refers the reader to the page and line(s) in my edition.

to Aristotle, that sodomy causes mental illness. From the *Compendio Theo-logie* comes the notion that while the devil seeks to instigate humans to any and all evil, he draws away from sodomy himself, which "he abomi-nates because of the nobility of his nature" (76–78). Thus a sin against nature was abhorrent even to the demon, and yet people today are not ashamed to practice sodomy, the author says, but rather glory in it, excus-ing themselves because it is the custom. The author, however, knows that it is indecorous for one's member to be fit into the "office" or character-istic of another, meaning into his or her mouth or anus (87–100).

G. M. was capable of citing ancient authors to buttress his case. Hav-ing referred to Aristotle's *Nicomachaean Ethics,* and to a moralism of "Seneca," he three times in the treatise uses verses of the Roman satirist Martial to the same end (99–100, 113–118, 439–448). To this slight evi-dence of humanistic training can be added an equally scant willingness to incorporate historical materials into his account. Significantly these mater-ials are all drawn from the law rather than from historical sources them-selves. Thus it is on the basis of canonistic legal passages that he docu-ments the sodomitic behavior of the Saracens in Sicily, and the earlier sins of the English, the Spaniards, and even the Burgundians (101–109). He closes this first section of his work by targeting the active party to a homosexual act, who puts his penis into the "wrong receptacle," com-ments on the legal disabilities suffered by convicted sodomites, but insists that a person who is forced to receive an active's penis, like a vanquished soldier (*oppressione barbarorum*) is not guilty of a crime (121–159). Only a willing "passive" partner incurs that blame.

In a second section, G. M. proves that the "contagion" of crimes against nature is worse than fornication or adultery, or incest with one's mother, all of which are natural. His authority here is Thomas Aquinas, whose reasons for and against this position he details (163–226). Interest-ingly, the author overrules the argument that sodomy is not so bad be-cause it is a victimless crime, ruling that by preventing conception the sodomist makes God a victim, and this is even worse than sacrilege. By the same token, sodomy is even more harmful to a marriage than is adul-tery (169–172, 197–199, 200–203, 245–249).

The third section, again dependent on Thomas, rules that sodomy is as detestable in women as in men (265–281). In this unique reference to women's sexual activity, the author is describing heterosexual activity; les-bianism is nowhere mentioned. The passage is significant because it shows that contemporaries also found women guilty of sodomy, when males penetrated their "false vase" (mouth or anus). The author means that a woman is quite as sinful as a male passive, because her anal receptivity also prevents conception. A husband "abusing" his wife in this way is actually worse than if he abused a prostitute: obviously one cannot be irreverent toward a prostitute, but is certainly so towards one's wife (273–279). The author goes on to establish the significant principle that as a general rule, the active's role is more sinful than is even the consenting passive's (282–287).[6] Then implicitly talking about anal or oral reception, the author states that through such "extraordinary pollution," the penetrated person may impede his or her (?) right to contract marriage (297–298). The author appears therefore to address himself to young women wishing to indulge in heterosexual activity before marriage and not get pregnant.

The fourth section determines what judge is competent to try accusations of sodomy. He rules that sodomy being a crime of mixed forums, it may be tried by a secular court but is definitely also within the purview of ecclesiastical judges because, just like usury, which unnaturally germinates money from money, sodomy is against nature (310–313).

Section five deals with the punishment of sodomy. He lists first those punishments meted out by the civil law (372–382), then the burning mandated by municipal statutes (382–384), and finally those levied by the canon law (385–402).

The author next considers who is competent to absolve sodomites, and has a simple answer: either one's bishop or another person with special license to absolve (407–409). He follows this by asking what penances were to be assigned to those absolved (414). In this latter context, the author claims that sodomy is worse than bestiality, for no non-human male animal engages in same-sex activity (an old saw that had often been disputed) (421–430).[7] Thus while in other areas men may behave like beasts without being sinful, here they show themselves inferior to animals, indeed even go against the basic instincts of animals.

In the final argument of this work, the author explains in what ways humans (*homines*) sin against nature. Masturbation is against nature, but only minimally (449–450). Worse is insertion in a "false vase," and worse still sex with the wrong sex. Finally bestiality (that is, sex with another species) is placed at the top of the list as the worst of all such sins (459–

---

[6] In *Sex and Conquest*, I show that whatever the church and state's attitude, the general culture of the Middle Ages always considered the passive the more despicable.

[7] See e.g., Boswell, *Christianity*, 152–56.

460).[8] With this, the small treatise against the sodomite sinner comes to an end.

Text

Reverendus Dominus G. M. ad peccatorem Sodomitam, ut cognoscat quam ceteris criminibus crimen sodomiticum sit detestabilius.

[a i–r] Quoniam, ut ait Apostolus: Omnes stabimus ante tribunal Christi, recepturi prout in corpore gessimus, sive bonum fuerit, sive ma-
5   lum; c. Cum ex eo, de pen. et remis. [X.5.38.14]. Ideo, ne brevis vite voluptas eterna maledictione pensetur, oportet nos diem messionis extreme carentia vitiorum prevenire. Et quia nonnulli sicut pecudes absque ulla discretione indesinenter vitio sodomitico deserviunt[9] (C.32 q.7), Non solum [c.15], per quod venit ira dei in filios diffidentie, c. Clerici, de exces. pre-
10   lat. [X.5.31.4], c. Ut clericorum mores, de vita et hon. cler., quam ceteris criminibus detestabilius sit, et sit magis fugiendum legibus aperiatur.

Legitur enim tres civitates apud Jordanem hoc scelesto genere fedatas, et duas ex vicinitate inextinguibili igne consumptas, quarum nomina hec sunt: Sodoma, Gomora, Seboim, Segor, et Oleale, vel Eschale, ut est tex-
15   tus iuncta glose in dicto c. Clerici, de exces. prelat. [X.5.31.4]. Licet glosa iuncto texto in c. Sed et continuo, de pen., D. 1 [c.46], voluerit illas esse sex, id est, et Adoma. Sed Hostiensis in dicto c. Clerici dicit quod in historia non reperiuntur nisi quinque. Sed cum Segor plura nomina secuta fuerit, forte unum Oleale vel Eschale fuit, idcirco sex videntur.

20   Sed illud minime pretereamus quod dicit glosa in dicto c. Sed et continuo, licet in totum ad materiam non faciat, quae apud illas civitates locus est, cuius nomen est Aspala, vel secundum alios Asfaltes, qui dicitur mare mortuum, cuius aqua potabilis non est, neque natabilis humano generi. Mirabile quidem ferrum natat, pluma mergitur, ibi poma nonnulla exterius
25   pulcherrima reperiuntur cinerem [a i–v] et favillam interius habentia, et simili modo luxuriam pingendam exclamat glosa. Unde dicit ibi Archidiaconus, quod ille locus dicitur aqua luxurie, et ideo non natabilis, quia homines illaqueat non potabilis, quia non recreat. De qua dicit Hieronimus: Libido transacta semper relinquit plenitudinem, nunquam satiatur, et ex-

---

[8] Cf. Boswell, *Christianity*, 323; T. Tentler, *Sin and Confession on the Eve of the Reformation* (Princeton, 1977), 186–208; J. Brundage, "Let Me Count the Ways: Canonists and Theologians Contemplate Coital Positions," *Journal of Medieval History* 10 (1984): 81–93.

[9] The text actually reads: indesinenter libidini serviunt.

tincta semper reaccenditur. Ideo ferrum natat, quia constans et firmus su-   30
perat luxuriam, et ideo pluma mergitur, quia levis et fragilis superatur et
vincitur. Poma exterius pulcherrima dicit, quia forma apparens est pulchri
et deceptrix. Sed interius sunt plena cinere et favilla, quia peccato et im-
munditia, de quibus Genesis 19.

Refert enim Augustinus super Genesi, libro primo, quod cum santus   35
[sic] Loth cogitaverit luxuriam non humanam sed bestialem, ut dixit Philosophus in 7 Ethicorum, et probatur in c. Non solum (C.32 q.7 [c.15]), in
finem, ut hospites a sodomitis liberaret dixit: Sunt mihi due filie que non-
dum viros noverunt, peducam illas ad vos, et illis utimini. Voluit enim fi-
lias suas potius prostituere hac compensatione ut a sodomitis nihil in   40
hospites perpetraretur, de quo facit textus (D.15), Quod ait [c.1]. Unde
Ambrosius in libro de Abraam dixit quod licet illa fuerit flagitiosa puritas,
tamen minus putavit secundum naturam coire quam adversus naturam de-
linquere (C.32 q.7), Offerebat [c.12].

Legitur enim quod ea nocte qua Christus natus est, omnes qui reperti   45
sunt illo vitio laborantes mortui sunt, ut dixit Hieronimus super Isaiam.
Non enim voluit pati tantam ignominiam in natura nostra reperiri quam
assumpserat. Etenim propter sui abominationem ad divinam ultionem pro-
clamatur. Unde Genesis 19 dixit dominus: Clamor sodomorum et gomor-
reorum multiplicatus est, et peccatum eorum aggravatum est nimis, in   50
vitium quod agunt clamat vindictam. Duo dicit scriptura peccatorum ge-
nera clamare ad deum propter sui [a ii–r] horrorem, homicidium videlicet
et vitium sodomiticum, quia utrunque destruit speciem humanam quantum
in se est, sed tamen peiori me do [sic] sodomita. Nam homicida destruit
separando animam a corpore, que tamen remanet immortalis et corpus de-   55
mum reassumit. Sed sodomita destruit impediendo ne sit homo in ne gene-
retur. Unde Apostolus primo Cor., 6 [.10] Neque molles neque masculo-
rum concubitores regnum dei possidebunt.

Tanta enim est huius sceleris enormitas ut sepe numero pestilentias,
tempestates, terremotus, necnon fames contigisse probetur, ut in Autentica   60
Ut non luxurientur contra naturam, collat. 6 [Nov. 77], et Archidiaconus,
(C.3 q.7), Infames [c.2], ad que facit glosa in c. Flagitia in verbo perver-
sitate, (C.32 q.7 [c.13]). Hinc pullulant infirmitates ac mentis varias per-
turbationes, argumento eorum que dicta sunt, ad quod facit textus c. Cum
infirmitas, de pen. et remis. [X.5.38.13]. Unde et Philosophus in 6 Ethico-   65
rum clare denotat, homines fortitudinis et animositatis virtutem hac morbi
contagione perdere. Nam dum inclusi in secretis cubilibus vitio sodomitico
indulgent molles et effeminati efficiuntur, quod probatur in c. Si gens An-

70 glorum (D.56 [c.10], et ibi per dictum Guidonis elucum [sic]. Quare Augustinus in libro 3 Confessionum dixit naturam homines non creasse ut simili modo uterentur, de quo facit textus in dicto c. Flagitia.

    Violatur quippe societas que cum deo nobis esse debet cum eadem natura cuius ipse est auctor libidinis perversitate maculetur. Ex quo Bartholus in l. Cum vir, Cod. de adulterio [C.9.9.31], dixit quod adeo hoc crimen
75 est abominabile, quod cum lex illa loquatur de sodomia, cum de ea loqui non sit honestum, legi non consuevit. Dicitur enim in Compendio Theologie quod postquam diabolus induxit homines ad huiusmodi scelus, ex nobilitate sue nature abominans, hoc vitium fugit. Contagiosa enim est illorum familiaritas, ideo evitanda. Nam unus deditus huic vitio totam civi-
80 tatem inficere suffi[a ii–v]ciens est; Genesis 19. Et ideo in lege mandabatur tales sequestrari a conversatione ceterorum ne alios inficerent. Ideo Apostolus ait, Roma 1 [1.32], quod qui filios familias et subditos non corrigunt de hoc vitio maculatos, digni sunt morte cum eadem pena; consentientes teneantur ubi prohibere possunt. Unde Seneca: Qui non vetat peccare
85 cum possit, iubet. Hinc est quod Joseph cum puer esset, fratres suos cum masculis et cum iumentis coeuntes accusavit patri ut punirentur (19 Gen.).[10] Sed hodierno tempore homines ita cecantur, quod nedum de vitio hoc erubescant, sed gloriantur, et se propter assuefactionem et consuetudinem excusant, non advertentes ad Augustini dictum libro 3 Confes-
90 sionum, ubi dixit quod flagicia contra naturam qualia sunt sodomitarum semper repudianda sunt. Et licet omnes homines simili vitio uterentur, tamen divina lege tenerentur; de quo facit textus C.32 q.7, Flagicia [c.13]. Nam tanto sunt graviora peccata contra naturam quanto diutius infelicem animam detinent alligatam, et sic consuetudine hoc tale vitium non tolera-
95 tur, facit textus in c. Quanto, loco 2, de consuetudine [X.1.4.4].

    Satis enim indecorum est quod unum membrum officio alterius fungatur (D.89, Singula [c.1]). Et clarius per Marcialem, disticho uno [XI, 22], dum scribit in pediconem masturbatorem his verbis:

        Divisit natura marem:[11] pars una puellis,
100   Una viris genita est. utere parte tua.

    Scribitur quondam Sarracenos tantam sceleris ignominiam parvipendentes in partibus Sicilie masculis et feminis abuti presumpsisse, quod probatur in c. [In] Archiepiscopatu, de raptoribus [X.5.17.4]. Nec minus

---

[10] Actually Gen. 37.2.

[11] In text: mares.

Anglicos alio tempore huiusmodi morbo inquinatos reperimus: Nam hi, spretis legalibus conubiis, ad instar gentis sodomitice luxuriando fedam 105 vitam ducebant. Nec minus hoc Hispanis et Burgundorum populis conti[a iii–r]git, qui adeo fornicati sunt donec Sarracenorum impetum, deo permittente, senserint, et penas vitio sodomitico condignas reportaverint, ut est textus D. 56, Si gens anglorum [c.10].

Convincitur et auctoritate Romanorum vituperium qui, lege matrimoni- 110 ali dote constituta antiquitus, cum maribus palam contrahere procurabant. Unde Martialis libro 12 [42]:

> Barbatus rigido nupsit Callistratus Aphro
> hac qua lege viro nubere virgo solet.
> preluxere faces, velarunt flammea vultus, 115
> . . . .[12]
>
> dos etiam dicta est. nondum tibi, Roma, videtur
> hoc satis? expectas nunquid ut et[13] pariat.

Ve inquam miseris natura abutentibus. Nam ubique reperio iura tam canonica quam civilia contra eos armari, ut dicit textus in lege Cum vir, 120 Cod. de adulteris [C.9.9.31]. Eum nanquam infamem faciunt qui, vase naturali obmisso, ad extraordinarium progreditur; C.3, q.7, Infames [c.2]. Nam rates, ut ibi Archidyaconus, non possunt pro aliis postulare, cum etiam ad ferendum testimonium inhabiles reputentur. Nec eos testari permittit lex, ut est textus Inst., de testamentis ordinandis, § Testes [I.2.10.6], 125 quod tamen singulariter intellexit glosa, si convicti et condemnati fuerint de tali crimine. Sed hoc secundum leges. Alius vero forte secundum canones, per textum in c. Testimonium, de testibus [X.2.20.54], et c. 1 [Denique] de exceptionibus [X.2.25], et ibi glosa in verbo hactenus, ubi satis esset si convictus foret ita ut crimen esset notorium. 130

Plus dixit dominus Antonius in c. Nisi cum pridem [X.1.9.10], in verbo Coll., de renuntiatione, quod ius adeo abhorret hoc vitium, ut etiam post peractam penitentiam executionem ordinis impediat, ad quod facit Speculum,[14] in titulo 2, § Vix, versi Sunt quoque. Et hec procedunt tam in agentem quam in patientem, ut dicit Archidiaconus (C.3, q.7), Infames 135 [c.2], quod tamen limitandum esse duxi, ubi voluntate spontanea aguntur. Nam si oppressione barba[a iii–v]rorum vel aliorum incurvati fuissent, eis

---

[12] Missing from text: nec tua defuerunt verba, Talasse, tibi.
[13] In text, reversed: et ut.
[14] *Speculum judiciale*, of Guillaume Durand (1271).

non esset imputandum, ut dicit textus (C.3, q.7), Infames [c.2]. Nam qui
violentiam passus est, pudicitiam amisisse probari non potest, nec ullo
140   modo convincitur crimen sodomie incurrisse. Ad quod dictum Augustini
in libro De bono coniugali, qui dicit adulterium cum vel proprie libidinis
instinctu vel aliene consensu cum altero vel altera contra pactum coniu-
gale concumbitur; facit textus in c. Ille autem, C.32, q.5 [c.14]. Et Isidorus
in Synonimis, libro 6. Non potest corpus corrumpi nisi prius corruptus fue-
145   rit animus; c. Non potest, ea causa et questione [c.8]. Et Hieronimus in
epistola ad romanos, libro primo: Non potest fieri ut nisi quis mechetur
prius in corde, quod mecha sit in corpore; c. Preposito, § non potest, ea
causa et questione [c.6]. Et Augustinus in libro De duabus animabus: Non
nisi voluntate peccatur, dicto c., ea causa et questione, § non [. . .] nisi.

150   Ex quibus omnibus infertur, quod ubi quis opprimitur violentia precisa
et absoluta, ei non est imputandum si quid turpe contra eius voluntatem
sequatur. Ad quod facit Augustinus in libro primo De libero arbitrio: De
pudicitia quis dubitabit, quin ea sit in animo constituta, quandoquidem
virtus est? Unde a violento stupratore eripi non potest; ea causa et ques-
155   tione, c. de pudicitia [C.32 q.5 c.6]. Et Hieronimus in libro Hebraicarum
questionum: Corpus mulieris non vis maculat, sed voluntas; ea causa et
questione, De pudicitia, § Corpus mulieris. Et Ambrosius in libro quinto
De virginibus: Revera non potest caro ante corrumpi, nisi mens fuerit ante
corrupta; c. Revera, ea causa et questione [c.2].

160   Quod turpior est usus contra naturam
                         quam fornicationis et adulterii,
                                etiam cum matre.

        Solet queri an labes et sodomitici criminis contagio, [a iv–r] sacrile-
gium, fornicationem, adulterium, et incestum superare dicatur. Et videtur
165   dicendum quod sic, per textum in c. Adulterii malum (C.32 q.7[15] [c.11]),
ibi: Sed omnium horum est pessimum, quod contra naturam sit.
        Sed contra, ne sicco pede transeamus, tribus mediis arguendum duxi, et
primo sic:[16] Tanto est aliquod peccatum gravius quanto magis contrariatur caritati. Sed magis videntur adulterium, stuprum, et raptus contrariari
170   caritati, cum vergant in iniuriam proximi quam peccatum contra naturam,

---

[15] In text: ii.
[16] The following is all taken from Thomas Aquinas, *Summa theologica*, 2.2.154.12.1
seq.

per quod nullus alteri iniuriatur. Ergo peccatum contra naturam non dicitur maximum inter species luxurie.

Secundo sic: Illa peccata videntur graviora que contra deum committuntur; sed sacrilegium contra deum directe committitur, quia vergit in iniuriam divini cultus. Ergo sacrilegium est maius peccatum quam vitium contra naturam. 175

Tertio sic: Tanto aliquod peccatum est gravius quanto exercetur in personam quam magis diligere debemus. Sed secundum ordinem caritatis magis diligere debemus personas coniunctas que per incestum polluuntur quam personas extraneas, que maculantur per vitium contra naturam. Ergo 180 incestus est gravius. His tamen non obstantibus puto procedere dictum c. Adulterii malum (C.32 q.7). Patet conclusio vera ex illo Gn. 19: Homines sodomite erant pessimi etc. Secundo ratione iuxta beatum Thomam in secunda secunde, questione 154[17] [12 Resp]: "Sicut enim in speculativis error circa ea quorum cognitio est homini naturaliter indicta, est gravis- 185 simus et turpissimus; ita in agendis agere contra ea que secundum naturam determinata sunt, est gravissimum et turpissimum. Quia ergo in vitiis que sunt contra naturam transgreditur homo id quod est secundum naturam determinatum circa usum venereum, inde est quod in tali materia hoc peccatum est gravissimum" plusquam incestus. Nam "per alias [a iv-v] [autem] 190 luxurie species preteritur solum id quod est secundum rectam rationem determinatum, ex [pre]suppositione [tamen] naturalium principiorum." Unde quia "magis [autem] repugnat rationi quod aliquis venereis utatur non solum contra id quod convenit proli generande, sed etiam cum iniuria alterius. [Et] ideo fornicatio simplex," dicitur "minima inter species luxurie" 195 si "committitur sine iniuria alterius persone."

Ad rationes vero in oppositum adductas primo respondetur sic: Nam quantum ad primum fundamentum negatur consequentia, quia peccatum contra naturam contrariatur caritati et reverentie que debetur ipsi deo.

Ad secundum respondetur negando etiam consequentiam, quia vitium 200 contra naturam est contra deum, ut est iam dictum, et tanto est gravius sacrilegio quanto ordo nature est prior et stabilior quam quilibet alius ordo supradictus.

Ad tertium respondetur et sic negando etiam consequentiam. Et ratio, quia minor est falso, quia unicuique individuo magis est coniuncta natura 205 speciei quam quodcumque aliud individuum, et ideo peccata contra natu-

---

[17] A printer's error has the edition read: xliiii. A "c" thus became an "x."

ram que fiunt speciei sunt graviora quam commissa contra individua. Et
sic ex supradictis remanet conclusio quod sodomia sive peccatum contra
naturam est maior incestu, fornicatione, et adulterio, ut in dicto c. Adul-
210 terii malum.

Ex supradictis omnibus infertur ad duo principaliter notanda. Et primo,
quod quemadmodum propter adulterius licitum est coniuges separari et sic
divortium fieri (c. Uxor a viro non discedat, C.32 q.7 [c.17]) cum simili-
bus, eodem modo propter delictum sodomie, cum vitium contra naturam
215 sit maius adulterio, ut iam in precedentibus clare probatum est et ostensum
per textum in dicto c. Adulterii malum (C.32 q.7 [c.11]), ubi textus dicit:
"Adulterii malum vincit fornicationem; vincitur autem ab incestu. Peius
est enim cum matre, quam cum aliena uxore [a v–r] concumbere. Sed omnium horum est pessimum, quod contra naturam sit." Hanc opinionem
220 sensit textus notatus in c. Omnes causationes, in verbo Sodomita, ea questione et causa [C.32 q.7 c.7], quod dictum sequitur Hugolino et Laurentio,
ut refert dominus Cardinalis ibi. Idem sensit beatus Thomas in quarto distinctione, 35,[18] dicens quod "propter hoc vitium [contra naturam] ita potest procedi ad divortium" quoad thorum quemadmodum propter adulte-
225 rium. "Sed iura de hoc vitio non faciunt mentionem, [tum] quia est passio
innominabilis, tum etiam quia raro accidit."

Sed contra hoc fortiter opponi potest de textu in c. Si uxorem (C.32
q.5 [c.18]), ubi dicitur quod propter aliam causam quantumcunque horri-
bilem non potest quis dimittere uxorem, excepta causa fornicationis, pro
230 quo facit etiam textus in c. 2, de divortiis [X.4.19]. Et hanc partem sensit
Innocentius in c. primo de adulterio [X.1.14], limitando tamen nisi maritus
vellet uxorem ad illud crimen trahere, quia tunc posset fieri divortium et
coniugum separatio, per textum in c. Idolatria (C.28 q.1 [c.5]). Item facit
quia pene sunt molliende, non autem ampliande; regula In penis, de regu-
235 lis iuris, in Sextus [VI.5.13.49]. Et sic cum fuerit dictum excepta causa fornicationis, ergo non in alia. Nam inclusio unius est exclusio alterius; c.
Nonne, de presumptionibus [X.2.23.5]. Johannes Andree in c. Maritus, de
adulteriis [X.5.16.4], simpliciter referendo transit, licet dominus Abbas in
dicto c. Maritus dicat Johannem Andree transire cum opinione Innocentii.
240 Et sic dicunt intelligendam esse glosam in dicto c. Omnes causationes
(C.32 q.7 [c.7]), ubi etiam tractat et ponit quid de pollutione manuali et
de pollutione extra claustra pudoris, que glosa diffuse circa hec pro et contra allegat.

---

[18] The modern reference in the *Summa theologica* is: Suppl. 62. 1 Resp.

Sed hac contrarietate non obstante, prima opinio putatur verior et communior, quia nomine adulterum [a v–v] seu fornicationis comprehendi- 245 tur omnis illicitus coitus (C.32 q.7) c. Non solum [c.15], et ea causa, questio 4, c. Meretrices [c.11]. Nam maior iniuria infertur matrimonio ex nefando crimine contra naturam, quam ex crimine naturaliter commisso. Cum autem Christus dixerit quod ex causa fornicationis licitum est uxorem dimittere, videtur intelligere de qualibet fornicatione. Nam satis videtur 250 fornicari iste in corpus suum. Et hanc opinionem tanquam veriorem sequi- tur dominus Antonius, Johannes Calderini, et dominus Abbas in dicto c. Maritus, de adulteriis [X.5.16.4], et Abbas in c. 2 de divortiis [X.4.19], et Archidyaconus in dicto c. Omnes causationes [C.32 q.7 c.7]. Quod verum credo si fuerit notorium. Cogita tamen quia pulcher est articulus. 255

Secundo principaliter infertur ex superioribus, quod cum incestus sit coire cum matre, et incestus sit minus malum quam vitium contra natu- ram, ut supra monstratum est, quod coire cum matre sit minus peccatum quam vitium contra naturam, et hoc videtur velle textus in dicto c. Adul- terii malum (C.32 q.7 [c.11]) ibi: "Peius est enim cum matre quam cum 260 aliena uxore concumbere. Sed omnium horum est pessimum, quod contra naturam fit."

Quod vitim contra naturam ita sit detestabile
in feminis quemadmodum in masculis.

Videamus an abuti masculis et feminis iudicetur a pari. Et videtur di- 265 cendum quod sic, quod probatur in c. In archiepiscopatu, de raptoribus [X.5.17.4], et ibi per doctores, pro quo facit glosa in dicto c. Omnes causa- tiones (C.32 q.7 [c.7]), et quod habetur in Autentica, Ut non luxurientur contra naturam, coll. 6 [Nov. 77]. Unde Augu[a vi–r]stinus contra Jo- hannem libro primo dixit, quod Apostolus tam in masculis quam in femi- 270 nis vehementer hoc arguebat, ut probatur in c. Usus naturalis, ea causa et questione [C.32 q.7 c.14]. Usus enim naturalis licitus est sicut in coniugio, illicitus sicut in adulterio, contra naturam vero semper illicitus, ut ibi. Et licet hoc in meretrice execrabile sit, in uxore tamen execrabilius reputatur, et sic maius peccatum, ut dicto c. Adulterii malum [C.32 q.7 c.11]. Ratio 275 est quia bonum prolis periclitatur inter coniuges, quod sic non est inter adulterum et meretricem, cum ille coitus sit illicitus et a lege damnatus, tum etiam quia maior reverentia debetur uxori quam quis tenetur diligere, quod sic non est in meretrice. Et ideo magis peccat, ut dixi, qui abutitur uxore quam si abuteretur alia in eodem genere peccati, secundum Lauren- 280 tium, quem dominus Cardinalis refert in dicto c. Adulterii malum.

Et licet hoc vitium tam agenti quam patienti detestabile sit, tamen minus videtur peccare patiens quam agens, ut sensit glosa in dicto c. Adulterii malum, in verbo naturam, ibi. Malo vinci quam vincere, ea causa et
285   questione, ea ratione, quia qui agit non solum peccat in personam propriam: sed etiam in personam patientis, cum ad vitium succumbentem induxisse presumatur. Ad quod facit textus in c. Noli putare, et in c. Homicidium (D. 1 [cc. 28, 27] de pen.). Dicunt aliqui glosatorem non advertisse ad id quod legitur Levitici 20 [.13]: "Qui dormierit cum masculo coitu
290   femineo, uterque operatus est nephas, ideo morte moriantur," et sic videtur equaliter peccare cogita. De materia huius vitii vide per beatum Thomam in secunda secunde questione 154,[19] articulo penultimo et ultimo [11, 12], et textum Institutionis de publicis iudiciis, § Item lex Iulia [I.4.18.4], et ibi per Augustinum, et in c. Nonne [C.1 (q.1) c.37] et in c.
295   Sunt plures, §[a vi–v] Auctoritas (D.3 [c.42] de pen.) et glosa in verbo Sepius, Extraordinaria [C.35 q.3 [c.11]), que ultra alia videtur velle quod extraordinaria pollutio in non naturali membro propter criminis enormitatem impediat matrimonium contrahendum.

Ad quem spectet cognitio criminis sodomitici

300   Dubium restat: An hoc crimen sit mere ecclesiasticum. Et quia pulchrum scire est, ideo examinabo. Et primo quod sit ecclesiasticum secura via monstrabitur. Licet enim Bartolomeus Brixiensis, in suo dignissimo Repertorio, in littera Sodomia, dixerit hoc vitium secundum aliquos dici non contra naturam, sed preter. Tamen contrarium sapit textus in c. Adul-
305   terii malum (C.32 q.7[20] [. 11]), ibi: "Sed omnium horum est pessimum, quod contra naturam fit."

Modo sic: Crimen directe nature contrarians cadit in iurisdictionem ecclesiasticam. Ista est doctrina Johannis Andree in c. primo de usuris in Sexto [VI.5.5.1], quam refert Abbas in c. Cum sit generale, in 9 coll. [sic],
310   de foro competenti [X.2.2.8]. Quia cum usura sit contra naturam, iudex ecclesiasticus est competens, sed cum sodomia sit vitium contra naturam, ideo ecclesiasticum erit hoc crimen, et sic per iudicem ecclesiasticum iudicari poterit.

Item quod sit ecclesiasticum probo per textum in c. Clerici, de exces.
315   prelat. [X.5.31.4], ubi ecclesia laicos deprehensos laborare morbo sodomitico excommunicat, sed ubicunque reperitur iudicem ecclesiasticum posse

---

[19] As indicated above, the same erroneous "xliiii" for "cliiii."
[20] In text: iiii.

excommunicare. Concluditur ex hoc iurisdictio sua in illo casu. Et hoc corroboro sic: Excommunicatio est pena (c. Sacro, de sententia excommunicationis [X.5.39.48]), qua nulla pena maior in ecclesia [b i–r] reperta est, (C.24 q.3): Corripiantur [c.17]. Sed cum pena non sit alicui infligenda nisi per iudicem (C.33[21] q.2) § In hoc capitulo [c.4], et ferri non debeat sine cause cognitione (C.2 q.1), Nemo [c.11], et c. primo, de sententia excommunicationis, in Sextum [VI.5.11], et per solum iudicem, ut in dicto c., ubi ter verbum iudex repetitur. Ergo per excommunicationem concluditur iurisdictio, facit capitulum Novit, de iudiciis, ubi papa procedebat contra regem Francie ad interdictum et excommunicationem [X.2.1.13]. Nec per hoc dicitur alterius iurisdictionem turbare nec ponere in messem alienam falcem, quoniam spectabat ad eum iudicare de peccato. Si ergo non spectasset ad eum tanquam iudicem, turbasset alterius iurisdictionem illum excommunicando, ex quibus verificatur dicta conclusio quam sequitur Lappus Allegatione 67, et Johannes Andree, In re, ea que fiunt a iure, libro Sexto [VI.5.13.56].

Sed contra hoc adduco textum notabilem in c. Dilecto, de sententia excommunicationis, in Sexto [VI.5.11.6], ubi excommunicatio fertur pro defensione iuris sui. Idem sensit Innocentius in c. Venerabili, de censibus [X.3.29.34]. Sed cum clarum sit quod quis non possit esse iudex in facto proprio, ut volunt doctores in c. Cum venissent, de iudiciis [X.2.1.12], maxime per dominum Antonium et Lappum consilio 39, ergo per excommunicationem non concluditur iurisdictio. Et sic hac ratione hoc vitium non erit ecclesiasticum indistincte.

Sed hac contrarietate non obstante, procedit ipsa conclusio. Et ad textum in dicto c. Dilecto [VI.5.11.6], respondeo quod ibi excommunicatio fertur non ut a iudice sed ut a parte, quo casu iurisdictio non concluderetur. Sed ubi fertur a iudice ut a iudice, ut est in dicto c. Clerici, de exces. prelat. [X.5.31.4], bene concluditur tali modo iurisdictio per ipsam excommunicationem. Et sic aperte probatum est vitium contra naturam esse ecclesiasticum. Dominus Antonius in dicto c. [b i–v] Clerici intellexit, quod hoc crimen non erat ecclesiasticum, sed ideo iudex ecclesiasticus ibi impediebat se propter perseverantiam in delicto. Sed hoc dictum damnat dominus abbas in dicto c. Clerici, asserens quod ista est divinatio ad illum textum. Unde dicit ipse quod qualitercunque peccent homines contra naturam, ut in actu venereo vel adorando idola vel alio modo contra naturam, semper ecclesia potest iurisdictionem suam exercere in laicos, ita

---

[21] In text: xxiii.

quod crimen erit ecclesiasticum. Et hoc videtur sensisse Innocentius in c.
355   [Quod] super his, de voto [X.3.34.8], ubi dicit quod ecclesia contra infi-
deles peccantes contra naturam potest suam exercere iurisdictionem. Nam
etiam deus punivit, ut Gn. 19, eodem modo ipse vicarius, et per conse-
quens eius prelati, qui sunt assumpti in partem solicitudinis. Nam ex hoc
peccato leditur ipse deus qui est auctor nature, ut est textus in c. Flagi-
360   tia[22] (C.33 q.7 [c.13]).

Et per hanc rationem sensit Johannes Monachus, ut refert ipse Abbas
in dicto c. Clerici [X.5.31.4], quod ideo ecclesia punit usurarios et non
fures sive latrones, quia usurarii delinquunt contra naturam, ut dictum est,
facientes germinare pecuniam que naturaliter non germinat. Non tamen
365   intelligas per superiora quod hoc crimen sit mere ecclesiasticum, quia hoc
esset falsum, cum sit mixti fori, cum ita per secularem sicut per ecclesiasticum possit cognosci. Unde dixit dominus Abbas in c. In archiepiscopatu,
de raptoribus [X.5.17.4], in fine, quod locus erit perventioni. Idem sensit
Johannes de Anania, ibi, et dominus Abbas in c. Clerici, de exces. prelat.

370   Sequitur de pena sodomiticorum
                        [b ii–r] De pena sodomiticorum.

Qua vero pena veniant puniendi qui vitio contra naturam irretiti sunt
et maculati, adhuc ostensum non est. Nam aliud secundum leges et aliud
secundum canones. Voluit enim Imperator in lege Cum vir, Cod. de adul-
375   teris [C.9.9.31], et in Autentica Ut non luxurientur contra naturam,
collat. 6 [Nov. 77], quod propter tale vitium delinquens gladio feriatur, et
sic capite punitur. Hoc idem sensit glosa in c. Clerici, de exces. prelat.
[X.5.31.4], et textus de penitentia, D. 1 [C.33 q.3], § Qui puero [c.15].
Idem voluit etiam glosa in c. Flagitia (C.32 q.7 [c.13]). Plus dico quod
380   eadem pena punitur qui ad hoc vitium perpetrandum commodat domum
vel mediator est, ut voluit textus in lege Qui puero, Cod. De extraordina-
riis criminibus [D.47.11.1.], et in § Qui puero, de penitentia, D. 1. Sed
hodiernis diebus, secundum leges municipales, huiusmodi morbo inquinati
comburantur.
385   Secundum vero canones alia pena feriuntur, de qua per textum in dicto
c. Clerici [X.5.31.4]. Nam si sunt laici, excommunicantur et a cetu fidelium separantur. Et dicit Hostiensis in dicto c. Clerici quod tales compel-
luntur agere penitentiam, alias vindictam regie potestati reservandam esse

---

[22] In text: flatia.

dicit, et hoc per textum in c. In archiepiscopatu, de raptoribus [X.5.17.4], in fine, que secundum legem suam iudicabit. 390

At vero si clerici fuerint contra naturam incontinentes, a clero eiiciendi sunt, et in monasterio ad agendam penitentiam detrudantur; si fuerint incorrigibiles, secundum aliquos, ut in dicto c. Clerici [X.5.31.4]. Unde dicit Hostiensis per illum textum, quod talis poterit privari beneficiis suis, quod militare posse credimus si de hoc fuerint convicti vel condemnati, 395 cum tunc tales efficiantur infames. Ita glosa notabilis, in § Testes, Inst. de testamentis ordinandis [I.2.10.6]. [b ii-v] Et quia "infamibus porte dignitatis non pate[a]nt," regula Infamibus, de regulis iuris (VI. [5.13.87]), ad quod facit textus in capitulo Tantis Daniel (D.81 [c.3]), et c. Inter dilectos, de exces. prelat [X.5.31.11]. Unde dicit lex: "Quos scelus aut[23] vite turpitudo inquinat, et quos infamia ab honestorum cetu segregat, dignitatis 400 porte non patebunt," ut Cod. de dignitatibus (C.12.[1].2).

Ad quem spectat absolutio vitii sodomitici.

Cuius auctoritate autem fiat absolutio a casu sodomitico aperiendum est. Hostiensis in Summa, de penitentiis et remissionibus [X.5.38.], § Cui 405 confitendum, retulit esse de casibus episcopo reservatis, quem sequitur Zabarela, in Clementinis, Dudum, in § Hac deinde, circa finem de sepulturis [Clem. 3.7.2]. Unde per solum episcopum tractanda est, vel per alium ad hoc speciali licentia habita. Nam in generali confessione, ista non veniunt que speciali privilegio episcopo reservantur, ut est textus in c. Si epis- 410 copus, de penitentiis et remis., in Sexto [VI.5.10.2]. Pro quo etiam facit textus in c. finali de officio vicarii, eo libro [VI.1.13.3], et regula In generali, de regulis iuris, in Sexto [VI.5.13.81], cum si.

Que penitentia sodomiticis sit iniungenda.

Restat examinari de penitentia pro vitio sodomitico iniungenda. Regu- 415 lariter enim per legem ecclesie pro mortali peccato septennis penitentia imponitur, c. Hoc ipsum (C.32 q.2 [c.11]). Sed propter enormitatem criminis contra naturam, maior pro hoc vitio imponitur pe[b iii-r]nitentia, ut notatur in dicto c. Hoc ipsum, circa finem. Magnitudo vel excellentia criminum excedens vulgare, peccatum maiorem ultionem expectat (D.82), 420 Presbyter [c.5], et (C.27[24] q.1), Devotam [c.27]. Hoc enim crimen bestialem conditionem excedit. Nam nulla bestia hoc agere reperitur; non enim

---

[23] In text: et.
[24] In text: xxii.

commiscetur animal masculum cum masculo eiusdem speciei vel alterius.
Unde per alia vitia homo efficitur similis bestiis cum agat contra rationem
425   naturalem. Per hoc autem vitium efficitur inferior omni bestia, quia non
solum agit contra rationem vel instinctum naturalem, sed etiam contra instinctum bestialem seu animalem, ex quo agit contra naturam generis, ut
est textus in c. Non solum (C.32 q.7 [c.15]), ibi: "Qu[a]s ego nec mutis
pecudibus comparaverim. Pecora enim cum conceperint ultra non indul-
430   gent maribus copiam sui."

Quot modis dicatur quis peccare contra naturam.

Ultimo finem faciendo, non omittam quod contra naturam peccari plu-
ribus modis dicitur.
Primo modo ubi absque omni concubitu causa delectationis veneree
435   vitium procuratur, quod ad immunditiam pertinet, quam mollitiem voca-
mus que fit manibus, de quo Apostolum (1 Cor. 6. [9-10]): Molles non
possidebunt regnum dei. Unde Martialis in Ponticum [IX, 41] scribens ostendit delicti magnitudinem:

Pontice, quod nunquam futuis, sed pellice leva
440   uteris et Veneri servit amica manus,
hoc nihil esse putas? scelus est, mihi crede, sed ingens,
quantum vix animo concipis ipse tuo.
[b iii–v]nempe semel futuit, generaret Oratius ut tres;
Mars semel, ut geminos Ilia casta daret.
445   omnia perdiderat, si masturbatus uterque
mandasset manibus gaudia feda suis.
ipsam crede tibi naturam dicere rerum:
"istud quod digitis, Pontice, perdis, homo est."

Hoc tamen peccatum est minimum inter ea que fiunt contra naturam. Ita
450   dixit Johannes in Summa Confessorum, in secundo libro, in titulo de raptoribus, questione 2, in fine.
Secundo modo contra naturam peccatur ubi non servatur debitus
modus concumbendi quantum ad instrumentum, vel vas non debitum, aut
quantum ad alios modos monstruosos. Et hoc peccatum superat mollitiem.
455   Tertio modo contra naturam peccatur quando fit per concubitum ad
non debitum sexum, ut quando masculus masculum incurvat, quod vitium
dicitur sodomiticum. Et hoc peccatum est gravius supradictis peccatis.
Quarto modo contra naturam peccatur quando fit per concubitum ad
rem non eiusdem speciei, ut masculus cum bestia. Et tunc iste superlative

peccat respectu omnium supradictorum. Ita dicit Thomas secunda secunde, 460
questione 154, quarto articulo.[25] Nam iste peccat duplici ratione. Primo
quia non servatur debitus sexus, secundo quia non servatur species; ita
Iohannes in Summa Confessorum, libro 3, titulo 34, de penitentiis et remissionibus, verbo 40, Qui cum brutis. Ad quod facit Leviticus secundo:
Qui cum [iumento et pecore][26] coierit morte moriatur [Lev. 20.15], facit 465
textus in c. Mulier (C.15 q.1 [c.4]). Et iste est de casibus episcopo reservatis, ut est glosa in c. Se episcopus, de penitentiis et remissionibus, in
Sexto (VI.5.10 [c.2]). Et de excellentia huius delicti, vide textum in dicto
c. Hoc ipsum (C.33 q.2 [c.11]), circa finem.

Finis. 470

---

[25] The actual reference in the *Summa theologica* is 2.2.154.11 Resp., whence come the four modes and their language.

[26] In text: brutis.

Dressing Like a Woman:
The Case of the Berdache*

THE AMERICAN BERDACHE[1] was not completely foreign to late fifteenth-century explorers who knew their travel literature. From the Near and Middle East had come stories of corporeally integral males who dressed and acted like women their life long, a feature that distinguished them from European "sodomites." Still, the conquerors of America were amazed to find such transvestites among almost every people they encountered: perhaps three or four per village, many more in the cities. Women dressed like men, so-called "female berdaches," were rare in this part of the hemisphere. Some of the interlopers thought that these berdaches, and the passive "sodomy" or receptive sexual role they indulged, afforded the Europeans a just *titre de conquête*, like cannibalism and human sacrifice. But as one Spaniard put it, if that measure was applied, then some European nations would lose their right to govern themselves. And so it was that many of these early ethnographers, even while ruthlessly suppressing the berdaches of the New World, also sought to describe them for their readers. As a result, we know a good deal about them, or so it might seem.

---

* This essay appeared previously in *L'Histoire* (May, 1998): 41.
[1] Mistakenly labeled "hermaphrodites" by early French explorers. Delia Cosentino confirms that this originally Persian word, Italicized as *bardascio,* is still used in the Montopolese dialect of the Sabine Mountains to refer to pubescent boys.

For in recent times the berdache has become a subject of hot debate, being cast either as primordial gay heroes or as the victims of child abuse that our sources suggest most of these berdaches to have been.[2] The berdaches no longer exist, but a dispute over their significance rages.

European missionaries and lay writers portray the berdaches clearly enough. While an occasional adult warrior became a berdache to avoid war, most berdaches were children or adolescents, and certainly less than twenty-five years of age. They dressed and spoke like, and usually spent their time among, women, and could not easily be distinguished from them by outsiders. Berdaches rarely fought, or at least could not carry men's weapons. Sometimes the native word for "berdache" is the same as that for "coward," and indeed like the Europeans, Americans insulted their war enemies by dressing and otherwise insulting them as women. Nor do the berdaches at the time of European contact seem to have had any priestly or consultative roles. Instead, the berdaches did "women's things" although, being "more robust" than women, in the sources' words, they often headed women's work groups. One of these "things of women" was sexual reception rather than penetration. Though integrally male, berdaches were forbidden to act heterosexually but were expected to receive any male who sought their attention. We find them employed as village prostitutes, who helped keep braves away from marriageable girls, and in various economic roles such as wives, where they were often preferred by men because of their strength, and even as religious figures of a sort, being ceremonially mounted in sacrificial prayer. Thus the homosexual behavior of the berdaches in the sixteenth through eighteenth centuries, rather than being the decisive element of their makeup, was only one, albeit important feature of a social being whose essence lay in subordination to (penetrative) men on the basis of the female gender s/he represented.

How then did the male child become a berdache, for once and ever? The answer is that he was usually forcibly converted to womanhood either by big men who raped him — to then build their retinues with such figures and then sell their services — or by parents who, having sired only boys, needed girls to serve them. This "appointment to office," as I have called it, was still common among the Zuni in the early twentieth century. In-

---

[2] The outline of this debate is to be found in my "Gender Subordination and Political Hierarchy in Prehispanic America," elsewhere in the present volume. It commenced after the publication of R. Trexler, *Sex and Conquest: Gendered Violence, Political Order, and the European Conquest of the Americas* (Ithaca, 1995).

deed, parents and communities already during pregnancy had often decided to convert a male fetus into a girl once born. Passive sexual reception was one ultimate result of that conversion.

Needless to say, the berdaches should be viewed as one part of a larger political and cultural reality. Thus among the eighteenth-century Iroquois, not just individuals but a whole subordinate people like the Lenape was labeled as a "woman" over and against the "men people" who made up the heart of the Confederacy. Certainly the berdache was one American means of representing all those males who were not "men," that is, those males who were in fact dependent on other men. Thus these men were made out to look like these societies' images of women so as to represent, in gendered form, the principle of dependence in society. They helped to express the relation between force and masculinity on the one hand, dependence and femininity on the other.

Gender Subordination and
Political Hierarchy
in Prehispanic America*

IT IS A WIDESPREAD CHARACTERISTIC of patriarchal conceptions of political order that power in polities is said to belong to males or those perceived as male, while dependency is said to be the fate of the female. Not for nothing did the half-native Garcilaso de la Vega, historian of the collapse of the Inca empire at the hands of macho Spaniards, insist that there never was a more manly people than his beloved Inca![1] Indeed, in traditional societies, the very notion of independence is commonly glossed as something masculine and that of dependence as feminine or as childish, so that those lowest in the political echelons or excluded from them are viewed as "girls," to use a term employed in today's armies, prisons and

---

* This essay appears concurrently in *Infamous Desire: Male Homosexuality in Colonial Latin America*, ed. P. Sigal (Chicago, 2002), chap 2.

[1] *Comentarios reales de los Incas*, 3 vols., Biblioteca de Autores Españoles [hereafter BAE] 133–135) (Madrid, 1960–1965), 133:226 (bk. 6, chap. 25). See also R. Trexler, *Sex and Conquest: Gendered Violence, Political Power, and the European Conquest of the Americas* (Ithaca, 1995), 150. I would like to thank my friend Jean Quataert for reading a draft of this article.

offices, even though they may be biologically male.[2] In short, whatever their lineage arrangements or the symmetry of their cosmologies, most societies, for all their variety, in what touches political power and order are at one in assigning femininity to what is further down, masculinity to what is up.[3] Obviously, like the husband who is conceptualized as a "girl" at work or as unemployed, but as a male as head of a household, that person may be simultaneously gendered in both directions depending on the social context. To be sure, there is much contingency in matters of gender, which it is the task of the historian to ferret out. But the general rule enunciated above — that the exercise of power is perceived as totally male in patriarchal societies — should not be ignored or forgotten. That way lies the land of Cocaigne, where the suffusive ubiquity of power itself may be doubted, and, for those with their own agendas, what is down may be made up.

To be sure, in every political entity, as well as in personal relations, there is a process at work by which persons and corporations are judged to be in concord or at odds with either their biological sex or, in the case of corporations, with a male or female gender said to be "natural" to them. Now, one problem in studying this gendering process is that, as a general rule, patriarchal societies limit formal political, and often ritual, participation to men; that is, they exclude all females and young males. Yet — what is less often recognized — that male political institution itself soon

---

[2] Only recently (July 1996) the press reported that Joe Arpaio, the sheriff of Maricopa County (Phoenix, AZ), famous for his gendered treatment of prisoners, had forced the latter to wear pink clothing. Typical uses of the term "girl" to address prisoners occur in the film *The Shawshank Redemption* (dir. Frank Darabont). See further A. Scacco, ed., *Male Rape: A Casebook of Sexual Aggression* (New York, 1982), and recently S. Donaldson, "The Deal Behind Bars," *Harper's Magazine* (August 1996): 17, 20, an insider's description of sexual strategies and tactics, kindly brought to my attention by Jim Senter. A broad survey of such gendering behavior, across the animal kingdom, is in the papers of a symposium on this subject: R. Trexler, ed., *Gender Rhetorics: Postures of Dominance and Submission in History* (Binghamton, 1994).

[3] S. Brandes provides an excellent example in his *Metaphors of Masculinity: Sex and Status in Andalusian Folklore* (Philadelphia, 1980), chap. 8, especially 144, where he observes that during the olive harvest in "Monteros," women are invariably down, picking olives from the ground, men always up, reaching into the trees. I distinguished between dualistic symbolic systems in highland Peru and the de facto power monopoly of men in my *Sex and Conquest*, 218, n. 29; cf. however I. Silverblatt, *Moon, Sun, and Witches: Gender Ideologies and Class in Inca and Colonial Peru* (Princeton, 1987), and B. J. Isbell, "De inmaduro a duro: lo simbólico femenino y los esquemas andinos de género," in *Más allá del Silencio: las fronteras de género en los Andes*, ed. D. Arnold (La Paz, 1997), 253–301.

takes on a gendered character: the adult political males build or define hierarchy within their male polis in part by assigning a feminine gender in that hierarchy to males who by reason of status or age are lower down the political scale. A political hierarchy is thus imagined and characterized at one level as the corporation of males, who defend all the women and children outside, but at another as a register that has males at the top and male "females" and "children," or those addressed and insultable as such, at the bottom. In patriarchal ideology, "women" appear within, though women are outside, the political hierarchy, just as "women" may appear in, though women may be excluded from, for example, a dance. How then is such an obvious political inconsistency or ambiguity — gender is, after all, ambiguous by definition — represented in human societies?

After studying the gendering of politics in late medieval and early modern Europe,[4] I became interested in the same process when after 1980 I turned my attention to American studies and especially to the pre-Hispanic period in the area we today call Latin America. Given my previous study of collective insults in late medieval Italy, I was hardly surprised to find that participants in the wars of conquest between the Spaniards and the indigenous Americans, and subsequent commentators, genderized those conflicts. It soon became clear to me that military and diplomatic activities were the most obvious areas in which relations between people were expressed in gendered language, and that realm of political relations will also come first in the present paper.

It was when I turned to descriptions of political and social relations in inner-political native contexts that I encountered something new to me. At the time of contact, the majority of American tribes in what comes to be called Latin America possessed a particular social figure, the berdache, who may be defined as a transvested biological male who till death represented himself as a female in all possible ways, usually including his sexually receptive or "passive" self-"presentation" to other, penetrating, males. One of this figure's prime functions in that place and time was, I would ultimately argue, to serve as a visual embodiment of the gender hierarchy, to express to the whole community just what I have stated above: the relation between force and masculinity on the one hand, de-

---

[4] See specifically "Ritual in Florence: Adolescence and Salvation in the Renaissance," now in my *Dependence in Context in Renaissance Florence* (Binghamton, 1994); "*Correre la Terra*: Collective Insults in the Late Middle Ages," in *Dependence in Context*, and "Bending Over Backwards," elsewhere in the present volume.

pendence and femininity on the other. The following paper continues my discourse on the subject of the berdache.

The berdache, it seems, was one American means of representing all those males who were not "men," that is, those males who were in fact dependent on other men. The trivial admonition that if you weren't on top you would be on bottom was embodied in a particular social creature, the berdache. This figure, as he was encountered during the Spanish conquests of what we today call Latin America, became the subject of my 1995 book, *Sex and Conquest: Gendered Violence, Political Order, and the European Conquest of the Americas*, and that work in turn has become the object of some heated dissent, especially by Michael Horswell, both in his Ph.D. dissertation "Third Gender, Tropes of Sexuality and Transculturation in Colonial Andean Historiography" (1997) and now in a chapter of *Infamous Desire*, cited above, and by Will Roscoe, in his *Changing Ones: Third and Fourth Genders in Native North America* (New York, 1998). Both of these works have helped me to focus some of my findings better, for which I am thankful. But what follows will also show the price these and other researchers pay when they allow their own personal search for identity to determine their reading of the past.[5]

In the following pages I want to bring the figure of the "Latin American" berdache, that is, the figure encountered by the Iberians at the time of their conquests, to the foreground once again.[6] This is not a paper about women, nor does it discuss the Spaniards' sexual treatment of the Americans,[7] nor is my work concerned with mentalities, that is, with

---

[5] Horswell's dissertation was done at the University of Maryland at College Park. In what follows, I cite from this work, rather than from his chapter in *Infamous Desire*, which summarizes part of the dissertation. St. Martin's Press published Roscoe's work. The author had finished a draft of his work when he received my work. Unfortunately he chose not to incorporate information from my text into the body of his own work, merely adding a critique of my work and that of two other authors as the last chapter of his book.

[6] The parameters I set are important. For instance, Roscoe writes that "Trexler argues that *throughout the Americas* berdaches were 'young men forced to dress as women ...,'" whereas I actually said that "*in different parts of Mexico and the Andes* we encounter young men forced to dress as women. ..." (my italics). Thus for reasons I will examine later, Roscoe purposely misstates the parameters I set. I have now, in fact, addressed the general problem of the berdache "throughout the Americas" in "Making the American Berdache: Choice or Constraint?" *Journal of Social History* 35 (2002), 613–36. In the present article, however, I refer to Roscoe only as his work touches on the berdache during the periods and in the spaces of the Iberian conquests, which is the focus of my book, and of this article.

[7] On this subject, see A. Barbosa Sánchez, *Sexo y conquista* (Mexico City, 1994); and

native mythology or philosophy, which were, after all, attempts to explain established behaviors. This paper is about native American power, which may be suggested in thought but is manifested in the indigenous behavior of men made out to look like these societies' images of women so as to represent, in gendered form, the principle of dependence in society.[8] Specifically, it will describe the political significance of the berdache, understanding the word "politics" in the broadest sense.[9] Needless to say, political power is not the only force that peoples represent in gendered fashion. So once we have described this outright political figure, I will try to place the image of the berdache alongside some other gendered representations in Middle America.

Of all areas of social and political life, certainly the military and diplomatic spheres are those where the influence of gendering is most quickly and keenly recognized. For perhaps universally in the heat of battle and in the first flush of victory, engaged warriors defame their opposite numbers by calling them women. Yet interestingly, as time passes after a war, these gender assignments lose their military aggressiveness and yield to diplomatic considerations: victors and losers are forced by circumstances to become different grades of "brothers" if they are to live in comity with each other.[10] This general dynamic certainly matches the behavior of the Spaniards and the Americans in confronting and later coming to terms with each other. But more important to our present theme, it concurs with what we know of military and diplomatic relations between the

---

R. Herren, *La conquista erótica de las Indias* (Barcelona, 1992).

[8] Roscoe thinks that "power in native societies is first and foremost spiritual and supernatural": *Changing Ones*, 190. Theology not being my strong suit, I will have to leave that notion of power to someone else.

[9] Much of the large literature on the berdache is cited in the bibliography of my *Sex and Conquest*. Literature since I finished *Sex and Conquest* includes a survey by W. Roscoe, "Was We'wha a Homosexual: Native American Survivance and the Two-Spirit Tradition," *Gay and Lesbian Quarterly* 2 (1995): 193–235. The recent collection of S. Jacobs, W. Thomas, and S. Lang, eds., *Two-Spirit People: Native American Gender Identity, Sexuality, and Spirituality* (Urbana, 1977), has little of historical significance. Exceptions are the articles by A. Pilling, cited further below, and S. Lang, whose dissertation, *Männer als Frauen — Frauen als Männer: Geschlechtsrollewechsel bei den Indianern Nordamerikas* (Hamburg, 1990), 310–57, provides the best overview of the literature on the much rarer, so-called female berdaches. Like much of the literature on the berdaches, these works pay no real attention to historical change.

[10] Juan Ginés de Sepúlveda provides one good example of this postbellum reassessment, in his *Crónica Indiana* (Valladolid, 1976), 442 (bk. 7, chap. 26); others are in my *Sex and Conquest*, 72–74.

American peoples themselves. In sum, in the military sphere gender assignments are often not fully definitive, but can change to accommodate shifting political conditions. This is true not only of individuals but of gendered corporations as well. It is well known, for example, that in another part of the Americas at a later point, corporate relationships between whole peoples were described in gendered fashion, with the subordinate tribe of the Delaware being "the woman" and the superior tribes of the Iroquois being made up of "the men."[11]

Moving now from verbal to bodily gendering, we can quickly pass in review some of the actions taken in warfare and diplomacy. They ranged from practices carried out on corpses to castration and sodomitic rape through depilation and the like. These practices usually had a gender insult at their base, and even when none is mentioned, the "womanly" character of a person or tribe who would let such things happen to him was clear to one and all. Nor were the Americans unique in these regards.[12]

But the most relevant practice of this type for our purposes is that victors forcibly transvested losers as women to emphasize their subordinate status, a habit the Spaniards were well acquainted with from Europe. Thus in the pre-Hispanic tradition of the Aztecs, written down after the Conquest, we find the ruler of one Valley political unit forcing the ambassador of another to dress as a woman for the return home to Tenochtitlan.[13] Let us not surmise, however, that warriors only perpetrated this insult against military enemies. Within the same ethnic unit, we find forced transvestism visited upon subordinates by superiors. Thus in the Andes, Inca Huascar is said to have forced his general to dress up as a woman

---

[11] The seventeenth-century Delaware's structural subordination to the Iroquois in gendered form was, I argue, manifested by the former dressing like women when they received the latter. Though the principle of diplomatic gendering that I will presently describe is comparable, I have not found such a corporate institution of cross-gendering at the state level in Meso-America. An extended look at these similarities and differences is given in Trexler, *Sex and Conquest*, 74–79, and see especially the excellent article by F. Speck, "The Delaware Indians as Women: Were the Original Pennsylvanians Politically Emasculated?" *Pennsylvania Magazine of History and Biography* 70 (1946): 377–89.

[12] The readiest overview of such practices is in antiquity, through the relevant articles in *Paulys Realencyclopädie der classischen Altertumswissenschaft, neue Bearbeitung*; see also my *Sex and Conquest*, 12–37.

[13] H. Alvarado Tezozomoc, *Crónica Mexicana* [and the] *Códice Ramírez* (Mexico City, 1975), 263f., 54, 57.

because he had lost a battle.[14] Other examples of this behavioral humiliation by gendering are common enough, and Cecelia Klein has found convincing evidence in the Aztec record showing this culture's soldiers being
spurred on to heroism with threats to the effect that otherwise, they would
be denounced as women,[15] a threat which, as we have seen, did at times
include forced transvestism. The derision of women implicit in this practice will hardly surprise anyone familiar with the treasury of misogyny in
the oral traditions of these, and other, American peoples.

Let us be clear: in these military-diplomatic examples, we are talking
predominantly about forced transvestism that could have been only temporary in nature. Of course a humiliated soldier returning home accused of
cowardice would never again be thought of as fully male, and just as
probably, some prisoners who had been "made women," perhaps through
rape or depilation, remained so. Yet the evidence does not allow the presumption that berdaches, who were permanent transvestites, were usually
products of the battlefield.[16] I believe only that the creation and maintenance of political authority within the polities derived from the same principle of violent transformations of gender that we have now seen outside,
on the battlefield. Just as contestants on the battlefield gendered losers female, so were polities capable of forcing their own domestic "cowards"
(the native word for "berdache" sometimes was identical to that for "coward") into womanhood in the context of civil life, to which we now turn.

In this world where gendering was so ubiquitous in inter- and intratribal relations, we have now come finally to the berdaches who were a

---

[14] M. Cabello Balboa (fl. 1576–1586), *Historia del Perú bajo la dominación de los Incas*,
pt. 2 of *Miscelanea Austral* (Lima, 1920), 155 (chap. 19). For no apparent scholarly reason,
Horswell essentially dismisses this account, as he will others that he thinks dishonor
Andean, not to say contemporary American women, berdaches, and "homosexuals."
Here as elsewhere, he fails to mention my evidence that the identical practices — in this
case insult transvestism — was practiced in the Valley of Mexico, not to mention in
North America as well. Instead, he suggests that here the Inca may actually have been
bestowing a gift of cloth upon his (losing) general!: "Third Gender," 32–33.

[15] "Fighting with Femininity: Gender and War in Aztec Mexico," in Trexler, *Gender
Rhetorics*, 113.

[16] C. Callender and L. Kochems, "The North American Berdache," *Current Anthropology* 24 (1983): 451, also caution against such an assumption; see further Trexler, *Sex
and Conquest*, 217, n. 22. Alas Horswell misreads me, to then proclaim that it is "non-
sensical" of me to say — as I did not — that berdaches are "products of conquest politics in the Andean context": "Third Gender," 25. My point that war provided a template for the erection of civil institutions was lost on him.

fixture across the Americas as well as among various Middle Eastern and east Asian peoples. How do we know about the American berdaches? At the time and in the geographical region that are our sole concern — the Latin American world before and during the contact period with the Spaniards — Spanish writers, both ecclesiastical and lay, are our most important sources, followed by several mestizo writers. There are obvious advantages in this fact, especially because churchmen wrote about these cultures to the end of more successfully converting the natives, and thus filled their accounts with sound ethnographic information. But there are also disadvantages because, as with sources in general, those used in this study are interested, that is, they write about these cultures — which were largely alien to them — from a particular point of view.

Thus, historians have the duty to read sources carefully, and to evaluate their promise and problems. They will begin with a study of European sexual discourse at the time of the conquests, so as to recognize the conventional shibboleths used by European sources, and the first two chapters of my *Sex and Conquest* do precisely that.[17] They will of course dismiss generalizations to the effect that Americans were "all sodomites." When dealing with other sources on the Americas where ideology is at play, the historian will also seek out primary-source authorities with polarized opinions, such as those separating Fernández de Oviedo and Las Casas, cited below. The latter for instance give fairly detailed information on such homosexual behavior and on cross-dressing, often distinguishing between the two acts, as sources inexperienced in the Americas do not, all in the attempt to refute each other's notions as to the extent of homosexual behavior. Yet as the most reliable sources, the student will prefer those off-hand observations of sexual behavior whose point of emphasis lies elsewhere, that is, upon those observations that are not directly ideological in nature. This is regularly the case with references to sodomy in the New World record. Scholars unfamiliar with the primary sources may imagine that the Europeans regularly combine the "crime" of sodomy with cannibalism and human sacrifice into a package whose purpose was merely to justify conquest, but in fact, the overwhelming number of references to sodomy in this record occur alone, with no link to those other, more serious "crimes."[18]

---

[17] See my categorization of the primary sources according to their value and demerits in *Sex and Conquest*, 3–5.

[18] See Peter Mason's "Sex and Conquest: A Redundant Copula?" *Anthropos* 92

Perforce, in the absence of police records the information at the historian's disposal will be largely anecdotal in nature, because there were no scientific studies of sexuality in these ages.[19] But nonetheless, from such anecdotes comes a trove of knowledge of undoubted value precisely because it is not trying to make a large point and is so commonly devoid of any reference to larger questions. Given the off-handedness of so many of these records, and the fact that they commonly were set down by people with no interest in such questions, one marvels at the naiveté of the notion that the Spaniards referred to the berdache so often merely because "the conquerors were collecting evidence to justify their conquest."[20] This trove of information I have collected will not of course answer all or even most questions about the American berdache of these contact centuries; the sources are too fragmentary for that. But the historian will bear in mind what it is that he or she sets out to demonstrate, and be sure that the sources used are adequate to prove that point. They will prove to be fully adequate on that score.

We should be clear that for all their problems, there is no alternative to the use of these European records, because no purely American record from the time of the Spanish conquests exists regarding the berdaches and their role in society. One may hope that some day such indigenous sources on the berdache in native languages will come to our aid. But certainly, no one will wait for them, or be so naive as to believe that a native American source would be any less interested. Nor can we uncritically project backwards into Hispanic colonial times the more available information on berdaches gathered by nineteenth- and twentieth-century ethnographers of North America, much less retroject into the contact past the concerns of today's sexual identity groups; I will return to this point at the end of this paper. It is reckless to disregard the historical nature of these contact-period human beings. Once the European materials are understood, bemoaning their problems is mere provincial bathos, and a waste of time.[21]

(1997): 577–82, with my rejoinder in *Anthropos* 93 (1998): 655–56. This was followed by Mason's response and my closing observation, *Anthropos* 94 (1999): 315–16.

[19] The exception are the records of the city of Florence, Italy, masterfully studied by M. Rocke, *Forbidden Friendships: Homosexuality and Male Culture in Renaissance Florence* (New York, 1996).

[20] Roscoe, *Changing Ones*, 194.

[21] My experience is that some Americanists cite European sources profusely — what else is there? — until they encounter statements they do not like, at which point they declaim against European sources, which don't understand Americans, etc. Thus Roscoe

A second historiographical problem must also be addressed, and that is the relative scarcity of source materials for the berdaches among any particular people. Needless to say, if more were known at the ethnic level from the historical period that interests me — the period of contact and colonization — the position of the pre-Conquest berdache among any given people might form the subject matter of who knows how many dissertations. But in fact, the material referred to in my recent book contains everything I could find available on this figure for the period in question. Certainly someone — like Michael Horswell elsewhere in *Infamous Desire* — mainly interested in the mentality or cosmology of a given people can use the behavioral material s/he encounters in this article and in my monograph to develop a broader understanding of gender within that given ethnic group; such an effort is to be encouraged. But my concern has been with the berdache as a living individual, and that led me perforce to a large range of (mostly) Spanish sources from across the Latin-American world as it is defined today. To be sure, there were substantial differences among the berdaches of that world, and I have insisted upon them in earlier work when I found them, as I will here. But the bulk of these sources also reveals strong similarities, which I want to emphasize in this paper. These similarities are so fundamental and straightforward as to allow the general argument I shall present.

We begin by noting that sixteenth-century Iberian and mestizo chroniclers quickly labelled the subject of this paper and the objects of their curiosity "berdaches," a term that was current in the Old World. Roscoe and others claim to the contrary that the term was applied to our figure only in the eighteenth century. However, the evidence is clear that this originally Persian word meaning a servant or slave boy — the word is still used in vernacular Italian with the same connotation of dependence — was a rooted part of the historical literature of Meso-America at the end of the sixteenth century.[22]

---

refs to the "cant of conquest" even while citing it affirmatively: *Changing Ones*, 189. This practice is the more blatant among deconstructionists like Mason, for whom there is no there there.

[22] Roscoe (*Changing Ones*, 173) has the word used for the first time in the New World by the Frenchman Deliette in 1704, even though my book shows "berdache" being used by the writer Diego Muñoz Camargo ca. 1576. See the text in *Sex and Conquest*, 259, n. 86. The word was promptly reemployed by J. de Torquemada. This Franciscan first referred to the famous boy Antinous whom the Emperor Hadrian "le servia de bardaje," and then made a god (*Monarquia Indiana*, 3 vols. [Mexico City, 1975], 2:393), and then a few pages later, in a long description of the berdaches of the New World,

Turning now to the vital statistics of these persons, we ask if these berdaches, who may have numbered three or four to a village but whose number in cities proves impossible to estimate, played any significant role in
group politics narrowly defined. Horswell has laid out a vast claim in this
regard, going so far as to state that "castrated or transvested, [third gender
persons] participated in the power structure of Tawantinsuyu" or the Inca
state.[23] What are we to make of such a claim? Transvestites at least do
in fact occasionally appear as actors in military and diplomatic contexts,
and describing them will plunge us quickly into the berdaches' intra-group
social significance. A more cautious reading of the evidence will not sustain broad claims.

The all but universal rule for the berdaches described in this paper is
that they did not take part in actual warfare.[24] Like the Floridian Tumu-
cua, they carried provisions and gathered up the wounded. But they did
not carry arms, or to be still more precise, they did not bear the arms proper to male warriors.[25] The exception that proves the rule in Meso-
America is in a report of Nuño de Guzmán, writing in 1530 and describing
a "Chichimec" he encountered at Cuizco west of Tenochtitlan. The
Spaniards thought he was a woman because of his clothing, and were
dumbfounded to find this "woman," (armed in the same way as the other
combatants?), the last to surrender. They soon enough discovered that he
was a man in women's clothing, and killed him.[26] The exceptional nature of this report is the more clearcut because those relatively few men I
found assuming the role of berdache only at an advanced age did so, if we
are to credit later records, to avoid fighting in any more wars.[27]

---

came back to the same boy, and the same Hadrian who "tenia un moçuelo de estos por
muger (como en otra parte diximos) . . .": *Monarquia*, 2:427. My thanks to Delia Cosentino for her information on the contemporary Italian use of *bardasso(a)*.

[23] "Third Gender," 156.

[24] Obviously, the explanation that they were cowards cannot be actually credited; the
allegation must rather be understood as a formal quality of their condition. For Roscoe's
view to the contrary, see further below.

[25] Thus Marquette in describing the Illinois in 1673 says that that tribe's berdaches
did fight, but with clubs, not bows and arrows, which were the arms of men: R. Gold
Thwaites, ed., *The Jesuit Relations and Allied Documents: Travels and Explorations of the
Jesuit Missionaries in New France, 1610–1791*, vol. 59 (New York, 1959), 128ff.

[26] Presumably this warrior was a permanent, not a temporary, transvestite; see the account in *Colección de documentos ineditos relativos al descubrimiento, conquista y organización
de las antiguas posessiones españoles en America y Oceania*, vol. 13 (Madrid, 1870), 367f.

[27] The existence of such "senior berdaches" is implied by Las Casas. I have gathered
the evidence in my *Sex and Conquest*, 96–101.

Not surprisingly, Latin American sources in this period never document these men who did not fight as ever having provided counsel to those responsible for the tribe's or village's military and diplomatic policy. Berdaches were neither counselors nor politicos, to judge by the sources for this time or place. Even outside the Latin-American area, it is not until 1673 that we encounter any sign of berdaches being relied upon for military or diplomatic advice.[28] Significantly, that source suggests that the Illinois consulted their berdaches on military matters because of their spiritual powers. They were "Manitous, c'est à dire des Genies ou des personnes de consequence."[29]

We turn now to the question of the berdache's possible role in native religion, to find that almost from the beginning of the conquests in Latin America, the berdaches played a significant religious role in intratribal social life. Yet we must be clear what that role was, and when it is that we encounter changes in this regard presumably brought about by the Spanish occupation. Let it be said first of all that the occult powers ascribed to the Illinois berdaches in 1673, mentioned above, are nowhere to be found in the contact period in Latin America. One of the first European sources on America, Peter Martyr, mentions one group, the *piaches* of the South American Tierra Firme, who did indeed function as *curanderos* by recourse to spirits, and who also prognosticated for their people (and soon for the Spaniards).[30] But unfortunately, in these early sources the *piaches* are not said to have transvested or engaged in homosexual acts. During the sixteenth century, there is no indication that Latin American berdaches claimed any occult powers.

At a later date, however, the berdaches did begin to have occult powers attributed to them. In the very year 1673 when the Illinois berdaches were said to have charisma, far to the south and this time within our Latin-American sphere, the writer Nuñez de Pineda published an account

---

[28] Writing about the Illinois and Nadouessi in 1673, Marquette at first provides a classic description of the berdache: they assume the role when young, and they do all those debased things one would think only women are capable of, etc. They do fight, as we saw above, but not with men's weapons. Interestingly, they sing in the festivals honoring the tribal god Columet, but cannot dance. Then he adds the novelty: the berdaches *are* summoned to councils, where "nothing can be decided without their advice." Marquette concludes. "They are considered Manitous, that is, spirits or persons of consequence": Gold Thwaites, *Jesuit Relations*, 59:128.

[29] Gold Thwaites, *Jesuit Relations*, 59:128.

[30] Peter Martyr d'Anghiera, *Opera* (Graz, 1966), 255–62 (dec. 8, chaps. 8–9).

of the Araucanians, including a description of two types of shamans (*machis*).[31] One such, called *hueyes* or *weye*, were berdaches, that is, transvestites engaging in passive homosexual acts. These were identifiable by their ugliness, said Nuñez de Pineda, but tolerated by the Araucanians because they were said to have a pact with the devil, which made them effective *curanderos*. This singularly important information was, of course, clearly influenced by Christianity. The "devil" is a Christian deity, not an American one. In any case, what is to be emphasized is that nowhere else, in the century and a half before the Araucanian description, could I find berdaches who, from occult resources, cured the sick and spoke to the politicos about the future.[32] In large parts of Latin America, the end of the third quarter of the seventeenth century seems to mark a divide between the world of the berdache as he was at contact and a new world in which, in certain tribes at least, s/he had occult powers and some limited political weight.[33]

What then was the berdaches' religious role on contact with the Spaniards? Rather than being prophetic politicos, the berdaches seem to have held a role best described as sacrificial. The stage for this discussion may be set by an insightful, but to date unreplicated statement of Las Casas, who claims that natives in the Tierra Firme thought the gods were pleased if young boys were prettified as girls before they were sacrificed.[34] Sacrifice appears close to the surface in much that touches on the berdache in religion. As we shall see in the Andes, mid-sixteenth-century berdaches were ceremonially and sacrificially raped by big men during temple ser-

[31] F. Nuñez de Pineda y Bascuñan, *Cautiverio feliz y razón de las guerras dilatadas de Chile* (Santiago, 1863), 107, 164, 157–59.

[32] There are many reasons for the changes in the berdaches' roles in modern times. Perhaps the most practical has been the change in the sexual division of labor brought on by the European-imposed absence of men from native villages due to mining and other factors. The impact of Western sexual and gender notions certainly played a key role as well. That is a problem for another historian or anthropologist to tackle.

[33] One is reminded of the new roles of Andean women as priests once their men had been neutralized by colonialism: Silverblatt, *Moon, Sun, and Witches*, 198–207.

[34] This cross-dressing was not for reasons of sodomy, he insisted, "sino solamente por hacerles sacrificio agradable": B. de Las Casas, *Apologética Historia Sumaria* (Mexico City, 1967), 2:232 (chap. 180). The context: Las Casas speculated that wanting to be part of any and all sins, the devil had "introducido y enseñado otro peor género de sacrificio, como fue . . . que ofrecían los moles y afeminados, porque se hallaron (según dijeron algunos españoles) algunos mozos vestidos como mujeres": *Apologética*, 2:232 (chap. 180).

vices, while the nineteenth-century Pueblo Americans still practiced something similar on their berdaches during corn festivals. In such instances, the berdaches appear to have been sacrifices to the deities, and in my view, this practice is at one with the sexual sacrifice accorded the Peruvian god Pachacama, which seems to have consisted in bent-over subjects at prayer presenting their hindquarters for anal penetration to the God, that is, to his priests.[35] In New Spain, as we shall also see, the information linking berdaches to sacrifice appears in Mexico before the Spaniards ever set foot in Peru. Further, the repeated Spanish claim that the "devil" encouraged the natives to engage in homosexual behavior in the temples — a claim probably also put forward by savvy natives as well — when rightly understood, does argue for "sodomy" being at least partially sacrificial in character, as does the claim that sodomitic activity in the temples was routine.[36] The question then becomes, was the position of the sacrificed an honorable one?

It is Michael Horswell's merit to have pointed out that in the Andes, according to the Jesuit Blas Valera, to whom this anonymous source is ascribed, eunuch priests prayed for the Inca and the community, and that when they went through the streets they were followed by the people, "who considered them saints."[37] Alas, this author wants these honored priests, whom Valera does not say were transvested, to be the more exotic, unmutilated berdaches, assuring readers that "Valera is careful to use terms [like 'eunuch'] that the European reader could understand." Yet even if these men were eunuchs and not berdaches — and Valera leaves no doubt on that score — Horswell can make them serve his purpose. In a flash and uniquely, eunuchs join berdaches in the ranks of Horswell's "third gender" (!) because both, he says, assume "the effeminized position," a position whose honor Horswell is determined to defend throughout his work.[38]

---

[35] On the Pueblo, see W. Hammond, "The Disease of the Scythians (Morbus feminarum) and Certain Analogous Conditions," *American Journal of Neurology and Psychiatry* 1 (1882): 339–55, and the same author's *Sexual Impotence in the Male and Female* (Detroit, 1887), 157–73. On the relation between prayer and sexual postures in the Pachacama rites, as well as in other devotions, see further Trexler, "Bending Over Backwards," and *Sex and Conquest*, 102–9.

[36] See further the Guatemaltecan Maya divinity Tohil soliciting (sexual?) embrace: Trexler, "Bending Over Backwards."

[37] "Third Gender," 156. Horswell notes that I did not cite this passage. In fact, I did not pursue it because the author was, as we shall see, talking about (eunuch) priests and not about berdaches.

[38] "Third Gender," 156.

All Horswell's effort with this source proves vain. First, Valera specifically says that these castrated priests were virgins (who would not have assumed the effeminized position). And second, once Valera is rightly read, it is clear he was not stating that these figures were honored because they were either berdaches or eunuchs. In fact, the author only means to tell his Christian readers that the Andean priests as priests were considered saints. That is, this Jesuit was making the usual missionary observation that, so much superior in this to lax Christians, these non-Christian people considered their priests, "prideful pharisees" though the Jesuit knew them to be, saints.[39]

Such veneration is scarcely surprising for any sacrificial figure. It was after all common for the Aztecs before the Conquest to worship those they would sacrifice, and in the later history of the berdache, we encounter many an abused berdache simultaneously honored. As I showed in my book's dustcover reproduction of George Catlin's striking painting of the Sauk or Fox "Dance to the Berdash," there was no incoherence between violating the berdache and venerating him, indeed, the one might be a condition of the other. Horswell's fancy to the contrary, Valera's text does not in the least show that even these eunuchs, and definitely no berdache as berdache, were participants "in the power structure of Tawantinsuyu."[40]

Thus within our time frame and area, the berdache played no significant role in the formal political life of these nations and assumed a largely passive one in the latter's religious life. Clearly, few young boys would choose this type of life, and none are said or intimated to have done so. We have come now to the question of how one became a berdache, and the picture that will emerge from our sources is one in which young boys were forced into the life of a berdache either by older men or by circumstances beyond their control. The following pages will document that claim.[41]

---

[39] Cf. e.g., Peter of Ghent in 1529 observing that the pueblo "considered as saints" the priests of Tenochtitlan: below, n. 43.

[40] The sources being fruitless, Horswell first equates the berdache with woman, and then, to sustain his argument about berdache "power," notes that two tombs of rich Moche women have been unearthed. By Horswell's reasoning, the many women's tombs in, say, Renaissance Florence surely prove that that sex was a part of that city's power structure!

[41] For the apparently less sizable number of those who entered the estate when full-grown adults ("senior berdaches"), see my *Sex and Conquest*, 96–101.

An important early source concerned with the religious role of berdaches provides us with the beginning of an answer to this question of
origins: becoming a berdache was predominantly a social process. Said
otherwise, in this process berdaches were not usually atomized individuals,
but social creatures. Writing in mid-sixteenth-century Peru, the linguist-
missionary fray Domingo de San Tomas introduces us to the coercion that
was commonly present in the making of a berdache in conquest Latin
America. On interrogating two berdaches in a temple practicing the sexual
aspect of their craft, San Tomas found them of course quick to resist any
responsibility for their status or their passive homosexual behavior:

> They answered me that it was not their fault, because from child-
> hood they had been put there by the caciques to serve them in this
> cursed and abominable vice [of sodomy], and to act as priests and
> to guard the temples of their idols.[42]

Presumably the boys said in 1529 by a missionary in Tenochtitlan to
have been "abused" by priests in the temples of Tenochtitlan — a claim
backed up by two other independent sources of these years — would have
pleaded the same guiltlessness.[43] They were doubtless right to do so. On

---

[42] P. Cieza de León, *Crónica del Perú*, 3 vols. (Lima, 1984), 1:200 (pt. 1, chap. 64).

[43] "Algunos de estos sacerdotes no tenían mujeres, sino en lugar de ellas muchachos
de que abusaban": the full text of Peter of Ghent's 1529 report on sodomy in Tenochtitlan temples perpetrated by some priests on young boys [*muchachos*] is in J. García Icazbalceta, *Bibliografía Mexicana del siglo XVI* (Mexico City, 1886), 398. The sodomitic substance of this report was then independently confirmed first by the conquistador Bernal
Díaz del Castillo: "Aquellos papas eran hijos de principales y no tenían mujeres, más
tenían el maldito oficio de sodomías": *Historia verdadera de la conquista de la Nueva
España*, 2 vols. (Mexico City, 1968), 1:162 (chap. 162), and by Tomás López Medel, the
royal *oidor* in Mexico City who, according to some accounts, declined to succeed Archbishop Zumárraga in 1546: "Tenían los mexicanos y guatemaltecas grande copia de sacerdotes en aquellos templos y allí era su perpetual mansion y morada, a donde se ejercitaban en tan abominables lujurias y pecados que es cosa abominable y torpe decir. Y tenían
éstos ya adquiridos tantos derechos o, por mejor decir, introducidas tan nefandas y espur-
císimas costumbres en este caso con el pueblo que, por no ofender las orejás castas, se
han de pasar con silencio": López Medel, *De los tres elementos: Tratado sobre la naturaleza
y el hombre del Nuevo Mundo*, ed. Berta Ares Queíja (Madrid, 1990), 233 (pt. 3, chap.
20). See also the entry on López in the *Enciclopedia universal ilustrada*, 3:167. In 1593,
Thomas de Bozius declared the same from Europe in his *De signis ecclesiae dei* (Cologne,
1593), 1:519 (bk. 7, signum 29). In the light of this evidence, the burden of proof rests
with those who would dispute these sources. For Cieza de León's observation that sodomy might be considered wrong in Peruvian villages in whose temples it was licit, see
Trexler, *Sex and Conquest*, 106. In his letter cited above, Peter of Ghent was also disturbed that fathers sacrificed or mutilated their own sons — out of fear not love — and

the other hand, still another source, a *relación* of fray Diego de Loaysa written in 1528, which I discovered after the publication of my *Sex and Conquest*, seems to say that the Mexican priests hated same-sex sodomy even more than they did heterosexual coitus. Alas, upon closer examination this reading, as discordant as the source as a whole, proves to be of such poor quality and so ambiguous as to be all but worthless.[44] In Tenochtitlan as in the Inca realm, priests sodomized berdaches.

The forced disposition of children for purposes of tribute, or as hostages, or as temple servants, is not unknown in these American or in many other cultures. At the very beginning of the Spanish Conquest, Campeche natives offered the conqueror Grijalva a boy as a gift. The early historian Oviedo narrates how Muiscan (northern Colombian) caciques returned from their temple with at least one small boy each whom they raised to puberty before sacrificing to the sun. And Guatemaltecans told the late sixteenth-century historian fray Juan de Torquemada that the ancient Olmecs had required conquered villages to surrender on demand two

---

that the priests serving the "idols," considered saints by the populace, "se alimentaban solamente de niños cuya sangre bebían." See above and in the following text for other indications of young males similarly sacrificed, a theme that informs much early Spanish reporting on Tenochtitlan.

[44] "Muchos de ellos [que tienen cargo de los uchilobos] no comían sino solamente la sangre de los que sacrificaban. Estos aborrescían el coito e no conversaban con mujeres, e mucho más el pecado de la sodomía": cited in G. Fernández de Oviedo, *Historia general y natural de las Indias*, BAE 117–21 (Madrid, 1959), 120:243, and for Loaysa's whole *relación*, 237–45. This odd sentence is in fact a correct transcription of Oviedo's ms. at the Real Accademia in Madrid, which I checked. Still, we know Loaysa only from Oviedo, and I suspect an original meaning that the priests were more accustomed to sodomy than to heterosexual coitus, a conventional polarization of the time. In any case, the Dominican Loaysa's account, as far as I can tell unnoticed by modern historiographers, does not inspire confidence, though Oviedo himself thought the friar credible. Only recently landed in America, Loaysa accompanied Julián Garcés, the new bishop of Tlaxcala, to Mexico City and then promptly, in March 1528, accompanied Cortés (on his way to Spain) as far as Havana. From Havana Loaysa went to Honduras and thence to Leon, Nicaragua, where he encountered Oviedo and wrote his *relación*. Loaysa was not well acquainted with the Aztecs. As seen above, he repeatedly says their temples were called Huitzilopochtli (the God of war). He says that Montezuma's father and uncle left their distant homeland in 1439 for the trip to Mexico. He misnames the famous Franciscan Martin of Valencia "Juan," and calls Zumárraga, the bishop of Mexico City, "fray Juan de Carraba." See also C. Gibson, *Tlaxcala in the Sixteenth Century* (Stanford, 1952), 54, and F. López de Gómara, *Cortés* (Berkeley, 1966), 385, copying Oviedo.

boys each, perhaps for sexual purposes.[45] In the light of this type of evidence, the fact that Peruvian caciques consigned the two berdaches interviewed by fray Domingo to perpetual rape hardly comes as a surprise.

This evidence has been inadequately credited in the literature. Horswell, for example, will not accept Santo Tomas's witness, thorough kenner and supporter of the Andeans though the latter may be. In the first place, this author intimates, the fact that young people so quickly adopted their sex's division of labor shows that at just as early an age, such youngsters were themselves "responsible" for the passive sexual roles they adopted! This ideologically driven opinion is not unique in the literature. Compare Horswell's statement, for instance, to Roscoe's argument that the rape of a Mohave *girl* would have had no negative psychological effect because rape was no different from many other things a tribal member was constrained to do or undergo.[46] Horswell continues: The source itself is not reliable. Because Santo Tomas was a friar and the boys were natives, "his two punished [sic! (actually *castigado* means 'reprimanded')] and *perhaps* repentant subjects *naturally* would blame their 'errors' on others. . . ." (my italics). Thus Horswell seeks to dismiss a first-hand, knowledgeable, primary source, one sympathetic to the Andeans, just as he wants the Inca Huascar to have gifted rather than transvested his losing general, and just as he leaves unmentioned the humiliating obeisance that Pachacamac's subjects, presumably old and young alike, paid the God through their presentations. Of course Horswell ignores the imposing evidence of constraint

---

[45] On the offer, see Peter Martyr D'Anghiera, *Opera*, 150 (dec. 4, chap. 4). Oviedo implies that the boy was used homosexually during that year. In the meantime, the boy, as an orant, represented his master to the Gods at temple: Oviedo, *Historia general*, 119:127f. (bk. 26, chap. 30), and cf. above Blas Valera's "eunuchs" praying for the community. Torquemada: "Asimismo les demandaban cada día, que se les diesen, de cada pueblo, dos niños; no supieron declarlos Indios, que dieron essa relación, si querían estos para sacrificar, o para comer, o para servicio": *Monarquia*, 1:332 (bk. 3, chap. 40).

[46] The argument runs: The source to the contrary, "it is risky to say that the youths truly considered themselves 'forced' into their sacred roles. . . . Furthermore . . . the practice of young children taking on responsibility, both mundane and sacred, was (and still is) the norm in Andean society. . . . The ethics of reciprocity in Andean communities is what motivated service, an ethics that the youth learned from an early age": "Third Gender,"154f. This writer, on the contrary, considers it risky *not* to say that the youths "truly considered themselves forced." See also Roscoe, *Changing Ones*, 95. In both these utterances regarding children's "responsibility," the reader recognizes the language not of the scholar of juvenile development, but, *inter alia*, of NAMBLA, the North American Man/Boy Love Association, on which see the concluding part of this article.

exercised against these youngsters beyond the Andes, for he studies the Andes alone, and in them, so he wants the reader to believe, "the passive sodomical role and to cross-dress were not considered inferior activities."[47]

There were in my view no laws against sodomy in these lands,[48] and some of those with power sequestered or seduced boys as well as girls to their own ends then, much as they so evidently do now in some developing as well as in some developed countries.[49] An occasional Iberian source of the time describes young American boys who of their own free will market their wares to all comers, but we must dismiss this perverse notion of *children's* free will then — "agency," Roscoe calls it — as most of us would now.[50] In full awareness that many cultures justify such practices and call them by another name, the scholar must not hesitate to label as force or constraint the transvestism and sodomization of the young here, any more than we want to call female clitoridectomies a mere expression of African custom there. Nor is this just an historiographic difference of opinion. Our sources repeatedly point out the coercive sociality that was at the origin of becoming a berdache. Thus according to his first letter from the American mainland, Hernan Cortés warned the caciques of Zempoala that they must not just break their images, but

---

[47] "Third Gender," 154. Horswell presents no evidence to that effect, and indeed, as I have indicated, the misogynistic strain in Peruvian culture in no way lags behind that in other traditional cultures.

[48] Claims that such laws did exist are post-conquest constructions with obvious ideological purposes; see Trexler, *Sex and Conquest*, 156–61, 257. In the Nahuatl realm, one can trace the claim of anti-sodomy laws not to Tenochtitlan (!) but to ca. 1538 Texcoco (see *Sex and Conquest*, 257, nn. 61 and 63). A further link in that Texcocan string of claims is in F. de Alva Ixtlilxochitl, *Historia de la nación chichimeca*, in his *Obras Historicas*, ed. E. O'Gorman, 2 vols. (Mexico City, 1977), 2:101. It appears that the Franciscans imputed anti-sodomitic enlightenment to Texcoco because that town was the home of the acclaimed philosopher-king Nezahualcoyotl, whose family would quickly convert under the influence of Peter of Ghent, who often lived in Texcoco.

[49] The discourse in this paper can scarcely surprise anyone aware of the massive reality of (male as well as female) child abuse in our own contemporary world. My conclusions about pre-Hispanic child abuse in the person of the berdaches are by now much like those of scores of studies of sexual abuse of children, including some of a historical character, emerging almost daily in the periodical and monographic literature.

[50] Absurdly, this author imagines me horrified that berdaches, exerting "agency," may have wanted to be penetrated: *Changing Ones*, 196. This and a score of other insults in his pages do nothing for his argument. My point is that both the context of their being "brothelized," and the age of the youngsters, prohibit talk of free will.

... that also, they had to be pure of sodomy. Because they keep [*te-nian*] *muchachos* in women's clothes who go about profiting in that infamous office.[51]

Thus boys sounding like entrepreneurs turn out to be kept by caciques, part of their retinue and, as I argue elsewhere, a model protostructure of the patriarchal state in formation. Berdaches were not isolated individuals of the Western stamp. They were created and raised within a social nexus. Repeatedly, the berdaches of the Spanish conquest centuries, who earn their keep through prostitution, turn out to belong to lords, who "kept them" in their possession.[52]

The actual process by which a young boy attained this status of berdache seems to have occurred in either a societal or a familial context. The societal procedure may in turn be further subdivided. Either an older man dressed the boy up as a woman and then violated him — since in the native view "women," not men, were meant to be penetrated or to fellate — or the older male first raped the boy, and then dressed him up as a woman as punishment for not being male. The late sixteenth-century Peruvian historian Murúa provides the most straightforward formulation of the former scenario with his description of Cuzcenans who first appointed males to be women, then dressed them as such, then penetrated them.[53] But the evidence for the latter scenario comes from the much earlier royal historian Oviedo, who resided for years in the Tierra Firme and thus deserves all the greater attention. He says that sodomy was common among many native peoples, then immediately contextualizes this remark as follows:

---

[51] Díaz del Castillo, *Historia*, 1:162 (chap. 52).

[52] See the repeated cases of this in *Sex and Conquest*, 94–95 and passim. Obviously, the fact that these boys were constrained to become berdaches did not preclude some developing into self-confident adults capable of handling the wrong done them as children. Unfortunately, in our period no such accounts survive.

[53] M. de Murúa, *Historia de los Incas, Reyes del Perú* (Lima, 1922), 122f. (bk. 2, chap. 4). On appointment to the status of berdache, see below. Juan Ossio is preparing an important new edition of Murúa replete with many original drawings. Embarrassingly, Will Roscoe in his attempt to discredit Murúa's account while reviewing my book characterizes the friar, well-known to historians of the period, as an "obscure" source: W. Roscoe, "Mapping the Perverse," *American Anthropologist* 98 (1996): 861. Cf. above for the Andeanist Horswell's no less embarrassing determination that Cabello Balboa, another Peruvian historian whose message did not please, was also "obscure." Apparently for them, once so labeled, (alleged) obscurity equals falsity.

And the Indians who are *señores y principales* and who sin in this way keep young men [*tienen mozos*] publicly with whom they consort in this infamous sin. And once they fall into this guilt [of sodomy], these passive *mozos* then are dressed in *naguas*, like women. . . .[54]

Unsurprisingly, Roscoe will not have such a translation, straightforward though it may seem, and he quickly reassures his readers, without explaining how he does so, that "there is no mention of rape or force, however, and the wording clearly indicates that the acts were voluntary."[55] In fact, Oviedo and Murúa only disagree on whether the boy got his woman's skirt before or after being sodomized. As do all the sources that comment on the matter, both agree that the initiation to the estate of berdache was coercive, carried out, that is, within the company of older men. Indeed, as I have already indicated, in 1529, years before even Oviedo set pen to paper, the famous Texcoco-based Franciscan lay missionary Peter of Ghent called these actions against Tenochtitlan boys at times under six years of age by their proper name, "abuso."

Let us be clear. To speak of children exercising free will, now or then, is itself a type of abuse. Yet Roscoe and Horswell repeatedly insist that, to use the former's words, "the large majority of those who became berdaches did so entirely of their own volition."[56] Indeed, Roscoe goes further, at more than one point excluding forced or coerced boys from the very ranks of "true berdaches."[57] The reader may rightly be perplexed by a self-proclaimed social constructionist like Roscoe vehemently proclaiming that his berdaches made choices that were free, but the deeper irony is that both

---

[54] "Entre los indios en muchas partes es muy común el pecado nefando contra natura, y publicamente los indios que son señores y principales que en esto pecan tienen mozos con quien usan este maldito pecado; y los tales mozos pacientes, asi como caen en esta culpa, luego se ponen naguas, como mujeres . . .": *Sumario de la natural historia de las Indias*, BAE 22 (Madrid, 1946), 508 (chap. 81). With no justification, Roscoe says the text suggests that the boys rather did this voluntarily. Oviedo, however, clearly has cacique power coming first and last: the principal's sodomitic will, then the construction of a brothel, then the same principal's penetration of these boys. But Roscoe's mistake was predictable, since he also misunderstood who Oviedo was talking about. He says that Oviedo was describing Cueva-speaking people, but Oviedo was clearly referring to "los Indios en muchas partes": Roscoe, "Mapping the Perverse," 861.

[55] *Changing Ones*, 193.

[56] *Changing Ones*, 200.

[57] *Changing Ones*, 9, 194.

he and Horswell, who imagine themselves latter-day *defensores indorum* against the sexual repression they (rightly) impute to "the Europeans," actually adopt the thoroughly Pauline or European view that, because man has free will, each person is responsible for his own immortal soul, or body, in the process merrily abandoning the context which must be the basis for such constructionism.

But the Latin American sources, Oviedo and Murúa, Domingo de San Tomas, Peter of Ghent, and many others, all describe young boys below the "age of reason" being coerced into homosexual activity by a *Herr*, while no source of the time describes an autonomous *Knecht* "willingly" becoming a berdache — whatever that might mean for a youngster.[58] I will later explore why these authors adopt this stance. But it must be said that those who would argue the free will of these boys in "Latin America" at the time of the conquests must come up with some evidence to support their belief. *All* the Latin American documentation in the conquest centuries points decisively in the opposite direction.

But the evidence presented so far only scratches the surface of the berdaches' originological history of subordination. Regularly, sources like Oviedo and Murúa speak of the "office" filled by such children, and on careful examination, a picture emerges of them being *appointed* to the role of women. What could be more illustrative of appointment to gender than Cieza de León's Andean report that

> ... [the devil] made it understood that service to him could properly take the form of some boys [*mozos*] of childhood age [*niños*] being kept in the temples, so that at times, and when sacrifices and solemn festivals were executed, the lords and other principals would copulate with them in the notorious sin of sodomy.[59]

Once we have grasped this quite structural indigenous approach to gender — one the Andeans shared with their cousins across the Americas[60] — we can begin to comprehend how a social-political entity might make these appointments not only after a boy was born, but when the fetus was still in the womb, where there can be no talk of youngsters choosing to

---

[58] Generally speaking, males were thought able to resist coercion after they were fourteen or fifteen years old; details are in Trexler, *Sex and Conquest*, 201–3, nn. 28, 29, 41.

[59] Cieza de León, *Crónica*, 1:199 (pt. 1, chap. 64).

[60] A point I examine in detail in "Making the American Berdache."

become berdaches. A description and analysis of such appointments will not only confirm the presence of constraint in the making of berdaches, but begin to highlight the significant social roles that the berdaches did play in their respective societies. For if the berdaches were not military, diplomatic, political, or charismatic figures in the time and place under consideration, they definitely did play significant social roles, which will emerge in what follows.

The Conquest evidence for the practice of appointing a male fetus to be a berdache once born features the community as the decision-making agent. While traveling among the Yuma in the lower Colorado River valley in 1541, Hernándo de Alarcón encountered a village which maintained four berdaches. After one died, the next-born male was appointed to be converted into a woman for life, joining his three existent fellows.[61] As Alarcón makes clear, these berdaches were a public sexual resource, providing hospitality to visitors to be sure, but also procuring peace and tranquility within the group. The four berdaches, he says, could "be used by all marriageable youths of the land."[62] Obviously, this communal institution aimed to discourage young unmarried males from having relations with girls and women of the tribe, which would have complicated social relations. We may characterize this berdache function as demographic in nature, and re-emphasize that in such cases, obviously no talk of free will may be entertained. Needless to say, Roscoe passes over in silence the significance of this document of Alarcón,[63] while Walter Williams, another gay who has engaged himself in the study of the berdache, obviously "doubts the validity" of sources to this effect.[64]

---

[61] "E che la prima di esse [donne] che partoriva mascio, era deputato a dover far quell'esercizio muliebre": G. Ramusio, *Navigazioni e viaggi*, 6 vols. (Turin, 1985), 6:652 (the oldest text is in Italian).

[62] "Questi tali non possono aver commercio carnale con donna alcuna, ma sí ben con essi tutti i giovani della terra che sono da maritarsi": Ramusio, *Navigazioni*, 6:652.

[63] Instead, he imagines that the authorities were replacing a dancer! Obviously, Roscoe says only that the "antierotic lens of counter-reformation Catholicism" produced Alarcón's "distorted account of this process," without stating what that process was: *Changing Ones*, 143–44. I need hardly point out that the Counter-Reformation had not begun in 1541, that Alarcón was a soldier not a priest, and that as such he betrays no antieroticism in his account.

[64] *The Spirit and the Flesh: Sexual Diversity in American Indian Culture* (Boston, 1992), xii, and for where Williams stands in the historiography of the berdache, see Trexler, *Sex and Conquest*, 6. A rarity in this regard, G. Bleibtreu-Ehrenberg recognized that young boys were reclassified as girls "bereits vor der Geburt eines Kindes": *Der Weibmann* (Frankfurt am Main, 1984), 104.

Turning now to the familial context from which berdaches might emerge, we immediately reencounter this phenomenon of appointment, but now in a post-natal context where parents are determined to control the gender of their offspring. Surely the most characteristic source of this particular demographic phenomenon in Latin America is the learned and seasoned bishop Fernández de Piedrahita, in his mid-seventeenth-century report on the Laches of Colombia. Our author says that fathers among this people took into account the sex distribution of their children, and if they found there to be too many males (to be specific, five) and no females, they were permitted to change one of those boys, once he reached one year of age, into a girl (to use Piedrahita's words), because fathers obviously desired to be served.[65] Comparable motivations for such a switch are found elsewhere in the ethnographic literature, and indeed, outside Meso-America can be found applied to girls where there were no boys in a family.[66] But to the point: in the early Meso-American record, cases like the one involving one-year old Laches leave no room for talk of choice.

What is so impressive about this practice of appointing unborn or infant males to the role of berdaches is its tenacity, for in fact, the same procedure was still being effected in the Hispanic sphere in modern times. Thus in the 1820s the Franciscan friar Boscana, in his masterful ethnography of the natives of the San Gabriel Valley in the Mexican province of California, describes how "while yet in infancy [chiquitos] were selected, and instructed as they increased in years, in all the duties of the women. . . ."[67] Displaying the same historical romanticism from which Horswell

---

[65] "Ambición que tienen de estar bien servidos. Tienen por ley que si la mujer paría cinco varones continuados, sin parir hija, pudiesen hacer hembra a uno de los hijos a las doce lunas de edad": L. Fernández Piedrahita, *Historia general del nuevo reino de Granada* (Bogotá, 1942), 1:25.

[66] In "Making the American Berdache," I study this phenomenon across the hemisphere and beyond, to Greenland. For general ethnography, the verification in southern climes of such gender switching at or near birth may prove to be the most significant discovery I have made regarding the berdache; it was widespread in arctic climes.

[67] G. Boscana, *Chinigchinich*, trans. A. Robinson (Banning, CA, 1978), 54. Cf. H. and P. Reichlen, "Le manuscrit Boscana de la Bibliothèque nationale de Paris: Relation sur les indiens Acâgchemem de la mission de San Juan Capistrano, Californie," *Journal de la société des Américanistes* 59 (1970): 233–43, 252–53, containing the variant Harrington translation. Boscana's work was originally entitled *Relación historica de la creencia, usos, costumbres, y extravagancias de los Indios de esta Mision de S. Juan Capistrano, llamada la Nacion Acâgchemem.*

and Roscoe ultimately descend, Alfred Kroeber, no matter how much he admired Boscana, could not accept the straightforward lesson of the learned and experienced friar. Twice in his authoritative *Handbook of the Indians of California*, the great anthropologist returned to his master Boscana's troubling lines, to assure his readers that Boscana to the contrary, the berdaches were "not delegated to their status, but entered it, *from childhood on, by choice* or in response to an irresistible call of their nature" (my italics). He insists again: "That they were deliberately 'selected' in infancy as stated [by Boscana], seems inconceivable." Alas, the only evidence Kroeber presents for his conviction is "the lack of repression customary in Indian society," a perfect example of circular reasoning.[68] Kroeber concludes therefore that femininity could come to the surface unimpeded, where it was not discouraged by adults. Again, we see free will thoughtlessly imputed to children, a train of thought Kroeber would never have used in referring to Anglo children. Such is the "cant of the [anthropological] conquerors," to echo Roscoe, that the best of scholars may bring to the study of native Americans.

Yet another case in Hispanic America where female gender was assigned to infants or children is encountered in the ethnographic record of early-twentieth century Zuni — near enough to the Yumas who had indulged in the practice three and a half centuries earlier. According to the anthropologist Clews Parsons, "if a household was short on women workers, a boy would be more readily allowed to become a *lámana*" — without any compulsion, her sources predictably assured the Anglo anthropologist. How old might such a boy be? Without a trace of curiosity, Parsons says that the youngest of that tribe's four berdaches, one Lasbeke, was only six years old, not at all an age at which an Anglo mother would have spoken of her own child's "free will."[69] And in fact, Arnold Pilling has recently determined that in that very time frame, at the end of the nineteenth century, "the emergence of a cross-dresser in a Zuni household was nearly always a response to the lack of a sister or female matrilateral cousin in the household."[70] Roscoe himself cites Edward Gifford to the effect

---

[68] A. Kroeber, *Handbook of the Indians of California* (Berkeley, 1953), respectively 497, 647.

[69] E. Clews Parsons, "The Zuñi La'mana," *American Anthropologist* 18 (1916): 521, 525–26.

[70] A. Pilling, "Cross-Dressing and Shamanism among Selected Western North American Tribes," in *Two-Spirit*, 72.

that as late as 1940, the same Zuni might bring up a boy as a girl if there was no girl in the family.[71] Thus well into this century, at least this American people was still assigning female gender to male children for social and economic reasons.

In all these "appointments to office," either the community or a household was the active party, with the child obviously constrained by force and circumstances to do their bidding. With this background in mind, then, we can readily understand the forces at work behind fray Bernardino de Sahagún's mid-sixteenth-century dramatic description of parents deciding what was to be the gender of their "small boy." What "should [they] make of him," he has the parents ask themselves, and one possibility ran as follows: "Is he perchance a woman? Shall I place, perchance, a spindle, a batten, in his hands?"[72] To answer that question, the parents may well have weighed this small boy's limited past behavior, but what is more decisive here as elsewhere is that the executive power to assign gender was vested in those parents, rather than being the boy's own choice. Indeed, this passage of Sahagún's hints in the sixteenth century at a means of parental decision-making found repeatedly in later times: the test. In different variations, parents presented children with some emblem of masculinity, like a bow and arrow, alongside another that stood for femininity, like a spindle or beads. Then in reaching for one or the other, the child — and the context regularly makes clear this was commonly a child — would betray his or her "true" gender and the parents would then raise the young person in that gender.[73] I need hardly point out that such a ritual procedure is a fine example of parental or communal control — for these authorities prescribed the meanings of such symbols — rather than of free choice by the child.[74] This would be true even if Sahagún had said that the parents proceeded with the rite only after the child betrayed "womanly" behavior — which neither he nor any other of the

---

[71] Roscoe, *Changing Ones*, 199.

[72] B. Sahagún, *Florentine Codex: General History of the Things of New Spain* (Santa Fe, 1980), bk. 9:14. This "small boy" was clearly a child: when he accompanied the older merchants, he bore nothing on his back except the group's drinking vessels.

[73] See for example S. Jacobs, "Berdache: A Brief Review of the Literature," in *Ethnographic Studies of Homosexuality*, ed. Wayne R. Dynes and Stephen Donaldson (New York, 1992 [originally 1968]), 276. A study of these tests is needed.

[74] In "Making the American Berdache," I suggest that the famed visions of the Plains Indians, which are sometimes understood as free-will exercises leading some adolescent boys to become berdaches, are better viewed as exercises in which the communities controlled the substance and meaning of what was viewed.

sources of this time and area does — for in any case, such an action still comes down to an assertion of parental authority. What the orthodox defenders of (Occidental) free will among the native Americans fail to keep in mind is the extremely widespread native American perception that at certain times they themselves control and assign the (malleable) gender — what they called sex — of their children. The artisanal role of the parents in shaping the gender of their children is not open to dispute.

I have argued that the phenomenon of appointing young children to the office of berdache unavoidably involved coercion. Some last, but no less significant pieces of evidence in this regard concern the Meso-American institution of same-sex marriage, as it is portrayed for us first in the mid-sixteenth century by Bartolomé de Las Casas. This scholar/bishop describes how highland Maya fathers provided their (unmarried) youth with *niños* or young boys, whom they would treat as wives, presumably until the youth married and cohabited.[75] Clearly, such an arrangement helped preserve the honor of the future bride and groom, as well as order within the community at large.[76] But it also coerced youngsters into the life-long position of berdaches, either through the force of circumstances — if the boys had no one to defend them — or through outright gifting of such *niños* by their parents to the families of such young men. Thus Las Casas not only documented the self-evident fact that, here as elsewhere,[77] younger boys in the nature of things were (and are) at the sexual mercy of older boys, but he saw that in Guatemala, at least, this disadvantage had been institutionalized.

The experienced Franciscan ethnographer Geronimo Boscana documented a similar case in the San Gabriel Valley in the early nineteeth century, that is, a half century after the conquest of that area of Mexico by the Spaniards. Recall Boscana's infants mentioned above whom adults selected to be berdaches and then instructed over the years in the duties of women. They then assumed one of two assignments, according to our source. Some became public prostitutes (*rameras*), while others were claimed by chiefs (*capitanes*), who married them, not just for sex, Boscana

---

[75] Las Casas, *Apologética*, 2:522 (chap. 239).

[76] A cautionary note: Elsewhere in the ethnographic literature (including Europe) there is evidence of young *girls* of low status being provided to nubile young men of a better social standing for sexual purposes, obviously to comparable ends of avoiding the violation of "honest" nubile young women.

[77] I encountered similar problems, and practices, in late medieval and early modern Florence, Italy: R. Trexler, *Public Life in Renaissance Florence* (New York, 1980), 382.

says, but to prepare their meals and other domestic tasks, for "the ber-daches were always stronger."[78]

Looking back over the foregoing material, we see in the contact period in the area we today call Latin America a social figure who is significantly sacrificial in nature, a condition seen not least in the fact that circum-stances or big men usually forced boys into accepting this estate. Further, the data so far show a figure who has a set of social roles to which he is willy-nilly appointed, but which have still not been systematically enumer-ated. Let me do so at this point, summarizing these social roles or tasks as prostitutional, economic, and demographic in quality.

By a prostitutional role in political society I mean to describe the ber-dache's sexual functioning as an exchange object in the political realm, and it is because of this political angle that I place this role first. I have described groups of berdaches who remain in the sexual and other service of their lords. They might reside in male brothels or they might live with an ally of the lord, but in any case their sexual and other services could be rented out by a cacique or a curaca.[79] To be sure, this situation can only be clearly documented in a handful of Latin-American situations, and no transregional claim is made in this regard. Nevertheless, there can be little doubt that in many tribes of this expansive realm, berdaches were under the control of political figures who used them as instrumentalities of their power. In fact, I have shown by evidence describing Peru that these trans-vested, yet corporeally powerful "women" in fact formed the retinue of such powerful men.[80] If a retinue of powerful men — even without "mas-culine" arms — was an early form of the primordial state, as I have sug-gested it was, then the berdaches, dressed as women but as men fully capa-ble of defending their lord, represented one type of state formation and ex-pression in the Americas. Comparable to the youth of many societies who are dressed up in ornamental uniforms and then brutally lord it over the dependents of the Señor, these berdaches exercised a certain political authority, at sufferance, even if it was not institutionalized.

I have already described what I call the demographic role of the ber-daches, who, as we have seen, were sometimes the product of gender-distribution practices aimed at guaranteeing either the legitimacy of family

---

[78] In Reichlen, "Le manuscrit Boscana," 252–53.

[79] The evidence is provided in Trexler, Sex and Conquest, 90–94.

[80] "No ay principal que no trayga quatro o cinco pajes muy galanes. Estos tiene por mancebos": J. Ruíz de Arce, Servicios en Indias (Madrid, 1933), 32.

members or the "unbalanced" family's attainment of a normative sexual distribution of male and female children. So we may turn now to the economic role of many berdaches. What were these "women's" tasks? Two Spanish historians of the sixteenth century, describing the Tierra Firme and Nicaragua, listed them as sweeping and washing, grinding corn, spinning and cooking, thus reinforcing a gender hierarchy that was surely more flexible.[81] But there were other tasks assigned different berdaches, and the anthropological literature raises the possibility that because of their strength, berdaches were often put in charge of village production units otherwise made up of females. I have been unable to confirm the idea through the conquest literature, but it may well be sound. Thus in the mid-nineteenth century William Hammond encountered a dozen Pueblo women working together on their metates, and because of their identical appearance, he was amazed when his host pointed to one of them as actually a berdache, with whom Hammond could "do what [he] pleased."[82]

However, another type of evidence is at hand that does tend to confirm this view, and it is domestic rather than communal in nature. As early as Piedrahita in the mid-seventeenth century, Latin American sources refer to the "robustness" of the berdaches, and the Franciscan Boscana in early nineteenth-century California followed up with almost identical language. Piedrahita pointed out that because of this robustness, men preferred the Laches berdaches as wives, and Boscana's observations of San Juan Capistrano natives in 1822 confirmed that for California. "Being more robust than the women," the friar noted, berdaches, *who had been selected as infants*, "were better able to perform the arduous duties of the wife, and for this reason they were often selected *by the chiefs* and others. . . ."[83] Once again, the sociopolitical importance of some of these berdaches is obvious.

---

[81] Oviedo, *Somario*, 508 (chap. 81); A. de Herrera, *Historia general de los hechos de los castellanos en las islas y tierrafirme del mar Océano*, 10 vols. (Madrid, 1934–1957), 8:339 (dec. 4, bk. 6, chap. 1).

[82] "I observed that he used the masculine pronoun *el* in referring to the individual," said Hammond, "Disease," 343f.

[83] My italics. "Ejercitaban los oficios de mujeres con robustecidad de hombres": Fernández Piedrahita, *Historia general*, 1:25, and Boscana, *Chinigchinich*, 54. George Catlin said the same of the Mandan berdaches later in the century: "[The berdaches] performed the duties of women with the robustness of men": *Letters and Notes on the Manners, Customs and Conditions of North American Indians* (New York, 1973), 2:15.

§

The previous pages, and the book that lies behind them, offer the first study of the institution of the berdache in Latin America before the nineteenth century. In that work I insisted that this early history may be different from the profile of the berdaches elsewhere in the eighteenth through twentieth centuries. Yet several of the commentators on this work have failed to keep these distinctions of time and place clearly in mind — one thinks immediately of Roscoe's intentional misstatement of the time and place of my argument which I quoted at the beginning of this paper. Roscoe and others have gone on from there to wildly denounce this work. Whence this heat?

Some part of such behavior is, to be sure, mere professional jealousy at a perceived outsider (historian) who dared address a topic that had been ignored by early Colonial scholars. I am repeatedly identified in the reviews as a "European historian" who, in one reviewer's words and typical sentiment, "has undertaken to become a Latin Americanist," even though I have been writing and publishing colonial American history for a score of years.[84] More interesting are the critiques of those who put themselves forward on the one hand as modern-day defenders of past "homosexuals," and on the other as *defensores indorum*, or modern-day historical romanticists. I have touched on this latter problem of romanticism as regards Native Americans earlier in the paper, so here I will limit my remarks to the former — gay defenders of past homosexual behavior. One such scholar, Randolph Trumbach, in a discussion following a public paper I delivered, announced that my approach to the pre-Conquest berdache "hurts us," meaning today's gays.[85] But most germane of all are those writers who, like Walter Williams, Horswell, and particularly Roscoe, look back, determined to find a non-repressive and thus non-Anglo historical past when "homosexuals" were allowed their freedom.[86]

---

[84] The characterization is by E. Couturier, in *The Americas* 55 (1998): 144.

[85] This occurred at the Columbia University Seminar on Gay and Lesbian Studies in spring 1996; I have verified Trumbach's statement with others at the gathering. The basic argument of this point of view, silly as it sounds, is that any historical study of homosexual activity that determines that the passive was not doing what he wished to do implies that the modern gay in pursuing his life-style is not freely doing what he does; see further at the conclusion of this paper. The upshot of all this is that in such authors' works, they presumably carefully excise anything in the past that, in the authors' view, might "hurt" today's gays.

[86] My criticism of Williams's work is in *Sex and Conquest*, 6.

The quasi-monopoly that gays have on studies of historical homosexual behavior in general and berdaches in particular is understandable enough. The former have been marvelously productive — one thinks of the work of Michael Rocke and John Boswell — but, as Boswell's work itself shows, one's own status can complicate the pursuit of historical truth.[87] As an example, modern gay studies spend much time on the notion of homosexuals as a third or fourth sex. Of course humans represent a myriad variety of genders. Let a thousand genders bloom! But a review of the literature on third genders shows that that notion often is little more than an identity politics within a discourse meant to circulate mainly among other gays. This is not the place to critique the notion, only to state that, whatever the situation may be later and elsewhere, I have seen no source of the period and in the places I have studied which supports the notion of a third or fourth sex or gender among these berdaches.

If the notion of a third gender is primarily a discourse with the like-minded about the writer's own identity, it is not surprising that that search for positive identity is too often transformed into a false understanding of the past. In his recent book, Roscoe provides nothing short of a road map on how such anti-history is done. I point out in my work that there was no "homosexuality," there were no "homosexuals," in this period. Homosexuality as a life-style is at most an eighteenth- or nineteenth-century notional innovation, and for that reason, as I explained, I avoided those terms and referred at most to "homosexual behavior," while also allowing the sources their customary use of the word "sodomy," meaning (usually same-sex) anal or fellative intercourse.[88] But Roscoe has an agenda, and it is not that of the professional historian — or anthropologist. History, says this author, "provides the models and language for lesbian and gay natives to open dialogues about homophobia and (re)claim a place in their communities."[89] Now, the professional may be charmed to

---

[87] I refer of course to Boswell's unfounded conviction that there was a "gay" culture in the Middle Ages, that is, partners whose relationship was equal rather than pederastic in character.

[88] Unfortunately, Roscoe proves himself ill-equipped to discuss this language. He defines "sodomites" as "males who were receptive in sex with other males" — whereas, as I clarified in my *Sex and Conquest*, 169, "sodomite" usually refers in the sources to the active party: *Changing Ones*, 181. Our critic then proceeds to define sodomy as "an act that in European societies was usually understood as a rape of a younger man by an older man": *Changing Ones*, 182, 186. News indeed. Such is the expertise Roscoe brings to reading historical sources, all of which routinely describe homosexual behavior as "sodomy."

[89] *Changing Ones*, 198.

find this white man putting himself forward as a defender of Native Americans. As we have seen, that lineage reaches back to Kroeber, and beyond. But for those who think history must provide first and last the elements for arriving at past truths, Roscoe's assertion is a recipe for mere historical propaganda. First, Roscoe wants to convince his (gay) readers that an essential identity exists between the berdaches of yesteryear and the (native American) gays of today.[90] And so, ignoring the reasoning I and others have given for avoiding the terms "homosexual" and "homosexuality" in dealing with earlier centuries, and indeed bizarrely misunderstanding what early modern Europeans meant by "sodomy,"[91] this author continually employs the former usages. His agenda explains why: using the terms homosexual etc. solves both Roscoe's own identity problem and that of other contemporaries, including, he hopes, any of his Native American gays. Since in today's parlance the modern life-style word "homosexual" refers both to the gay who penetrates and the one who receives, by using that term to describe berdaches Roscoe leaves the impression that this historical figure might both receive and penetrate. Indeed, Roscoe positively states at one point that the berdache was "sexually active"![92] Yet Roscoe knows perfectly well that the berdache was a male who, in whatever cavity, *only* received, and did not advance, the penis.

This is the second point of Roscoe's agenda, which reflects the author's inability to meld his own sense of contemporary gay self-assertion with the reality of his historical berdaches' passivity. The astonishing thing about Roscoe's work, in fact, is that he regularly represses, if he does not omit altogether, the fundamental fact that berdaches were as good as always sexually passive. Failing to distinguish between the berdache active in other areas of life, yet — to use the the technical term — "sexually passive," Roscoe rails against those whose descriptions of berdaches make them seem, well, passive, indeed even "slaves."[93] Still more astounding: in his latest work, Roscoe spends more than a chapter in proving that berdaches were militarily valorous, "great warriors." Now, I myself referred earlier to a case in which the Spaniards encountered a berdache warrior. But where-

---

[90] *Changing Ones*, 10, chap. 8, 183–87.
[91] See above, n. 88.
[92] *Changing Ones*, 9.
[93] I am said to describe slavery in describing berdaches: *Changing Ones*, 191. The institution of slavery plays no part in my book's discussion of the berdache. Roscoe's passionate use of the term shows how far his book strays from scholarly discourse.

as I labeled this the exception that proves the rule, pointing out that the berdaches in warfare were used all but exclusively as provisioners, porters, cooks — in short, in the roles of women, Roscoe labors to leave the impression that his later berdaches were often involved in actual warfare as warriors,[94] apparently finding it hard to imagine a person who is courageous yet does not want to engage in warfare. Yet there is no doubt whatever that across the hemisphere — and here I do for once exceed my self-imposed boundaries — Roscoe's claim of berdache militarism is nonsense. From then till now, with the rarest of exceptions, berdaches across the hemisphere almost never lifted manly arms, because that was not their assignment.

From these previous elements proceeds a third part of Roscoe's — and of Horswell's — agenda, which is to deflate the evidence that coercion and force were common elements in the making of the berdache by the pre-Columbian peoples in today's Latin America. The reasoning is evident, as I have previously suggested. If it can be shown that at the time of contact with the Spaniards, natives had mostly entered the berdache status through political or familial constraint, that might be taken to mean that today's homosexual also became so through constraint, rather than having become "what he is." What follows is predictable. My repeated insistence that I could only speak for the situation in Latin America in the early centuries of conquest, and specifically not speak for the later history of the American berdache, was beside the point. The Latin American berdache must also have entered his status voluntarily. Contradictions do not stand in the way. If Roscoe once affirms that "most tribal cultures, especially those in which visions are credited with bestowing skills and inclinations, do *not* view gender identitites as being chosen" (my italics), he soon enough doubles back, vaunting the fact that these "individual[s] [do] choose or desire an alternative gender identity."[95]

---

[94] Cf. *Changing Ones*, 31f., chap. 2, 148, 197f.

[95] *Changing Ones*, 130, 196. In this latter context Roscoe claims that "whether or not berdache status was coercively imposed, the rules of European discourse required that berdaches be described as if it were and that the possibility of an individual choosing or desiring an alternative gender identity never be represented." He added that "Europeans never sympathized with berdaches as victims. . . ." But as I pointed out above and in my book, European sources did occasionally refer to just such entrepreneurs who had (allegedly) chosen their way. And as I explained in detail in my book, there is a clear pattern in late medieval Spanish law that exempts passives beneath ca. fifteen years of age precisely because they were victims who could not freely choose. The persecution of berdaches by both their own peoples and the Iberian conquerors is of course a matter of

So central has the (Western, Pauline) notion of free will become for Roscoe that at one point he is driven to use a non-source to make his point. He cites the 1985 memoir of the eighty-five-year old Carolyn Reynolds (b. 1900), who recalls how the aged Crow berdache Maracota Jim "was probably glad to get away from his native tribe ... [because] at home, he was forced to dress like a woman. ..."[96] Troubled by this text (Reynolds's "understanding of the Crow third-gender role was [obviously] faulty"), Roscoe cites what he calls a keepsake that had been inserted into this book by its publisher to the effect that Reynolds, after completing her memoirs, did after all conclude that "Crow mothers would not force cross-dressing on their children; this would be contrary to the 'free and easy life.'" Instead, Maracota Jim — Roscoe's erstwhile "third-gender warrior" Osh Tisch — "was garbed like a woman, and Crow friends tell me, he dressed like a woman because he wanted to." Roscoe's invincible naiveté here becomes pulp fiction. Of course the Crow would deny constraint, as native Americans long ago were taught to deny such matters to the white man. But in the teeth of his source, Roscoe does not hesitate to convert this guilty, romantic, white publisher's word into ethnography!

I hope that this critique of other scholars has served its purpose, which is to illustrate the perils of making one's own life-style the point of departure and the predominant reason for research into the past. It really will not do in the absence of evidence to have one gay arguing for the "effeminate position" as having been honored in the past, while another lays claim to the berdache's "third gender warrior" position knowing that warring was foreign to the berdaches. I would indeed welcome more straight scholars in this field — to establish its bona fides — but I nonetheless believe deeply that the eros that gays bring to the study of historical sex and gender can and often does contribute to first-class historical scholarship. Not for nothing did I thank the gay and lesbian rights movement for inspiration in introducing my *Sex and Conquest*, even if its dedication was "For the Children" who have so commonly been the victims of these and other adult societies.

There are so many questions to which a dispassionate study of the berdaches can still contribute. Certainly foremost among these is a better understanding of early American women. Of course the comparison between

---

fact, but self-persecution as a modern historiographical strategy surely diminishes this type of work.

[96] *Changing Ones*, 37.

the male berdache and the so-called female berdache is one such area, and it has been getting increased attention recently. But what I have in mind is a subject that lies in the interstices between the berdaches and the broad mass of early American women, viewed and treated as dependents. It cannot be too forcefully stated that most boys in the time and place I have studied were made and kept "girls" as an expression of processes of humiliation that helped inform and define social structure. The treatment of the (male) berdaches documented in my work is in fact also about the native treatment of, and attitudes toward, women, attitudes that, by the way, struck the Spaniards (!) as starkly misogynous.[97] The information on treatment of the berdaches is the more valuable for the history of women in this age because women themselves so rarely appear in the historical record of the Conquest and early colonial period.

Two further areas of needed research beckon strongly. As has often been pointed out, an analytically fundamental distinction needs to be made between berdaches, who their lives long played the roles of women to the nines, and several other native American types who transvested, to be sure, but only for limited periods of time.[98] Yet as far as I know, no real study of this matter has been done: we have a long way to go before a broader picture of cross-gender representations is possible in these societies. Then there is the matter of the often striking difference between how peoples imagined or ritually represented the gendered organization of their universes and the way they manifested power.[99] This disparity continues to bedevil historical studies — how could it not? — but, especially in a world like that of the Aztecs where philosophical and cosmological rather than historical documents are most of what we have for the contact period, the de facto centrality of behavior over thought as an etiological principle needs always to be asserted, and that disparity more seriously investigated.

Penultimately, let me address a matter of anthropological debate. At the time native Americans came into contact with the Spaniards in

---

[97] Such observations were made of Mexico and of the Tierra Firme: Trexler, *Sex and Conquest*, 122, 162. Needless to say, these (male and foreign) assertions must be treated with care. But they also should not be ignored as part of an historical romanticism privileging the alleged better position of women in the good old days.

[98] Such transvestisms, in festivals or as the result of battlefield "cowardice," may have remained temporary because they did not proceed to rape.

[99] In a different time and place, I studied this problem: *Public Life in Renaissance Florence*.

today's Latin America, what was the relative importance of the berdache's sexual behavior in comparison to his/her other behaviors and functions? Recently, a debate whirled about studies of the berdaches of Oman and Mombasa by Wikan and Shepherd, the one arguing that questions of gender and sexuality were the primary motivations in homosexual "marriages," the other asserting that the moving force was not sexual but economic: commonly, poor passives joined with actives of greater affluence and often more elevated social station for economic reasons. Questions of sexuality and gender were secondary.[100]

Alas, our Spanish sources so despised merchandising that they say little enough about the economic role of the berdaches, so we are hamstrung indeed for this period, and cannot contribute much to the debate. However, I do think that my approach to the berdaches calls for a broadening of the Wikan-Shepherd argument. In my view, the Latin American institution of the berdache during the contact period was significantly a phenomenon of representation, and specifically the representation of political and social dependence. The berdache's public representation of his/her sexual and economic activities is in my view marked enough in these early sources that the question might more properly be phrased: Are not the gender and economic frames of Wikan and Shepherd rather themselves epiphenomenal expressions of a dominant need to portray the hierarchy of political and social power? The meaning of the American berdaches at the time of the Conquest is certainly rooted both in sexual and economic activity — the former the better documented — but all such activities of these "appointed" berdaches proclaimed a hierarchy of power and dependence. It may well be asked how personages who conceal the fact they are male can be representational. I would reply that what berdaches in fact represented was the political reality that all men, though they may have called themselves brothers, were not. Rather, the berdaches were the patriarchy's girls.

Finally, let me once again position the research in the present paper within the more general study of the berdache. Throughout this paper, I have insisted that my subject has been the berdache in those areas conquered by the Spaniards during the conquest periods. I have made few claims regarding the North American berdache, and certainly not regarding those of more recent times. Yet on the surface, an impressive degree of similarity, further documented in my "Making the American Berdache,"

---

[100] The Wikan–Shepherd debate is in *Man*, n.s. 12 (1977): 304–19; n.s. 13 (1978): 663–71.

seems to link the Meso-American berdache of the fifteenth and sixteenth to those of North America during the eighteenth and nineteenth centuries. How then can we ultimately come to an evaluation of the perceived similarities among berdaches who lived among hunter-gatherers, sedentary agrarians, and even city dwellers?

My hypothesis for explaining that perceived similarity is already a matter of record: a male figure whose female gender expresses the ideological basis of a certain type of early state formation, the berdache appears so similar across the American oecumene because in general, the level of state formation of the various peoples of the Americas was roughly comparable. Yet clearly, this hypothesis is inadequate. What is needed now are discrete *historical* studies of the berdache among the North American peoples comparable to my own on Meso-America, to create the basis on which a more substantial comparative hypothesis could first be formulated. The limited sources are not the only obstacle to carrying out such a study, however. What is no less necessary is the determination to look at the past dispassionately, free of the narcissism the present — that ultimate guarantor of historiographic eros and curiosity — can bring to its study.

§

Everywhere, the Europeans soon put an end to the culture of the berdache, and nowhere sooner than in Meso-America. Yet in any corner of that vast region where the Spaniards did not penetrate, old cultural institutions persevered, as becomes clear in a document brought to my attention since the publication of *Sex and Conquest*. It is 1702, almost two centuries since the fall of Mexico. The place is the area around Lake Petén (in today's Guatemala), the people are the Itzas, who still openly resisted the invaders. A Spanish army chaplain writes to the crown about a recently conquered site:

> Lord, the perversity of [this] miserable people is such that next to their main temples they had a large set-off house of very decorous construction solely for the habitation of sodomites. Into it entered all of those who wished to have their sodomitic copulations with [the inhabitants], and especially [with] the very young ones. Thus [the visitors] learned [how to fornicate] there. The [passives], ministers of the demon, wore women's clothes. Their sole occupation was making bread for the priests, and their obscenities.[101]

---

[101] "Señor, a tanto la perversidad de esta misera gente que tenían al lado de sus prin-

As usual, the source is antagonous, but with the ring of authenticity for all that. At this late date, temple-based brothels for young males were still in place among these Maya. The ministering boys' purpose was not only to provide customary sexual satisfaction, but to teach (ultimately hetero-) sexual behavior to young men, just as other passives were found teaching that behavior two centuries earlier. And like earlier berdaches, through manufacture of "bread" these transvested passives still contributed to the economic welfare of the temple community. But does their residence in a large, "decorous" walled-around house hard upon temples mean that these berdaches served a religious purpose in the narrow sense of the term, part of a three-way sacrificial exchange system of the type we found earlier and elsewhere? Alas, once again a source on the berdache leaves much unanswered. What leaves us impressed and respectful, however, is the rooted, tenacious nature of the institution of the berdache in this Meso-American region.

---

cipales mesquitas una casa grande, de fabrica muy decorosa como prebilejiada, solo para la habitación de los someticos, en donde entraban todos los que querían tener con ellos sus nefandos ayuntamientos, y en especial los de poca edad para que alli aprendiesen, usando estos ministros del demonio trajes de mujeres y ocupandose solo en hacer pan para los sacerdotes y en sus torpezas": letter of 12 March 1702 by Francisco de San Miguel y Figueroa, cited in G. Jones, *The Conquest of the Last Maya Kingdom* (Stanford, 1998), 499, n. 45. My thanks to Peter Sigal for the reference, and to Grant Jones for discussing it with me, as well as for a transcription of the Spanish original. On the reputation of the Itzás for sodomy, see P. Sigal, *From Moon Goddesses to Virgins. The Colonization of Yucatecan Maya Sexual Desire* (Austin, TX, 2000), 217f., 223–27.